Science Instruction in the Middle and Secondary Schools

Developing Fundamental Knowledge and Skills

Seventh Edition

Eugene L. Chiappetta
University of Houston

Thomas R. Koballa, Jr.
University of Georgia

Allyn & Bacon

Boston New York San Francisco
Mexico City Montreal Toronto London Madrid Munich Paris
Hong Kong Singapore Tokyo Cape Town Sydney

Series Editor: *Kelly Villella Canton*
Editorial Assistant: *Annalea Manalili*
Senior Marketing Manager: *Darcy Betts*
Production Editor: *Gregory Erb*
Production Management and Composition: *Progressive Publishing Alternatives*
Composition Buyer: *Linda Cox*
Manufacturing Buyer: *Megan Cochran*
Interior Design: *Progressive Publishing Alternatives*
Cover Designer: *Elena Sidorova*

For related titles and support materials, visit our online catalog at www.pearsonhighered.com.

Library of Congress Cataloging-in-Publication Data

Chiappetta, Eugene L.
Science instruction in the middle and secondary schools: developing fundamental knowledge and skills. — 7th ed. / Eugene L. Chiappetta, Thomas R. Koballa, Jr.
p. cm.
Includes index.
ISBN-13: 978-0-13-715304-6
ISBN-10: 0-13-715304-X
1. Science—Study and teaching (Secondary)—United States. I. Koballa, Thomas R.
II. Title.
Q183.3.A1C637 2010
507.1′2—dc22

2009002125

Photo Credits: p. 100, photo courtesy of Martin Haswell; p. 261, MODIS Rapid Response Team, NASA Goddard Space Flight Center; Classroom Snapshot, Michael Newman/PhotoEdit, Inc.; all other photos appear courtesy of the authors.

Printed in the United States of America
10 9 8 7 6 5 4 3 2 BRG 13 12 11 10

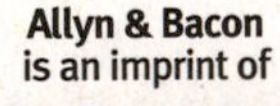

www.pearsonhighered.com

ISBN 10: 0-13-715304-X
ISBN 13: 978-0-13-715304-6

We dedicate this edition to Marcile Hollingsworth and the science teachers who have devoted their lives to making school science interesting and applying effective teaching methods in their courses.

About the Authors

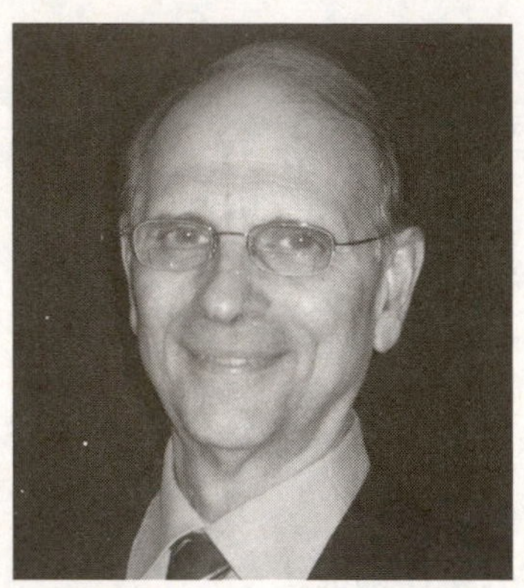

Eugene L. Chiappetta is a professor of science education in the Department of Curriculum and Instruction at the University of Houston. Dr. Chiappetta holds a bachelor's degree in Biology from Allegheny College and master's degree in General Science, and a Ph.D. in Science Education from Syracuse University. He has coauthored many textbook analysis research studies, using the nature of science as a framework. Recently, a recipient of the National Association for Research in Science Teaching Paper Award for *Examination of Science Textbook Analysis Research Conducted on Textbooks Published over the Past 100 Years in the United States,* The "Skoog Cup" for Significant Contributions and Leadership in the Development of Quality Science Education in Texas, and "Teaching Excellence" Award in the College of Education. Professor Chiappetta teaches undergraduate and graduate courses in science education and has coordinated teacher certification and science education programs for over three decades.

Thomas R. Koballa, Jr. is a professor of science education in the Department of Mathematics and Science Education at the University of Georgia. Dr. Koballa holds a bachelor's degree in Biology and master's degree in Science Education from East Carolina University, and a Ph.D. in Curriculum and Instruction from the Pennsylvania State University. He is past president of the National Association for Research in Science Teaching and the recipient of the Association of Science Teacher Education's Outstanding Mentoring Award. He teaches undergraduate and graduate classes in science education and has authored or coauthored more than 50 journal articles and chapters. His current research foci include science teacher learning and mentoring.

Brief Contents

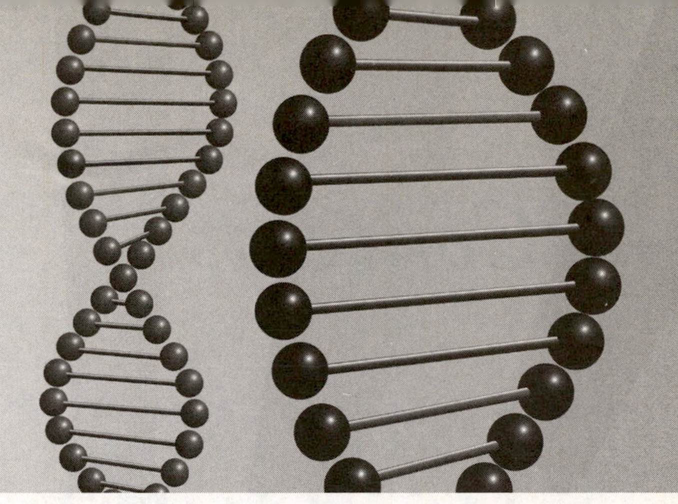

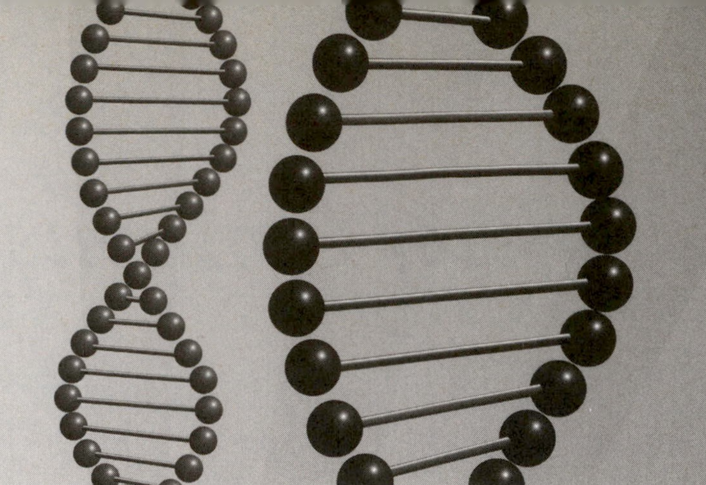

Contents

Part Three

Strategies for Science Teaching

Preface

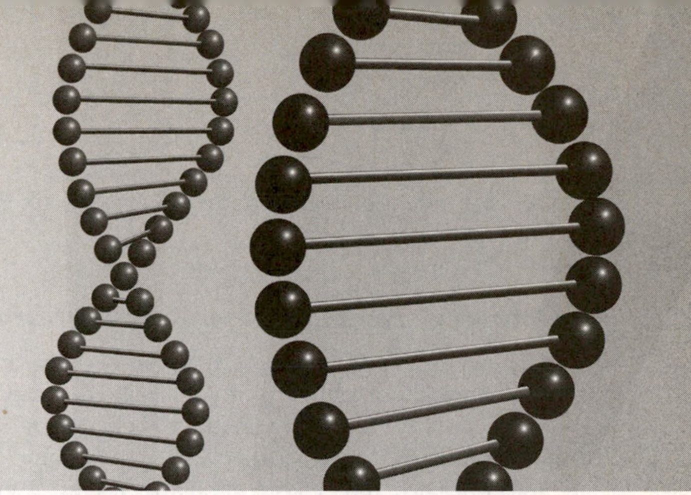

Today, science teaching is both exciting and challenging. The current advancements in science and technology are almost miraculous regarding their impact on individuals and society. Advances in biotechnology have provided insights into the function of the human genome that were unknown a few decades ago. Advances in the field of digital electronics have resulted in enormously capable devices such as the handheld cell phones that were only the dreams of science fiction writers of the past. However, school science has not experienced similar advances. From multiple vantage points, the teaching of science has not changed significantly over the past half century. Too many students continue to find school science unappealing and fail to see its relevance to their personal lives and to society. But unlike the past, school science is now challenged to address the needs of an increasingly diverse population of students and measures of educational accountability that are most visible in new state and national standards and the accompanying standardized tests.

In today's age of scientific and technological wonders, how does science education develop a scientifically literate citizenry that can appreciate, understand, participate in, and contribute to science and technology? The answer to this question resides within the individuals who are now entering the science teaching profession. These men and women want to know how to use their understandings of science and technology to prepare the next generation of Americans for life in the twenty-first century. In readying for this responsibility, they need to develop understandings about how to help students see science as a way of thinking and investigating as well as an accumulated body of knowledge. Furthermore, these men and women need to understand how to help students see the wonderment of science, and recognize the relationship between science and their daily lives, a healthy environment, and a productive society. This seventh edition of *Science Instruction in the Middle and Secondary Schools* is designed to provide individuals with the guidance for addressing both the excitement and challenges associated with entering the science teaching profession.

New to This Edition

This new edition is organized into three parts. The first part, Getting into Teaching, includes Chapters 1–6. These chapters provide information that will enable readers to grasp the essentials of science teaching. The second part, Foundations for Science Teaching, includes Chapters 7–10 and addresses basic understandings critical to the planning of science instruction and science teaching. The final part, Strategies for Science Teaching, includes Chapters 11–15, which emphasize the themes of argumentation, modeling and investigation, bringing coherence to the activities of science teaching and learning. The applicable National Science Teachers Association (NSTA) Standards for Science Teacher Preparation are discussed in each of the chapters of this edition.

Part One: Getting into Science Teaching

Modifications in the first six chapters aim to get individuals new to science teaching familiar with basics of purposeful science teaching and learning. Each chapter opens with a new vignette designed to draw the user into the chapter and to serve as a referent for many of the points of discussion. Others substantial modifications have been made to Chapters 3, 4, and 6.

Chapter 3, Planning to Teach Science, has been revised to emphasize unit planning in the context of critical questions: What are you planning to teach? Who are you planning to teach? How are you planning to teach? How are you planning to assess? In addition, the chapter uses the NSTA Standards for Science Teacher Preparation as organizers for unit design and assessment.

Chapter 4, Assessing Science Learning, has been moved forward from the position it occupied in the previous edition because of the importance of assessment in the learning process and its current emphasis in public schooling across the nation. This chapter stresses the centrality of continuous assessment and presents the science learning assessment system as a means for aligning learning goals with diagnostic, formative, and summative assessments.

Chapter 6, The Science Learning Environment, has a new focus that emphasizes teacher leadership rather than disciplinary management. This emphasis is reflected in the addition of discussions of democratic practices in the classroom as well as in discussions of the importance of relationships between teacher and students, and among students in a healthy learning environment. In addition, attention is given to the influence of culture on the science learning environment.

Part Two: Foundations for Teaching Science

Chapter 7, The Nature of Science, has been expanded, with the addition of new sections. New to the chapter is the section, What is Not Science?, to help readers better understand the differences between science, nonscience, pseudoscience, and junk science. Further, a discussion of the NSTA Standards for Science Teacher Preparation has been added and the discussion of the Scientific Enterprise has been strengthened.

Chapter 8, Inquiry and Teaching Science, has been moved forward from the previous edition to reflect its status as more than a set of instructional strategies. Because of its history in science education, inquiry is truly a foundational concept with many facets and meanings. Readers of this textbook can benefit from the broad presentation of inquiry-based teaching and learning in school science.

Chapter 9, Diverse Adolescent Learners and Differentiated Instruction, sports a new title that reflects the addition of sections addressing how the needs of today's diverse student population can be approached through differentiated learning and assessment activities.

A section on using modeling to learn has been added to Chapter 10, Learning in Middle Grades and Secondary Schools. This new section illustrates how to engage students' thinking and prompt their expression of ideas. This chapter concludes with a significantly modified section on learner motivation.

Part Three: Strategies for Science Teaching

The themes of argumentation, modeling, and investigation bring coherence to the chapters of Part Three. For example, in Chapter 11, the instructional strategies of demonstration, discussion, and lecture are presented as tools for promoting science talk and scientific argumentation among learners. Similarly, the presentation of socioscientific issues in Chapter 12 highlights opportunities for scientific argumentation as a vehicle for understanding the activities of scientific communities as well as developing science understandings. Further, Chapter 12 has been expanded with attention to the ruling from the recent *Kitzmiller v. Dover Area School District* case, which discounts intelligent design as a topic appropriate for school science. Chapter 13, Laboratory Work and Fieldwork, now includes new examples of strategies for encouraging meaningful learning when students are engaged in laboratory and fieldwork.

Chapter 14, Safety in the Laboratory and Classroom, has been revised to specifically address the NSTA Safety and Welfare Standard for Science Teacher Preparation. This chapter includes a rubric that can guide the learning and assessment of these important learning outcomes. Finally, Chapter 15, Computers and Electronic Technologies, gives greater emphasis to the technological tools that enable the investigation of scientific questions and the computer-based simulations that aid students' learning about scientific phenomena.

Alignment with the NSTA Standards for Science Teacher Preparation

This edition of *Science Instruction in the Middle and Secondary Schools* is strategically designed to aid science teacher education programs to prepare teacher candidates to demonstrate the knowledge, skills, and dispositions called for in the NSTA Standards for Science Teacher Preparation. As the foundation for a performance assessment system, the Standards describe expectations for teacher performance in science content, science pedagogy, and their students' learning. These expectations are communicated as a matrix that indicates the alignment between the standards and eight assessments. It is these eight assessments through which science teacher education programs are able to demonstrate the competence of program completers, and in so doing are recognized by NSTA and accredited by the National Council for Accreditation of Teacher Education (NCATE). The Standards are available at www.nsta.org/pdfs/NSTAstandards2003.pdf and the Standards/Assessment matrix can be found at www.nsta.org/pdfs/NCATEAssessmentsAndNSTAStandardsChart.pdf.

The assessments and how the chapters of this edition support their attainment by science teacher candidates are described below. However, Assessments 1, 2, and 7 will not be discussed further here. Assessments 1 and 2 target students' science content knowledge, specifically performance on state content licensure tests (e.g., PRAXIS II) and grades in science content courses disaggregated by licensure levels and area (e.g., secondary biology). Assessment 7 addresses teacher candidates' understandings of scientific research and investigation developed through participation in authentic scientific research. It is assumed that teacher candidates will have achieved competence in the content areas in which they will seek licensure and have experiences in science research before enrolling in the course or courses where this text is used.

Assessment 3: Unit Plan. This assessment targets unit plans developed by teacher candidates. Specifically, the candidates' units must be assessed on the following standards:

- Science Concepts and Principles (Standard 1a)
- Unifying Concepts of Science (Standard 1b)
- Technology in Science (Standard 1c)
- Nature of Science (Standard 2c)
- Inquiry (Standard 3b)
- Issues in Science (Standard 4b)

- Curriculum (Standard 6)
- Science in the Community (Standard 7b)
- Assessment (Standard 8)

Chapter 3, Planning to Teach Science, is specially designed to guide candidates through the process of unit development, with attention given to each of the standards identified above. In addition, Chapter 4, Assessment of Science Learning; Chapter 7, The Nature of Science; Chapter 8, Inquiry and Teaching Science; Chapter 12, Science, Technology, and Societal Issues, and other chapters in Part Three of this text provide important information to support the unit development process.

Assessment 4: Safety and Welfare Performance. This assessment addresses teacher candidates' classroom teaching performance, with specific attention to matters of safety and welfare. Chapter 14, Safety in the Laboratory and Classroom; Chapter 13, Laboratory Work and Fieldwork; Chapter 6, The Science Learning Environment; and Chapter 9, Diverse Adolescent Learners and Differentiated Instruction, present information that will prepare candidates to organize a safe and effective science learning environment and advance the welfare of organisms and student learning (Standards 9a, b, c, and d). It is recommended that the assessment of candidates' performance relative to safety and welfare be nested within an overall assessment of effective teaching practice. (See Example Assessment 4: Student Teaching Assessment at www.nsta.org/pdfs/NCATE-Assessment4StudentTeachingRubric.pdf.)

Assessment 5: Evidence of Student Learning. This assessment targets the learning of students taught by teacher candidates relative to the following standards:

- Science Concepts and Principles (Standard 1a)
- Nature of Science (Standard 2c)
- Inquiry (Standard 3b)
- Issues in Science (Standard 4b)

Chapter 10, Learning in Middle Grades and Secondary Schools; Chapter 7, The Nature of Science; Chapter 8, Inquiry and Teaching Science; and Chapter 12, Science, Technology, and Societal Issues, provide teacher candidates with information and teaching suggestions to guide students' science learning relative to these standards. In addition, Chapter 6, Assessing Science Learning, addresses the fundamentals of assessing students' learning and offers strategies for documenting student learning and using assessment to modify instruction. It is recommended that evidence of student learning be presented in portfolios developed by teacher candidates. (See Example Assessment 5: Evidence of K–12 Student Teaching Assessment at www.nsta.org/pdfs/NCATE-Assessment5EvidenceOfStudentLearningInScience.pdf.)

Assessment 6: Safety and Welfare Knowledge. This assessment addresses teacher candidates' knowledge and skills of classroom safety and welfare. Chapter 14, Safety in the Laboratory and Classroom; Chapter 13, Laboratory Work and Fieldwork; Chapter 6, The Science Learning Environment; and Chapter 9, Diverse Adolescent Learners and Differentiated Instruction, provide information that will prepare teacher candidates to construct understandings about safety and welfare and reflect on practices that would promote safety and welfare in the science classroom (Standards 9a, b, c, and d). Evidence of teacher candidates' knowledge and skills of classroom safety and welfare may be demonstrated by a test or module or portfolio assessed using a rubric. It is important to note that while both Assessment 4 and Assessment 6 target safety and welfare, the two assessments differ in their focus. Assessment 6 calls on teacher candidates to demonstrate their knowledge and skills related to safety and welfare, which should exceed that actually demonstrated in observations of candidates when teaching.

Assessment 8: Contextual Content. This assessment focuses on teacher candidates' understanding of science in the context of human culture. It specifically attends to how unifying concepts distinguish science from other ways of knowing, how science is a way of thinking and investigating, and how science is related to societal issues and technology (Standards 1b, 2a, 2b, 3a, and 4a). Chapter 2, The Purpose of Teaching Science; Chapter 7, The Nature of Science; Chapter 8, Inquiry and Teaching Science; Chapter 11, Discussion, Demonstration, and Lecture; Chapter 12, Science, Technology, and Societal Issues; and Chapter 15, Computers and Electronic Technologies, provide teacher candidates with information about the many facets of science that contribute to its unique character. Evidence of teacher candidates' knowledge of the contextual content of science may be demonstrated through written or performance assessments.

Acknowledgments

With the current edition, this science methods book will have been in print for over 50 years—a remarkable achievement. We thank Alfred Collette and Walter Thurber for initiating the book with its first edition in 1959 and setting the tone for its style of informing preservice and inservice teachers about science teaching and how to be effective in the classroom. We also thank Alfred Collette for giving us the opportunity to continue the revision and publication of this valuable teaching resource. In addition, we thank our colleagues who have published their excellent works in the science education literature on teaching and learning science and science teacher education. The following are some of the individuals to whom we are indebted for the important ideas they provided for the current edition and for assisting us in our professional work.

Co-author Eugene Chiappetta would like to give special thanks to the following individuals:

Jill Bailer, a middle school science teacher in the Houston Independent School District, has co-taught secondary methods with me for many years at the University of Houston. She has provided me with many insights on teaching science at the middle school level. Robert Dennison, a biology teacher facilitator in the Houston Independent School District, has kept me informed about the evolution versus creationism controversy, and the work of Charles Darwin. In addition, Robert has assisted me in teaching a biology methods course at the university.

David Fillman, Director of Science for the Galena Park Independent School District, has conducted many science textbook analyses with me, which have provided validation for the nature of science framework that is a central theme of this textbook and the national science education reform movement. David has also supported many funded programs that I have coordinated at the University that have impacted many science teachers in the Houston area.

Patricia Harrison, Director of Secondary Science for the Alief Independent School District, has been instrumental in providing many ideas that align with effective science instruction. She has helped to validate the multi-instructional approach that is evident in this science methods textbook.

Thanks also to the science department at Spring Woods Senior High School, Spring Branch Independent School District, especially the Science Department Chairperson, Virginia Tucker; science teachers Ann Brown, Robin Kohler, and Gina Disteldorff, and the principal Wayne Schaper, Jr. These educators have permitted me to study science in their classrooms, take photographs of students engaging in the study of science, and allowed me the opportunity to teach science methods courses in their classrooms in order to provide an authentic setting for preparing preservice and inservice science teachers. I am forever indebted to Spring Woods High School.

My wife, Barbara, is always willing to proofread yet another chapter or paper. She has been a great supporter of my professional work and a wonderful partner in my personal life. I am forever grateful.

Co-author Tom Koballa would like to thank the following individuals:

Al Schademan, Assistant Professor of Science Education at California State University, Chico, for his guidance in the preparation of Chapter 9, Adolescent Learners and Differentiated Instruction, and Steve Thompson, an extraordinary Georgia physics teacher, for his insights regarding classroom leadership presented in Chapter 6, The Science Learning Environment. Steve Kuninsky, Robert Willis, Laura Crowe, and Donna Governor for sharing their thinking about science teaching and learning with me and for their assistance with photographs of science teachers and students.

Also, special thanks to Dava Coleman for proofreading chapters multiple times and suggesting numerous improvements, and to Kristi Leonard of the University of Georgia College of Education's Office of Instructional Technology for formatting many of the table and figures that appear in this textbook.

Finally, we would like to thank the reviewers of the Seventh Edition for providing valuable feedback: Wendy Michelle Frazier, George Mason University; Paul Narguizian, California State University, Los Angeles; and José M. Rios, University of Washington Tacoma.

Chapter

1

Thoughts and Actions of Beginning Science Teachers

Beginning teachers have a great deal to consider as they prepare to teach today's students.

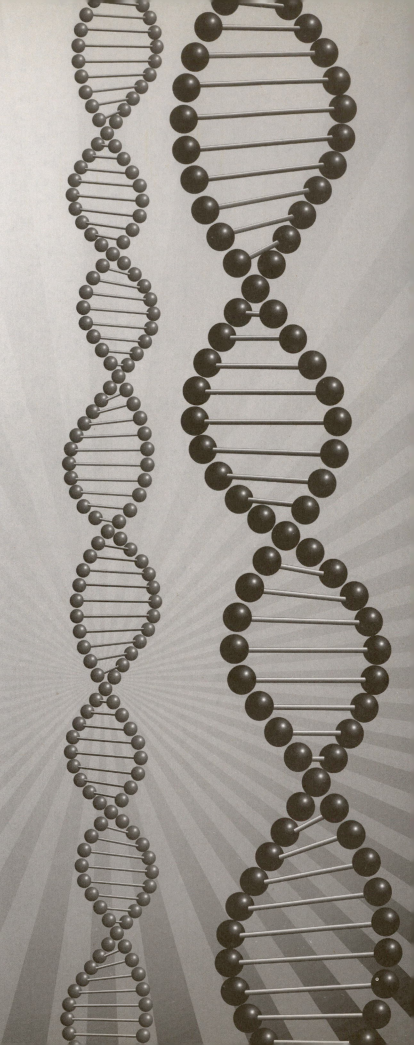

The setting of this vignette is the classroom of a beginning science teacher who is teaching ninth-grade physical science in a large urban high school. Mr. Clay has a degree in physics and is assigned to teach several physical science classes in addition to one physics class. The teacher is presenting the first lesson of a two-week unit on Newton's laws of motion, which is one of the physical science course topics. The first semester of physical science is devoted to physics, the second to chemistry.

Mr. Clay: Students, today we are going to begin the study of mechanics. We will focus mainly on Newton's laws of motion and then move on to speed, velocity, and acceleration. I will write the laws on the board and I would like you to copy them into your notebook.

Law 1—A body at rest tends to remain at rest unless acted on by an unbalanced force, and a body in motion will continue in motion unless acted on by an unbalanced force.

Law 2—The acceleration of a body is proportional to the force acting on it and inversely proportional to the mass of the body.

Law 3—Every force is accompanied by an equal and opposite force.

Mr. Clay: Franklin, what is the key concept related to the first law?

Franklin: I don't know.

Mr. Clay: Celia?

Celia: I don't know either. We have never studied physics before in science class.

Sammy: Yes, we have. Isn't Newton the guy who was hit on the head with the apple?

Mr. Clay: Well, there is a story about Sir Isaac Newton observing an apple falling to the ground. However, the historical figure that could inform us concerning the development of Newton's first law is Galileo, a scientist who studied motion and inertia. Inertia is related to mass, and mass is a measure of inertia. Now remember, mass and weight are not the same. Weight is a measure of the force on an object due to gravity, and mass is the amount of matter an object possesses. We will come back to this later.

Mr. Clay: Who knows what the second law means? [No one responds.] Let me help you then. Simply stated, acceleration is related to the force required to set an object in motion divided by the mass. I will write this relationship on the board.

$$a = F/m$$

For example, if you want to push this empty student desk five feet across the floor, how much effort would you exert? Now, if Clifford were sitting in the desk, how much effort would you have to exert to start moving him five feet across the floor?

Mr. Clay: Angela, what do you think?

Angela: I would have a hard time moving Clifford around on that desk.

Mr. Clay: Why?

Angela: He is too big.

Mr. Clay: Yes, you would have a difficult time moving the desk with Clifford sitting in it. Now, can someone tell me about Newton's third law?

Silence falls over the classroom.

Mr. Clay: Look at the textbook on the front desk. Is the book exerting force on the desk? Tonja?

Tonja: I think so.

Mr. Clay: Good. What force is acting to pull the book down on the table? Benny?

Benny: Mr. Clay, we did not study this before in science.

Mr. Clay: Okay, I will help you. The force pulling down on the book is gravity. What force is acting in the opposite direction of gravity? What force is pushing up on the book? Sally?

Sally: I'm not sure what you are asking. I don't see any force.

Mr. Clay: Generally forces are invisible. In this case, the table is exerting an upward force on the book.

Mr. Clay: Can anyone tell me what is speed?

Roger: I guess speed is how fast you are going.

Mr. Clay: Can you give us the formula for calculating speed?

Roger: No way.

Mr. Clay: Here, I will write the formula for computing speed on the board.

$$s = d/t$$

Have you ever seen this equation before? We will come back to this later in the week. How about acceleration? Can any one give me the formula for acceleration?

Again, silence falls over the classroom.

At this moment, the assistant principal's voice booms over the intercom, informing students that they should go to the gym for the pep rally rather than to their next period class. As the bell rings and students rush for the door, Mr. Clay announces that he will continue with Newton's laws tomorrow.

AIMS OF THE CHAPTER

Use the questions that follow to guide your thinking and learning about some fundamental aspects of science teaching:

- What beliefs do many *uninformed* beginning science teachers hold that may lead to ineffective teaching?
- What beliefs do many *informed* science teachers hold that result in successful science teaching?
- What five basic teaching functions must beginning teachers develop competence in if they desire to be effective in the classroom?

Most people with a college degree feel that they can teach. This view is reasonable because it has been formed as a result of at least 16 years in the classroom. Those who have logged thousands of hours in classes have formed many ideas about teaching based on a great deal of experience. A common belief among these educated people is

> "I can teach, probably better than most of the teachers who have taught me."

However, in reality, successful teaching is far more complex and challenging than most people realize.

As the stories of classroom veterans as well as people who have quit teaching make clear, teaching, especially teaching science, is not an easy task. Beginning science teachers often struggle in the classroom. Some of their beliefs concerning how students learn and how to instruct students may be skewed, resulting in ineffective teaching. This is evidenced by student behavior during instruction and student performance on different kinds of assessments, including unit tests. Students may be inattentive and disruptive in the classrooms of new teachers. Further, assessment results may be lower than desired.

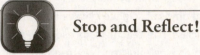

Stop and Reflect!

- What are some of the challenges that you associate with being a beginning science teacher?
- Why do you think that beginning teachers find teaching so challenging? Make a list of your reasons.
- Make a list of the beliefs about science teaching that may cause a beginning science teacher to be successful or unsuccessful in his or her work.

Aligning Thoughts and Actions of Beginning Science Teachers with the Basic Teaching Functions

The challenges facing beginning science teachers are many, but not insurmountable. The remaining sections of this chapter will highlight critical features of science teaching that beginning teachers should consider. These features are *purpose, assessment, planning, teaching,* and *management*. In order to help develop a mindset for effective teaching, the discussions will contrast the thoughts and actions of many uninformed preservice teachers, as well as some who are beginning their career in the classroom, with those who are more informed and experienced. Please reacquaint yourself with the vignette at the beginning of this chapter to prepare for a discussion of how this beginning science teacher instructs students and how he might have instructed them.

The Purpose of the Lesson

To benefit from this discussion, write down several sentences that you think capture the purpose of Mr. Clay's lesson on Newton's three laws of motion. Then, let's listen in on a conversation between Mr. Clay and his school-based mentor, Mrs. Bebee, to learn what Mr. Clay's thoughts were concerning the lesson's purpose.

Mrs. Bebee: Mr. Clay, how do you think your lesson went today?

Mr. Clay: I felt a little uncomfortable. I don't think the students were with me and I was taken aback by how little they know about force and motion.

Mrs. Bebee: What do you mean?

Mr. Clay: The students have not had much physics before in middle school. I thought they studied physical science each year and would have some idea about forces.

Mrs. Bebee: Well, you are experiencing the same problem that we all experience, expecting students to have learned the most basic skills and concepts that are part of or are supposed to be part of science courses in earlier grades. It just doesn't always happen for a variety of reasons, and it is discouraging. Let's discuss what took place this morning in your physical science class. Could you tell me the purpose of your lesson and how you prepared for it?

Mr. Clay: I read through the textbook chapter and my college notes to identify what I thought these kids should know. I wanted to give them an overview of Newton's three laws of motion so that I could go into the laws in more depth later.

Mrs. Bebee: That is a reasonable approach, but let's back up and think about teaching science in general to these teenagers. What were your initial thoughts for this lesson?

Mr. Clay: I wanted to touch on the key concepts associated with each of the three laws, and to cover them during the period. But it didn't go as well as I expected. I could sense students' attention waning after about 15 minutes into the lesson.

Mrs. Bebee: Why do you think students were becoming uninterested?

Mr. Clay: I'm not sure. This is how I introduce the study of mechanics in my physics course.

Mrs. Bebee: While I have never taught a high school physics course and do not have your background in physics, my experiences with ninth-graders on this topic have given me a different perspective. Could I share my thoughts with you, regarding how I see your lesson on mechanics fitting with what I view as the primary purpose of middle school and high school science teaching?

Mr. Clay: Sure.

Mrs. Bebee: My overall purpose for all physical science units is to help students develop understandings that they can use outside of school in everyday life. In my lessons, I strive to maximize student engagement and to hook them at the very start with activities that interest them in the subject. With this in mind, I try to be creative, to come up with instruction that centers on one of the major concepts or principles during the first lesson. I address only one or two of the main ideas and spend most of the class period on it. In the case of your lesson today, I probably would have focused on Newton's first law and inertia. Most important, I want students to feel comfortable with the science concepts they are about to learn. I'm always trying to focus on students as learners and individuals, as much as and often more than the subject matter when introducing a topic.

Mr. Clay: In other words, I should have attempted to teach only about inertia and to leave the other two laws, and speed, velocity, and acceleration, for another time.

Mrs. Bebee: Yes. Give this approach some more thought. Oh, have you examined the physical science syllabus that the physical science teaching team revised last year for this course?

Mr. Clay: Well, I was given one, but I haven't had a chance to really study it. Perhaps I was relying too much on what I do in my physics course.

Mrs. Bebee: Would you like to go over the physical science syllabus with me for the force and motion topics? Perhaps I can share some of my experiences and insights with you. As I have pointed out, you have an excellent science background on which to draw from in teaching physical science.

Mr. Clay: Sure. Can we meet during fifth period tomorrow?

At this point, it should be evident that the beginning teacher holds beliefs concerning the purpose of this introductory lesson that caused him to be less effective than desired. He thought the purpose for the introductory lesson was to touch on key concepts of mechanics, which has merit in some instructional settings. However, a major purpose of teaching science is to interest *all* students in the study of science by engaging their thinking and encouraging them to want to learn more about the subject matter under study. With this orientation, critical content and cognitive connections should be woven into the lessons to build understanding of natural phenomena. This serves to link science instruction with students' lives outside of school, helping them to build the understandings, skills, and dispositions associated with a scientifically literate citizenry.

The purpose that a teacher has for a science lesson directly affects how she will plan and teach and also what students will learn. We delve into a more in-depth discussion of the purposes and many aspects of science teaching in the middle and secondary schools in the next chapter.

The Assessment of Learning

Based on their own school experiences, most people think of assessment as testing and giving grades. Often, this is a teaching function that is considered only at the end of a lesson or an instructional unit. Testing requires administering and scoring a paper-and-pencil test that includes a selection of multiple-choice and true-false items along with a few short-answer or essay questions. Test development may involve writing questions or choosing items from a test bank provided with the textbook program.

And grading is often thought of as a bias-free way of segregating students along the A to F continuum.

In actuality, assessment must be an ongoing activity that is an integral part of the teaching and learning process. A beginning teacher may wish to check on student progress or may wish to diagnose students' understanding about a topic before beginning a new unit of instruction. These kinds of assessments provide the teacher with feedback useful for determining which students need help and for improving the quality of instruction. A comprehensive assessment effort couples these formative assessment strategies with summative assessments, and the overall determination of achievement and grades.

Let's listen in on another part of the postlesson conference between Mr. Clay and Mrs. Bebee in which they discuss issues of assessment:

Mrs. Bebee: Mr. Clay, can you tell me how you might have determined what your students learned about force and motion during this lesson?

Mr. Clay: Well, I had not planned an assessment at the end of this lesson, but I was planning to give them a test next week. That would give the class seven days on Newton's laws, with one of those days spent in the lab. By then, the students should know the three laws.

Mrs. Bebee: So, what do you think your students learned from today's lesson?

Mr. Clay: To be honest, I'm not really sure what they learned today.

Mrs. Bebee: Okay, let's think about what you could have done to find out what they learned as a result of your teaching.

Ms. Clay: Well, I guess I could have given them a pop quiz at the end of the period. But, in order to do that, I would have had to restructure my lesson to allow time for the quiz.

Mrs. Bebee: A short quiz at the end of the period is not a bad idea, and you are right about the need to restructure your lesson to allow time for the quiz. You could carry out the quiz in five minutes or less. Some of the teachers in the department regularly give short quizzes at the end of class. Ms. Bennett, who teaches chemistry, calls her end-of-class quiz the students' "ticket out the door." Her students must hand in their quiz papers before they leave the classroom. Other teachers in our department don't give end-of-class quizzes. Instead, they ask questions throughout their lessons, ask students to construct concept maps or drawings, or allow students to perform dramatic role-playing to demonstrate learning.

But since you suggested giving a pop quiz, let's think about questions that you might have asked to determine what your students learned during the lesson.

Mr. Clay: I might ask students to write a definition for each of the three laws. As an alternative, I could present a scenario illustrating one of the laws, then ask students to identify the law illustrated and to write a short explanation supporting their answer.

Mrs. Bebee: Very good! Student answers on a quiz can tell you what they learned and more. Say, 28 out of the 32 students in the class performed well. What does this tell you about your teaching?

Ms. Clay: Unfortunately, that probably would not have happened with this lesson. However, I get the idea. I'm beginning to understand that assessment has multiple purposes. Assessment is not only for giving student grades, but it can help me to improve my teaching as well. I should probably plan to give some quizzes and use other kinds of assessments before the unit test—for sure students will do better and I can monitor their progress.

As the conversation between the beginning teacher and the mentor teacher reveals, assessment is one of the most important of the teaching functions. Well-constructed assessments can serve many purposes, including improving instruction, reinforcing learning outcomes, and evaluating student understandings and skills. As you will learn further on in this textbook, there is no best way to assess the outcomes of learning. A multitude of assessment methods exists for use in science classrooms.

The Planning of the Lesson

Appropriate planning certainly ranks as one of the most important teaching functions. This activity provides a scheme for accomplishing a set of learning outcomes. A teaching plan lays out a blueprint that gives vision, organization, and coherence to classroom instruction and student learning. This activity requires considerable thought and creativity. It is obvious when a teacher has not planned well, because the instruction results in a lack of student engagement and little learning.

Science teachers must plan frequently and thoroughly to be successful. Further, their goal must be to engage students in activities that are instructive and meaningful, which help students to construct important concepts, and to develop life-long understandings, dispositions, and skills. In addition, with very abstract subject matter, one goal might be to focus on a limited number of key concepts, rather that an overview of many.

Stop and Reflect!

- What and who might the beginning teacher turn to when planning the lesson on Newton's laws of motion?

During the postlesson discussion between Mr. Clay and the mentor teacher, Mrs. Bebee, it became evident that the beginning teacher's planning may have benefited from a different direction. When Mrs. Bebee asked Mr. Clay how he planned the lesson, the response was that he (a) referred to his college physics notes, and (b) modeled his teaching based on what he would do in his physics course. Mrs. Bebee responded to this plan by suggesting that Mr. Clay take a different approach when introducing a new topic to ninth-grade physical science students.

The mentor teacher emphasized that Mr. Clay should develop his lesson around the lives of the students, by identifying what students might find meaningful in the content of the lesson and how they might use what they learn in life; then, he can begin with what students can relate to, given their prior experiences inside and outside of school. With this in mind, select more than one instructional activity to engage students. Then, outline the instruction for the activities in order to project how long they might take, identify the resources needed, and note other considerations for the lesson. Finally, check the alignment between the lesson assessment and the student learning experiences specified for the lesson. In other words, will the learning experiences enable students to demonstrate what they should know or be able to do?

Reflect on this brief discussion on planning and determine the extent to which it matches with what you believe about planning and the thoughts of a beginning science teacher. Your thinking will likely reveal the close link between lesson purpose and assessment and how the teacher would plan for the lesson. Further on in this textbook, you will find an entire chapter devoted to planning to teach science, which goes into greater depth on this aspect of teaching, and can prepare you for lesson and unit planning in the middle and high schools. A central feature of this discussion will be how planning instruction is based on the identification of desired learning outcomes and determining acceptable evidence to demonstrate if students have achieve the desired outcomes.

The profession needs many highly motivated individuals to fill the science teaching positions in the nation.

The Teaching of the Lesson

Most people consider teaching as *the* major activity of a teacher. Teaching, or instruction, as it is often called, is what people usually think of when they visualize the classroom. Teaching initiates and guides learning. This basic function can take many forms, such as lecture, discussion, demonstration, laboratory work, guided reading, simulation, and so on. Let's return to the conversation between the beginning science teacher, Mr. Clay, and his mentor in order to understand his thinking with regard to the instructional activities for the lesson.

Mrs. Bebee: Mr. Clay, what was your instructional plan for this lesson?

Mr. Clay: Well, I wanted to define some basic concepts related to force and motion.

Mrs. Bebee: What methods or techniques did you use to accomplish this?

Mr. Clay: I used the board to present the information and asked students questions.

Mrs. Bebee: I think you used the board effectively and your questions were clearly stated and focused, all of which demonstrate effective teaching skills and strategies. Now let's step back and consider the purpose for the lesson that we discussed earlier, where you might teach only about inertia. How might you teach the lesson?

Mr. Clay: Well, if I were to focus only on inertia for the lesson, there are several demonstrations that I could conduct to illustrate this concept.

Mrs. Bebee: Great! That is how I would approach the lesson. What else would you do?

Mr. Clay: I would ask more questions.

Mrs. Bebee: Yes. Now you are thinking differently about this lesson. Let me build on your ideas. When I initiate the force and motion unit, I show two YouTube video clips—one of an automobile crash where the passenger dummies are not wearing seat belts, the other of a large linebacker tackling a small running back. These videos combined with strategically placed questions help to contextualize the lesson, since most of our urban students have witnessed or heard news reports of car crashes and many of them enjoy football. Then I conduct demonstrations that illustrate inertia, whereby I invite many students to the front demonstration table to assist or to conduct a given demonstration. Further, I direct students to read selected passages from the textbook about the first law and to take notes, explaining key concepts. We spend the entire period on inertia and the first law. I try to build many mental connections between the first law and students' everyday lives before moving on to the second law. In addition, I have students participate in a very short laboratory exercise that I have developed to reinforce their understanding of inertia.

When we analyze the instruction of the beginning science teacher, it becomes evident that his approach is different from the experienced teacher. To maximize student learning, many methods and techniques are used during a science lesson. Note that the mentor teacher indicates that she uses demonstration, lecture, question-and-answer, reading in the textbook, and note taking as well as laboratory work when introducing force and motion. Effective instruction necessitates careful consideration of students' prior knowledge, abilities, and context. While there is no best approach to teaching, some approaches are better than others for a given situation, depending on the students and the desired learning outcomes. You will learn more about teaching skills, instructional strategies, and learning techniques further on in this textbook in Chapter 5 on teaching science. You will also learn more about how instruction can be designed to address the learning needs of students in Chapter 9 on adolescent learning.

The Management of the Learning Environment

Classroom management is the number one concern of beginning teachers. Although teachers who are new to the classroom have spent many years learning about the content they will teach and perhaps many years using science knowledge in the workplace, most beginning teachers have had little practice at managing the learning of others and dealing with adolescent students from many cultural backgrounds. The task of guiding the learning of 25 or 30 middle or high school students in a science classroom or laboratory can be extremely challenging, requiring refined understandings in order to make good management decisions.

Many classroom management decisions must be made in advance of the actual lesson as part of lesson planning. Others are more appropriately made in the midst of instruction. In either case, the teacher's decisions must be directed toward developing a classroom environment where students learn, feel safe, and assume responsibility for their own actions.

Mr. Clay and Mrs. Bebee also addressed issues of classroom management during their postlesson conversation. Let's eavesdrop in on a part of their conversation.

Mr. Clay: I am really disappointed in the students' behavior. Some of them were talking and not taking notes while I was lecturing. And did you see how they all ran for the door as soon as the bell rang? I didn't even have a chance to tell them what I wanted them to do for homework.

Mrs. Bebee: Yes, I observed that and I share your disappointment. You know, it would be so easy to blame the students for their actions and come down on them hard tomorrow, but let's think about some of the things that you could have done to make the class run more smoothly. For instance, you said you didn't have time to give the homework assignment. What could you have done to provide yourself with more instructional time? Begin by telling me how you started the class period.

Mr. Clay: Well, I started by calling the roll. It took me exactly five minutes. I know it took me five minutes because I checked my watch when I got to Jessie Young's name, the last one on my grade roll.

Mrs. Bebee: That's quite a lot of time to check attendance, even though you have 32 students in the class. Now, tell me what the students were doing while you were calling the roll.

Mr. Clay: Most were taking out their textbooks and notebooks, and talking. A couple of students were sharpening pencils, and I saw Ken and Marvin arguing about something. I had to stop twice and tell Marvin to return to his seat on the other side of the room.

Mrs. Bebee: I hear you saying that the students were not engaged in any learning activities during the first five minutes of class. If you check attendance this way every day, you will have lost, let me do the math here, 900 minutes or 15 hours of instructional time by the end of the school year. Is this a good thing?

Mr. Clay: Of course not. I never thought of calling roll in terms of lost instructional time. Perhaps I should develop a seating chart and check attendance using it, like I saw Mr. Jefferson do when I observed his biology class.

Mrs. Bebee: Good idea! Checking attendance using a seating chart is exactly what I would recommend. However, this will also take some time. What could students be doing while you're checking attendance?

Ms. Clay: Well, I guess I need to give them something to do. But, I'm not sure what.

Mrs. Bebee: One strategy is to have students respond to a few questions on previously studied material that pertains to the day's lesson. You can write the questions on the board or an overhead transparency before the tardy bell rings, and instruct students to begin answering the questions. With students engaged, you should have time to check attendance and deal with other housekeeping chores at the start of the period. This means no lost instructional time.

Mr. Clay: I could also write the day's homework assignment on the board or transparency and tell students to copy it into their notebooks. This would solve the problem of students leaving class without their homework assignment.

Mrs. Reed: I think this would be a productive approach to managing your teaching and learning environment.

You can sense from this exchange that classroom management has a lot more to do with making decisions about classroom procedures and routines than it does with disciplining students who misbehave. When students know what is expected of them and clear procedures and routines are in place, students often will rise to meet those expectations, resulting in a more effective lesson. More information about how to manage the science-learning environment is presented further on in this textbook.

Stop and Reflect!

- If you were in Mr. Clay's place, how would you have responded to Mrs. Bebee's recommendations for improving the classroom environment?
- What recommendations would you add to those offered by Mrs. Bebee?

Informed and Uninformed Science Teaching

Mr. Clay's lesson on force and motion along with his postlesson conversation with his mentor, Mrs. Bebee, reveal much about science teaching. Science teaching is much more than asking questions and giving information. Teaching science in middle school and high school also involves considering the lesson's purpose; planning carefully, zeroing in on the objectives and assessment; managing the learning environment; as well as thinking about the lesson in the broader context of being nested within one of several units that make up a science course.

The postlesson conversation between the two teachers also highlights differences in understanding and skills associated with science teaching. Mrs. Bebee's classroom experience and ability to reflect on her teaching enable her to see lesson strengths and potential weaknesses, and to make decisions that will likely lead to greater student learning. This knowledge base for science teaching is called *pedagogical content knowledge*, a special amalgam of content and pedagogy that is uniquely the province of teachers (Shulman, 1987, p. 8).

Of course, it is not expected that a beginning teacher will think about teaching and student learning in the same way that a veteran teacher would. However, by carefully considering the five basic elements of teaching discussed in this chapter, the beginner will be more apt to enter the science classroom prepared to meet the many challenges associated with teaching. These fundamental teaching functions provide a set of lenses through which one can focus on student learning. It is the nature and depth of understanding associated with the five aspects of teaching that distinguishes the *informed* science teacher from one who is *uninformed*. The thoughts and actions about science teaching commonly associated with informed beginning science teachers and uninformed beginning science teachers are presented in Table 1.1.

Finally, teacher beliefs influence all aspects of their work. Beliefs play a critical role in how you and other science teachers view science, approach instruction, and set expectations for student learning (Jones & Carter, 2007). Beliefs about planning, assessing, teaching, and managing the learning environment, as well as other aspects of schooling can be viewed as an individual's belief system. Therefore, it is prudent to be aware of your own beliefs and the beliefs of others regarding many aspects of the educational process. As you learn about new ways of teaching and learning, you may experience dissonance between how you believe instruction *should* take place in the classroom and how it *is* taking place. This is a natural aspect of professional growth, and calls for sensitivity in dealings with others in the schools you visit and in which you work.

Not all of what you learn through participating in a science teacher education program will fit well in all school settings. The sociocultural context of public and private schools may be different from that of a teacher preparation program. For example, teachers in the school where you work or student teach may view assessment differently from what you will learn about in this text and in your science teacher preparation program. Further, your work in schools will shape your thinking about teaching and learning as much as a teacher certification program will. Nevertheless, the understandings, skills, and dispositions that you construct by reading this text and participating in a teacher certification program can serve you well as a middle or high school science teacher.

TABLE 1.1 Comparisons Between the Thoughts and Actions of Beginning and Experienced Science Teachers

Thoughts and Actions of Beginning Science Teachers	Thoughts and Actions of Experienced Science Teachers
Purpose	
Focus on teaching subject matter. Convey chunks of subject matter from the textbook. Get right into the details of the subject. Cover a certain amount of material.	Focus on teaching students. Teach a few concepts or principles from the course syllabus. Provide meaningful overviews of course content to be studied. Help students grasp a few concepts well and to spark interest.
Planning	
Focus on covering textbook chapter material. Organize lecture notes over the content. Assume students understand what should be learned. Plan for the students who will most likely learn what will be taught during the lesson.	Identify what students may find meaningful about the core concepts or principles. Outline several instructional activities. Specify intended learning outcomes for each lesson. Plan to accommodate students who will learn lesson content as well as less able students.
Assessment	
Rarely check for student learning during instruction. Use mostly paper-and-pencil tests to determine what students know and can do. Fail to use test results and grades to evaluate teaching effectiveness.	Review frequently to check for student learning. Use multiple methods to determine grades. Consider student performance to gauge teaching effectiveness and improve instruction.
Teaching	
Attempt to transfer information to students. Ask students to take notes and to remember what they hear and see written. Use few teaching skills and strategies.	Engage students in thinking and finding out with questions and other means. Ask students to explain their understandings. Use many teaching skills and strategies.
Management	
Attempt to keep students in their seats. Make students listen and follow instruction. Discipline students who misbehave.	Provide opportunities for active student learning. Give students opportunities to express their ideas. Encourage students to monitor their own behavior.

Assessing and Reviewing

Academic Considerations

1. Respond to the Science Teaching and Learning survey presented in Figure 1.1. What do your responses tell you about your own thoughts concerning science teaching and possible actions in the science classroom? See how your responses compare with those of other beginning science teachers.
2. Suppose you are in a teaching position similar to that of Mr. Clay's and you are teaching the first lesson in a science unit (you pick the topic). Describe your lesson purpose, assessment, and possible student learning experiences. Include in your description some ideas about how you might align your purpose, instruction, and assessment.
3. Many individuals who choose to become teachers performed well in school and have developed an interest in the content they hope to teach. Think about a science topic that you find particularly

FIGURE 1.1 Science Teaching Inventory.

Science Teaching Inventory

This inventory was developed for individuals interested in a career in science teaching to assess their beliefs about science teaching and learning. The inventory assumes that beginning science teachers believe and act based on recollections of their own science learning experiences and their knowledge of today's adolescent learners, schools, and contemporary thinking about science teaching and learning. The inventory is intended to be self-administered and self-scored. Find the scoring key in Appendix D.

Directions: Choose either A or B for each item. Even though you may not completely agree with either choice, select the one that mostly closely matches your thinking.

1. A. The purpose of science teaching is to transmit subject matter knowledge to students.
   B. The purpose of science teaching is to help students develop science understandings.
2. A. Science lessons should be content-focused and sequential.
   B. Science lessons should be flexible and inquiry-centered.
3. A. The teacher is solely responsible for science lesson and unit planning.
   B. The teacher should solicit input from students when planning science lessons and units.
4. A. The big ideas of science should be the focus of science instruction.
   B. The focus of science instruction should be students learning chunks of content.
5. A. The starting point for instruction should be students' science misconceptions.
   B. When starting a lesson, a teacher should assume that students have no understanding of the content to be taught.
6. A. The outcome of science teaching is students knowing more science content.
   B. The outcome of science teaching is students understanding science content in depth.
7. A. The subject matter students learn in science class is applied in the class context, including tests and projects.
   B. The subject matter students learn in science class is used to make sense of the world.
8. A. In science class, assessment is distinct from learning.
   B. In science class, assessment is integrated with learning.
9. A. The purpose of assessment is to understand students' constructions of knowledge.
   B. The purpose of assessment is to measure science learning and grade students.
10. A. The function of laboratory and fieldwork is to verify concepts taught in class.
    B. Through laboratory work and fieldwork students can explore concepts they will encounter in life.
11. A. Student obedience is the centerpiece of science classroom management.
    B. Science classroom management emphasizes student responsibility.
12. A. Sound instructional planning will lessen classroom management problems.
    B. Student discipline problems can be curtailed by establishing strict classroom and laboratory rules.

interesting. What life events triggered your interest in the topic? How might you go about developing interest in this topic among middle or high school students? What relationship do you see between interest and learning?

4. Read Lee Shulman's seminar article, "Knowledge and Teaching: Foundations of the New Reform" (see References to this chapter). What is your understanding about the knowledge base for science teaching? How is your understanding similar to and different from those presented by Shulman? Write a report that summarizes your thoughts about the information presented in this article.
5. Write an autobiographical essay in which you discuss your experiences in school and work that led you to consider science teaching as a profession. Conclude your essay by speculating about the influence of your background on your career as a science teacher.

Practical Considerations

6. Prepare for and teach a 20-minute lesson on a science topic that you know a lot about. The students for your lesson could be other beginning teachers or adolescents. (Adolescents willing to collaborate as students may be identified by contacting leaders of after-school programs and youth centers.) Video-record the lesson and view it by yourself or with a friend. Write a short critique of the lesson. Then put both the recording and the critique aside. You will want to view your teaching and read your critique several months from now to gauge your development as a science teacher.
7. Make arrangements to observe a lesson taught by a veteran middle or high school science teacher and to speak with that teacher after the lesson. Ask the teacher about the lesson's purpose, assessment, planning, instruction, and classroom management. Write a paragraph about your experience in which you compare your thoughts about the lesson with those of the teacher. Share your paragraph with other beginning teachers.
8. Conduct interviews with two first-year science teachers and ask them about the joys and challenges that they associate with their jobs. Write a report summarizing the teachers' responses and giving your opinion about whether you share their ideas regarding the joys and challenges of science teaching.
9. Interview a science teacher who has served as the mentor for beginning teachers in the past. Ask the teacher about his or her expectations for a beginning science teacher in the areas of lesson planning, assessment, instruction, and classroom management. Prepare a report summarizing your findings, drawing conclusions regarding your own preparation for science teaching.

Developmental Considerations

10. The National Science Teachers Association (NSTA) is the largest organization in the world committed to the advancement of science teaching. Access the NSTA Web site [www.nsta.org] and check out its teacher resources, events for science teachers, and professional journals—*The Science Teacher*, for high school teachers, and *Science Scope*, for middle school teachers. Join NSTA as a student member.
11. Begin a journal of how your teacher education classes and school-based experiences affect your thinking about science teaching and student learning. Make entries into the journal throughout your teacher education program.
12. Start a notebook of science teaching ideas and materials. Organize your notebook into sections (e.g., classroom management, assessment, safety, demonstrations, etc.) and add your reflections regarding the usefulness of ideas and materials included.

References

Jones, G. M., & Carter, G. (2007). Science teacher attitudes and beliefs. In S. K. Abell & N. G. Lederman (Eds.), *Handbook of research on science education* (pp. 1067–1104). Mahwah, NJ: Lawrence Erlbaum.

Shulman, L. (1987). Knowledge and teaching: Foundations of new reform. *Harvard Educational Review, 57*(1), 1–22.

Chapter

2

The Purpose of Teaching Science

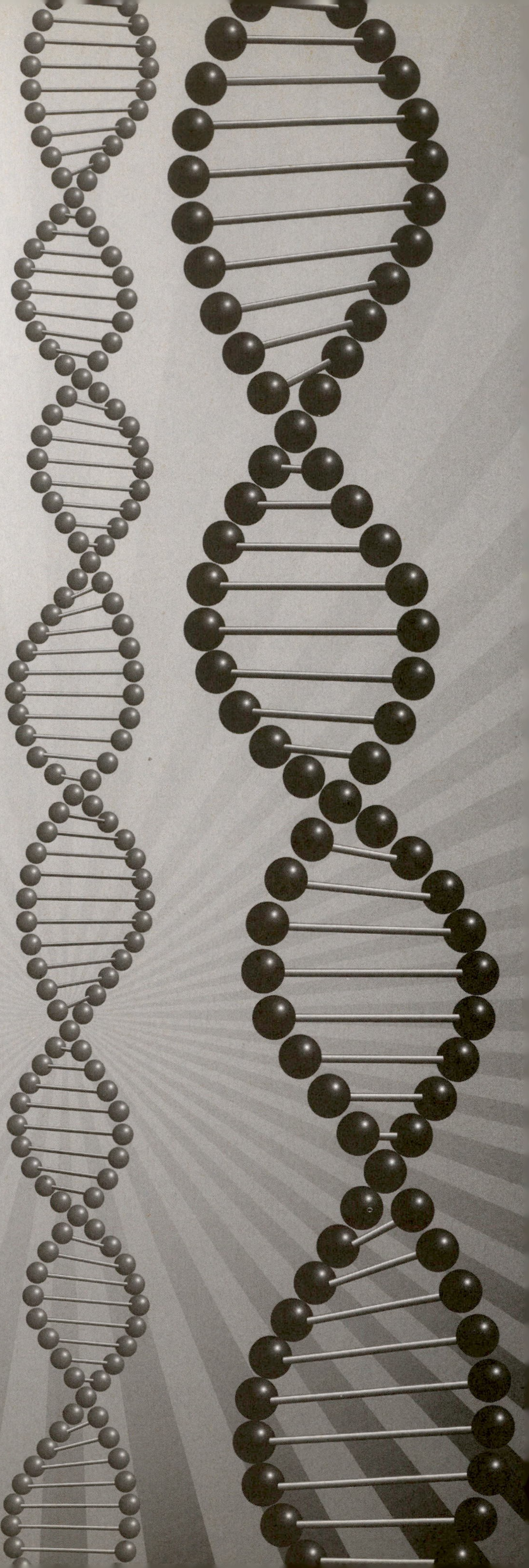

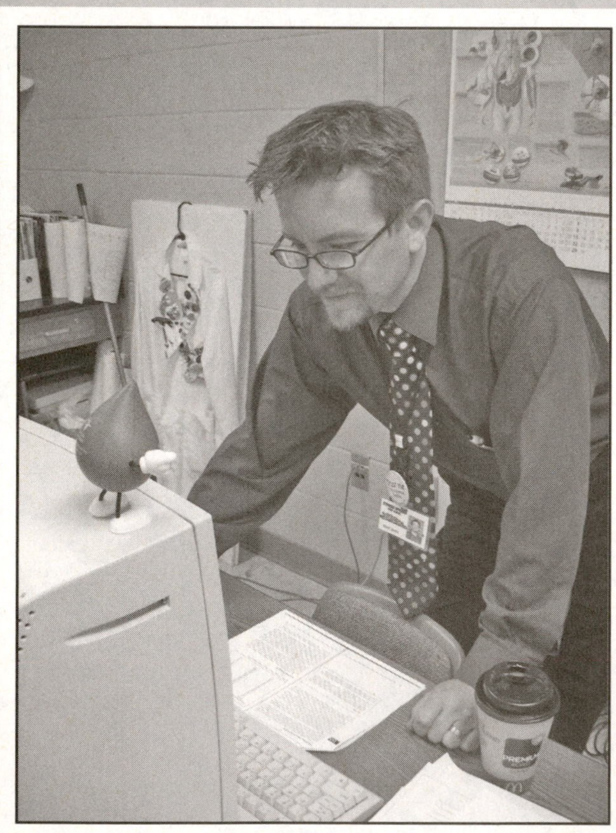

Science teachers should frequently refer to national and state standards to guide and inform their instruction.

This vignette is a conversation between Mr. Long, a newly hired sixth-grade science teacher, and Ms. Roberts, a veteran middle school science teacher and science department head. Mr. Long has no teacher-education training and was hired by the district on an emergency certification basis because of the need for science teachers. Before taking this teaching position, he worked for an aerospace contracting company. Mr. Long has gotten off to a bumpy start in his first few weeks of teaching and has been approached by the science department head for some guidance. Before examining Mr. Long's planning, teaching, and classroom management, Ms. Roberts has decided to give the new teacher an orientation on the U.S. educational system and science education.

Ms. Roberts: Mr. Long, have you had an opportunity to observe middle schools and middle-grade students recently?

Mr. Long: No, as I indicated in my interview for this position, I was with an aerospace company for the past 20 years traveling all over the world. When my daughter was growing up, my wife spent more time with her than I, going to school and church activities, because I traveled so much, troubleshooting for the company. When I married my second wife, her children were already in high school. Therefore, I have spent no time in public schools after graduating from high school myself. I think that I will learn about schools in the alternative certification program in which I am enrolled.

Ms. Roberts: OK. I am going to give you a crash course on the U.S. educational system and the purpose of science teaching. You will need this background to orient your thinking about this school, the curriculum, and the students. So tell me, what is our job with these students?

Mr. Long: I feel that these kids need to be prepared for college and to learn science, engineering, and computer technology. They need to be taught a lot of science and math so that they can get into the hard stuff and learn to solve problems like I did when I was their age. I don't want them flipping hamburgers for a living.

Ms. Roberts: This district has changed greatly over the past 20 years. When I began teaching in this school, the student body was mostly white and middle class. About 60 percent of the students went on to college. Today, the school is attended by students from many ethnic backgrounds and socioeconomic levels, a large percentage of whom are eligible for free or reduced lunches. A significant percentage of the students who start the school year in the fall move elsewhere with their family before the end of the year. We worry about these kids staying in school and graduating, let alone going to college. We try to provide a learning environment that will encourage them to want to come to school. Yes, we would like all students to learn science, but we also would like them to appreciate science and how it may lead to job opportunities. The curriculum is broader than I believe you experienced in your schooling. We spend a great deal of time designing science courses that are tailored to the abilities and backgrounds of these students. All of the sixth-grade teachers collaborate to provide our students with a well-rounded education. We try to balance general education goals with subject matter goals that are specifically related to science.

Mr. Long: I am here to teach science, not reading, writing, and civics.

Ms. Roberts: I can appreciate your feelings, and I think many individuals enter the teaching profession with that point of view. May I lend you a textbook describing the foundations of U.S. education and ask you to read just the first chapter? This may give you a different perspective concerning general education in the public schools.

Mr. Long: Sure, it can't hurt me to read one chapter.

After listening in on the conversation between the inexperienced and the experienced teacher, it should be obvious that Mr. Long must change his beliefs and orientation regarding the purpose of schooling. Without a sense of the broad goals that should be used to guide a general education, the uninformed science teacher, Mr. Long, will experience more difficulty in his first year of teaching middle-level students. Further, without this orientation to the U.S. public school system, Mr. Long will be out of line with the expectations of the school and the district in which he teaches.

> *"The American Public School has always carried a heavy burden of responsibility."*
>
> *—Hlebowitsh (2001, p. 4)*

AIMS OF THE CHAPTER

Use the following questions to guide your thinking and learning about the many purposes of science teaching, from those that are related to general education to those that are specific to science education:

- What are some of the expectations of the U.S. educational system for all students who attend public schools?
- What are major differences in the public school system in the United States versus some western European and Asian countries?
- What are some of the goals that have been laid down for science education that are evident in *Science for All Americans*, the *National Science Education Standards*, and the *National Standards for Science Teacher Preparation*?
- How does student test performance in the United States compare with those in other countries?
- How would you approach the organization of a science lesson or unit, after studying the contents of this chapter?

As stated in the quote by Hleblowitsh, the U.S. educational system asks a great deal from pubic schools and its teachers. While the general public views education as teaching the three Rs along with academic preparation, much more is expected. The system must consider individual and personal growth so that each student can maximize his or her potential, both personally and as a member of society. Therefore, society wants its citizens to understand the democratic process and to be socially active in their communities. In addition, many would like schools to provide vocational education in order to prepare students to take their place as skilled workers in a communication/technology-based society. The list is long regarding the demands that society, especially politicians, have placed on public education.

Indeed, the U.S. public school is a comprehensive system of education. Elementary, middle, and high school teachers are expected to do a great deal for all students. They must increase student understanding of fundamental knowledge and skills related to language arts, mathematics, science, and social studies. Further, teachers are expected to ensure mastery of core content for all students on standardized tests. Many states have implemented statewide testing programs at the middle and high school levels to determine student readiness to advance to the next grade level and to graduate from high school. Further, teachers are being held accountable for the success or failure of their students.

In contrast to the U.S. system of schooling, the educational systems in other first-world countries are remarkably different from ours. For example, in western European countries such as Austria, Germany, France, and Italy, vocational as well as academic preparation is a standard option of public education. At the fourth grade level, students take an examination that determines their educational track for part or all of their mandatory schooling. The system attempts to match the backgrounds, interests, and especially the maturity levels of students with an appropriate educational experience.

Many western European countries use test results for student placement in the high school, which begins in grade 5 and terminates in grade 12, where an academic curriculum stresses mathematics, science, languages, history, and so on. Those not entering the high school academic track go into the middle school, which extends from grades 5 to 8. The middle school focuses on vocational studies along with basic academic subjects. Middle-grade students can take an examination at the end of the eighth grade for entrance into an academic high school. However, most of the middle-level students continue on in the vocational school for the remainder of their public education.

In vocational schools, students learn practical knowledge and skills related to many businesses and trades. These students can choose to be a bookkeeper, sales clerk, chef, baker, mechanic, electronic technician, and so on. Vocational schools in Europe have been in place for a long time and fulfill their purpose well.

In addition to providing two educational paths, the European educational system attempts to teach less subject matter content over the school year. For example, consider the academic track where students participate in physics instruction throughout the middle and high school grades. The instruction each year addresses a smaller number of topics than one year of physics in the United States. Further, the European textbooks in physics, as well as in the other science subjects, have fewer pages of text than those used in the United States. Also, the major content areas—biology, chemistry, and physics—are taught each year during grades 5 through 12.

Schooling in India is much more specialized than in the United States. At the middle level, each science field—biology, chemistry, and physics—is taught each year separately. Students receive instruction in each field by a different teacher with an undergraduate degree in that field. At the end of grade 10, students take an examination that directs their education either into commerce (business) or math/science. They then follow this track in grades 11 and 12 and into college, but only if they are fortunate enough to earn high scores on high school exit and college entrance exams.

In China, an examination is administered to students at the end of middle school. The majority of students fail to earn a minimum score on the exam, which signifies the end of their formal schooling. A vast majority of these individuals enter the workforce as unskilled laborers. The remaining minority of students, who earned a minimal science score, go on to either a trade school or a high school. Those entering high school specialize in either the liberal arts or the hard sciences (math, physics, chemistry, biology, etc.).

The comprehensive nature of middle and secondary schools in the United States presents a big challenge to inexperienced as well as experienced science teachers. In addition to working in an educational system that requires all students to participate in a comprehensive curriculum and to learn a great deal of subject matter during each school year, teachers are expected to accomplish these varied goals with a diverse student population, consisting of individuals who come from very different ethnic, socioeconomic, and educational backgrounds. Many school districts in large urban areas report over 50 different languages and dialects spoken by students in their schools.

A substantial percentage of students in our society are from low-income families. These children lack the resources of children from middle- and high-income families. You are unlikely to find computers, Internet connections, books, educational magazines, and desks to complete homework in homes of students from low-income families. Many of these children have never visited a zoo or a museum, nor have they traveled to other parts of their home state to visit places of historical importance or educational value. Yet, the U.S. educational system asks the same from the disadvantaged children as from the advantaged in terms of the acquisition of basic skills.

Given the broad and varied purposes imposed on the pubic schools by society, what has society asked of science education and science teachers? As you might expect, science education also has a long list of goals and purposes. Back in the 1940s, The National Society for the Study of Education (1947) identified many outcomes for science teaching in the *Forty-Sixth Yearbook, Part 1*, which are summarized as follows:

- knowing facts
- understanding concepts
- understanding principles
- acquiring skills
- adjusting attitudes
- fostering appreciations
- furthering interests

In the 1980s, Project Synthesis (Yager, 1982) produced a cluster of science education goals that grouped together many of the purposes of science education. The project was carried out to increase science teachers' awareness that there is more to science teaching than focusing on content mastery of the subject matter and organizing courses that stress academic preparation. These four goals are:

- understanding personal needs
- examining societal issues
- preparing adequately academically
- shaping career education

More recently, during the 1990s, the National Research Council (1996) in their publication *National Science Education Standards* stresses the importance of producing a scientifically literate society. This widely circulated publication emphasizes the importance of educating students to encourage their curiosity about the world in which they live so that they ask questions about nature and answer those questions as the result of their investigative actions. Further, this publication indicates that students should examine science and societal issues in order to become knowledgeable about the interactions among science, technology, and society.

Let's return to a brief conversation between Mr. Long, the new science teacher, and Ms. Roberts, the experienced science teacher, after the beginning teacher read the introductory chapter in the foundations of American education textbook.

Ms. Roberts: Mr. Long, did you learn anything from the chapter that might give you a different perspective regarding the purpose of middle school education?

Mr. Long: Yes, I think so. Now I realize that we are expected to teach these students a lot more than the science in their textbooks. We need to prepare them for life. Perhaps I'm starting to think about what I teach from a different angle. I realize that I must make the material in the textbook relate to the student's entire life and to what a student will be doing after high school graduation.

Ms. Roberts: Good! If you don't mind, I would like to introduce you to the long and rich history of science education. This may give you a better idea about the purpose of science teaching in middle schools and secondary schools. However, what I give you to study will focus only on the recent past.

Stop and Reflect!

Before going on to the next section, list the goals or purposes of education, in general, for grades 6 to 12, that you believe have been set down for our nation's school. How do you think the general education goals might be similar to the science education goals that you will read about below?

Goals and Purposes of Science Education from 1980 to the Present

The Period Between 1980 and 1989

A great deal of criticism and controversy occurred during the 1980s regarding the status of science education. *A Nation at Risk* (National Commission of Excellence in Education, 1983) clearly states that "our educational system has fallen behind and this is reflected in our leadership in commerce, industry, science, and technological innovations which is being taken over by competitors throughout the world" (p. 5). Many of the reports and discussions that appeared in the literature were drawn from a multitude of studies conducted in the 1970s. The more than 2,000 pages of reports from the professional groups were synthesized and interpreted by Norris Harms and other science educators in Project Synthesis (Yager, 1982).

As pointed out previously, Project Synthesis called for a more balanced science curriculum for the nation's youth, which should consider personal and societal needs of students as well as their academic preparation and potential careers. Out of Project Synthesis and many other studies came a movement that has directed science education beyond its discipline base, which is something politicians and others never seem to get beyond. This led to a science educational reform aimed at strengthening the economic viability of the nation, which in turn necessitated a scientifically literate populace.

Today, the electronic-, communication-, and information-age society in which we live requires citizens who can develop technology as well as live with it. Science teachers have been given the challenge of educating the youth of America to participate in a technology-based world economy in which they must gather and use information from computers and other electronic devices. However, in order to profit from this information, students must possess a knowledge base that will permit them to assimilate information from printed and electronic sources and to make sense out of it. During the 1980s, as well as today, there is a body of fundamental knowledge that students should master related to biology, chemistry, earth science, and physics in order to use that knowledge in their daily lives and in their future workplace.

The Period Between 1990 and 1999

During the 1990s, the education reform gained momentum as it spread across the nation. School systems moved in many directions in their attempt to improve education, experimenting in many areas, from trying to help bilingual students learn content to creating alternative forms of education through charter schools. However, what stands out as most memorable from this period is the sincere attempt to (a) focus on the education of all students, especially students of color and those traditionally underrepresented in all aspects of society; (b) specify higher standards for learning; (c) promote a broader-based assessment process; and (d) establish tougher accountability for teachers and students. These aspects of the general educational reform are evident in the writings of the professional organizations representing the various subject matter disciplines.

With regard to science education, a bold initiative was announced in the 1990s when national guidelines were published that were meant to not only set the philosophical tone for learning science in grades K–12, but to identify the content to be learned. The time had arrived when policy makers believed that a country with 50 states could benefit from the thinking of national committees of educators and scientists. The nation's schools needed goals and directions with more specificity than they had ever had during any period in the past. Now, perhaps, the national policies could better guide local and state boards of education in their attempt to achieve science literacy for all Americans.

Given the large number and heterogeneity of the school districts across the United States, science teachers need standards for subject matter content in order for students to learn a similar body of knowledge by the time they complete their high school education. Adopting commercially produced textbook-based curricula or innovative instructional materials do not offer that direction. This was evident during the science education reform movement of the 1960s and 1970s that relied heavily on instructional materials, funded by the government, to initiate changes in school science programs. The curriculum materials of the past that went under acronyms, such as SAPA, ISCS, BSCS, ISIS, and HHP, differed significantly in their content as compared with what appeared in traditional textbooks that were used widely in the schools. We are optimistic that the national guidelines of the 1990s will provide a better outline of critical content and a clearer picture of the nature of science than the reform movements of the past half century.

Three prominent organizations have given the profession sets of standards to guide the science education reform. The American Association for the Advancement of Science (AAAS), The National Research Council (NRC), and the National Science Teachers Association (NSTA). The AAAS produced a large set of reform documents called Project 2061—Science for All Americans. The NRC published a booklet called the *National Science Education Standards*. The NSTA calls their project Scope, Sequence, and Coordination.

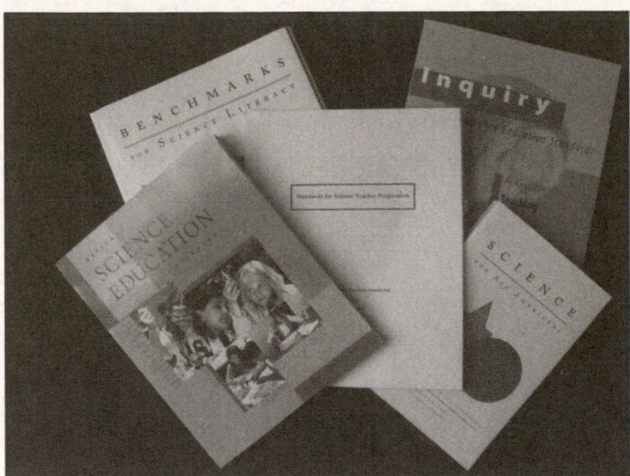

All science teachers should study the national science education reform documents.

Project 2061

In the mid-1980s, the American Association for the Advancement of Science (AAAS) spearheaded the science reform movement by initiating Project 2061. The central theme of this reform effort is to produce a scientifically literate society by the year 2061 when Halley's Comet will be visible from Earth. The AAAS is taking the long view with its reform effort because it posits that important societal changes require a great deal of time to achieve. One of the first documents it produced is titled *Science for All Americans* (AAAS, 1990). As the name implies, the intent is for *all* students to receive an education in science.

The AAAS reform project stresses the critical need to produce a scientifically literate society so that individuals can deal with the problems they will face in the new millennium. Many of the problems with which U.S. citizens must concern themselves are global, such as population growth, destruction of tropical rain forests, extinction of plant and animal species, scarce natural resources, and nuclear war. Science can provide knowledge and understanding about natural phenomena and social behavior that can benefit society. However, it will take an educated society, versed in science and technology, to comprehend societal problems and deal effectively with them. "The life-enhancing potential of science and technology cannot be realized unless the general public can understand science, mathematics, and technology, and acquires scientific habits of mind. Without a science-literate population, the outlook for a better world is not promising" (AAAS, 1990, pp. xiv–xv).

Science for All Americans identifies serious shortcomings of our educational system, which science teachers must address in order for a successful science education reform to take place. It reminds us that a great deal of instruction that takes place in science classrooms centers around learning answers rather than exploring questions. Memorization is emphasized at the expense of critical thinking. Often, reading about science takes the place of doing science. Students are not encouraged to work together on problems or to discuss their findings with others.

> *The present curricula in science and mathematics are overstuffed and undernourished.... Some topics are taught over and over again in needless detail; some that are of equal or greater importance to science literacy—often from the physical and social sciences and from technology—are absent from the curriculum or are reserved for only a few students. (AAAS, 1990, p. xvi)*

The idea that science courses cover too much material is a serious problem. This situation must be changed by focusing on less material and studying it in greater depth, which will actually result in students learning more. The "less-is-more" idea has become a slogan in the reform and should be taken seriously by all science teachers.

The recommendations in the *Science for All Americans* document are clear about the education that a student must receive in order to be scientifically literate. Indeed, it is a comprehensive and interdisciplinary education that is proposed. Students must come to understand the nature of science, mathematics, and technology as well as how these enterprises function separately and together. They must be versed in the physical, life, and social sciences from which they gain fundamental knowledge and understanding of reality. Students must study the world that has been shaped by human action to further the progress of society. Great importance should be placed upon providing students with a historical perspective of how the fundamental science ideas have evolved, such as the place of the earth in the solar system, matter and energy, fire, the atom, germs, and the diversity of life. Importantly, this reform project places a premium on the development of habits of mind that stress useful values, attitudes, and skills that students must acquire as they become versed in science, mathematics, and technology.

In addition to *Science for All Americans*, Project 2061 has produced another important document titled *Benchmarks for Science Literacy* (AAAS, 1993). *Benchmarks* specifies a common core of learning for students to master specific points in their K–12 education. The document lists learning outcomes that all students should know or be able to do in science, mathematics, and technology by the end of grades 2, 5, 8, and 12. The objectives identify fundamental ideas that *all* children can attain. However, the document reminds us that many students are capable of going beyond these outcomes. Further, science teaching can use many methods and approaches to help students achieve these literacy goals.

National Science Education Standards

The National Research Council (NRC) produced a publication titled *National Science Education Standards* (NRC, 1996). This document stresses the importance for every citizen to become scientifically literate. Individuals need a background in science in order to evaluate technical information and make informed decisions. They need to reason logically and think scientifically about problems that confront them in their daily lives. The knowledge and skills that are central to science also are necessary for many jobs and careers, whether or not they are in scientific fields. The following quote by the NRC (1996) reflects the intent of the *Standards*:

> *The National Science Education Standards are designed to guide our nation toward a scientifically literate society. Founded in exemplary practice and research, the Standards describe a vision of the scientifically literate person and present criteria for science education that will allow that vision to become a reality. (p. 1)*

The *Standards* make it clear that scientific literacy is at the center of the reform movement. A scientifically literate person is identified as one who is curious about the world and desires to ask questions and find answers to those questions. These individuals can describe and explain natural phenomena as well as predict their behavior. They can also deal with science and societal issues by expressing them from an informed point of view, using their knowledge to evaluate the issues.

Knowledge and understanding of science are important guidelines for the realization of a scientifically literate society. Students must learn fundamental scientific facts, concepts, principles, laws, theories, and models. These ideas must be integrated into students' cognitive structures so that they can be recalled and applied in their decision-making activities. Further, students must be able to use this understanding to distinguish between scientific information that is valid and that which is unsubstantiated.

Inquiry is a theme that runs through the *Standards*. This concept is defined relative to scientific inquiry, which centers on humankind's probing the natural world in search of explanations, based on evidence, leading toward an understanding of reality. Scientific inquiry includes both the ideas under study as well as the way in which those ideas come to be known. The *Standards* make it clear that there are many ways to inquire and to find out, from conducting firsthand investigations to reading about what others have found. Further, "conducting hands-on science activities does not guarantee inquiry, nor is reading about science incompatible with inquiry" (NRC, 1996, p. 23). Table 2.1 presents the changing emphases that are recommended by the science reforms regarding how to teach science *as* inquiry.

Science and technology are seen as compatible and necessary to the development of scientific literacy. They are closely tied together and should be part of reform science programs. However, they are different enterprises. The major aim of science is to understand nature, whereas the major aim of technology is to create devices and systems to assist society.

The *National Science Education Standards* provide science teachers as well as the entire profession with important guidelines that they can use to plan, organize, develop, implement, and evaluate science programs, which will make a difference in reforming science education. There are many dimensions to science teaching, and they must be considered in the development of effective science programs that will produce scientifically literate citizens.

Scope, Sequence, and Coordination

During the 1980s, the National Science Teachers Association initiated a science reform project for grades 6–12. The project is called Scope, Sequence, and Coordination (SS&C), and its aim is to change the structure of science curricula in the middle and senior high schools. The rationale for altering the content structure that exists is a belief that teaching the separate disciplines—biology, chemistry, earth/space science, and physics—each year in a separate year, is inefficient and does not integrate the sciences so that they make sense to the students. With the "layer cake" curriculum that has been in existence for over a century, students take earth science for one year, biology for one year, and perhaps chemistry one year. This yearlong, concentrated approach does not lend itself to building upon what the students have studied in previous science courses. Further, the one-year science courses that are traditionally taught are usually textbook-based experiences that are heavy on content and learning large numbers of vocabulary terms. The one discipline-based science course often results in students memorizing many terms, taking factually oriented paper-and-pencil tests, and remembering very little fundamental science.

Scope, Sequence, and Coordination's recommendation for reforming middle and senior high school science is to teach all four of the major science disciplines—biology, chemistry, earth/space science, and physics—each year in grades 6–12. In this manner, students would be able to connect the sciences and learn through a coordinated sequence the fundamental principles of the four major disciplines of science. Further, if the curriculum adheres to the less-is-more notion that covering fewer topics can help students learn more about a given area, then students will develop a deeper understanding of a given set of important ideas.

The term *scope* refers to the coherence of the curriculum that can be achieved by studying a set of fundamental ideas over six or seven years of school science. The word *sequence* addresses student learning with the

TABLE 2.1 Recommendations for Teaching Science from National Science Education Standards

Changing Emphases

The National Science Education Standards envision change throughout the system. The science content standards encompass the following changes in emphases:

Less Emphasis on	*More Emphasis on*
Knowing scientific facts and information	Understanding scientific concepts and developing abilities of inquiry
Studying subject matter disciplines (physical, life, earth sciences) for their own sake	Learning subject matter disciplines in the context of inquiry, technology, science in personal and social perspectives, and history and nature of science
Separating science knowledge and science process	Integrating all aspects of science content
Implementing inquiry as a set of processes	Studying a few fundamental science concepts
Covering many science topics	Implementing inquiry as instructional strategies, abilities, and ideas to be learned

Changing Emphases to Promote Inquiry

Less Emphasis on	*More Emphasis on*
Activities that demonstrate and verify science content	Science as exploration and experiment
Investigations confined to one class period	Activities that investigate and analyze science questions
Process skills out of context	Investigations over extended periods of time
Individual process skills such as observation or inference	Process skills in context
Getting an answer	Using multiple process skills—manipulation, cognitive, procedural
Providing answers to questions about science content	Science as argument and explanation
Individuals and groups of students analyzing and synthesizing data without defending a conclusion	Communicating science explanations
Doing few investigations in order to leave time to cover large amounts of content	Groups of students often analyzing and synthesizing data after defending conclusions
Concluding inquiries with the result of the experiment	Doing more investigations in order to develop understanding, ability, values of inquiry, and knowledge of science content
Management of materials and equipment	Applying the results of experiments to scientific arguments and explanations
Private communication of student ideas and conclusions to teacher	Management of ideas and information
Using evidence and strategies for developing or revising an explanation	Public communication of student ideas and work to classmates

Reprinted with permission from National Science Education Standards. *Copyright 1996 by the National Academy of Science. Courtesy of the National Academy Press, Washington, DC.*

belief that students should be taught beginning with concrete ideas and moving toward the abstract as they advance through the grade levels. In addition, science programs should space the learning so that fundamental ideas are studied over many years rather than many days or weeks. Also, the curriculum should provide application of knowledge so that it is relevant to students' lives. The word *coordination* refers to the continuity of studying the four basic science disciplines.

Science teachers should examine the publication *Scope, Sequence, and Coordination of Secondary School Science, Volume 1: The Content Core* for a thorough description of the recommendations that the National Science Teachers Association (1992) has put forth to change the way science is organized in the secondary schools. More recently, this project has coordinated its efforts with the *National Science Education Standards,* producing a curriculum framework called *Scope,*

Sequence, and Coordination: A Framework for High School Science Education (Aldridge, 1996), which lists content standards and implementation guidelines for reforming science education.

Science Test Performance in the United States and Other Nations

Third International Mathematics and Science Study

During the 1990s, the Third International Mathematics and Science Study (TIMSS) was conducted. The test results for elementary, middle, and senior high school students were reported, comparing the United States with 41 countries. With regard to science performance of eighth-grade students, the United States falls approximately in the middle when assessed for their general knowledge about science. Schmidt (1997) summarized these results as follows:

- The United States is in the middle regarding test performance in earth and life sciences when compared to other countries, and significantly lower in physics.
- The United States does not do as well in mathematics as it does in science.
- Math and science curricula are grouped differently in different countries.
- Achievement scores reflect the curriculum. Students did better in countries where they were tested on ideas taught in science.
- The United States has no single vision for math and science, which appears to be problematic in a country with approximately 15,000 school districts.
- In the United States, there is grand dialog regarding education, but the results never seem to improve.
- More topics are taught in the United States in a given school year than in many other countries. For example, in Germany and Japan, 10 topics may be covered versus 65 in the United States.
- Most reform ideas merely add to the curriculum rather than replace or reduce subject matter content.
- Teachers seem to do what they believe they are being asked to do, which is to teach all of the topics.
- U.S. textbooks have 700 to 800 pages, while those in other countries might have 150 to 200 pages.
- U.S. textbooks are too long and are not focused on fundamental principles.
- The U.S. educational system needs a set of national standards to specify fundamental principles that all students should learn.

The science test performance of U.S. students at the end of high school is more toward the bottom quartile than in the middle with respect to other countries. Further, high school science textbooks are much thicker in our public schools than in other countries. Most high school students in the United States study only one of the major science fields (biology, chemistry, and physics) each year, while in many other countries students study each of the major scientific fields during the ninth, tenth, eleventh, and twelfth grades. Schmidt's (1997) comment below captures well the type of curricula most often observed in school across the nation.

> *"U.S. education in math and science is a mile wide and an inch deep. It never gets off the surface level of knowledge."*
>
> —*Schmidt (1997)*

Program for International Student Assessment (PISA)

At the turn of the twenty-first century, the Organization for Economic Co-Operation and Development (2007) undertook the Program for International Student Assessment (PISA) by initiating a series of worldwide surveys of school learning in mathematics, reading, and science. The triennial surveys (2000, 2003, and 2006) sought to determine the attitudes, knowledge, and skills of 15-year-old students in 57 countries; a large cooperative effort, producing useful comparisons of educational performance across countries and cultures. The assessment in science focused on students' attitudes toward science, identifying scientific issues, explaining phenomena scientifically, using science evidence, and demonstrating knowledge of science and knowledge about science.

The 2006 PISA report (OECD, 2007) for science shows similar findings to the TIMSS report conducted over a decade earlier. The performance of 15-year-old students in the United States was approximately in the middle of the 57 countries taking part in the study in 2006 with a mean score of 489 (Table 2.2). Finland was at the top with a student mean score of 563. Countries in which students also performed well were Canada, Japan, Australia, Korea, Germany, and the United Kingdom. In many of the countries males and females showed no difference in average score. However, socio-economic differences accounted for a significant proportion of school performance in some countries, such as in the United States, Germany, and Argentina.

With all the talk about crisis, reform, standards, and test scores, one might get the impression that science education is in a sad state with little hope for change. However, in the 1990s, the United States led the world in scientific and technological advancement. Its economy was exceptional. Consequently, the prosperity of the country, up until now, has not been tied exclusively to the scientific literacy of the general public nor to the number of scientists and engineers that it produces. However, this could change in the future. Much of the prosperity in the communication and technology industry has resulted

TABLE 2.2 Mean Science Score Performance for 15-Year-Old Students in 57 Countries

Country	Mean	Country	Mean
Finland	563	Slovak Republic	488
Hong Kong-China	542	Spain	488
Canada	534	Lithuania	488
Chinese Taipei	532	Norway	487
Estonia	531	Luxembourg	486
Japan	531	Russian Federation	479
New Zealand	530	Italy	475
Australia	527	Portugal	474
Netherlands	525	Greece	473
Liechtenstein	522	Israel	454
Korea	522	Chile	438
Slovenia	519	Serbia	436
Germany	516	Bulgaria	434
United Kingdom	515	Uruguay	428
Czech Republic	513	Turkey	424
Switzerland	512	Jordan	422
Macro-China	511	Thailand	421
Austria	511	Romania	418
Belgium	510	Montenegro	412
Ireland	508	Mexico	410
Hungary	504	Indonesia	393
Sweden	503	Argentina	391
Poland	498	Brazil	390
Denmark	496	Columbia	388
France	495	Tunisia	386
Croatia	493	Azerbaijan	382
Iceland	491	Qatar	349
Latvia	490	Kyrgyzstan	322
United States	**489**		

from many factors such as a democratic government, a free economy, global competition, and technically skilled workers from other countries. The present reform is about helping all students to study science and technology so that they can appreciate these enterprises, and to apply the knowledge and skills in their everyday lives as well as in the workplace.

National Science Teachers Association Standards for Science Teacher Preparation

As we have discussed previously, the American public education system expects a great deal from students, who are all expected to exhibit many different learning outcomes in each school year. No doubt these goals present a big challenge to educators as well as to students. However, many professional organizations have responded by developing national frameworks and standards to guide school science programs and science teacher preparation. The National Science Teachers Association (NSTA) in conjunction with the National Council for Accreditation of Teacher Education (NCATE) has prepared 10 standards to guide in the preparation of science teachers. Figure 2.1 presents brief descriptions of each standard. The standards pertaining to the nature of science, inquiry, issues, curriculum, science in the community, assessment, and safety and welfare are part of the learning outcomes in many of the chapters in this textbook to assist those desiring to achieve national recognition and accreditation or to improve their science teacher preparation program.

FIGURE 2.1 *Standards for Science Teacher Preparation* from the National Science Teachers Association and the National Council for Accreditation of Teacher Education.

Standards for Science Teacher Preparation

Standard 1: Content—Teachers of science understand and can articulate the knowledge and practices of contemporary science. They can interrelate and interpret important concepts, ideas, and applications in their fields of licensure; and can conduct scientific investigations.

Standard 2: Nature of Science—Teachers of science engage students effectively in studies of the studies of the history, philosophy, and practice of science. They enable students to distinguish science from non-science, understand the evolution and practice of science as a human endeavor, and critically analyze assertions made in the name of science.

Standard 3: Inquiry—Teachers of science engage students both in studies of various methods of scientific inquiry and in active learning through scientific inquiry. They encourage students, individually and collaboratively, to observe, ask questions, design inquiries, and collect and intepret data in order to develop concept and relationships from empirical experiences.

Standard 4: Issues—Teachers of science recognize that informed citizens must be prepared to make decisions and take action on contemporary science-and technology-related issues of interest to the general society. They require students to conduct inquiries into the factual basis of such issues and to asses possible actions and outcomes based upon their goals and values.

Standard 5: General Skills of Teaching—Teachers of science create a community of diverse learner who construct meaning from their science experiences and possess a disposition for further exploration and learning. They use, can justify, a variety of classroom arrangements, groupings, actions, strategies, and methodologies.

Standard 6: Curriculum—Teachers of science plan and implement an active, coherent, and effective curriculum that is consistent with the goals and the recommendations of the National Science Education Standards. They begin with the end in mind and effectively incorporate contemporary practices and resources into their planning and teaching.

Standard 7: Science in the Community—Teachers of science relate their discipline to their local and regional communities, involving stakeholders and using individual, institutional, and natural resources of the community in their teaching. They actively engage students in science related studies or activities related to locally important issues.

Standard 8: Assesment—Teachers of science construct and use effective assessment strategies to determine the backgrounds and achievements of learners and facilitate their intellectual, social, and personal development. They assess students fairly and equitably, and require that students engage in ongoing self-assessment.

Standard 9: Safety and Welfare—Teachers of science organize safe and effective learning environments that promote the success of students and the welfare of all living things. They require and promote knowledge and respect for safety, and oversee the welfare of all living thinks used in the classroom or found in the field.

Standard 10: Professional Growth—Teachers of science strive continuously to grow and change, personally and professionally, to meet the diverse needs of their students, school, community, and profession. They have a desire and disposition for growth and betterment.

From www.nsta.org/org/ncate.

In conclusion, many uniformed beginning science teachers rarely consider the ideas discussed in this chapter. They are interested in getting right into the subject matter, often teaching as telling, just as they might have experienced during their education. These individuals are intent on covering a certain amount of subject matter during the class period, and carrying out all the duties required of teachers. Unfortunately, beginning science teachers often experience many setbacks and frustrations in their initial teaching because of their approach and mind-set regarding the purpose of science teaching and the nature of public schooling. We think that it is advisable for inexperienced science teachers to reflect on the history and goals of the American public school system, the recommendations from national science education reform committees, and the results of international assessments in mathematics and science. This background provides a perspective of science education and an orientation of how to think about science instruction to help all students become productive citizens in a communication/information-age society.

Assessing and Reviewing

Analysis and Synthesis

1. Go back over the first section of the chapter where the U.S. public school is discussed. What did this section reveal to you regarding: (a) the demands that are placed on schools in the United States and (b) how the educational system in the United States differs from that in other countries, such as those in western Europe and Asia?
2. Write statements that capture the recommendations of national committees regarding the purpose of science education and the implications of national assessments of student performance. Construct bulleted phrases under the following headings to capture the essence of these recommendations.
   The period between 1980 and 1990
   Project 2061
   National Science Education Standards
   Scope, Sequence, and Coordination
   Third International Mathematics and Science Study (TIMSS)
   Program for International Student Assessment (PISA)
3. Write a few paragraphs reflecting your thinking regarding the purpose of science teaching for the level at which you are planning to teach, that is, middle school or high school. In your thinking, consider not only the subject matter content, but also the diversity and ability of the students and the performance of students in the United States versus other countries.
4. Revisit the vignette at the beginning of the chapter, which describes a conversation between a beginning middle school science teacher and a veteran science teacher.
   a. Do you believe that individuals, who are new to science teaching, have a similar orientation to school science as Mr. Long?
   b. Do you believe that teachers, like Mr. Long, will change their views regarding the many purposes of science education after reading and discussing them with veteran teachers?

Practical Considerations

5. Now that you have studied the goals and purposes of science education, describe, in a few paragraphs, how you would approach a science lesson that introduces a particular unit of study.

Developmental Considerations

6. Either borrow or purchase for your professional library some of the science education reform documents, printed in paperback, that were discussed in this chapter and listed in this chapter as Resources to Examine. Read some of the chapters in these books and reflect on the recommendations for science education in the United States. Further, obtain a copy of the science standards for the state in which you intend to teach.

Resources to Examine

Benchmarks for Science Literacy. 1993. American Association for the Advancement of Science, New York: Oxford University Press. Address for ordering: 2001 Evans Road, Cary, NC 27513-2010. Phone: (800) 451-7556.

All school science departments should have a copy of this book, which contains general statements of learning for 12 areas of science education, such as the nature of science, the physical setting, the living environment, the human organism, the designed world, historical perspective, habits of mind, and more. The generalizations ar arranged into what students should know by the end of grades K–2, 3–5, 6–8, and 9–12. Science teachers can compare what they expect students to learn at the end of their course with these standards.

National Science Education Standards. 1996. National Research Council, Washington, DC: National Academy Press. Address for ordering: 2101 Constitution Ave., NW, Box 285, Washington, DC 20055. Phone: (800) 624-6242 or (202) 334-3313 (in the Washington area).

This is a 243-page booklet that gives an overview of what should take place to achieve a successful science education reform. It gives science standards for teaching, professional development, assessment, science content, and science programs. All science teachers should have a copy of this booklet for frequent reference.

NSTA Standards for Science Teacher Preparation. (2003). The standards can be accessed electronically at the National Science Teachers Association Web site. Locate the Standards for Science Teacher Preparation.

The 41-page professional standards document gives the background and evolution of the standards, and the many professional organizations involved in its development. It provides a detailed description of the 10 standards for science teacher preparation and how to apply them. This information reinforces the importance of master science content, teaching science as inquiry, focusing on science/societal issues, using a variety of teaching skills, learning about science curricula, assessing student performance, attending to the safety and welfare of students, and growing professionally.

References

Aldridge, B. G. (Ed.). (1996). *Scope, sequence, and coordination: A framework for high school science education.* Arlington, VA: National Science Teachers Association.

American Association for the Advancement of Science (AAAS). (1990). *Science for all Americans.* New York: Oxford University Press.

AAAS. (1993). *Benchmarks for science literacy.* New York: Oxford University Press.

Dow, P. B. (1991). *Schoolhouse politics: Lessons from the Sputnik era.* Cambridge, MA: Harvard University Press.

Hlebowitsh, P. S. (2001). *Foundations of American education: Purpose and promise.* Belmont, CA: Wadsworth.

National Assessment of Educational Progress (NAEP). (1998, September). Long-term trends in student science performance. *NAEPFACTS.* Washington, DC: U.S. Department of Education Office of Educational Research and Improvement.

National Commission of Excellence in Education. (1983). *A nation at risk: The imperative for education reform* (Stock No. 065-000-001772). Washington, DC: U.S. Government Printing Office.

National Research Council (NRC). (1996). *National science education standards.* Washington, DC: National Academy Press.

National Science Teachers Association. (1992). *Scope, sequence, and coordination of secondary school science. Volume 1: The content core.* Arlington, VA: Author.

National Society for the Study of Education (NSTA). (1947). *Forty-sixth yearbook, part 1.* Chicago: University of Chicago Press.

Organization for Economic Co-operation and Development. (2007). *PISA 2006: Science competencies for tomorrow's world—Executive summary.* Retrieved December 26, 2007, from, www.pisa.oecd.org

Schmidt, W. (1997, March). *A report on the third international mathematics and science study, conducted at the eighth-grade level.* Speech at the Annual Meeting of the National Association for Research in Science Teaching.

Yager, R. E. (1982). The current situation in science education. In J. R. Staver (Ed.), *1982 AETS yearbook.* Columbus, OH: ERIC Center for Science, Mathematics and Environmental Education at Ohio State University.

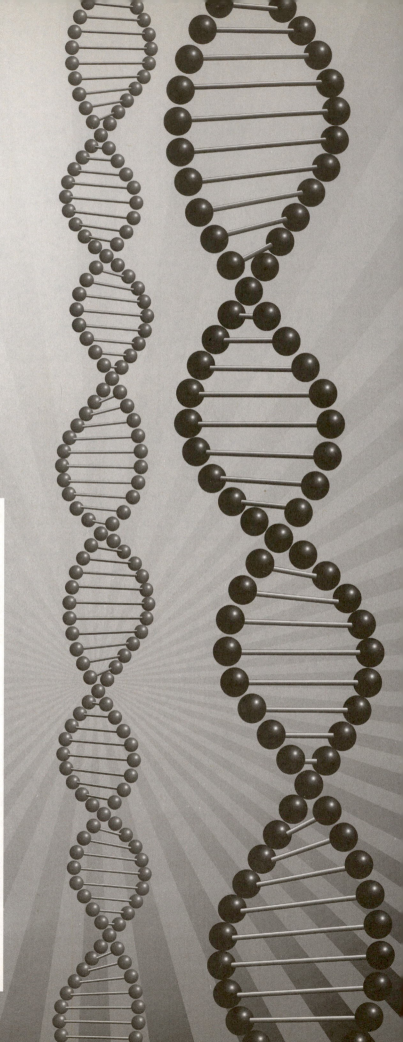

Chapter 3

Planning to Teach Science

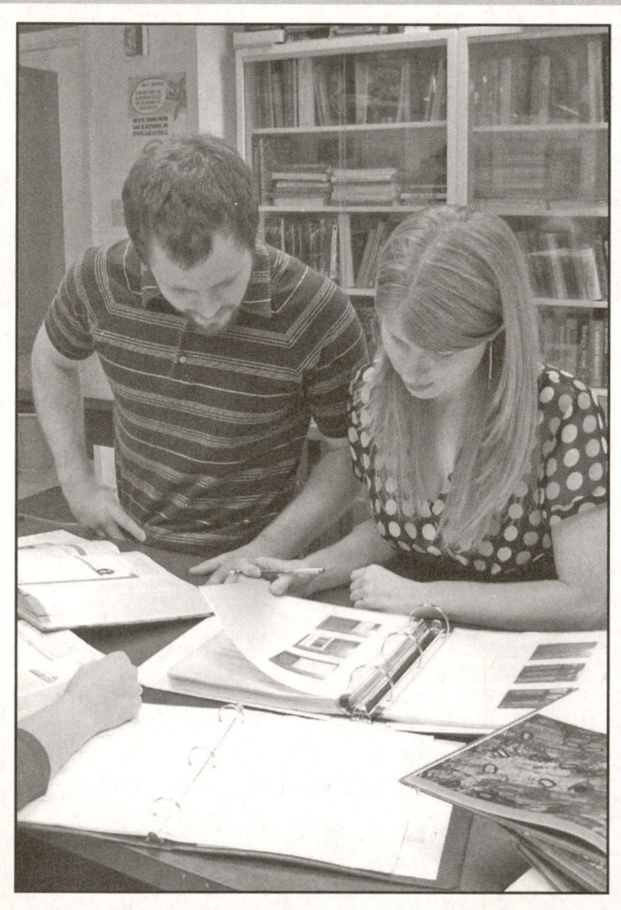

Beginning teachers must devote a great deal of time to plan instruction.

Ms. Thompson is a first-year biology teacher at a large urban high school. She has completed several education courses and has been given a temporary teaching permit with the expectation that she will complete her certification program in her first three years of teaching. Ms. Thompson is working after school with her mentor, Mr. Lee, who has been a biology teacher at Central High for 18 years. Mr. Lee has mentored many new teachers during his career and often has a student teacher in his classroom. Let's listen in on a conversation between these two teachers.

Mr. Lee: Ms. Thompson, next week we'll begin teaching about the cell, which is used as a foundation for the rest of the biology course. What are your thoughts on how to teach the cell unit?

Ms. Thompson: I would like to begin by teaching about the discovery of cells, cell structure and function, organelles, and mitosis. Then I'd move on to energy transfer, photosynthesis, glycolysis, respiration, and fermentation. If the kids know this material, they will have little difficulty with the rest of the course.

Mr. Lee: How long will you spend on this?

Ms. Thompson: I can probably cover these topics in six or seven days. There is a great deal to cover this semester and I must get through this material quickly. My friend Alice teaches biology in the district, at Perimeter High, and that is what she does.

Mr. Lee: Yes, I know Alice. She has been teaching about as long as I have, and I believe the biology teachers at Perimeter have a different approach to biology course instruction than some of us here at Central. The student population in this school is much more diverse than where Alice teaches. Can you believe that there are over 30 different languages and dialects spoken by students here at Central High? Do you have time for me to describe how I would organize the cell unit?

Ms. Thompson: Sure, I would like to learn more about teaching and to benefit from your experience. My first year has been a challenge. Anything that you can do to help me would be appreciated.

Mr. Lee: OK! Let's get started on this unit. Before we talk about lessons and activities, let's consider what you want the students to learn from the unit—you know, those understandings that they won't forget.

Ms. Thompson: I'm confused. I just told you what I plan to cover: discovery of cells, cell structure and function, mitosis, and so on. But I guess you're asking about something different.

Mr. Lee: Yes, I am. Teachers here at Central have decided to focus our cell unit on the similarities and differences between prokaryotic and eukaryotic cells, diversity and variation within eukaryotic cells, and about cell specialization. We also want students to understand how the cell membrane functions. There is more to it than this, but my point is that we begin our planning by thinking about what we want the student to know and be able to do. We use a conceptual framework approach to the study of biology, which begins with the cell and reflects learning outcomes similar to those presented in Benchmarks for Science Literacy (1993), which is a national science education standards document.

Ms. Thompson: Your unit certainly takes a different approach and includes fewer topics than what I was thinking about. Now I'm beginning to understand your point about considering what students should learn from the unit rather that what topics to cover. But, what else should I be considering as I plan for this unit?

Mr. Lee: Well, one part of unit planning is to consider where a unit fits within a course. For instance, we'll want to talk about how our cell unit fits into our high school biology course and how it contributes to students' overall learning in biology. The other part of unit planning involves refining the student learning goals, like the ones I mentioned, in order to articulate the essential understandings that students should take away from the unit. Then, before designing lessons that address these understandings, we'll also need to consider the kinds of assessments that will provide evidence of student learning.

Ms. Thompson: Wow! I never really thought about planning from a unit planning perspective. It seems like a lot of work.

Mr. Lee: When carried out alone, unit planning can be a daunting task. Fortunately, there are many resources to help teachers with this type of planning. Science teachers in our state, like most others across the county, have developed frameworks for middle school and high school science courses. These frameworks are built around both state and national standards. They illustrate many ways that courses can be organized into units and the understandings that students should gain from the units. Many frameworks also include unit assessment tasks as well as suggested lessons and laboratory activities. If you'd like, I can show you the biology course framework tomorrow and point out how teachers here at Central have used it to design lessons that meet the needs of our students, while also addressing state and national standards.

Ms. Thompson: That sounds great! I've heard stories of teachers who were just given a book and told to start teaching. I'm glad to know about these frameworks, and I appreciate your willingness to help me learn how I can use the biology framework to guide my unit planning. I feel a lot better knowing that it seems possible to design units and lessons that are based on the standards and that meet the needs of our students. See you tomorrow after school.

Mr. Lee waved goodbye to Ms. Thompson as she left the room. He sat quietly, reflecting on how times have changed since he began teaching. Back then, there were no standards and no statewide science testing. The student population at his first school was very homogeneous compared with the students he teaches today. The focus of science teacher planning was more about topic coverage and classroom instruction than student learning.

AIMS OF THE CHAPTER

Use the questions that follow to guide your thinking and learning about planning to teach science:

- Why is planning so important?
- What are the major aspects of planning to consider when making decisions about a course, a unit, and a lesson?
- What are the basic components of a science unit plan?
- How can you begin to plan a science unit that includes lessons that will enable middle school and secondary school students to build enduring science understandings?

Planning is one of the most important teaching functions. This activity provides a "game plan" of what to teach and how to teach. The process of thinking through a science course, its units, and the lessons nested within each unit gives you opportunities to sequence instructional events that hold the potential to initiate and sustain learning. Architects use blueprints, conductors follow music scores, and teachers use unit and lesson plans. All teachers plan. However, some plans are more carefully and thoroughly conceived than others.

Those who plan well will likely be more effective in helping students to learn. These teachers will be in a better position to specify learning outcomes that all or most students can achieve. They will be prepared to manage a learning environment where students are expected to be more responsible for their own learning. Teachers who plan well can teach for student understanding rather than for rote memorization.

The most critical ingredient in planning is *taking time to plan*. Without taking the time to individually or collaboratively think about a unit or lesson, it is unlikely that a teacher can orchestrate a coherent set of experiences that will engage most students in learning. In our busy, hectic society many beginning as well as experienced teachers are overwhelmed by the multitude of after-school responsibilities that demand their time. Some teachers have a second job, church activities, young children to care for, coaching duties, cheerleading practice, and so on, all of which compete with planning for their time.

Also, there are in-school tasks that add to a teacher's instructional planning responsibilities and those that steal precious planning time. Special provisions must be *provided* and *documented* to show that each special education student is being accommodated by plans that will aid his or her learning. This additional planning also is required for English as Second Language (ESL) students. Moreover, the amount of testing and student progress reporting has become burdensome. The list of noninstructional tasks that face teachers is large and growing. For example, teachers may need to use their designated planning time to meet with parents, write reports, or cover the classes of sick colleagues. Regardless of the circumstances that make planning a challenge, we cannot overemphasize the importance of being prepared when the bell rings to begin class.

An experienced teacher can play an important role in providing a beginning teacher with emotional support and ideas for successful planning and teaching. Veteran teachers have developed ideas about course organization and unit and lesson sequencing, with an eye toward achieving student learning outcomes that reflect state and national standards. To this end, they have collected and built unit and lesson plans that incorporate laboratory exercises, simulations, demonstrations, CDs, PowerPoint presentations, videos, textbooks, Web sites, reviews, tests, and so on. It is important for an individual who is new to science teaching to access and incorporate such curriculum resources as these into his or her planning. It is not unusual for a new or even an experienced science teacher to feel isolated (Guarino & Watterson, 2002). Therefore, it is necessary for new teachers to reach out to those who have been teaching for many years and ask for their assistance with planning.

The remaining sections of this chapter will help you think about some fundamental aspects of science unit and lesson planning. More details about assessment, instructional practices, how students learn, and other considerations of unit and lesson planning will be taken up in subsequent chapters of this textbook. As you explore the fundamentals of planning in this chapter, it is important that you keep student learning in the forefront of your thinking. Planning for effective teaching is what enables student learning. Consider the following questions to guide your thinking about planning:

- Whom are you planning to teach?
- What are you planning to teach?
- How are you planning to teach science?
- How are you planning to manage the science learning environment?
- How are you planning to assess student learning?

Whom Are You Planning to Teach?

It has been said that *students* are more important than *science* in the science classroom. The reasoning behind this statement is that without student engagement and cooperation, there can be no science teaching and learning. Yes, it is the students that make teaching the challenging and enjoyable profession that it is. Therefore, you must think twice, three times, or more about the students you teach. How will these young and impressionable people receive you as a teacher as well as the instruction you have planned? With perhaps over 100 students a day in your classes you can be certain that there will be many individuals you will not reach unless you plan carefully.

You must continually remind yourself that diversity characterizes today's U.S. school population, and you must address this diversity in your planning, teaching, management, and assessment. You must think ahead and predict how students will respond to your instruction, especially those who are less than proficient in speaking, reading, writing, mathematics, and study skills. Also, how will you deal with boys and girls who do not participate in instruction because they have little interest in formal schooling or come to school hungry? Will there be students in your classes who are unable to hear you speak or unable to read what you are writing on the board or projecting on a screen? How will you react to students who take pleasure in being disruptive and those who are poorly mannered?

Think about the realities of the classroom and reflect on the following questions as they relate to your science instructional planning:

Language Skills

- How will you accommodate the learning needs of students who have recently arrived in the United States from Mexico, Brazil, Russia, Romania, China, or Korea, for instance, who are unable to easily communicate in English?
- How will you modify your instruction for students who have been in the U.S. school system for many years, yet they are unable to read at grade level and unable to write a coherent paragraph?
- How will you plan science learning experiences that require the use of simple mathematical formulas for students who have not mastered basic algebra?

Classroom Behavior

- What classroom management challenges should you anticipate when instructing many students each day?
- How will you respond to students who thrive on being disruptive?
- How will you help students take responsibility for their own learning?

Physical and Learning Challenges

- How will you modify your teaching plans for students who have difficulty seeing the board or projection screen?
- How will you accommodate students with hearing impairments or mobility challenges?
- What must you do to enable a dyslexic or attention-deficit student to be successful in your class?

Cultural diversity and student attributes will be discussed in more detail in later chapters. Nevertheless, these matters should be of paramount consideration in your planning to teach science.

What Are You Planning to Teach?

"As a result of your teaching, what should students know and be able to do?"

Only your consideration of the students who will populate your classes is more central to the planning process than this question. When you have decided what

Understanding the relationships among concepts is critical to a teacher's planning of science units and lessons.

students should know and be able to do as a result of your teaching, you are well on your way to effective planning. But, your answer to this question is highly dependent on your views of the purpose of general education in the United States. If you think the purpose is to train all students to become scientists or engineers, then you will probably aim to teach a high-powered science course, covering large amounts of subject matter and requiring students to understand the content as a scientist or engineer might, down to the smallest details. If you think the purpose is to educate all students so that they understand certain fundamental science concepts and develop an understanding of the scientific enterprise, then your planning will involve the careful selection of subject matter and skills for students to master.

The vignettes that open the preceding chapters provide examples of the thoughts and beliefs of inexperienced science teachers whose first instinct urged them to cover a large number of abstract science concepts that were presented to them in college science courses or that are found in science textbooks. If that is your orientation, stop and think! The chances are great that the students in the classes you will be assigned to teach will have a wide range of abilities. Some common statements from beginning science teachers regarding the abilities of their students include:

- "What did they teach these kids in science in the earlier grades? They cannot read and interpret graphs."
- "I overestimated the ability of these students. I thought they could use fractions."
- "Most of my students failed the first test, and I thought I made it so easy."
- "My students are not able to write a coherent paragraph."

Recall the opening vignette in Chapter 1 in which Mr. Clay began the unit on mechanics by trying to cover Newton's three laws of motion in one day. When this approach did not work well, the mentor teacher suggested that Mr. Clay begin at a more concrete level, focusing on only Newton's first law and inertia and using demonstrations that the students can observe firsthand. In the opening vignette in Chapter 2, Mr. Long, the aerospace engineer, was eager to jump into some heavy-duty problem solving with his sixth-grade students until his mentor teacher came to the rescue. Ms. Roberts awakened Mr. Long to the type of students in their middle school and the purpose of the U.S. educational system. Both of these snapshots of teaching, along with the one involving Ms. Thompson at the beginning of this chapter, reveal that the planning efforts of beginning teachers tend to be guided by past science learning experiences rather than considerations of the adolescent learners that populate their classes. They also reveal uninformed notions of what counts as science learning. The focus of the vignettes' lessons and conversations suggest the beginning teachers view science learning as students memorizing facts and reproducing information rather than as students being able to understand, organize, and retrieve science concepts in a meaningful way and to use their science understandings to solve problems in novel situations (Abell & Volkmann, 2006).

While we do not wish to paint a bleak picture of students and teaching situations in the middle and secondary schools, we wish to encourage you to think about the primary purpose of science education at this level of schooling and its bearing on instructional planning. It is our hope that people going into science teaching will seriously consider the fundamental purpose of science education in U.S. schools and its relationship to their planning efforts. Even with students who are enrolled in advanced classes or attending private schools, you will likely find those who need help to develop understandings and skills considered necessary for further learning. Please keep in mind, *you are teaching science for all Americans.*

Study Figure 3.1 to orient your thinking regarding what an uninformed, beginning science teacher might choose as appropriate learning outcomes for an instructional unit versus a more informed and experienced science teacher. Note the difference in the concrete/abstract nature of the subject matter given in the examples of sound and hearing and weather at the middle school level, and photosynthesis and respiration as well as induced electromagnetic force at the high school level. Further, note the differences in what counts as science learning. Are students being asked to memorize and reproduce facts or to organize, retrieve, understand, and apply their understandings in new contexts?

Those who are preparing to become science teachers must come to view teaching in a different way from what they likely experienced over many years of schooling (Lederman & Gess-Newsome, 1999). They must develop *pedagogical content knowledge* and apply it in their teaching. Pedagogical content knowledge is a special amalgam

FIGURE 3.1 Comparison of learning outcomes that an uninformed, beginning science teacher might select for a unit versus a more informed, experienced science teacher.

Uninformed, Beginning Teacher	Unit Topic	Informed, Experienced Teacher
• Label the structures of the outer, middle, and inner ear. • List the steps through which a mechanical disturbance is changed into chemical and electrical impulses in the auditory cortex of the brain.	Middle School Integrated Science—Sound and Hearing	• Describe the similarities and differences between the structures of the human ear and a simple condenser microphone. • Demonstrate and explain how a blind or blindfolded person might locate the origin of a nearby sound.
• Describe the kinds of data gathered from a hygrometer, barometer, and anemometer. • Define relative humidity.	Middle School Earth Science—Weather	• Collect weather data and use the data to forecast the weather. • Develop a human "comfort index" that can be used to inform people of the influence of temperature and humidity on personal comfort.
• Write chemical formulas for photosynthesis and respiration. • Outline the steps in the light and dark reactions of photosynthesis.	High Science Biology—Photosynthesis and Respiration	• Explain why photosynthesis and respiration are considered complementary processes. • Describe how bacteria that live near sulfur vents and active volcanoes on the lightless ocean floor can create carbohydrates used for respiration.
• Define magnetic flux and magnetic field. • State Faraday's law.	High Science Physics—Induced Electromagnetic Forces	• Demonstrate different ways to produce an electric current using a magnetic field and other materials. Then, relate the findings to Faraday's law. • Give examples of how inducted magnetic forces are used in devices that serve society.
Uninformed, Beginning Teacher	Unit Topic	Informed, Experienced Teacher

of content and pedagogy that is uniquely the province of experienced teachers (Shulman, 1986). The pedagogical content knowledge that a teacher builds over a career goes well beyond the basics of knowing science content well enough to explain it. Pedagogical content knowledge fuses the *what* and the *how* of instruction in a way that facilitates learning.

Following is a short checklist of resources to help you make wise decisions regarding *what* to teach when planning a science lesson or unit.

_____ Course syllabus prepared by the school or district

_____ Teacher and student copies of the assigned textbook, laboratory manual, and ancillary materials

_____ Guidance from experienced teachers in the school building, district, and elsewhere

_____ Course frameworks prepared by state committees or local teacher teams

_____ Innovative curriculum materials and other related resources

_____ The Internet for all types of teaching resources and information about science

_____ *National Science Education Standards* and *Benchmarks for Scientific Literacy*

Stop and Reflect!

Working with a classmate, identify a topic that you are teaching or may teach in the future. List two or three learning outcomes associated with the topic that you believe an uninformed science teacher might use when building a unit and contrast these with what an informed and experienced teacher might use.

How Are You Planning to Teach Science?

Effective teaching is a complex set of actions that is based on thoughtful planning and sound decision making. If you observe an effective teacher in practice, you will observe certain actions that facilitate student learning. Figure 3.2 presents a menu of teaching skills, strategies, and techniques that hold great promise for engaging students in thinking and learning. These aspects of teaching are overviewed here in order to set the stage for planning science units that will be taken up later in this chapter.

Units bring coherence to a science course by the way in which they are related through the structure of the discipline. For example, a physics course might consist of units on forces, linear motion, magnetism, and electricity. Units include multiple lessons, or learning experiences, through which students build understandings. It is when engaging students in science learning experiences that teachers employ these skills, strategies, and techniques.

When organizing learning experiences for students, you will want to employ a number of *teaching skills*. There are questions to be asked during the lesson. These must be planned beforehand so that they can be used instantly to draw students into the learning process. Also to be considered are the directions and

FIGURE 3.2 Menu of skills, strategies, and techniques to engage students in science learning experiences that lead to understanding.

Employ many teaching skills
- Initiating instruction
- Giving directions
- Asking questions
- Giving feedback
- Bringing closure to instruction

Use a variety of instructional strategies
- Demonstrating
- Discussing
- Lecturing
- Reading
- Role-playing
- Simulating
- Working in the laboratory and field
- Writing

Incorporate techniques to enhance learning
- Identifying similarities and differences
- Using graphic organizers
- Note-taking
- Practicing
- Reviewing

feedback that must be given to students in order to keep them safe and productively engaged. Experienced science teachers acknowledge that their ability to employ these skills is largely dependent on their science content knowledge and an understanding of the students in their classes.

An *instructional strategy* is the manner in which an entire lesson or a major part of it is approached. Experienced teachers tend to use multiple teaching strategies to gain students' attention and to involve them in learning. Using two or more strategies during a class period is much more effective than using only one (Rosenshine, 2002). They often divide the class period into two or more segments, and move fluidly from one strategy to another and to yet another to facilitate learning related to a particular topic.

Educational researchers have learned that it requires more than teaching skills and instructional strategies to facilitate student learning. They have assisted the profession greatly by identifying *techniques* that have shown to increase student achievement (Marzano, Pickering, & Pollock, 2001). For example, note-taking, identifying similarities and differences, using graphic organizers, reviewing, and practicing are among some of the most powerful techniques to enhance learning in any course. We urge that you make these techniques part of your teaching repertoire by planning for their inclusion in your lessons.

Sections in several subsequent chapters of this text are devoted to in-depth discussions of teaching skills, strategies, and techniques useful for facilitating students' science learning. As you contemplate the application of these skills, strategies, and techniques, think about how they contribute to thoughtful and effective teaching and student learning.

 How Are You Planning to Manage the Science Learning Environment?

Almost every beginning teacher experiences classroom management challenges. While thorough planning will eliminate many management concerns, it will not ensure that all students will be on task and behaving appropriately. As you plan instruction, begin to reflect on at least these aspects of classroom management:

- creating a positive learning environment
- guiding student learning
- addressing student misbehavior

Is your lesson planned so well that you will be able to interact with the students during the instruction? Effective teachers know all their students by name and call on them to answer questions and to take part in the instruction. They have high expectations and communicate this fact to the students. These teachers focus on the students they are teaching as well as the subject matter they wish students to master.

Can you visualize the classroom setting where the instruction will take place? Think about the seating arrangement, the laboratory benches or tables, the white board, projection screen, and where you will position yourself throughout the lesson. These considerations and other aspects of the instructional environment should facilitate the learning that you envision for the students. And, of course, be sure to have all the materials on hand and ready to go before the lesson is to be taught.

Later in this textbook you will find a complete chapter devoted to managing the science learning environment. However, you might give some thought to dealing with challenging students and how you would respond to students who disrupt the learning of others. Will you ignore disruptive behavior, signal students to stop, move closer to them, speak directly to the situation, send the students to the office, or take some other action? Your goal is to foster a learning environment that promotes student engagement and learning.

 How Are You Planning to Assess Student Learning?

Although assessment is often conceptualized as a test that comes at the end of a lesson or unit, assessment should occur frequently during instruction and involve more than testing. Effective assessment is a process that is both seamless and balanced. Assessment is considered *seamless* when it is difficult to determine when instruction ends and assessment begins (Abell & Volkmann, 2006). In other words, assessment is an integral part of instruction and occurs throughout a lesson and unit. Seamless assessment is facilitated by the use of a balanced approach to assessment. By *balanced*, we mean that assessment involves a mix of alternative and traditional assessment techniques. So, in addition to using tests and quizzes, a balanced assessment approach might employ such assessment techniques as performance tasks, graphic organizers, observations, and interviews along with a host of others.

When science assessment is both seamless and balanced, having students memorize facts and reproduce information is no longer considered evidence of science learning. The focus of assessment is on students being able to demonstrate that they are able to make sense of and appreciate the science they are learning and apply their understandings in real-world contexts. This shift in focus makes clear that tests and quizzes alone are insufficient means for assessing student learning and that assessment cannot be thought of solely as the culminating experience of a lesson or unit.

Assessment that is seamless and balanced serves to provide accountability information about what is happening in science classes to parents and other stakeholders and about the extent to which students have achieved understandings specified in standards. More important, assessment provides information that is useful for students to gauge their own learning progress and to teachers in order to improve their instruction.

Before studying assessment in more depth in a later chapter, we encourage you to begin to think about how to plan for assessment that is both seamless and balanced by contemplating the following questions:

- How can students' knowledge about the topic of a lesson or unit be determined before teaching begins?
- How might assessment be embedded into the lessons of a unit?
- What different kinds of assessment techniques are appropriate for assessing students' understandings at the end of a unit?
- How can assessment results be used to improve a teacher's teaching and students' learning?

Constructing Science Instructional Units

As was mentioned earlier in this chapter, the first step in planning is to decide what you want students to know and be able to do. As we think about the cell unit described by Mr. Lee, students' learning should center on the similarities and differences between prokaryotic and eukaryotic cells, diversity and variation in eukaryotic cells, and cell specialization and the functions of the cell membrane. From the perspective of someone with a strong biology background, many learning outcomes related to these topics might be identified. However, the teacher of an introductory high school biology course, or any middle school or secondary science course, needs to specify learning outcomes that are appropriate for today's students. This calls for an examination of national and state standards documents and locally developed course frameworks that are keyed to standards. National and state standards present a vision of a scientifically literate adult citizenry by outlining what students should know and be able to do at different grade levels. In many cases, state standards are interpretations of national standards, with contextual modifications based on regional and cultural differences. We encourage all beginning teachers to carefully read their state and national standards documents and to discuss their implications for course and unit planning with fellow students, classroom teachers, and course instructors. However, we recommend that beginning science teachers start their unit planning efforts in earnest by consulting state and locally developed course frameworks that are keyed to state or national standards.

Course Frameworks

A well-developed course framework provides two kinds of information critically important to unit planning. First, the framework provides an overview of the science course by outlining the units that make up the course and the topics or concepts addressed in each unit. This information may be presented as a *curriculum map* or in some other form that indicates relationships among units and course topics. Second, the framework provides a description of each unit, understandings that students should take from the unit, and the multiple standards that the unit is intended to meet. When unit development is guided by backward design strategies (Wiggins & McTighe, 2005), units also may contain essential questions to guide instruction, learning outcomes that are described in terms of key knowledge and skills that students will develop, and summative assessment tasks that provide evidence of student learning. The elements typically found in course frameworks are identified in Figure 3.3 and online sources of frameworks for middle school and secondary science courses are provided in Table 3.1.

Frameworks have not been developed to tell teachers how to teach, but to provide a structure for planning instruction to meet standards. For this reason, lessons and laboratory experiences are described in some frameworks and in others teachers are provided only with information about instructional resources available in print and online. When using frameworks to guide your instructional planning, recognize that they may include imperfections and may not present a structure that is totally compatible with your thinking about a course or the units within a course. However, frameworks are a good starting point for planning units and for contemplating how units are related to one another in a course. After examining one or more frameworks developed for middle school or secondary science courses, you will have a sense of how others have planned for standards-based instruction and how you might use their work to jumpstart your own thinking about student learning and unit planning.

Science Literacy Maps

As a science teacher, your instructional planning needs to consider not only the course or courses you will teach, but how your planning relates to the science understandings that students will construct before entering and after leaving your classroom. The science literacy maps created by the National Science Digital Library (NSDL) (http://strandmaps.nsdl.org) are an online resource developed for just this purpose. The science literacy maps are based on strand maps published in the *Atlas of*

FIGURE 3.3 Elements likely found in state and locally developed science course frameworks.

Course Description	Tells what the course is about and how the course is related to other science courses.
Course Map	Outlines the units or concepts that make up the course and the relationships among them.
Learning Outcomes	Specifies the understandings that students should construct as a result of instruction.
Unit Overview	Describes in general the focus of the unit and the standards or more specific learning outcomes that the unit is intended to address.
Essential or Guiding Queations	These bring focus to students' learning experiences.
Summative Assessment Task	Makes explicit what counts as evidence of student learning.
Knowledge, Skills, and Dispositions	Describes the building blocks of understanding and often the target of learning experiences.
Learning Experiences	Lays out the lessons in which students engage to build knowledge, skills, dispositions, and ultimately understandings.

Science Literacy, Volumes 1 and 2 (AAA Project 2061, 2001; 2007) and show relationships among concepts and how concepts build upon one another through the elementary, middle, and secondary grades. The literacy maps can be accessed by drop-down topic menu (e.g., The Living Environment, The Physical Setting, The Nature of Science) and by selecting specific concepts. Figure 3.4 shows a screen capture for the Physical Setting domain that can be traced through grade-level bands in the science literacy map accessed at the NSDL Web site. By examining literacy maps, you can consider how the learning outcomes that will be the focus of your unit are related to learning outcomes associated with students' prior and future science learning experiences. Careful study of selected literacy maps will also provide you with insight into the potential usefulness of available frameworks and how they might be used as starting points to address the learning needs of the students for whom you are planning instruction.

Learning Outcomes

Earlier in this chapter, learning outcomes likely chosen by uninformed beginning science teachers and more experienced science teachers were contrasted to highlight differences in what counts as meaningful science learning. We wish to extend this conversation here. Several authors (Bransford, Brown, & Cocking, 1999; Wiggins & McTighe, 2005) describe facets of understanding that have direct implications for science unit planning. Their message is that to truly understand a science phenomenon involves being able to use knowledge about

TABLE 3.1 Online Sources of Frameworks for Middle School and Secondary Science Courses

District of Columbia Public Schools
www.K12.dc.us/dcps/standards/science.html

Tools for planning and teaching five high school science courses and science at grades 6–8 are found here. The tools for each course include standards and sample learning activities, a course map, and unit road maps that include a rationale for connecting standards into units, and standards-based worksheets.

Georgia Standards.Org
www.georgiastandards.org/scienceframeworks.aspx

This site contains course maps for an array of middle school and secondary science courses. Learning outcomes and summative assessment tasks are presented for units within the courses.

Indiana's Academic Standards and Resources
http://indianastandardsresources.org/about.asp

Resources for middle grades and secondary science include scope and sequence for courses, classroom activities, and classroom assessments. Links to standards are shown for all activities and assessments.

Kentucky Department of Education, Curriculum Document and Resources
www.education.ky.gov/KDE/Instructional+Resources/Curriculum+Documents+and+Resources/Teaching+Tools/

Teaching tools useful for unit planning include combined curriculum documents, curriculum maps, and units of study. Combined curriculum documents for middle grades and secondary science courses describe science big ideas, as well as enduring understandings, skills and concepts, and core content assessments. Curriculum maps offer suggestions for organizing courses around units of study.

Massachusetts Science and Engineering/Technology Framework
www.doe.mass.edu/frameworks/current.html

Standards are presented with suggested learning activities for middle school and secondary science courses. Sample lesson vignettes describe learning experiences aligned with multiple standards and suggested assessment strategies. Strand maps in appendices show relationships between standards and broad topics in the biological, physical (chemistry and physics), and earth and space sciences.

North Carolina Standard Course of Study
www.ncpublicschools.org/curriculum/science/

Middle grades and secondary resources include support documents for individual science courses. The support documents for each course outline course goals, provide one or more course scheduling schemes and suggestions of weaving unifying concepts through the course, and offer a host of inquiry support activities linked to guiding questions.

Ohio Department of Education, Science
www.ode.stae.oh.us/GD/Templates/Pages/ODE/ODEPrimary.aspx?Page=2&TopicID=1697&TopicRelationID-1705

Accessible at this site are traditionally organized and integrated high school science program models and sample scope and sequence for model courses along with resources for model implementation. Also, accessible through Ohio's Instructional Management System are standards-based unit and lesson plans for middle grades and high school courses.

Virginia Department of Education Science Curriculum Framework
www.doe.virginia.gov/VDOE/Instruction/Science/sciCF.html

Frameworks are presented for middle school and high school science courses. The framework for each course shows how standards are linked to essential understandings as well as knowledge and skills.

the phenomenon and related skills to solve problems in context, to answer *how* and *why* questions about the phenomenon, and to provide convincing explanations for answers about the phenomenon. In addition, understanding in science involves becoming aware of personal dispositions—attitudes, beliefs, and values—that can facilitate and impede science understanding and of dispositions associated with the scientific enterprise. Important for science unit planning, these understandings are reflected in goals for science learning outlined in the *National Science Education Standards* (National Research Council, 1996):

- science content
- science inquiry and inquiry skills
- history and nature of science
- issues of science, technology, and society

Maneuvering from this broad range of understandings and goals for science learning to units and lesson plans is a challenging task for experienced teachers, let

FIGURE 3.4 Screen capture showing a portion of the science literacy map for the Physical Setting domain accessed at the National Science Digital Library Web site.

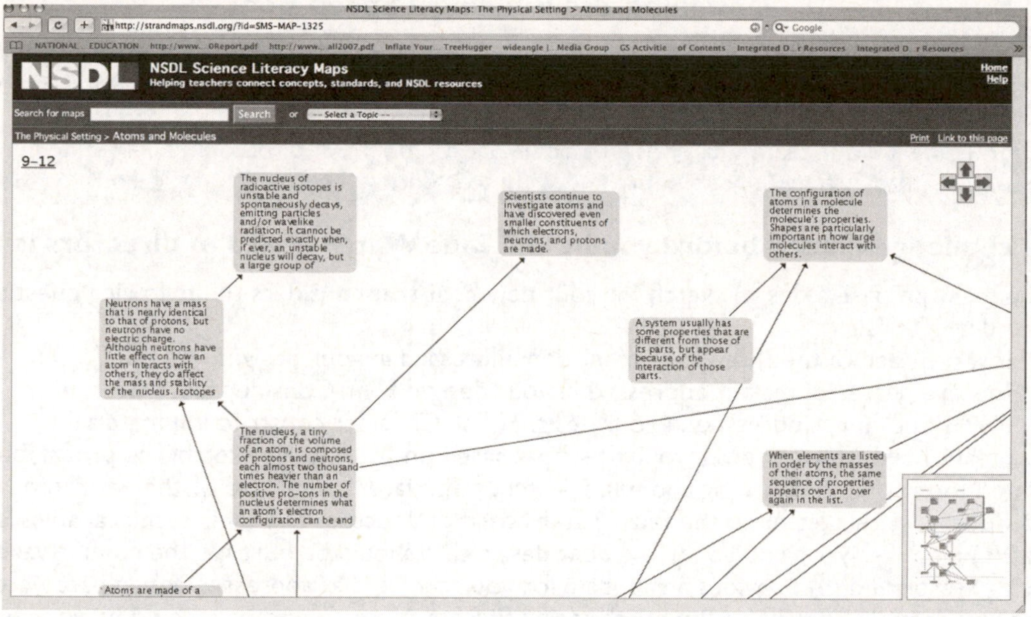

Reprinted with permission of the National Science Digital Library (NSDL. org).

alone someone who is new to science teaching. For this reason, we urge you to use state and locally developed frameworks to guide your quest for appropriate learning outcomes for the students you will teach.

In frameworks, you will find statements of understandings that are positioned as the centerpiece of units as well as "essential" or "driving" questions that help bring focus to students' learning experiences. These statements and questions reflect the efforts of many competent and well-intentioned educators to interpret standards in terms of what they mean for students becoming scientifically literate adults. Here are examples of these understandings and questions from two state frameworks:

> *Understanding:* All organisms transfer matter and convert energy from one form to another. Both matter and energy are necessary to build and maintain structures within the organism. *Question:* How is matter transferred and energy transferred/transformed in living systems? (Delaware Life Processes, Grade Level Expectations Grades 9–12, www.doe.k12.de.us/files/pdf/science_Standard6.pdf)

> *Understanding:* Because Earth turns daily on an axis that is tilted relative to the plane of Earth's yearly orbit around the Sun, sunlight falls more intensely on different parts of the Earth during the year. The difference in heating of Earth's surface produces seasons and weather patterns. *Question*: How does the tilt of Earth affect the seasons and Earth's climate? (Georgia's Grade 6–8 Earth Science, www.georgiastandards.org/scienceframework.aspx)

Using statements and questions like these, framework developers have selected or built summative assessment tasks to use in providing evidence of student understanding and to articulate the knowledge and skills, and sometimes the dispositions, that enable students to achieve success on the assessment tasks. These statements of knowledge, skills, and dispositions also offer suggestions for student learning experiences that address not only science content, but also inquiry; the history and nature of science; and issues of science, technology, and society. These statements also may bring into focus unifying concepts of science, such as systems, order, and organization; evidence, models, and explanation; constancy, change, and measurement; and evolution and equilibrium (NRC, 1996).

Evidence of Learning

Once you have decided what students should know and be able to do as a result of your unit, you must decide how students will demonstrate their understandings. In other words, what counts as evidence of science learning? Since science units tend to have multiple learning outcomes that address content knowledge, skills, and occasionally learner dispositions, the preferred summative assessment of student learning for science units is a performance task rather than a paper-and-pencil test or exam. Through the performance task, the teacher makes explicit what counts as evidence of learning for the unit and how students will demonstrate their learning.

Presented in Figure 3.5 is a performance task for a physical science unit on force and motion. Accompanying the task is a rubric that is given to students at the time

FIGURE 3.5 Performance task for a physical science unit on force and motion and accompanying rubric.

Designing and Building a Speed Boat

You are a member of the Blue Water powerboat racing team. Your sponsor, Blue Water Manufacturing, the world's leading marketer of bottled water, is threatening to withdraw its sponsorship because your team did not win a race during last year's competition season. To maintain your team's sponsorship your team must design a boat that the board of directors and their technical advisors believe can successfully compete and win races during the up-coming season.

The challenge placed before you by the Blue Water board of directors is to:

1. As a team, prepare a design sketch for your new boat that considers the following questions regarding its design:
   - How are each of the three laws of motion addressed in your design?
   - How are phases of matter addressed in your design? Hint: Consider fuel types.
   - How is buoyancy addressed in your design? Hint: Consider construction materials.
2. As a team, build a prototype of your new boat based on your design sketch. The prototype can be no more than 1 meter long and must present no hazards to humans or the environment.
3. Individually, write a letter to the Blue Water board of directors and their technical advisors that (a) identifies your choice for the boat design that should be built for the coming year's racing season and (b) provides a rationale for your choice that addresses design parameters that you deem important to the boat's racing success. Note: Your choice could be your team's boat design or the design of another team.

Task Rubric

Criteria	Does Not Meet Expectations	Meets Expectations	Exceeds Expectations
Design sketch	Design sketch includes inaccuracies about laws of motion, phases of matter, and/or buoyancy.	Design sketch accurately portrays the laws of motion, phases of matter, and buoyancy.	Design sketch accurately portrays the laws of motion, phases of matter, and buoyancy AND considers at least one other design feature.
Prototype	The prototype does not match the parameters specified in the design sketch.	The prototype matches the parameters specified in the design sketch.	The prototype exceeds the parameters specified in the design sketch.
Letter	The choice of boat design is not explained in terms of laws of motion, phases of matter, and buoyancy.	The choice of boat design is explained in terms of laws of motion, phases of matter, and buoyancy.	The choice of boat design is explained in terms of laws of motion, phases of matter, and buoyancy AND at least one other design feature.

Based on a description of a performance task presented at the Georgia Performance Standards Framework for Science—Physical Science (High School), www.georgiastandards.org/scienceframeworks.aspx

the task is introduced. The rubric serves to tell students what is expected of them and can be used by a teacher to scaffold students' learning as well as to assess their mastery of the unit's learning outcomes.

In contrast to traditional unit planning practices, where what counts as evidence of student learning is typically considered only after the unit is taught, we encourage you to consider selecting or developing a performance task for use as the summative assessment for your unit early in the planning process. Doing this will ensure that the performance task does in fact provide evidence of student learning that is aligned with your intended learning outcomes for the unit; it will also allow you to modify the assessment task if the intended learning outcomes are adjusted as the unit is taught.

Learning Experiences

The most prominent activity of unit planning has tended to be the development of lesson plans. However, in this discussion of unit planning, we choose to emphasize the selection and adaptation of learning experiences in which students will engage to develop understandings over the development of discrete lesson plans. The distinction that we make between learning experience and the traditional lesson plan is, we believe, an important one for beginning teachers to understand. Historically, the focus of lesson plans has been on what teachers do, rather than on what students do and what they learn. As a result, lesson plans have become, for too many beginning teachers, inflexible scripts to follow. When a unit consists of a strung-together series of lesson plans, each intended to represent a day's worth of instruction, the overarching learning goals for the unit tend to be forgotten and replaced with discrete learning aims.

Our intent here is to encourage you to think differently about lesson planning. Make the focus of your lesson planning efforts student learning experiences that are tied to the learning outcomes of your unit. Consider planning for learning experiences that span multiple class periods. Plan with an eye toward learning experiences that go beyond the recall of facts and information, that actually scaffold students' development of understandings needed to analyze, argue about, and apply science content. It is these kinds of learning experiences that will enable students to achieve the learning outcomes specified for your unit as reflected in your summative assessment task.

As you contemplate the planning of lessons to support student learning, please be mindful of the fact that lessons, because of their focus and level of student interactivity, serve different purposes within the context of a science unit. According to Abell and Volkmann (2006), lessons can *engage* students, that is, pique their interest in the topic of the unit. They can allow students to *explore* science concepts, the relationships among concepts, and ideas about science and the work of scientists that are central to the unit. Lessons can also help students *explain* their developing science understandings and to *elaborate* on their understandings by applying what they are learning to contexts outside of school. Finally, lessons can enable students to *evaluate* their own learning and, in doing so, make modifications to enhance their understandings. It is possible that one lesson can serve multiple purposes. For example, a laboratory lesson that allows middle school students to explore weather vane design and operation could also be used to engage them in a unit on weather and climate.

There is no one accepted format for constructing a lesson plan. The sequence, number of elements, and amount of detail in a lesson plan vary considerably. Besides lesson plans, some school systems require teachers to keep daily plan books. A daily plan book is sometimes confused with a lesson plan, which it is not. The plan book merely presents a sketch of what will occur during each class period, and provides the minimum detail and number of elements. A daily plan book gives the teacher, administrators, or a substitute teacher an idea of the learning experiences that the teacher has planned for the week. Figure 3.6 is an example of a daily plan book for five class sessions of a unit on chemical periodicity. The main reason for beginning teachers to construct lesson plans over merely outlining their teaching intentions in a daily plan book is to engage in in-depth thinking about how learning experiences can help students achieve the outcomes specified for the unit. When this in-depth thinking is made explicit through written lesson plans, veteran teachers and college instructors are better able to provide assistance that will enable you to address many questions about the lesson and this most important one: How does the learning experience of the lesson prepare students to achieve success on the unit's culminating assessment? If the culminating assessment was developed to reflect the unit's standards-based learning outcomes, then every lesson planned with this question in mind should engage students in learning experiences that address the knowledge, skills, and dispositions required for success on the culminating assessment task for the unit.

Resources from which to select and build lessons for inclusion in science units abound. Complete science lesson plans and lesson ideas are presented in textbooks, laboratory manuals, activity books, trade books, and science teacher journals. Moreover, the Internet contains thousands of Web sites where science lesson plans are available, and the number of these sites continues to grow daily. By typing "science lesson plans" into any Internet search engine, you will likely retrieve more sites containing science lesson plans than you could examine in weeks. Listed in Table 3.2 are a few sources that we recommend for initiating your search for science lesson plans and lesson idea.

 Making Your Teaching Ideas Explicit

As a beginning teacher, you will want to seek guidance when planning units. No one expects you to be able to plan and teach like a veteran teacher. Making your thinking explicit by preparing written unit plans, starting with the identification of standards-based learning outcomes and culminating assessments and ending with descriptions of student learning experiences, will enable college instructors and experienced teachers to understand what you are attempting to accomplish with your units and to help you improve them and enhance your teaching.

Consistent with the National Science Teachers Association (NSTA) *Standards for Science Teacher Preparation,* we encourage you to construct unit plans to teach science concepts and principles associated with a specific science discipline and the unifying concepts of science that help distinguish science from other ways of knowing. In addition, we encourage you to incorporate into your units other elements that are considered fundamental to helping young people develop the understandings needed to be

FIGURE 3.6 Daily plan book for one week of instruction.

Monday

Guiding Question: How is the periodic table organized?

Procedures: Students read and discuss Section 14.1 "Classification of the Elements." Students locate groups, periods, representative elements and transition elements.

Instructional Materials: Addison-Wesley Chemistry: Chapter 14, pp. 390–394. PowerPoint of Periodic Table.

Assessment: Have students annotate a paper copy of the Periodic Table to show how elements vary from one side of the table to the other and from top of bottom.

Tuesday

Guiding Question: How can properties of halide ions be used to predict trends?

Procedures: Students read and complete lab, "Chemical Properties of the Halides." Students analyze data and predict trends in reactivity of halide ions.

Instructional Materials: Addison-Wesley Chemistry: Chapter 14, p. 397. Chemicals shown in Figure A on p. 397 along with HNO_3 and NaOCl.

Assessment: Have students look up reduction potential values of I_2, Br_2, Cl_2, and F_2 in Section 23.2 of Addison-Wesley Chemistry and explain the reduction potential values.

Wednesday/Thursday

Guiding Question: What are the trends for atomic radii and ionization energy and how are they related?

Procedures: Students define and discuss atomic radii and ionization energy. Teams complete lab on graphing periodic trends and explore trends in electronegativity.

Instructional Materials: Teacher developed lab and lab procedure sheet, graphic paper, pencils, and rulers.

Assessment: Have students write responses to the following questions: What is responsible for the trend in atomic radii down a group and across a period? Why is group 18 (Nobel Gases) not included in your graph?

Friday

Guiding Question: How can the charge on an ion be inferred from the periodic table?

Procedures: Students construct a table of ionic charges of representative elements by group.

Instructional Materials: PowerPoint of Periodic Table.

Assessment: Have students name the ionic charge of an element when given its group.

Based on information from *Addison-Wesley Chemistry*, by A. C. Wilbraham, D. D. Stanley, M. S. Matta, and E. L. Waterman, 2002, Needham, MA: Prentice Hall.

scientifically literate citizens of the twenty-first century. In Figure 3.7, we identify these desirable unit elements, the NSTA *Standards* to which they correspond, and how they might be evident in your planning and teaching. The development of a unit with these elements is required in order for you to meet the expectations for science teacher candidates set forth in the NSTA *Standards*.

By now, you should recognize that planning to teach science requires time and effort. But, without adequate planning, your teaching effectiveness will suffer, as will your ego. The more attention you give to planning, the easier it will become and the better you will teach.

TABLE 3.2 Internet Sources for Science Lesson Plans and Lesson Ideas

American Association of Physics Teachers
www.aapt.org
Lesson plans that feature laboratory experiences for teaching a variety of physical science and physics concepts can be accessed through this site.

American Chemical Society
www.acs.org
Lesson plans for a variety of chemistry lesson are available along with information about *Chem Matters*, the ACS magazine for high school students.

National Aeronautics and Space Administration
www.nasa.gove
Type "science lesson plans" or a specific topic into the site's search engine to find hundreds of lesson plans. Also check out the many images and video clips available.

National Association of Biology Teachers
www.nabt.org
Lesson ideas for middle school life science and high school biology can be found by clicking on "Resource Links."

National Oceanic and Atmospheric Association
www.noaa.org
The onsite search engine provides access to hundreds of lesson plans about topics ranging from ocean currents and tides to non-source point pollution. Some lessons emphasize the use of online data resources.

National Science Digital Library
www.nsdl.org
Use the site search engine to find lesson idea or click on "K–12 Teachers" to access science teaching resources.

National Science Teachers Association
www.nsta.org
Information about journals for middle school and high school science full of lesson plan ideas are available. The most recent issues of the journals can be accessed online.

Public Broadcast System
www.pbs.org
Type "science lesson" into the site search engine to find lesson plans on a wide range of science topics, many of which are associated with PBS broadcasts.

FIGURE 3.7 Unit plan considerations as recommended by the National Science Teachers Association *Standards for Science Teacher Preparation.*

1 Science concepts and principles–	A science unit must address the concepts and principles central to a section of a middle school or secondary science course. These concepts and principles must reflect contemporary understandings and practices of the discipline on which the course is based.
2 Unifying concepts of science–	A science unit must help students develop understandings about concepts that transcend and unify the science disciplines. One or more of the following unifying concepts should be highlighted in the learning experiences of a unit: • systems, order, and organization • evidence, models, and explanation • constancy, change, and measurement • evolution and equilibrium • relationship of form, function, and behavior
3 Technology in science–	A science unit must help student recognize the role that technological advancements have played in scientific progress and challenges, while at the same time understanding the distinctions between science and technology.
4 History and nature of science–	A unit must engage students in the study of the history of scicnce and the nature of the scientific enterprise. Coming to view science as more than a body of facts is critical to the science education of all students.
5 Inquiry–	There are many goals for inquiry teaching within a science unit. The goals may include students learning about the scientific enterprise, learning to inquire, learning science concepts and principle, learning about science as argumentation, and learning about the culture of science. A science unit must address one or more of these goals while taking into account factors likely to influence the success of inquiry teaching.
6 Issues–	A science unit must provide opportunities for students to engage in decision-making relative to contemporary science- and technology-related issues that affect their lives or community. Stem-cell research, drought-relief, global-warming, robotics, and evolution are examples of contemporary issues germane to science teaching in middle school and secondary science classes.
7 Curriculum–	Science unit planning must begin with the identification of standards-based learning outcomes. The culminating unit assessment must reflect these desired learning outcomes, and learning experiences must be designed to help students achieve the learning outcomes as demonstrated by their success on the culminating assessment.
8 Science in the community–	A science unit must contextualize science learning for students by relating science concepts and principles to the students' personal lives and the communities in which they live.
9 Assessment–	Assessment in the context of a science unit is multifaceted. Student learning should be assessed often and with multiple formats, not just tests and exams. Besides generating grades, assessment must provide students with a means of gauging their own learning and give the teacher information to guide instruction.

For a copy of the *Standards* go to: www.nsta.org/pdfs/NSTAstandards2003.pdf.

Assessing and Reviewing

Analysis and Synthesis

1. Explain the meaning of the phrase "planning with the end in mind." Then, construct a rationale for this approach to planning that indicates why it is preferred to a planning approach that begins and ends with the collection of lesson plans and laboratory investigations.
2. Examine two or more state or locally prepared frameworks for a science course that you hope to teach. While examining the frameworks, look specifically for the elements identified in Figure 3.3. Share your findings with your instructor and other students in your class.
3. Evaluate a unit that is part of a state or locally prepared framework or found elsewhere for alignment among learning outcomes, culminating assessment tasks, and learning experiences. Write a paragraph that describes your findings and, if appropriate, offer suggestions for enhancing the alignment among these unit components.
4. Explore the science literacy maps available at the National Science Digital Library Web site (http://strandmaps.nsdl.org). From the maps, develop a mental model for the sequencing of science concepts and principles for the science course or courses that you hope to teach.

Practical Considerations

5. Construct a checklist of reminders that you will make a part of your unit planning. Organize the list by using the headings that follow. For each heading, add several phrases that elaborate your thinking.
   Whom are you planning to teach?
   What are you planning to teach?
   How are you planning to teach science?
   How are you planning to manage the science learning environment?
   How are you planning to assess student learning?
6. Begin the development of a unit plan for a course that you hope to teach. To initiate your planning, consider what should be the learning outcomes for your unit and how the learning outcomes might be assessed using one or more culminating assessment tasks. Additionally, consult the unit plan considerations presented in Figure 3.7 to guide your thinking about what a science unit should included. Note: Many of these considerations are addressed in later chapters of this textbook to further aid your unit planning efforts.

Developmental Considerations

7. Identify a few science teachers who are regarded as very effective in their work. Discuss unit planning with them and ask them for suggestions about how to use state and locally developed frameworks to construct science units. Also, ask the teachers to share with you some of their best unit plans.

Resources to Examine

Gender and Science Digital Library [Online]. Available: http://eecgsdl.edc.org

The site provides links to most state science standards and frameworks. Standards and frameworks can be accessed by typing "science standards and frameworks" into the site search engine.

Understanding by Design. 2005. Grant Wiggins and Jay McTighe. Alexandria, VA: Association for Supervision of Curriculum Development.

This 13-chapter book addresses aspects of unit construction following a backward design approach. Many examples and unit construction templates are also provided.

Understanding by Design Exchange [Online]. Available: http://ubdexchange.ascd.org

Available at this site are unit plans for many middle school and secondary science courses developed following the backward design approach described by Wiggins and McTighe in *Understanding by Design*. A reduced registration fee is charged when multiple teachers are registered by a school or school system.

"Those Who Understand: Knowledge Growth in Teaching" (1986). *Educational Researcher, 15*(2), pp. 1–32.

Lee Shulman presents his thoughts about pedagogical content knowledge—the unique knowledge base that teachers develop as a result of experience and reflection. This is a seminal paper about the special knowledge that effective teachers possess that combines subject matter knowledge and ways of teaching the content.

Cases in Middle and Secondary Science Education: The Promise and Dilemmas. 2004. Thomas Koballa Jr. and Deborah Tippins, Eds. Upper Saddle River, NJ: Merrill

This paperback contains over 30 classroom cases about science planning and teaching. The text is an excellent resource for beginning and experienced teachers and those who prepare science teachers. It serves as a companion text for this science methods textbook.

References

Abell, S. K., & Volkmann, M. J. (2006). *Seamless assessment in science: A guide for elementary and middle school teachers*. Portsmouth, NH: Heinemann.

Bransford, J. D., Brown, A. L., & Cocking, R. R. (1999). *How people learn: Brain, mind, experience, and school.* Washington, DC: National Academy Press.

Guarino, F. L., & Watterson, S. M. (2002, September). You are not alone. *The Science Teacher*, 40–41.

Lederman, N. G., & Gess-Newsome, J. (1999). Reconceptualizing secondary science teacher education. In J. Gess-Newsome & N. G. Lederman (Eds.), *Examining pedagogical content knowledge* (pp. 199–214). Norwell, MA: Kluwer.

Marzano, R. J., Pickering, D. J., & Pollock, J. E. (2001). *Classroom instruction that works: Research strategies for increasing student achievement*. Alexandria, VA: Association for Supervision of Curriculum Development.

National Research Council. (1996). *National Science Education Standards*. Washington, DC: National Academy Press.

Project 2061. (2001). *Atlas of science literacy*. Washington, DC: American Association for the Advancement of Science.

Project 2061. (2007). *Atlas of scientific literacy*, Volume 2. Washington, DC: American Association for the Advancement of Science.

Rosenshine, B. (2002). Converging findings on classroom instruction. In A. Molnar (Ed.), *School reform proposals: The research evidence* (pp. 175–196). Greenwich, CT: Information Age.

Shulman, L. S. (1986). Those who understand: Knowledge growth in teaching. *Educational Researcher, 15*(2), 1–32.

Wiggins, G., & McTighe, J. (2005). *Understanding by design* (2nd ed.). Alexandria, VA: Association for Supervision of Curriculum Development.

Chapter 4

Assessing Science Learning

Students require diagnostic and formative as well as summative feedback to be successful science learners.

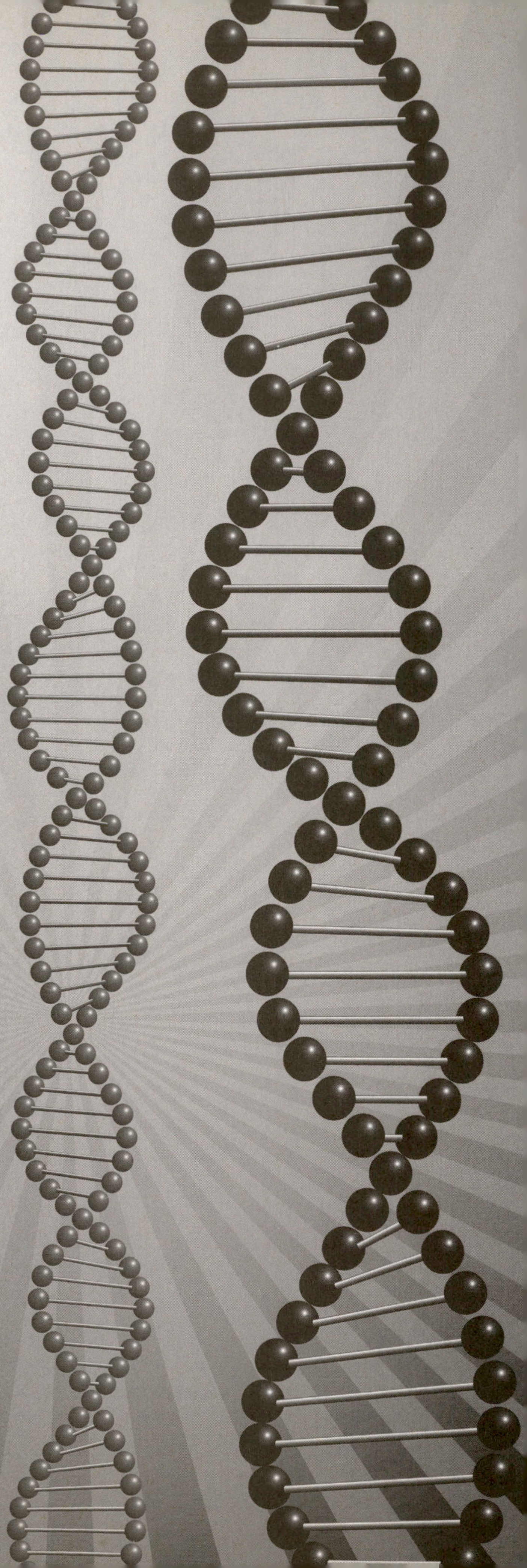

The Troops-to-Teachers program at State University enabled Mr. James Tyson, recently retired from the military, to secure a middle school physical science teaching position as he completed a teacher-credentialing program. On this afternoon, Mr. Tyson enters the classroom of a fellow science teacher, Mrs. Johnson, with frustrations about the poor performance of his students on a test that addressed their understandings of the properties of matter.

Mr. Tyson: I can't believe my students did so poorly on my test. My lessons were well planned and I think I did a good job of teaching. What could I have done differently?

Mrs. Johnson: I believe you are asking the right question, Mr. Tyson. Rather than blaming students for their poor test performance, as sometimes teachers do, you are thinking about what you can do to help your students learn. This is commendable! Tell me about what you did to help your students learn about properties of matter, and I'll try to be of help.

Mr. Tyson: Well, I first identified the state standard. It's Standard 6A, which indicates that students should understand the properties of matter and how matter is classified. Then, I searched the Internet and asked other teachers for activities that address this standard. In addition to having students read our textbook and answer questions at the end of the chapter on properties of matter, I involved the students in a laboratory activity and several demonstrations. In one demonstration, that I felt really helps students understand chemical change, I contrasted chemical change and physical change. I used cutting paper and chewing food as examples of physical change. Then I used burning a candle, digesting food, and burning paper as examples of chemical change. Of all the questions on the test, students performed the worst on the ones dealing with chemical change.

Mrs. Johnson: From your description, it seems that you did a good job teaching. But, what did you do before the test to find out about your students' learning?

Mr. Tyson: I'm not sure what you mean.

Mrs. Johnson: Think about our visit to Mr. Martin's class last week during your planning period. You wanted to visit the classes of other physical science teachers to see how they teach about properties of matter. Do you recall what Mr. Martin did after he demonstrated and discussed several examples of chemical and physical change?

Mr. Tyson: Yes, he held up a stick of melting butter and asked the students to close their eyes. Then, he said:

- Hold up one finger if you think melting butter is a physical change
- Hold up two fingers if you think melting butter is a chemical change
- Hold up three fingers if you are not sure.

He did the same thing when he showed the students a piece of spoiling meat. And he followed the finger count by asking students to explain their votes.

Mrs. Johnson: Why do you think that Mr. Martin did this finger exercise with his students?

Mr. Tyson: I think he used it to find out which students understood the difference between chemical and physical change and which ones didn't. So, this was a way for Mr. Martin to find out if his teaching was effective.

Mrs. Johnson: You are exactly right. Mr. Martin assessed his students' learning during the lesson, long before giving them the unit test. The data Mr. Martin gained from the finger exercise gave him feedback on his students' learning. Using these data, he was able to make decisions about future instruction.

Mr. Tyson: So, your point is that I don't have to wait until the end of the unit to assess my students' learning. I can assess as I teach.

Mrs. Johnson: I think you have solved your own problem about students' poor test performance. And, there are many different ways to assess students' learning while teaching. You may remember seeing Mr. Martin systematically recording his observations on a checklist as he walked among the lab groups asking questions on the day of our visit to his classroom.

Mr. Tyson: I want to learn more about how to help my students. Can we meet tomorrow after school to brainstorm how I can make assessment a part of my teaching routine?

Mrs. Johnson: By all means. Come by my room tomorrow afternoon at 3:30.

As Mr. Tyson left Mrs. Johnson's classroom, she began to think about the many facets of assessment that teachers need to understand. There is assessment for accountability that centers on standardized tests. But, more important is assessment that focuses on learning. It can provide teachers with feedback to guide instruction and aid student understanding.

AIMS OF THE CHAPTER

Use the questions that follow to guide your thinking and learning about science assessment:

- How are learning, assessment, and teaching related?
- What are the features of a balanced and seamless assessment system?
- How can assessment be used to improve science teaching and learning?
- What are some useful procedures for assigning grades?

Any discussion of assessment should begin with a consideration of learning. As described in the *National Science Education Standards* (National Research Council [NRC], 1996), the goals for science learning include science content; science inquiry and inquiry skills; history and nature of science; and issues of science, technology, and society. Evidence of learning within these domains for middle school and secondary students goes beyond memorizing facts and regurgitating what is found in textbooks. Evidence of learning centers on students being able to use knowledge about a science phenomenon and related skills to solve problems in context, to answer how and why questions about the phenomenon, to recognize what they do not know, and to provide convincing explanations for answers about the phenomenon. It also includes personal dispositions—attitudes, beliefs, and values—that can facilitate and impede science understandings and dispositions associated with the scientific enterprise.

Science Learning Assessment System

When considered from the perspective of student learning, assessment is the means of determining the extent to which students achieve the learning goals specified in standards documents and frameworks. This places assessment not as an isolated event that occurs at the end of instruction, but as an important consideration of planning and teaching. Your thoughts of assessment as applied to science teaching and learning should include four components.

1. **Learning Goals.** General learning goals for a science course or unit may come from national standards or state or locally developed frameworks. Specific learning goals, perhaps stated as questions, benchmarks, or objectives, may also be found in state or locally developed frameworks. Learning goals are linked to assessment by indicating what students should know or be able to do or what dispositions they should hold at the end of instruction.
2. **Beginning-of-Instruction Assessment.** The diversity of today's middle school and secondary population virtually ensures that all students will not come to science classes with the same understandings, skills, and dispositions. Early assessment may facilitate differentiated instruction to meet the needs of diverse learners.
3. **During-Instruction Assessment.** Assessment need not wait until the end of instruction, but can be woven into science learning experiences. Much information about student learning and the quality of teaching can be gathered during instruction.
4. **End-of-Instruction Assessment.** At the conclusion of an instructional sequence, it is important to determine what students have learned. Assessment that occurs at the conclusion of an instructional sequence is often used for assigning grades.

These four components comprise the features of a science learning assessment system. No one component is more important or less important than the others. Planning instruction with assessment in mind will contribute to your teaching success and to the success of your students as science learners. Let's now look at each of these four components of the system in turn, using the chapter's opening vignette as a context for the discussion.

Learning Goals

In Chapter 3, you learned about course frameworks and took the opportunity to explore several state and locally developed examples online. As a result of your exploration, you should have recognized that a powerful feature of frameworks is their translation of standards into descriptions of what students should know and be able to do at the end of a science course or unit. As you can well imagine, it is a harder task to develop an assessment that stays true to the developers' intention when a standard addresses a broad content area or is vaguely worded. A number of frameworks include statements of learning outcomes that are more precisely worded than standards, sometimes called essential questions, benchmarks, or objectives. These statements help to explain the standards and to guide teachers' decisions about what students should learn.

If you think back on this chapter's opening vignette, you will recall that Mr. Tyson spoke about the standard that was the primary focus of his unit, but he did not mention how he moved from standard to learning experiences for his students. More important, absent from his discussion with Mrs. Johnson was how he translated the standard into exactly what he expected students to learn from his unit on matter and how his students' learning would be assessed. It is possible that Mr. Tyson was not clear on what he expected his students to know or be able to do as a result of his teaching. This might have contributed to his students' poor test performance. In contrast to what Mr. Tyson seems to have done, we encourage you to plan with the end in mind (Tileston, 2004; Wiggins & McTighe, 2005).

The idea of planning with the end in mind has powerful implications for the alignment of learning goals, instruction, and assessment. Determining what you want students to know or be able to do as a result of instruction, or planning with the end in mind, provides guidance for your design and selection of assessments and learning experiences. Figure 4.1 presents two different descriptions of assessments, learning goals, and learning experiences that could be derived from Mr. Tyson's discussion of properties of matter.

FIGURE 4.1 Assessments, learning goals, and learning experiences.

	Teaching and Learning Condition 1
Assessment	Students will perform the operations described below and then indicate if each operation is an example of a physical change or chemical change and provide at least one reason for each answer. • Mix salt, sand, and water • Mix of sodium hydrogen carbonate and hydrochloric acid
Learning Goal	Determine if mixtures show a physical or chemical change and provide reasons to support the decisions.
Learning Experience	Students should be provided with guidance and practice in carrying out laboratory procedures that lead to chemical and physical changes. They must also be provided with opportunities to observe the physical properties of matter that will allow them to determine if a physical or chemical change has occurred (e.g., physical state, color, odor, solubility in water, effect of magnetism). In addition, students should practice constructing criteria based on their observations that will enable them to distinguish between a physical change and a chemical change. Finally, the students should be reminded of safe laboratory practices.
	Teaching and Learning Condition 2
Assessment	Students will write definitions for physical change and chemical change and give two examples of each kind of change.
Learning Goal	Define physical change and chemical change and give examples of each kind of change.
Learning Experience	In a class lecture, students would be given definitions of physical change and chemical change and provided with examples of physical change and chemical change to memorize. Additionally, students would be given opportunities to generate their own examples of physical change and chemical change that would be checked by the teacher.

You will note that the two assessments place different expectations on students. The level of cognitive demand required of students is much greater for Condition 1 than for Condition 2, with Condition 1 better reflecting the nature of science learning expectations described in the *National Science Education Standards*. This difference in intellectual activity is also reflected in the learning experiences for the two conditions. The understanding that you should take from examining Figure 4.1 is that aligning assessment with learning goals is critical to the success of your teaching and your students' learning.

Stop and Reflect!

Examine frameworks to locate a culminating unit assessment or lesson assessment along with the learning goal(s) and learning experiences to which it is matched. Share your thoughts about the alignment between assessment, goals, and learning experiences with a classmate.

Beginning-of-Instruction Assessment

A significant influence on students' science learning is what they already know and can do, as well as how they feel about school science. For this reason, it is important to gather information from students about these important considerations near the beginning of instruction.

At the start of a unit, a teacher could gauge students' prior knowledge and readiness for instruction in a number of ways. Students could be introduced to the topic of a unit through an engaging activity, perhaps centering on a discrepant event or a natural anomaly that will invoke student responses and questions. A problem-based dilemma that highlights important ideas from the unit could also be used to reveal students' strongly held assumptions and misconceptions. Alternatively, students could be given a brief ungraded pretest that addresses key concepts and major ideas from the unit.

Whether informal, like an engaging activity, or a more formal pretest, these assessments serve a diagnostic purpose. By *diagnostic*, we mean that the assessment is intended to reveal students' understandings in order to better meet group and individual needs through instruction. Information from beginning-of-instruction assessments may be extremely useful to teachers planning instruction for today's middle school and secondary students, with their diverse academic backgrounds, abilities, interests, and skills. Thinking about Mr. Tyson's students, we can only speculate about how their test performance may have been affected had their learning needs been diagnosed at the beginning of the unit on the properties of matter.

During-Instruction Assessment

There is much information about student learning that can be gathered during instruction. Recall from the opening vignette how Mr. Martin assessed his students' understanding of chemical change by presenting them with a melting stick of butter and a sample of spoiling meat. He asked his students to close their eyes while holding up fingers so that each student's response would not be biased by the responses of their classmates. Also, Mr. Martin's request for students to explain their votes provided insight into the signs of chemical change that his students were cueing on when raising their fingers.

A key feature of during-instruction assessment is its seamlessness (Abell & Volkmann, 2006), meaning that instruction flows naturally into assessment and assessment flows back into instruction. And, when cast as virtually indistinguishable from instruction, assessment can take many forms. As suggested in the opening vignette, asking students questions is one form of during-instruction assessment. Students could also be asked to jot down two or three key concepts from a lesson or to draw a picture to show their thinking. Student oral responses to questions as well as writing and drawing tasks can tell a lot about what understandings they are constructing. Inaccurate and incomplete responses or representations suggest that differentiated group instruction may be appropriate, particularly if the responses seem to cluster in discernable patterns.

You may also find that questions and response tasks are not necessary to gauge students' learning and their feelings about your teaching. Students will often tell teachers when they need further clarification and assistance or if they do not like something that has occurred in class. In addition, student inattentiveness or off-task behavior can indicate that students find a lesson boring or that a learning task is too easy or too difficult. As a teacher of middle and secondary school students, you will need to become attentive to such signals and be prepared to modify your teaching.

Assessment during instruction is considered *formative* because its primary purpose is not to generate grades. Its primary purpose is to provide teachers with information that will enable them to make adjustments to their instruction that reflects the progress and needs of their students. By assessing student learning during instruction, you are helping yourself be an effective teacher and communicating to students that you value them as individuals and want them to experience success.

End-of-Instruction Assessment

An appropriate way to bring closure to instruction is to allow students to show what they have learned. When considered in the context of a single or multi day lesson, end-of-instruction assessment could be done in as little as five minutes by giving a short quiz or asking students,

"What have you learned today?" or "What about this lesson was unclear to you?" But when thought about as the concluding experience of a unit, the assessment will take longer, could include multiple parts, and may be initiated well before the final days of the unit. Preparing an assessment that reflects students' learning from a unit is an important part of the unit planning process. As was discussed earlier in this text, when planning with the end in mind, your end-of-unit assessment should not only reflect the desired learning goals for the unit, but also guide the selection and development of unit-learning experiences.

End-of-instruction assessment is considered *summative* because it is applied at the conclusion of an instructional sequence and is used to indicate accomplishment, typically in the form of a grade. More important, end-of-instruction assessment provides students with the opportunity to demonstrate their learning as described in the *National Science Education Standards*. Rather than just showing the ability to retrieve facts and recognizing bits of information, end-of-instruction assessment should allow students to show how scientific knowledge can be utilized and how information can be reorganized to generate new understandings.

Tests have long been used to assess student learning at the end of an instructional sequence, but this tradition is giving way to alternative forms of assessment, including performance tasks, portfolios, presentations, and long-term projects. The use of alternatives to paper-and-pencil tests are encouraged because they provide students with ways to demonstrate their understandings that may not be revealed by tests alone. As will be discussed in the next section of this chapter, both traditional and alternative forms of assessment have a place in the science classroom.

The assessment of science learning involves the integration of multiple parts. Assessment must reflect the goals of science learning in addition to serving multiple purposes—diagnostic, formative, and summative. Often a single assessment can serve multiple purposes. Ideally, assessment will also enhance the ability of students to monitor, evaluate, and regulate their own learning (Marzano & Kendall, 2007).

Balanced Assessment

Understanding assessment as part of the process of unit planning and teaching means that testing and assessment are not synonymous. Teachers have long recognized that multiple-choice, fill-in-the-blank, true–false, and short-answer questions included on paper-and-pencil tests do not assess all that students are learning in science classes. Rather than abandoning tests altogether and using only alternative forms of assessment, many informed teachers have chosen to employ a *balanced assessment* approach (Balanced Assessment Group, 1998). In a balanced assessment approach both traditional and alternative assessment formats are employed to gather information about student learning for diagnostic, formative, and summative purposes. The learning assessed using a balanced assessment system includes what students should know and be able to do as a result of science instruction as well as students' science-related dispositions.

We recommend that the assessments, in either traditional or alternative formats, that comprise a teacher's balanced assessment approach be viewed as the recipes in a cookbook. Just as the cook selects the recipe that best matches the occasion and the palettes of his guests, the science teacher should select the assessment format that best matches his intended learning goals and provides the desired information to chart student learning. What follows is a discussion of both traditional and alternative assessment formats along with assessments of students' dispositions.

Science Tests

Tests are an important part of science assessment. Science teachers need to be able to construct tests that do an effective job of assessing students' learning. Test construction may involve teachers writing test items or selecting items from test banks. Most new science textbook and kit-based programs come with tests banks that provide a wide array of items. Teachers must prepare or have access to a variety of test items that can be used to assess different levels of student thinking and skills. To effectively assess student learning, the tests that teachers use must be *valid*, measure what they are supposed to measure, and be *reliable*—provide consistent information over time (Borg & Gall, 1983). Test reliability can be improved by including multiple questions to assess students' understandings, and validity can be ensured by aligning test items with learning outcomes presented in standards and frameworks.

Science teachers use a variety of item formats when constructing tests for their students. Among the most frequently used item formats are multiple-choice, true-false, matching, completion, and essay questions. The challenge for teachers when using these formats is to select items that assess students' higher order thinking required to utilize scientific knowledge and generate new understandings, not just their abilities to recall facts and recognize bits of information. Identified in Table 4.1 are resources that can help you to write and select test questions that assess students' higher order thinking.

An important part of testing is preparing students to be successful test takers. In addition to helping students review materials that will be assessed on a test, informed teachers provide students with practice answering questions similar to those that they will see at test time. They also teach students how to strategically respond to test

TABLE 4.1 Resources for Writing and Selecting Test Items

Alabama Professional Development Modules
http://web.utk.edu/~mccay/apdm/

Five separate modules provide detailed instruction on the construction and use of true–false, short-answer, matching, multiple-choice, and essay questions. Each module includes practice item–construction tasks, self-assessment, and suggestions for classroom applications.

Center for Teaching Excellence, University of Illinois at Urbana-Champaign
www.oir.uiuc.edu/dme/exams/ITQ.html

Advantages and limitations of using seven different test item types are presented along with sample items identified as desirable and undesirable. Also discussed are performance items, useful for testing the application of knowledge, and strategies for assessing the quality of multiple-choice, true–false, sentence completion, and essay questions.

Center for the Enhancement of Teaching, San Francisco State University
http://oct.sfsu.edu/assessment/measuring/htmls/construct_test.html

Guidelines are given for constructing multiple-choice, matching, true–false, and essay questions. Suggestions are also offered for formatting, administering, and scoring tests.

Construction of Objective Tests
www.clt.cornell.edu/campus/teach/faculty/Materials/TestConstructionManual.pdf

Written by professors Marjorie Devine and Nevart Yaghlian of Cornell University, this manual provides detailed suggestions on preparing for testing, constructing test items, and using test results to revise test items.

Dr. Robert Runte, Faculty of Education, University of Lethbridge
www.uleth.ca/edu/runte/tests

Recommendations for constructing multiple-choice, true–false, matching, sentence completion, short-answer, and essay questions are offered. Issues addressed for each question type include appropriate use and placement on tests. A glossary of testing terms and references is provided.

How to Prepare Better Multiple-Choice Test Items
http://testing.byu.edu/info/handbooks/betteritems.pdf

Prepared by faculty at Brigham Young University, this guide discusses the anatomy of a multiple-choice item, advantages and limitations of multiple-choice items, and different response formats for multiple-choice items, including "best answer," "multiple response," and "combined response." A checklist for reviewing multiple-choice items is also provided.

How to Write Better Tests: A Handbook for Improving Test Construction Skills
www.indiana.edu/~best/write_better_tests.shtml

Written by Dr. Lucy Jacobs, this book is provided online by Indiana University. Chapters cover test planning, test formats, and the writing of five types of test questions.

Preparing Effective Essay Questions
http://testing.byu.edu/info/handbooks/WritingEffectiveEssayQuestions.pdf

Prepared as a support for the efforts of the Brigham Young University Testing Center, this handbook reviews advantages, limitations, and common misconceptions about essay questions. Also included are suggestions for use and construction of essay questions as well as a checklist for assessing them.

Study Guides and Strategies
www.studygs.net/tsttak1.htm

A wealth of information about the development of different types of test questions can be found at this site. Additional guidance is offered about test administration and strategies for preparing students for testing.

Test Construction: Some Practical Ideas
www.utexas.edu/academic/cte/sourcebook/tests.pdf

Marilla Svinicki of the Center for Teaching Effectiveness at the University of Texas provides recommendations for writing test items and essay questions and for matching a test with a unit's learning goals.

questions and write essays. General guidance centers on teaching students to read through test questions carefully, while looking out for keywords and qualifiers, such as "sometimes," "always," and "never." Students are also taught to formulate a likely question response, before looking at the response choices listed below the stem of a multiple-choice item and the word list provided with matching items. Informed teachers may also encourage students to budget their time when answering an essay question, construct an outline before writing, and proofread the essay before handing it in. Sources of information about tips for test taking and sample science items useful for preparing students for unit tests and high stakes graduation and end-of-course tests are presented in Table 4.2.

Alternative Science Assessments

Alternative assessments tend to enable teachers to gain richer understandings of what students are thinking and how they construct meaning than is typically possible

TABLE 4.2 Sample Science Test Items and Test-Taking Tips

California Standards Tests Released Test Questions
www.cde.ca.gov/ta/tg/sr/css05rtq.asp

Released science test questions from the 2003, 2004, 2005, 2006, and 2007 California Standards Tests for grade 8 and secondary biology, chemistry, earth science, and physics.

EDinfomatics
http://edinformatics.com/testing/testing2.htm

Links are provided to tests of student learning proficiency based on state frameworks. Released tests and test items for middle school and secondary science can be accessed through the links.

National Assessment of Educational Progress
http://nces.ed.gov/nationsreportcard/itemmaps/index.asp

Released items from the 2005 administration to 8th and 12th grade students are available at this site. Multiple-choice and written response items are provided along with national data on student responses.

Oswego City School District Regents Prep Exam Center
http://regentsprep.org/regents.cfm

Offered at this nonprofit site are review materials and sample questions aligned with science content addressed in all science areas of the New York State Regents Exam—Earth Science, Living Environment, Chemistry, and Physics. Links to old Regents Science Exams and answer keys are also available at this site.

PISA Released Items—Science
www.oecd.org/dataoecd/13/33/38709385.pdf

Sponsored by the Organization for Economic Co-Operation and Development, the Programme for International Student Achievement (PISA) assesses science achievement internationally. Available are more than 90 pages of released science items that cover a wide range of topics, including biodiversity, ozone, and evolution.

Test Taking and Anxiety
www.ulc.psu.edu/studyskills/test_taking.html

From Penn State University's Learning Center, the suggestions offered address students' test preparation, test taking, and test anxiety.

Test-Taking Tips
www.testtakingtips.com/test/index.htm

Specific test-taking tips are provided for multiple-choice, true–false, short-answer, open-book, and essay tests.

Tips on Writing the Essay-Type Examination
www.csbsju.edu/academicadvising/help/essayexm.htm

Prepared by the Academic Advising Center of the College of St. Benedict at St. John's University, this site offers seven tips for writing essay responses. Also included is a list of keywords (e.g., analyze, illustrate, trace) often used in essay questions and the types of responses that each is intended to elicit.

Top Ten Test-Taking Tips for Students
www.teachervision.fen.com/study-skills/teaching-methods/6390.html

Tips for test taking and test preparation are offered at this *TeacherVision*-sponsored site.

when using only tests. Many alternative assessments focus on student performance and on task authenticity by asking students to use knowledge and skills that are applicable to real-life situation and problems. Several alternative assessment formats are presented in Table 4.3.

Developing alternative assessments is very different from constructing tests, and in many respects more demanding. Concerns associated with alternative assessments tend to be more apparent than is the case with tests. The authenticity and complexity of the tasks increase the possibility for students to misinterpret directions and questions. Scoring inconsistencies are possible when scoring criteria are poorly developed. Also, unfamiliarity with the nature of the tasks, special tools, or language may disenfranchise some learners. Fortunately, a growing number of educators are building alternative assessments, testing them with science learners, and making them available for science teachers to use and modify.

TABLE 4.3 Alternative Assessment Formats

Concept Map

A concept map graphically shows meaningful relationships among scientific concepts. Students may be asked to generate the map without assistance or provided with a partially completed map or list of concepts. Concept maps can be used to reveal student misunderstandings at the beginning of instruction or at the end to assess student learning. Information about concept mapping and software that supports the construction of concept maps can be found at the Concept Mapping homepage (http://users.edte.utwente.nl/lanzing/cm_home.htm) and at a site sponsored by the Florida Institute for Human and Machine Cognition (http://cmap.ihmc.us/Publications/ResearchPapers/TheoryCmaps/TheoryUnderlyingConceptMaps.htm).

Drawing

Drawing exercises are useful for assessing the understandings of students for whom English is their second language and for students who find writing challenging. Drawing can be used to reveal students' understandings before and after instruction. Seventh-grade students' before and after drawings show how their visit to Fermilab affected their understandings of scientists and the work they do (http://ed.fnal.gov/projects/scientists/).

Interview

An interview can be conducted with individuals or small groups of students. It can be centered around a set of questions constructs in advance or be very informal, with questions emerging directly from the learning context. Interviews can be used to assess student learning during and at the end of instruction. When conducted while students are problem solving, interviews can provide insights into their thinking about the problem. Information about the interview as an assessment tool is available at the Alaska Department of Education and Early Development site (www.eed.state.ak.us/tls/Frameworks/mathsci/ms5_2as1.htm#interviews) as well as at National Institute for Science Education's Field-Tested Learning Assessment Guide site (www.flaguide.org/cat/interviews/interviews1.php).

Journal

A journal may include responses to questions given by the teacher, questions written by students that they wish to have answered, reactions to class activities and homework, or spontaneous reflections. Writing prompts keep journals from becoming diaries, where students simply recount daily events without reflection. Charts, drawings, and graphs also may be included in journals. Journals need to be read periodically if they are to be a useful assessment tool. To keep journals from becoming burdensome, consider reading only a dozen or so journals a week. Journals are appropriately used for diagnostic and formative assessment. More information about journal writing can be found at the online instructional strategies page of Saskatoon Public Schools' Web site (http://olc.spsd.sk.ca/DE/PD/instr/strats/journal/index.html).

KWL Chart

Originally conceived as a reading strategy, KWL stands for "know," "want or will," and "learned." Using a three-column chart, students are asked to write what they know about a topic in the left column, what they what want to or will learn about a topic before instruction in the middle column, and what they learned after instruction in the right column. Information about uses for the KWL chart and examples can be found at the Web site of North Central Regional Educational Laboratory (www.ncrel.org/sdrs/areas/issues/students/learning/lr2kwl.htm) and at the site of ReadingQuest.org (www.readingquest.org/strat/kwl.html).

Laboratory Report

The traditional lab report allows students to report the findings of their work and to discuss the significance of the findings. The traditional report is usually organized into sections, with such titles as Purpose, Materials, Procedures, Data, Data Interpretation, and Conclusion. An alternative to the traditional report is the narrative lab report. A narrative report may take the form of a letter to a parent or friend in which the student describes the lab experience. Licata (1999) recommends the following questions as prompts to guide students' writing of narrative lab reports: What was I looking for? How did I look for it? What did I find? What does it mean? Information about constructing tradition laboratory reports can be found at the Web site of the University of Toronto's Engineering Communication Center (www.ecf.toronto.edu/~writing/handbook-lab.html) and information about constructing narrative lab reporting can found in Ken Licata's 1999 article in *The Science Teacher* (www.nsta.org).

TABLE 4.3 *(Continued)*

Model Construction
Models may be physical, such as Watson and Crick's model of DNA, conceptual, such as the Bohr model of the atom, mathematical, or portrayed as computer simulations. Models can reveal what students know and what they have learned. Students' science understanding is often revealed as conceptual models that employ analogical reasoning, such as when a student describes the structure and function of a cell in terms of the services provided by a municipality. Information about models can be found at sites of the Stanford Encyclopedia of Philosophy (http://plato.stanford.edu/entries/models-science/#PhyObj) and the Science Education Resources Center at Carlton College (http://serc.carleton.edu/introgeo/models/index.html).

Oral Presentation
Oral presentations involve students speaking to peers on a topic about which they have developed expertise. Organization, knowledge of the topics, and preparedness are among the criteria considered when evaluating oral presentations. Information about using oral presentation for assessment and rubrics can be obtained from the Science Education Resources Center at Carlton College (http://serc.carleton.edu/introgeo/campusbased/presentation.html).

Performance Assessment
In performance assessment, a student works to solve a problem or generates a product that illustrates the application of certain understandings and skills. A performance task often involves the student manipulating materials or equipment in an authentic laboratory or field context, and can be used to diagnose and monitor students' developing competency. Performance assessments can be modified versions of science instructional activities. Sample performance assessments and additional information about uses of performance assessment are available at the National Institute for Science Education's Field-tested Learning Assessment Guide Web site (www.flaguide.org/cat/perfass/perfass7.php).

Portfolio
A portfolio presents evidence of student capability or progress and can be used in formative assessment, to stimulate reflection, or as a summative evaluation of student work for a semester or an entire course. A portfolio may include items that make use of many of the assessment formats described in this table. Written captions accompany items included in a portfolio to explain how the items serve as evidence of learning. Information about the uses of portfolios and their contents is available at the National Institute for Science Education's Field-Tested Learning Assessment Guide Web site (www.flaguide.org/cat/portfolios/portfolios7.php) and at Jon Mueller's Authentic Assessment Toolbox (http://jonathan.mueller.faculty.noctrl.edu/toolbox/portfolios.htm). Information about helping students build online portfolios is available at a Web site sponsored by Penn State University (http://portfolio.psu.edu/about/index.html).

Venn Diagram
This graphic organization makes use of overlapping circles to highlight similarities and differences among two or more topics. For examples, characteristics of vascular and nonvascular plants could be presented in a Venn diagram, with similarities among the two shown in the overlapping area. Information about Venn diagrams is available at the Graphic.org Web site (www.graphic.org/venbas.html).

The instructional materials provided by school science publishers are the first place to look for assessments that make use of the various formats described in Table 4.3 and many others. Assessments may be found among the plethora of supplementary materials provided by publishers. Trade books and journal articles are additional sources of alternative assessments that can be used with middle and high school science students. The National Science Teachers Association (NSTA) and the Association for Supervision and Curriculum Development (ASCD) frequently publish trade books on issues of assessment and include assessment articles in their journals, *The Science Teacher, Science Scope,* and *Educational Leadership*. In addition, the Internet is a growing resource for science alternative assessments. An increasing number of Internet sites display alternative assessments that can be used as shown or modified by science teachers to better match their assessment needs. Two excellent sites to search for assessment tasks are the Center for Technology in Learning's *Performance Assessment Links in Science* (PALS) (www.pals.sri.com) and *Alternative Assessment* (www.miamisci.org/ph/lpdefine.html) maintained by the Miami Museum of Science. Assessment tasks found at these sites use a number of assessment formats, including journals, portfolios, concept maps, and performance assessments.

Providing feedback to students regarding their performance on alternative assessments requires making explicit the criteria by which students' work will be judged. This typically involves the use of a *scoring rubric* or *checklist*. For a rubric, the criteria are shown as lists of descriptors along a graduated scale. The scale for most scoring rubrics has between three and five points. On a scale that runs from 1 to 5, a score of 5 would represent the highest level of performance, and a score of 1, the lowest level of performance. Many

Balanced assessement includes performance tasks in addition to paper-and-pencil tests.

teachers set a minimal acceptable level of performance, such as 3 on a 5-point scale or assign point values to performance levels. In contrast, a checklist consists of a description of the desired performances and a scale to score the performances. The typical scale includes only "yes" and "no" options to indicate whether or not the performance was observed. Other checklist formats include space for comments about the performance to be recorded and scales that provide a range of options to score the performance.

Before a rubric or checklist can be used effectively, the task to which it will be applied must be known. Specified in the description of the task are the learning outcomes that students are expected to meet. Students are usually given the task and the scoring rubric or checklist at the same time. Doing this makes the scoring criteria explicit and eliminates the need for students to ask what they need to know or be able to do in order to perform well on the assessment. Table 4.4 shows a scoring rubric for assessing students' chemistry laboratory reports. Figure 4.2 on page 60 shows a checklist for assessing students' use of the microscope and how to prepare and stain materials for observation. This checklist provides a range of options—excellent, adequate, and inadequate—for scoring the performance.

The process of transforming an instructional activity into an alternative assessment task can be accomplished by marrying the instructional activity with an appropriate rubric or checklist. This can be done by accessing rubric and checklist templates available online and modifying them to match the tasks. Templates from which task-specific rubrics and checklists can be developed for assessing a variety of performances are available at:

- Rubristar (http://rubistar.4teachers.org/index.php)
- iRubric (www.rcampus.com/indexrubric.cfm)
- Project Based Learning (http://pblchecklist.4teachers.org/checklist.shtml)

The value of scoring rubrics and checklists lies in their ability to communicate information about students' performance to teachers, parents, and students themselves.

Assessing Science-Related Dispositions

The focus of science tests and alternative assessments tends to be on students' understandings and skills. Assessing students' science-related dispositions, that is their beliefs, attitudes, and values, requires the use of other methods. The importance of assessing students' dispositions and making use of the information provided by the assessments is two fold. First, dispositions have a powerful influence on student's engagement and science learning (Koballa & Glynn, 2007). Second, favorable dispositions toward science are an important goal of science education; students who leave school with favorable science-related dispositions are likely to be lifelong science learners and informed science-related decision makers (Koballa, Kemp, & Evans, 1997).

There are three methods that are commonly used to assess students' science-related dispositions. The first method involves the use of self-report scales. Likert scales, to which students indicate agreement or disagreement with statements, and semantic differential scales, where bipolar adjectives are used as scale anchors, are examples of this method. The second method involves students providing open-ended responses to questions. Questionnaires along with individual and group interviews are examples of this method. The third method of assessing students' science-related dispositions involves the teacher observing students as they work, with an eye toward specific science-related behaviors. Checklists, where a series of specific behaviors are described, can guide a teacher's observations. Observations of the behaviors associated with science-related dispositions are often recorded as a tally or as a rating that denotes frequency of occurrence (e.g., 3 = often, 2 = occasionally, 1 = rarely, 0 = not observed). Sources of materials for assessing students' science-related dispositions are presented in Table 4.5 on page 61.

TABLE 4.4 Chemistry Laboratory Report Rubric

Category	Accomplished	Acceptable	Unacceptable (Must Redo)
Title and Purpose (10 points)	Title and purpose are clearly stated. (8–10 points)	Title and purpose are stated, but lack clarity. (5–7 points)	Title or purpose is missing. (0–4 points)
Procedure (15 points)	Stated in concise numbered steps and described in sufficient detail to replicate. (13–15 points)	Stated in concise numbered steps, but includes minor omissions. (5–12 points)	Steps are omitted and/or missing details. (0–4 points)
Observations (15 points)	Data are recorded completely and organized appropriately in a table. (13–15 points)	Data are recorded and organized in a table with some errors. (7–12 points)	Data are incomplete and/or not recorded in a table. (0–6 points)
Calculations (20 points)	Calculations are accurate and complete with proper units. (16–20 points)	Calculations are complete with minor errors or with missing or incorrect units. (10–15 points)	Calculations are incomplete, contain serious errors, or include no units. (0–9 points)
Results (20 points)	Results are summarized by correctly answering all the questions in the laboratory handout. (16–20 points)	Results are summarized by correctly answering most of the questions in the laboratory handout. (10–15 points)	Most questions are not answered correctly. (0–9 points)
Conclusion (20 points)	Results are discussed in terms of the purpose of the lab, reasonable sources of error, and the effect of the error on the results. (16–20 points)	Results are discussed in terms of the purpose of the lab and sources of error. However, the discussion of the sources of error is not reasonable or it is limited. (10–15 points)	The results are not discussed in terms of the purpose of the lab, reasonable sources of error, and the effect of the error on the results. (0–9 points)

Based on a rubric written by Dava C. Coleman that appears on page 249 in T. R. Koballa and D. J. Tippins (Eds.) (2004), Cases in middle and secondary science Education, *Upper Saddle River, NJ: Merrill/Prentice Hall.*

Each method has strengths and limitations that should be considered when assessing students' dispositions. Scales are easy to score, but challenging to develop. Similarly, questionnaires are easy to administer and interviews are relatively simple to conduct. However, a rubric is often needed to guide the analysis of questionnaire and interview responses. Further, scales, questionnaires, and interviews rely on student self-report, which may lead to inaccurate conclusions if care is not taken when interpreting the results. Observations are not affected by the limitations associated with the other methods for assessing students' dispositions, but reliable conclusions may require looking for the same behaviors multiple times.

Information collected using the three methods, despite the associated challenges, can help teachers determine the nature of the science-learning environment they are providing for students. The information can also tell teachers about the effectiveness of their teaching and the beliefs, attitudes, and values of their students regarding the course or specific instructional units. Making use of the information about students' science-related dispositions can lead to improved instruction, enhanced student learning, and adults who value science and use their understandings of science in their daily lives.

 Coherent Assessment

As was mentioned earlier, assessment must be a central element of science teaching, not an afterthought. Assessment should be balanced, involving a mix of tests, alternative formats, and assessment of dispositions, and assessment should also be seamless, integrated with instruction. Teachers can make this happen by considering how assessment, as discussed earlier in this chapter, can be matched with different lessons within the context of a science unit.

Say you are constructing a unit on genetics for the purpose of having students develop understandings about the roles of genes and chromosomes in passing traits from one generation to the next. The early lessons of the units will likely be ones that engage students, piquing their interest in the topic. Assessment in these early lessons should have a *diagnostic* focus, with the

FIGURE 4.2 Example of a checklist to assess students' use of the microscope.

E = excellent; A = adequate; I = inadequate

Gross body movements

1.	Removes microscope from its case or space in the storage cabinet. Grasps the arm of the instrument with one hand and places the other hand under the base.	E	A	I
2.	Sets the microscope down gently on the table with the arm toward student and stage away from student. The base should be a safe distance from the edge of the table.	E	A	I
3.	Uses a piece of lens paper to wipe the lenses clean.	E	A	I
4.	Clicks the lower power objective into viewing position.	E	A	I
5.	Adjusts the diaphragm and mirror for the best light.	E	A	I
6.	Places a prepared slide of human hair on the stage so that it is directly over the center of the stage opening.	E	A	I
7.	Secures the slide in place with the stage clips.	E	A	I
8.	Looks to the side of the microscope and slowly lowers the low-power objective by turning the coarse adjustment wheel until the objective almost touches the slide.	E	A	I
9.	While looking through the eyepiece, with both eyes open, slowly turns the coarse adjustment so that the objective rises. The hair should become visible.	E	A	I
10.	Brings the hair into sharp focus by turning the fine adjustment wheel.	E	A	I
11.	Shows the properly focused slide to teacher.	E	A	I
12.	Focuses the hair under high power and shows this properly focused slide to teacher.	E	A	I
13.	Prepares to return microscope to storage area; turns the low-power objective into viewing position and adjusts it approximately 1 cm above stage.	E	A	I
14.	Returns the microscope, handling by the arm and base, to storage place.	E	A	I

Finely coordinated movements

The following observations are made by the teacher, who judges how well a student can prepare and stain materials for observation under a microscope.

Preparation and staining of an onion cell wet mount slide

1.	Rinses a microscope slide with water and wipes both sides with a clean, soft cloth.	E	A	I
2.	Rinses and dries a cover glass.	E	A	I
3.	Cuts an onion lengthwise and removes a thick slice.	E	A	I
4.	Peels the delicate tissue from the inner surface.	E	A	I
5.	Uses a medicine dropper to place a drop of water in the center of slide.	E	A	I
6.	Places a small section of onion tissue in the drop of water.	E	A	I
7.	Lowers the cover glass over the onion skin.	E	A	I
8.	Staining the specimen: adds a drop of iodine stain along the edge of the cover glass.	E	A	I
9.	Places a small section of a paper towel on the opposite side of the cover glass. This will draw the stain across the slide by capillary action.	E	A	I

intent of gathering information about students' readiness for learning. Using the first two questions of a KWL chart (What do you KNOW? What do you WANT to know? What have you LEARNED?), questionnaire, or other assessments, information about students' knowledge of genetics and dispositions about, for example, genetically modified foods or cloning might be gathered. Information obtained through this kind of assessment may offer ideas about appropriate learning experiences and how to differentiate instruction. Other lessons of the unit will involve students exploring genetics concepts and principles through laboratory experiences or computer simulations, and developing meaningful explanations of, for example,

TABLE 4.5 Scales, Questionnaires, and Protocols for Assessing Students' Science-Related Dispositions

Classroom Observation Protocol

This is a six-part observation tool designed by Frances Lawrenz, Douglas Hoffman, and Karen Appeldoorn for use in science classrooms and laboratories. Accompanying the protocol are directions for interviewing the teacher prior to the observation in order to understand the context and goals of the lesson.(http://cehd.umn.edu/carei/CETP/Handbooks/COPHandbook.pdf)

Classroom Observations—What Will You Look For?

Laura Henriques provides suggestions for focused classroom observations and observation sheets as part of assignments for her science teacher education classes. (www.csulb.edu/~lhenriqu/300obs.htm)

Draw a Scientist or a Science Teacher

Students' drawings reveal their feelings and beliefs about scientists and science teachers. The checklist that accompanies the Draw-A-Science-Teacher-Test suggests how students' drawings could be scored.

Finson, K. (2002). Draw a scientist: What we do know and do not know after fifty years of drawing. *School Science and Mathematics, 102*(7), 335–245.

Thomas, J. A., Pedersen, J. E., & Finson, K. (2001). Validating the Draw-A-Science-Teacher-Test Checklist (DASTT-C): Exploring mental models and teacher beliefs, *Journal of Science Teacher Education, 12*(3), 295–310.

Science Attitude Scale for Middle School Students

The scale was designed to gather data on five components of students' science attitudes, including science investigations and reading and talking about science. The developers suggest that the scale also can be used with secondary students.

Misiti, F. L., Shrigley, R. L., & Hanson, L. (1991). Science attitude scale for middle schools students. *Science Education, 75*(5), 525–540.

Science Classroom Observation Form

Designed by Richard Butts and Marvin Wideen to assess inquiry orientation, this observation protocol focuses attention on the interactions among students, the teacher, and the classroom environment. (http://eric.ed.gov/ERICDocs/data/ericdocs2sql/content_storage_01/0000019b/80/39/60/ea.pdf)

Science Laboratory Environment Inventory

This 35-statement instrument assesses students' dispositions about five dimensions of the science laboratory environment. The instrument has been extensively field tested with high school biology students.

Fisher, D., Henderson, D., & Fraser, B. (1997). Laboratory environments and student outcomes in senior high school biology. *The American Biology Teacher, 59*(4), 214–219.

Students' Attitudes Toward Scientific Fieldtrips

This questionnaire was designed to collect data on four dimensions of field trips: the learning aspect, the social aspects, the adventure aspect, and the environmental aspect.

Orion, N., & Hofstein, A. (1991). The measurement of students' attitudes toward scientific field trips. *Science Education, 75*(5), 513–523.

Survey of Public Attitudes Toward and Understanding of Science and Technology

Questions included in this national survey administered by the National Science Foundation address a wide array of science-related topics and issues. Survey questions selected from the survey could be asked of middle school and secondary students to gauge their disposition toward school science and relevance of science to their daily lives. (www.nsf.gov/statistics/question.cfm#17)

how a Punnett square can be used to predict the results of monohybrid and dihybrid crosses. Students' lab reports, results for Punnett square problem sets, responses to questions, concept maps, quizzes, along with other assessments, can serve a *formative* function, providing information useful for making instructional adjustments to better address the learning needs of students. Finally, assessment toward the end of a unit might take the form of a unit test or a performance task that engages students over several days. A task, such as one that asks students to apply their understandings of genetics to create an offspring of two cartoon superheroes that exhibits traits to thwart an antagonist's evil deeds, would also enable students to elaborate on their understandings of genetics in addition to serving as the *summative* assessment for the unit.

This example, situated in the context of a genetics unit, illustrates the alignment of learning experiences and assessment that should be part of a teacher's thinking when planning for instruction. How can you begin to make this kind of thinking a part of your repertoire of unit planning and teaching?

Stop and Reflect!

With a classmate, examine a unit that you developed or one developed by others.

- What assessments in the unit serve a diagnostic or formative function?
- What is the nature of the unit's summative assessment? If it is a test, suggest an alternative form of assessment.
- How are students' dispositions assessed in the unit? Do assessments of students' dispositions serve a diagnostic, formative, or summative function?

Grading and Reporting Grades

A serious responsibility for all science teachers is grading and reporting grades. Teachers grade student work in order to communicate with students and their parents about students' performance. Grades serve as indicators of student learning and thus "should be based on solid, high-quality evidence about student achievement" (Brookhart, 2004, p. 11). But not all of what students do in a science class should be graded. While student dispositions, ability, effort, and attendance do influence achievement and should be assessed, most teachers agree that these factors should not be considered in determining grades. Nonjudgmental, formative feedback to students about these and other achievement-related factors is best provided by written or oral means. Grades are meaningful and defensible when they are derived from assessments, either tests or alternative formats, that match the course's curricular aims in terms of content, level of required thinking, and mode of response (Brookhart, 2004).

Determining Grades

An important consideration of teachers when thinking about grading is whether grades should reflect what a student has actually learned or how the student's performance compares with the performance of classmates. This is the main difference between *criterion-referenced* and *norm-referenced grading*. In criterion-referenced grading, student achievement is judged relative to performance against an established set of criteria. Following this system, grades are not adjusted in any way. The teacher will allow as many As, Bs, Cs, Ds, and Fs as students earn. The same would be true for scores of 1, 2, 3, 4, and 5 obtained using a scoring rubric or checklist.

In norm-referenced grading, a student's grade is dependent on how well he or she has performed relative to other members of the class. When using this system, the teacher has in mind a predetermined percentage of students who will receive As, Bs, Cs, Ds, and Fs. This procedure, sometimes called *grading on the curve*, assumes that students in a typical class can be categorized in a normal distribution.

Both criterion-referenced and norm-referenced grading present challenges for teachers. The assumption underlying criterion-referenced grading, that all students can earn As if they achieve at the established performance level, is occasionally questioned. Some administrators and parents expect to see a distribution of grades in a class and may insist that grading practices be altered to produce a certain number of As, Bs, Cs, Ds, and Fs. In contrast, the criticisms of norm-referenced grading are greater in number and tend to be more persuasive. One criticism is that teachers seldom produce tests or other assessments that yield normally distributed scores. Another criticism is that the sizes of most middle and high school classes in which the procedure may be used are too small to expect a normal distribution. This is particularly true in advanced classes where students are homogeneous, with similar aptitudes. More important, norm-referenced grading does not match the model of science learning proffered in the National Science Education Standards (NRC, 1996), where all students are given the opportunity to achieve at high levels. If all students master the expected learning standards, how can a teacher justify giving the majority Cs, Ds, and Fs? Clearly, the criticisms of norm-referenced grading make criterion-referenced grading the obvious choice for most middle and high school science teachers.

Grading Accommodations

Students with special needs may require considerations that go beyond the decision to adopt a criterion-referenced or norm-referenced grading scheme. It may be necessary to accommodate the needs of students with learning disabilities by making modifications to grading criteria, such as changing the grading weights for different assessments or including extra credit activities. Also, these students could be given extra time to complete assessments, or contracts could be used that specify individualized expectations. For students whose first language is not English, less emphasis might be placed on grammatical correctness when grading assessments that involve writing or oral interviews could be substituted for written products. When considering grading accommodations for students, keep in mind that not all disabilities require accommodations. Special education teachers, students' Individualized Education Programs (IEPs), and lists of approved grading accommodations prepared by school districts may be your best sources of information about how to accommodate the needs of these students. More information about how to accommodate the needs of students with exceptionalities is presented in Chapter 8.

Assigning Grades

Ideally when using criterion-referenced grading, the teacher would identify the standards and describe the students' performance relative to the standards. This approach would yield written statements of students' attainment on report cards rather than As, Bs, and Cs. Whereas a few middle and secondary schools use criterion-referenced report cards to indicate student progress toward specific standards, the vast majority of schools require that students' grades be reported as numerical scores or letter grades.

The numerical or letter grade recorded on most report cards is a summary score, derived from the combination of several scores. This summary score is intended to provide the best representation of the teacher's evaluation of a student's performance. Combining scores of different kinds, whether percentages from tests or rubric scores from projects, lab work, or portfolios, to arrive at a summary score is indeed a challenging task. Fortunately, there are several methods for arriving at a report card grade.

Woolfolk (2004) describes two systems for combining grades from different assignments to arrive at a numeric grade—percentage grading and the point system. Percentage grading involves assigning grades based on the percentage of an assignment a student has accomplished or mastered. Using this system, the teacher gives percentage scores for class tests, performance tasks, and other assignments, and computes an average for these scores to arrive at a final grade. Suppose a student's test score was 85%, her lab report score was 93%, and her microscope performance score was 61%. Assuming the scores are weighted equally, her average grade is 78% and would be recorded as a C if the following percentage categories were applied:

A	90–100%
B	80–89%
C	70–79%
D	60–69%
F	below 60%

Applying this system with rubric scores is problematic. For instance, a rubric score of 2 on a 4-point scale may indicate a performance much better than the 50% that this score would generate by percentage grading.

In contrast, the point system is adaptable for use with grades generated from tests as well as rubrics. When using the point system, a total number of points is awarded for each assignment, determined by its value (Woolfolk, 2004). For example, a maximum score of 15 points could be awarded for a performance task worth 15% of the term grade; a maximum score of 20 points could be awarded for a unit test worth 20%; and a maximum score of 30 points could be awarded for a portfolio worth 30%. A portfolio meeting all the criteria would be given a score of 30 points, while one that meets some but not all the criteria would be given a score of less than 30 points. To calculate report card grades using this system, the teacher would simply add up the points for each student. Letter grades could be given by using an established scale. If required, a percentage grade could be calculated using this system by dividing a student's actual points by the maximum possible points and multiplying by 100. An established scale might look something like this:

Term Scoring Scale

Maximum possible points = 250

A	250–200 points
B	199–150 points
C	149–100 points
D	99–50 points
F	below 50 points

Expectations for Grading

Before adopting any grading system, it is important to understand the expectations for grading that might be placed on you by the school where you are employed. Much can be learned about those expectations by studying the school's grading policies and examining the report card format used to communicate student grades. Grading policies tend to specify what should be taken into account when grading, whether grades are reported as letters, numbers, or written descriptions of performance, and how final exam grades should be weighted in calculating course grades (Brookhart, 2004). In addition, a school's grading policy may provide information about how grades should be interpreted (e.g, A = Excellent), what grading accommodations are appropriate for students with special needs, and how grades should be reported to the school administration. Many middle and secondary schools now require teachers to report grades in an online grading system that allows for storage and easy retrieval of students' grades, communication with parents, and the printing of report cards. The report card provides other useful information, including the number of grading periods, if a mark for conduct, effort, or attitude must be reported, and whether a space for teacher comments is provided. All of the information gleaned from these sources is vitally important to you in considering decisions about grading and grade reporting practices.

Brookhart (2004) urges teachers to not allow grading to be an afterthought, but to think about it well in advance of the deadline for turning in report cards. In addition to communicating with students about what is expected of them to achieve at high levels, she suggests that teachers reflect about their own grading practices and offers the following questions to guide that reflection:

- How do you assess tests, quizzes, lab reports, performance tasks, homework, class participation, effort, cooperation, etc.? How do these items contribute to a report card grade?

- What methods do you use to calculate or assign report card grades?
- What meaning do you try to encode in your grades? Student achievement? Student progress? Student improvement?
- What do you do when a student's grade is just below (or just above) the borderline or cutoff for a letter grade?
- How should failure, Fs and zeros, be handled in determining final grades?

Grading, regardless of the system used, is always a challenge for teachers. Students are concerned about their grades and want to know how they will be graded. Grades can motivate students as well as turn them against science and science teachers. It is important that teachers inform students about their grading system.

Demonstrating Your Understandings of Assessment

As a beginning science teacher, you will be expected to demonstrate your understandings of assessment both in your planning and in practice. *Standard 8: Assessment* of the National Science Teachers Association (NSTA) *Standards for Science Teacher Preparation* states:

> *To show that they are prepared to use assessment effectively, teachers of science must demonstrate that they:*
>
> *a. Use multiple assessment tools and strategies to achieve important goals for instruction that are aligned with methods of instruction and the needs of students.*
>
> *b. Use the results of multiple assessments to guide and modify instruction, the classroom environment, and the assessment process.*
>
> *c. Use the results of assessment as a vehicle for students to analyze their own learning, engaging students in reflective self-analysis of their own work.* (NSTA, 2003, p. 26)

It is recommended that your understandings of assessment be revealed in an instructional unit. Specifically, a unit that you develop should include multiple assessments that may serve diagnostic, formative, and summative functions. Furthermore, your unit should show conceptual alignment between standards, assessment, and learning experiences, which can be achieved when planning with the end in mind.

In practice, you should be able to demonstrate that you can assess students' science learning and dispositions and to translate assessment results into student grades. You will also be expected to demonstrate your ability to use assessment results to guide the instructional experiences in which you engage students and to help students use assessment results to analyze and modify their own learning.

Realizing these expectations is not simple, and will require the support of university instructors and experienced science teachers over a period of time. But, developing understandings of assessment and being able to apply your understandings in the science classroom is critical to your success as a science teacher and to the success of your students as science learners.

Assessing and Reviewing

Analysis and Synthesis

1. Describe in your own words the relationships among the components of the science learning assessment system: learning goals, beginning-of-instruction assessment, during-instruction assessment, and end-of-instruction assessment.
2. Construct or locate several examples of traditional and alternative assessments and measures that could be used to assess students' dispositions. Discuss the assessments with classmates and evaluate their potential usefulness in assessing student achievement relative to your state or national standards.
3. Suppose a teacher told you that she does not have time for formative or diagnostic assessment in her science classes. What would you say to try to convince her to include these forms of assessment in her teaching plans?
4. Write three questions that could be used to assess student learning while you are teaching. What information would you be likely to obtain from students' responses to these questions that would help you modify your instruction?

Practical Considerations

5. Use an online design tool to build a rubric or checklist for a particular science performance. Test the rubric or checklist with a class and solicit student feedback regarding its appropriateness. Then, revise the rubric or checklist based on the students' feedback.

6. Study a teacher's test recently administered to a class of students. Talk to the teacher about the items included on the test, how instruction prepared the students to succeed on the test, and how the test results will be used to inform instruction and by students to modify their learning.
7. Examine a school's grading policy and report card format. What do these sources of information tell you about the grading system used by teachers at the school? Then, talk with a teacher at the school about his or her grading practices to verify your assumptions.

Developmental Considerations

8. Discuss assessment with science teaching colleagues and ask them for suggestions about how to include diagnostic, formative, and summative assessments in a unit. Also, ask the teachers to share how they plan for assessment and how they use assessment results to help students modify their learning.
9. Read an article from *Science Scope* or *The Science Teacher* that focuses on assessment. Discuss the article with others interested in science assessment. Devise a plan to implement a suggestion from the article in your planning and teaching.

Resources to Examine

Classroom Assessment and the National Science Education Standards. 2001. Washington, DC: National Academy Press.

A supplement to the National Science Education Standards, this book offers arguments for strengthening assessment in the science classroom. It contains sections on summative and formative assessment, school system level support for assessment, and teacher professional development for improving science classroom assessment.

Grading. 2004. Upper Saddle River, NJ: Merrill/Prentice Hall.

This 11-chapter book written by Susan Brookhart provides a wealth of information about grading and its relationship to student assessment. The book is organized around three themes: understanding grading, integrating assessment and instruction, and combining grades into marks for report cards.

Uncovering Student Ideas in Science: 25 Formative Assessment Probes. 2005. Arlington, VA: NSTA Press.

Page Keeley, Francis Eberle, and Lynn Farrin present detailed descriptions of easily administered assessment probes for physical, life, and earth science topics. The probes encourage students' oral and written responses that reveal their underdeveloped science conceptions and are accompanied by suggestions for instruction.

Seamless Assessment in Science. 2006. Portsmouth, NH: Heinemann Press.

In this paperback, Sandra Abell and Mark Volkmann provide a strong learning-based rationale for seamless assessment and discuss a variety of assessment strategies appropriate for middle school and secondary science. Many examples of seamless assessment, with accompanying illustrations of student responses, are presented in the text.

What Every Teacher Should Know About Student Assessment. 2004. Thousand Oaks, CA: Corwin Press.

Chapter 7 of this book by Donna Tileston provides detailed instructions for building aligned assessments. The instructions are presented as six steps for teachers to follow. Other chapters address teacher-made tests, performance tasks, and state and national assessments.

References

Abell, S. K., & Volkmann, M. J. (2006). *Seamless assessment in science: A guide for elementary and middle school teachers.* Portsmouth, NH: Heinemann.

Balanced Assessment Group. (1998). *Balanced assessment for the mathematics curriculum: High school assessment.* White Plains, NY: Dale Seymour.

Borg, W. R., & Gall, M. D. (1983). *Educational research* (4th ed.). New York: Longman.

Brookhart, S. M. (2004). *Grading.* Upper Saddle River, NJ: Merrill/Prentice Hall.

Koballa, T. R., & Glynn, S. M. (2007). Attitudinal and motivational constructs in science learning. In S. K. Abell and N. Lederman (Eds.), *Handbook for research in science education* (pp. 75–102). Mahwah, NJ: Earlbaum.

Koballa, T. R., Kemp, A., & Evans, R. (1997). The spectrum of scientific literacy. *The Science Teacher, 64*(7), 27–31.

Licata, K. P. (1999). Narrative lab reports. *The Science Teacher*, *66*(3), 20–22.

Marzano, R. J., & Kendall, J. S. (2007). *The new taxonomy of educational objectives* (2nd ed.). Thousand Oaks, CA: Corwin Press.

National Research Council. (1996). *National Science Education Standards*. Washington, DC: National Academy Press.

National Science Teachers Association. (2003). Standards for science teacher preparation. Retrieved November 30, 2008, from www.nsta.org/pdfs/NSTAstandards2003.pdf

Tileston, D. W. (2004). *What every teacher should know about student assessment*. Thousand Oaks, CA: Corwin Press.

Wiggins, G., & McTighe, J. (2005). *Understanding by design* (2nd ed.). Alexandria, VA: Association for Supervision of Curriculum Development.

Woolfolk, A. (2004). *Educational psychology*. Boston: Allyn & Bacon.

Chapter

5 Teaching Science

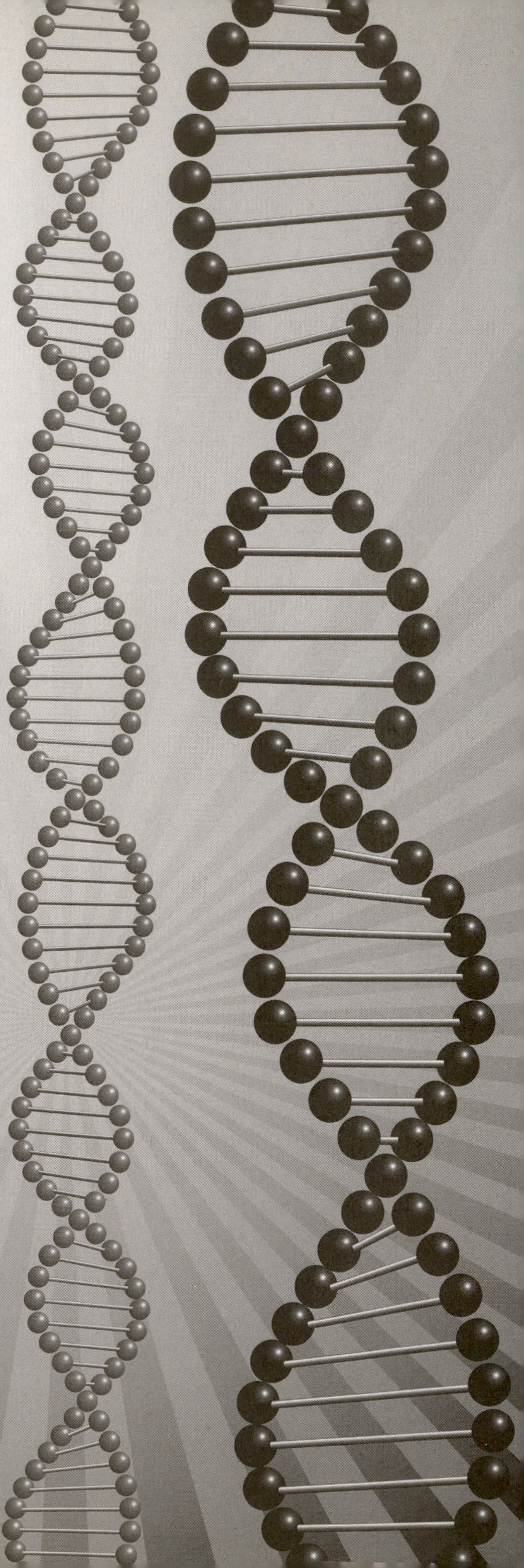

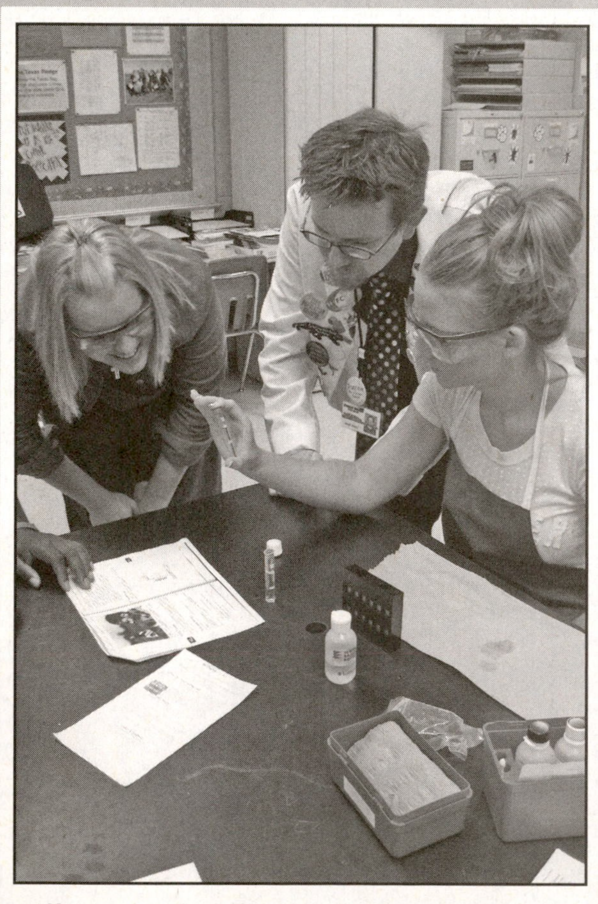

Effective teachers engage students as active learners.

Mr. Palmer completed his student teaching during the previous school year and is a new teacher assigned to teach eleventh-grade chemistry at Spring High School. The school is located in a suburban district about 20 miles west of a large mid-western city. The student population composition is about 15% from lower-middle-class families, 60% from middle-class families, and 25% from upper-middle-class families. Approximately 70% of the students who graduate from high school go on to college. Mrs. Oliver is the assistant principal for instruction; she has scheduled a visit to Mr. Palmer's classroom in order to observe his teaching and to determine how he is getting along as a first-year teacher. The observation session is taking place during the second month of the school year.

Mr. Palmer greets the students by name as they enter the classroom. When all students are in their seats, he moves to his computer to take roll, using an online grade book and attendance roster. Then he immediately begins the lesson.

Mr. Palmer: Class, I want you to observe carefully what I am about to do. Therefore, would you stand and come within about six feet of the demonstration table.

Then Mr. Palmer calls one of the students to the demonstration table to weigh a handful of steel wool. He calls on another student to record the mass of the steel wool on the board. After the teacher puts on safety goggles, he places the steel wool on a square of aluminum foil and ignites it by touching the positive and negative contacts of a 9-volt battery to the metal fibers of the steel wool. The glow and flame from the reaction causes a great deal of excitement among the students, who did not expect the steel wool to burn. The teacher plunges the 9-volt battery into many areas on the surface of the steel wool to ensure that most of the iron fibers have ignited. After all the flames die out and the steel wool appears darker in color, the teacher calms the students down and calls for silence. He asks the class members to take their seats and to make an inference regarding the mass of the steel wool by requesting a show of hands.

Mr. Palmer: Students, as the result of setting the steel wool on fire, does it weigh: (a) less, (b) more, or (c) the same?

He calls for a show of hands for each category and records the results on the board:

Less	More	Same
26	0	2

Mr. Palmer invites one of the students to the front demonstration table to place the burned, or oxidized, steel wool on the balance to determine its mass. He calls on another student to record the mass of the steel wool on the board. Needless to say, the students are surprised to observe that the steel wool is heavier after it has been burned. The students respond with looks and comments of disbelief. After the talking dies down, Mr. Palmer states that he wants students to explain why the steel wool weighs more after it is burned. He urges them to form their explanations carefully. After waiting for a few minutes, Mr. Palmer calls on several students to explain their thinking regarding the mass of the steel wool in order to support their votes.

Mr. Palmer: Class, I have drawn a greatly enlarged strand of the steel wool on the board. Tammy, would you go to the board and measure the diameter of this strand of steel wool.

$$\text{———} + \text{heat} + O_2 \rightarrow$$

Tammy: It's about 2 mm wide.

Mr. Palmer: Good! Thank you. Class, what happens to each fiber of the steel wool when it is set on fire? Does the mass (a) decrease in mass, (b) increase in mass, or (c) remain the same? Please, I want a show of hands.

After some friendly argumentation among the class members, some of the students seem to accept the fact that the mass of the steel wool increases as the result of burning. Nevertheless, many students still seem perplexed about this and hold onto their idea that burning causes matter to disappear, resulting in a decrease in mass.

Mr. Palmer then directs students to copy the diagram on the board of the steel fiber that Tammy measured and to draw what that fiber might look like after it is ignited. The teacher encourages the students to use the drawing pencils and markers that he supplies for making the drawings. As students attempt to complete their sketches of an iron fiber increasing in diameter and mass, Mr. Palmer walks among them, asking questions and guiding thinking. He spends most of his time interacting with a few English as a Second Language (ESL) students, giving them cues so that they can show an increase in the size of the fiber. After students complete their diagrams, Mr. Palmer asks for a few volunteers to sketch their "ignited fibers" on the board, which is accompanied by a brief question-and-answer session to illustrate visually how the mass increases and how one form of chemical change takes place as the result of oxidation.

Mr. Palmer hands out a two-page explanation of the oxidation that occurs when iron is set on fire. The handout also includes a diagram of the oxidation process that was scanned and pasted into the text. The teacher asks the students to silently read the handout and to underline key ideas. Then he conducts a guided read-aloud activity of the two-page handout, placing key terms and phrases on the board. After Mr. Palmer brings the session to a close, he announces that the class period is going to end in 10 minutes and that before they review what has been learned during today's lesson, he wants to call attention to the homework assignment that is written on the side board:

- Read pages 246 to 554 in the textbook. Write down the headings and subheadings, and under each, briefly write key ideas about chemical change and oxidation.
- Go to the NOVA Web site and find the program that recently aired on PBS, "Interior of the Earth," which is about chemical and physical changes, but do not view it.

Mr. Palmer: Now let's review what you have learned today before the bell rings. First, write a paragraph to describe the chemical process that took place when I ignited the steel wool. I'll help some of you with the paragraph.

Stop and Reflect!

Before going on in this chapter, please respond to the questions and statements below.

1. What is the science content focus of the lesson?
2. In what way does the content focus of the lesson reflect content recommended by national standards?
3. With which NSTA/NCATE *Standards for Science Teacher Preparation* does the instruction or pedagogy of the lesson correlate?
4. Which part of the science unit would the lesson fit into, the beginning, middle or end?
5. What does the teacher do to engage students in the lesson?
6. Name the instructional strategy used to begin the lesson.
7. List and briefly describe all the instructional strategies used in the lesson.
8. Describe the technique used by the teacher to help students represent or visualize their knowledge regarding the change in the mass of the steel wool.
9. How does the teacher attempt to accommodate ESL and learning-disabled students?
10. How does the teacher use technology in the course?
11. Describe the extent to which the teacher asks students to explain their ideas.
12. How well does the teacher attempt to relate the concepts under study to everyday life?
13. Rate the lesson with regard to key ideas associated with science learning.

The extent to which the students were engaged in the lesson.

1 2 3 4 5 6 7 8 9 10

Very little Somewhat A great deal

The extent to which the students represented their knowledge.

1 2 3 4 5 6 7 8 9 10

Very little Somewhat A great deal

The extent to which there was consideration for diverse learners.

1 2 3 4 5 6 7 8 9 10

Very little Somewhat A great deal

The extent to which students were asked to explain ideas.

1 2 3 4 5 6 7 8 9 10

Very little Somewhat A great deal

AIMS OF THE CHAPTER

Use the following questions to guide your thoughts and actions about teaching science:

- To what extent can you design a science lesson that will highly engage student learning, teach for understanding, stress the representation of student thinking, and accommodate diverse learners?

- How many different instructional strategies can you incorporate into a science lesson, moving seamlessly from one strategy to the other, during class period?
- Which of the teaching skills will you become proficient in when teaching science lessons?
- Which reinforcement techniques will you use to enhance learning when you teach science, especially those that accommodate diverse learners who are learning English as a second language or who have some learning disability?
- On a scale of 1 to 10, what teaching effectiveness score would you receive from your instructor or peers if you taught a science lesson to middle school, high school students, or to adult peers preparing to become science teachers?

The act of teaching is familiar to all of us. After 16 or more years of education, all college graduates possess some knowledge of how to instruct students because they have observed and participated in thousands of hours of instruction. We would also venture to say that most individuals with a baccalaureate degree believe they can teach well. The time has come for you to test this assumption.

The written materials and exercises that follow in this chapter focus on helping you to become an effective science teacher: one who is informed about good teaching practices, knowledgeable enough to explain and recognize them, and able to implement them in a variety of classroom settings. The focus will be on teaching in front of students in grades 6–12, as well as with adult peers in the science methods class. Teaching "science as inquiry" is our philosophical position with regard to instruction, which includes a variety of skills, methods, and techniques (National Research Council, 1996; NSTA/NCATE *Standards for Science Teacher Preparation*, NSTA, 2003). The research literature is clear that quality teaching makes a difference in what students learn (Lumpe, 2007).

Further on in this textbook, you will encounter entire chapters that address: (a) inquiry-based teaching and learning, (b) laboratory exercises and fieldwork, and (c) science/technology/society approaches to science teaching. For now, let's examine teaching science lessons by focusing on four aspects of teaching effectiveness: the personal characteristics of the teacher, the use of teaching skills, the implementation of instructional strategies, and the incorporation of learning techniques.

 Personal Characteristics

The attributes of a teacher are critical to success in the classroom. The most capable science teachers that we have observed possess a great deal of energy that translates into their classroom teaching. These individuals are more likely to engage students in thought-provoking instruction and to *teach science as inquiry* than those who expend a minimal amount of energy in their planning and teaching. Instead of presenting students with a large body of organized information, the more experienced and informed science teachers engage students in a variety of thinking processes and ways to help them construct their own science understanding and to consider how these understandings can be used to enhance their lives.

A competent science teacher must possess a good *understanding of the subject* he or she teaches. Only with this level of knowledge will a teacher be able to ask good questions, probe for student understanding, and stimulate class discussion. The body of scientific knowledge is large, and comprehending even a small amount of core content in the fields of science that you are assigned to teach requires a good background. Students quickly realize when their teacher lacks subject matter competence. Therefore, all science teachers must maintain continuous study of science, especially in the areas that they are assigned to teach.

An individual who can *make the subject interesting and relevant to the audience* holds the potential to engage students in learning and remembering the content under study. The teacher with a baccalaureate degree in science who attempts to merely cover the content of a science lesson does not fare well in his or her teaching. Lessons need to be tailored to the prior knowledge and abilities of the audience. You are expected to bring your own special twist to teaching a given topic, which must include minds-on activities as well as information.

Teachers who are *enthusiastic* about teaching science are apt to motivate students. Their understanding about natural phenomena and the stories about how this knowledge has been constructed over time are evident by their interest in teaching as well as the topic under study. And, of course, exceptional science teachers are passionate about their work. These educators exude their knowledge and understanding of science, which in turn infects their students.

You must be "with it" in order to be successful in the classroom. "Withitness" is the ability to teach students and to know what is taking place in all areas of the classroom (Brophy, 1983). Teachers who exhibit this ability can manage student activity and instruct at the same time. They know if students are misbehaving and off-task, and students are aware that the teacher knows what they are doing at all times. Therefore, you must be prepared to move from one instructional strategy to another, keeping an eye on all students and engaging them in learning. Withitness is a personal characteristic that may be difficult to develop, but it is essential to managing a productive learning environment.

You must show *interest in helping students to learn*, not merely in communicating what students should learn. Audiences of all ages can sense the difference between a teacher who covers the subject matter and one who is focused on how well they are grasping the material. An effective teacher is a guide and a facilitator, encouraging students to learn and to be successful (Rogers & Freiberg, 1994).

Stop and Reflect!

Return to the scenario of the first-year teacher described at the beginning of this chapter and to your analysis of his teaching. Considering the personal characteristics of an effective teacher, how would you describe and rate Mr. Palmer on these elements?

1. How interested is the teacher in teaching science to young people and helping them to be successful in learning science?
2. Does Mr. Palmer make the subject matter interesting?
3. Is the teacher "with it"?

Teaching Skills

Teaching skills are specific behaviors that teachers use to conduct lessons and implement instructional strategies. These skills are needed to introduce lessons, ask questions, give directions, provide feedback, interact with students, and end lessons. Teaching skills must be developed in order to conduct effective science lessons. These are the behaviors that promote student engagement during instruction.

Introduction

The introduction prepares students for learning. It focuses attention on what will be taught and attempts to interest students in the lesson. Other labels given for the lesson introduction are set induction, anticipatory set, and attention grabber.

Directions

Directions communicate what is expected and guides students to proper and productive behavior. Directions are given in a manner that ensures all students know what to do and how to perform. Directions are generally given orally and written on the board. Questions asked by the teacher can be used to determine how well students comprehend what it is they are requested to do.

Questions

Questions involve students in learning by causing them to think and respond. Student responses to questions aid in the development of understanding. Teachers can ask many types of questions beyond the one-answer type, such as higher-order, open-ended, and probing questions. They can use questions that encourage students to: be *engaged* in the lesson, *explore* their own thinking, *explain* their ideas, *evaluate* their findings, and *elaborate* on what they have learned. Further, teachers can demonstrate appropriate wait time, giving students opportunities to think about the questions posed and the responses given by other students.

Teaching Aids

There are many teaching aids that facilitate the presentation of ideas and information, and which promote student learning. These instructional devices, when coupled with good questions and clear explanations, are very effective. The chalkboard and whiteboard, found most often at the front of the classroom, are common fixtures in most classrooms. The overhead may also be found in the classroom. Teacher-made posters are effective teaching aids. Today, many schools have electronic projection systems in classrooms to show pictures and text from computer files, PowerPoint presentations, CDs, and DVDs.

Management

Good classroom management includes everything that a teacher does to create and sustain a productive learning environment. The skills that lead to a productive learning environment can be observed in teachers who develop positive relationships among all students and between students and the teacher. It also can be observed in those who transition efficiently from one activity to another. The good classroom manager keeps students on task and is quick to address disruptive behavior. Further, these teachers consciously position themselves in the classroom in order to maximize student engagement.

Closure

The closure brings a lesson or a teaching segment to an end. This act helps students to review what has been presented and reinforce main ideas. Student achievement of the intended learning outcomes also can be ascertained during closure. Asking students to respond orally to questions, complete a worksheet, or construct a diagram or concept map are effective ways to both assess and reinforce learning.

Assessment

An essential aspect of a successful teaching and learning experience for students is to measure and evaluate their learning, during and at the end of the lesson. When all is said and done with regard to a teaching session, a legitimate question to ask is, to what extent did the students achieve the instructional objectives? A complete teaching and learning experience should provide evidence of student learning, whether it takes the form of questions to answer on paper or a paper-and-pencil quiz, or drawing a concept map. The assessment process should provide teachers and students with a clear idea about the success of the lesson and what future lessons should be addressed.

The effective use of many teaching skills during a period of instruction, while seemingly simple and straightforward, is not easy to carry out well. The development of these skills is a life-long pursuit. In busy, complex classrooms, many teachers are not aware of how well they open a lesson, engage students, close the lesson down, and so on, because: "(a) classroom events are complicated, (b) communication is rapid, (c) teachers generally do not study their classroom behavior (d) rarely do they receive good, objective feedback" (Good & Brophy, 2000, p. 23).

Stop and Reflect!

Think back to your assessment of the teaching skills used by Mr. Palmer in the opening vignette.

1. Which teaching skills were used in the teaching session?
2. How would you judge the effectiveness of this beginning science teacher with regard to his use of specific behaviors to conduct the lessons?
3. Do you think that this teacher uses teaching skills automatically, or does he make a conscious effort to use them in lessons?

Instructional Strategies

An instructional strategy is the way in which a major segment or an entire lesson is approached. It is the general teaching plan for achieving a given set of learning outcomes. Some lessons are planned around the presentation of information, and thus the lecture may be used. Some lessons are planned around activities that require students to develop abstract ideas from firsthand laboratory experiences. Some lessons are planned around the illustration of science principles or laws through the use of a demonstration. Some lessons are planned around reinforcing what has been learned over several lessons by recitation that incorporates questioning and reading selected passages from the assigned textbook, while other lessons are designed around two or more instructional strategies.

Let's review the instructional methods discussed earlier in this textbook so that you will get into the habit of carefully selecting, planning, and implementing these approaches in your science lessons.

Lecture

Lecture involves the presentation of information. Lecturing is an efficient way to instruct a large group of students. It should involve carefully organized information communicated in an articulate manner. Further, a lecture should be interesting and informative, advancing the audience's understanding of the topic, not merely covering large numbers of terms to be memorized. Lectures should be planned based on the attention span, background knowledge, and interests of the audience.

Discussion

Discussion permits students to express their views and clarify their ideas. This is a good strategy for promoting student involvement in the classroom. Discussion groups can be organized with the entire class, small groups, or in student pairs. However, in order for discussions to be productive and focused on the intended learning outcomes of the lesson, their purpose must be made clear. Students must listen carefully, and responses must focus on the important content that is being discussed. Panels can be organized in order to debate and discuss issues. Also, informal discussion groups can be formed for the purpose of brainstorming to generate ideas.

Demonstration

Demonstrations illustrate ideas through concrete means. They focus attention on key aspects of a concept and can be an effective means for guiding student thinking. Demonstrations are often of high interest to students. This is a strategy that teachers can use to illustrate science concepts or principles that may not be desirable to study in the laboratory because of expense or safety. Science demonstrations are instructive when conducted in a skilled manner.

Laboratory Work

The laboratory involves students in firsthand experiences to study natural phenomena. Laboratory exercises also are used to teach laboratory techniques and inquiry skills to students. This strategy can be approached in a variety of ways, such as initiating laboratory experiences with an inductive or a deductive activity or by focusing on a problem to be solved. Laboratory exercises should be used frequently throughout a science course to promote interest and develop comprehension of abstract concepts.

Reading

Reading is a way to promote many aspects of science by forming ideas and grasping meaning from the printed word. Directed reading activities in science textbooks or other printed materials can be implemented frequently as a whole-class, small-group, or independent activity. One type of content reading strategy might include the following activities: (a) pre-reading exercises to identify what students know, (b) during-reading exercises that focus on key terms and important ideas, and (c) after-reading exercises that summarize main ideas.

Group Work

Group work is an excellent way to engage students in learning science. This strategy encourages students to work together, sharing ideas and working cooperatively at tasks that lead to a common product. Cooperative grouping is designed to assign different roles to individual students with guidelines to carry out specific tasks. This can be a powerful strategy to learn science content and process, promote good working habits and cooperation, and to build a positive classroom atmosphere.

Simulations and Games

Simulations and games are designed to illustrate events and processes that occur in the real world. They help students to visualize objects and events that cannot be observed in the classroom, laboratory, or nearby community. Today, there are many computer simulations that provide rich learning experiences for students. Good, short science simulations should be part of all units and courses of study, but must not to be confused with laboratory work that is firsthand experience.

Computers and Internet

The computer and the Internet hold enormous potential to engage students in learning about phenomena, answering questions, and solving problems. Students can search thousands of science topics on the Internet and even find scientific data to analyze and study. They can use e-mail to contact scientists and others for information. Many government research facilities and science museums can be accessed for information related to science. Students can use word processing and graphics programs to organize and present their ideas and findings. The instructional possibilities are unlimited with computer and Internet technology.

Recitation

The recitation session requires students to demonstrate their knowledge through their responses to teacher questions. It usually takes place toward the end of a lesson with the teacher calling on certain students to answer questions that pertain directly to the learning outcomes of the lesson. However, recitation can take place during lessons. Recitation is an excellent strategy for incorporating formative assessment into instruction.

Stop and Reflect!

- List the instructional strategies that were used by Mr. Palmer during his science lesson, and compare your list with those of other participants in the methods course. How much agreement is there among your analyses?
- Which instructional strategies would you use to teach chemical changes to middle school or to high school chemistry students?

Teachers should provide students with frequent feedback about their learning.

Learning and Reinforcement Techniques

When you teach a science lesson that incorporates many teaching skills and instructional strategies, you may feel confident about the success of your teaching. And indeed, you should feel good about this. However, there is more to the teaching effectiveness equation that must be considered in order to reinforce student learning. Remember, we want students to understand what they are expected to learn and to explain this understanding in an articulate manner. Teaching and learning for understanding is a major goal for science education, just as the aim of science is to understand natural phenomena. Teaching for understanding sets the stage for moving on to applying what is being studied. Further, many in our professions believe that students who understand the conceptual knowledge they are expected to learn will perform better on district, state, and national standardized texts.

Today, educators realize that a teacher must cause students to use learning techniques that organize and reinforce the knowledge they are constructing. Research on cognitive learning processes has advanced our understanding on how to help students develop knowledge structures that promote understanding and retention of subject matter (Rosenshine, 2002). Following is a list of some of the techniques to incorporate into your instruction. While you may not be able to use all of these techniques in a given lesson, you should implement most of them within a unit of study.

Note taking should be a standard practice in science course learning. This process causes students to focus on the important ideas and information. Students must keep a science notebook of useful information that they will commit to memory and refer to when reviewing for tests, doing homework, and completing assignments. Also, you must teach students how to take notes and monitor their note taking so that feedback can be given on how well this is being done.

Writing summaries and short papers to organize ideas is critical to the understanding of abstract science subject matter. Writing requires students to think deeply to recall what they know, organize what they are expected to learn, and to write their thoughts on paper. Students should be required to write often about their science learning. Writing is one of the most powerful mental tasks in which teachers can engage students (Wallace, 2004).

Identifying similarities and differences is a technique that appears to have one of the strongest effects on learning (Marzano, Pickering, & Pollock, 2001). When you call on students to compare science concepts, they must know their attributes and indicate how they are similar and what distinguishes them. It is essential that students possess a clear idea of how fundamental science concepts are similar, yet different, such as mitosis and meiosis, mass and weight, and speed and acceleration. Analogies are powerful tools for helping students to learn abstract ideas.

Concept mapping supports visual learning. It helps students to organize information by showing the relationships among key concepts. This graphic learning technique can facilitate the meaningful learning of abstract and complex ideas when students are actively engaged in forming their own concept maps of important subject matter content. You should frequently ask students to construct concept maps, webs, and diagrams to demonstrate their knowledge of the subject under study.

Practice and feedback must be an integral part of all science instruction. There is always the danger of covering too much subject matter in science courses and not providing enough instruction of main ideas to ensure mastery. Students need to practice the cognitive skill of articulating their understandings of science in order to integrate their knowledge into long-term memory. Teachers must monitor these learning activities and provide feedback to ensure that students are forming ideas correctly and staying on the task of learning.

These and other learning techniques will be taken up in Chapter 10. Nevertheless, we hope that you will be motivated to use them in your teaching. Your commonsense knowledge about these techniques will get you started.

Stop and Reflect!

Go back and examine the instruction that took place in Mr. Palmer's classroom.

1. Which learning reinforcement techniques did Mr. Palmer use during his science lesson?
2. How might Mr. Palmer improve his teaching in order to ensure greater understanding of chemical changes among his students?
3. Name several learning reinforcement strategies that you have observed in the classrooms of effective science teachers.

Summary

This chapter has provided a brief description of many aspects of teaching that relate to student learning. You know about these elements of teaching because of the many years you have spent in school. Now, you must incorporate these teaching skills, instructional strategies, and learning techniques into your teaching, and you must become more aware of the personal characteristics of good teachers that also impact student success. Figure 5.1 summarizes these ideas and you should refer to them often as you plan and teach science lessons.

FIGURE 5.1 A menu of personal characteristics, teaching skills, instructional strategies, and learning techniques to engage students in learning science for understanding.

Be Aware of Personal Characteristics

- ✓ Inclines toward inquiry-based instruction
- ✓ Demonstrates knowledge and understanding of the subject
- ✓ Makes the subject interesting and relevant to the audience
- ✓ Enthusiastic about teaching science
- ✓ Exhibits "withitness" in the classroom
- ✓ Shows interest in helping students to be successful

Employ Many Teaching Skills

- ✓ Introductions that grab attention and provide a foundation for the lesson
- ✓ Directions that are clear and concise
- ✓ Questions directed toward students to stimulate thinking and reasoning
- ✓ Teaching aids to facilitate the presentation of ideas and information
- ✓ Management that keeps students on task and minimizes disruptions
- ✓ Closure to summarize and review main ideas
- ✓ Assessment linked to reinforce learning and linked to instructional objects

Use a Variety of Instructional Strategies

- ✓ Lectures that promote organization of ideas and stimulate interest
- ✓ Discussions that stimulate thoughtful dialog among students
- ✓ Demonstrations that spark interest and illustrate key concepts
- ✓ Laboratory work that provides firsthand experiences with laws and principles
- ✓ Reading that helps to build knowledge
- ✓ Group work that promotes cooperation and collaboration
- ✓ Simulations/games that illustrate important concepts and principles
- ✓ Recitation that reinforces learning

Incorporate Techniques to Enhance Learning

- ✓ Note taking that organizes and summarizes information to be learned
- ✓ Writing that stimulates deep thinking and mental processing of ideas
- ✓ Identifying similarities and differences among key concepts
- ✓ Concept mapping to facilitate visual learning
- ✓ Practice and feedback for mastery

Many lessons that form a unit plan should be planned to incorporate several teaching skills, instructional strategies, and learning reinforcement techniques, but certainly not all of them in a single period of instruction. Once again, analyze the science lesson illustrated in the chapter opener and identify which of the specifications stated in the NSTA/NCATE *Standards for Science Teacher Preparation*, Standard 5: General Skills of Teaching, stated below.

> *Teachers of science create a community of diverse learners who construct meaning from their science experiences and possess a disposition for further exploration and learning. They use, can justify, a variety of classroom arrangements, groupings, actions, strategies, and methodologies. (NSTA, 2003)*

Now Let's Teach Science

The time has arrived when you should teach a science lesson and receive feedback and evaluation on your performance. Develop a science lesson to be given to your peers, adult science majors, preparing to become science teachers. (Refer to an earlier chapter on planning science instruction.) Construct a lesson plan for a 50-minute period of instruction. Conduct the first 20 minutes of the lesson and receive feedback from your peers and instructor. The instructor can provide the overall rating of the teaching, or this can be achieved by the collective ratings of the peer group. Of course, if time permits, the teaching session can extend for the full 50-minute lesson. Following are some guidelines for this exercise, which can be modified to suit your situation.

1. Design a science lesson to be taught to a group of *peers* that is appropriate for this audience. The lesson must be one that:
   - actively engages the audience in thinking
   - is perceived by peers and the instructor to be interesting and meaningful
   - is challenging for the adult science majors in the audience
   - focuses on a science concept, principle, law, or theory
   - does *not* involve laboratory work, *nor* does it attempt to teach science process skills or about the nature of science
2. Construct a detailed, long-form lesson plan for a 50-minute class period. The lesson must be typed, single-spaced, and include:
   - cover page with the title of the lesson and your name
   - paragraph giving the purpose
   - list of materials and equipment that are needed to deliver the lesson
   - instructional objectives that state precisely what the peers will learn from the lesson
   - detailed descriptions of the instructional activities

   Be sure the first instructional activity (often called a *set induction* or an *anticipatory set*) grabs the attention of the learners and provides them with a mental set for the lesson. End with a closure and review of key ideas.
   - Attach handouts that will be used in the lesson.
   - Provide an assessment of the instructional objects at the end of the lesson plan.
3. Teach part of the lesson (approximately 20 minutes) to peers. This teaching exercise is only for the first part of the lesson, and the individual teaching must not attempt to teach the entire lesson during this period of time because it would result in a fast-paced lesson that would minimize learner engagement.
4. Following the 20-minute teaching session, the individual who was teaching can participate in the feedback of the lesson by going to the board and writing the comments of the audience as suggested in Figure 5.2.
5. After reflecting on the lesson for several days, write at least one paragraph stating the strengths of the lesson and one paragraph indicating aspects that might be modified or improved.

Figure 5.2 presents a feedback and evaluation form that can be used for this teaching exercise. The form lists some of the personal characteristics, teaching skills, instructional strategies, and learning techniques that might be used during a science lesson. Note there is a place for observational notes. In addition, there are spaces at the bottom of the form to list the *effective aspects* of the teaching and *suggestions for improvement*. At the end of 20 minutes of teaching, the individual who taught can place the labels on the board as shown on the form and list statements given by the peers and instructor. The individual who teaches may also list his or her reflections regarding the teaching.

NOTE:

The first 20 minutes of the teaching should be very engaging, interesting, and challenging to the audience, teaching them something that they did not know about the science topic. This segment of the lesson should be a "knock your socks off introduction" that leaves the audience saying: "I did not know that" or "I never thought of it that way." Further, the session should be an invitation to inquiry, whereby the audience wants to learn more about the topic.

Begin the feedback with the effective teaching behaviors that were demonstrated, followed by a list of suggestions for improvement that should have been present during this lesson to this group. Avoid the use of the term *criticism* or a discussion that is critical in nature. List only suggestions for improvement that identify teaching behaviors that were absent and detracted from the lesson. You should not bring up trivial aspects of the teaching or suggestions that pertain to teaching a younger audience. Keep the feedback positive!

The form also has a place at the top to rate the lesson. The rating scale scheme is a holistic approach to assessment, not one where you add up points for each behavior observed. At the end of the session, you form an overall impression of the teaching. This scale can be modified for a 50-point, 100-point, or other range.

All teachers can profit from a short 20-minute teaching session with feedback and evaluation from adult peers. After success with this short, practice teaching approach, lessons can be given to middle and high school students in local school classrooms. The classroom science teacher can provide feedback and a rating score on the lesson. The lessons can also be taped and analyzed after the lesson has been conducted.

FIGURE 5.2 Feedback and evaluation form for a teaching session.

Title of Lesson: ____________________

Name of Teacher: ____________________ Date: __________

Rating of Lesson: ------Poor------ ------Fair------ ------Good------ ------Excellent-----

6.0 6.5 7 7.5 8.0 8.5 9.0 9.5 10

Elements to Look for During the Lesson

A. *Personal Characteristics*

___ Demonstrates understanding of subject
___ Exhibits enthusiasm for teaching
___ Maintains student's interest
___ Plans a challenging lesson

B. *Teaching Skills*

___ Provides an attention-grabbing introduction
___ Asks thought-provoking questions
___ Gives students time to think about their answers
___ Paces the lesson well
___ Uses a variety of teaching aids

C. *Instructional Strategies*

___ Implements more than one instructional strategy
___ Uses instructional strategies well
___ Results in great deal of student engagement

D. *Learning Techniques*

___ Note taking and writing are encouraged.
___ Explaining ideas is stressed.
___ Feedback is given.
___ Reinforcement and praise are observed.

Notes on Teaching Observed During the Lesson

Summary of Post-Lesson Feedback

Effective Aspects of the Teaching *Suggestions for Improvement*

Assessing and Reviewing

Analysis and Synthesis

1. Name the four categories of teaching that were discussed in this chapter. Within each category, which descriptors do you feel are most critical to effective science teaching?

Practical Considerations

2. Consider a situation where a colleague or peer asks you to observe a science lesson that he or she will teach and to provide feedback and an evaluation of the lesson. Based on the discussion of science teaching in this chapter, design a feedback and evaluation form that you would use in observing your colleague or peer.
3. Make arrangements to observe an inexperienced and an experienced science teacher instructing middle or high school students. Use a feedback and evaluation form that you developed or the one presented in this chapter to make notes and to summarize the teaching behaviors observed during the lessons. After you have listed the effective aspects of the teaching and suggestions for improvement for each lesson, compare the lessons taught by the inexperienced and experienced teachers.
4. Choose the science subject that you are most comfortable in teaching to a class of middle or high school students. Then, make an arrangement to teach a science lesson in a public or private school. Ask the cooperating teacher to use the feedback and evaluation form, which you designed or the one in this chapter, to record observations and to identify effective aspects of your teaching as well as suggestions for improvement. Spend some time discussing the instrument with the cooperating teacher in order for him or her to understand the purpose of this exercise and how to assess it.

   Remember to do the following in preparation for your teaching: (a) determine what the cooperating teacher would want you to teach; (b) find out the number of students in the class, the arrangement of the classroom, and the characteristics of the students; (c) prepare a long-form, detailed lesson plan and share it with the cooperating teacher for his or her suggestions; (d) gather all materials needed for the lesson well in advance of the session; and (e) practice the lesson before you deliver it.

   After the lesson, discuss the teaching of the lesson with the cooperating teacher. Several days after the lesson, reflect on your instruction and write a few paragraphs highlighting the effective aspects of your teaching and those that need more work.

Developmental Considerations

5. Find one or more books or papers that address teaching-effectiveness research. Summarize for your professional files teaching behaviors and strategies that might be useful to you in becoming a successful science teacher.

Resources to Examine

Qualities of Effective Teachers. 2002. Alexandria, Virginia: Association for Supervision and Curriculum Development, Alexandria, Virginia.

This short paperback by James Strong addresses many aspects of effective teaching. The chapter "The Teacher as a Person" discusses the personal aspects of a teacher that influence teaching and learning. The book gives many bulleted lists containing tips on the teaching skills and instructional strategies discussed in this chapter on teaching science. It also gives a long list of the research studies that support the ideas put forth in this paperback.

Classroom Instruction That Works: Research-Based Strategies for Increasing Student Achievement. 2001. Alexandria, Virginia: Association for Supervision and Curriculum Development, Alexandria Virginia.

This is a valuable resource for teachers and educators. The book describes many of the instructional strategies and learning techniques that have been successful in promoting learning, such as cooperative learning, reinforcement, homework, practice, cues, questions, and advanced organizers. Furthermore, the instructional effect of each factor on learning is given.

Universal Teaching Strategies. 2005. Boston: Allyn & Bacon.

This book by Jerome Freiberg and Amy Driscoll goes into depth in discussing many instructional strategies and management strategies. It describes the strategies and offers examples on how to implement them in the classroom. The chapters often provide some historical research background of effective teaching.

An Illumination of the Role of Hands-On Activities, Discussion, Text Reading and Writing in Constructing Biology Knowledge in Seventh Grade. 2004. *School Science and Mathematics, 104*(2), 70–77.

Caroline Wallace's study highlights the efficacy of engaging students in expressing their thoughts in writing when learning science. The research study shows that the students who used the techniques called Science Writing Heuristic did better on a conceptual test than those students who did not benefit from this aid for their learning. Reading, writing, and discourse should be implemented more frequently in the science classroom.

References

Brophy, J. E. (1983). Classroom organization and management. *The Elementary School Journal, 83*(4), 265–285.

Good, T. L., & Brophy, J. E. (2000). *Looking into classrooms.* New York: Longman.

Lumpe, A. T. (2007). Application of effective schools and teacher quality research to science teacher education. *Journal of Science Teacher Education, 18*, 345–348.

Manning, L. M., & Bucher, K. T. (2005). *Teaching in the middle school.* Upper Saddle River, NJ: Merrill Prentice Hall.

Marzano, R. J., Pickering, D. J., & Pollock, J. E. (2001). *Classroom instruction that works: Research-based strategies for increasing student achievement.* Alexandria, VA: Association for Supervision and Curriculum Development.

National Research Council (NRC). (1996). *National science education standards.* Washington, DC: National Academy Press.

National Science Teachers Association (NSTA). (2003). *Standards for science teacher preparation.* Arlington, VA: Author.

Rogers, C., & Freiberg, H. J. (1994). *Freedom to learn.* Upper Saddle River, NJ: Merrill Prentice Hall.

Rosenshine, B. (2002). Converging findings on classroom instruction. In A. Molnar (Ed.), *School reform proposals: The research evidence* (Educational Policy Research Unit, pp. 175–196). Tempe, AZ: Arizona State University, College of Education.

Wallace, C. S. (2004). An illumination of the role of hands-on activities, discussion, text reading and writing in constructing biology knowledge in seventh grade. *School Science and Mathematics, 104*(2), 70–77.

Chapter 6

The Science Learning Environment

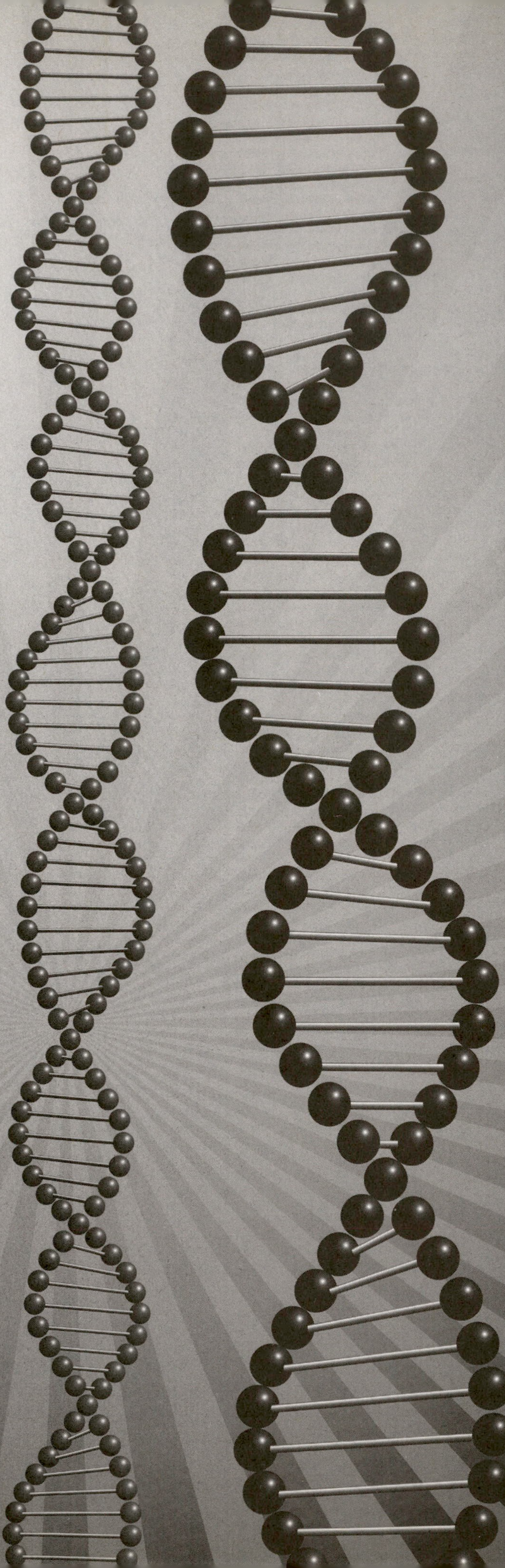

When teachers show a personal interest in science, they demonstrate instructional leadership.

First-year teacher Ms. Melissa Nelson decided to seek advice from her mentor, Mrs. Reed, before she left school for the day. Ms. Nelson had heard from other teachers that Mr. Henderson, the assistant principal, was observing science classes this week, and she wanted him to see a flawless lesson.

Mrs. Reed: So, you've also heard the rumors that Mr. Henderson is making his rounds. I'm glad you stopped by to talk. Tell me what you are planning for tomorrow.

Ms. Nelson: Well, my plan is to begin the period as you suggested. I'll have the warm-up questions and homework assignment written on the white board at the front of the classroom as students flood in. As students are working on the questions during the first five minutes of class, I'll check attendance.

Mrs. Reed: So far, so good.

Ms. Nelson: Then after going over the warm-up questions, I'll introduce the lab that I've planned, making sure to address safety concerns.

Mrs. Reed: Tell me about the lab.

Ms. Nelson: I plan to have students determine which of five antacids works best to neutralize hydrochloric acid. This lab follows today's discussion of the digestive system and heartburn, which is caused by hydrochloric acid from the stomach seeping into the esophagus. I'd like to have the students work in four-person lab groups and test the antacid solutions using both pH test paper and pH meters. This lab will enable me to help students think about controlling and manipulating variables, in addition to learning about antacids. And, I've already prepared the 0.10 M hydrochloric acid.

Mrs. Reed: I'm impressed with your planning. It sounds like you have everything set to go. So, let's talk a little about your classroom management. You know that Mr. Henderson is a real stickler when it comes to classroom management, especially when observing first-year teachers.

Ms. Nelson: I've heard from other teachers that he zeros in on students being familiar with routines and following rules as measures of a teacher's classroom control. It's like he thinks of students as factory workers and the teacher as their boss.

Mrs. Reed: I agree with you. Mr. Henderson holds a view of classroom management that is shared by many other teachers and school administrators. He seems to believe that teacher authority and discipline are the keys to a first-year teacher's success. But, as you and I have discussed there are other management approaches that may be more powerful for working with the diverse learners that we teach in our classes. What do you remember about those different approaches?

Ms. Nelson: Well, one that we talked about is focusing on personal relationships. You know, relationships between my students and me and relationships among the students in my classes. Your suggestion to get to know my students as individuals and to use my knowledge of their personal needs and unique characters to build a caring, family-like environment in my classes has really made a difference. Students that I thought were incorrigible, like Jennifer and Oscar, are actually OK kids, just going through some tough times. Once I got to know them and tried to address their needs in my teaching, things got better.

Mrs. Reed: Yes. Your work with Jennifer and Oscar is indeed a success story. Rather than trying to control their every move in the hope of soliciting acceptable behaviors, you were able to reframe the way you looked at their actions.

Ms. Nelson: Yeah. I feel very proud of my success with Jennifer and Oscar. But, I'm still feeling challenged by students in my second period class, and this is the class that, given my luck, Mr. Henderson will observe. As we've discussed, I'm trying to incorporate more democratic practices, like allowing the students to vote on the order of topics addressed in a unit or the day that lab reports are due. Students seem to be responding well to having a voice in classroom decisions, but I know I still have a long way to go.

Mrs. Reed: I think you have nothing to worry about when Mr. Henderson comes to observe you teach. Your management approach tells me that your students will be engaged in a meaningful and challenging laboratory experience.

Further, I'm pleased to hear that you are framing your classroom context in terms of personal relationships and democratic decision making rather than just maintaining order through classroom control.

Ms. Nelson: Thanks, Mrs. Reed, for listening and your continuing support. I've worked hard to build the relationships that I enjoy with my students and to identify opportunities I can use in making class decisions. I know that you are right; I'm ready for Mr. Henderson to experience the learning environment that my students and I have created.

AIMS OF THE CHAPTER

Use the questions that follow to guide your thinking and learning about some fundamental aspects of managing the science learning environment:

- What should science teachers know about the first days of school?
- What are some causes of middle and high school students' inappropriate behaviors?
- How can science teachers build culturally responsive science learning environments and help students develop productive learning habits?
- What factors influence students' motivation and engagement in science learning?

The science learning environment consists of the interpersonal, physical, and instructional aspects of the classroom that affect students' science learning. Teachers tend to view their students and the learning environments in which they function in one of three ways (Achinstein & Barrett, 2004). The view that is prevalent among beginning middle school and secondary science teachers is the *managerial view*, which emphasizes the teacher's role in managing student behavior through the use of rules, procedures, and discipline. The two other views, the *human relations view* and the *political view*, highlight the need to build relationships among individuals and engage students in democratic practices, respectively. Your understanding of these views and their implications for science teaching and learning is critical to your success as a science teacher in today's schools. When considered from the perspective offered by the combination of these three views, *classroom leader* rather than classroom manager more aptly describes the teacher's role in fostering a positive, culturally responsive learning environment. The teacher functions as more than the manager of an efficiently run classroom. The teacher also works as a collaborator to build a caring community of diverse science learners and as a change agent who engages students in decision-making practices that affect the entire classroom community.

This view of teacher as classroom leader reflects a significant shift in thinking about the teacher's role in guiding students' actions and the relationship between teacher and students and among students. The shift is from a paradigm of obedience, where the teacher uses authority to maintain order in the classroom, to a paradigm of responsibility, where the teacher helps students to develop inner self-guidance (Brophy, 2000). Important changes reflective of this paradigm shift are presented in Table 6.1.

Consistent with this paradigm shift, disciplining students is done only when all means for enabling students to make appropriate decisions are unsuccessful. The major focus of the teacher's work as classroom leader is developing and implementing a plan that encourages appropriate student actions rather than figuring out how to deal with behavioral problems once they have erupted. This plan must consider the three views of students and the learning environments in which they function as discussed above

TABLE 6.1 Changing Emphasis in Classroom Management

Less Emphasis on	More Emphasis on
• Management as a bag of tricks and recipes to follow	• Leadership as thoughtful decision making
• Student obedience	• Student self-regulation and responsibility
• Teaching rules and procedures	• Developing trust and caring
• Short-term responses to misbehavior	• Long-term solutions to personal and classroom challenges
• Work-oriented, autocratic environment	• Learning-oriented, democratic environment
• Adopting a behavioral management plan	• Developing a personalized instructional plan
• Behavior dictated by majority norms	• Behavior as culturally influenced

Based on information from "Reflections on best practice and promising programs" by C. S. Weinstein, 2000, in H. J. Freiberg (Ed.), Beyond behaviorism: Changing the classroom management paradigm *(pp. 147–163), Boston: Allyn & Bacon.*

while being consistent with the educational aims of the school. From the managerial view, the teacher may consider what rules and procedures are needed for student safety and classroom decorum. From the human relations view, the teacher may contemplate how each student can be recognized as a unique individual while at the same time developing a sense of class cohesiveness. And from the political view, the teacher may consider how can students be given a voice in classroom decisions that may help them develop as responsible individuals. An effective plan will lead to the establishment and maintenance of a culturally responsive learning environment that supports academic success and well-being of all students.

 The First Days of School

The first days of school are critically important. The year's success or failure is largely determined by what the teacher says and does during the first days of school (Evertson & Emmer, 1982; Sanford & Evertson, 1981). By and large, beginning science teachers will not have experienced the excitement and stress associated with starting the school year, at least not from the teacher's side of the desk.

Your memories of the first days of school as a middle or high school student probably include visiting with friends, scoping out the new kids, and meeting your teachers. You may recall how your new teachers introduced themselves and explained their expectations. Your first impressions of those teachers likely told you a great deal about how the class would operate, what you would learn, and what would be expected of you throughout the year.

Observations indicate that the learning environments initiated by beginning teachers during the first days of school vary considerably. Some may be academically oriented and stress the socialization of students into a learning community, while others may discourage students' questions, emphasize grades over learning, and foster competition rather than cooperation. Helen Patrick and her colleagues (2003) provide insights into the messages conveyed by teachers during the first days of school. The instructional practices used by teachers who cultivate a supportive learning environment, one that considers each of the three views of classroom leadership mentioned earlier in this chapter are summarized in Table 6.2. It is these instructional practices associated with a supportive, culturally response learning environment that enable all students to achieve academically.

TABLE 6.2 Instructional Practices of Teachers in Supportive Environments During the First Days of School

Learning and Expectations for Students	Relationships Between Teacher and Students	Relationships Among Students	Democratic Practices	Rules and Management Strategies
• Express enthusiasm for the curriculum and learning	• Introduce themselves in personal and caring ways	• Promote an atmosphere of community	• Acknowledge traditional power differential in classrooms	• Identify classroom rules and explain the reasons for them
• Discuss the empowering nature of learning	• Share some information about themselves and families	• Discuss the importance of respect among students	• Discuss how students can be involved in instructional decisions	• Give clear examples of appropriate and inappropriate behaviors
• Present learning as an incremental process	• Use humor that is developmentally appropriate	• Encourage thoughtfulness of others and consideration for the feelings of all students	• Express interest in negotiating conflicting points of view	• Stress students acting responsibly and with self-control
• Portray learning as enjoyable, valuable, and worthwhile	• Convey a sensitivity to students' needs	• Express enthusiasm for the different cultures and languages represented in the class	• Emphasize fairness and equity in access to instructional materials and support for learning	• Share expectations that students will act appropriately and show respect for others
• Exude confidence in your ability to teach and help students learn	• Show genuine respect for students	• Encourage inclusive rather than exclusive behaviors		• Enforce expectation in instances of student misbehavior

Based on information from "How teachers establish psychological environments during the first days of school: Associations with avoidance in mathematics," by H. Patrick, J. C. Turner, D. K. Meyer, and C. Midgley, 2003, Teachers College Record, 105*(8), 1521–1569.*

Stop and Reflect!

Today is the first day of school and as a beginning biology teacher Jennifer Kilborn wants to get off to a good start. She arrives in her classroom at 7:45 a.m. to make sure that everything is ready. After straightening the rows of student desks and hanging the large poster of Dian Fossey and her gorillas on the wall, Jennifer sits nervously at her desk watching the clock in anticipation of the first-period bell. As she stares at the clock's second hand sweep around the dial, her mind is filled with the stories told by two veteran teachers she met during the district's pre-planning days. Her thoughts keep returning to the teachers' parting words: "Start out the year by showing them who is boss," "As a young teacher, you'll need to be extra tough," and "Don't even think about smiling until Christmas." Jennifer is very anxious. She knows she is not a mean person by nature and does not want to appear to be mean spirited to her students, but feels that she must be firm with her students during the first days of school to avoid the problems that can befall beginning teachers.

What advice would you give Jennifer to calm her nerves and help her get the school year off to a good start?

Understanding Student Behavior

Before addressing teacher actions that can foster a supportive learning environment, it is important to reflect on personal biases that may lead to inaccurate interpretations of student behavior in the classroom as well as to consider the possible causes of student misbehavior.

Cultural Influences On Student Behavior

Students in today's schools reflect the diversity of a multicultural society and exhibit behaviors that are influenced by their cultural backgrounds. Teachers who do not share the cultural backgrounds of their students may not be aware of how their own culturally based expectations influence their interpretation of students' classroom behavior. For example, a Latino student's attempts to offer help to a classmate during a test would be viewed as cheating by most teachers. But this behavior is likely to stem from having been taught the importance of assisting others in need, hardly a reason for being reprimanded when viewed from the norms of the student's culture. Simply put, different cultures hold different views about appropriate behavior and these differences must be taken into account when teaching in today's schools (Weinstein, Curran, & Tomlinson-Clarke, 2003). Consider the behaviors identified in Figure 6.1. What might be acceptable expressions of these behaviors for students who share your cultural background and for students whose backgrounds are different from yours?

As a person responsible for the learning of students from diverse ethnic, socioeconomic, language, and racial backgrounds, what can you do to become a culturally responsive classroom leader? Weinstein and her colleagues (2003) recommend that teachers reflect on how their classroom leadership decisions promote or obstruct students' access to learning through the lens of cultural diversity. Questions based on the work of these authors to guide your reflection are as follows:

- How does my own cultural background influence the behavioral expectations I have for students?
- What do I know about my students, the communities in which they live, their culture's norms for interpersonal interactions, and their parent's expectations for proper behavior in school?
- How might the norms of schooling reflected in my classroom marginalize or privilege individuals or groups of students?

Reflecting on these questions should help to place you in a mind-set for making classroom decisions that promote equal access to science learning for the diverse communities of students that you are teaching or will soon teach. Strategies for culturally responsive classroom leadership are found throughout the subsequent sections of this chapter.

Possible Causes of Student Inappropriate Behavior

The forces and pressures that students encounter in and out of school can be the cause of behaviors considered inappropriate or undesirable for the classroom. And, as just discussed, seeming misbehavior may well reflect cultural norms that the teacher does not understand. Common causes of student misbehavior may include family pressures and expectations, student academic abilities and motivation toward schoolwork, involvement in after-school activities, as well as health and personality factors. In addition, the school administration and the science teacher may unwittingly contribute to student misbehavior, perhaps by imposing expectations that are in conflict with a student's cultural worldview.

A useful tool for understanding the motives behind student misbehavior is Abraham Maslow's (1968) theory of a hierarchy of human needs. According to Maslow, humans are motivated by unsatisfied needs and certain lower needs must be satisfied before higher needs can be considered. His hierarchy includes four general types of needs—physiological, safety, love and belonging, and esteem—that must be satisfied before a

FIGURE 6.1 Assessing your cultural content knowledge.

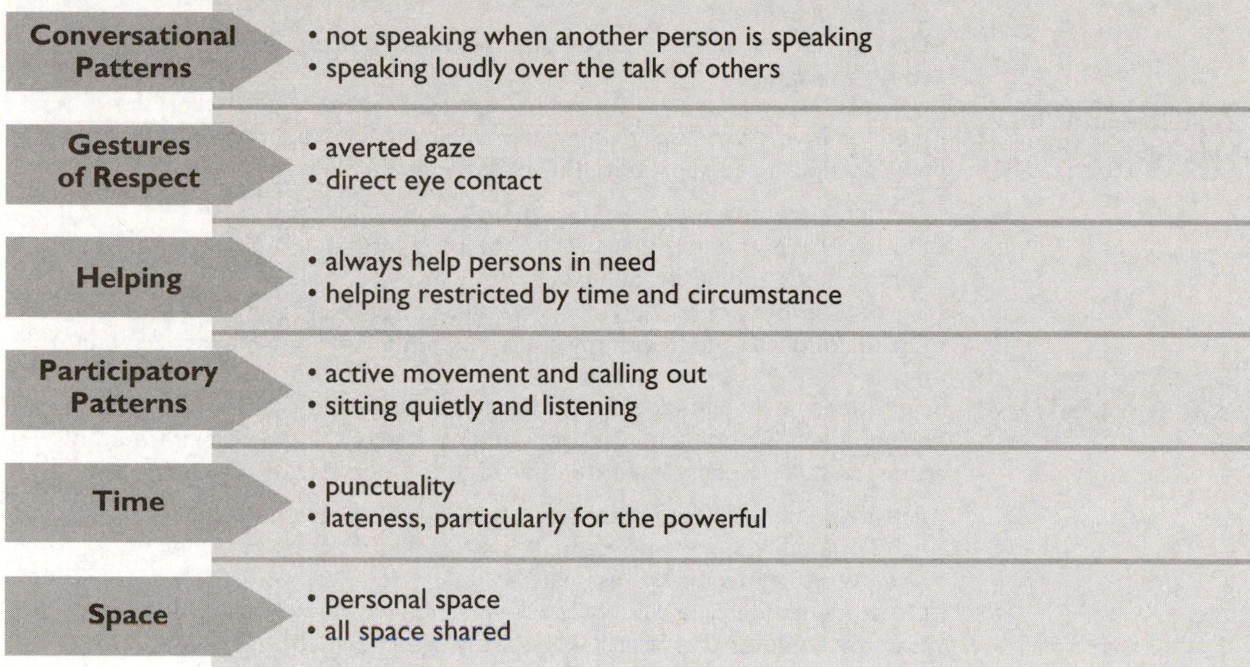

person can address his or her need for self-actualization. The need for self-actualization is the desire to achieve one's full potential and is often fulfilled through learning (Maslow, 1968). Thus, middle and high school students' basic physiological needs along with their needs for safety, love and belonging, and esteem must often be met in order for them to be engaged science learners. As a teacher, there is much that you can do to enable students to meet many of the needs that will allow them to be engaged learners. The information presented in Figure 6.2 may help you think about inappropriate behavior as a student's response to the frustrations associated with being in a learning environment in which his or her basic needs are not being met. The questions in the figure may also help you consider the actions that you might take as a teacher to help students become self-actualized learners.

What might be acceptable expressions of behavior for people who share your cultural background and for people whose backgrounds are different from yours? Examples of behavioral expressions that might be considered acceptable in different cultures are presented to initiate your thinking. Add to these lists.
What does the influence of culture on expressions of behavior suggest to you about why teachers should be explicit about their expectations for classroom behavior?
Conversational Patterns
• not speaking when another person is speaking
• speaking loudly over the talk of others
Gestures of Respect
• averted gaze
• direct eye contact
Helping
• always help persons in need
• helping restricted by time and circumstance
Participatory Patterns
• active movement and calling out
• sitting quietly and listening
Time
• punctuality
• lateness, particularly for the powerful
Space
• personal space
• all space shared

A teacher's knowledge of cultural influences on student behavior in addition to an understanding of unmet personal needs that may prompt episodes of misbehavior can be a tremendous help in providing a supportive learning environment for all students. Viewing misbehavior as a student's response to a vexation associated with being in an uninviting environment may enable a teacher to think about long-term solutions to inappropriate behavior rather than just short-term ones.

Stop and Reflect!

- Think of a culturally influenced behavior in which you engage that might be misinterpreted by a person who does not understand your culture. How could you help a "cultural outsider" come to understand your behavior?
- What unmet needs might be prompting the misbehaviors exhibited by the two students described below?

Sam Johnson often falls asleep during class. When he is not sleeping, he bullies smaller boys in class and demands money from them. He says he needs the money to buy lunch.

Jane Morris recently moved to the school district. On the first biology test, she performed poorly and has not spoken to anyone in the class since. When she is asked by her teacher to participate in a lab group, Jane refuses.

FIGURE 6.2 Questions to help address students' unmet needs.

Esteem Needs

Self-esteem may be met through achieving proficiency on an assignment or piece of work. Esteem coming from others in the form of recognition or admiration may fullfill a student's craving for power or might.

- Do I provide opportunities for students to show competence or mastery of learning tasks?
- Do all my students participate in group activities and class discussions?
- Do I listen to students' suggestions for improving my teaching and the class environment?
- Do I praise my students' accomplishments and encourage their classmates to do the same?

Love and Belonging Needs

Need for love and belonging may be met through group membership and by being accepted and appreciated by peers and adults.

- Do my students know that I like them?
- Do my students know that I accept them as individuals regardless of their personalities and backgrounds?
- Is my classroom organized to encourage camaraderie and teamwork?
- Do I take time to talk with my students about their out-of-class activities?

Safety Needs

Safety needs may be met by providing for a stable and consistent learning environment. School administrators and counselors should be informed of students' safety needs that extend beyond the purview of the classroom.

- Are students free from teasing and bullying in my classroom?
- Am I equitable in my enforcement of school and classroom rules?
- Are my assignments and tests fair?
- Do students feel free to express their feelings about my teaching?
- Can my students trust that I will not divulge information shared in confidence unless I am legally obliged to do so?
- Can my students get help from me when they need it?

Physiological Needs

Unmet needs for water, food, sleep and the like can make learning impossible. Some students' physiological needs can and should be addressed by the teacher, while others are better left to school administrators, counselors and parents or guardians.

- Are my students seated in the classroom where they can hear me and see the whiteboard or projection screen?
- Is the temperature of my classroom too hot or too cold?
- Is my classroom well lit and free of unnecessary distractions?
- Do I inform school administrators or counselors if I suspect that physiological needs are impeding a student's class performance?

Creating Culturally Responsive Science Learning Environments

A learning environment in which students' cultural backgrounds are considered and their personal needs are met is one in which the relationships between the teacher and students and among students are positive. The relationships that teachers build with their students are ones that encourage students to feel significant and take responsibility for their own actions. In building a culturally responsive learning environment, the teacher also has the responsibility of creating positive relationships among students. Instituting democratic classroom practices that are based on shared understandings of freedom, justice, and equality can help foster positive relationships between the teacher and students and among students. The time spent developing positive personal relationships and helping students to understand the operations of the classroom in terms of democratic principles is indeed worthwhile. Research clearly shows that the quality of classroom relationships and student empowerment in classrooms guided by democratic principles can have a significant influence on student behavior and academic success (Good & Brophy, 2000; Gradmont, 2003; Gross, 2006; Hoover & Kindsvatter, 1997; Marzano, 2003; Matsumura, Slater, & Crosson, 2008; Purkey & Novak, 1996).

Teacher–Student Relationships

The foundation for positive teacher–student relationships is teachers communicating to students that they are interested in them and have concerns for them as people and learners. Learning students' names is one way to initiate positive relationships because it communicates the teacher's interest in them. However, it is not easy to quickly learn 30 or 40 names, and if a science teacher has five classes, then he or she must learn 150 or more names. Seating charts and photographs of students from old yearbooks are helpful in learning names quickly and in associating names with individuals.

In addition to learning names, it is important to learn something about students' interests, aspirations, and academic backgrounds. This is particularly true for students whose cultural backgrounds are different from that of the teacher. It may be helpful to learn more about a student's family structure, ideas about acceptable behavior and punctuality, food preferences, and thoughts about science activities or topics that may be in conflict with religious beliefs (Jones & Jones, 2004). These "getting to know you" conversations may occur during individual or group conferences, perhaps while eating lunch in the school cafeteria or after school. Teachers sharing information about their own families and hobbies, inviting students to place their questions and ideas for changing the class environment in a suggestion box, and sending letters and memos to students that include information about what they will learn in class are all great ways to initiate open, professionally appropriate dialogue with students.

Building positive teacher–student relationships also has a lot to do with expectations. Middle and high school students may well expect their science teacher to direct learning in the classroom, to provide challenging assignments, and to be firm, compassionate, and interesting. And, of course, teachers have expectations for their students that are associated with academic achievement, good manners, and personal growth. Students in one teacher's high school science classes are reminded each day about expectations. Posted on the wall in this teacher's classroom are two charts that detail the expectations that he holds for his students and himself.

My job as a teacher is to . . .	**Your job as a student is to . . .**
• present information in an enthusiastic and organized manner. • return all graded activities in one day. • help students become problem solvers at home and at school. • give no busywork. • hold students responsible for their actions and inactions.	• be present in school and on time for class. • be in charge of your learning and growth. • complete all work to the best of your ability. • recognize that performance counts. • be successful, which requires consistent and dedicated work.

Teachers who are explicit about their expectations, communicate to students that they care about them as persons and learners.

Positive teacher–student relationships also develop when teachers give encouragement and praise and when they project personality and enthusiasm. It is important for a teacher to acknowledge that a class performed well on a test, a student did outstanding work on a project or homework, or a class was well behaved for a substitute teacher. It is also important for a teacher to recognize that for students with certain cultural backgrounds praise should be accompanied by expectations of even higher levels of accomplishment. Acknowledgements should be made as frequently as opportunities arise, and students should understand that they are sincerely given.

Teachers also can strive to build positive teacher–student relationships in other ways. They can listen carefully to what students have to say about themselves and the class. Listening carefully shows respect and caring, and provides students with the opportunity to share their thoughts with an adult. A teacher's listening and careful questioning may enable students to clarify problems and arrive at productive solutions. Teachers also should strive to be positive in their interactions with students and give meaningful feedback. Students, like all people, are more apt to respond positively when they are requested to do something in a pleasant and courteous manner.

Similarly, students respond more favorably to teacher verbal and nonverbal behaviors that they perceive as inviting, such as when they are told they are valued members of the class and are given responsibility for deciding how they should tackle a laboratory task or decide when an assignment is due. The feedback that science teachers provide should be specific rather than general and focus on aspects of learning that students are able to control. It is helpful for teachers to reinforce through their feedback that science achievement and success in science class have more to do with effort than with luck or innate ability.

Positive relationships among students are critical to a healthy science learning environment.

Student–Student Relationships

Peer relationships can make a classroom a comfortable and exciting place where students want to be or an uninviting environment where students feel unsafe, insignificant, and disrespected. It is the job of the science teacher to ensure that peer relationships are positive and contribute to a supportive, interactive, and culturally responsive learning environment. This job starts with understanding how classroom groups are formed and how functioning classroom groups can lead to positive peer relationships.

It is unrealistic to expect middle and high school students to start the school year with a sense of group cohesiveness. They will need to get to know one another and understand each other's strengths and limitations before they can be expected to develop a class identity or work effectively as learning teams. To help students move toward developing a class identify, some science teachers encourage students to adopt a class motto. "Work Hard, Play Hard" is the motto adopted by an Advanced Placement physics class whose teacher rewards students' hard work with a 30-minute game of Ultimate Frisbee one Friday each month. Other teachers incorporate acquaintance activities into their classes at the beginning of the school year. For example, a biology teacher may ask students to find their "genetic twins" in the class based on observable hereditary traits such as tongue-rolling, free earlobe, widow's peak and mid-digital hair. Common hereditary traits can be the starting point for conversations between students of diverse backgrounds who might otherwise not speak. This acquaintance activity can also serve as an advance organizer for studying human genetics later in the year.

Science classes provide numerous opportunities for group work. Students of diverse backgrounds and abilities can be assigned to study groups responsible for checking each other's homework and making sure that assignments are understood. In addition, students will work in laboratory groups, where they may be assigned different tasks that support the group's overall efforts. By involving students in collaborative learning activities throughout the year, group cohesiveness can be enhanced. Group cohesiveness is likely to foster peer-helping relationships, even among students who might not ordinarily be friends, and group cohesiveness can improve the quality of the learning environment. Group cohesiveness in a class is also likely to enable the teacher to work more effectively with parents and other family members. Parents who understand from their children that good things are happening in a teacher's class are more receptive to meeting with the teacher and providing support when needed to encourage appropriate behavior.

Democratic Classroom Practices

Science learning environments are further enhanced when students are allowed to make decisions about their own learning. Allowing students to make decisions about their learning shows respect for them and ensures that their concerns are taken seriously. Empowering students by involving them in democratic practices can be seen as a challenge to the legitimate authority of the teacher, but it need not be if classroom actions are based on ethical reasoning and democratic principles.

Democratic classroom practices are evident in policies that guide student class activities. During the first days of school in a classroom guided by democratic principles, a teacher would not just present students with rules to follow, but would discuss a proposed set of rules with the class and modify them to achieve class consensus. Classroom rules that acknowledge the democratic principles of personal freedom, justice, and equality proposed by Grandmont (2003, p. 100) are the following:

1. Act in a safe and healthy way.
2. Treat all property with respect.
3. Respect the rights and needs of others.
4. Take responsibility for learning.

Classroom practices stemming from the first rule would logically include wearing safety goggles and not eating in the laboratory. Practices related to the second rule might include students assuming responsibility for the proper use of classroom computers and laboratory equipment in addition to taking care with the personal belongs of classmates. The third rule would provide guidance for students working in groups and individually. Practices stemming from the fourth rule might include students assuming responsibility for adequately preparing for tests and other assessments and bringing textbooks and supplies to class. Rules developed with student input and based on democratic principles tend to be seen as fair and are more compelling than rules just generated by a teacher and presented to students (Gathercoal, 1997).

Democratic classroom practices are also evident in a teacher's instructional decisions. Teachers can convey personal freedom, justice, and equality in a number of ways. For example, a teacher may provide students with choices for how and when to demonstrate their learning. Demonstrating science understandings by developing a PowerPoint presentation, a video, or a rap song is encouraged in some science classes. These demonstrations can be scheduled to allow parents as well as other students and community members to participate.

Project work, problem-based activities, and guided inquiries are among the many science learning opportunities where, after being provided with the learning goals, students are allowed to decide what methods and materials to use and how much time is needed in achieving the goals. Compared to students given cookbook directions for a lab activity to be completed in a single period, students can be allowed to design and carry out their own laboratory experiments over several class periods. With this approach students become more likely to exhibit greater interest and stay on task longer.

When dealing with inappropriate behavior, a teacher guided by democratic principles would ask questions about an incident rather than assigning blame. Questions that help students think about their actions encourage responsibility and tend to promote respect between student and teacher rather than hostility. Leaders in the field of democratic education posit that creating classroom environments that provide opportunities for individual and collective decision making not only makes classrooms places that students want to be, but also prepares students to function as adults in a democratic society (Gathercoal, 1997; Pryor, 2004).

Stop and Reflect!

- What might you do to develop positive relationships with your students or to develop positive relationships among students in a class?
- What democratic practices would you consider implementing in your teaching? Why?

Organizing and Leading Science Learning Experiences

There are patterns of organization and behavior that are characteristic of successful, culturally responsive learning environments. As Brophy (2000) described, the classroom is arranged to facilitate defined learning activities and that needed equipment and supplies are stored within easy reach of students. Movement of students around the classroom is orchestrated by a set of routines that requires only minimal directions from the teacher. Students are engaged in learning experiences with an understanding of what they are doing and what materials are needed to achieve the intended learning goals. By attending to the classroom setting—procedures and routines—the informed beginning teacher is able to be a classroom leader that facilitates these patterns of organization and behavior and, in doing so, increases the time students spend actively engaged in science learning.

Classroom Setting

Elements to consider within the learning space include the dimensions of the classroom as well as the position of laboratory workstations, storage closets and shelves, fixed safety equipment, and exits from the classroom. Within this physical space, the teacher can position the active elements of the environment to make them responsive to the learning needs of students. For example, students' desks can be formed into a circle to facilitate class discussion, or they can be arranged so that all students can see the teacher and whiteboard without twisting and turning during whole-class instruction. The teacher's strategic arrangement of the physical space is of great importance because it communicates to students how materials are to be used and what is expected of them as learners.

The physical space of the learning environment is an important consideration in all aspects of science teaching, but especially when engaging students in laboratory work. Laboratory work may be done in the classroom that is used for general instruction, in a special area within the classroom, or in a separate laboratory room. Conducting laboratory work in the same classroom space used for general instruction requires attention to special details. Furniture may need to be moved to accommodate the demands of space and student movement that accompany most laboratory activities. Since desks or chairs must often be moved within a single class period, students must be instructed how to arrange the room for laboratory work. The placement and use of laboratory materials and equipment must be considered. Frequently used materials such as thermometers, rulers, small beakers, test tubes, and graph paper should be readily accessible, while often-used equipment such as electronic balances and microscopes should be kept in a location easy for students to reach. Answers to questions such as the following can help the teacher plan for the spatial organization of the laboratory work area, the arrangement of materials, and other aspects of the physical environment.

- How many students will be at a laboratory station at one time?
- Will students sit, stand, or move about?
- Will they talk, work cooperatively, or work independently?
- Will they use gas and electrical outlets?
- Will students need to move from one location to another to gather materials?
- How will chemicals and laboratory materials be set out for students to use?
- How should students exit the laboratory work area in case of emergency?

Procedures and Routines

According to Wong & Wong (2001, p. 167), "The number one problem in the classroom is not discipline; it is the lack of procedures and routines." Activities such as passing out papers, organizing students into groups, and assigning student tasks are routines that can create problems unless they are handled efficiently. Teachers who spend unnecessary amounts of time passing out papers and collecting them create situations in which students keep themselves occupied by talking loudly and engaging in play. Many routine situations can cause a great deal of confusion unless simple procedures are established beforehand. Simple procedures that communicate the teacher's expectations for starting and ending class, whole-group instruction, grading, and laboratory work can prevent inappropriate behavior.

Most teachers believe that how they start class sets the tone for the entire class period. For this reason, many teachers insist that students are seated and prepared to learn when the bell rings. However, starting class at the sound of the bell is not always possible due to the administrative duties that must be performed by the teacher, such as checking attendance. Informed beginning teachers plan activities that engage students as soon as the bell rings, allowing time to deal with the necessary administrative tasks. Informed beginning teachers also favor the practice of dismissing students themselves rather than allowing students to leave the classroom when the bell rings. When students are dismissed by the teacher, final instructions regarding classroom clean up or the next day's assignment can be given with the assurance that all students have received the information.

With science classes exceeding 25 students in many schools, teachers need to establish procedures for ensuring that large-group instruction goes smoothly. Students will want to know when and how the teacher will call on them to respond to questions. They will want to know when talking among students is permitted. Students also will want to know under what conditions they may leave their seats to sharpen pencils, collect papers, and go to the restroom. In many classrooms, students must raise their hands and be recognized before asking a question or making a comment during a lesson. A no-talking policy is enforced in some science classrooms, while in other classrooms students are allowed to talk quietly to others seated around them. Some teachers insist that students sharpen pencils and collect papers before the bell rings and allow students to go to the restroom during class only in an emergency.

In the laboratory, students will encounter many practices that are new to them. It is for this reason that science teachers need to attend to procedures related to appropriate dress, disposal of chemicals and specimens, keeping a notebook, and laboratory clean up. Standards established by the National Science Teachers Association (NSTA) and the Occupational Safety and Health Administration (OSHA) provide guidance for many aspects of laboratory work. More information about these standards is presented in Chapter 13 to help teachers formulate their laboratory procedures to ensure student safety and effective learning. This information includes discussions of appropriate dress and the disposal of chemicals and used laboratory specimens. For many students, keeping a science notebook will be a new experience, and they will need to be told how to do so. Informed beginning teachers will provide guidance regarding notebook form and neatness. For example, some teachers require students to record procedures and results on the left page of the notebook and inferences and conclusions on the right page. Many experienced teachers also establish procedures for directing other aspects of laboratory work, including how students should make up missed labs, what to do when equipment is broken or chemicals are spilled, and when to begin to clean up the lab area in preparation for the end of class.

Consideration also should be given to procedures related to grading. Students will want to know and should be allowed to have input into how their work will be graded. The informed teacher will be prepared to discuss personal grading practices with students. A grade book, perhaps on the computer, will need to be established and a system developed for recording daily grades, scores for major tests and projects, and student absences and tardies. A decision will also need to be made regarding how different assignments and tests will be weighted. Finally, it is important to explain major class assignments and grading practices to parents and guardians. This information will enable parents and guardians to monitor their children's progress better and to assist with learning problems that may arise.

Without a doubt, classroom procedures and routines are important considerations of the science learning environment. According to Wong & Wong (2001, p. 194), a teacher who is the leader of a positive learning environment:

1. Has well-thought-out and structured procedures for every activity
2. Teaches the procedures for each activity [to students] early in the year
3. Rehearses the class so that the procedures become class routines
4. Reteaches a procedure when necessary and praises to reinforce when appropriate

Teaching to Motivate and Engage Students

Effective instruction and desirable student behavior go hand-in-hand. Productive student behavior can often be traced to a teacher's success in planning science learning experiences and teaching in ways that enhance student motivation and engagement. Student motivation and engagement are influenced by the teacher's instructional practices, the curriculum, and other factors that are related to a student's self-esteem. These other factors include students' confidence in their abilities to succeed, the value they find in the work to be done, and their feelings of safety and support (Jones & Jones, 2004).

Instructional Practices

Beginning teachers must enter the classroom with the confidence of knowing what is to be done during each minute of the teaching day. Over-planning can provide the confidence needed to enter the classroom with a feeling of comfort. It is good practice to always plan more activities than can possibly be done by the students during a single class period. It is also good practice to have an alternative plan available in case of emergency. Poor planning is often cited as the number one cause of students becoming disinterested and uninvolved, which in turn leads to student inattention, off-task conversation, and class disruption. However, teachers who communicate organization and confidence as a result of their planning can avoid many behavioral problems. When planning for instruction, teachers must decide how students will be engaged to achieve different standards-based learning outcomes. These outcomes will need to be matched with the most appropriate instructional format for student academic activity.

Additionally, teachers must consider in their planning how to begin and end learning activities, how to transition from one learning activity to another, and how to begin and end the class period. One way to think about organizing instructional activities is to break the class period into smaller segments and plan for each. The class period might begin with students doing a warm-up activity, consisting of copying the day's essential questions and agenda, while the teacher takes attendance and deals with other administrative tasks. Next, the student's initial work could be quickly checked before beginning the day's primary learning experience, which may consist of one or more activities. Finally, the class period is closed with the teacher giving students homework instructions, reviewing the day's learning experience, and presenting an overview of future class sessions.

Two critical times during group instruction are when transitioning from one activity to the next and when communicating directions and information (Emmer, Evertson, & Clements, 1994). To prevent inappropriate behavior and wasted time, transitions should be planned to be smooth and brief. Informed beginning teachers establish procedures for students to follow during transitions. For example, when moving from desks to lab stations, students know to go directly to their lab stations without visiting with friends. Smooth transitions are also more likely to occur when planning has taken place to ensure that materials and equipment needed for the next activity are at hand. The possibility of student inappropriate behavior is further reduced when planning has occurred to ensure that intended learning outcomes are clearly communicated, activity directions are presented in an orderly sequence, and students understand the purpose of the learning experience (Emmer et al., 1994).

Curriculum

The curriculum describes what is taught in science class and what students are expected to learn. It is a central element of the science learning environment. Good classroom leaders recognize this fact and use their knowledge of students and their culture to make sure that what is taught matches their abilities and interests. When the curriculum is too difficult, too easy, or perceived as boring or irrelevant by students, they give up on learning and find something else to do in class. Often the "something else" is considered by the teacher to be inappropriate behavior.

Making changes to the curriculum is often no simple matter. Today, state legislatures, school boards, and administrators have as much to say about what is taught in science classes, as the teachers do. Nevertheless, teachers must consider the relationship between what is taught and student behavior. Minor adjustments to the curriculum that consider students' interests and cultural backgrounds can mean the difference between having to constantly reprimand students for being off task and inattentive and having a lively discussion among a class of enthusiastic adolescents. The importance of the curriculum to a well-managed classroom cannot be overstated. According to Kohn (1996, p. 21), "How students act in class is so intertwined with curricular content that it may be folly even to talk about classroom management or discipline as a field unto itself."

Student Readiness for Learning

Students' motivation and engagement in science class has as much to do with their readiness to learn and their feelings of comfort as the teacher's instructional practices and the curriculum. Far too many students in middle and high school today are unable to succeed because they lack the basic skills necessary to do so (Cummings, 2000). These students need to be taught basic study skills such as how to take notes, organize a notebook, and keep up with assignments and graded papers. They also need help in learning how to manage their time and work, to prepare for different kinds of tests and alternative assessments, and to engage in academic reading. In addition, some middle and high school science teachers find that their students also need help with developing the mathematical skills needed to succeed in science.

If teachers see their job as helping all students succeed, they will do all that they can to ensure that students develop these skills as they learn science. For example, many middle school teachers require their students to keep assignment books in which homework and due dates are recorded on a daily basis. To help students prepare for tests, some teachers reserve 15 minutes of class time every Friday to review sample test items and discuss test-taking strategies with their students. Other teachers teach multiplication, ratio and proportion, and algebra when understanding science concepts requires these mathematical skills. And, still other teachers, in attempting to improve academic reading proficiency, teach students to read textbook chapter headings, photograph captions, and summaries for contextual clues before reading a chapter page for page.

While helping students develop these necessary skills, the informed science teacher communicates to students that they are capable of performing at high levels (Jones & Jones, 2004). By breaking learning tasks into smaller steps and providing feedback on students' learning, teachers can help students experience success and at the same time teach them strategies that will enable them to achieve success again and again. Especially for students learning English and with other special learning needs, experiencing success is important because these students may have fewer opportunities to experience success in school compared to other students. Modifications to instruction and assessment activities can be especially helpful to them. Dropping nonessential topics from the curriculum, assigning fewer homework problems, and constructing tests and other assessments so as to reduce the demands on verbal or mathematical skills are examples of modifications that are likely to lead to students feeling successful. Feelings of success are also associated with working in groups, especially for African-American, Hispanic, and Native American students (Banks & McGee Banks, 1993; Freeman & Freeman, 2002). Science teachers should consider using cooperative learning in their classrooms and laboratories to enhance the learning experience. There is no doubt that teaching students who are motivated by their own successes is far more pleasant than dealing with the disruptive behavior of students who are frustrated by their inability to cope with the demands of learning.

Relevance of Learning Experiences

Students are also more likely to value their science learning experiences when they see the content as personally relevant. When introducing course content during the first days of school, informed teachers will ask students what they want to learn about the different course topics. They will then construct learning experiences to take advantage of students' interests and cultural backgrounds. For example, to capitalize on a class's diversity and interest in snakes, a life science teacher might introduce a unit on reptiles by having students report on different culturally based attitudes toward snakes and the roles of snakes in different world cultures.

The value that students place on science learning is also associated with their understanding of the learning goals and the standards on which the goals are based. Teachers can help students understand the goals of science learning by explaining the purpose of instructional activities in language that is easily understood and in ways that are meaningful to them. As discussed in Chapter 2 of this text, the overarching goals of science learning encompass personal and societal needs, career education, and academic preparation. An informed teacher knows that science course learning goals emphasizing only academic preparation will not be valued by most of today's students. Teachers can help students understand the purpose of instruction by telling them what they need to accomplish and why it is important to them as adolescents and as future adults.

When students feel safe and supported, they are also motivated to focus on the tasks of learning. Central to student safety and its implications for motivation are problems that may arise from bullying or teasing of students by other students. The psychological trauma associated with bullying and teasing can be debilitating for some students. Teachers may be unaware of the bullying going on among students they teach (Barone, 1997), making it important to help "students develop empathy for their peers and improved skills in interacting with others" (Jones & Jones, 2004, p. 151).

Dealing with Student Inappropriate Behavior

The recommendations and suggestions made up to this point in the chapter will likely enable the majority of students to engage in appropriate classroom behavior. However, even under the best classroom conditions, student misbehavior will occur. When student inappropriate behavior disrupts the learning environment, then it is time to use disciplinary interventions (Zuckerman, 2007). *Disciplinary interventions* are "actions taken by the teacher to bring about changes in the behavior of students who do not conform to class or school expectations" (Brophy, 1996, p. 5).

Some student behaviors that warrant disciplinary actions include:

- continually disrupting classroom routines and procedures
- repeatedly preventing other students from conducting normal classroom activities
- cheating on tests
- swearing
- being disrespectful to the teacher
- deliberately destroying or damaging laboratory equipment, school property, or the property of other students
- endangering the safety of the teacher or fellow students.

Of course, some of the behaviors listed are more inappropriate and serious than others, but they all must be dealt with in one way or another. The teacher can deal with most misbehavior in the normal course of daily activity, while the more serious behaviors that violate the school's code of conduct are better handled by the school administration. In cases where student misbehavior involves the violation of law, school administrators will request the assistance of law enforcement officials to deal with the problem.

Disciplinary interventions that range from preventive to remedial are set out in Shrigley's (1979, 1985) list of coping skills. Presented in Figure 6.3, this list is a guide for beginning teachers when attempting to curb student misbehavior in the science classroom and laboratory. Research indicates that 40% of 523 classroom disruptions investigated were curbed when teachers used the first four coping skills—ignoring behavior, signals, proximity control, and touch control (Shrigley, 1985). Teachers considering the use of Shrigley's coping skills should also heed his warning, "The teacher majoring in coping skills and minoring in excellent teaching will wind up constantly reacting, constantly putting out brush fires. Coping skills serve to rescue the teaching act, and they usually focus on the symptoms. They may do little to answer the deep-seated problems of disruptive individuals" (Shrigley, 1979, p. 3).

It is desirable at times to ask students who continuously exhibit inappropriate behavior to remain after class or discuss the reasons for their persistent disruptions after school (Zuckerman, 2007). Individual conferences avoid student embarrassment and teacher-student confrontation during class. Students will regard the situation seriously when the teacher asks for a private conference to discuss inappropriate behavior. Conferences are particularly effective for addressing behavioral problems that cannot be settled quickly and reasonably when they occur. During a conference, both the teacher and student can discuss the situation amicably and reasonably to correct the behavior. Under certain circumstances, individual conferences are more effective if school administrators and parents are involved. Some students may require this type of conference to realize the seriousness of the situation.

Punishment is a special type of disciplinary intervention that is perceived as adverse by students. Punishment should only be considered when all other disciplinary interventions have failed. If it is decided that punishment must be used, Shrigley (1979, p. 6) recommends that it be "legal, infrequent, prompt, appropriate, impersonal, private, just, and mild." Punishment can have unexpected negative side effects. When students are unable to see the relationship between their behaviors and the punishment, hostility and aggression toward the teacher may result.

Of course, there are a host of disciplinary interventions in addition to those mentioned that can be used to curb students' inappropriate behavior. Others that have

FIGURE 6.3 Shrigley's coping skills useful for curbing inappropriate behavior.

Coping skill	Description
1. Ignore behavior	An annoying behavior will often subside if ignored by the teacher.
2. Signal interference	Body language, such as a stare, can indicate that a behavior is inappropriate.
3. Proximity control	The teacher moves about the classroom and stands near a misbehaving student to provide the adult support needed to diffuse a disruption.
4. Touch control	By placing a hand on the shoulder of a student, the teacher can relieve tension and anger. Discretion must be used when employing this coping skill.
5. Gordon's active listening	The teacher listens carefully to a student's description of the problem and acknowledges the student's concern and frustration.
6. Gordon's I-messages	An I-message reveals the problem along with the teacher's feelings and is best used when rapport exists between teacher and student. "When students play around Bunsen burners in the lab (behavior), I fear (feeling) that someone will be burned (effect)."
7. Speak to the situation	The teacher describes the problem, but does not directly address the student. "Shoving discs into the DVD player can break the machine."
8. Direct appeal	Often in the form of a question, the statement attempts to appeal to the students' sense of logic and fairness. Two examples are, "John, do you realize that you're disturbing other students with your singing and drumming?" and "Is it fair to disrupt the work of others because you feel the urge to sing and drum on your books?"
9. Interrogative	A question can be used to indicate that the student has a choice regarding his or her behavior. "Will you stop arguing with Jane and return to your desk?"
10. Glasser's questions	"What are you doing? What should you be doing?" When used in combination, these questions can help a student analyze his or her behavior and take corrective action.
11. Logical consequences	The teacher responds directly and logically to the student misbehavior. If two students make a mess of the classroom by throwing paper, a logical consequence would be to have them clean up the paper.
12. Contrived consequences	This teacher response to student behavior is punitive. If two students make a mess of the classroom by throwing paper, a contrived consequence would be to assign the students to in-school suspension for three days.
13. Canter's broken record	The teacher repeats an assertive statement two or three times rather than arguing or trying to reason with the student. "Michael, put down the beaker and return to your seat...put down the beaker and return to your seat."
14. Compliance or penalty	The student is given the choice to comply with the teacher's request or accept the penalty. "Michael, put down the beaker and return to your seat or go to the office...Michael, if you don't put down the beaker and return to your seat, I'll call for Mr. Rigs who will help me escort you to the office."

Based on "Strategies in Classroom Management," by R. L. Shrigley, 1979, *NASSP Bulletin*, 63, 1–9; and "Curbing Student Disruptive Behavior in the Classroom—Teachers Need Intervention Skills," by R. L. Shrigley, 1985, *NASSP Bulletin*, 69, 26–32.

been used successfully by experienced teachers include changing seating assignments, removing seductive objects, and sending a note to parents. Regardless of the interventions used, Brophy's (1996, p. 21) timeless principles for effectively handling student misbehavior may prove to be a helpful source of guidance:

- Minimize power struggles and face-saving gestures by discussing the incident with the student in private rather than in front of the class.
- Question the student to determine his or her awareness of the behavior and explanation for it.
- Make sure that the student understands why the behavior is inappropriate and cannot be tolerated.
- Seek to get the student to accept responsibility for the behavior and to make a commitment to change.
- Provide any needed modeling or instruction in better ways of coping.
- Work with the student to develop a mutually agreeable plan for solving the problem.
- Concentrate on developing self-regulation capabilities through positive socialization and instruction rather than controlling behavior through power assertion.
- Emphasize that the student can achieve desirable outcomes and avoid negative consequences by choosing to act responsibly.

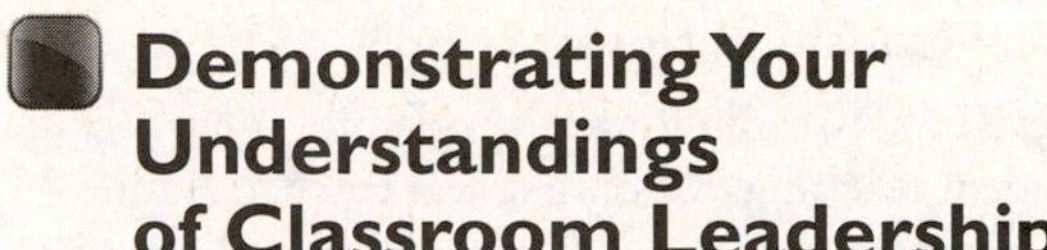

Demonstrating Your Understandings of Classroom Leadership

As indicated in *Standard 5: General Skills of Teaching* of the National Science Teachers Association (NSTA) *Standards for Science Teacher Preparation*, you will be expected as a beginning teacher to demonstrate your ability to "create and maintain a psychologically and socially safe and supportive learning environment" (NSTA, 2003, p. 21). This can be done when engaging students in science learning experiences by attending to the matters addressed in this chapter. First of all, make classroom leadership rather than classroom management the focus of your efforts. Do this by planning for and enacting teaching practices that lead to building interpersonal relationships between you and students and among students. Also, base your decisions about student learning and behavior on democratic principles and strive to understand your students' cultural backgrounds. Finally, teach in ways that establish classroom routines while enhancing student motivation for science and for learning. Your careful consideration of these factors in planning and teaching will convey to students that they and their ideas are important and lead to the increased occurrence of appropriate student behavior.

Assessing and Reviewing

Analysis and Synthesis

1. Prepare a list of things that you would say or do during the first days of school to build rapport with middle or high school science students. Share your list with classmates and discuss disagreements.
2. Revisit the behavioral patterns identified in Figure 6.1. First, assess how your own cultural background might bias your expectations for student behavior in a science class. Then, construct a plan for presenting your expectations for appropriate classroom behavior to students that takes into account your own biases.
3. After reading the following vignette, work with a partner to devise a plan for involving Mr. Bell's students in the construction of rules and procedures that you believe will lead to a more efficient and effective end to the class period.

   Five minutes before the bell rang to dismiss the class, Mr. Bell told his students to stop their work, return the microscopes to the storage area, and clean up their work areas. The students rushed to the storage cabinet to see who could get their microscopes put away first. A few students neglected to remove the microscope slides from the stage of the microscope. Others did not lower the body of the microscope completely so that the eyepiece struck the lower part of the shelf above, possibly doing damage to the microscope. As students were about to return the slides to the box on Mr. Bell's lab desk, the bell rang. As a result, some students returned the slides in a disorderly fashion, and many simply left the slides at their worktables. Mr. Bell also attempted to announce the next day's assignment, but half the class had already left the room.

4. Select a concept or topic from a middle school or secondary science course that you believe students will find boring. Develop a plan to teach the concept or topic in a way that will likely motivate students to be engaged science learners.

Practical Considerations

5. Devise a classroom leadership plan for use when student teaching or as a first year teacher. Address in your plan how you will consider the following in your efforts to create and maintain a psychologically and socially safe and supportive learning environment for your students.

   Cultural influences on student behavior
   Relationships between the teacher and students and among students
   Classroom practices that convey personal freedom, justice, and equality
   Organization of the classroom setting

6. Talk with a veteran science teacher about students' readiness for science learning. During your discussion, seek information about how the teacher works with students who need help with reading and basic mathematics, test preparation, and study skills, including taking notes, organizing a notebook, and keeping up with assignments.
7. Observe two or more middle or secondary school science classes and pay attention to how the teachers deal with inappropriate student behavior. Map your observations on Shrigley's coping skills presented in Figure 6.3. Discuss with a classmate the teacher's uses of coping skills to curb inappropriate student behavior.

Developmental Considerations

8. Form a reading group of science teachers who read and discuss articles and books about classroom leadership. Focus your reading selections on articles and books that emphasize the paradigm shift from teacher authority to student responsibility as described by Brophy (2000) and that highlight the *human relations view* and the *political view* of classroom leadership studied by Achinstein & Barrett, (2004).
9. Keep a journal of your science classroom leadership successes and challenges. Reflect on your journal accounts and devise a plan for sharing your successes and strategies for overcoming challenges with science teachers at your school or at a professional meeting.

Resources to Examine

The First Days of School. 2001. Harry Wong Publications, 1030 W. Maude Ave., Suite, Sunnyvale, CA 94086.

Written by Harry and Rosemary Wong, this book should be required reading for beginning teachers. It is full of illustrations and pithy advice about how to become an effective instructional planner, teacher, and classroom leader. Inspiring students to want to learn is a central theme of this book.

Culturally Responsive Classroom Management: Awareness into Action. 2003. *Theory into Practice, 42*(4), 269–276.

In this article, Carol Weinstein, Mary Curran, and Saundra Tolinson-Clarke offer suggestions for enacting culturally responsive classroom leadership in addition to discussing three prerequisite understandings that underlie teachers' ability to lead classrooms in culturally competent ways.

Classroom Management that Works: Research-Based Strategies for Every Teacher. 2003. Association for Supervision and Curriculum Development. 1250 N. Pitt Street, Alexandria, VA 22314

Robert Marzao's book addresses the major areas of classroom leadership discussed in this chapter. In addition, it highlights the research and theory that supports many practical recommendations for classroom rules and procedures, teacher–student relationships, students' management responsibilities, and disciplinary interventions.

Comprehensive Classroom Management: Creating Communities of Support and Solving Problems. 2004. Allyn & Bacon. 75 Arlington Street, Boston, MA 02116

This is a 10-chapter volume on classroom management by Vern Jones and Louise Jones. Creating positive interpersonal relationships, increasing student motivation, minimizing disruptive student behavior, and altering unproductive student behavior are among the topics addressed. Cartoons and questions to prompt reader reflection are found in every chapter.

Judicious Discipline: A Constitutional Approach for Public High Schools. 2003. *American Secondary Education, 31*(3), 97–117.

Richard Grandmont reports on a study to examine the influence of the democratic practices of *Judicious Discipline* developed by Forest Gathercoal on the behavior of high school students. The findings suggest that implementing democratic practices help students take responsibility for their actions and develop feelings of respect. Grandmont concludes that the use of democratic practices by teachers can benefit the culture of any high school.

References

Achinstein, B. & Barrett, A. (2004). (Re)Framing classroom contexts: How new teachers and mentors view diverse learners and challenges of practice. *Teacher College Record, 106*(4), 716–746.

Banks, J., & McGee Banks, C. (1993). *Multicultural education: Issues and perspectives* (2nd ed.). Boston: Allyn & Bacon.

Barone, F. (1997). Bullying in the classroom: It doesn't have to happen. *Phi Delta Kappan, 79*, 80–82.

Brophy, J. (1996). *Teaching problem students.* New York: Guilford Press.

Brophy, J. (2000). Perspectives of classroom management: Yesterday, today, and tomorrow. In H. J. Freiberg (Ed.), *Beyond behaviorism: Changing the classroom management paradigm* (pp. 43–56). Boston: Allyn & Bacon.

Brownstein, E., Jones, & Meissner, (2007). *Pedagogical and professional knowledge, skills and dispositions, NSTA Assessment #4: Sample Student Teaching Evaluation Rubric.* Retrieved May 7, 2008, from www.nsta.org/pdfs/NCATE-Assessment4StudentTeachingRubric.pdf

Cummings, C. (2000). *Winning strategies for classroom management.* Alexandria, VA: Association for Supervision and Curriculum Development.

Emmer, E. T., Evertson, C. M., Clements, B. S., & Worsham, M. E. (1994). *Classroom management for secondary teachers.* Boston: Allyn & Bacon.

Evertson, C. M., & Emmer, E. (1982). *Preventive classroom management.* In D. Duke (Ed.), *Helping teachers manage classrooms* (pp. 2–31). Alexandria, VA: Association for Supervision and Curriculum Development.

Freeman, Y., & Freeman, D. (2002). *Closing the achievement gap: How to reach limited-formal-schooling and long-term English learners.* Portsmouth, NH: Heinemann.

Gathercoal, F. (1997). *Judicious discipline* (4th ed.). San Francisco: Caddo Gap Press.

Good, T., & Brophy, J. (2000). *Looking into classroom* (8th ed.). New York: Longman.

Grandmont, R. P. (2003). Judicious discipline: A constitutional approach for public high schools. *American Secondary Education, 31*(3), 97–117.

Gross, L. A. (2006). Using classroom space and routines to promote democratic opportunities. *Social Studies and the Young Learner, 19*(1), 24–27.

Hoover, R. L., & Kindsvatter, R. (1997). *Democratic discipline: Foundation and practice.* Upper Saddle River, NJ: Merrill.

Jones, V., & Jones, L. (2004). *Comprehensive classroom management: Creating communities of support and solving problems.* Boston: Allyn & Bacon.

Kohn, A. (1996). *Beyond discipline.* Alexandria, VA: Association for Supervision and Curriculum Development.

Marzano, R. J. (2003). *Classroom management that works: Research-based strategies for every teacher.* Alexandria, VA: Association for Supervision and Curriculum Development.

Maslow, A. (1968). *Toward a psychology of being.* New York: D. Van Nostrand.

Matsumura, L. C., Slater, S., & Crosson, A. (2008). Classroom climate, rigorous instruction and curriculum, and students' interactions in urban middle schools. *The Elementary School Journal, 108*(4), 293–312.

Patrick, H., Turner, J. C., Meyer, D. K., & Midgley, C. (2003). How teachers establish psychological environments during the first days of school: Association with avoidance in mathematics. *Teachers College Record, 105*(8), 1521–1569.

Pryor, C. R. (2004). Creating a democratic classroom: Three themes for citizen teacher reflection. *Kappa Delta Pi Record, 40*(2), 78–82.

Purkey, W., & Novak, J. (1996). *Inviting school success: A self-concept approach to teaching, learning, and democratic practice* (3rd ed.). Belmont, CA: Wadsworth.

Sanford, J. P., & Evertson, C. M. (1981). Classroom management in a low SES junior high: Three case studies. *Journal of Teacher Education, 32*(1), 34–38.

Shrigley, R. L. (1979). Strategies in classroom management. *NASSP Bulletin, 63*(428), 1–9.

Shrigley, R. L. (1985). Curbing student disruption in the classroom—teachers need intervention skills. *NASSP Bulletin, 69*(479), 26–32.

Weinstein, C., Curran, M., & Tomlinson-Clarke, S. (2003). Culturally responsive classroom management: Awareness into action. *Theory into Practice, 42*(4), 269–276.

Wong, H. K., & Wong, R. T. (2001). *The first days of school.* Sunnyvale, CA: Harry Wang Publications.

Zuckerman, J. T. (2007). Classroom management in secondary schools: A study of student teachers' successful strategies. *American Secondary Education, 35*(2), 4–16.

Chapter

7
The Nature of Science

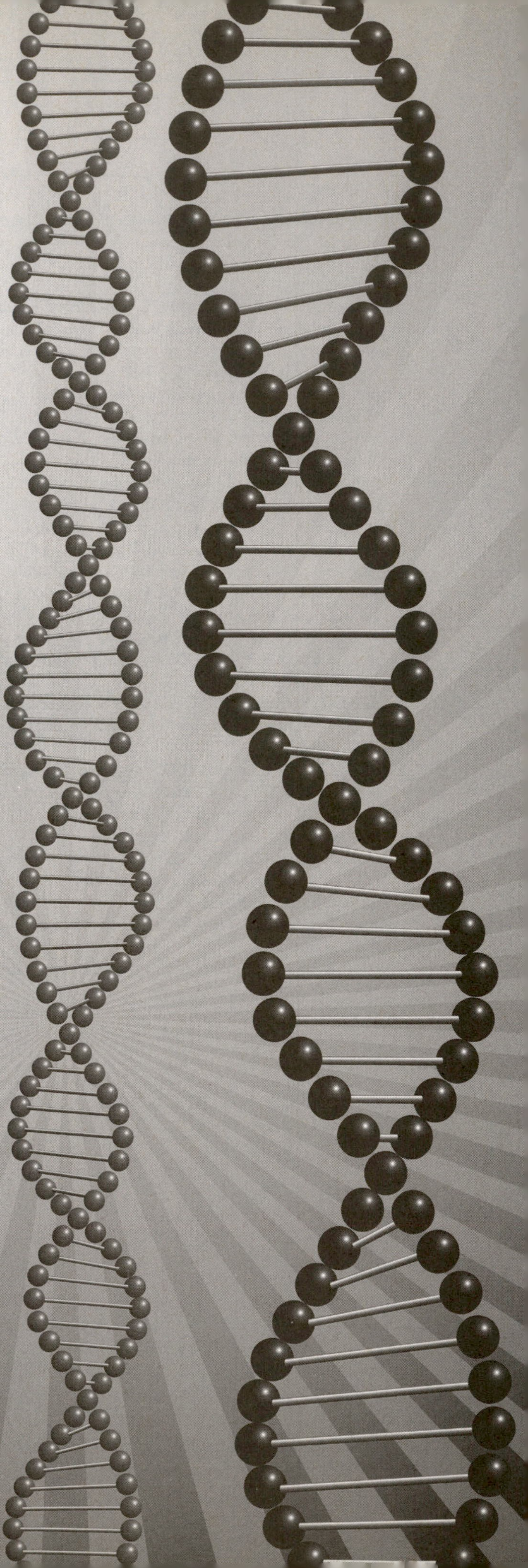

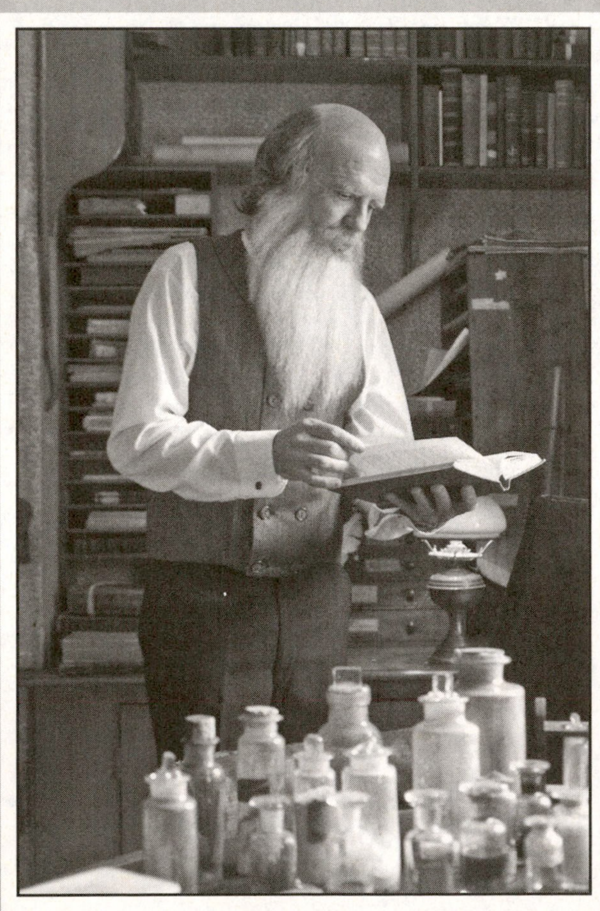
Some science teachers role-play famous scientists to increase student interest in the subject matter under study.

Science teaching must reflect correct views of the nature of science. Lectures, classroom discussions, laboratory activities, assigned readings, long-term investigations, and examination questions should correspond to what is generally accepted as scientific knowledge and process. Erroneous beliefs about how scientists go about their work must be eliminated, as must simplistic instruction of concepts, laws, principles, and theories that distort scientific knowledge. Science teachers must possess a broad understanding of the nature of science in order for them to make accurate interpretations and coherent presentations of the discipline. The challenges are great for making curricular decisions about school science in order for the subject to be appropriate for the cognitive abilities of adolescents yet distinguishable from the authentic science that is carried out by adults. Further, science teachers must help students to appreciate the value of science and how it benefits their lives by teaching science within relevant, real-life contexts.

AIMS OF THE CHAPTER

Use the questions that follow to expand your understanding about the nature of science:

- Why is it important for a science teacher to understand the nature of science?
- How will you define science when speaking with students?
- How well can you explain the scientific enterprise by describing what scientists do in their work?
- Which criteria would you use to distinguish among authentic science, pseudoscience, and junk science?
- How familiar are you with the nature of science put forth in some of the science education reform documents?

Before you begin reading this chapter, please engage in a preassessment to determine your understanding of the nature of science. Figure 7.1 presents 12 statements, some of which are considered myths of science. Respond to the true–false quiz; then write a brief paragraph to support your response to each item. When you have

FIGURE 7.1 A true–false quiz to assess understanding of the nature of science.

Myths of Science Quiz

Directions: Each statement that follows is about science. Some statements are true and some are false. On the line in front of each statement, write a "T" if it is true and an "F" if it is false. Then support your response to each statement with at least one paragraph on a separate sheet of paper.

____ 1. Science is a system of beliefs.
____ 2. Most scientists are men because males are better at scientific thinking.
____ 3. Scientists rely heavily on imagination to carry out their work.
____ 4. Scientists are totally objective in their work.
____ 5. The scientific method is the accepted guide for conducting research.
____ 6. Experiments are carried out to prove cause-and-effect relationships.
____ 7. All scientific ideas are discovered and tested by controlled experiments.
____ 8. A hypothesis is an educated guess.
____ 9. When a theory has been supported by a great deal of scientific evidence, it becomes a law.
____ 10. Scientific ideas are tentative and can be modified or disproved, but never proved.
____ 11. Technology preceded science in the history of civilization.
____ 12. In time, science can solve most of society's problems.

completed the quiz and written explanations, read the chapter to see how well you understand the nature of science and the beliefs or myths of science that are held by many individuals.

 What Is Science?

"Science is a particular way of knowing about the world. In science, explanations are limited to those based on observations and experiments that can be substantiated by other scientists. Explanations that cannot be based on empirical evidence are not part of science."

(The National Academy of Sciences, 1999, p. 1)

Toward a Definition of Science

Science is a broad-based human enterprise that is defined differently depending on the individual. A layperson might define science as a body of scientific information. A scientist might view it as a set of procedures by which hypotheses are generated and tested. A philosopher might regard science as a way of questioning the truthfulness of what we know. Prospective science teachers might put forth the following phrases when asked for a definition of science:

- To discover nature
- Using scientific methods
- A process of finding out
- A study of the universe
- Organizing facts into theories
- A method of discovery
- A body of organized knowledge
- Problem solving
- A search for truth

All these ideas have some connection with science, but each is limited. Only collectively do they begin to portray the breadth and complexity of the scientific enterprise.

Science is the study of nature in an attempt to understand it and to form an organized body of knowledge that has predictive power and application in society. This definition parallels a statement by Edward Teller (1991), an eminent nuclear physicist: "A scientist has three responsibilities: one is to *understand*, two is to *explain* that understanding and three is to *apply* the results of that understanding" (pp. 1, 15). Further, science is based on observation and experimentation, relying heavily on carefully collected data, strong evidence, and persuasive conclusions. Terms such as *understand*, *explain*, and *apply*, along with *observation*, *experimentation*, *data*, *evidence*, and *conclusion*, can be used to form a coherent explanation of science. Further, these ideas can be used to plan and teach science where students are expected to understand science concepts, to explain them in writing and orally, and to apply them in the laboratory and in everyday life through an active learning process that resembles authentic science.

The assertion that scientists try to understand, explain, predict, and apply offers science teachers a simple and clear idea of the scientific enterprise. Scientists strive to understand the phenomena that make up the universe—from the beating of our hearts to the migration of birds to the explosion of stars. Their aim is to describe the internal and external structure of objects, the mechanisms of nature, and the occurrence of events to a measurable degree of accuracy. Scientific understanding goes beyond description to the deeper level of explanation, which combines many observations, facts, laws, and generalizations into coherent theories that accurately present reality, not only specifying what is occurring, but how and why it is occurring. Scientific inquiry aims at determining cause and effect relationships, as well as investigating relationships among phenomena whose links may not be causal.

 The Scientific Enterprise

Scientists go about their work in many ways, creating methods and techniques to study the aspects of nature that interest them. Some scientists are more theoretical, others are more experimental, and still others are more technologically minded. When envisioning how new knowledge is produced by science, one could say that scientists decide on what they are looking for and study it vigorously. Scientists usually use theories to *guide their observations and thinking, pose researchable questions,* and *design ingenious experiments* to test out their ideas. They rely heavily on *empirical data* to settle claims about nature, and use *logic and reasoning* to develop evidence and form conclusions.

Scientists *make public* their understanding through carefully written papers, posters, and reports. Their technical results are presented at professional meetings and manuscripts submitted for publication in professional journals. In both cases, especially the latter, research is carefully reviewed by colleagues, who make critical comments and suggestions, recommending the work for publication or rejection. Published works are open to *additional examination* by the scientific community whereby the logic and reasoning can be evaluated, and procedures and results can be tested by additional observation and experimentation. Scientists deal harshly with colleagues who misrepresent their research by "fudging" data, "cooking-the-books," or taking credit for discoveries that others have claimed. These individuals are ostracized by their professional peers and lose opportunities for grant funds.

Making public the work of scientists provides a system of checks and balances. By bringing their work into the public domain, the scientific community is usually able to identify the violation of *ethical principles* and *poor science*. Therefore, scientific claims must be articulated in a manner that permits other scientists to *confirm* or *disprove* these assertions or eventually to translate them into useful products. At any time during the journey to understand nature, the most cherished ideas can be *disproved, falsified, or modified*. Scientists must remain open-minded and willing to change their ideas, based on new data and compelling arguments, all of which serve to maintain the tentative nature of scientific knowledge and the forward progress of science.

In addition to understanding and explaining phenomena, scientists strive to apply the knowledge that they construct about the world. Many scientists, along with engineers and technologists, spend a great deal of their time designing and producing *useful products* for society. Most of these products hold the potential to improve the quality of life, such as manufactured drugs, genetically engineered hormones, electronic communications, and superconducting materials. The number of ways in which science and engineering add to the quality of our lives is incalculable, and the fact that they have done so has earned them high esteem in society. Unfortunately, the products of science and engineering can be misused, such as drug abuse and deadly weapons, causing some to criticize science and technology.

Often scientists are presented as brilliant, bespectacled, white males in lab coats, who work alone, making major discoveries that revolutionize a scientific field. This is an inaccurate stereotype. The scientific community reflects considerable diversity, in gender, ethnicity, and culture. While textbooks usually highlight the most famous scientists whose work revolutionized some area of science, most of the advancements in science are the result of individuals who contribute incrementally to a particular field, adding facts and supporting theories—by conducting normal science (Kuhn, 1962). Most scientific work is a team effort with collaboration among many scientists, technicians, assistants, and editors, and so forth. Research is expensive, tedious, and sometimes dangerous, and often very competitive.

Sometimes science textbooks "color" the work of scientists, which distorts students' perceptions of the scientific enterprise. These resources incline toward a popularized view of the history of science that "romanticizes scientists, inflates the drama of their discoveries, and casts scientists and the process of science in monumental proportions" (Allchin, 2003, p. 329). Allchin gives us the story of Alexander Fleming, who is often credited with the discovery of penicillin. While Fleming did stumble on to the effects of penicillin and followed up on its effects on the growth of bacteria, he did little to take that finding to the production of a drug that has been used to save tens of millions of lives. It was actually Howard Florey and Ernst Chain at Oxford University, with the help of many technicians, who worked out the production of penicillin for commercial use—a long laborious process.

Many stories about the advancement of science in textbooks center on male scientists, giving the impression that this type of work is best carried out by men. However, many women, such as Marie Curie, Rosalind Franklin, Barbara McClintock, Lisa Meitner, and Rosalyn Sussman Yalow, have contributed significantly to the advancement of science. Textbooks must include the achievements of women and many others who are underrepresented in science in order to present a more balanced view of the nature of science.

Lastly, the statement "science is a way of knowing" implies that science is only one of many ways to establish knowledge about the world and that it competes with other ways humans establish knowledge. We must be mindful that other cultures—African, Asian, Hispanic, and Native American—have their own worldviews that differ from the Western view of science (Stanley & Brickhouse, 1994). Among these cultures there may be alternative views, for example, of medicine and astronomy. For many people, these alternative views and practices do not seem to offer a serious challenge to the contemporary scientific establishment when it comes to understanding and explaining nature (Loving, 1995). However, we do not want to assert that science can solve all problems, because many societal problems are political in nature and difficult to resolve in spite of the availability of valid scientific knowledge.

 What Is Not Science?

In some instances, determining what something "is not" helps to better understand what that something "is." At first glance, this idea appears quite simple for distinguishing science from nonscience. For example, most scientists will be quick to say that astronomy and psychology are different from astrology or parapsychology. However, it may be more difficult than you think to identify a single criterion (or several for that matter) to distinguish science from mythology or pseudoscience.

Morris (1991) presents the example of distinguishing between superstring theory and the claims of astrologers. He points out that if subjecting a theory to empirical testing is used as the criterion for being scientific, then astrologers fare even better than the superstring theorists. Most physicists would agree that it is virtually impossible to observe a superstring, because this fundamental entity is hypothesized to be many millions of times smaller than a proton, for whose existence superstrings are theoretically responsible. On the other hand, one can set up tests to determine the apparent influences that heavenly bodies exert on human affairs, even if the results may provide little data to confirm these relationships. Morris points out that both scientific and nonscientific theory seem to be the result of thought, imagination, speculation, and problem solving. Both enterprises put forth new and sometimes seemingly bizarre ideas. In the final analysis, however, scientific theories are supported by a great deal of evidence and generally offer clear and logical explanations of phenomena and useful understandings of phenomena.

In spite of some of the difficulties in attempting to differentiate among science, nonscience, and poor science, it is important to gain some competence in identifying what is not authentic science. Shermer (2001) offers some help with this problem by categorizing normal science, nonscience, and borderlands science:

Normal science: Heliocentrism, evolution, quantum mechanics, big bang cosmology, plate tectonics, and neurophysiology of brain function

Nonscience: Creationism, remote viewing, astrology, alien abduction, UFOs, Freudian psychoanalytic theory, and recovered memories

Borderlands science: Superstring theory, inflationary cosmology, theories of consciousness, search for extraterrestrial intelligence, and chiropractic

Nonscience or pseudoscience presents itself as science, making claims that are unsupported but which are believable. A characteristic of these claims is how little they have changed over the past in spite of the scientific advancements in the field. Pseudoscientific claims often rely heavily on authority, do not explain or predict well, and lack supporting evidence and consensus from the scientific community (Ben-Ari, 2005). However, remember that many notable scientists of the past held pseudoscientific ideas, such as Newton who practiced alchemy and Galileo who gave horoscopes.

Today, *junk science* is as much a troubling matter as nonscience and pseudoscience. Junk science is "extensively corrupted science, science corrupted in objectivity and/or method, the corruption either deliberate or involving sloppy methods or due to ignorance of what science is about, the outcome of useless conclusions that make false statements about the natural world" (Agin, 2006, p. 4). Junk science is commonplace in society and used to promote thousands of products and services. This type of science is evident in commercial industries, such as food products, nutritional supplements, herbal medicine, talk therapy, cosmetics, and age prevention. These multi-billion dollar businesses take advantage of a scientifically illiterate society where advertisement pays for television programs, magazines, and newspapers. Fortunately, our understanding of the nature of science can help us pose some questions to evaluate "scientific claims" and nonscientific theories.

- How well is the mechanism of the science explained?
- How well does the claim predict the results of the product or service?
- To what extent have the claims been supported by other sources, especially scientific research?

The Nature of Science and National Standards

Science distinguishes itself from other ways of knowing and from other bodies of knowledge through the use of empirical standards, logical arguments, and skepticism, as scientists strive for the best possible explanations about the natural world.

(National Research Council, 1996, p. 201)

The quote from the *National Science Education Standards* (National Research Council [NRC], 1996) indicates that science is a way of coming to understand the world in which we live. Although there are other ways of knowing, science is unique in that it has standards and practices that generate ideas to explain phenomena and to predict outcomes. Regardless of their durability and utility, scientific theories can be rejected with new findings.

The *Standards* (NRC, 1996) remind us that scientific explanations must meet certain criteria, which distinguish science from myth, personal belief, religious values, mystical belief, superstition, and authority. Scientific explanations must accurately reflect empirical observations and experimental results. The knowledge generated must also be formed from logical reasoning that conforms to rules of evidence. Further, the knowledge is made public so that it can be scrutinized and challenged, resulting in a continual process of confirmation, modification, or rejection.

The national reform document *Science for All Americans* (American Association for the Advancement of Science [AAAS], 1990) emphasizes the importance of understanding the nature of science. This document reinforces the NRC quote that science employs certain ways of finding out as evidenced by the ways in which the scientific community gathers data and puts forth logical arguments to explain ideas, while reserving the right to reject any of its theories or principles. *Science for All Americans* stresses that teaching science should be consistent with the nature of scientific inquiry and that instruction should (a) begin with questions about nature, (b) engage students actively, (c) concentrate on the collection and use of evidence, (d) provide historical perspective, (e) insist on clear expression, (f) use a team approach, (g) not separate knowing from finding out, and (h) de-emphasize the memorization of technical vocabulary (AAAS, 1990, pp. 202–203). That said, explicit instruction must be included along with investigative experiences in order to develop students' understanding of the scientific enterprise (Abd-El-Khalick, Bell, & Lederman, 1998). However, in order for this to occur, science teachers must understand how valid knowledge about nature is constructed and how it has evolved over time.

Themes of Science and Science Literacy

Standard 2: Nature of Science. Teachers of science engage students effectively in studies of the history, philosophy, and practice of science. They enable students to distinguish science from nonscience, understand the evolution and practice of science as a human endeavor, and critically analyze assertions made in the name of science. To show they are prepared to teach the nature of science, teachers of science must demonstrate that they:

(a) understand the historical and cultural development of science and the evolution of knowledge in their discipline.

(b) understand the philosophical tenets, assumptions, goals, and values that distinguish science from technology and from other ways of knowing the world.

(c) engage students successfully in studies of the nature of science, including, when possible, the critical analysis of false or doubtful assertions made in the name of science.

(Standards for Science Teacher Preparation, *NSTA 2003)*

Sometimes reading about the philosophy of science can become confusing and leave the impression that science is not much different from mysticism or religion. Further, this literature presents many discussions on what science is not, obscuring the intent of science education, which is to promote an appreciation of science and to help people learn more about this enterprise. Fortunately, there are dimensions of science that scientists and science educators readily recognize and accept as useful. These dimensions or themes can be used to plan, carry out, and analyze science instruction.

We will refer to these dimensions or facets as *themes of scientific literacy* and state them as follows: (1) science as a way of thinking, (2) science as a way of investigating, (3) science as a body of knowledge, and (4) science and its interactions with technology and society. These major areas of science can be used to analyze what is being emphasized in a teaching session, laboratory exercise, or textbook chapter. Figure 7.2 emphasizes that science content is often given more consideration than the other dimensions.

FIGURE 7.2 Four themes or dimensions of science that should be evident in science instruction to various degrees.

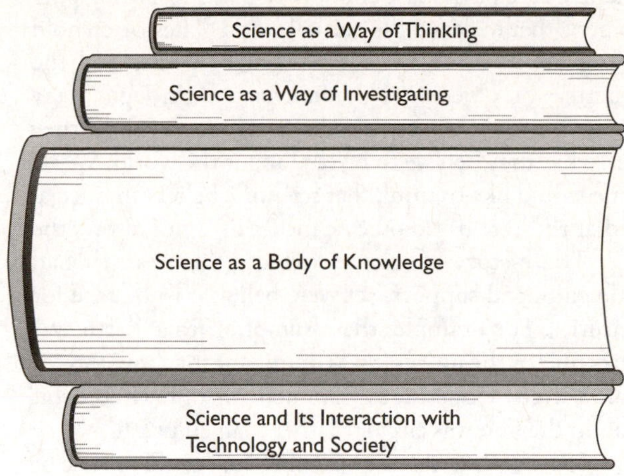

Before reading further, recall your experiences as a student in a college science class. What stands out in your mind regarding these experiences? Did the instructors get you to think about the topic under discussion? Did they spend time explaining to you how ideas were invented and their related phenomena discovered? Were major investigations or experiments discussed, illustrating how they contributed to the establishment of the laws and theories under study? Was class time spent on the applications of the subject matter or their relevance to society? Did a particularly interesting demonstration illuminate the lecture material? The chances are high that many of the science classes in which you enrolled in college or took in high school were comprised mostly of lectures that presented a large body of information.

We believe strongly that science lectures at the middle school, high school, and college levels must go beyond the presentation of technical information. These sessions should be more balanced, showing how scientists go about their work and how their results impact the work of other scientists, as well as that of society. Science textbooks must also convey a more balanced view of science than they have in the past. If the presentation of science content comprises 80% or 85% of a given textbook, little text is left to help students understand how ideas were formed (Lumpe & Beck, 1996). The four themes we will discuss here—thinking, investigation, knowledge, and science/technology/society—can help science teachers to become more sensitive to the importance of balance in the curriculum (Chiappetta & Fillman, 2007).

Science as a Way of Thinking

"The whole of science is nothing more than a refinement of everyday thinking."
—Einstein (1954, p. 283)

Beliefs

Scientists are passionate about their ideas regarding phenomena that make up the natural world. They often hold strong beliefs as to the mechanism of events and the structure of objects in the universe. Although many scientists would reject the idea of absolute truth, they seek what they believe to be true about the world. While some would like to think that scientific beliefs are special in that they are based on evidence, this is not always the case. The history of science includes theories that had little empirical support, yet were believed to be true for centuries. For example, the assumption that Earth was the center of the universe was dominant for thousands of years. Even Copernicus assumed that Earth's orbit around the Sun was circular rather than elliptical.

Not everyone agrees that belief is a part of science or that scientists should even hold beliefs in the body of scientific knowledge. Some define belief as faith, asserting that religious belief is different from scientific belief. Others suggest that scientists should be "forbidden to express belief in the absolute truth of any of the scientific observation statements that make up the body of science. There is always the possibility, no matter how small it may be that a scientific statement will be shown to be false" (Strahler, 1992, p. 22).

Scientists are humans and they do believe in their ideas. Even particle physicists, who theorize about realms of reality smaller in scale than a proton, believe they are getting to the bottom of it all. Steven Weinberg, a Nobel laureate in physics, says, "What drives us onward in the work of science is precisely the sense that there are truths out there to be discovered, truths that once discovered will form a permanent part of human knowledge" (Weinberg, 1998, p. 7). Therefore, science teachers should discuss the beliefs of scientists in order to illustrate how they view the world and what underlies their dispositions and curiosity. However, the body of scientific knowledge that becomes durable is based more on compelling evidence than on the beliefs of individual scientists.

Curiosity

Scientists are very curious about nature. They frequently ask the question: Why? This curiosity often manifested the many interests of scientists, even beyond that of unraveling the mysteries of natural phenomena. Nicholas Copernicus (1472–1543), for instance, who caused a scientific revolution by placing the Sun at the center of our solar system, pursued many vocations. "Copernicus was a churchman, a painter, a poet, a physician, an economist, a statesmen, a soldier, and a scientist" (Hummel, 1986, p. 55). Benjamin Franklin (1706–1790) likewise demonstrated his many interests as a printer, writer, publisher, inventor, statesman, and scientist.

Jean Henrie Fabre (1823–1915) began his insatiable fascination with insects at a young age in the French countryside. His studies remained within the enormous field of insects where he produced volumes, describing the anatomy and behavior of many insects including bees, wasps, gnats, dung beetles, spiders, and scorpions. Leonardo da Vinci (1452–1519) epitomizes the curiosity and creativity of the human mind. Not only was da Vinci regarded as a great artist, but his accomplishments extended into science and technology. From his sketchbooks, we observe the study of gears, hydraulic jacks, flying machines, parachutes, cranes, pulley systems, drilling machines, and underwater breathing apparatus. However, not all scientists are insatiable.

"Scientists—that is, creative scientists—spend their lives trying to guess right" (Polanyi, 1958, p, 143) because they are motivated to get to the truth. For them, the truth is a deeper understanding of the world. This is a creative process that is fueled by personal passion to find out. Some scientists are so driven by their curiosity to explain their ideas that they may risk ridicule, discrimination, and persecution to continue their work.

Imagination

In addition to being curious, scientists rely heavily on imagination. Albert Einstein asserted, "Imagination is more important than knowledge." He evidences his thinking in many ways, especially when he put forth his theory of special relativity. Einstein imagined himself riding on a beam of light while holding a mirror in front of him, reasoning how long it would take a light beam to register his image back to him and to a stationary observer. The early Greek philosophers and scientists tried to visualize a harmonious universe with heavenly bodies moving in a particular manner. James Clerk Maxwell formed mental pictures of the abstract problems that he attempted to solve, especially electromagnetic fields. Many students in a college organic chemistry course have listened to the story of how August Kekule came to visualize the benzene ring during a dream:

> *The atoms flitted before my eyes. Long rows, variously, more closely, united; all in movement wriggling and turning like snakes. And see, what was that? One of the snakes seized its own tail and the image whirled scornfully before my eyes. (Cited in Beveridge, 1957, p. 76)*

In the development of the atomic model, J. J. Thomson put forth the "raisins in a bun" model. His conception of the atom shows a ball of positively charged matter with negatively charged electrons embedded in it, similar to raisins in a bun. Although this model did not last very long, it was a useful way to explain the charged nature of the atom. A great deal of scientific and technological knowledge is based on models of phenomena generated by imaginative thinking on the part of scientists and engineers.

Reasoning

Associated with imagination is reasoning. The history of science provides many examples of how those who participate in the scientific enterprise study phenomena with considerable reliance on their own thinking as well as that of others. According to Albert Einstein, science is a refinement of everyday thinking. This belief becomes evident when one studies the work of scientists in their attempt to construct ideas that explain how nature works. Science teaching can benefit greatly from the inclusion of narratives about the development of the major theories of the natural and physical world, illustrating how these explanations evolved and changed over time (Duschl, 1990).

Examples of science courses that focus on the nature of scientific thinking can be found among the national curriculum projects produced during the 1960s. Harvard Project Physics, in particular, centered its textbook and supplemental reading on historical accounts of how scientific principles and theories were put forth by various individuals. A classic example of how a scientist used a thought experiment to illustrate correct and incorrect reasoning about the motion of celestial bodies is given in Galileo's *Two New Sciences,* in which he presents a conversation between three characters: Simplicio, who represents the Aristotelian view of mechanics; Salviati, who represents the new view of Galileo; and Sagredo, who represents a man with an open mind and eager to learn. Such literary constructions were a necessary and clever way to put forth their reasoning regarding a belief that was offensive to the current political and religious powers of the period (Project Physics Course, 1975).

If educators turn to the history of science, they will find many examples of thought experiments that illustrate creativity, imagination, and reasoning. The writings of Ernst Mach contain numerous examples of puzzles that inspired thinking deeply about physical phenomena. Mach (1838–1916), a great scientist and philosopher, presented thought experiments for his readers to perform in each edition of his Zeitschrift. One such brain teaser asks, "What happens when a stoppered bottle with a fly on its base is in equilibrium on a balance and the fly takes off" (cited in Matthews, 1991, p. 15). Einstein formulated his theories of relativity following concepts he conceived during his thought experiments.

Scientists engage in a variety of reasoning behaviors to elucidate patterns in nature. Sometimes they use inductive thinking; at other times they use deductive thinking. Through inductive reasoning, one arrives at explanations and theories by piecing together facts and principles, generalizing from specific instances to broader circumstances. Sir Francis Bacon did a great deal to promote this approach. He argued strongly that the laws of science are formed from data collected through observation and experimentation (Bruno, 1989). In doing so, he stressed empiricism over deductive logic. Nevertheless, deductive thinking is no less important in the processes of science.

Deductive thinking involves the application of general principles to specific instances. The deductive process makes inferences about specific situations from known or tentative generalizations. This form of reasoning is often used to test hypotheses, either confirming or disproving them. Deduction is frequently used in astronomy to predict events from existing theories. It also has been used extensively in the area of theoretical physics to predict the existence of certain subatomic particles, many of which have been discovered years after their announcements. The hypothetical-deductive approach is also a suggested strategy to use for instructing students in biological sciences to help them better understand these disciplines (Moore, 1984).

Cause-and-Effect Relationships

Scientists often seek to establish cause-and-effect relationships to advance their understanding of the world. The search for cause and effect is central to experimentation and to modern science. Further, this conceptual relationship helps to explain the mechanism by which cause produces effect. Many events can stimulate cause-and-effect reasoning, from the very common to less frequent, such as:

- Why do cats give birth only to kittens?
- Why do some people who smoke develop lung cancer?
- Why do tornadoes form?
- Why do comets reappear every so many years?

In concept, the logic of the cause-and-effect relationship is simple. "A" is shown to cause "B." A common example of this simple relationship can be observed by plucking a guitar string. If you shorten the string and pluck it, the string produces a higher pitched sound. Consider human respiration. If you cut off all oxygen to the human body, the person will die. Cells need oxygen to carry out important processes, which, in humans, enters the body by way of the lungs. Thus the phrase: Oxygen supports life.

The cause of an event must provide the antecedent conditions that are necessary and sufficient for the event to occur. For example, we often hear the comment that cigarette smoking causes lung cancer. Some scientists, as well as tobacco company representatives, object to that statement. Not every person who smokes gets lung cancer. Some people smoke for 50, 60, 70, or 80 years and never contract lung cancer. Smoking may more correctly be termed a risk factor for lung cancer, because we cannot say that tobacco is the sole agent for causing this disease or that smoking tobacco will always result in lung cancer. However, smoking increases the probability of lung cancer. Today, scientists often use statistical probability to predict and explain events.

With living organisms, cause-and-effect relationships are very difficult to establish. The problems involved in the search for causes in living organisms are formidable. Ernst Mayr (1961, p. 1503) posits the cause for a single bird's migration from New Hampshire in late August:

> *There is an immediate set of causes for the migration, consisting of the physiological conditions of the bird interacting with the photoperiodicity and drop in temperature. We might call these the proximate causes of migration. The other two causes, the lack of food during the winter and the genetic disposition of the bird, are the ultimate causes. . . . There is always a proximate set of causes and an ultimate set of causes; both have to be explained and interpreted for a complete understanding of the given phenomenon.*

Do not assume that physical scientists have an easier task determining causation than biological scientists. Consider investigations into the nature of subatomic particles. Physicists have turned to probability and complex mathematical formulas to explain the behavior of electrons and dozens of other subatomic particles, rather than determining the exact nature of a given particle. The Heisenberg uncertainty principle limits the extent of our knowledge regarding the position and momentum of a particle along any axis. Further, those in the historical sciences (evolutionary biology and geology) are very hard pressed to establish cause-and-effect relationships in their work.

Self-Examination and Skepticism

Scientific thinking is more than an effort to understand nature. For centuries, philosophers of science have examined the ways in which scientists have arrived at their conclusions about nature. To paraphrase Poincare (1854–1912) the French mathematician, an intelligent person cannot believe everything or believe nothing. What then can intelligent persons believe, what must they reject, and what can they accept with varying degrees of reservation?

Scientists have always concerned themselves with these questions. Indeed, physics was once called "natural philosophy." But never have scientists spent more effort than today in examining their processes of reasoning. Investigations into the particulate nature of matter, quantum mechanics, and acceptance of the principle of indeterminacy have undermined our earlier notions of the predictability and well-behaved order of nature that once were never questioned. Even the more reluctant scientists have been forced to look closely at their ways of thinking.

Along with self-examination, skepticism is a healthy disposition that every citizen should possess, not only the scientist. Everyone should be skeptical about the many claims made about products, events, and phenomena we hear and read about. We should question advertisements and commercials offering herbs and pills that will cause weight loss or cure cancer. We should question claims from those who say they can detect your thoughts. We should also observe how the scientific community reacts to claims, such as those reporting energy from cold fusion, a human clone, or a perpetual motion machine. When a claim is made about a *too good to be true* product or event, a skeptical reaction should be in order as well as a call for the evidence to support the claim.

Objectivity and Open-Mindedness

Many more characteristics than those mentioned above can be assigned to scientific thinking. For example, objectivity and open-mindedness are often ascribed to the scientific attitude. Although these images of scientists are put forth in textbooks, they may not necessarily represent the manner in which all scientists conduct their work. Scientists are no more dispassionate about their life's work than are other people. Holton (1952) reminds us about the distinction between public and private science that challenges the empiricist stereotype of the detached objective researcher who the public sees in the final edited version of the scientist's work.

Gauld (1982) cautions science educators about their beliefs regarding the empiricist conception of the scientific attitude and suggests perhaps eliminating it from science education. "Teaching that scientists possess these characteristics is bad enough, but it is abhorrent that science educators should actually attempt to mold children in the same false image" (Gauld, 1982, p. 118).

If scientists do not have great conviction in the ideas they are pursuing, they would lack the drive necessary to carry out their research. Scientists must believe in the theories that guide their research agenda for which they have a strong allegiance (Kuhn, 1962). However, some of their scientific beliefs create personal biases that interfere with their progress, because their interpretation of data and reasoning causes them to view the phenomenon under study less objectively. While complete objectivity by individual scientists is not possible, it is this personal view of the world that makes science productive, especially when it is mixed in with the views of other scientists working on the same problems.

Polanyi (1958, p. 18) states the notion of scientific objectivity in his book *Personal Knowledge*:

> *The purpose of this book is to show that complete objectivity, as usually attributed to the exact science, is a delusion and is in fact a false idea. But I shall not try to repudiate strict objectivity as an idea without offering a substitute, which I have called 'personal knowledge'.*

Science as a Way of Investigating

"The Scientific Method expressed in that way haunts the introductions of textbooks, lab report guidelines and science-fair standards. Yet we consider it a poor model for learning about method in science."
—Wivagg & Allchin (2002, p. 2)

The preceding quote highlights what Wivagg and Allchin (2002) call "The" dogma of the scientific method. These writers, as well as others who have studied the history and philosophy of science, point out a myth in science education that continues in spite of the historical record of how science actually takes place. You can still find in science classrooms a poster that lists the five or six steps of the scientific method. Although scientific reports follow a format similar to the steps listed in the scientific method, this procedure is a standardized way of preparing scientific papers for publication. The actual research often takes a very different path than what appears in print.

The work of Karl Pearson (1937) and others, who believed that they could capture the scientific method in the five steps that follow, is still taught in some science courses and it sometimes appears in the introductory chapter of many elementary, middle, and high school science textbooks:

1. Observing
2. Collecting data
3. Developing a hypothesis
4. Experimenting
5. Concluding

Science as a way of investigating utilizes many approaches to constructing knowledge. Science has many methods, which demonstrates humankind's inventiveness for seeking solutions to problems. Some of the approaches used by scientists rely heavily on observation and prediction, as in astronomy and ecology. Other approaches rely on laboratory experiments that focus on cause-and-effect relationships such as those used in microbiology. Percy Bridgman's (1950) comment reinforces this idea: "The scientific method, as far as it is a method, is nothing more than doing one's damndest [sic] with one's mind, no holds barred." Alan Chalmers (1982, p. 169) stresses that "there is no timeless and universal conception of science or scientific method" that can distinguish science from other forms of knowing or make science superior to other human enterprises. Some scientists are experimenters who do the investigating, while others are theorizers who attempt to explain data and pose interesting questions to guide inquiry. Among the many processes often associated with science and inquiry are observing, inferring, hypothesizing, predicting, measuring, manipulating variables, calculating, experimenting, and creating models. While these are useful skills to possess, a more realistic view of investigative science might be in these ideas offered by Franz (1990):

experimentation
reason
chance
observation
hypotheses
strategy
intuition
overcoming difficulties
serendipity

Student investigation is an important element in learning about the nature of science.

In spite of what is often reported about scientific investigations, especially in science textbooks, the inquiry process is rather idiosyncratic—there is no simple linear account of how science proceeds. Furthermore, because there is no "scientific method," the current science education reform documents avoid using the term "the scientific method," instead using the terms *scientific methods* and *scientific methods of inquiry* (AAAS, 1990, p.1). The *Standards* (NRC, 1996) state:

> *The importance of inquiry does not imply that all teachers should pursue a single approach to teaching science. Just as inquiry has many different facets, so teachers need to use many different strategies to develop the understandings and abilities described in the Standards. (p. 2)*

James Conant, chemist and president of Harvard University, asserted, "There is no such thing as *the scientific method.* If there were, surely an examination of the history of physics, chemistry, and biology would reveal it" (1951, p. 45). Harvard historian of science, Gerald Holton, supports this sentiment as follows:

> *All too often the suggestion has been made that the successes of science are the results of applying "the scientific method." But if by "scientific method" we mean the sequence of and rule by which scientists now and in the past have actually done their work, then two things soon become obvious. First, as for every task, there are here not one but many methods and unaccountable variants, and second, even these different methods are usually read into the story after the work has been completed, and so reflect the actual working procedures only in a rather artificial and debatable way. The ever-present longing to discover one master procedure or set of rules underlying all scientific work is understandable, for such a discovery might enormously benefit all fields of scholarship; but like the search for the philosopher's stone, this hope had to be abandoned. (Holton and Roller, 1958, p. 216)*

Among the contemporary philosophers of science in the twentieth century, Paul Feyerabend has voiced, perhaps, the most vehement position against a scientific method. His sentiments are expressed in a notable book titled *Against Method* (Feyerabend, 1993). Feyerabend goes so far as to say there is not one science, but many sciences, which proceed in radically different ways. In fact, we might think of this enterprise as many different science projects. Feyerabend proclaims, "there is no common structure to the events, procedures and results that constitute science" (1993, p. 1). Therefore, one cannot explain progress in science in a simple, one-method manner.

Hypothesis

A hypothesis is an investigative tool that helps the inquirer to clarify ideas and state relationships so they can be tested. A hypothesis is a concise statement that attempts to explain a pattern or predict an outcome. Hypotheses stem from questions that a scientist asks concerning a problem under study. A hypothesis is a generalization to be tested by additional observation or experimentation. It is tentative and therefore can be rejected or modified. Hypotheses set the stage for challenging an idea in order to determine if it merits at least a temporary place in the fabric of scientific knowledge.

Even though a situation can be set up that could disprove a hypothesis, contrary evidence may not necessarily lead to the complete rejection of a hypothesis. Revision of the hypothesis rather than rejection may be appropriate.

> *If the generalization has any reasonable body of supporting data, the finding of new facts which do not fit usually leads to the refinement or elaboration of the original hypothesis. . . . On the other hand, if the original basis for the hypothesis was slender, the unfavorable instances may so outweigh the favorable ones as to make it reasonable to believe that the earlier agreement was a matter of pure chance. Also, a new hypothesis may be developed which fits the original data as well. (Wilson, 1952, p. 28)*

Scientists who engage in experimentation probably do so from a more optimistic point of view rather than attempting to discredit their ideas, as suggested by Popper (1963). In reality, they are betting on their hypotheses, hoping their experiments will confirm their predictions. However, sometimes unexpected results occur that are difficult to explain. Chamberlin (1965) urges researchers to propose not just one hypothesis but as many as the mind can invent, thus freeing the mind from bias that might result from excessive love of one's intellectual child. With many hypotheses, the researcher can be somewhat more objective and increase the probability for identifying several causes, knowing that some of the hypotheses will not survive. Nature is complex; attempting to explain it by limiting ourselves to one hypothesis is too narrow and self-defeating.

The term *hypothesis* poses a problem in science education, because it is used differently and often misunderstood. For example, consider science fair competitions where the term hypothesis usually appears in the project report as one of the steps of the scientific method. Many of these student-generated hypotheses are not tied to a body of knowledge that is understood by the student. A better choice to guide these investigations might be a set of questions or predictions. With many science fair projects it is doubtful that students create statements that apply to a general class of objects and events to be tested. This shortcoming is evident by sampling that took place as well as the lack of understanding of how the sample fits with the population of objects or events under study.

Some science educators object to defining a hypothesis as an "educated guess," a term often expressed by preservice and in-service science teachers. They realize that scientists carefully study phenomena and problems before they launch their research projects. Why would a scientist devote a great deal of energy and money pursuing a guess? Galus (2003, p. 10) states: "In the scientific world, the hypothesis is formulated only after hours of observation, days of calculating and studying, and sometimes years of research into the phenomena of interest."

Observation

Observation is certainly one of the cornerstones of science. Although most observations are carried out through the sense of sight, other senses like hearing, feeling, smelling, and tasting also can be part of the observation process. Through observation, data and information are gathered and organized in order to make sense out of reality. This is how facts are established so that hypotheses can be tested to support theories. The body of knowledge formed by scientists is the result of extensive observation, reading, imagination, and reasoning, which eventually coalesce into concepts, principles, and theories.

The list of individuals who have made significant contributions to science as the result of their keen observations is long. Among those worth mentioning is Tycho Brahe, who amassed the most important early observations regarding the motion of stars and planets during the Middle Ages. These observations, in turn, were used by Kepler to produce the now-accepted idea that planets move in elliptical orbits around the Sun. Tycho used his eyes as well as a few simple devices to study the movement of celestial bodies. Tycho made his observations with scrupulous regularity, repeating them, combining them, and trying to allow for the imperfections of his instruments. As a result, he reduced his margin of error to a fraction of a minute of an arc and provided the sharpest precision achieved by anyone before the telescope (Boorstin, 1985).

Although observation plays a central role in scientific investigation, this skill is tied closely to the knowledge, thinking, and motivation of the observer. As Goethe said, "We see only what we know." The scientist as well as the layperson sees with the mind. Beveridge (1957) points out that what people observe in a situation depends upon their interests and expectations. Furthermore, he claims that false observations occur when the senses provide the wrong information to the mind or when the mind plays tricks on the observer by filling in information from past experiences. Often, the observer focuses attention on what is expected, thus missing unexpected occurrences and valuable facts. Although observation is one of the most fundamental inquiry skills, it is a complex activity that merits careful study in and of itself. Further, scientific observation is guided by theory.

Experimentation

Along with observation, experimentation is another cornerstone of modern science. Through experimentation, ideas can be confirmed or supported and erroneous beliefs that have been passed down by authority can be discarded. Experimentation permits us to probe nature's secrets, which seem to be tightly guarded and often disguised. The controlled experiment offers the scientist an opportunity to test ideas and determine cause-and-effect relationships. Experimental activities range from using a match to burn a peanut to using a particle accelerator to smash a proton.

Modern science came into being in the sixteenth century when Galileo and others built upon Greek science, which was dominated by philosophers who distrusted experimentation. Greek philosophers relied primarily on reasoning to develop their ideas. Some of these individuals placed little value upon practical activities that could reveal the obvious. They shunned the technologies of the craftsman, such as mechanical and optical devices that could provide accurate observations (Aicken, 1984).

When one experiments, events are initiated, producing relationships that can be studied carefully. The conditions of these interventions are known and controlled. In this manner, the procedure is documented and can be reproduced by others. The controlled experiment is often used to test a hypothesis concerning cause-and-effect relationships. Condition A, for example, is altered to determine its effects on condition B. The situation that is manipulated by the researcher is called the *manipulative* or *independent variable*, and the resultant variable is called the *predicted* or *dependent variable*. Other variables are held constant and their conditions noted. In situations where living organisms are under study, randomization of organisms or subjects into experimental and control groups is most desirable.

We must guard against placing ultimate trust in experimentation for evidence. Beveridge (1957) warns not to put excessive faith in experimentation because the possibility of error in technique always exists, which can result in misleading outcomes. "It is not at all rare for scientists in different parts of the world to obtain contradictory results with similar biological material. Sometimes these can be traced to unsuspected factors; for instance, a great difference in the reactions of guinea pigs to diphtheria toxin was traced to a difference in diets of the animals. In other instances, it has not been possible to discover the cause of the disagreement despite a thorough investigation" (Beverage, 1957, p. 34).

Science teachers should be mindful that, although the intent of scientific investigation is to gather evidence to support a hypothesis or to answer a question, the process leaves open the possibility for error and misinterpretation. Scientists can collect faulty data—the initial information taken by observation. Then they can make errors in transforming data into evidence when they construct graphs, charts, diagrams, mathematical formulas, and other types of models in order to form arguments to verify or discredit ideas. Because human judgment is involved in these steps, the process leaves open the possibility for faulty conclusions.

Mathematics

Roger Bacon expressed it well when he said, "Mathematics is the door and the key to science." His quote suggests that mathematics is necessary to the understanding of nature's clockworks and without it we cannot get inside to find out what is taking place. The formulas and symbols assist us when we describe relationships that represent laws and patterns in nature. Mathematics is often referred to as the *language of science*.

At a very deep level, mathematics helps us to express models of phenomena that we cannot possibly observe directly or in their entirety. The atom, for example, is so small that we cannot see it or the electrons and protons that form its structure. The simple planetary models that we often see in textbooks or the packet of pulsating wave models may be inaccurate models of the atom. According to scientists who study atoms and subatomic particles, the atom may be an entity that we cannot visualize. Nevertheless, mathematical models have been devised that predict well the behavior of groups of atoms and subatomic particles. Mathematics has been used as a tool to provide useful representations of nature for objects and phenomena that are out of our direct perceptual reach.

The power of numbers and the intimate association between mathematics and the evolution of science is evident throughout recorded history (de Santillana, 1961). For example, Pythagoras, in his studies of nature, mingled astronomy, geometry, music, and arithmetic. He indicated that numbers were special and that the universe produced harmonious melody. He described the motion of the stars in terms of rhythm and melody. Pythagoras's one physical discovery had to do with the patterns of sound produced by changing the length of a plucked string. He noted that moving an instrument's bridge to different locations or intervals on the string changed the sound. The ratios 1:2, 4:3, and 3:4 were important numerical relationships that resulted in distinct sounds. He further discovered that the numbers 1, 2, 3, and 4, which formed these ratios, added up to 10, the "perfect number."

Galileo, it is often said, made significant contributions to modern science because he attempted to explain phenomena with evidence, using mathematical relationships. Many connect Galileo with the falling stone controversy. Those who subscribed to Aristotle's notion of falling bodies believed that a heavier object falls at a faster rate than a lighter object. Galileo probably said, "Wait a minute." If you try this out, you will find that they both fall at the same rate, provided that air resistance is minimized. His work on this problem eventually resulted in the celebrated formula,

$$s = 16t^2$$

which states that a falling body has traveled a certain distance, s, after falling t seconds. Galileo also demonstrated that the trajectory of a ball thrown in the air follows a parabolic path.

Science as a Body of Knowledge

The body of knowledge produced from many scientific fields represents the creative products of human invention that have occurred over the centuries. The enormous collection of ideas pertaining to the natural and physical world is organized into astronomy, biology, chemistry, geology, physics, and at the interfaces of these disciplines. The result is a compilation of catalogued information containing many types of knowledge, each of which makes its own unique contribution to science. The facts, concepts, principles, laws, hypotheses, theories, and models form the content of science. These ideas possess their own specific meaning, which cannot be understood apart from the processes of inquiry that produced them. Therefore, the content and methods of science are tied together, and teaching one without the other distorts the learner's conception and appreciation of the nature of science.

Facts

The facts of science serve as the foundation for concepts, principles, and theories. A fact is often thought of as truth and the state of things. Facts represent what we can perceive through our senses and with instruments, and they are usually regarded as reliable data. Often, two criteria are used to identify a scientific fact: (1) it is directly observable and (2) it can be demonstrated at any time. Consequently, facts are open to all who wish to observe them. We must remember, however, that these criteria do not always hold, because factual information regarding a one-time event, such as a volcanic eruption, may not be repeatable. In addition, uncertainty and limitation are inherent in measurement that accompanies facts. Therefore, data can never be considered absolutely pure and unequivocally true, because they contain a probability of error.

The presentation of facts alone in a science course is not enough, because the receiver of the information should know how the facts were established. For example, it is widely known that food can spoil in the presence of microorganisms, causing whoever eats it to become very sick or even die. This fact becomes intelligible and meaningful when students learn how evidence for various types of food poisoning has been established. For example, one of the most deadly food poisonings is botulism, which is caused by the anaerobic bacteria *Clostridium botulinum*. A tiny amount of toxin produced by this organism is deadly. A lethal dose of the *botulinum* toxin is approximately .0000001 g—one ten-millionth of a gram (Black, 1994). Therefore, one gram of this compound is enough to kill about 10,000,000 people. The toxin acts by paralyzing muscles, blocking the neurotransmitter acetylcholine, thus stopping breathing. Canned foods, such as beans, corn, and beets, must be heat-treated to prevent this bacterium from multiplying while in an airtight container.

The historical accounts of food poisoning from bacteria and fungi are numerous. Microbial contamination of milk, cereal, and bread, for example, provide a meaningful context for explaining the mechanisms that have established the causal factors of food poisoning. Therefore, it is a fact that microorganisms can impart toxins to food, causing sickness or death. Perhaps not all the facts given in a science course can be taught within the context of how they were discovered, but many can and should be.

Concepts

Many facts have little meaning by themselves. They are raw material, in a sense, and must be examined to form meaningful ideas and relationships. Thinking and reasoning are required to identify patterns and make connections with the data that form relationships we call concepts. A concept is an abstraction of events, objects, or phenomena that seem to have certain properties or attributes in common. Fish, for example, possess certain characteristics that set them apart from reptiles and mammals. Most bony fish have scales, fins, and gills. According to Bruner, Goodnow, and Austin (1956), a concept has five important elements: (1) name, (2) definition, (3) attributes, (4) values, and (5) examples. The process of concept formation and attainment is an active process and requires more than simply conveying these elements to the learner. The students must establish some of the attributes and discover some of the patterns in data if the concepts are to become linked to other meaningful ideas in their minds. In addition, concepts can be affective as well as cognitive.

Many of the terms associated with scientific fields represent concepts. They are ideas used to form categories. In biology, for example, tree, grass, insect, ape, gene, and enzyme, each represent a class of entities that share common characteristics. In chemistry, element, molecule, compound, mixture, acid, base, and isotope can be considered concepts. There are physics concepts, such as electron, proton, neutron, wave, solid, and X-ray. Concepts become meaningful to learners when they have had many opportunities to experience examples or instances of them. For example, we describe the class of animals called fish by observing a variety of fish and noting that they live in water, take in water through their mouths, and have fins. Categorizing observations aids scientists and the public at large to form knowledge about the world in which we live.

Laws and Principles

Laws and principles also fall into the general category of concepts. Although they can be considered broader than a simple concept, principles and laws are often used synonymously. These higher-order ideas are used to *describe* phenomena and patterns in nature. Laws and principles state that which exists. They are often accepted as facts. Nevertheless, their distinction and empirical basis must be remembered. Laws and principles are supported concepts and facts. They are more general than facts, but they are subject to limiting conditions and are related to observable phenomena. For example, gas laws and laws of motion specify what can be observed under certain conditions. The principles that regulate growth and reproduction provide reliable information regarding changes that take place in living systems.

Theories

When science goes beyond the classification and description of phenomena to explanations, it moves on to the level of theory. Scientists use theories to *explain* underlying patterns and forces. A scientific theory is an explanation of a phenomenon that is well supported. Theories are ambitious intellectual endeavors, because they deal with the complexities and obscurities of reality — that which is hidden from direct observation. Theories are concerned with magnitudes of time, distance, and size that defy ordinary perception; therefore they are a special type of knowledge. "When a theory explains a large and diverse body of facts, it is considered robust; if it consistently predicts new phenomena that are subsequently observed, then it is considered reliable. Facts are the world's data; theories are explanatory ideas about those facts. An explanatory principle is not to be confused with the data it seeks to explain (Shermer, 2002, p. 167).

Consider the theory of the atom, which states that all matter is made up of tiny particles called *atoms*, many millions of which would be required to cover the period at the end of this sentence. This conception becomes even harder to grasp when we consider the aspect of the theory that suggests an atom is mostly empty space with a small, dense, positively charged center surrounded by a cloud of negatively charged particles moving in certain regions of space far out from the center.

Theories have a different purpose than facts, concepts, and laws. They incorporate many types of knowledge into explanations of why phenomena occur as they do. Theories are of a different nature; they never become fact or law, but remain tentative until disproved or revised.

> *Any physical theory is always provisional, in the sense that it is only a hypothesis: you can never prove it. No matter how many times the results of experiments agree with some theory, you can never be sure that the next time the results will not contradict the theory. On the other hand, you can disprove a theory by finding even a single observation that disagrees with the predictions of the theory. As philosopher of science Karl Popper has emphasized, a good theory is characterized by the fact that it makes a number of predictions that could be disproved or falsified by observation. Each time new experiments are observed to agree with the predictions the theory survives, and our confidence in it is increased; but if ever a new observation is found to disagree, we have to abandon or modify the theory. At least that is what is supposed to happen, but you can always question the competence of the person who carried out the observation. (Hawking, 1988, p. 10)*

Theories are of great importance to science. They represent some of the most monumental and creative works of humankind, which are evident in the theory of the atom, special and general relativity, plate tectonics, and natural selection. These inventions of the mind incorporate a great deal of thinking, imagination, writing, and modeling. Consider natural selection, for example. Darwin used domestic breeding as a model for selection and used Malthus's notion of a struggle for survival of the fittest (Harre, 1970). Recall the four postulates of natural selection: (1) all organisms produce more offspring than can survive, (2) overproduction occurs that leads to a struggle for survival, (3) individuals within a species vary, and (4) those organisms best adapted tend to survive. Overproduction, competition, variation, mutation, struggle for existence, and adaptation are just some of the concepts and principles that are used in Darwin's theory for explaining the evolution of life on this planet, which has been changing for some 3 billion years. Science educators have the responsibility to help others to comprehend the nature of theories by showing how they explain complex phenomena that cannot be observed directly, and that a scientific theory has much more support than a guess or speculation used in everyday conversation.

Models

The term *model* is often used in scientific literature. A scientific model is a *representation* of phenomenon that we cannot see or observe directly. These models are mental images or constructs that are used to explain abstract ideas and come in many forms: physical structures, diagrams, graphs, and mathematical formulas. They include the most salient features of an idea or theory that the scientist is attempting to make understood. The Bohr model of the atom, the planetary model of the solar system, the wave and particle models of light, and the double helix model of DNA all have been represented in material and visual forms as well as in mathematical expression. While not a replica of reality, these abstractions are invaluable to the progress of science.

Sometimes there are no sharp distinctions among models, hypotheses, and theories. Textbooks are the major referent for most of our ideas about scientific models. They are useful in helping us to become familiar with important ideas. Unfortunately, many people come to believe that the models presented in science textbooks are the real thing, forgetting that they are used only to help the learner conceptualize the salient features of a principle or theory, and that the mental picture is not what exists in reality McComas (2000).

Remember that because models are not perfect, they are problematic in teaching science. Too often, the model becomes the reality that is under study. Students rarely see the limitations of these analogies, which result in a highly simplistic representation of a phenomenon. Amdahl (1991, p. 18) advises that when devising a concrete model of the universe, for example: "Don't mistake your watermelon for the universe."

In closing this section on science as a body of knowledge, science teachers must be alerted to the problems associated with the categorizations and definitions of science content. There is no standardized or universally accepted definition for the terms scientific fact, concept, law, principle, theory, or model. Often, these ideas are poorly defined and used interchangeably. After an analysis of 12 introductory college biology textbooks, Kugler (2002) points out how many biologists/authors disagree on the definitions of these science terms and how they provide examples that are inconsistent with their own definitions. Therefore when teaching science, we must strive to define terms carefully and to use them in a consistent manner.

Science and Its Interactions with Technology and Society

A great deal of scientific work that is conducted today is a collaborative effort, carried out by many individuals working as a team within a societal context whose progress is influenced greatly by society and the availability of technology. Consequently, science, technology, and society influence one another, causing each to advance or to make little progress. Basic science could not advance without the use of highly sophisticated equipment, such as particle accelerators, chromatographs, spectroscopes, electron beam microscopes, space telescopes, electrophoresis apparatus, lasers, and integrated circuits. These and thousands of other technological products help us to answer questions about nature. Questions posed about nature give rise to the necessity for developing equipment that can help to answer these inquiries. For example, there have been great advances in the sophistication of chromatographic instruments over the past half century to determine the composition of complex substances. Computer software programs have been developed to advance understanding of the human genome, weather patterns, changes in the oceans' floors, and the structure of the universe.

Society also plays a key role in the progress of science and technology. Society, through governmental organizations such as the National Science Foundation and the National Institutes of Health, exerts a large influence on the funding for science, engineering, medicine, agriculture, and mathematics. Business and industry carry out research and development programs that expend billions of dollars each year to improve on their products, employing many scientists, engineers, and technicians.

Technology

Technology advances when both science and society have needs and problems to solve. For example, the desire to travel long distances in a short period of time, to process enormous amounts of data, to build light-weight structures, and to diagnose deadly diseases have stimulated the creation of products that are very advanced technologically from those available only 25 years ago. The production of jumbo jets can carry thousands of people daily across continents and the oceans. Cell phones are common in most nations across the globe, providing instant communication to all parts of the world. Medical imaging can detect significant changes in organ tissue. Special polymers are being produced that have exceptional properties, some of which are stronger and much lighter than steel. Technology has been around longer than science. It began when people fashioned tools to carry out everyday tasks, such as cooking, hunting, and making shelters. However, today's technology is very sophisticated and coupled tightly with science as evidenced with nanotechnology.

Nanotechnology is a relatively new field of research and product development. This multidisciplinary field draws on many areas of applied science and technology such as applied physics, chemical engineering, biological engineering, electrical engineering, and material science. At the ultra-small nanoscale, materials show different properties than at the macroscale, which enable unique applications. The development of materials, atom–by-atom or molecule-by-molecule, can produce extraordinary products. "Electric power can be converted to motion and vice-versa, with 10 times the efficiency and about 10^8 (100,000,000) times more compactly. Computers can be 10^{12} times smaller and use 10^6 times less power. Materials can be about 100 times stronger" (Center for Responsible Nanotechnology, 2008, p. 1). The field is and will continue to produce products that benefit society in the areas of electronics, cosmetics, transportation, medicine, agriculture, and many more.

Society

Just as scientific knowledge impacts society, society impacts science. A large amount of scientific work is funded through governmental grants and private business. The money is generally targeted for projects that study important societal problems, such as cardiovascular disease, cancer, and national defense. The Manhattan Project, which produced the first atomic bomb, serves as an example of how national security stimulated scientific and technological advances in capturing the power of the atom. The mapping of the human genome is another project that succeeded as the result of large funding from society. The great advances that have occurred in molecular biology and biotechnology over the past half century are the result of large governmental funding.

Generally, significant sums of money are required to support every phase of large scientific research projects, from writing grant proposals, to conducting research, to communicating results. Politics play an important part in determining which research areas to support and how much funding is provided. Usually, politicians are interested most in research and technology that can solve problems of high public interest, especially if it can benefit the citizens in their home states. Most people would rather see their tax dollars go into cancer and cardiovascular research than the more theoretical exploration of tiny particles that constitute the atom. The religious convictions of politicians can impact funding, as evidenced by the government withholding funds for embryonic stem cell research. More than ever before, science is rooted in society and intertwined with technology. This topic will be taken up in greater detail in Chapter 12, which addresses science, technology, and society.

Assessing and Reviewing

Analysis and Synthesis

1. How did you score on the true–false quiz (Figure 7.1) with regard to identifying some myths of science? Compare your true–false answers with this key: 1-F, 2-F, 3-T, 4-F, 5-F, 6-F, 7-F, 8-F, 9-F, 10-T, 11-T, and 12-F. In order to better understand the 12 statements, go back through the chapter and look for discussions of the nature of science that pertain to each quiz item. The 12 statements parallel the development of the chapter from beginning to end.
2. Present a definition of science. How does science differ from other ways of knowing such as myth and religion?

Practical Considerations

3. Let's evaluate a science teacher's approach to experimentation in order to determine the extent to which it reflects authentic science to the students, considering that school-based science carried out by adolescents may differ to some degree from authentic science conducted by adults.

   Teacher: Today, class, you are going to conduct an investigation to determine how many paper clips you can hang on the end of a magnet before the force gives way and the clips fall off. I want you to follow the scientific method that we use to guide our laboratory work. Remember the steps of this method listed on the poster.

   The Scientific Method

   1. Problem
   2. Hypothesis
   3. Procedure
   4. Results
   5. Conclusion

   a. Evaluate this approach to teach science by writing one sentence indicating the extent to which it reflects the way scientists go about their work.

   b. In one or two paragraphs, substantiate your evaluation of this teaching episode from what you read in this chapter.

4. Analyze a teaching situation or instruction materials to determine which dimension(s) or theme(s) of science discussed in this chapter is emphasized. Make an outline of the major terms associated with (a) science as a way of thinking, (b) science as a way of investigating, (c) science as a body of knowledge, and (d) science and its interactions with technology and society. Use these categories to determine the science curricular emphasis in the following paragraphs that you might find in a science textbook:

   i. Bones are a complex tissue. The outer covering is composed of a tough membrane called the *periosteum*, which aids in nourishing the bone. The periosteum contains a rich supply of blood and is where muscles are attached to the bone. Beneath the periosteum is a bony layer that contains mineral matter. This layer can range from very hard material to spongy material. Many channels, called the *Haversian canals* that carry nourishment to the living cells of the bone, penetrate the bony layer.

   ii. There is a global debate taking place concerning the rain forests that are being cut down in South America. The people of that region believe it is their right to clear the trees so that they can cultivate the land and grow crops to feed themselves. People in other parts of the world are distressed to learn of the rain forest destruction; they want the trees to take in carbon dioxide from the atmosphere and give off oxygen. Further, they fear that many species of plants and insects will become extinct with the disappearance of the rain forest habitat.

5. Identify the ideas that you will use in planning and teaching science to help students understand and appreciate this enterprise. Construct a visual representation of major terms that presents your conception of science. You might begin by placing "The Nature of Science" at or near the center of your graphic organizer and connect it with lines to the key terms.

Developmental Considerations

6. Begin or add to your professional library, paperback books on the nature of science. These can be purchased from the Internet at bookseller Web sites and in local bookstores. In some cities, there are half-priced bookstores where science and nature of science books can be purchased for very little money.

Resources to Examine

The Dogma of "The" Scientific Method. Nov./Dec., 2002. *The American Biology Teacher.*

The authors, Wivagg and Allchin, write a clear, crisp, two-page article about the naïve conceptions of a scientific method. The article should convince most readers that science is a creative enterprise and scientists use many tools in their quest to understand nature. The authors also point out that scientific papers, although appearing to follow the scientific method, are written to fit a standard publication format.

Quizzing Students on the Myths of Science. Nov., 2004. *The Science Teacher.*

The authors, Chiappetta and Koballa, explain each of the 12 myths of science in order to provide science teachers with a better understanding of science. They address important aspects of authentic science such as method, controlled experiment, law, theory, and the tentativeness of scientific knowledge. The article provides a good advanced organizer for the information presented in the nature of science chapter.

Just a Theory: Exploring the Nature of Science. 2004. Amherst, NY: Prometheus Books.

Moti Ben-Ari has written a useful paperback book that can inform science teachers about science. The book addresses many areas of the nature of science that teachers should be informed about such as theory, pseudoscience, science and religion, logic and mathematics, and the future of science. This book is an easy read and can be useful in sharpening one's thinking about the scientific enterprise.

Skeptic Magazine. Skeptic at P.O. Box 338, Altadena, CA; Phone: 626-794-3119; Fax: 626-794-1301; E-mail: skepticmag@aol.com

Skeptic Magazine offers science educators and the general public many resources for better understanding science, pseudoscience, and nonscience. The magazine's articles address many topics, such as science and religion, creationism and evolution, fad diets, paranormal claims, astrology, and alien abductions. In addition, many resources are listed in the magazines that readers can obtain, such as the Skeptics' Lecture Series at Caltech, *Skeptic Magazine* back issues, the Skeptic's Book Club, and *The Skeptic Encyclopedia of Pseudoscience.*

What's in a Word? *Science Scope.* October, 2007.

Renee Schwartz has written an informative article for science teachers about the importance of using correct terminology in science courses. She discusses words that should be avoided and those that should be used in their place, providing reasons for these choices. The article reinforces the ideas discussed in this chapter, and is one that secondary school students can read to improve their understanding of the nature of science.

References

Abd-El-Khalick, F., Bell, R. L., & Lederman, N. G. (1998). The nature of science and instructional practice: Making the unnatural natural. *Science Education, 82,* 417–436.

Aicken, F. (1984). *The nature of science.* London: Heinemann Educational Books.

Agin, D. (2006). *Junk science: How politicians, corporations, and other hucksters betray us.* New York: St. Martins Press.

Allchin, D. (2003). Scientific myth-conceptions. *Science Education, 87,* 329–351.

Amdahl, K. (1991). *There are no electrons.* Arvada, CO: Clearwater Publishing Co.

American Association for the Advancement of Science (AAAS). (1990). *Science for all Americans.* New York: Oxford University Press.

American Association for the Advancement of Science. (1993). *Benchmarks for science literacy.* New York: Oxford University Press.

Angier, N. (2007). *The canon: A whirligig tour of the beautiful basics of science.* Boston: Houghton Mifflin.

Ben-Ari, M. (2005). *Just a theory: Exploring the nature of science.* Amherst, NY: Promethus Books.

Beveridge, W. I. B. (1957). *The art of scientific investigation.* New York: Vintage Books.

Black, H. (1994, December). Poison that heals. *Chem Matters,* 7–9.

Boorstin, D. J. (1985). *The discoverers.* New York: Vintage Books.

Bridgman, P. W. (1950). *The reflections of a physicist.* New York: Philosophical Library.

Bruner, J. S., Goodnow, J. J., & Austin, G. A. (1956). *A study of thinking.* New York: John Wiley.

Bruno, L. C. (1989). *The landmarks of science.* New York: Facts on File.

Center for Responsible Nanotechnology. (2008). Powerful products of molecular manufacturing. Retrieved June, 26, 2008, from www.crnano.org/products.htm

Chalmers, A. F. (1982). *What is this thing called science?* Portland, OR: International Specialized Book Service.

Chamberlin, T. C. (1965). The method of multiple working hypotheses. *Science, 148,* 754.

Chiappetta, E. L. & Fillman, D. A. (2007). Analysis of five high school biology textbooks used in the United States for inclusion of the nature of science. *International Journal of Science Education, 15,* 1847–1869.

Conant, J. B. (1951). *On understanding science.* New York: A New Mentor Book.

de Santillana, G. (1961). *The origins of scientific thought.* New York: New American Library of World Literature.

Duschl, R. A. (1990). *Restructuring science education.* New York: Teachers College Press.

Einstein, A. (1954). *Ideas and opinions.* New York: Dell.

Feyerabend, P. (1993). *Against method.* London: Verso.

Franz, J. E. (1990). The art of research. *ChemTech, 20*(3), 133–135.

Galus, P. J. (2003, May). A testable prediction. *The Science Teacher,* p. 10.

Gauld, C. (1982). The scientific attitude and science education: A critical reappraisal. *Science Education, 66,* 109–121.

Harre, R. (1970). *The principles of scientific thinking.* Chicago: University of Chicago Press.

Hawking, S. W. (1988). *A brief history of time.* New York: Bantam Books.

Holton, G. (1952). *Introduction to concepts and theories in physical science.* Reading, MA: Addison-Wesley.

Holton, G., & Roller, D. H. D. (1958). *Foundations of modern physical science.* Reading, MA: Addison-Wesley.

Hummel, C. E. (1986). *The Galileo connection.* Downers Grove, IL: InterVarsity Press.

Kugler, C, (2002). Darwin's theory, Mendel's laws: Labels and the teaching of science. *The American Biology Teacher, 64,* 341–351.

Kuhn, T. S. (1962). *The structure of scientific revolutions.* Chicago: University of Chicago Press.

Loving, C. C. (1995). Comments on multiculturalism, universalism, and science education. *Journal of Research in Science Teaching, 79,* 341–348.

Lumpe, A. T., & Beck, J. (1996). A profile of high school biology textbooks using scientific literacy recommendations. *The American Biology Teacher, 58,* 147–153.

Matthews, M. R. (1991). Ernst Mach and contemporary science education reforms. In M. R. Mathews (Ed.), *History, Philosophy, and Science Teaching* (pp. 9–18). New York: Teachers College Press.

Mayr, E. (1961). Cause and effect in biology. *Science, 134,* 1503.

McComas, W. F. (2000). Elements of the nature of science: Dispelling the myths. In W. F. McComas (Ed.), *The nature of science in science education: Rationales and strategies* (pp. 53–70). Dordrecht: Kluwer.

Moore, J. A. (1984). Science as a way of knowing. *American Zoologist, 24,* 467–534.

Morris, R. (1991). How to tell what is science from what isn't. In J. Brockman (Ed.), *Doing science.* New York: Prentice Hall.

National Academy of Sciences. (1999). *Science and creationism: A view from the national academy of sciences.* Washington, DC: National Academy Press.

National Research Council (NRC). (1996). *National science education standards.* Washington, DC: National Academy Press.

Pearson, K. (1937). *The grammar of science.* London: Dutton.

Polanyi, M. 1958. *Personal knowledge.* Chicago: University of Chicago Press.

Popper, K. (1963). *Conjectures and refutation: The growth of* scientific *knowledge.* New York: Harper & Row.

Project Physics Course. (1975). *Project physics.* New York: Holt, Rinehart and Winston.

Shermer, M. (2001). *The borderlands of science: Where sense meets nonsense.* New York: Oxford Press.

Shermer, M. (2002). *Why people believe weird things: Pseudoscience, superstition, and other confusions of our time.* New York: Henry Holt.

Stanley, W. B., & Brickhouse, N. W. (1994). Multiculturalism, universalism, and science education. *Journal of Research in Science Teaching, 78,* 387–398.

Strahler, A. N. (1992). *Understanding science.* Buffalo, NY: Prometheus Books.

Teller, E. (1991, March 12). Teller talks. *The Daily Cougar, 57*(83), pp. 1, 15. Houston: University of Houston.

Weinberg, S. (1998, Oct. 8). The revolution that didn't happen. *New York Review of Books.* [Online]. Available at: www.nybooks.com/nyrev/

Wilson, E. B., Jr. (1952). *An introduction to scientific research.* New York: McGraw-Hill.

Wivagg, D., & Allchin, D. (2002). The dogma of the scientific method. *The American Biology Teacher, 64,* 484–485.

Chapter

8

Inquiry and Teaching Science

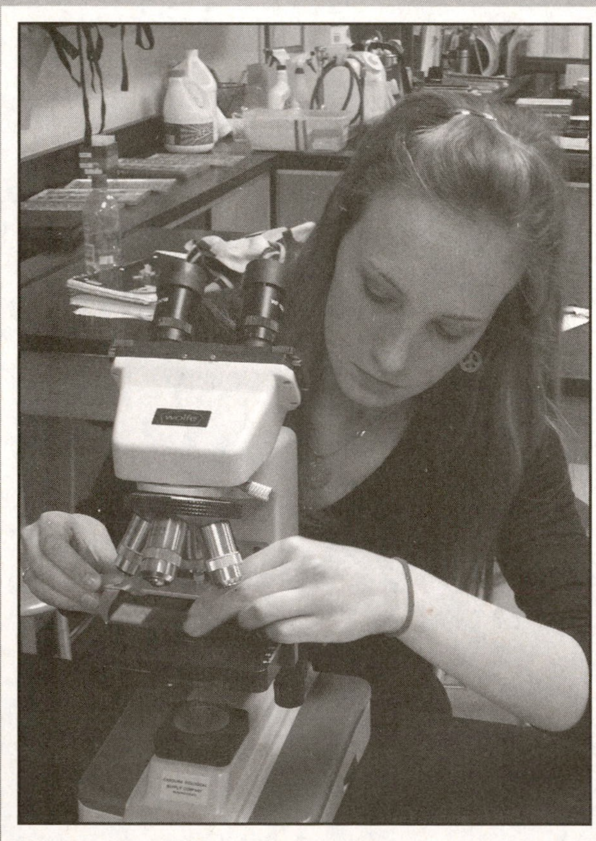

Students benefit greatly by learning about natural phenomena through investigation.

All students must be provided with many opportunities to explore the natural world in order to learn how it works. Student interest in and understanding of science increases when they are placed in situations where they are actively involved in the study of natural phenomena. However, in order for school science to resemble authentic science, to some degree it must reflect how science is practiced. For this to occur, teachers and textbooks must illuminate the thinking and investigative activities that scientists use to construct knowledge. The term *inquiry* has been used for over a half century by educators to refer to the investigative approach to learning with the belief that the inquiry-based instruction will result in many valued learning outcomes, such as:

- understanding the nature of science and investigative processes
- in-depth knowledge of scientific concepts, laws, principles, and theories
- reasoning, thinking, and computational skills
- attitudes, interests, values, and "habits of mind" related to mathematics and science

Unfortunately, inquiry-based school science has so many facets and interpretations, all of which have led to a great deal of confusion and misunderstanding regarding this approach to school science, as shown by the many facets of inquiry-based school science that are shown in Figure 8.1.

AIMS OF THE CHAPTER

Use the questions below to guide your thinking and learning about inquiry-based science instruction and how you can be successful in its implementation.

- How would you distinguish between everyday inquiry conducted by laymen and scientific inquiry conducted by scientists?
- Can you give the distinctions among expository teaching, reception learning, discovery learning, open inquiry, and guided inquiry?
- How would you explain the differences between traditional science instruction and inquiry-based instruction?
- Which one of the following instructional approaches is recommended by many of the national science education reform documents, teaching science *by* inquiry or teaching science *as* inquiry, and how would you explain these important approaches to school science?
- Can you describe the components of instructional approaches to inquiry-based instruction, such as the Learning Cycle, 5E Instructional Model, and 7E Instructional Model?
- How would you describe eight strategies and techniques to initiate and sustain inquiry-based science?
- What would your teaching plan look like if you intended to demonstrate a certain instructional strategy and set of techniques to engage students in finding out about a given phenomenon?
- What concerns and problems can you cite that are associated with science teachers' attempts to implement inquiry-based science programs?

Read the vignette below and determine the extent to which it is an invitation to inquiry.

At the beginning of the period, toward the end of winter, one of the students in Mrs. Long's seventh-grade life science class asked a question that got the entire group thinking. This situation was a surprise, because for a majority of the school year most of the students were apathetic, causing the teacher to initiate the instruction with questions and prompts in order to get them involved with the course material. Here is how the students, all of a sudden, became interested in science and how the teacher handled the situation.

Rickie: Why do blackbirds sit on the telephone lines at the intersection of the Interstate and Spencer Road at about suppertime?

Mrs. Long: Rickie, that is an interesting question. Can anyone think of a reason why these birds gather together at the intersection?

Marci: There is a shopping center there.

Mrs. Long: Yes, but how would the shopping center attract the birds to this location? Tom, you have your hand up.

Tom: There are lots of lights at the shopping center. Maybe the birds like the light.

Mrs. Long: Good thinking. Let's place some terms and ideas on the board. First, would someone tell me the question that we are trying to answer?

FIGURE 8.1 Many facets of inquiry-based school science.

Rationale for Inquiry-Based Instruction

- Understanding the nature of science and investigative processes
- In-depth knowledge of scientific concepts, laws, principles, and theories
- Better reasoning, thinking, and computational skills
- Improved attitudes, interests, values, and "habits of mind" related to science

What Are Inquiry and Inquiry-Based Instruction?

General Inquiry School-Based Inquiry NSES NSTA/NCATE

Critical Elements of Inquiry from National Standards

Questions Evidence Explanations Evaluation Communication

Instructional Distinctions

Expository Teaching Discovery Learning Open Inquiry Guided Inquiry

Amount of Structure

- Level 1—Pose problems and describe methods, but leave solutions to students
- Level 2—Pose problems, but leave methods and solutions to students
- Level 3—Leave the identification of problems, methods, and solutions to students

Specific Aims

- Science *as* Inquiry—Focus on the understanding of a phenomena through active student engagement
- Science *by* Inquiry—Focus on investigative methods and processes of science
- Three Families of Science Activities—Knowledge building, support activities, and practices to be reconsidered
- Talk and Argumentation—Focus on the use of argumentation to advance science understandings and practice

Assessing Inquiry Learning

Understanding Inquiry Ability to Conduct Inquiry Conceptual Understanding

Instructional Approaches and Lesson Cycles

- Learning Cycle—Exploration, concept introduction, and concept application
- 5E Instructional Model—Engage, explore, explain, elaborate, and evaluate
- 7E Instructional Model—Elicit, engage, explore, explain, elaborate, evaluate, and extend

Supporting Strategies and Techniques

Asking Questions Science Process Skills Discrepant Events Inductive Activities
Deductive Activities Gathering Information Small-Group Investigations Science Fair Projects
Grouping Techniques

Concerns Associated with Inquiry-Based Instruction

Understanding Learning Terms Testing Time Materials and Equipment Facilities
Hands-On Activities Covering the Curriculum Discipline
Colleagues Administration Parents

Regina: Why do the blackbirds sit on the wires near the interstate?

Mrs. Long: Good, Regina. I'll place the question at the top of the board, your reasons for this phenomenon at the left, and factors that affect bird behavior on the right. Please think of more reasons why the birds congregate at this location toward the end of the day.

Linn: There are many cars that pass through this area. But I would think the cars might scare the birds.

Mrs. Long: Okay, I'll write traffic as one possible reason. Can some of you other students think of reasons for the gathering of the blackbirds on the lines? Sammy.

Sammy: What about the dumpsters? I see birds picking up food around them.

Mehja: Mrs. Long, why don't the birds gather in the trees in front of the apartments that are up the road from the shopping center? They like to be around trees.

As the students continue to give reasons for a situation they have observed in their community, the teacher places their ideas on the board. Then she asks class members to come up with factors related to bird behavior and survival, which she places on the right side of the board. By this time the students are getting interested in the problem. Now, the teacher has a smile on her face. Although the life science course will include the study of ecology toward the end of the semester, a student's question initiated a situation that will stimulate the study of ecology in the urban environment. A teachable moment has presented itself in Mrs. Long's life science class with an opportunity to engage students in science inquiry.

Stop and Reflect!

Before reading further in the chapter, respond to the following:

1. How did the science teacher handle the student's question about the flocking of the birds near the intersection of the interstate and the shopping center?
2. Describe how the teacher might continue this point of interest with the students.

What Are Inquiry and Inquiry-Based Instruction?

Standard 3: Inquiry. *Teachers of science engage students both in studies of various methods of scientific inquiry and in active learning through scientific inquiry. They encourage students, individually and collaboratively, to observe, ask questions, design inquiries, and collect and interpret data in order to develop concepts and relationships from empirical experiences.* (Standards for Science Teacher Preparation, *NSTA 2003)*

Science courses must reflect many elements of the nature of science in order for them to be justified as teaching and learning science, as stated above in the *Standards for Science Teacher Preparation.* Science is generally characterized as an active process whereby men and women, curious about nature, contribute to humankind's understanding of objects and events that surround them. Inquiry is a word that has been used over and over in the science education literature to characterize the active processes involved in scientific thinking, investigation, and the construction of knowledge. For the past 50 years, the term *inquiry* has been used frequently to develop national, state, and local science curriculum guidelines and course materials as well as to promote certain instructional approaches. However, defining inquiry-based instruction and assessing its use in the classroom has become a big problem because of the many views and understandings that surround this idealized form of science teaching.

In general, inquiry is finding out about something. It centers on the desire to answer questions and to learn more about an object or event. Humans have always been inquirers, searching for food and places to live. People from all walks of life inquire on a routine basis. Parents search for the best bargains when purchasing food and clothing for their families, and businesspeople look for customers who need their products and services. Journalists seek out people who can provide them with information to produce a good story, and detectives look for clues to the causes of accidents and homicides. Teenagers try to find friends with whom they like to associate. Inquiry, in general, is used by people around us all the time.

Scientific inquiry also takes place in society, but it has a specialized focus and is conducted by a group of people called *scientists.* As stated often in this textbook, scientific inquiry centers on natural phenomena and is an attempt to *understand* nature, to *explain* that understanding, to make accurate *predictions* from the knowledge, and to *apply* the knowledge to societal needs. However, the knowledge has to be more than personally satisfying; it has to pass the scrutiny of other scientists through the processes of argumentation and verification. Scientists take many paths in their quest to answer questions. Scientific inquiry is a creative process that is fueled by curiosity and hard work, often resulting in frustration and sometimes leading to useful knowledge. Scientific inquiry has at least two critical aspects: the process of finding out and the product of the search. Further, scientific work is centered on the development of models of reality that guide thinking and investigation. This approach to science education can take place in the classroom, the laboratory, the field, the community, museums, and zoos.

A great deal of the science teaching that occurs in middle and senior high schools, as well as at the collegiate level, can be characterized as teaching the products of science. This mode of teaching is designed to present a body of information that has been organized by the teacher or the textbook. Unfortunately, this approach often omits the thinking that was used and the paths that were taken to form the knowledge. The approach also minimizes the firsthand and minds-on experiences that students should be provided. Teaching science as a body of knowledge results in conveying the abstracted, distilled, polished, and pristine outcomes of the learning process that others have gone through to construct new knowledge. As a consequence, this approach often produces learning outcomes that have little meaning to students, resulting in the memorization of ideas that are learned poorly. Content with little or no process is not the recommended approach for science education.

Critical Elements of Inquiry from National Standards

Because of its importance, inquiry-based science instruction has been addressed throughout the *National Science Education Standards* (1996). In addition, the National Research Council (2000) produced an entire document *Inquiry and the National Science Education Standards: A Guide for Teaching and Learning*. The guide provides descriptions of many K–12 classrooms where inquiry science is occurring. The document focuses on five essential features of inquiry-based science, which informs good science teaching.

1. **Learners are engaged by scientifically oriented questions.** Questions are used to begin the inquiry process by stimulating interest and determining what students know about a given phenomena. A question-asking session can begin by calling on students to present their knowledge and mental models of a concept. Here is where students' *why* questions can be guided toward *how* questions, which in turn can be used to plan investigations that will result in useful data and informative explanations. Good questions initiate thinking and stimulate the need to find out.
2. **Learners give priority to evidence, which allows them to develop and evaluate explanations that address scientifically oriented questions.** Empirical and observational data are two pillars of modern science, which advanced science beyond natural philosophy where logic and reason dominated the quest to understand nature. Measurement and numbers, derived from rigorous experimentation and observation, are formed into evidence for convincing arguments that support scientific thinking. This type of knowledge construction advanced the understanding of natural phenomena far beyond approaches that relied solely on reasoning and existing knowledge.
3. **Learners formulate explanations from evidence to address scientifically oriented questions.** Scientific explanations include evidence and reasoning, both necessary in forming an understanding of reality. They are used to describe complex cause-and-effect relationships inherent in the biological and physical universe. The establishment of scientific explanations goes beyond what is currently known to form new ideas that are open to examination by the scientific community for comments and criticism—often leading to revision and even rejection of the proposed ideas.
4. **Learners evaluate explanations in light of alternative explanations, particularly those reflecting scientific understanding.** The establishment of science explanations requires more than an amalgamation of reasoning and evidence; it requires an evaluation of the proposed ideas. Just as one or more controls are used to weigh the effect of a treatment or to ascertain a cause and effect relationship, alternative explanations should be considered when assessing the validity of explanations and conclusions derived from an inquiry-based investigation. Students should develop "habits of mind" for asking: "What else might be the cause?"
5. **Learners communicate and justify their proposed explanations.** Written communication is the culminating product of scientific investigations. Letters, papers, and monographs are used to make public findings for others to examine, challenge, and replicate. Scientists spend a great deal of time summarizing their investigations and modifying them from critical reviews by other scientists. Likewise, students need practice in communicating the questions they form, the procedures they use, the data they gather, and the explanations they generate. Language and the clear expression of ideas must be essential aspects of school-based science inquiry.

 Important Distinctions

An explanation of certain terms can help to better understand the distinctions between traditional and inquiry-based science instruction. Traditional science courses exhibit a great deal of *expository teaching* where information is organized and packaged for students to receive. While expository instruction and *reception learning* are useful, they are often overused in teaching science at many levels, especially in survey science courses at the secondary and collegiate levels. The intent of inquiry-based teaching and learning is to moderate expository teaching by also engaging students in the act of finding out information and making sense out of firsthand experiences through guided instruction.

Discovery learning is often used synonymously with inquiry. However, these two ideas have a different meaning. Discovery is more limited in scope than inquiry, and it pertains to the act of figuring out something for one's self—"Aha, I've got it" or "Now I see it." Discovery learning places more emphasis on the methods and techniques of the investigative process to the neglect of the content under study. In contrast, inquiry should focus on the content under study just as much as the process of finding out. Therefore, inquiry-based science learning includes many elements, some of which do not involve self-discovery. Scientists often call upon others for information to assist them in solving a problem. They read professional journals to gather information in order to gain insights into their problem solving. Scientists do not often make discoveries. Much of their work centers on inventing ideas, as well as testing and refining models. Further, pure discovery learning is not a very effective way to promote the construction of knowledge (Meyer, 2004).

Experience and research support the *guided inquiry* approach where students are given structure, directions, and cues during the learning process. The guided inquiry approach aims at keeping students mentally engaged so that they are learning core content, which includes active participation and learning how to learn. The challenge for science teachers is how to regulate the amount of information and expository instruction, when to give answers to students, and when to withhold answers. All of the national standards promote the guided approach to science learning. The amount of guidance that a teacher provides is dictated by the nature of the content, students' abilities, resources available, and having enough time to carry out the investigation.

Given the importance of inquiry in science teaching, all science teachers must understand this idea in order to advance scientific literacy. Unfortunately, inquiry is often misunderstood and leads to unintended outcomes (Abrams, Southerland, & Silva, 2008). For this reason, many aspects of school-based inquiry are discussed in the sections that follow.

 Amount of Structure

Joseph Schwab, a curriculum theorist at the University of Chicago, exerted enormous influence on teaching science *as* inquiry, describing the structure and essence of school-based inquiry (Chiappetta, 2008). As a member of the Biological Sciences Curriculum Study Committee in the late 1950s and early 1960s, he discussed the "enquiry approach" (the term he used for inquiry) and how to use it in the classroom. At the time, Schwab urged science educators to take a different approach to

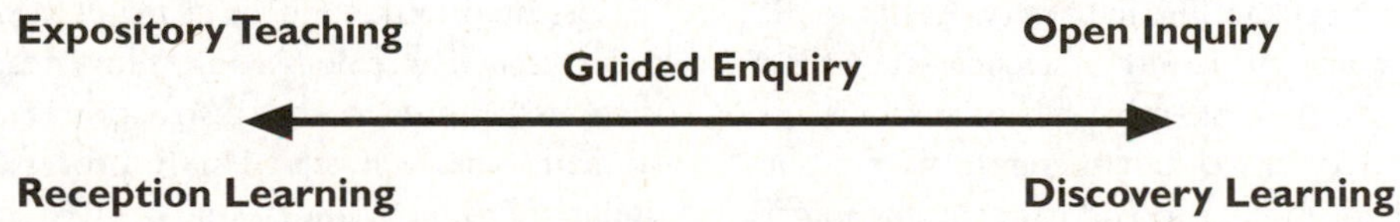

The preceding diagram shows a continuum of emphases in science instruction, pointing out extreme positions with expository teaching and reception learning on one end and open inquiry and discovery learning on the opposite end. Guided inquiry occupies the middle range of the instructional continuum. While one might get the impression that *open inquiry* is the ideal or best form of inquiry-based instruction, this is not an accepted belief of informed educators (Settlage, 2007). Turning students loose to carry out investigations is a misguided notion. Most students need guidance—many require a great deal of guidance.

science teaching and to adopt one that better reflects the ways in which scientists go about their work. He stressed the belief that "scientific research has its origin, not in objective facts alone, but in a conception, a construction of the mind" (Schwab, 1962, p. 12). Schwab proposed that we should help students to realize how scientists interpret information and form ideas. Textbooks, as well as science teachers, should go beyond merely presenting the facts and the outcomes of scientific investigations; they must show how these products were derived by scientists—how a body of knowledge grows and how new conceptions come about. Schwab felt that to teach science *as* inquiry would show students the following:

1. How knowledge arises from interpretation of data.
2. That the interpretation of data—indeed, even the search for data—proceeds on the basis of concepts and assumptions that change as our knowledge grows
3. That because these principles and concepts change, knowledge also changes
4. That though knowledge changes, it changes for good reason—because we know better and know more than we knew before (BSCS, 1978, p. 306).

Examination of these recommendations clearly shows that Schwab believed the aim of science is to produce content, but that it can only be understood by examining the process and evolution of a given body of knowledge. Schwab (BSCS, 1978) went further in his recommendations to stress the importance of student-conducted research to further their understanding of science and the development of skills and habits of an inquiring mind. The spirit and the phrase, teaching science *as* inquiry, can be found today in the *National Science Education Standards* (NRC, 1996). Schwab (1960, p. 9) also suggested three levels of inquiry that science teachers can consider for their courses:

Level 1—Pose problems and describe methods, but leave the solutions to students.

Level 2—Pose problems, but leave methods and solutions to students.

Level 3—Leave the identification of problems, methods, and solutions to students.

Specific Aims

The purpose of scientific inquiry is to understand nature and to apply that understanding in society. As discussed earlier in the chapter on the nature of science, science is a broad-based discipline that has many facets. Similarly, inquiry is a multifaceted activity and, therefore, we must be cautious not to define inquiry too narrowly by aligning it only with knowledge or only with investigation. Natural phenomena and ideas about them are central to inquiry, and the pursuit of these ideas is driven by interest and fascination that scientists have for understanding nature. Scientific inquiry, in its simplest form, is about the *what* and the *how* of understanding the world in which we live. One way to conceptualize inquiry as it relates to teaching science is to analyze it by using the terms content (what) and process (how). Figure 8.2 shows four conceptualizations of science teaching: (a) content, (b) content with process, (c) process with content, and (d) process (Chiappetta & Adams, 2004).

Content is the body of knowledge that results from scientific activity as well as the ideas upon which knowledge is built. It consists of facts, concepts, laws, principles, and theories that are used to explain objects and events. Knowledge and understanding about the world is *the major goal of scientific inquiry.* The knowledge forms the major truths upon which science builds and progresses. However, a major problem arises when science is presented as a body of knowledge that is lacking in how scientific ideas were arrived at during human history. The reasoning, methods, techniques, experiments, and the like are also important to the development and understanding of scientific knowledge. Further, it is necessary for students to engage in active learning in order for them to reconstruct scientific knowledge and to find meaning in it, which requires them to go through a rather lengthy conceptual change process in order to form correct ideas about nature.

Content with process is another way to view science teaching (Figure 8.2). This conception brings into science teaching the process of finding out about something, and reflects an important way to teach science *as* inquiry. Again, the goal is to learn about phenomena by bringing into instruction the ways and means that are used to arrive at various understandings. The methods, techniques, and apparatus are all important aspects of the scientific process. The paths scientists have taken to discover objects and events, and the explanations they have created can be taught in many ways, including lecture, discussion, role-playing, films, readings, and simulations. However, the instruction must go further; students must be involved in the processes of finding out about the subject under study. They should engage in laboratory and firsthand investigations of ideas, sometimes replicating the activities scientists use to study nature and sometimes designing investigations to answer

FIGURE 8.2 Four ways to view inquiry and science instruction.

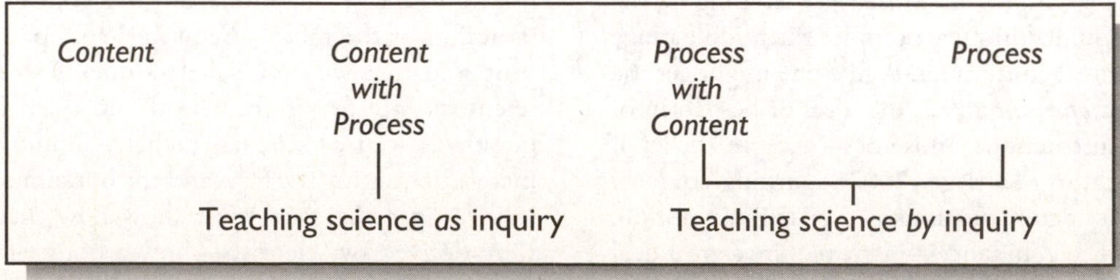

questions that are of special interest to them but have not been answered by others.

Process with content is a third way to view science teaching (Figure 8.2). Its main focus is to engage students in finding out about many phenomena and events. The purpose is to promote active student engagement and to teach students how to inquire. The curriculum includes a variety of content that supports student investigation. The content serves as the context for the investigation. Hands-on activities are the focus, along with some student understanding of the content. This approach is found in the elementary and some middle school science classrooms. However, it must be evaluated because students can be physically busy, yet learning very little content. Science-process skills and scientific reasoning are best learned within a context of important science content. Further, there must be a focus on the ideas that form our knowledge about nature, which are the critical issues that scientists think about.

A *process* approach has been used in science teaching to promote inquiry and discovery learning. Its main intent is to teach students investigative skills purported to be used by scientists. Among the science process skills that serve as the main focus of process-based science programs include observing, inferring, measuring, using numbers, hypothesizing, experimenting, and interpreting data. This type of curriculum can be found in the elementary school and in aspects of middle school science programs. The process approach omits or de-emphasizes critical science content. Such programs are *not* aligned with the national standards that view content knowledge to be an essential learning outcome of inquiry-based science. Further, it is not supported by decades of research in cognitive science, which indicates students learn important skills within the context of learning about "something." This is not to say that science teachers should avoid all instruction unless it is aimed at teaching content. There is a place for special emphasis on process skill instruction, for example, to help students to practice graphing, designing experiments, and identifying variables. However, a heavy emphasis on process without content is not a defensible position for science teaching at any level of schooling.

Two phrases that have been used in science teaching can help educators to better understand the purpose and history of the content/process dichotomy associated with inquiry. These phrases are "teaching science *by* inquiry" and "teaching science *as* inquiry." The terms "by" and "as" connote important differences between these phrases, as shown in Figure 8.2.

In addition to the aims and distinctions of inquiry-based science described above, Windschitl (2008) offers a framework that can further our understanding of this often misunderstood topic, which he classifies into *three families of science activities*. The first are the *core knowledge building activities* that align with the content with process idea and stress the importance of model building during the inquiry process. The second are *activities that support the work of inquiry*—gathering information, participating in teacher-conducted demonstrations, carrying out laboratory exercises, and developing laboratory and technical skills. The third are *practices that need to be reconsidered* when they are purported to be the focus of authentic inquiry, such as the scientific method, investigating arbitrary questions, studying ideas outside of the natural world, and substituting isolated science-process skills for authentic inquiries.

If student inquiry is to mirror what scientists do, then a significant part of their investigative activity should include *talk* and *argumentation*. Scientists spend a great deal of time presenting arguments to support their findings. Scientific arguments differ from everyday argumentation that is often acrimonious and used to support an opinion. Scientific argumentation is the use of reason that is based on evidence to form understanding. Observations and data are not the final piece of scientific inquiry, but require further thinking, discussion, and argumentation among scientists to establish the validity of their ideas.

In order to structure investigative experiences to reflect authentic science, students should be encouraged to talk about their ideas and form arguments to support them. This element of the inquiry process supports the modeling to learn strategy presented in Chapter 10. Students, like scientists, should be given more opportunities and time to discuss their ideas, write about them, develop PowerPoint presentations, and to communicate with others via the Internet (Michaels, Shouse, and Schweingruber, 2008). Below are some suggestions to facilitate talk and argumentation in the science classroom:

- Restate student responses.
- Ask for clarification of student responses.
- Call on several students to respond to a given question.
- Provide students with time to think about a question before responding.
- Encourage students to focus on evidence in their arguments.
- Incorporate the use of models and visuals to facilitate discussion.

Stop and Reflect!

Before going further, respond to the following:

- Describe four conceptions of science teaching and their purpose: (a) content, (b) content with process, (c) process with content, and (d) process.
- List several reasons why teaching science *as* inquiry is recommended by the science education reform movement rather than science *by* inquiry.

 Assessing Inquiry Learning

The assessment of inquiry-based learning is, perhaps, among the most difficult student outcomes to measure. As discussed in this chapter, inquiry is a multifaceted educational goal that has many dimensions. You may have difficulty keeping all of these ideas in mind when you sit down to plan what to teach, how to teach, and how to assess. Below are three dimensions of inquiry assessment from which you can draw ideas to measure student learning and your success with teaching science as inquiry (Van Scotter & Pinkerton, 2008).

1. **Understanding Inquiry.** Ask students to write reflections in their notebooks of some of the difficulties and some of the rewarding moments that they experienced during their investigations. Place a few questions on paper-and-pencil tests to measure students' general knowledge and understanding of the inquiry process and the nature of science. Also ask students to describe how their investigations mirror the inquiries that scientists conduct.
2. **Ability to Conduct Inquiry.** Ask students to write investigation reports that present how the inquiry was conducted and what was found. Provide a rubric or scoring device to measure the use of questions, the presentation of data, and the number of resources used to expand their knowledge. Be mindful of the critical elements of inquiry: question, evidence, explanations, evaluation, and communication. Along with written reports, urge students to develop PowerPoint presentations to augment their investigative reports.
3. **Conceptual Understanding.** Determine the conceptual change or growth of knowledge that occurs during the study of a phenomenon. Pre- and posttests and quizzes can be used to measure the change of knowledge from the beginning of the study to its completion. Journal entries and short papers are also useful for this purpose. These can document the conceptual change process.

 Instructional Approaches and Lesson Cycles

Inquiry is a philosophical stance regarding how to teach school science, which encompasses more than a set of steps or procedures carried out in a laboratory exercise or a long-term investigation. The spirit of inquiry should pervade all aspects of science instruction, including lecture, discussion, and writing. Science teachers should view inquiry strategies developed by educators as more than a series of steps or as a cookbook recipe for how scientists go about their work.

Lesson cycles are useful to beginning as well as experienced science teachers for adding depth and engagement to the learning process. They provide a framework of steps or lesson components to guide planning, teaching, and assessment. Three lesson cycles are presented below that science teachers can use to implement inquiry-based instruction, which are the Learning Cycle, the 5E Instructional Model, and the 7E Instructional Model.

The Learning Cycle

The genesis of these strategies originated from the inductive approach to school science inquiry that was organized into a teaching cycle called the Learning Cycle, originally intended for use in elementary school science instruction. The method has been used and researched at many levels, including the middle school, high school, and college levels. Results have shown that the Learning Cycle promotes inquiry and perhaps intellectual development (Fuller, 1980; Renner et al., 1985). The Learning Cycle has three phases: exploration, invention, and application.

Exploration

The exploration phase allows students to experience objects and events in order to stimulate their thinking about a concept or principle. Students are engaged in activities that permit them to discover patterns and relationships. During this phase, students are given some guidance to keep them focused on the learning task. Questions are posed and cues are given to guide thinking. However, students are not given answers or labels.

Invention

The invention phase allows students to determine relationships between objects and events that they have experienced. Initially, the teacher serves as a guide to channel thinking and encourage students to construct appropriate labels for the relationships they have just discovered. Then, the teacher provides key terms to explain the concept under study.

Application

The application phase allows students to apply their knowledge of a given concept or principle. The teacher encourages the students to find or discover examples to illustrate the concept they have just experienced. In addition, the ideas are discussed in terms of their application in everyday life. This phase permits students to generalize their learning, thus reinforcing newly acquired knowledge.

The 5E Instructional Model

The three-phase learning cycle has been expanded to a five-phase approach to science inquiry, called the 5E Instructional Model (Trowbridge & Bybee, 1996). This strategy incorporates more instruction than the learning cycle, therefore, it engages students in more learning opportunities. Study Figure 8.3 for a summary of the 5E Instructional Model phases, which are engagement, exploration, explanation, elaboration, and evaluation.

The 7E Instructional Model

Lesson and teaching cycles can be expanded beyond the 5E Instructional Model in order to increase the number of elements by introducing additional components or even repeating existing components. This will serve to expand and reinforce student-learning opportunities. The 7E Instructional Model was proposed to enhance the 5E Instructional Model as follows (Eisenkraft, 2003):

- Elicit
- Engage
- Explore
- Explain
- Elaborate
- Evaluate
- Extend

Here the engage component has been expanded to include an *elicit* component in order to access student prior knowledge. The elaborate phase has been expanded to include the *extend* component, intended to provide more practice and transfer of learning.

Supporting Strategies and Techniques

Science teachers have many pedagogical strategies and techniques available to help them plan and conduct inquiry-oriented science. These pedagogical tools have been used successfully by many science teachers to initiate student thinking and to sustain their interest during instruction. You should master these approaches and use them to support the content/process focus that you believe appropriate for a given group of students. For the

FIGURE 8.3 The 5E Instructional Model for engaging students in inquiry-based instruction.

Engagement

Introduce students to the concept or topic under study. Pique their interest. Determine what the students know about the topic and motivate them to learn more about it. Give the learners a good sense for what they will be studying without telling them too much about the ideas or subject matter to be learned. Stimulate interest to the point that students might say: I wo uld like to find out more."

Exploration

Design an instructional event that gives students concrete experiences with the key concepts or principles of the topic. Guide their thinking toward the attributes and patterns of the phenomenon, which should be evident from their firsthand experiences. Ask students to carefully record what they see and to organize their data/information.

Explanation

Call on students to describe their experiences and findings. Ask for deep reasoning by encouraging them to explain what they have found. Provide plenty of time for discussion before presenting the scientific labels and terms for the ideas under study. Build from students' findings toward defining, describing, and explaining the concepts that are the focus of the investigation.

Elaboration

Give students more instruction so that they might form rich connections with what they know and what they are expected to learn. Implement many instructional strategies and learning techniques to expand and reinforce learning. In addition, show applications of the concepts and principles, especially as they pertain to everyday living.

Evaluation

Assess what students are learning at many points during the instruction to determine how well they are grasping main ideas. Solicit oral and written responses to gauge learning. Conclude the five-phase instructional cycle with an assessment to measure how well students have mastered the instructional objectives of the mini-unit or major unit of study.

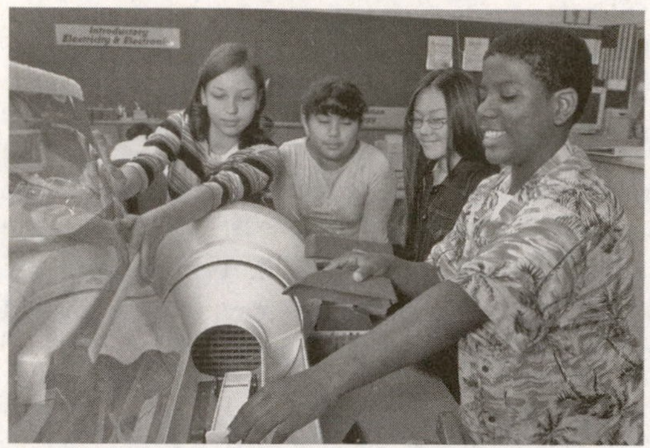

Classroom Snapshot 8.1

A Questioning Technique

Ms. Sanchez placed a small transparent container filled with water before the class. She held up a paper clip and directed students' attention to a question on the chalkboard.

What Will Happen When I Place This Paper Clip on the Water?

The class was silent for a short time, then one hand went up. When the student was given permission to answer, she indicated that the paper clip would drop to the bottom of the pan. The rest of the class seemed to support this prediction. With that, the teacher asked all of the students to write their prediction in their notebook. Then she requested every student to go back to the laboratory tables to test their prediction. She provided each student with a small container of water and three different sizes of paper clips. At first, all of the paper clips were sinking to the bottom of the container when the students placed their clips on the water. With some guidance, most students were able to float the small paper clip on the water.

When most of the students were successful in floating the paper clip, Ms. Sanchez directed student attention to another question that she had written on the board.

What Variables Are Related to Your Success in Floating a Paper Clip on the Water?

Answering this question caused students to think hard because they had three paper clips to work with and their manual dexterity to consider as variables. When the hands-on part of the activity concluded, the teacher discussed the properties of water and surface tension as she guided students' explanations regarding the floatation of a metal paper clip more dense than water. Then the discussion was directed toward the scientific reasoning students used to determine how to float a paper clip.

beginning science teacher, the following is a list of strategies and techniques to begin to master. These strategies and techniques can be incorporated into many instructional approaches to promote inquiry-oriented science. Questions can be asked during lecture, discrepant events make wonderful demonstrations, and laboratory and field experiences provide opportunities for gathering information.

- Asking questions
- Science process skills
- Discrepant events
- Inductive activities
- Deductive activities
- Gathering information
- Small-group investigations
- Science fair projects

Asking Questions

Questions are fundamental to scientific inquiry as well as to science instruction. Asking the right question is critical in investigative work. Questions can engage thinking and orient mental activity toward meaningful ends. For instructional purposes, questions can be classified in many ways. For example, there are the *what, where, which, when,* and *why* types of questions. The questions can be phrased to match Bloom's taxonomy—knowledge, comprehension, application, analysis, synthesis, and evaluation. Further, questions can be used to direct students' thinking along the lines of the science process skills such as observing, inferring, hypothesizing, and experimenting. More about questions is presented in Chapter 11.

One questioning technique that some science teachers use is to write questions on the board for the students to answer. These questions, generally small in number, can guide the instruction toward the intended learning outcomes. Examine the questioning techniques used by Ms. Sanchez in Classroom Snapshot 8.1. Science teachers who encourage students to state what they think, to test their ideas, and to explain their findings are using pedagogy that reflects scientific inquiry and strategies recommended by cognitive psychologists.

Yes/No Questioning Technique

Richard Suchman (1966), who created the Inquiry Development Program in the 1960s for the middle school, offers many suggestions to teachers who want to implement inquiry in their classrooms. His six rules for inquiry sessions reflect the openness and freedom that he believed students should be given in order to develop their inquiry skills.

Rule One: Encourage students to ask questions that the teacher can answer with a "yes" or "no" response.

Rule Two: Permit students to ask as many questions as they wish when they initiate their question asking.

Rule Three: Avoid evaluating the worth or accuracy of students' explanations.

Rule Four: Allow students to test out their own ideas at any time.

Rule Five: Encourage interaction and discussion among students.

Rule Six: Permit students to "mess around" with lots of materials connected with an inquiry session.

Suchman's suggestions provide us with one way to promote inquiry in the science classroom. This approach places the learner in the position of having to find out and explain how, and shifts the responsibility for learning away from the teacher to the student. Perhaps this is a questioning technique to practice and use for certain inquiry sessions.

Science teachers have many other types of question-asking techniques that can cause students to think and to respond in meaningful ways. Experienced teachers use questions to probe students' responses and to ask for clarification. The following are some questions that you can use to focus student learning and the representation of knowledge:

- Can you give me an example?
- What do you mean by that?
- Can you explain?
- Why do you say that?
- What led you to that answer?
- What is your evidence?
- Can you give me your reasons for that statement?
- Are there other possible reasons for that occurrence?
- Can anyone else explain this?
- Is there anyone who disagrees with that?
- How many of you agree with what she says?

Science Process Skills

One way to actively engage students and to help them become more proficient in representing the world around them is to focus the instruction on science process skills. A process skill approach stresses the development of investigative skills that are often associated with scientific inquiry. These skills are called *observing, classifying, inferring, measuring, using numbers, predicting, defining operationally, forming models, controlling variables, interpreting data, hypothesizing,* and *conducting experiments*. Many educators hold the belief that the development of these skills will better enable students to solve problems, learn on their own, and appreciate science. Table 8.1 presents a list of many commonly used science process skills in science programs.

Many middle school science programs use process skill development as one of the primary learning goals along with science concepts. They use a variety of content and contexts within which students practice scientific skills during hands-on instruction. Scientifically literate students must be competent in using science process skills. For example, graphing is an essential skill for all students to develop. Graphs organize information efficiently. Graphing is a communication skill that is used throughout school science, from elementary school through college. It also is used in the business world to convey information concisely. Middle school science programs must ensure that all students are proficient in graphing before they enter high school. The following are some of the graphing sub-skills:

- Identifying the appropriate type of graph—bar or line—to represent data
- Providing a useful title for a graph and correctly labeling the x and y axes
- Constructing a bar or line graph when given a data table
- Interpreting a graph by communicating its significance
- Interpolating and extrapolating information from a line graph

At first thought, graphing seems so simple to the college science major who is preparing to become a science teacher. This is deceiving because graphing is tied closely to the context in which it is used. Change the context or content, and many students are lost and unable to demonstrate the skill. While this mental activity may appear simple for an adult teacher who has majored in science, it is not as easy for many middle and high school students to perform, especially those students who are learning English as a second language.

In addition to the basic science process skills, inquiry is carried out using integrated process skills or more advanced reasoning skills. Let's read about the process/content emphasis used by Mr. Roosevelt, a middle school science teacher, who wants students to better understand how to manipulate and control variables (see Classroom Snapshot 8.2).

Analyze Mr. Roosevelt's use of the string telephone laboratory. Identify which of the four perspectives of teaching science and inquiry that were discussed at the

TABLE 8.1 Basic and Integrated Science Process Skills

Process Skill	Definition
Basic Skills	
Observing	Noting the properties of objects and situations using the five senses
Classifying	Relating objects and events according to their properties or attributes (This involves classifying places, objects, ideas, or events into categories based on their similarities.)
Space/time relations	Visualizing and manipulating objects and events, dealing with shapes, time, distance, and speed
Using numbers	Using quantitative relationships, for example, scientific notation, error, significant numbers, precision, ratios, and proportions
Measuring	Expressing the amount of an object or substance in quantitative terms, such as meters, liters, grams, and newtons
Inferring	Giving an explanation for a particular object or event
Predicting	Forecasting a future occurrence based on past observation or the extension of data
Integrated Skills	
Defining operationally	Developing statements that present a concrete description of an object or event by telling one what to do or observe
Formulating models	Constructing images, objects, or mathematical formulas to explain ideas
Controlling variables	Manipulating and controlling properties that relate to situations or events for the purpose of determining causation
Interpreting data	Arriving at explanations, inferences, or hypotheses from data that have been graphed or placed in a table (this frequently involves concepts such as mean, mode, median, range, frequency distribution, t-test, and chi-square test)
Hypothesizing	Stating a tentative generalization of observations or inferences that may be used to explain a relatively larger number of events but that is subject to immediate or eventual testing by one or more experiments
Experimenting	Testing a hypothesis through the manipulation and control of independent variables and noting the effects on a dependent variable; interpreting and presenting results in the form of a report that others can follow to replicate the experiment

Data compiled from Science: A Process Approach, Commentary for Teachers, *by the American Association for the Advancement of Science, 1965, Washington, DC.*

beginning of this chapter Mr. Roosevelt is using: content, content with process, process with content, or process. Explain your answer and whether you feel the teacher is using an appropriate instructional approach with his middle school students.

Discrepant Events

An attention-getting, thought-provoking approach to initiate inquiry is through the use of discrepant events. A discrepant event *puzzles the observer*, causing him or her to wonder why the event occurred as it did. These situations leave the observer at a loss to explain what has taken place. Discrepant events influence equilibration and the self-regulatory process, according to the Piagetian theory of intellectual development. Situations that are contrary to what a person expects cause him or her to wonder what is taking place, resulting in cognitive disequilibrium. With proper guidance, the individual will attempt to figure out the discrepancy and search for a suitable explanation for the situation. When a person arrives at a plausible explanation for a discrepant event, he or she will establish cognitive equilibrium at a new level. The individual is now better equipped mentally to approach new situations that cause curiosity and puzzlement (Piaget, 1971).

An inquiry session initiated with a discrepant event can begin with a demonstration or film, preceded by directions to focus students' attention on what they are about to observe. Discrepant-event demonstrations of the laws of motion, center of gravity, Pascal's principle, density, and vacuum, to mention just a few, can be used to initiate inquiry sessions. The use of discrepant events receives support from cognitive psychologists, because of its potential impact on learning.

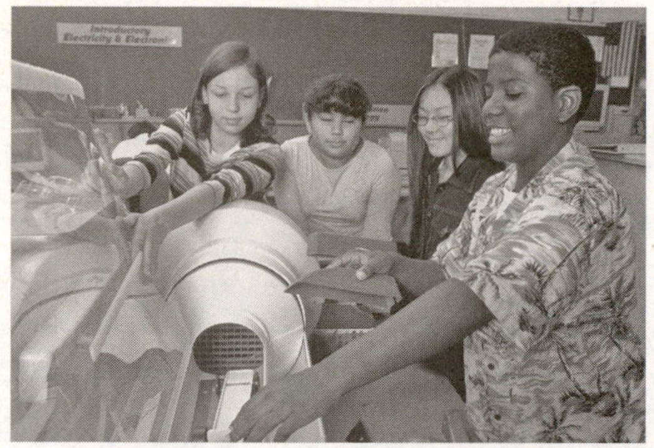

Classroom Snapshot 8.2

Manipulating Variables

Mr. Roosevelt engages his middle school students in an extensive laboratory investigation with the "string telephone." Mr. Roosevelt initiates this activity by demonstrating how two metal soup cans connected with a wire transmit voice sounds between two people. He challenges the students to construct many different phones to determine which pair will transmit the clearest voice messages. He also asks them to predict which phones will work best and to explain why. Working in groups, the students bring to class many cans and containers of various sizes and composition—from small metal cans to large coffee cans, from small paper cups to giant soft drink containers, and from Styrofoam cups to plastic dairy food containers. The students also bring to class a variety of lines to connect the phones, such as thread, string, monofilament fishing line, and wire.

After the students have tested many combinations of phones and lines, they select a set of phones that produces very clear voice sounds. For example, a pair of paper cups connected by carpet thread produces amazing results. Mr. Roosevelt asks his students to identify the variables that seem to produce good sounds through these simple devices. He guides students' thinking so that they realize they were conducting an experiment and controlling variables. The students come to realize not only that the size and composition of the phones are important but also that these variables affect the vibration of the transmitting material. Even though the students lack the scientific terminology to explain the effects of elasticity on vibration, they feel good about conducting an investigation that seems scientific. Mr. Roosevelt continues the discussion of vibration and sound quality by asking students to demonstrate pleasing sounds and music with musical instruments they play, such as guitars, pianos, and drums.

Here is a discrepant event you can try right now. Go to the kitchen and cut an approximately 4 × 4 piece of wax paper. Place a drop of water in the center of the wax paper. Tilt the wax paper until the drop of water moves down the paper. Continue to tilt the wax paper so that the bead of water can move down its surface. Observe carefully the downward movement of the drop. Then ask whether the drop of water rolls or slides down the wax paper.

After you have committed yourself to an answer, try to support your inference with an explanation. When you have "experimented" with this little puzzler and are confident that you can describe and explain the movement of the drop of water, go to Appendix A and read "A Drop of Water" in the section "Little Science Puzzlers." Then, present the problem to a group of adults or middle or high school students and determine the extent to which this activity is a discrepant event for them and how well they can explain the movement of the drop of water across the wax paper.

Inductive Activities

The inductive strategy provides students with learning situations in which they can *discover* a concept or principle through experiences in the laboratory, field, or classroom. With this strategy, the attributes and instances of an idea are encountered first by the learner, followed by naming and discussing the idea under study. The inductive approach provides students with concrete experience whereby they obtain data from objects and events, which in turn gives them a foundation upon which to anchor information and build new knowledge. Inductive activities can be thought of as an experience-before-vocabulary approach to learning. Note the sequence of this instructional format in Classroom Snapshot 8.3.

Deductive Activities

In contrast to the inductive strategy, deductive thinking is used often in science courses. It is the traditional lecture/laboratory sequence with which most science majors are familiar. This strategy is commonly observed in the middle school through college science teaching. With the deductive strategy, a concept or principle is defined and discussed using appropriate labels and terms, followed by experiences to illustrate the idea. The deductive approach is a vocabulary-before-experience model of teaching where lecture and discussion precede firsthand or concrete experiences. It can also involve hypothetical-deductive thinking, whereby the learner generates ideas

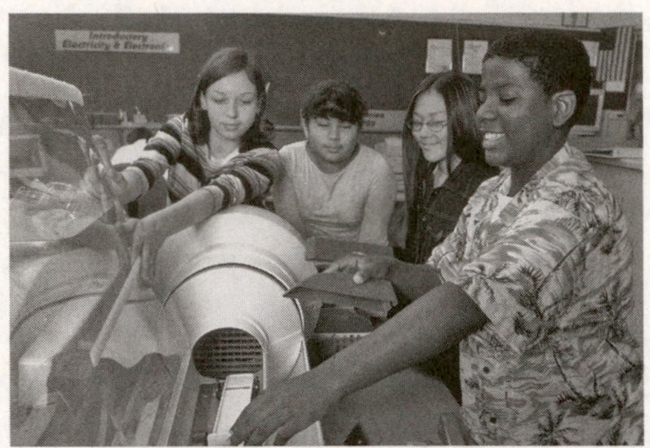

Classroom Snapshot 8.3

An Inductive Activity

Mrs. Talbert often initiates the study of a topic with an inductive activity in order to stimulate student thinking and to establish a concrete reference for understanding the principle under study. For example, she begins the study of ocean currents with a laboratory exercise that has students examine the movement of colored solutions, each with a different density, as they mix with tap water. Mrs. Talbert gives each lab group a set of the following solutions:

1. A blue solution of tap water
2. A green solution that is partially saturated with salt
3. A red solution that is saturated with salt

Mrs. Talbert directs her students to carefully pour each of the colored solutions into a separate beaker of clear tap water and observe the movement of the solutions as they mix. She does not tell students that the colored solutions are of different densities. After the students have made their observations and attempted to explain how the colored solutions mix with the tap water, the teacher initiates a discussion about ocean currents and the density of salt water. She place key terms on the board, calling students' attention to the science behind the differential mixing of solutions. This is followed by sending the students back to the lab tables to prepare salt solutions of different densities, adding food coloring and observing what occurs when they are poured into plain water. In addition, Mrs. Talbert asks students to indicate where in the science classroom the air-conditioned cold air moves when it is forced out of the ventilation ducts located near the ceiling. Then, the class discusses the density of cold and warm air masses and how it relates to weather conditions.

to be tested or discovered or the teacher makes explicit what it is the students should be looking for in the laboratory or field.

Consider teaching part of an acid–base unit using deduction. The instruction might begin with a discussion of acids and bases— their properties, occurrence in everyday life, pH, and indicators. This might be followed by a laboratory activity to classify solutions as either acidic or basic, and to order them according to their pH. This deductive activity would conclude with a post-laboratory discussion of students' findings and their comprehension of the content under study.

Gathering Information from Many Sources

Scientific inquiry includes more than constructing knowledge through hands-on activities. Laboratory work and hands-on activities are not the only ways in which scientists and others expand their knowledge. A great deal of the inquiry that scientists and engineers carry out involves reading and conversing with others. Many of these professionals probably spend more time gathering ideas and information from literature sources and other people than they spend in their laboratory. Information gathering is one of the most important inquiry-supporting activities.

Science teachers must encourage students at many points during the inquiry process to obtain information from a variety of sources. Information gathering can occur during the explanation and elaboration phases of a teaching cycle by assigning certain pages to read in the assigned textbook and outlining key points. In other instances, the teacher may ask students to bring in newspaper clippings on a topic or to search the Internet for information. Reading and writing are essential to the inquiry learning process.

Reading Printed Material

Newspapers and magazines are rich sources of information that students can use to improve their scientific knowledge. A science course requirement might involve students to cut out or photocopy articles and organize them into a notebook. Another technique to improve knowledge and understanding of a given topic is to require a short written report. These reports can be compiled from a single source or a few sources. When long reports are desired, students should be required to use a variety of sources for their write-ups, such as newspapers, textbooks, magazines, encyclopedias, journals, and the Internet. Students can research information in their home, the school library, and the public library. They should be taught how to cite information sources in their reports. Effective science teachers require information gathering throughout the school year, but they are careful not to burden students with this type of work. In addition, experienced teachers have found ways to help students who lack reading and writing skills.

Assignments of this nature are not always successful because of lack of student motivation and competence. Therefore, some science teachers identify topics they are familiar with before giving the assignment to students. They arrange topics on 3×5 index cards, and along with a topic title, they list appropriate literature sources that are readily available to the students. Also, there may be duplicate index cards with the same topic title, because there may be a limited number of topics that can be researched on a given subject for a class of 30 students. Using this strategy, students are guided during their information-gathering experiences. However, as students gain more experience and competence with this procedure, they require less direction and guidance.

Seeking Information from Individuals

People are a rich source of information and ideas. They can explain concepts to teenagers and improve students' understanding of these ideas, often better than a textbook or science classroom explanation. Older siblings, parents, aunts, uncles, pharmacists, lawyers, nurses, doctors, firefighters, engineers, construction workers, electricians, bakers, farmers, mechanics, coaches, musicians, and florists are among those with whom science students can interact to learn more about a topic. These people are often willing to spend time with adolescents to explain how something works or to clarify their ideas.

Inquiry techniques that engage students in gathering opinions of others are an excellent way for students to find out what others believe about issues and problems. This approach can also teach students how to develop questionnaires and survey instruments. Furthermore, this is an excellent way to make science relevant and to illustrate its relationship to society.

Accessing Information from the Internet

The Internet is one of the great human inventions of the twentieth century. This electronic network is an almost infinite source of information that is at the fingertips of anyone using a personal computer. The Internet consists of massive quantities of information available electronically from locations across the globe. It also provides access to people through e-mail and chat rooms. This gigantic electronic network is giving information a new meaning. Most university scientists and science departments have Internet sites, as do exploratoriums, museums, planetariums, zoos, and government research facilities. Individuals at these sites will respond to inquiries pertaining to science. In addition, these sites offer instructional materials that can be downloaded to personal computers.

Small-Group Investigations

Science teachers have successfully used small-group investigations for decades to engage students in inquiry. The synergy of students working in groups of four or in pairs, pursuing questions of interest, can motivate them to work on a problem for an extended period of time. This type of problem solving engages students in investigations where they *raise questions*, *plan procedures*, *collect information*, and *form conclusions*. These learning experiences can be short or long, taking up to several months to complete. This approach is the type of inquiry-based teaching and learning recommended by the *National Science Education Standards*.

An example of a small group, long-term investigation is given in Classroom Snapshot 8.4 and the rubric to score students' performance is given in Table 8.2. Examine the investigation and the rubric in order to analyze the degree to which they focus on:

1. the teaching science as inquiry approach to school science
2. the alignment of the assessment with the purpose of the instruction
3. the NSTA *Standards for Science Teacher Preparation*, specifically:
   - Standard 2: Nature of Science. c. Engage students successfully in studies of the nature of science including, when possible, the critical analysis of false or doubtful assertions made in the name of science.
   - Standard 3: Inquiry. a. Understand the processes, tenets, and assumptions of multiple methods of inquiry leading to scientific knowledge.

Science Projects

Science projects are science course experiences that require many hours of student involvement. They take place over many weeks and even months. Some science projects reflect "true" inquiry whereby students identify a topic to study, propose questions to be answered, designate procedures for carrying out a project, gather information and data, present the results, and form the conclusions. These projects entail a great deal of effort on the part of students, as well as guidance from teachers

Classroom Snapshot 8.4

Small-Group Investigation

One day during the study of plants in Mr. Grady's biology class, a student asked, "Can garlic cure cancer?" The question sparked some interest among class members, which brought forth more claims about the medicinal effects of garlic, such as lowering cholesterol and blood pressure, and curing colds. Mr. Grady immediately realized that he could turn this situation into a group investigation to study the biological effects of garlic, which would provide a foundation to explore the questions students raised about the medicinal effects of garlic and other foods further on in the course when health product claims will be taken up.

The teacher introduced the class to *allelopathy*, which he defined as the beneficial or harmful effect of one plant on another. Before he proposed an investigation of this concept with plants, the teacher elaborated on garlic's colorful folk history and why it is an interesting plant to study, especially its allelopathic effects. He pointed out that garlic has been used to ward off vampires and witches, as an aphrodisiac, as a folk remedy for fevers and other ailments, and in cooking. Of course, there are other medicinal claims for garlic such as lowering blood pressure and cholesterol and preventing cancer. Further, it is claimed that garlic can stimulate the immune system and lower blood sugar. Does it not appear to be a miracle drug? Because of the many claims for garlic and the ease with which it can be obtained, this condiment is ideal for experimentation and learning about a biological concept like allelopathy.

With this background and apparent interest in the topic, Mr. Grady organized the class into groups of four students each. He asked the students do some reading about allelopathy and garlic before they state their research questions. Also, he told the students that they should develop some tentative ideas, in the form of statements and diagrams, about the relationships they are proposing to study. Then Mr. Grady indicated he would familiarize the class with the rubric that would be used to score the investigations.

and parents. A science project can be undertaken individually, by a pair of students, by a group of students, or by an entire class. Science projects should be a common component of all science courses, whether or not they are tied to a science fair competition. Figure 8.4 on page 138 lists the titles of many science fair projects.

In many schools, students are encouraged to complete a project for a science fair. These are big events for science teachers, students, parents, and members of the community. Science fairs stimulate enormous interest in science. They provide students with incentives to study problems in depth and to communicate their findings. Further, they give students an opportunity to pursue investigations that they would not ordinarily be able to carry out during regular science class periods because of limitations of equipment, space, and time. In addition to identifying the gifted science students, these events encourage all students to get involved in inquiry and to design products. Science fairs not only display the talents and interests of students, but they also reveal the orientation of a school's science program, the type of science teaching that is occurring, and the type of students in the school.

Science fair projects can take many forms, such as:

1. **Hobby or pet show-and-tell:** A display of items of special interest to the student, such as arrowheads; seashells; bee hives; or photographs of animals.
2. **Display of a natural phenomenon:** Pictures and descriptions of lightning, a volcano, an earthquake, a hurricane, a tornado, and the like.
3. **Model:** A three-dimensional model of a volcano, a brain, a heart, an internal combustion engine, a rocket, a space station, a 35-mm camera, the solar system, and the like.
4. **Report and poster:** Photographs and pictures of objects with explanations and information taken from literature sources on such topics as nuclear power, HIV infection, movement of Earth's continental plates, how a computer works, living in space, a rain forest habitat, a biome, and the like.
5. **Laboratory exercise:** The presentation of a laboratory exercise that illustrates a concept, principle, or law such as the frequencies of a pendulum, osmosis, crushing metal cans with air pressure, chemical and physical properties of acids and bases, behavior of

TABLE 8.2 Rubric for Investigating Allelopathy with Garlic

Criterion	3 points	2 points	1 point	0 Point
Questions to guide the investigation	Poses specific questions to elucidate the effects of garlic on plant growth and viability	Poses one specific question to elucidate the effects of garlic on plant growth and viability	Poses a general question to elucidate the effects of garlic on plant growth and viability	No questions are posed to guide the investigation
Discussion of allelopathy and garlic to demonstrate their understanding	Extensive discussion of allelopathy and garlic that illustrates good understanding of their effects on plant growth and viability	Succinct discussion of allelopathy and garlic that illustrates some understanding of their effects on plant growth and viability	Very little discussion of allelopathy and garlic that illustrates some understanding of their effects on plant growth and viability	No discussion of allelopathy and garlic that illustrates some understanding of their effects on plant growth and viability
Experimental design of the investigation	Uses many controls or conditions to examine relationships between allelopathic effects of garlic	Uses two controls or conditions to examine relationships between allelopathic effects of garlic	Uses one control or conditions to examine relationships between allelopathic effects of garlic	Uses one control or conditions to examine relationships between allelopathic effects of garlic, which is flawed
Presentation of data and findings	Data and findings are presented in a clear manner, which might include tables, charts, photos, etc., all of which provide an exceptional display of results	Data and findings are presented in clear manner, which might include tables, charts, photos, etc.	Data and findings are presented in a succinct manner	Data and findings are poorly presented
Discussion of results that integrates understanding of allelopathy with evidence and argumentation that support the findings	An extensive discussion of results that integrates understanding of allelopathy with evidence and argumentation that support the findings	A brief discussion of results that integrates understanding of allelopathy with evidence and argumentation that support the findings	A sketchy discussion of results that reiterates the findings with little integration of findings and content understanding	No discussion is provided that integrates understanding of allelopathy with evidence and argumentation that support the findings
Evaluation and conclusion of investigation	Captures the essence of the experiment with accurate and informative generalizations that identify other possible relationships between allelopathic effects of garlic and plant growth and viability	Captures the essence of the experiment with accurate and informative generalizations, but no consideration for other possible relationships between allelopathic effects of garlic and plant growth and viability	The conclusion is a restatement of the findings	No conclusion is offered

light rays, determination of electrical current and resistance, and the like.

6. **Observational study:** Extensive observations of a situation or phenomenon and reporting the findings, such as bird counting, whale reporting, weather conditions and patterns, driving behavior and accidents at a busy intersection, changes in ozone levels and pollution counts in an urban area, and the like.
7. **Experimental study:** Manipulating a situation to determine the results of the intervention, such as the effects of fertilizer on plant growth, temperature on food spoilage, moisture on the amount of corrosion, and other experiments.

There are many types of science projects that students can complete, but some students are eager to carry out more challenging projects. Some challenging projects re-

FIGURE 8.4 Examples of titles for science fair projects or long-term science investigations.

The Effects of Electricity on Seed Germination
Electromagnetic Radiation and Bacterial Growth
The Study of Oral Bacteria
Does Music Affect Memory?
Fluoride in Your Water
How Does Food Spoil?
Antioxidants and Your Health
Pheromones and Ant Behavior
How Much Bacteria Is on Your Kitchen Dishrag?
The Association Between Alzheimer's Disease and Aluminum
Do We Need Food Additives?
Bugs That Eat Oil
Aerodynamics and Automobile Design
Which Flashlight Batteries Last the Longest?
Light and Photography
What Variables Contribute to the Strength of an Electromagnet?
What Does UV Radiation Do to Organic and Inorganic Materials?
Determining the Viscosity of Lubricants
How Does Acid Rain Affect the Growth of Plants?
Effects of Waves on Beaches

quire more imagination, tenacity, and adult guidance. When grading these projects for a course grade or judging them in a fair competition, it is best to form separate project categories because they should not be evaluated under one category. For example, a model cannot be judged with the same criteria used to judge an experimental study. This should be evident from the following categories and points that are often used to judge experimental science projects:

- Creativity (20 points)
- Investigative procedure (30 points)
- Understanding of the topic (20 points)
- Quality of the display (15 points)
- Oral presentation (15 points)

Although experimental projects are a good way to promote inquiry, discretion must be used in determining what each student can accomplish, considering the availability of resources and adult assistance. Some students may not have the resources available to compete with students whose parents are professionals. Further, science teachers should help these students to learn about the content of their investigations before they undertake their experiments in order for the inquiry process to improve their conceptual knowledge. If science fairs are to reflect scientific investigation, you must keep in mind what has been discussed in this chapter about inquiry.

Grouping and Cooperative Learning

Placing students in groups to work on a problem or to conduct an investigation is a practice supported by research findings as well as observations of classrooms of effective science teachers. The dynamics of group work can stimulate and sustain inquiry in many situations better than individual work. Not only can group work enhance student problem-solving ability, but it can also

Inquiry learning can be facilitated by students working in groups.

improve concept development (Lumpe, 1995). Students find a great deal of meaning in science courses when their knowledge is constructed during productive, small, cooperative group activities.

Effective science teachers often group students and assign them tasks in order to facilitate inquiry-based learning. This approach seems to increase student involvement in the learning environment. When students have a specific task to carry out, they seem to have more direction and interest in their own learning. Grouping and the assignment of group roles are useful management strategies that change the role of the teacher from a dispenser of information to a manager of student-directed learning where students tend to be more productive with fewer behavioral problems. Further, these techniques develop in students a feeling for "doing" science. Cooperative learning also can improve achievement and mastery of content (Slavin, 1989/1990), as well as develop a positive classroom environment (Kagan, 1989/1990). Cooperative learning, as its name implies, gets students to work together, eliminating some of the competitiveness and isolation that can exist in most academic environments.

A variety of roles can be assigned to students working in small groups. The following is a list of roles commonly assigned by science teachers to facilitate group work:

- **Leader,** who organizes and keeps the investigation moving
- **Manager,** who gathers and maintains materials and equipment
- **Recorder,** who records data and seeks information
- **Reporter,** who prepares the written report

Cooperative instruction can take many forms with no set number of steps to follow. Nevertheless, the following steps are discussed to highlight important aspects of this strategy.

Step 1 Organize students into groups, using criteria to make decisions regarding this process. Determine the desired cognitive and affective outcomes for the investigation, and then place students into groups accordingly. For example, if you wish to assign tasks to individual students, identify students in each group who can carry out a particular task and who also work well together with others in the group.

Step 2 Identify ideas or topics that will motivate student inquiry. Some science teachers provide a preliminary list of ideas for their students that relate to the course unit. However, this approach should also encourage brainstorming in order to identify additional ideas for student investigation. Group problem solving can focus on many ideas, such as science concepts or principles, science topics, socio-scientific issues and problems, products and services, and technological devices.

Step 3 Ask each group to provide a preliminary outline of their project or study. This step immediately places students on a productive path. When you examine the outline, provide suggestions and guidance. Be sure each student in the group knows exactly what to do.

Step 4 Monitor the investigations. You should have a good idea where each group is while the investigations are carried out. Some inquiries and projects will be conducted during class time, making them easy to monitor. Other investigations will take place after school and on weekends. For this type of work, take some time during class to ask for information to determine how groups as well as individuals are progressing.

Step 5 Help students to prepare their final reports so that they do well and feel good about their work. Provide guidance in organizing an outline for the reports and designate who will write certain sections of the report. The report is an opportunity for students to demonstrate their science process skill reasoning through the questions they attempt to answer, the inferences and hypotheses they form, and the tables and graphs they construct to communicate their findings. This phase of the work is ideal for helping students represent knowledge, visualize models, give explanations, and demonstrate understanding.

Step 6 Assist each group to identify several, if not all, students to take part in presenting their report. This aspect of cooperative group work develops presentation skills and confidence in speaking in front of others. Try to avoid having the same students make all of the presentations.

Step 7 Evaluate the investigations and projects. This often takes the form of assigning points to groups and individual students and entering them into the grade book. Generally, students put a great deal of effort into the activities, and they should be rewarded accordingly.

Unfortunately, successful cooperative group instruction does not just happen according to the formula. The ability, maturity, and discipline of the students are big factors regarding how well the strategy will work. Therefore, you must think carefully about who is placed within each group. Since the leader is key to the productivity and success of a team, select students who can motivate and guide their peers in carrying out tasks. These individuals must have negotiating skills to keep fellow students on task and to complete the project on time.

Managers should be students who like to build things and gather materials. They are individuals who enjoy being physically active and working with their hands. Many of these students will go all out to find equipment and bring it to school or build projects at home. Often, these students get help from their parents. Recorders must be actively keeping track of group activities. They must take notes and record data, and they must be responsible individuals who will stay focused on their group's activities. Reporters must be students who have the maturity and skills to organize and prepare most of the report. While they do not have to write all of the report, they usually do the bulk of the project presentation. These students should be able to use word processing and organize PowerPoint presentations.

Concerns Associated with Inquiry-Based Instruction

In order for science teachers to make the transition from a traditional mode of instruction to an inquiry-based mode, they must understand scientific inquiry and its relationship to science teaching. This understanding will permit them to construct a personal rationale to justify the inquiry approach to themselves, other science teachers, administrators, and parents. An understanding of inquiry—its conceptions and strategies—is also necessary so that inquiry-based science can be adapted to the large differences among students and schools. The challenge that faces science teachers is to understand the meaning of general inquiry, scientific inquiry, teaching science *by* inquiry, and teaching science *as* inquiry, and in particular the content/process emphasis most appropriate for a given group of students.

There are many concerns associated with inquiry-based science teaching. Science teachers must be aware of these concerns as they move toward teaching science and inquiry.

1. **Understanding.** Science teachers must develop a clear conception of inquiry-based science and be able to explain it to administrators and parents. This conception should show how content and process are balanced to provide educational outcomes that support the science-literacy goals of the school, district, state, and nation.
2. **Assessment.** Assessment greatly influences the teaching and learning processes. If a large part of the course assessment focuses on science content, which is often the case, teachers may spend a great deal of instructional time teaching concepts and terms. Because of the accountability movement in education, science teachers are under constant pressure to help students pass standardized tests, which causes them to stress content at the expense of inquiry-based science instruction.
3. **Time.** Investigative science instruction does require more time than teaching science solely as a body of knowledge. Inquiry-based instruction requires more time to plan and far more time to conduct than traditional instruction. Those teachers who make inquiry an important part of their instruction must know how much time to invest in investigative experiences in order to help students master critical content and to appreciate the way scientific knowledge is constructed.
4. **Materials and Equipment.** Activity-oriented and hands-on experiences require materials and equipment. These items must be gathered together, purchased or constructed by teachers, which requires a large commitment of time and effort as well as money. Science teachers should know how much money is allocated to their school's science budget and become active in using the money to promote an activity-oriented science program. Further, they should try to increase the budget for science and purchase equipment that will be used frequently to support student inquiry.
5. **Facilities.** Teaching facilities that accommodate hands-on activities, group work, student movement, and storing projects are important to inquiry-based instruction. Many schools lack good science facilities, making it difficult to teach large classes of students in an activity-oriented mode of instruction. Teachers must employ a great deal of creativity as they arrange the learning environment in order for students to become active learners.
6. **Learning Terms.** Yes, science terms and vocabulary are important to all students' science education. Names give meaning to concepts and are essential for good communication. However, teaching and testing for a large number of terms can be a mind-numbing experience. The number of science terms to be learned in any given chapter of a high school biology textbook can be greater than what one would find in a given chapter of a foreign language textbook. This should be avoided.
7. **Hands-on Activities.** Hands-on activities hold the potential to actively engage students in learning science. However, these activities do not ensure that students are learning the knowledge and skills under study. While students may seem busy and engaged, their minds may be on matters other than gaining new knowledge and skills. Consequently, it is essential that the teacher make explicit, at many points during instruction, what students should be learning.
8. **Covering the Curriculum.** Science teachers often voice concern about covering the curriculum. They indicate that the district or the state requires them to cover too much content and there is no time for inquiry instruction. Remember, there are at least four ways to view inquiry-based instruction. Two of the approaches discussed, content and the content with process, focus on learning science subject matter. However, inquiry teaching is more than methods, approaches, and techniques. A major purpose is

aimed at encouraging students to wonder why and to want to find out more.

9. **Discipline.** There always exists the possibility for students to misbehave when they are given freedom to move around in a laboratory setting or to work in small groups. Considerable planning, structure, and rules must accompany investigations that permit students to get out of their seats and move around the classroom, laboratory, and areas in and around the school. Science teachers can withhold activities from students who misbehave. This often sends a message to students that they must behave in an orderly manner, and they must be productive if they desire to engage in interesting inquiry-oriented activities.
10. **Colleagues.** Often, the biggest roadblocks to inquiry-based instruction are the science teachers who primarily teach science as a body of knowledge and who have been doing this for many years. Experienced science teachers often are resistant to change. They are comfortable with lecture, one lab a week, drill-and-kill review sheets, and paper-and-pencil testing. Further, some teachers' students do very well on state and national examinations without the benefit of an inquiry instruction. Why should they change to a more student-centered, minds-on approach that requires more work?
11. **Administrators.** Many school-building principals and assistant principals like to see quiet, orderly classrooms. They react negatively to noise coming from classrooms and view this situation as a lack of teacher control. In addition, many administrators are interested in how well students perform on standardized science tests and support teacher-directed methods of instruction that will improve test scores. Science teachers must discuss their teaching philosophies and classroom activities with administrators in order to determine how these educators view the goals of the curriculum and the methods of attaining these goals.
12. **Parents.** Parents want their children to do well in school, and many want their children to be prepared well for college. Most adults identify with textbook-driven science courses and with teacher-assigned homework that can be completed by finding answers to questions stated at the end of the chapter. These parents are uncomfortable with schooling that deviates from what they were used to in their formal education.

Assessing and Reviewing

Analysis and Synthesis

1. Demonstrate your understanding of inquiry and science teaching by *explaining* the following concepts:
   a. inquiry in general
   b. scientific inquiry
   c. teaching science *by* inquiry
   d. teaching science *as* inquiry
   e. discrepant event
   f. science process skills
   g. inductive activities
   h. deductive activities
   i. gathering information
   j. small-group investigations
   k. science fair projects
2. Reflect on the science courses that you have taken during your schooling. Indicate which of these courses were inquiry-based and which were not. Further, explain whether these courses approached science *by* inquiry or science *as* inquiry or some other approach. In addition, support your analysis by indicating the type of instructional strategies used to instruct the classes.
3. Conduct an analysis of laboratory exercises and other science instructional materials in order to determine the type of inquiry strategies emphasized and the extent to which they engage students in learning science.

Practical Considerations

4. Organize a file of instructional activities that can be used to teach science as inquiry in your teaching area (i.e., life science, earth science, physics). These activities can be found in science textbooks, paperback books, and laboratory manuals. Some of the best inquiry-oriented activities will come to mind, however, when you reflect on what takes place in your everyday surroundings.
5. Build your professional library of textbooks, paperback books, magazines, journals, manuals, Internet sites, and so on in order to include many resources for inquiry-based science. The materials should be sources for discrepant events, laboratory exercises, inductive activities, demonstrations, puzzlers, and small-group investigations.
6. Plan and teach an inquiry lesson to your peers or to middle school or senior high school students that emphasizes one or more ways to initiate and carry out inquiry instruction: process skills, discrepant events, inductive activities, deductive

activities, and problem solving. Participate in the critique and feedback of this teaching session with others.

7. Develop an inquiry activity that uses grouping, role assignments, and cooperative learning. Try out your activity with peers or middle or high school students to determine the effectiveness of this technique.

Developmental Considerations

8. Make a practice of reading science textbooks, paperback books, and journals to gain a deeper understanding of scientific inquiry in order to implement a more authentic form of inquiry-based instruction.

Resources to Examine

Inquiry-Based Instruction: Understanding How Content and Process Go Hand-in-Hand with School Science. February 2004. *The Science Teacher*, 46–50.

The article by Chiappetta and Adams supplements the discussion of the relationships among science content, process, and teaching science found in this chapter. However, it goes further by giving four approaches to inquiry-based instruction with different science content/process emphases—content, content with process, process with content, and process. The context for each example is the topic of browning or oxidation of fruit that has been bruised.

Inquiry and the National Science Education Standards: A Guide for Teaching and Learning. 2000. Washington, DC: National Academy Press.

This NCR paperback book offers many useful examples of how to implement inquiry-based instruction in classrooms from elementary through high school. There is a useful chapter on preparing teachers for inquiry-based teaching. The chapters on frequently asked questions about inquiry and supporting inquiry-based teaching and learning also are informative.

The Current NSTA Catalog for Membership and Publications. National Science Teachers Association. 1840 Wilson Boulevard, Arlington, VA 22201-3000. Phone: (800)722-NSTA. www.nsta.org

This catalog contains hundreds of booklets, teaching guides, and resources for science teaching in grades K–12. These materials address the major science disciplines, providing background information as well as inquiry-oriented activities. All science teachers should possess this publication and be a member of the National Science Teachers Association.

Inquiry in the Classroom. 2008. Charlotte, NC: Information Age Publishing. www.infoagepub.com

This book, edited by Abrams, Southerland, and Silva, provides many perspectives on school-based inquiry, which can serve to improve understanding about this multi-faceted and often ambiguous idea. It focuses on the role of students and teaching, contexts for inquiry instruction, student diversity, standardized tests, and student-scientist partnerships. The text presents many vignettes that offer the reader an opportunity to reflect on school-based inquiry.

Ready, Set, Science! 2008. Washington, DC: The National Academies Press. www.nap.edu

The authors Michaels, Shouse, and Schweingruber provide a very informative paperback book that includes background information and vignettes on many ways to promote active learning in the science programs. They present excellent discussions on organizing science education around core concepts, making thinking visible via talk and argumentation, and making thinking visible through modeling and representation. The vignettes present in-depth views of many teaching and learning examples in science classrooms.

Science as Inquiry in the Secondary Setting. 2008. National Science Teachers Association. 1840 Wilson Boulevard, Arlington, VA 22201-3000. Phone: (800) 722-NSTA. www.nsta.org

Luft, Bell, and Gess-Newsome have edited a short paperback that provides conceptual understanding and examples of how to implement inquiry in the science classroom. The book can inform science teachers regarding what school-based inquiry might look like; its historical development; and how inquiry might be conducted in earth science, chemistry, and in the field. It also explains the place of interpretation and argumentation in inquiry and in questioning and assessment. The book also addresses students with disabilities.

References

Abrams, E., Southerland, S. A., & Silva, P. (2008). *Inquiry in the classroom.* Charlotte, NC: Information Age Publishing.

Biological Sciences Curriculum Study (BSCS). (1978). *Biology teacher's handbook.* New York: John Wiley & Sons.

Chiappetta, E. L. (2008). Historical development of teaching science as inquiry. In J. Luft, R. L. Bell, & J. Gess-Newsome (Eds.), *Science as inquiry in the secondary setting* (pp. 21–30). Arlington, VA: National Science Teachers Association Press.

Chiappetta, E. L., & Adams, A. (2004). Inquiry-based instruction: Understanding how content and process go hand-in-hand with school science. *The Science Teacher, 70*(2), 46–50.

Eisenkraft, A. (2003). Expanding the 5E model, *The Science Teacher, 70*(6), 56–59.

Fuller, R. G. (1980). *Piagetian problems in higher education.* Lincoln, NE: ADAPT, University of Nebraska.

Kagan, S. (1989/1990). The structural approach to cooperative learning. *Educational Leadership, 47*(4), 12–16.

Lumpe, A. T. (1995). Peer interaction in science concept development and problem solving. *School Science and Mathematics, 96,* 302–309.

Meyer, R. E. (2004). Should there be a three-strikes rule against pure discovery learning? *American Psychologist, 59*(1), 14–19.

Michaels, S., Shouse, A. W., & Schweingruber, H. A. (2008). *Ready, set, science!* Washington, DC: National Academies Press

National Research Council (NRC). (1996). *National Science Education Standards.* Washington, DC: National Academies Press.

National Research Council. (2000). *Inquiry and* the *National Science Education Standards: A guide for teaching and learning.* Washington, DC: National Academy Press.

National Science Teachers Association (NSTA). (2003). *National Science Teachers Association Standards for Science Teacher Preparation.* Arlington, VA: Author.

Piaget, J. (1971). *Biology and knowledge.* Chicago: University of Chicago Press.

Renner, J. W., Cate, J. M., Grzybowski, E. B., Atkinson, L. J., Surber, C., & Marek, E. A. (1985). *Investigation in natural science: Biology teacher's guide.* Norman, OK: Science Education Center, College of Education, University of Oklahoma.

Schwab, J. J. (1960). Enquiry, the science teaching and the educator. *The Science Teacher, 27*(6), 6–11.

Schwab, J. J. (1962). The teaching of science as enquiry. In J. Schwab & P. Brandwein (Eds.), *The teaching of science.* Cambridge, MA: Harvard University Press.

Settlage, J. (2007). Demythologizing science teacher education: Conquering the false ideal of open inquiry. *Journal of Science Teaching Education, 18,* 461–468.

Slavin, R. E. (1989/1990). Research on cooperative learning: Consensus and controversy. *Educational Leadership, 47*(4), 52–54.

Suchman, R. (1966). *Developing inquiry.* Chicago: Science Research Associates.

Trowbridge, L. W., & Bybee, R. W. (1996). *Teaching Secondary school science.* Englewood Cliffs, NJ: Merrill.

Van Scotter, P., & Pinkerton, K. D. (2008). Assessing science as inquiry in the classroom. In J. Luft, R. L. Bell, & J. Gess-Newsome, *Science as inquiry in the secondary setting* (pp. 107–120). Arlington, VA: National Science Teachers Association Press.

Windschitl , M. (2008). What is inquiry? A framework for thinking about authentic scientific practices in the classroom. In J. Luft, R. L. Bell, & J. Gess-Newsome (Eds.), *Science as inquiry in the secondary setting* (pp. 1–20). Arlington, VA: National Science Teachers Association Press.

Chapter

9

Diverse Adolescent Learners and Differentiated Instruction

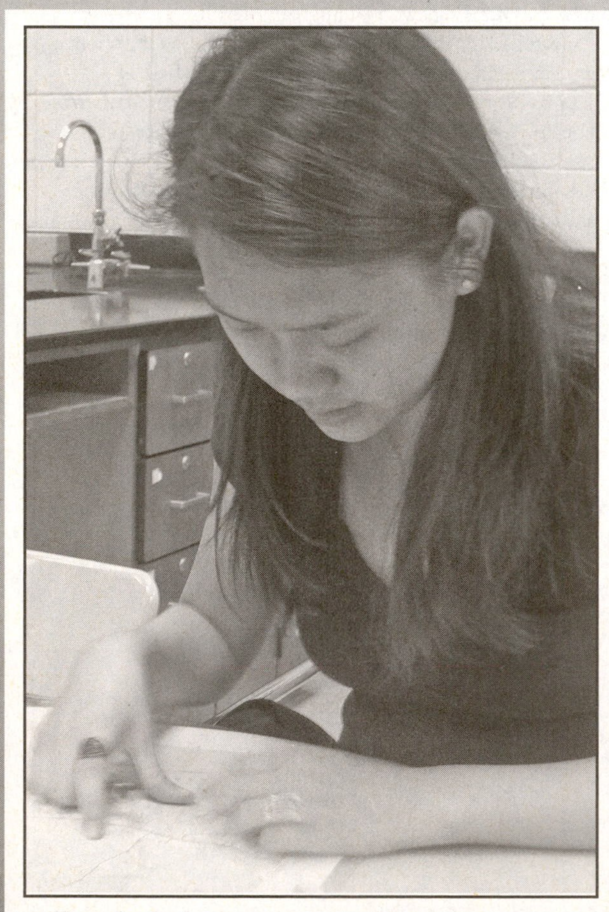

All students deserve an equitable education in science.

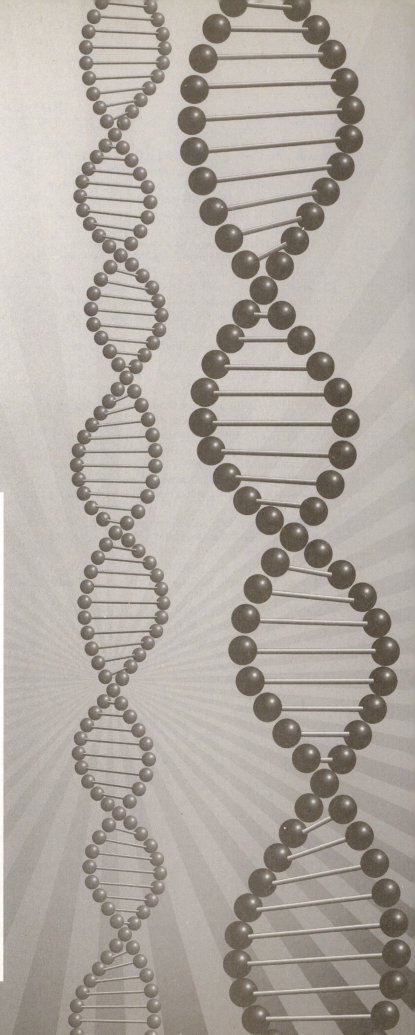

The U.S. educational system is being challenged to provide an equitable education for all students as the school-age population is becoming more diverse. Factors responsible for the growing diversity of this population include rising immigration, demographic shifts due to higher birth rates among some ethnic groups, and the inclusion of students with special learning needs into regular school classes.

The growing diversity of the school-age population is causing science teachers to rethink how they teach and what they teach. To meet the challenge before them, teachers must consider cultural background, home language, ethnicity, gender, disabilities, and student giftedness in their decisions about the science education they provide. They are recognizing that homogeneous instruction is not well suited for maximizing the learning potential of their students and are seeking ways to differentiate instruction to better serve the individuals that populate their classes. Today, science teaching and learning occurs in a context expanded by the diverse academic needs of individual students. An understanding of student diversity and how to differentiate instruction is needed to meet the demands of science teaching in today's schools.

AIMS OF THE CHAPTER

Use the questions that follow to guide your thinking and learning about important aspects of today's adolescent science learners and differentiated instruction:

- What are the demographics of today's school-age population and their teachers?
- How is multicultural science education different from the universalistic tradition of science education?
- What should teachers know about the diverse population of students in middle and secondary school science classes in order to serve their academic needs?
- What is differentiated instruction?
- How can differentiated instruction help today's diverse population of students excel in standards-based science classes?

Science Classroom Mosaic and Success in Science

The mosaic of American culture is clearly reflected in today's school-age population. Reports from a number of sources provide details about the changing demographics of this population and how teachers' views of cultural assimilation may affect their efforts to provide an equitable science education for all students.

Student Demographics

According to the U.S. Department of Education's National Center for Educational Statistics (2007), the white precollege school-age population was estimated at 28 million in 2005. While this number seems large, it reflects nearly a 20% decrease from 1972. During this same 33-year period, the population of African-American students increased from 15% to 16%. This increase brings the total school-age population of African Americans to more than 8 million. Also increasing in number was the population of other groups, mostly Asian but also Native-American students and students of more than one ethnicity. These populations increased to more than 3 million, or about 7% of the total school-age population. The largest increase was witnessed in the Hispanic population. From 1972 to 2005, the Hispanic school-age population increased from 6% to 20%. Hispanics are the fastest-growing segment of the school-age population and now number more than 9 million. These demographic shifts are most pronounced in urban areas, mainly in the southern and western regions of the United States, where African-American and Hispanic students, traditionally underrepresented in science, make up the majority of the public school population.

The same U.S. Department of Education (2007) report revealed that 6.7 million students, or roughly 14% of the school-age population, were served under the Individuals with Disabilities in Education Act (IDEA) in 2005. This number represents almost a 300% increase since IDEA compliance was first monitored in 1976. Disabilities covered by IDEA range from specific learning disabilities, emotional disturbances, and attention deficit disorder to orthopedic, hearing, and visual impairments. Students with disabilities are found among all demographic groups, adding to the diversity of middle and high school classes.

Teacher Demographics

In contrast to the school-age population, the teacher workforce is much less diverse. Data from the U.S. Department of Education (2007) indicate that of the 3.3 million teachers employed during the 2003–2004 school year, only 17% were racial or ethnic minorities. Teachers also tend to differ from the student population in terms of language and social status. The typical teacher speaks only English and is from a middle-class background (Villegas & Lucas, 2002). Moreover, enrollment in teacher education programs suggest that the racial and ethnic composition of the future teaching force is unlikely to change in the foreseeable future (Villegas & Lucas, 2002).

Factors Traditionally Linked to Success in Science

Diversity by itself does not affect students' success in science, but factors often associated with diversity do. For instance, socioeconomic status is viewed as the "single most powerful factor" that affects science performance and motivation (Lynch et al., 1996, p. 13). Students from low-income families who attend inadequately funded schools and are taught by less than highly qualified teachers do less well in science than their contemporaries (National Science Board, 2004). There is little doubt that poverty contributes to the poor science performance and lack of motivation among students from these ethnic groups. Children of low-income families lack many of the experiences that help other students succeed in school, and less than highly qualified teachers are ill prepared to help these children achieve their full potential. Many Asian Americans seem to have escaped the conditions of poverty through their educational achievements, but among recent Asian-American immigrants, particularly those from Southeast Asia, the problems of poverty are very evident (U.S. Commission on Civil Rights, 1992).

Many recent immigrants, particularly young Asians and Hispanics, come from homes in which English is not spoken (U.S. Department of Education, 2007). This places excessive demands on a student to learn English while at the same time trying to learn science. Poor science performance among these students is due to the high vocabulary demands and the abstract understandings associated with science learning (Lee, Fradd, & Sutman, 1995). Some Asian Americans seem to compensate for their limited English proficiency by excelling in school subjects that make low demands on their language skills (Lynch et al., 1996). Students from urban centers are not the only ones disadvantaged when their science experiences and curricular choices are compared with those students at schools in suburban communities. Students from rural areas, regardless of ethnicity, also may be disadvantaged science learners (U.S. Department of Education, 2003). The lack of high-quality educational opportunities in both urban and rural areas negatively impacts the science performance of these students.

Socioeconomic status, immigration status, English language proficiency, and geographic location are among the factors that teachers must consider in attempting to achieve the dual goals of academic excellence and equity set forth in state and national standards documents. But unlike guidelines for academic excellence that are laid out in detail in these documents, guidance for providing all students with the same opportunity to learn science and a rationale for doing so are not always made explicit.

Teachers' Beliefs About Culturally Based Deficiencies

Some teachers believe that equity in science education can be achieved by overcoming the deficits that are brought to school by diverse students. The lack of success among these students is assumed to be because their home life or cultural background is less advanced than that of students from the cultural mainstream. Remediation designed to compensate for their lack of knowledge and skills in science or less than favorable dispositions toward science is considered the solution to increasing science participation and performance in school, and ultimately, the number of culturally diverse people who pursue science and technical careers.

However, today more people are finding reasons to reject this deficit model. Instead, the focus is on the incompatibilities between the students' backgrounds and special needs and the expectations of the science classroom. As a microcosm of the school culture, science classes tend to promote the values ascribed to by the mainstream white, male-dominated, middle-class culture (Barton & Yang, 2000). For example, competition, fast work, and respect for the teacher are valued; rigid time schedules are followed; and students are expected to graduate from high school and go to college or seek work. In attempting to achieve equity in science education, teachers must recognize that these values are not shared by all cultures and that the related goals are not desirable for all students. Fairness and impartiality on the part of the science teacher are the keys to an equitable science education for all.

Stop and Reflect!

Before reading further, do the following:

- Write a brief description of a class of students that reflects the diversity of today's middle school or high school population. Then pick a student from the class description. What factors are likely to affect this student's success as a science learner?
- Read the excerpts from Ms. Kendal's journal in Classroom Snapshot 9.1. What ideas do you have for enhancing the likelihood that Ms. Kendal will be successful in helping all her students do well in physical science?

Classroom Snapshot 9.1

Excerpts from Ms. Kendal's Journal

Ms. Kendal is starting her first year of teaching at Riverview High School. She was an excellent student and decided to pursue a teaching career during her junior year in college. While feeling quite comfortable with the concepts addressed in the chemistry and physical science courses she was assigned to teach, she is not sure that she is ready to deal with the diverse needs of the students in her classes. Here are some excerpts from her weekly journal that reflect this uncertainty.

Preplanning

My teaching schedule was changed from what I was told when I was hired in June. I'm now assigned to teach three sections of physical science this semester. The names that appear on my class roles suggest that many different cultural backgrounds will be represented in my classes. There are many students with Hispanic surnames. The ESL [English as a Second Language] designation next to nine of the names means that these students will also be trying to learn English as they learn physical science. In addition, I have five students who require IEPs [Individualized Education Program], suggesting that they have some kind of disability. I sure hope that I can meet my students' learning needs.

Week 1

I feel that I got off to a good start with my classes. I was firm and took time to work with my students to establish a positive classroom environment. I met with Mr. Sanchez, our school's lead ESL teacher, and discussed ideas about how to best help my ESL students. His suggestions were consistent with what I learned in my college classes, but making time to plan for all the students' needs is my real challenge. It was also good to learn from Mr. Sanchez that students will not be pulled out of my physical science classes for special ESL sessions, but that Ms. Birdwell, an ESL, teacher, will periodically attend my classes and will be available to help me plan for the special language needs of these students during my planning period.

Week 5

The best thing that happened this week is that I met Ms. Jameson. We have the same lunch schedule. She is a very nice person and has taught physics and physical science at Riverview for the past nine years. She offered to help me develop lesson plans and to share her teaching materials. I'm hoping that she will be able to suggest ways to engage Josh and a couple of other students who have learning disabilities and seem disillusioned with school.

Week 10

Four students withdrew from my physical science classes this week. Their parents are migrant farm laborers. The students told me that they would return to the Riverview community in the spring when their parents are hired to plant next year's crop. The students were unsure about the schools they would attend in the locations where their families will live in the coming months. I feel sorry for these students. They seemed to be making such good progress in physical science and learning English.

 Equity in Science Education

Equity in science education means that all students regardless of cultural background, ethnicity, gender, or special needs have the same opportunity to learn quality science (Atwater, Crockett, & Kilpatrick, 1996). Lynch and her colleagues (1996) offer two compelling reasons for advancing equity in science education. The first is economic. Equity in science education will result in a workforce better prepared for the science- and technology-related jobs that are increasing in number. This highly skilled workforce will benefit the nation's economy as high-tech jobs are filled by U.S. citizens and not lost overseas. The second is based in social justice. We have the obligation to prepare all students to function in our modern science-based society. In addition, these authors advance the argument that equity in science education should be about educating students in the culture of power that permits access to scientific knowledge.

According to Delpit (1995), there is a culture of power that permeates schools through the voice and actions of teachers, who tend to reflect white middle-class values and traditions. The academic success of students from nondominant cultures is linked to understanding and acquiring the culture of those in power. For this to happen, Delpit contends that teachers must acknowledge the power they hold and directly inform students about such matters as interaction styles, dress, and other rules of the dominant culture.

Multicultural Science Education

Extending the notion of equity in science classrooms is multicultural science education. Nested within the larger framework of multicultural education, it is an ambiguous concept. Multicultural science education "can mean many things to many people" (Hodson, 1993, p. 688). According to Ogawa (1995), "Awareness of cultural diversity in science education seems to be at the crux of multicultural science education" (p. 584). Building on the work of James Banks, Atwater and Riley (1993) define cultural diversity in science education as "a construct, a process, and an educational reform movement with the goal of providing equitable opportunities for culturally diverse student populations to learn quality science in schools, colleges, and universities" (p. 664). Hodson (1993) warns about defining multicultural education too narrowly and contends that what constitutes multicultural science education will vary depending on the region, community, school, and classroom in which it is practiced. Today, multicultural science education is about providing equitable science learning opportunities for *all students*, regardless of cultural background, ethnicity, gender, or special educational needs.

Before addressing ways in which school science can be presented to make it attractive and accessible to all students, we will first turn our attention to the nature of science and how science is perceived from different cultural perspectives. In Chapter 7, you learned about science as a way of knowing and the need to be mindful of the worldview of other peoples. In the next section, that discussion is extended with attention given to a debate that has influenced current thinking about multicultural science education. The central tension of this debate is whether or not multiculturalism is at odds with a universalistic view of science.

Multiculturalism and Universalism in Science Education

Some people who write about the nature of science claim that science is universal. What is meant by this claim is that science, as a human construction, is a universal form of knowledge that transcends cultural interpretations (Matthews, 1994). This means that scientific knowledge has no national, political, or cultural boundaries. "Pure universalist science educators question the multiethnicity of atoms, quasars and quarks, while voicing a concern over the inaccuracies inherent in attempting to paint a social picture of science" (Weld, 1997, p. 265). An important tenant of the universalistic tradition is that the efficacy of humans' explanations of the natural world are grounded in reality.

The universalistic position has been challenged by multiculturalists on the grounds that it presents a biased interpretation of the nature of science. The universalistic position is considered biased primarily because it fails to consider knowledge systems developed by non-Western and ancient cultures as science (Luft, 1998). Multiculturalists claim that the universalistic position is only one among many possible scientific frameworks for investigating the natural world (Loving, 1995). By considering modern Western science as the only knowledge system, Stanley and Brickhouse (1994) warn that we run the risk of limiting our ability to generate new knowledge by destroying knowledge systems viewed as inferior. The consideration of non-Western science has recently spawned interest in the indigenous knowledge of science and technology held by Native Americans and other peoples in Africa and New Zealand.

Siegel's (1997) examination of the universalistic and multiculturalist perspectives on both epistemological and moral grounds has brought some clarity to the debate. His position is that multicultural science education cannot be justified from an epistemological basis because different knowledge systems are not equally valid. As Matthews (1994) points out, "no ethnic science is going to adequately explain how radios work, why the moon stays in orbit, why hundreds of thousands of Africans are dying of AIDS and so on. Mainstream science may not give us complete answers, but my claim is that it gives better answers than others" (p. 193).

However, Siegel argues in defense of multicultural science education from a moral stance. He urges that all students and the scientific ideas that reflect their cultures be treated with justice and respect in science classes. Referencing the work of Hodson (1993), Siegel goes on to remind the reader that Western science conceptions, including those of objectivity and rationality, are not shared by all peoples and that teachers need to be sensitive to this, but that exposure of all students, regardless of their cultural background, to Western science seems to be exactly what science education should be about (Siegel, 1997). The study of Western science affords students the opportunity to investigate ideas that are unfamiliar to them and to learn from their experiences. Siegel's position is that multiculturalism is very compatible with a universalistic view of science.

The debate between multiculturalists and universalists has mellowed in recent years, with both sides agreeing on salient points. One point is that not all knowledge systems developed by different cultures, and called science, are equally sound. A second is that students in the United States must come to understand modern Western science. The final point is that multicultural science education is a moral imperative, an imperative that has significant implications for the science classroom.

Cultural and Linguistic Diversity

Three approaches for promoting meaningful science learning among culturally and linguistically diverse students are described in the science education literature. Each approach has a different emphasis for addressing the needs of these students. Many of the instructional strategies associated with each approach are applicable to all students, regardless of cultural and linguistic diversity.

Content Integration

Baptiste and Key (1996) describe three levels of content integration appropriate for the science classroom. Levels one and two focus on multicultural awareness and integrating the contributions of many cultures and peoples into the curriculum. An example of level one integration is celebrating the scientific accomplishments of African Americans such as Charles Drew (blood groups) and Percy Julian (isolating sterols from soybeans) on the dates of their births. While an example of level two is the culminating experience in the *Chemistry in the Community* (American Chemical Society, 2006) unit "Understanding Food." The culminating experience for this unit asks students to compare the nutritional value of meals from several cultures, including Mexico and Japan, in terms of food energy, protein, iron, and vitamin B_1.

Diverse learners bring different perspectives to science learning tasks.

Level three requires making cultural and social issues the centerpiece of the curriculum. Farming practices, medicines used to treat diseases and other ailments, tools for making calculations, and chemical dyes are just a few examples of topics that provide ideas for science curricula that integrate information about ancient and modern cultures and may lead students to take socially responsible actions.

It is not always easy to develop learning experiences and units that integrate content reflecting different cultural perspectives. The good news is that more and more publishers are including suggestions for multicultural connections in the teacher editions of their texts and developing student readings, activity books, and supporting Web sites that highlight the scientific contributions of individuals and cultural groups. Information useful for developing science learning experience that reflect Baptiste and Key's upper levels can be found in such Web sites and books as:

- The Faces of Science: African Americans in the Sciences https://webfiles.uci.edu/mcbrown/display/faces.html
- Multicultural Education Internet Resource Guide http://jan.ucc.nau.edu/~jar/Multi.html
- *Blacks in Science: Ancient and Modern,* edited by Ivan Van Sertima (1983, Transaction Publishers)
- *Multicultural Science Education: Theory, Practice, and Promise,* edited by S. Maxwell Hines (2003, Peter Lang Publishing)

Cultural Harmony

For many culturally diverse students, particularly those who are recent immigrants, the culture of the science classroom is an unfamiliar one. For these students to be successful, school science must be related to their home culture and language. In *Science in the Multicultural Classroom* (1998), Roberta Barba writes about "culturally harmonious variables as those culture-of-origin beliefs, attitudes, and practices which influence (both positively and negatively, functionally and dysfunctionally) the teaching/learning process" (p. 14). These variables, Barba notes, affect students' interactions with teachers and classmates and how they go about constructing knowledge in the science classroom. Culturally diverse students develop meaningful science understandings when they see their culture and language facilitating learning rather than acting as an impediment to it.

Six culturally harmonious variables described by Barba (1998) that affect science learning are (1) format of print materials, (2) instructional language, (3) level of peer interactivity, (4) role models, (5) elaboration of context, and (6) interactivity with manipulative materials. Figure 9.1 describes ways in which these harmonious variables can be addressed in science classes to promote meaningful learning among culturally diverse students, especially those who are learning English.

The results of work by Aikenhead (1998) also suggest that the notion of "border crossing" is an appropriate way to frame the science experiences of culturally diverse students, particularly for those students whose home language is not English. These students have greater difficulty than their mainstream counterparts crossing the cultural boundaries between their everyday world and the world of science because the differences between everyday life and school science tend to be greater for them. For example, culturally diverse students may not:

- construct arguments based on logic
- tolerate ambiguity
- feel comfortable presenting evidence to support their ideas
- hold attitudes and values typically associated with Western science

For this reason it is important for science teachers to learn about their students' home languages and cultural experiences so that they are better positioned to make school science accessible to them.

Countering Racism and Stereotyping

Multicultural content reviewers check textbooks published today to ensure that racist language and stereotyping are not present and that photographs reflect the diversity of the student population. Teachers will want to keep these matters in mind when selecting and developing instructional materials for the classroom so as not to offend or make students feel uncomfortable.

Addressing racism and stereotyping in science classes also means that teachers need to consider the influence of their own expectations and perceptions on student learning and achievement. White teachers tend to expect African-American students to be less successful academically than white students (Fergusson, 2003). And, they may perceive the verbal interactions of students from diverse cultural backgrounds and for whom English is not their home language to mean that they lack the knowledge and cognitive skills to be successful in science (Holbrook, 2006). However, such perceptions are ill founded. Studies of recent Haitian immigrants and other culturally diverse student groups suggest that when science classrooms support culturally familiar environments, student learning is enhanced (Hudincourt-Barnes, 2003).

One way to support a culturally familiar environment for many diverse students is to shift the pattern of classroom interaction from the traditional teacher initiation, student response, and teacher evaluation to a form of classroom discussion that more closely matches cultural practices. For example, the discussion may include aspects of the free-flowing Haitian *bay odyan*, a mix of argumentation, joking, riddles, tales, and song (Hudincourt-Barnes, 2003). Also shown to support the science learning of diverse students while countering racism and stereotyping are the practices of cogenerative dialog and coteaching (Emdin, 2008). Cogenerative dialogue involves students and teachers discussing how to make the classroom environment more culturally familiar. And in coteaching, students use culturally familiar language and analogies to teach each other while schooling the teacher in their home culture.

FIGURE 9.1 Addressing harmonious variables in science classes.

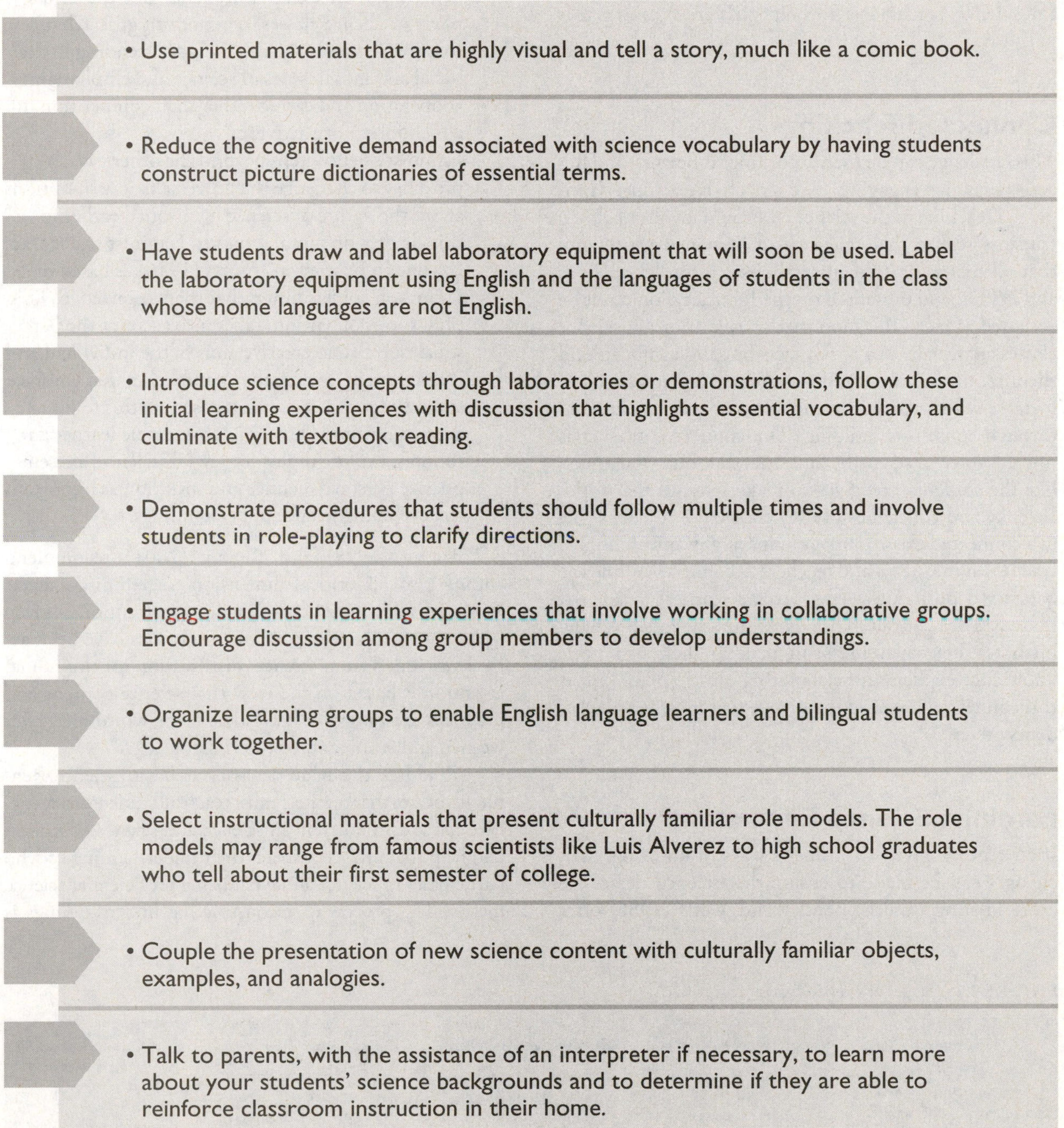

• Use printed materials that are highly visual and tell a story, much like a comic book.
• Reduce the cognitive demand associated with science vocabulary by having students construct picture dictionaries of essential terms.
• Have students draw and label laboratory equipment that will soon be used. Label the laboratory equipment using English and the languages of students in the class whose home languages are not English.
• Introduce science concepts through laboratories or demonstrations, follow these initial learning experiences with discussion that highlights essential vocabulary, and culminate with textbook reading.
• Demonstrate procedures that students should follow multiple times and involve students in role-playing to clarify directions.
• Engage students in learning experiences that involve working in collaborative groups. Encourage discussion among group members to develop understandings.
• Organize learning groups to enable English language learners and bilingual students to work together.
• Select instructional materials that present culturally familiar role models. The role models may range from famous scientists like Luis Alverez to high school graduates who tell about their first semester of college.
• Couple the presentation of new science content with culturally familiar objects, examples, and analogies.
• Talk to parents, with the assistance of an interpreter if necessary, to learn more about your students' science backgrounds and to determine if they are able to reinforce classroom instruction in their home.

Based on recommendations offered by Barba (1998); Simich-Dudgeon & Egbert (2000); Sutman, Guzman, & Schwartz (1993); and Watson (2004).

 Gender Inclusiveness

Equity in science education certainly extends to issues of gender. Viewing knowledge from the perspective of women is essential to an understanding of girls' beliefs and decisions regarding science. Belenky, Clinchy, Goldberger, and Tarule (1986) group women's ways of knowing into five stages that can be viewed as a developmental pathway beginning with silence and leading to constructed knowledge (Figure 9.2). The challenge for science teachers is to help girls move along this pathway.

Connected Teaching

This challenge can be met, according to Belenky and her colleagues, by engaging in connected teaching. Connected teaching in the science classroom involves helping students realize that science is a human construction, that all that is written in textbooks, recorded on CDs and DVDs, and presented on the Internet should not be accepted at face value, and that conversations in science classes are usually not about facts but about models and theories. In the connected classroom, students are comfortable with uncertainty and knowledge is constructed through consensus building. The connected teacher is not the voice of scientific authority, but one who, much like the students, struggles to make sense of the world. Belenky and colleagues (1986) clarify the teacher's role in a connected classroom by comparing the metaphors of teachers as midwives and teachers as bankers. "While the bankers deposit knowledge in the learner's head, the midwives draw it out. They assist the students by giving birth to their own ideas, in making their own tacit knowledge explicit and elaborating on it" (p. 217). It is this connected learning experience that most female students prefer.

Feminist Science Education

If credence is given to women's ways of knowing, then changes can be made to ensure that science classes are more inviting to girls. Bentley and Watts (1986) offer three approaches to consider: girl-friendly science, feminine science, and feminist science.

1. Girl-friendly science advocates making traditional science more attractive to girls by changing the image of science presented in classes. Challenging stereotypes, emphasizing the aesthetic appeal of science, and framing science curricula in a social context are all examples of ways to make science girl friendly.
2. Feminine science emphasizes changing the atmosphere of science classes to better suit girls. Changes to foster feminine science include attending to the social and moral issues of science and emphasizing cooperation and caring rather than competition in all school science activities.
3. Feminist science steps beyond the other two approaches to challenge the universalistic assumptions about the nature of science mentioned earlier in this chapter on moral grounds. Feminist science, according to Bentley and Watts (1986), is based on a philosophy of wisdom rather than knowledge. This philosophy of wisdom takes into account the personal, social, and creative aims of the individual and is reflected in investigative approaches that embrace subjectivity. A science class based on this feminist approach would allow for considerable learner autonomy, explore multiple views of science, and emphasize personal feelings and intuition as important to developing science understandings.

Barton (1998) and Rennie (2001) recommend adding a social–critical dimension to feminist science. With the addition of this dimension, attention is given to how women and also ethnic minorities have been actively excluded from science. Justification for this added attention is based on the view that science content and practices are biased in ways that favor white men over women and ethnic minorities (Barton, 1998).

To address the inequities associated with science, Rennie advocates that teachers must teach all students to recognize the sexism inherent in science and science education and help them to reconstruct their understanding of who participates in science and what being proficient at science means. The process of reconstructing understandings is

FIGURE 9.2 Stages of women's ways of knowing.

Silence	Received Knower	Subjective Knower	Procedural Knower	Constructed Knower
No voice in what constitutes knowledge and subject to the whims of outside authority	Recipient of knowledge, but incapable of creating knowledge	Creator of knowledge by objective systematic analysis	Creator of personal knowledge perceived as intuitive and subjective	Creator of conceptualized knowledge through the use of both subjective and objective procedures

From Belenky, B. F., Clinchy, B. M., Goldberger, N. R., & Tarule, J. M. (1986). *Women's ways of knowing*. New York: Basic Books.

virtually identical to that used in combating scientific racism and is intended to provide female students with a context for positioning themselves in school science and other science-related experiences (Barton, 1998). It is the feminist science approach aided by the use of a social critical lens that most closely aligns with the connected learning experience suggested by Belenky and her colleagues.

Teachers concerned with gender inclusiveness in science education should, according to Reiss (1993), view these three approaches as different answers to the question: What should science education for girls be like? While feminist science with emphasis on the sociocultural context of science might be the final answer, feminine science is seen as an acceptable answer, and girl-friendly science is better than doing nothing at all.

There are a number of strategies a teacher can use to move along the continuum from doing nothing to feminist school science. Listed in Figure 9.3 are several suggestions by Bentley and Watts (1986), Kahle (1996), Parkinson (1994), and Rennie (2001) for doing so. The list is not unlike excellent teaching strategies intended to ensure the inclusion of all students in science.

As powerful as these suggestions are, Tobin (1996) points out that teachers are unlikely to be successful in achieving gender inclusiveness in the classroom without the direct involvement of students. He recommends that students be taught to recognize gender inequities in the science classroom and be empowered to create learning opportunities that benefit all.

Stop and Reflect!

Before going on, do the following:

- Think of a personal science learning experience that you believe is a good illustration of compatibility between a student's culture and the expectations of the science classroom. What characteristics of the science learning environment discussed in the sections on cultural and linguistic diversity and gender inclusiveness do you associate with this science learning experience?
- Suppose that you questioned a student whose science grades and interest were declining. In response to your questioning, the student told you, "Science is not for people like me. So, why should I try?" What is one thing that you would tell or show the student to convey the message that science is socially constructed, subjective, and should be equally accessible to all?

FIGURE 9.3 Strategies for moving toward feminist school science.

- Choose science materials, such as case studies and life histories, to portray science as the subjective and passionate study of the natural world.
- Involve students in activities that emphasize visual and spatial skills, including constructing models and manipulating equipment and data.
- Using learning tasks with many approaches and that yield more than one correct answer.
- Engage students in learning experiences that examine myths and stereotypes about science and the people who do science.
- Be on the lookout for unintended biases in your classroom, such as calling on boys more than girls and allowing boys to dominate discussions and laboratory groups.
- Teach the skills of listening, supporting, and negotiating along with the more traditional skills of science.
- Use gender-sensitive language and encourage your students to do so.
- Invite women scientists and women studying science in college to visit your classes.
- Celebrate the contributions of women in science and other human endeavors.

 Exceptionalities

Although all students should be considered exceptional, there are some students who exhibit atypical performance. They deserve the same opportunities afforded all other students to learn quality science. For these students, equity in science education requires accommodating their exceptionalities.

The list of special needs is extensive, and therefore our focus will be on those students with special needs who are usually found in general education science classes. These include students with academic disabilities, the physically disabled, and the gifted and talented. Special education or resource teachers are sometimes assigned to help the science teacher address the special needs of these students. Four federal laws directly impact the teaching of students with special needs in science classes.

Inclusion and the Law

The first law passed by Congress in 1975 is Public Law 94-142, the Education for All Handicapped Children Act. This law, reauthorized as the Individuals with Disabilities Education Act (IDEA) in 1990 and amended most recently in 2004, requires that all schools must place students who have academic or physical disabilities in the "least restrictive environment." Least restrictive environment is usually interpreted to mean general education classes. Two other laws are Section 504 of the Rehabilitation Act of 1973 and the Americans with Disabilities Act, signed by President George H. W. Bush in 1990. These two laws assure the full civil rights of all persons with disabilities and have a broader interpretation of disabilities than does the IDEA. This broader interpretation provides students with learning disabilities, but ineligible for special education services, with access to "virtually anything that they could receive under the IDEA" (Bateman, 1996, p. 183). The most recently passed law that impacts the teaching of special needs students is No Child Left Behind (NCLB) signed by President George W. Bush in 2001. NCLB reinforces the goals of the other laws by directing additional funds to school programs that serve students with disabilities, but with the additional burden of demonstrating annual increases in students' academic performance.

Practically speaking, these laws have resulted in the inclusion of students with special learning needs in all school programs. Thus the likelihood is great that students who require accommodations for disabilities will be found in most science classes. Addressing the learning needs of these students presents the science teacher with unique challenges. What should you do when called upon to make accommodations for special needs students in science classes? Where can you obtain information about the appropriate accommodations for such students?

According to the IDEA, an Individualized Education Program (IEP) must be written for every special needs student, regardless of disability, who is placed in a general education class. A team of individuals is called on to develop the IEP. The team typically includes the student's parents or guardians, educational specialists, teachers, and school administrators. In many cases, the adolescent student also participates as a member of the IEP development team. The parents or guardians of the student as well as appropriate school personnel must approve the IEP before it can be enacted. The IEP for each student includes goals, instructional activities, and assessment procedures, which can guide the teacher as well as the student. Other information also may be included within the IEP that will assist teachers, including records relating to past performance and areas of needed focus and service. The Americans with Disabilities Act guarantees that the IEP and other records be maintained in confidence and be available to parents or guardians at their request. It also gives parents or guardians the right to challenge the IEP and to bring counsel, legal or otherwise, to meetings where the IEP is developed or discussed.

Once approved by appropriate parties, the IEP becomes mandatory and must be followed as closely as possible. An IEP may include information such as:

1. results of an assessment battery given to the student
2. interpersonal relationships with other students and adults
3. behavioral problems and recommendations for handling the problems
4. goals that have been set for the student
5. services that should be provided to help the student achieve his or her educational goals
6. procedures for evaluating goals and the timetable for evaluating them
7. a statement regarding the general health of the student as well as the disability or disabilities exhibited by the student
8. recommended instructional activities for various subject areas
9. when working with a student 14 years of age or older, transition activities intended to help him or her prepare for personal independence and employment or post-secondary education

When dealing with students with special needs in general education classes, teachers should refer to IEPs for assistance. It is also important for teachers to know that under a special regulation of the Family Educational Rights and Privacy Act, they may obtain access to a student's IEP without written permission from the student's parents or guardians. Access under these conditions is possible if it is determined by school authorities that the information in the IEP may help the teacher address the student's learning needs (Bateman, 1996).

Learning Disabilities and Behavioral Disorders

The term *learning disabled* is used to describe students of average or above-average intelligence with learning difficulties that result from some type of cognitive processing disorder. The processing disorder affects the person's ability to take in information and make use of it, and is often manifested in difficulties with reading and written language in addition to skills associated with mathematics, studying, organization, and social interaction (McNamara, 2007). In contrast, students with *behavioral disorders* are those who engage in disruptive or inappropriate behaviors that interfere with learning and relationships with other people (Smith, 1998). Characteristics of students with behavioral disorders include inability to concentrate, lack of motivation, aggression, and chronic disobedience. Contributing to behavioral disorders are biological influences as well as influences from home, community, and school.

Attention deficit hyperactivity disorder (ADHD) is not a special disability category, but a medical diagnosis made by a doctor (Beattie, Jordan, & Algozzine, 2006). Students with ADHD often experience challenges associated with learning disabilities and behavioral disorders. Inattentiveness and distractibility are characteristics associated with ADHD, along with impulsive behavior and incessant restlessness (Keller, 2003). Students with ADHD may be taking prescription medication like Ritalin to help them function in regular classes.

It is very likely that one or more students with these learning and behavioral challenges will be found in many science classes. As a teacher of these students, there are a few things to consider. First, it is important to learn as much as possible about the special needs student's abilities and disabilities. But rather than trying to accommodate the student's needs based solely on your own coursework and reading or past experiences, ask the student for help to devise individual learning accommodations. Students with special needs are perhaps the best sources of information about their learning challenges and should be consulted regularly about what they can and cannot do (Hofman, 1994).

Second, discrimination is too often associated with special needs students, some of whom are also racial or ethnic minorities (Donovan & Cross, 2003). Teachers may hold low expectations for students with learning disabilities or disorders and discourage them from enrolling in advanced science classes and pursuing science careers. The consequences of pullout programs and ability grouping can be particularly devastating to these students. Pullout programs, in which students with learning disabilities and disorders engage in special learning activities away from the general education classroom, often deprive these students of science learning opportunities. Low expectations are likely to become self-fulfilling prophecies when these students' access to challenging science experiences is limited by placement in general education courses.

Third, science instructional strategies that work well with students with learning disabilities and disorders are generally the same ones that work well with all types of students (Steele, 2008). This enables students with learning disabilities and disorders to participate in most general education class activities.

To address the special learning needs of students with learning disabilities and disorders in science classes, teachers often must modify their regular lessons. The following list includes examples of instructional modifications recommended by Mastropieri and Scruggs (1995), Keller (2003), Patton (1995), Steele (2008), and Watson and Johnston (2007) for teaching science to students with learning disabilities, behavioral disorders or ADHD:

- Choose approaches to teaching and learning that are activity oriented.
- Use teaching strategies that emphasize structure, clarity, redundancy, enthusiasm, appropriate pace, and maximum engagement.
- Partner students with learning disabilities or disorders with regular functioning students.
- Help students with learning disabilities and disorders to monitor their own behavior by using checklists.
- Adapt science activities by reducing the level of abstraction or breaking them into smaller parts.
- Make written instructions more accessible by translating text into symbolic and picture instructions using symbol- or picture-based communication software.
- Teach test-taking strategies, such as reading directions, skipping over difficult items and returning to them later, and budgeting time.
- Be flexible in deciding how students with learning disabilities or disorders are allowed to demonstrate their mastery of course content and skills.

Physical Disabilities

Students with physical disabilities are also present in general science classes. Participating in general classes ensures that these youngsters have the opportunity to develop useful science skills and understandings that will assist them in living fulfilling and productive lives. Many national science organizations, including the National Science Teachers Association, the American Association for the Advancement of Science, and the American Chemical Society, have affirmed the importance of science for students with physical disabilities by supporting the development of equipment and materials that enable them to be more successful in science classrooms.

Students with physical disabilities may lack the science experiences and understandings common to students without physical disabilities, because science may not have been part of the early schooling provided these students (Keller, 1994). If this is found to be the case, opportunities to involve students in these missed learning experiences will need to be built into the curriculum. Engaging students in activity-oriented science and using role models to inform students with disabilities that they are capable of performing well in science are important first steps in any accommodation effort (Scruggs, Mastropieri, & Boon, 1998). When making curricular accommodations, the teacher must develop an understanding of the student's disability and the implications of the disability for science instruction. More important, the teacher must actively solicit from the student with a physical disability ways to address his or her special needs.

It is becoming commonplace to find students with visual, hearing, orthopedic, and other health impairments in regular science classes. There are many accommodation and inclusion strategies appropriate for addressing the special learning needs of students with these physical disabilities. Table 9.1 presents characteristics associated with these physical disabilities and identifies sources that describe how to work effectively with these students.

Gifted and Talented Students

Often overlooked in science classes are the special needs of bright and highly motivated students. These so-called gifted students are not only the high academic achievers but also those who exhibit high levels of creativity and substantial task commitment (Renzulli & Reis, 1997). The abilities and special talents of these

TABLE 9.1 Physical Disabilities and Accommodations

Physical Disabilities	Sources of Information About Instructional Accommodations
Visual Impairments Some individuals are totally blind, whereas others can see outlines of objects to various degrees. Some individuals can see only objects and print that are within a few inches or feet of their eyes and then only with corrective aids.	• Science for Students with Visual Impairments: Teaching Suggestions and Policy Implications for Secondary Educators by David Kumar, Rangasamy Ramasamy, and Greg Stafanich. *Electronic Journal of Science Education*, 2001, *5*(3). Accessible at http://wolfweb.unr.edu/homepage/crowther/ejse/ejsev5n3.html • Perkins School for the Blind's Information Clearinghouse on Blindness and Visual Impairments in Science Education. Available at: www.perkins.org/clearinghouse/science/
Hearing Impairments Deaf people are disabled to the extent that they cannot understand speech through their ears, with or without the use of a hearing aid. People who are hard-of-hearing are disabled to the extent that they have difficulty understanding speech with or without a hearing aid.	• Strategies for Teaching Students with Hearing Impairments, West Virginia University. Available at: www.as.wvu.edu/~scidis/hearing.html • Teaching Chemistry to the Hearing Impaired by Edward Cain. *Journal of College Science Teaching*, 1981, *10*(6), 364–366. • Signing Science Dictionary Available at: http://signsci.terc.edu/dictionary/index.htm
Orthopedic/Motor Impairments The range of conditions included within orthopedic/motor impairments is enormous. The conditions affect the spinal column (spina bifida), brain function (epilepsy), muscles (muscular dystrophy), limbs (amputation), and joints (arthritis).	• Orthopedic Accommodations at Georgia Standards.Org Available at: www.glc.k12.ga.us/passwd/trc/ttools/attach/accomm/orthoimp.pdf • Strategies for Teaching Students with Orthopedic/Motor Impairments, West Virginia University. Available at: www.as.wvu.edu/~scidis/motor.html • Teaching Chemistry to Students with Disabilities edited by Thomas Kucera. Available at: www.rit.edu/~easi/easisem/chem.html
Other Health Impairments Included within the category are impairments that affect the respiratory system (asthma), the heart (heart disease), blood (sickle cell anemia), the immune system (HIV), and body systems (cancer, allergies). These impairments may cause students to miss class unexpectedly and for long periods of time.	• Students with Physical Disabilities and Health Impairments by John Venn. ERIC Clearinghouse on Handicapped and Gifted Children, Reston, VA. Available at: www.ericdigests.org/pre-9213/health.htm • Teaching Students with Other Disabilities by Cornucopia Of Disability Information. Available at: http://codi.buffalo.edu/archives/colleges/.gasouth/.other.htm • Band-Aids and Blackboard by Joan Fleitas, City University of New York. Available at: www.lehman.cuny.edu/faculty/jfleitas/bandaides/healthed.html

young people are often first noticed in the area of oral and written language, mathematics, music, and problem solving, but they are also evident in psychomotor ability and leadership.

Of course, no individual may be outstanding in all these areas. Youth who tend to exhibit any combination of special talents will need the curricular and instructional flexibility to demonstrate their unique skills. However, special attention to developing the talents of gifted students has lagged behind that for special needs students due to the virtual absence of U.S. legislation for gifted services and to the stigmas associated with gifted education, including that it is elitist, contributes to educational inequity, reduces the overall quality of general education, and represents a legal form of tracking (McGinnis & Stefanich, 2007; Smith, 1998).

These and other criticisms have led to a broader, more inclusive focus for gifted education that is reflected in the theme of *talent development*. According to Treffinger and Feldhusen (1996), the goal of talent development is to help able youth develop their abilities in all dimensions of human activity, not just intellectual and academic achievement. Coupled with this more inclusive focus for gifted education are broadened eligibility criteria for gifted programs. For example, in a number of states measures of creativity and motivation are used in addition to measures of mental ability and academic achievement for determining who should receive differentiated educational experiences and/or services beyond those normally provided by the general school program. The use of multiple measures, particularly ones that are sensitive to cultural and linguistic differences, has helped ensure that students from diverse populations are not overlooked when decisions are made about students' needs for certain levels and types of programs and services (Frasier, 1997). Thus, students selected to receive special programs or services will not only be those who have obtained high scores on tests of intelligence but also those who demonstrate potential to benefit from enhanced educational opportunities.

Once identified as able to benefit from special programs and services, Feldhusen (1997) recommends that adolescents work with school counselors, teachers, and parents to develop personalized, long-range talent development plans. Each student's plan is a way to focus more attention on talent development and may include information about the student's interests, prior experiences in gifted programs, standardized test scores, and current courses, as well as personal goals and recommendations for classes to be taken at school and extracurricular activities.

A number of programs, services, and opportunities that enable these bright and able students to carry out their development plans are provided in middle and secondary schools. Most involve some form of acceleration or enrichment. According to Schiever and Maker (1997), acceleration may take the form of service delivery or curriculum delivery. An example of acceleration as service delivery in middle school might involve a sixth-grader joining a seventh-grade class for science instruction. In high school it might involve a student passing a science course by examination or taking a science course on a part-time basis at a local college or university.

In contrast, an accelerated curriculum is one in which students move through the same subject matter as their peers but at a faster pace. When this type of acceleration occurs in a general education science class, it almost always involves providing differentiated instruction for the special students. Acceleration is sometimes scorned for interfering with students' social development; however, research indicates that acceleration does not impede social development. Acceleration does provide achievement gains beyond those possible when no special provisions are made for gifted students and tends to improve their motivation and confidence (Schiever & Maker, 1997; Van Tassel-Baska, 1986).

Enriched curricula or special enrichment programs permit gifted and talented students to have new experiences in addition to what is made available to other students. Enrichment can be provided by modifying or adding to the curriculum through activities such as field trips and WebQuests, science bowls, academic decathlons, and Saturday and summer mini-courses. Other forms of enrichment include mentor or apprenticeship programs that allow students to spend time working with scientists in the field or their laboratories. Science enrichment experiences are designed to develop students' thinking skills and to expand their content knowledge. Enrichment experiences may lead to the development of a product, such as a science fair exhibit or invention, that demonstrates creativity and cognitive growth (Schiever & Maker, 1997). Advanced Placement (AP) courses, which allow students to study college-level courses while still in high school, provide both acceleration and enrichment and exemplify the complementary nature of these two strategies to meet the needs of gifted students.

In heterogeneous classes, students of above-average intelligence and with special talents should carry out regular class work as well as special assignments. They can participate in introductory phases of units, fieldwork, and group work. Gifted students particularly benefit from student-centered instruction and the opportunity to investigate real problems.

The greatest help that can be given to gifted students is the opportunity to do original research. They prefer to investigate problems that have undisclosed outcomes. Their investigations may begin as an outgrowth of regular class work, but they should be encouraged to carry out their investigations in and out of school.

Stop and Reflect!

Before going on, consider the following questions:

- What purpose is served by an IEP? What information included in an IEP would be of benefit to a science teacher?
- What adaptations would make a science learning experience more suitable for a visually impaired student? For a student diagnosed with ADHD?
- How are accelerated and enrichment learning experiences different? Give an example of each type.

Differentiated Instruction

Our discussion to this point in the chapter makes it clear that diverse learners populate today's science classes. These students come to science classes with differences that influence their readiness to learn, their interests, and their learning preferences. These differences are significant enough to suggest that teachers must take them into account for all students to maximize their learning potential. Differentiation of teaching and learning routines is recognized as a means of providing for the learning needs of diverse students.

Tomlinson and her colleagues (2003) define *differentiation* as a teaching approach "in which teachers proactively modify curricula, teaching methods, resources, learning activities, and student products" (p. 120). Ideally differentiation would be applied to individual students, but in the context of science classes teachers' efforts to differentiate are most often directed toward groups of students, mainly for efficiency. For differentiation to be beneficial, it must be planned for and based on sound curricula and instructional practices.

To enhance the meaningfulness of our discussion of differentiation, a return to points made about unit planning in Chapter 3 is in order. Recall that a central theme of Chapter 3 was planning with the end in mind. We used this theme to argue that instructional planning should begin with the identification of the standards-based learning outcomes for a unit. This step should then be followed by the development of assessments that provide evidence of students' achievement of the learning outcomes. Finally, learning experiences should be selected or developed to enable students to perform well on the assessments.

Thus, in the context of unit planning and implementation, the focus of differentiation should be on (1) assessments that reflect the standards-based learning outcomes for the unit and (2) learning experiences that prepare students to perform well on the assessments. Making assessments and learning experiences the targets of differentiation will enable a teacher to attend to the diverse needs of students while preparing them to achieve the standards.

Before offering suggestions for making assessments and learning experiences responsive to the diverse needs of students, we say a few words about diagnostic assessment and its importance to differentiation. Tomlinson and McTighe (2006) point out the similar purposes served by diagnostics assessment and a medical examination. Just as a doctor needs information about patients' medical conditions in order to diagnose their illnesses, the teacher needs information about students' understandings, skills, and dispositions relevant to the unit's content in order to effectively differentiate. Recall from our discussion of diagnostic assessment in Chapter 4, that a pretest is one potential source of diagnostic information. Other sources of diagnostic information include concept maps, responses to problems and dilemmas, checklists, as well as interviews and journals. With information about students' strengths and preferences in hand, a teacher is ready to plan assessments and learning experiences that are responsive to their needs.

Assessment

Testing is the standard form of assessment in most science classes. Yet, many students would prefer to demonstrate their learning by different means. For example, some students might prefer to write stories, build models, or orally explain their thinking to demonstrate their learning. Differentiation of assessment is about providing students with options for demonstrating their learning. Of course, the options must provide evidence of learning consistent with standards-based learning outcomes.

One strategy for giving students options for demonstrating their learning is an adaptation of tic-tac-toe (Tomlinson & McTighe, 2006). As shown in Figure 9.4, a teacher could allow students to choose one of the twelve options to demonstrate their understandings or, to stress oral communication, a teacher might require students to choose one form of oral presentation and one other response mode from the visual or written options. The major challenge associated with providing students with such options is to devise a rubric that includes the criteria considered essential to the unit's learning goals. Fortunately, rubric builders, as discussed in Chapter 4, are available at several Web sites that can be used to construct rubrics that allow for varied response modes while including criteria that reflect essential learning goals.

The Differentiated Assessment Project (Bittel & Hernadez, 2006) offers other options for students to demonstrate their learning. Here, students choose from among a number of project ideas to demonstrate their learning associated with a unit. The projects are tied to letter grades that match levels of Bloom's taxonomy. Students choosing projects matched with the Analysis, Synthesis, and Evaluation levels of the taxonomy contract for As, while students choosing less cognitively demanding

FIGURE 9.4 Performance assessment options

Oral	Audio podcast	Lecture	Song	Story
Visual	Concept map	Photo gallery	Model	Cartoon
Written	Blog	"How to" manual	Poem	Fable

Based on information from Tomlinson, C. A., & McTighe, J. (2006). *Integrating differentiated instruction and understanding by design*. Alexandria, VA: Association for Supervision and Curriculum Development.

projects contract for Bs and Cs. Examples of astronomy project ideas that match the highest levels of Bloom's taxonomy include evaluating the astronomy content in a science fiction film and improving on a solar system model presented in a textbook.

As our examples suggest student performances allow for greater flexibility for differentiated assessment, but tests can also be differentiated by modifying test items based on such factors as reading level, mathematical difficulty, and cultural relevance. Whether performances or tests, differentiated assessment can allow students to demonstrate their learning in ways that play to their strengths.

Learning Experiences

Options for differentiating the science learning experiences in which students engage as part of a unit are almost limitless. Some options discussed in the previous sections of this chapter are appropriate for addressing the learning needs of culturally and linguistically diverse, female, and exceptional students. In addition, we encourage you to think about how the manipulation of key classroom elements can enhance the likelihood that diverse students will achieve success in a standards-based science classroom.

Tomlinson and McTighe (2006) identify the elements of time, space, resources, student grouping, instructional strategies, learning strategies, and teacher partnerships as elements over which teachers have much control and can manipulate on a daily basis to achieve desired student learning outcomes. Below we offer suggestions for flexibly using these seven elements to address specific learner needs in middle school and secondary science classroom.

Time

- Give students who work slowly due to language challenges or learning disabilities more time to complete assignments.
- Allow students who complete assignments early to enrich their understandings of the topic by examining related Web sites.

Space

- Set up learning stations in the classroom to enable students to learn concepts using a preferred learning style—visual, kinesthetic, or auditory.
- Permit easily distracted students to sit away from classmates during lectures and independent practice activities.

Resources

- Provide podcasts on topics addressed in assigned textbook sections for students who are struggling readers.
- Identify online and print sources in different languages of important science concepts for students who are English language learners.

Student Groupings

- Group students who are challenged by the same science concept or skill to allow for targeted instruction.
- Form groups based on differences in students' interests or cultural backgrounds to facilitate the sharing of perspectives.

Instructional Strategies

- Emphasize laboratory and field work to help students who learn by doing.
- Discuss the contributions of women and people of all cultural backgrounds to science in order to increase relevance and student motivation.

Learning Strategies

- Encourage students to discuss their science ideas with classmates as a way of checking for understanding.
- Promote the use of analogies, mnemonics, and songs that have special cultural associations as learning aids.

Teacher Partnerships

- Permit students who have mastered a concept to teach other students who find the concept challenging.

- Call on parents and community members from diverse groups who have science expertise to lead class sessions.

As you consider these seven classroom elements and the accompanying suggestions, you will no doubt think about other ways that they can be manipulated to address the diverse learning needs of today's students. Furthermore, as you spend time in middle school and secondary science classes you will begin to recognize patterns of student learning needs that can be addressed through differentiated instruction. For example, the need for targeted instruction is seen in just about all science classes. This need may be linked to student learning disabilities, excessive absences, or English language challenges. Providing differentiated learning experiences for students who need additional help to achieve the standards-based learning outcomes of a unit may occur through regular small-group meetings where key science concepts are addressed, special homework assignments, or online tutorials and practice sets.

Engaging Diverse Students As Science Learners

Consistent with the National Science Teachers Association (NSTA) *Standards for Science Teacher Preparation*, you will be expected to demonstrate your ability to plan for the needs of diverse learners in a unit and engage them in productive science learning experiences. NSTA Standard 5: General Skills of Teaching states:

> *To show that they are prepared to create a community of diverse learners, teachers must demonstrate that they:*
>
> a. *Successfully promote the learning of science students with different abilities, needs, interests, and backgrounds.*
> b. *Successfully organize and engage students in collaborative learning using different student group learning strategies.*
> c. *Understand and build effectively upon the prior beliefs, knowledge, experiences, and interests of students. (NSTA, 2003, p. 21)*

We recommend that you initiate your efforts at differentiating instruction with a unit topic with which you are very familiar and use diagnostic information to guide your planning and enactment of differentiated assessments and learning experiences.

Differentiating assessments and learning experiences is challenging and time consuming, but necessary for helping all students be successful science learners. While no one can expect you, as a beginning teacher, to be an expert at differentiation, it is reasonable to expect that you will make strides to provide for the learning needs of the diverse students in your classes. When doing so, please keep in mind that your first efforts can always be improved in the future.

ASSESSING AND REVIEWING

Analysis and Synthesis

1. In 2061 Halley's Comet will again be visible from Earth, and science education will be radically different than it is today, so say the framers of the Project 2061 *Benchmarks*. Given what you know about today's school-age population, what do you think will be the nature of this population in 2061? Are the factors that affect student success in science in 2061 likely to be the same as they are today? Explain.
2. A common medical practice today is for a physician to prescribe a calcium supplement for a new mother to replenish the calcium lost during childbirth. In China, new mothers have traditionally been fed a thick broth, high in calcium ions, prepared by boiling pig's feet in vinegar. Even today, many Asian-American mothers eat dishes of sweet-and-sour pork in the weeks following childbirth (based on a description by Barba, 1998, pp. 61–62). How could a science teacher use the information about this Chinese practice to formulate a multicultural science learning experience for students?

Practical Considerations

3. Use your local library and the Internet to develop a plan to differentiate instruction for a science concept that you will probably teach. Which key classroom element or elements (i.e., time, space, resources, etc.) could be manipulated in your differentiation plan?
4. Interview a teacher whose classes include students ranging from the learning disabled to the gifted and talented. Question the teacher about how he or she addresses the special learning needs. Share your findings with classmates.
5. Observe a science class that includes students who are English language learners. While observing, note the accommodations that the teacher makes to address the learning needs of these students. Talk with

the teacher after your observation to learn more about the accommodations you observed and the teacher's assessment of the accommodations' success.

Developmental Considerations

6. Start a collection of newspaper clippings, magazine articles, and Internet sites that present information about strategies for achieving equity among science learners.
7. Attend a regional or national conference of the National Science Teachers Association (NSTA). Participate in sessions that address differentiated instruction.
8. Search out funding agencies that support projects focusing on the science learning needs of diverse students. Work with colleagues to develop a proposal to support the implementation of a project to address the diverse learning needs of students at your school.

Resources to Examine

Inclusion in Science Education for Students with Disabilities. [Online.] Available at: www.as.wvu.edu/~scidis

This Web site is a comprehensive resource for teachers seeking suggestions for accommodating the science learning needs of students with disabilities. The site is organized into sections for easy access of information. One section provides more than 800 teaching strategies for students with learning disabilities and physical impairments. Other sections present suggestions for developing IEPs and general information about learning disabilities and physical impairments.

Other People's Children: Cultural Conflict in the Classroom. 1995. Lisa Delpit. New York: The New Press.

This book is a collection of essays that provides insights about how to navigate cultural differences in the classroom. It highlights inequities faced by poor and culturally diverse students brought about through stereotyping and the learner-deficit assumptions held by some teachers. Reading the book will instill a willingness to accommodate diversity.

Integrating Differentiated Instruction and Understanding by Design. 2006. Carol Ann Tomlinson and Jay McTighe. Alexandria, VA: Association for Supervision and Curriculum Development.

This book presents practical advice about how to differentiate instruction in a standards-based classroom. Chapters provide a rationale for the integration of differentiated instruction and core ideas from *Understanding by Design.* Also emphasized in the chapters are notions of responsive teaching that takes into account the diverse academic needs of today's students.

Inclusive-Classroom Problem Solver: Structures and Supports to Serve All Learners. 2007. Constance McGrath. Portsmouth, NH: Heinemann.

In addition to serving as a guide to learning disabilities, this book offers guidance for accommodating students with learning disabilities in regular classrooms. Chapters that address accommodations speak to the classroom layout, instruction and assessment, classroom climate, and relationships with parents.

White Teachers/Diverse Classrooms: A Guide to Building Inclusive Schools, Promoting High Expectations, and Eliminating Racism. 2006. Edited by Julie Landsman and Chance W. Lewis. Sterling, VA: Stylus.

This is a collection of essays that offers concrete and practical ideas for improving the school experiences of African Americans and other minority students. The essays approach the problem of poor academic performance among ethic minorities by encouraging teachers to consider the strengths that the students and their communities bring to the classroom.

References

Aikenhead, G. S. (1998). Border crossings: Culture, school science and assimilation of students (pp. 86–100). In D. A. Roberts & L. Ostman (Eds.) *Problems of meaning in science curriculum*. New York: Teachers College Press, Columbia University.

American Chemical Society. (2006). *Chemistry in the community* (5th ed.). New York: Freeman.

Americans with Disabilities Act, 42 U.S.C., sec. 121101. (1990).

Atwater, M. M., Crockett, D., & Kilpatrick, W. J. (1996). Constructing multicultural science classrooms: Quality science for all students. In J. Rhoton & P. Bowers (Eds.), *Issues in science education* (pp. 167–176). Washington, DC: National Science Teachers Association.

Atwater, M. M., & Riley, J. P. (1993). Multicultural science education: Perspectives, definitions, and research agenda. *Science Education, 77*, 661–668.

Baptiste, H. P. & Key, S. G. (1996). Cultural inclusion: Where does your program stand? *The Science Teacher, 63*(2), 32–35.

Barba, R. (1998). *Science in the multicultural classroom*. Boston: Allyn & Bacon.

Barton, A. C. (1998). *Feminist science education*. New York: Teachers College Press.

Barton, A. C., & Yang, K. (2000). The culture of power and science education: Learning from Miguel. *Journal of Research in Science Teaching, 37*(8), 871–889.

Bateman, B. D. (1996). *Better IEPs: How to develop legally correct and educationally useful programs*. Longmont, CO: Sopris West.

Beattie, J. R., Jordan, L. & Algozzine, R. (2006). *Making inclusion work: Effective practices for all teachers*. Thousand Oaks, CA: Corwin Press.

Belenky, M. F., Clinchy, B. M., Goldberger, N. R., Tarule, J. M. (1986). *Women's ways of knowing*. New York: Basic Books.

Bentley, D., & Watts, D. M. (1986). Courting the positive virtues: A case for feminist science. *European Journal of Science Education, 8*, 121–134.

Bittel, K., & Hernandez, D. (2006, December). Differentiated assessment. *Science Scope*, 49–50.

Delpit, L. (1995). *Other people's children: Cultural conflict in the classroom*. New York: New Press.

Donavan, S. M. & Cross, C. T. (Eds.) (2003). *Minority students in special and gifted education*. Washington, DC: National Academies Press.

Emdin, C. (2008). The three C's of urban science education. *Phi Delta Kappan, 89*(10), 772–775.

Feldhusen, J. (1997). Secondary services, opportunities, and activities for talented youth. In N. Colangelo & G. A. Davis (Eds.), *Handbook of gifted education* (pp. 189–197). Boston: Allyn & Bacon.

Ferguson, R. (2003). Teachers' perceptions and expectations and the Black-White test score gap. *Urban Education, 38*(4), 460–507.

Frasier, M. (1997). Gifted minority students: Reframing approaches to their identification and education. In N. Colangelo & G. A. Davis (Eds.), *Handbook of gifted education* (pp. 498–515). Boston: Allyn & Bacon.

Hodson, D. (1993). In search of a rationale for multicultural science education. *Science Education, 77*, 685–711.

Hofman, H. M. (1994). Learning disabilities (pp. 71–87). In J. Egelston-Dodd (Ed.), *Proceedings of a working conference on science for persons with disabilities*. Cedar Falls, IA: University of Northern Iowa.

Holbrook, C. L. (2006). Low expectations are the worst form of racism. In J. Landsman & C. W. Lewis (Eds.), *White teachers/diverse classrooms* (pp. 110–121). Sterling, VA: Stylus.

Hudicourt-Barnes, J. (2003). The use of argumentation in Haitian Creole science classrooms. *Harvard Educational Review, 73*(1), 73–93.

Kahle, J. B. (1996). Equitable science education: A discrepancy model. In L. H. Parker, L. J. Rennie, & B. J. Fraser (Eds.), *Gender, science and mathematics: Shortening the shadow* (pp. 129–139). Dordrecht, The Netherlands: Kluwer Academic.

Keller, E. C., Jr. (1994). Science education for the motor/orthopedically-impaired students (pp. 1–39). In J. Egelston-Dodd (Ed.), *Proceedings of a working conference on science for persons with disabilities*. Cedar Falls: University of Northern Iowa.

Keller, E. C. (2003). *Inclusion in science education for students with disabilities*. Retrieved June 4, 2008, from www.as.wvu.edu/~scidis

Lee, O., Fradd, S. H., & Sutman, F. X. (1995). Science knowledge and cognitive strategy use among culturally and linguistically diverse students. *Journal of Research in Science Teaching, 32*, 797–816.

Loving, C. C. (1995). Comments on "Multiculturalism, universalism, and science education." *Science Education, 79*, 341–348.

Luft, J. (1998). Multicultural science education: An overview. *Journal of Science Teacher Education, 9*, 103–122.

Lynch, S., Atwater, M., Cawley, J., Eccles, J., Lee, O., Marrett, C., Rojas-Medlin, D., Secada, W., Stefanich, G., & Willetto, A. (1996). *An equity blueprint for Project 2061, 2nd draft*. Washington, DC: American Association for the Advancement of Science.

Mastropieri, M. A., & Scruggs, T. E. (1995, Summer). Teaching science to students with disabilities. *Teaching Exceptional Children*, 10–13.

Matthews, M. (1994). *Science teaching: The role of history and philosophy of science*. New York: Routledge.

McGinnis, J. R., & Stefanich, G. P. (2007). Special needs and talents in science learning. In S. K. Abell & N. G. Lederman (Eds.), *Handbook of research in science education* (pp. 287–318). Mahwah, NJ: Erlbaum.

McNamara, B. E. (2007). *Learning disabilities: Bridging the gap between research and classroom practice*. Upper Saddle River, NJ: Merrill/Prentice Hall.

National Science Board. (2004). *Science and engineering indicators 2004*. National Science Foundation: Arlington, VA. Retrieved May 19, 2008, from www.nsf.gov/statistics/seind04/front/nsb.htm

Ogawa, M. (1995). Science education in a multiscience perspective. *Science Education, 79*, 583–593.

Parkinson, J. (1994). *The effective teaching of secondary science*. London: Longman.

Patton, J. R. (1995, Summer). Teaching science to students with special needs. *Teaching Exceptional Children*, 4–6.

Reiss, M. J. (1993). *Science education for a pluralist society*. Buckingham, England: Open University Press.

Rennie, L. J. (2001). Gender equity in science teacher preparation. In D. R. Lavoie & W-M. Roth (Eds.) *Models for science teacher preparation: Theory into practice* (pp. 127–147). Dordrecht, The Netherlands: Kluwer Academic.

Renzulli, J. S., & Reis, S. M. (1997). The schoolwide enrichment model: New directions for developing high-end learning (pp. 136–154). In N. Colangelo & G. A. Davis (Eds.), *Handbook of gifted education*. Boston: Allyn & Bacon.

Schiever, S. W., & Maker, C. J. (1997). Enrichment and acceleration: An overview and new directions. In N. Colangelo & G. A. Davis (Eds.), *Handbook of gifted education* (pp. 113–125). Boston: Allyn & Bacon.

Scruggs, T. E., Mastropieri, M. A., & Boon, R. (1998). Science education for students with disabilities: A review of recent research. *Studies in Science Education, 32*, 21–44.

Siegel, H. (1997). Science education: Multicultural and universal. *Interchange, 28*, 97–108.

Smith, D. D. (1998). *Introduction to special education: Teaching in an age of challenge*. Boston: Allyn & Bacon.

Stanley, W. B., & Brickhouse, N. W. (1994). Multiculturalism, universalism, and science education. *Science Education, 78*, 387–398.

Steele, M. M. (2008). Helping students with learning disabilities succeed. *The Science Teacher, 75*(3), 38–42.

Sutman, F. X., Guzman, A., & Schwartz, W. (1993). *Teaching science effectively to limited English proficient students*. ERIC Reproduction No. ED 357113.

Tobin, K. (1996). Gender equity and the enacted science curriculum. In L. H. Parker, L. J. Rennie, & B. J. Fraser (Eds.), *Gender, science and mathematics: Shortening the shadow* (pp. 119–127). Dordrecht, The Netherlands: Kluwer Academic.

Tomlinson, C. A. (2003). *Fulfilling the promise of the differentiated classroom: Strategies and tools for response teaching*. Alexandria, VA: Association for Supervision and Curriculum Development.

Tomlinson, C. A., & McTighe, J. (2006). *Integrating differentiated instruction and understanding by design*. Alexandria, VA: Association for Supervision and Curriculum Development.

Treffinger, D. J., & Feldhusen, J. F. (1996). Talent recognition and development: Successor to gifted education. *Journal of Education of the Gifted, 19*, 181–193.

U.S. Commission on Civil Rights. (1992). *Civil rights issues facing Asian Americans in the 1990s*. Washington, DC: U.S. Government Printing Office.

U.S. Department of Education, Center for Education Statistics. (2003). *The condition of education 2003*, NCES 2003-067. Washington, DC: U. S. Government Printing Office.

U.S. Department of Education, Center for Education Statistics. (2007). *The condition of education 2007*, NCES 2007-064. Washington, DC: U.S. Government Printing Office. Available at http://nces.ed.gov/pubsearch/pubsinfo.asp?pubid=2007064

Van Tassel-Baska, J. (1986). Acceleration. In C. J. Maker (Ed.), *Critical issues in gifted education. Defensible programs for the gifted* (pp. 179–196). Austin, TX: Pro-Ed.

Villegas, A. M. & Lucas, T. (2002). Preparing culturally responsive teachers. *Journal of Teacher Education, 53*(1), 20–32.

Watson, S. (2004, February). Opening the science doorway. *The Science Teacher*, 32–35.

Watson, S. & Johnston, L. (2007). Assistive technology in the inclusive science classroom. *The Science Teacher, 73*(3), 34–38.

Weld, J. (1997). Viewpoints: Universalism & multiculturalism in science education. *The American Biology Teacher, 59*, 264–267.

Chapter

10

Learning in Middle Grades and Secondary Schools

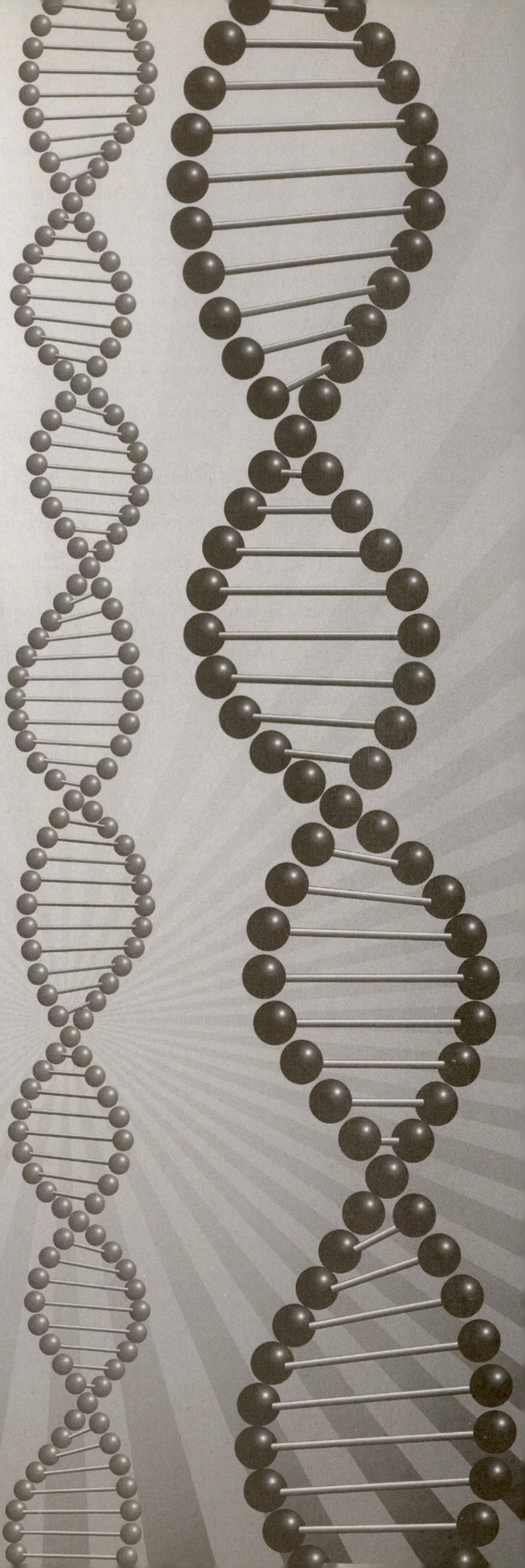

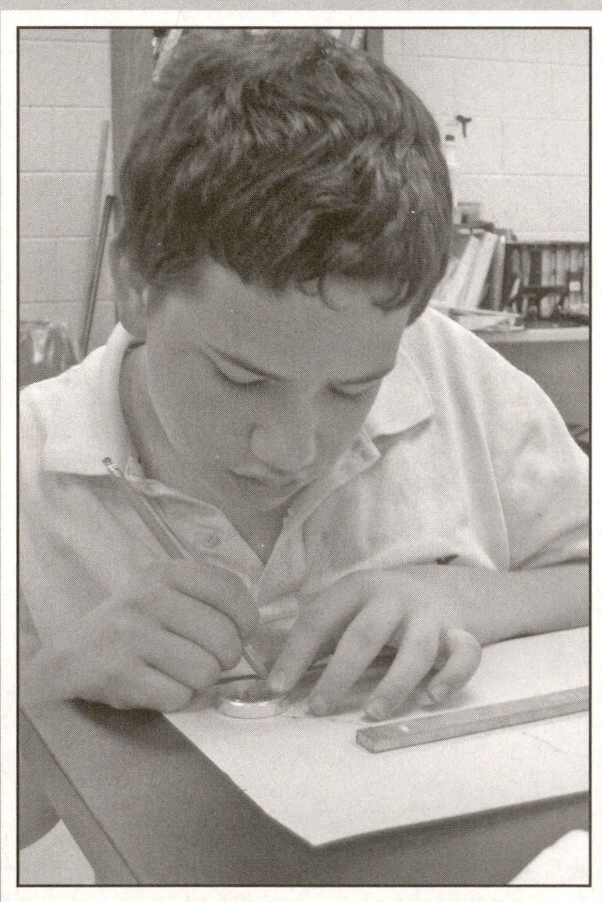

Meaningful science learning requires time for students to build their understanding.

Beginning science teachers often plan their instruction with the subject matter content in mind, identifying the knowledge they want students to learn. Because of this focus, they spend very little time considering what students know and the misconceptions students bring to science class. Without more attention paid to what students know and think, very little learning may occur. Further, there is more to effective teaching than focusing on the curricular content. While science teachers must understand a great deal about students' knowledge, they must also be sensitive to students' motivation to learn science. Science teachers must be aware that some students from diverse populations may hold negative feelings about school science and their teachers who are from the dominant socioeconomic class, all of which may be in conflict with their desire to learn. In order to advance scientific literacy among the nation's youth, science teachers must be knowledgeable about what learners bring to the science classroom: "their knowledge, language, beliefs, cultural practices, and roles in communities and power relationships" (Anderson, 2007, p. 6).

AIMS OF THE CHAPTER

Use the questions that follow to guide your thinking about student learning and how you can advance it during instruction:

- How would you distinguish cognitive psychology from behavioral psychology with regard to learning science subject matter?
- How would you explain the effects of students' alternative conceptions and motivation to learn science?
- How would you describe instructional practices that use the following techniques to improve student learning: prior knowledge, conceptual change, analogies, models, modeling to learn, and concept maps?

Introduction

The work of cognitive psychologists, learning theorists, and science education researchers can provide some understandings that can help science teachers to actively engage students in learning. One of the recommendations from cognitive psychologists is to view learning as an *active process* of student engagement with ideas and materials, rather than a process whereby students take in information passively. Also, they remind us that learning begins with what the student *knows*, which is the foundation of the learning process as well as the starting point. It follows then that students' ideas should be *modified* during instruction and become more complex and differentiated, building gradually over time through a series of small steps toward more coherent and correct scientific conceptions.

It is important to note that students must find the content and instruction *meaningful* in order for them to pursue learning with interest. Students must be encouraged to *represent their ideas*, often and in many ways. This view of learning is in contrast to one that considers learning as the acquisition of knowledge, mostly through the transmission of science content that has been organized by the teacher or the textbook, ready-made for internalization and retention for future use.

Today, many science educators believe constructivism is a good guide for teaching and learning science. They have adopted the recommendations from cognitive psychologists to focus on students' ideas. Science teachers are advised to incorporate into their instruction contradictions that puzzle students in order to cause them to modify their understanding. The use of concrete experiences and discourse is invaluable for the learning process. Conceptual mapping of key ideas can be useful in promoting the meaningful organization of science content. Images, analogies, models, and modeling to learn also can help students to make mental connections between what they know and the abstract concepts that we want them to learn.

Cognitive psychologists, science educators, and experienced science teachers have come to realize that learning science and becoming scientifically literate is a complex, slow process. These professionals have observed how difficult it is for some students to learn the most fundamental principles of biology, chemistry, physics, and earth and space sciences. They note that an understanding of this subject matter is formed over time through considerable experience, both inside and outside of school. Further, many students have not mastered the simplest science process skills, such as making accurate observations, graphing data, and designing investigations. Because of the difficulty some students have in learning science, science teachers must understand and use many strategies and techniques to guide their planning, teaching, and assessment of student learning.

Although constructivism is popular, behavioral principles and theories of learning are also important in education. Science teachers should use many of the principles learned from behavioral psychologists to complement what is now popular in cognitive psychology (Duit & Treagust, 1998). A previous chapter in this textbook focused on teaching science—teaching skills, instructional strategies, and learning techniques. In this chapter we will help you to form a deeper understanding for using these strategies and techniques in order to help students develop meaningful science understandings.

 Cognitive Approaches and Strategies for Teaching Science

Pupils come to science lessons with ideas about the natural world. Effective science teaching takes account of these ideas and provides activities which enable pupils to make the journey from their current understanding to a more scientific view. (Driver, Squires, Rushworth, & Wood-Robinson, 1994, p. xii)

Constructivism

Constructivism is a movement that has guided research and the teaching of science. The central thesis of the movement is that humans construct knowledge as opposed to knowledge being transmitted into the mind. Constructivism stresses the importance of considering what is already in the learner's mind as a place to begin instruction. Learning is regarded as an active process whereby students construct personal meaning of the subject matter through their interactions with the physical and social world. The student is the one who must make sense out of experiences. Knowledge is not just out there in textbooks or in teachers' heads ready to be transferred into the minds of students. Instead, "out there" is where one finds information and experiences that are incorporated into existing knowledge structures, which in turn are modified and expanded to reflect science.

A skilled teacher, who engages students in thinking, asking questions, testing ideas, representing thoughts, and explaining phenomena, can facilitate the learning process. As stated in the quote from Driver and her colleagues, effective science teaching must take into account what students know, then modify this knowledge so that it reflects scientific views.

The idea that the mind constructs useful ideas of reality has implications for instruction. If people have to conceptualize reality, they need to process, organize, and reflect upon it. Thus, learning becomes an active process that builds on prior knowledge. What learners know becomes as important as what we want them to know. Teaching and learning must be an interactive process that engages learners in constructing knowledge. Negotiation takes place between the teacher and students, whereby the teacher moves students toward greater understanding of reality. Often, these interactions take time, requiring many small steps toward reforming and building new ideas (Driver, Asoko, Leach, Mortimer, & Scott, 1994). Through this approach, students' ideas become more differentiated and more closely resemble scientific concepts.

There are at least two sources for constructing knowledge—personal experience with the physical world and interaction with the social world. Jean Piaget, Lev Vygotsky, and David Ausubel made significant contributions to these learning perspectives. During the last half of the twentieth century, Piaget's work on cognitive development provided educators with one foundation for constructivism. His theory of mental structures and logical mathematical operations has given us greater insight into development and learning. Importantly, the work underscores the significance of concrete experience in developing cognitive structures. Interaction with objects and events stimulates the construction of knowledge, as opposed to passive listening. For Piaget, it is the learner who brings to bear mental operations in reaction to the environment, engaging learning and furthering cognitive development. In translating this theory into practice, science teaching has promoted more experiences with concrete materials, emphasizing manipulation of objects, testing ideas, and organizing data. More emphasis has been placed on the use of contradictions and discrepant events to cause cognitive dissonance, motivating students to wonder why and find out how. Today, Piaget's equilibration concept provides teachers with a theoretical explanation of how assimilation and accommodation can advance learning.

Another dimension of learning and development is the role of others—peers and adults—in the construction of knowledge. Whereas Piaget focused his attention on physical interaction, Vygotsky focused much of his attention on social interaction and the importance to the process of communication. He believed that peers and adults greatly influence learning and the acquisition of science concepts. The organization of ideas by others has enormous influence on what people learn. Although Vygotsky believed, as Piaget proposes, that knowledge is constructed and developed over time, he stressed that the major contribution to cognition is social interaction. He used the idea of a *zone of proximal development* to focus attention on the potential (Sternberg, 1995) for learning and development via adult interaction. The zone of proximal (or potential) development is a range of possible development between what learners can do by themselves and what they can do with assistance from others who are at a more advanced level of thinking and possess more knowledge (Vygotsky, 1978).

For Vygotsky, direct instruction had a more influential role on the assimilation of ideas than for Piaget. Further, he stressed the importance of language in the mediation of ideas, which advances learning and development. Vygotsky emphasized that students learn about science from others. Similarly, scientists learn about their enterprise by interacting with other scientists and examining the ideas that they have contributed to the discipline. Thus, knowledge is also a product of culture that has been constructed over time, growing and changing as the result of human interaction with ideas that have been socially constructed.

David Ausubel also promoted a cognitive approach to learning, but he focused on the conceptual rather than the operative form of knowledge that was stressed by Piaget. Ausubel advocated that reception learning is directed toward discipline-based concepts that can be learned by students, and in fact most of what is learned, both in and out of school, is acquired through the transmission of ideas rather than through discovering them. However, he advised that reception learning must be meaningful in order for it to be effective. Ausubel cautioned educators that discovery as well as reception learning can be rote, and that they must avoid this situation and take every measure to make learning meaningful. However, he pointed out that students must relate the material under study to their existing cognitive structures of organized information (Ausubel, 1963). When students learn in a meaningful manner, they form mental connections between new ideas and the relevant elements within their existing cognitive structures. Ausubel's work has stressed the importance of logical organization of science content and the use of concept maps.

Today, constructivism has taken on a different meaning for many educators from the one widely used during the 1960s, 1970s, and 1980s. In the past, the Piagetian stage theory and his generalizable thinking skills dominated a great deal of teaching and learning in science education. The theory that developmental reasoning sets limits on what students can learn was central to the stage theory. As a result, considerable emphasis was placed on general reasoning ability with much less emphasis on learning specific concepts. This movement is evidenced by the importance placed on learning science process skills, which has been observed in science education over the past 50 years. For some science educators, this stance on separating content and process deemphasizes the importance of subject matter content and elevates the importance of science process skills. As a result of the stress placed on general reasoning skills and problem solving associated with the Piagetian psychology, neo-Piagetian researchers suggest that we modify our views regarding learning science and that we place more emphasis on the acquisition of subject matter content and science concepts.

Conceptual Change and Concept Development

A central element of learning science is what students *know* when they come to science class. All students have preformed conceptions about phenomena. Their minds are not empty, ready to be filled with a body of scientific knowledge. They already possess many ideas. Unfortunately, what students know frequently does not correspond well with scientific knowledge. Some researchers view students' ideas as primitive or naive or as misconceptions (errors in what has been learned). Others refer to students' knowledge as *alternative conceptions*, different from accepted beliefs, but nevertheless very important. Wandersee, Mintzes, and Novak (1994) provide science educators with an extensive review of alternative conceptions research in which they present a useful synthesis of eight knowledge claims (Figure 10.1). A brief discussion of these claims highlights important findings regarding students' scientific conceptions.

There is a strong consensus that students possess alternative conceptions about the natural world before, during, and after school science instruction (claim 1). For this reason, students' conceptions must become a focus of instruction and their ideas the starting point for instruction. The task of science teachers is to *change* students' ideas that are not in line with science, ideas that will be prevalent among many students of different ages, abilities, genders, and cultures (claim 2). Even the most capable students hold ideas about basic science that are not correct. We simply cannot cover up these alternative conceptions by piling on new information, nor can we erase them by logical presentation. For some of the most important concepts, alternative conceptions persist beyond formal instruction. Yes, these alternative conceptions "hang on" even after science course participation (claim 3). With certain natural phenomena, alternative conceptions parallel the growth of that knowledge as evidenced by explanations put forth by scientists and philosophers in earlier times (claim 4). This is especially evident when students are attempting to learn about abstract concepts such as force and motion.

Where do these alternative conceptions originate? In our diverse multicultural society, students from many different backgrounds arrive at the classroom. Their perceptions and beliefs vary widely (claim 5). Consider, for example, students' views of modern medicine. Those from families of means may hold the belief that going to the doctor for treatment of an illness is beneficial and is a common practice. Some students from poor immigrant families may hold the belief that doctors are to be avoided, and only in a life-and-death situation do they go to a doctor or hospital. Students from these different backgrounds and belief systems will interact with instruction on disease and medicine in different ways. Not only is family background a source for alternative conceptions, but textbooks, personal experiences, and teachers also contribute. Often science teachers possess the same alternative conceptions as do their students (claim 6).

The distressing fact is that students' alternative conceptions interact with the conceptions presented in school science, resulting in varied learning outcomes, some of which are not desired (claim 7). Today, researchers are coming to accept the idea that learning science is not a matter of simply adding information or replacing existing information. After many days and even

FIGURE 10.1 This set of knowledge claims derived from the research literature on alternative conceptions can be used to guide teaching and science learning.

Knowledge Claims About Alternative Conceptions

Claim 1: Learners come to formal science instruction with a diverse set of alternative conceptions about natural objects and events.

Claim 2: The alternative conceptions that learners bring to formal science instruction cut across age, ability, gender, and cultural boundaries.

Claim 3: Alternative conceptions are tenacious and resistant to extinction by conventional teaching strategies.

Claim 4: Alternative conceptions often parallel explanations of natural phenomena offered by previous generations of scientists and philosophers.

Claim 5: Alternative conceptions have their origins in diverse sets of personal experiences including direct observations and perceptions, peer culture and language, and in teachers' explanations and instructional materials.

Claim 6: Teachers often subscribe to the same alternative conceptions as their students.

Claim 7: Learners' prior knowledge interacts with knowledge presented in formal instruction, resulting in a diverse set of unintended learning outcomes.

Claim 8: Instructional approaches that facilitate conceptual change can be effective classroom tools.

From J. H. Wandersee, J. J. Mintzes, and J. D. Novak (1994), Research on alternative conceptions in science. In D. L. Gabel (Ed.), *Handbook of research on science teaching* (p. 195). Upper Saddle River, NJ: Merrill/Prentice Hall.

weeks of instruction, students fail to walk away with certain facts and beliefs because they are still grounded in what they knew prior to instruction. Further, that which takes place during science instruction sometimes merely serves to reinforce what some students believe. Attempting to teach about the evolution of animal species, from simple life forms to humans, is a good example of how personal belief in special creation is very resistant to change. However, for many science topics, there are change strategies that seem promising in moving students toward more scientifically accepted ideas (claim 8).

How do science teachers help students to understand and explain major science concepts? A teaching strategy recommended by Driver (1988) to facilitate conceptual change, from a constructivist point of view, is shown in Figure 10.2. In the teaching sequence presented in the figure, the teacher begins with a brief *orientation,* which introduces students to what they will be studying. This is followed by the *elicitation* phase in which students are asked to present their ideas. This activity is effective when conducted in small groups because all students can participate and put forth their conceptions. Each group can present its descriptions and explanations, placing them on flip charts for the entire class to view and discuss, which will help to *clarify* student understanding. Similarities and differences among ideas are noted. Here is where students' prior knowledge is made explicit and clear. This information is important because it is the knowledge base that must be restructured during the unit of study.

A powerful step in this sequence is the introduction of *conflict*. When students experience events that are contrary to what they believe or think, they take note. This can cause students to reconsider their ideas about phenomena.

The *construction* phase is where students engage in a variety of learning activities to attain the desired conceptions. It is essential that students verbalize their knowledge, using proper terms. They also can test ideas and compare and contrast the results with others in the class. Students can design experiments and engage in problem solving.

The teacher should *evaluate* students' understanding after the construction phase. How well have students learned the intended concepts or principles? Probably at this point it will be determined that some re-teaching needs to occur.

When most students have mastered the new content, they are ready to *apply* that knowledge to new situations. This step can lend greater meaning to the concepts, principles, and theories under study and help to form richer cognitive connections in the mind of the learner.

FIGURE 10.2 An instructional sequence to facilitate conceptual change of abstract science concepts.

Conceptual Change Instructional Sequence

Orientation:	Begin the instruction with a focus on what is about to be learned.
Elicitation:	Call on students to explain their ideas of the concept under study.
Clarification:	Probe students to clarify their understanding.
Conflict:	Create discrepant events that cause the learners to see that their conceptions may be incorrect.
Construction:	Help students to view their ideas differently and to provide more correct explanations.
Evaluation:	Assess student's understandings of the concepts under study.
Application:	Provide instances that apply what has been learned, especially in everyday life.
Review:	Ask each student to describe how his or her conceptions have changed from the beginning of the instructional sequence to the present.

From R. Driver (1988), Theory into practice II: A constructivist approach to curriculum development. In P. Fensham (Ed.), *Development and dilemmas in science education* (p. 141). Philadelphia: Falmer Press.

Finally, the teaching experience will end with a *review* of what was to be learned, permitting students to compare what they first thought regarding the concepts under study with what they learned from many instructional experiences.

The constructivist/conceptual change approach aims toward teaching a smaller number of science concepts, placing greater emphasis upon understanding. The teacher begins with students' prior knowledge, urging them to reflect on the ideas and beliefs they possess regarding a particular science concept or principle. Many opportunities are provided for students to find personal meaning from interacting with objects, events, and people. In addition, there is a deliberate attempt to utilize relevant contexts with which students can identify. Finally, there is a realization by the teacher that student misconceptions and naive ideas may continue after the completion of the unit of study.

Students come to science class with a "commonsense view of phenomena, which they have constructed through personal experiences and social interactions with others" (Driver et al., 1994). These commonsense views differ from scientific views and do not provide a coherent, accurate picture of the world. Nevertheless, these ideas serve the learner in everyday life and are difficult to replace. Science teachers can help students to acquire scientific conceptions with instruction that promotes both personal and social construction of knowledge through concrete experiences and teacher intervention. It is the teacher's role to introduce students to the culture of the scientific community, which cannot be discovered by students. The skillful teacher "introduces new ideas or cultural tools where necessary and provides the support and guidance for students to make sense of these for themselves" (Driver, Squires, et al., 1994, p. 11).

Stop and Reflect!

The section on alternative conceptions and conceptual change should impress upon you the significance of a psychologically based body of knowledge that relates to science teaching. Before going on to the next section in this chapter, do the following:

- Make a list of important assumptions regarding the alternative conceptions that you should consider when teaching science.
- Identify a scientific principle, law, or theory, and design a sequence of instructions that will help a given age group of students to change their ideas and guide them toward more correct scientific understanding. A beneficial approach to this activity might be to work with a partner or group of peers.

Contradictions and Equilibration

"Knowledge is not a copy of reality. To know an object, to know an event, is not simply to look at it and make a mental copy or image of it. To know an object is to act on it. To know is to modify, to

> *transform the object, and to understand the process of this transformation, and as a consequence to understand the way the object is constructed. An operation is the essence of knowledge; it is an interiorized action which modifies the object of the knowledge."*
>
> —*Piaget (1964)*

This quote by Piaget underscores a central theme in cognitive psychology: Learning is an active process. It is not a transmission process whereby knowledge is photocopied by the nervous system, but an interactive process whereby mental actions lead toward the understanding of objects and events that make up our world. The growth of knowledge is tied to internal mechanisms and cognitive organization. What implications do these views have for teaching science? What can science teachers do to encourage students to think deeply in order to construct a body of knowledge that they understand and can apply?

Piaget used the concept of *equilibration* to explain learning and cognitive development (Piaget, 1971). His conception of equilibration is that of a dynamic, continuous process that controls intelligence and learning (Furth, 1969). This process coordinates what infants, children, adolescents, and adults do when interacting with the world around them. It regulates their thinking and intellectual responses and does so by affecting what individuals can react to and how they respond. Piaget used the terms *assimilation* and *accommodation* to explain equilibration, suggesting how learning and development progress.

When an individual takes in information from objects and events, he or she assimilates it into existing cognitive structures. The cognitive organism perceives (assimilates) only what it can "fit into" the structures it already has (von Glasersfeld, 1995). Note that this notion is central to constructivist psychology, which stresses the belief that new knowledge builds upon prior knowledge. Constructivist thinking would question the value of a learning situation where the ideas to learn have no connection with existing ideas in the mind of the learner. For example, if a person were in a cafeteria line and saw a vegetable that she enjoyed eating, she would recognize it and perhaps take it. This individual would assimilate the idea right into her organization of foods. If she did not recognize a particular food, however, the chances are high that she would not place it on her tray. We would question a science teacher's effectiveness in trying to explain Einstein's theory of gravitation to a group of middle school students who have no sense or knowledge of space-time curvature. Where is the foundation for the geometry of curved space in the cognitive structures of these students? The presence of already existing knowledge increases the possibility for the learners to fit external ideas into their thinking, assimilate them into their schemata, and therefore find these ideas meaningful.

Along with assimilation, *accommodation* occurs (Piaget, 1971). When one assimilates information and events, he or she must also accommodate to it. Accommodation is the modification of existing cognitive structures to fit the ideas that one is internalizing. The degree to which individuals have to modify their existing beliefs and ideas depends upon the situation. Again, consider the cafeteria line. When people select a food that they eat regularly and place it on their tray, they accommodate the selection process with relative ease. However, if a friend suggests that you try an unknown vegetable, because it is a delicious food, you may try it. As you reach for the dish, you will be convincing yourself that this vegetable is going to suit your taste. Regardless of how the vegetable tastes, you will have learned something new about this food as well as the trust you place in the friend. Now you have accommodated, modifying your knowledge about eating this food.

The continuous equilibration process of assimilation and accommodation is one way to envision the growth and differentiation of knowledge as well as a mechanism for learning science. How does this theory assist us to teach science in a manner that will help students better understand important abstract ideas?

Piaget and others (Lawson, 1994; Fosnot, 1996) recommend the use of *contradictions* to stimulate assimilation and especially accommodation. Situations that contradict what students think or believe will get their attention. Discrepant events that challenge what people know or believe create puzzlement, causing them to think more deeply and to alter their worldview (Kasschau, 1986). Even classroom discussion can cause cognitive perturbation, creating cognitive disequilibrium.

Discrepant events are used by science teachers to challenge students to think and also encourage them to focus on a concept, law, or principle under study. For example, Bernoulli's principle is used to explain a phenomenon that many find difficult to comprehend. Demonstrations centering on this principle present contradictions to what people believe, thus putting them into a state of mental disequilibrium (Lawson, 1994). Note the demonstration setup in Figure 10.3 in which a sheet of paper is supported by two thick textbooks. Ask students what will happen to the paper when you blow hard between the two books. Many students will respond that the paper will fly off the books. Place the student responses on the board and take a count of the various predictions.

FIGURE 10.3 A discrepant event demonstrated by blowing under a sheet of paper supported by two books.

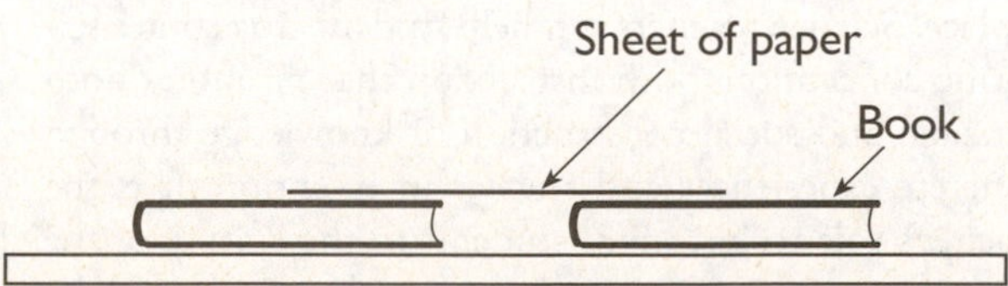

Demonstrate what happens when you blow vigorously beneath the paper. Ask a few students to come forward and do the same. Note the surprise and discrepancy between what most of the class believed would occur and what actually did occur. Now, how do you explain these results? Through a series of questions, develop a description of this event and an explanation of the principle involved. Many in the class will still be hooked to their beliefs with regard to the effects of rapidly moving air pushing directly on the paper. Write a scientific explanation on the chalkboard of what happened, then call on a few more participants to test the principle. Ask some individuals to blow under the paper and some to blow over the paper. Perhaps some participants will begin to incorporate a different view of a stream of air moving across an object.

Do not believe that this one demonstration will produce enough conceptual change for students to reach a level of equilibrium that solidifies scientific understanding of Bernoulli's principle. The task of the effective science teacher is to present many discrepant situations that produce disequilibrium, causing students to make many cognitive connections to accommodate to the events and information. For example, another demonstration that can be conducted in order to study Bernoulli's principle is to drop playing cards into a box. You can demonstrate this card drop one or two times and then call on some members of the class to try it. There is a certain way to hold the cards so that they fall into the box. Most students will not know this technique, so the cards they drop will fall away from the box when released. This activity generates cognitive dissonance, and the participants will need to examine what they know about air pressure to figure this out. Examine and try the several discrepant event demonstrations of Bernoulli's principle in Appendix B that are designed for use with inservice and preservice science teachers.

Meaningful Learning and Concept Mapping

Science teaching must complement discrepant-event and conceptual-change instruction with other strategies and techniques. One technique to help students to form relationships between ideas is called *concept mapping.* This approach to learning science began in the 1980s. The technique helps students to visually represent meaningful relationships between science concepts (Novak & Gowin, 1984). In Figure 10.4, a concept map is presented for the study of ecology in the middle school. The diagram in the figure presents the superordinate–subordinate relationships of the topic under study. The map graphically places the knowledge structure of ecology into a hierarchy, with broad general concepts at the top and the more specific concepts at the lower levels.

Novak and Gowin indicate that concept mapping promotes meaning through active learning because students must make connections between the new ideas that they are attempting to visually represent and those that already exist in their minds. They emphasize that students must participate in the creation of the concept map. Consequently, the new knowledge the students gain is constructed. The researchers state that "knowledge is not discovered like gold or oil, but rather it is constructed like cars or pyramids" (Novak & Gowin, 1984, p. 4).

FIGURE 10.4 A concept map for the study of ecology in middle school.

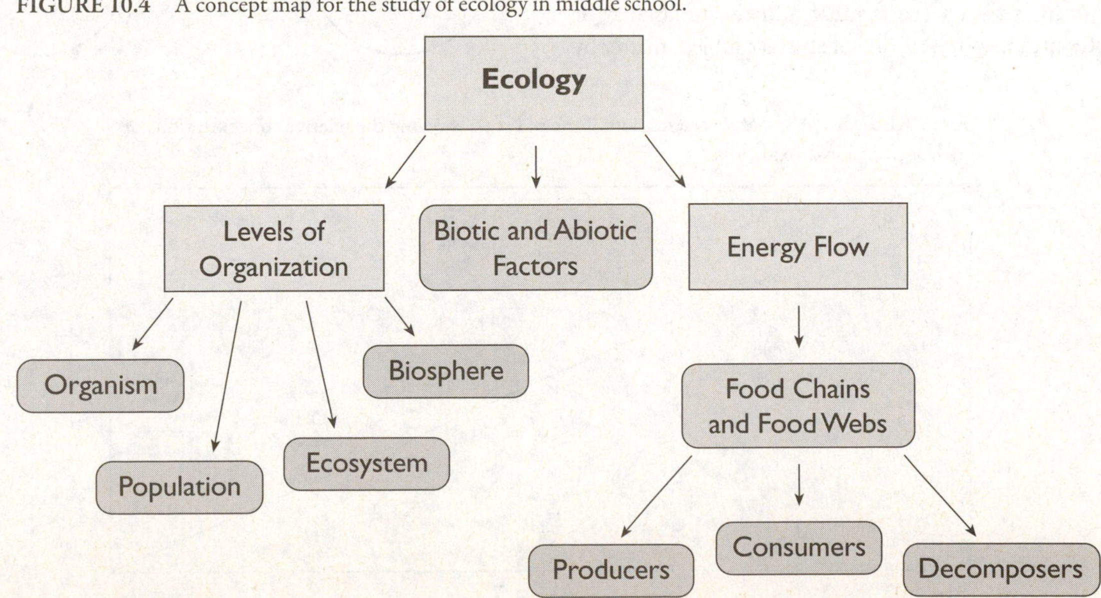

Novak and Gowin (1984) indicate that concept maps can be used to:

1. determine pathways for organizing meanings
2. negotiate meaning with students
3. point out misconceptions
4. promote higher-level thinking (p. 23)

Concept mapping is used in other fields besides science instruction. For example, it is used under the name *semantic mapping* for language arts instruction.

Images

The study of imagery has been part of the history of psychology from the early philosophers, who attempted to describe the mind, to current learning theorists (Kosslyn, 1980). Images can be thought of as thinking aids that help to transfer information. They are one way of representing objects that constitute the perceptible and imperceptible aspects of reality. The ability to produce images in the mind offers the possibility for humans to construct meaningful connections with ideas. The representation of phenomena and concepts are important for comprehending science.

Many scientific conceptions are very abstract and, therefore, difficult to imagine and represent pictorially. Nevertheless, these ideas are central to learning science and necessary for students to understand and explain. Science textbooks and teachers often present ideas with which students are familiar in order to make the unfamiliar comprehensible. You probably have heard the phrase "now picture this in your mind," used to encourage students to imagine what they are about to learn. This prompt requests students to represent in their minds relationships that will transfer knowledge from one domain to another. Analogical reasoning encourages students to construct cognitive connections between the familiar and the unfamiliar. It facilitates meaningful learning of abstract subject matter by helping students to integrate new information with existing knowledge, thus forming new conceptions.

Pictures and diagrams are used frequently during science instruction to represent concepts and principles. Science textbooks are filled with these teaching aids. Teachers use them in their lectures. Visualization provides students with cognitive aids that make abstract ideas more comprehensible. Because we cannot observe directly the movement of electrons or ions, for example, we must find ways to illustrate these concepts. Abstract ideas must be made accessible by visual representation through diagrams or other means. You can find experienced chemistry teachers who weave diagrams into their presentations to help students conceptualize concepts like pH. Some teachers use a diagram similar to the one shown in Figure 10.5 to illustrate how the acidity and basicity of a solution changes as the relative concentrations of hydrogen ions (H^+) and hydroxide ions (OH^-) change.

Analogies

The use of diagrams for instruction can further be enhanced by interactive techniques such as analogical reasoning. *Analogies* are one tool for getting students to make connections between what they know and what we want them to know. In some research studies, they have been reported to further students' comprehension of scientific concepts and to help them construct meaning (Dagher, 1995; Duit, 1991; Glynn, Duit, & Thiele, 1995). An analogy forms a relationship between what the learners are familiar with and what they are expected to learn (the unfamiliar).

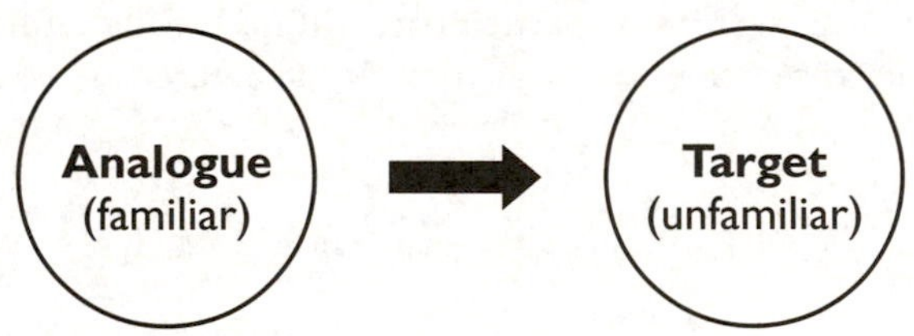

FIGURE 10.5 A visual representation of the pH scale showing the relative concentrations of hydrogen and hydroxide ions.

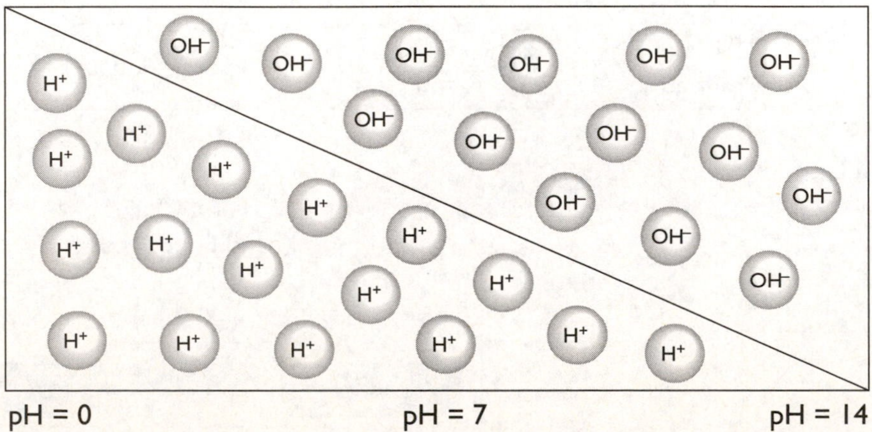

The familiar is referred to as the *analogue* and the unfamiliar the *target*. For example, science teachers have used the analogy of water flowing through a pipe (analogue) to help students comprehend electrical current (target).

Ausubel (1963) recommended the use of advanced organizers to facilitate the acquisition of knowledge. His idea of the comparative organizer serves to illustrate how we can show similarities and differences between what the students know and what they are expected to learn. This approach uses analogies to facilitate assimilation of new material into existing cognitive structures. Examine the analogy in Table 10.1. A life science teacher might use this table to help students learn about the structure of the cell from their knowledge of a car. We will examine six operations for teaching analogies, developed by Glynn (1995, p. 27) for his teaching-with-analogies model, to guide our discussion regarding this instructional strategy:

1. Introduce the target concept.
2. Review the analogue concept.
3. Identify the features of the target and analogue.
4. Map the similarities.
5. Indicate where the analogy breaks down.
6. Draw conclusions.

For the comparison given in Table 10.1 and the six operations just stated, let's examine a car analogy instructionally. A science teacher might begin by introducing the purpose of the exercise. This statement can be accompanied by listing the structures of the cell (target) on the chalkboard (operation 1). Information can be given regarding the structure and function of cellular parts, similar to those shown in the left-hand column of the table. The teacher can pose a question to prompt students to search for an analogy in everyday life that is similar to the workings of a biological cell. Students may or may not come up with the car as an analogy. They may provide an example that is more relevant to them than an automobile, which would certainly be an important path to pursue. In any event, if the students do not offer the car as a comparison, the teacher can present it (operation 2). Given the interest that adolescents show in driving automobiles, the car is likely to be familiar to them and a relevant analogue concept. The features of a car and a biological cell can be discussed (operation 3). A diagram of a cell can be constructed and a discussion of how its structures are related to a car can take place. In this manner, a comparison of key features of the analogue and target are mapped by bridging similar features (operation 4).

Many analogies can be discussed to help students widen their understanding of a living cell. For example, some life science teachers have used a house or a factory to provide an analogy for a living cell. Then, after students have had a variety of instructional experiences with cell analogies, using automobiles, houses, factories, and the like, the salient features of these objects should be critically analyzed to point out their limitations in representing a biological structure (operation 5). Finally, the teacher should draw conclusions about the cell that highlights the important functions carried out by this fundamental biological entity (operation 6).

The use of analogies is widespread in science lectures and textbooks. In some instances, these examples are beneficial to students; in others, they are less than effective. Glynn and colleagues (1995) have analyzed many textbooks for examples of analogies as well as analogies used by science teachers in their classrooms. These researchers report that textbooks and teachers who were judged to be effective with analogies used the six operations of the teaching-with-analogies model. Further, these authors and teachers carefully relate the familiar with the unfamiliar so that erroneous ideas do not come into their comparisons. Glynn and colleagues (1995) point out that Paul Hewitt's *Conceptual Physics* textbook contains many excellent analogies.

The idea of teaching abstract concepts and principles using analogies has great instructional appeal. Nevertheless, this approach is not always effective. Students can and often do miss the connection between the analogue and the target concept (Glynn et al., 1995). Pedagogical

TABLE 10.1 An Analogy of a Car and a Biological Cell

Structure or Function of the Concept to Be Learned	Structure of the Car Cell (familiar analogue)	Structure of the Biological Cell (unfamiliar target)
Outer structure	Body	Wall and membrane
Inner part	Interior	Cytoplasm
Control center	Driver	Nucleus
Communication	Electrical system	Endoplasmic reticulum
Energy	Engine	Mitochondria
Waste removal	Exhaust system	Vacuole

skill is needed to map the important features of analogical comparisons in order for conceptual bridges to be established by the learner. Remember that the student must be the one to make the key connections. Further, teachers must be on guard so that students do not form misconceptions (Thagard, 1992). For example, when using the flow of water through a pipe to illustrate electrical current, students as well as many elementary and middle school science teachers have formed the idea that electrons "zip" through a wire, similar to water shooting through a pipe. With direct electrical current, electrons move very fast in the spaces between atoms, but their net movement in the direction of the positive terminal is relatively slow. Many misconceptions have been found in textbooks and among teachers attempting to use analogical reasoning to explain concepts and phenomena whose features cannot be perceived directly.

Students must actively participate in the construction of mental models in order to learn abstract science concepts.

Models

Scientists frequently use physical and mathematical models to represent phenomena. These representations, especially the physical models, provide concrete means to view reality, offering science teachers and students a visual image to facilitate learning. Some common models are diagrams of the atom, the solar system, the cell, the DNA double helix, the water cycle, the Krebs cycle, structural chemical formulas, and the movement of electrical impulses along nerve cells. These and many other scientific models play an important role in conveying fundamental ideas to students. Without scientific models, teachers would experience considerable difficulty initiating student learning.

When using models to teach students about a theory or principle, we must remember that the model is a representation of a phenomenon and is referred to as the target. The target is the object, phenomenon, or system in nature. Because the target cannot be observed directly and photographed, it must be represented diagrammatically. Therefore, a scale model of a bridge or car, for example, may not be considered a typical scientific model. Most scientific models cannot be considered exact replicas of reality. They are working ideas that facilitate communication and guide research.

Science teachers must realize that although models may appear simple and concrete, students do not readily learn them. Students need to construct a mental model of the scientific model under study, a process that is incremental and takes considerable instructional time. Consider the following when teaching students about a model (Greca & Moreira, 2000):

- Students do not have the same background knowledge as the teacher; therefore, students do not visualize and understand a scientific model as readily as the teacher might expect.
- Students' conceptualization of a model is often incomplete, unstable, simplified, and unscientific.
- Mental modeling on the part of students is a very complex process and takes place over time through a series of small steps.
- Mental models are personal constructions for students as well as scientists.
- The acquisition of a mental model requires new language and involves a conceptual change process.

Modeling to Learn Science

Modeling to learn is an approach to instruction that focuses on the representation of students' ideas to advance their understanding of natural phenomena. The process organizes science course subject matter into fundamental scientific models, rather than topics. These models are used to guide the construction of students' ideas (mental models) toward more coherent scientific ideas (conceptual models) that scientists possess (Wells, Hestenes, & Swackhamer, 1995). The instruction is a highly interactive form of pedagogy that employs many strategies and techniques discussed in this textbook such as talking science, using discrepant events, concept mapping, forming analogies, conducting laboratory exercises, and making diagrams to expand students' mental models. Modeling is a powerful strategy that can be used in all science courses, not just physics where it has been extensively researched. Nevertheless, the journey from students' mental models or existing knowledge to more advanced understanding of scientific models requires a more carefully crafted form of instruction than that which is typically used in school science programs in grades 6–12 and at the college level. Conceptual change is difficult to achieve with many abstract and complex scientific ideas. The following vignette illustrates how a form of the modeling strategy might be used during a science classroom demonstration in preparation for subsequent laboratory work where students collect data to extend their conceptual models of diffusion and osmosis.

After participating in a workshop devoted to modeling to learn science, Mrs. Norton spends more than one class period on diffusion, a concept to which she formerly devoted only part of a high-school class period in biology. The teacher feels that students must have a good conception of the diffusion model in order to understand the passive transport of ions and molecules through a cell membrane. She wants students to realize the effects of toxic substances on the body and how they enter cells. The vignette below is an example of how a science teacher might initiate the study of movement across a cell membrane, using a modeling approach to teach diffusion.

Mrs. Norton: Class, please observe what I am about to do on the demonstration table. Can I have one volunteer to assist me? Thank you, George. Please stand here so that the class members can see what is taking place and hold open this dialysis tubing.

With all eyes toward the front of the room, Mrs. Norton pours some starch solution into a length of dialysis tubing that the student is holding and closes the tube off with a twist tie. Then Mrs. Norton places the tubing into a large beaker of water. She calls another student forward to pour some iodine-KI reagent into the beaker water. Mrs. Norton asks the two students to return to their seats. Now she asks a series of questions so that the class realizes that there is a starch solution inside the dialysis tubing and iodine surrounding the tubing. By now the starch solution begins to turn purplish/black, and Mrs. Norton asks the class why the starch solution turns dark.

Mrs. Norton: Alicia, your hand is up.

Alicia: I think something is happing to the solution inside the tubing.

Mrs. Norton: Good. But tell us exactly what is taking place in this system.

Thomas: There is a chemical reaction or something going on.

Mrs. Norton: Okay, but can you or someone else tell us what is taking place in the reaction? Dawn?

Dawn: The color is getting darker.

Mrs. Norton: How is that occurring? What is combining with what? Morgan?

Morgan: I think, but I am not sure. Somehow the iodine is getting into the tubing and reacting with the starch.

Mrs. Norton: How many of you think this is what is happening?

After Mrs. Norton feels that all the students realize that the iodine solution is seeping through the wall of the dialysis tubing and into the starch solution, she asks them to draw a diagram to illustrate how this is occurring. Mrs. Norton urges the students to be complete and to include all the substances and materials that are involved in modeling the diffusion that is taking place. Below is the first diagram that is placed on the board by one of the students.

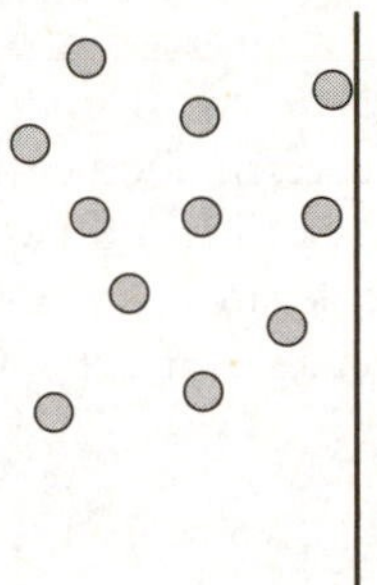

Mrs. Norton commends the student for the diagram, even though she realizes that the student's model is very incomplete. However, it serves as a starting point that causes a great deal of discussion among the students. During the discussion, the teacher places students' responses on the board. Some students agree with the responses, but some don't. As you can observe, the student's model lacks labels for the molecules and ions in solution, and shows no openings in the line that is used to represent the dialysis tubing or cell membrane. Now, Mrs. Norton calls on another student to place her diagram on the board and to give an explanation of the diffusion process.

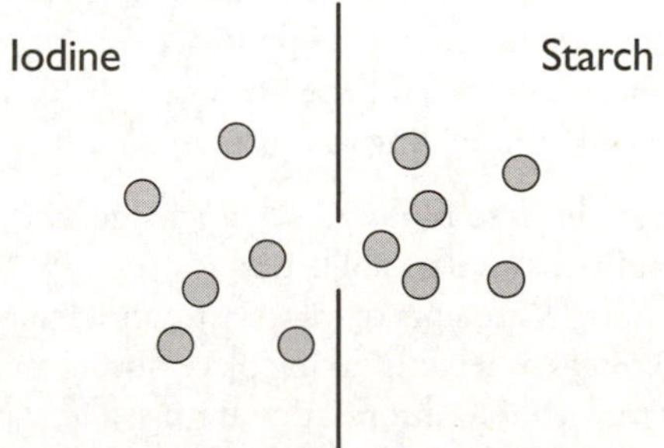

This student's model diagram has progressed from the first diagram; it has some labels for the molecules and an opening in the barrier between the iodine and starch solutions.

The teacher-to-student and student-to-student interaction continues until the end of the period and into the next class meeting with the teacher serving as a guide and mediator. She also provides some information and terms to help students build their mental models of diffusion toward a more conceptually correct model of this scientific principle.

At the beginning of the second class period devoted to diffusion, the student who drew the first model on the board was asked to diagram her current conception of diffusion. Below, you can observe that the student's mental model shows considerable growth from the first diagram. Note the openings in the dialysis tubing that permit the iodine ions to move across the membrane. Further, you can note that the triangles representing the starch molecules are too large to get through the openings in the membrane. The teacher continues the modeling process until the student diagrams and labels provide a reasonably good representation of the scientific process of diffusion before she adds and modifies the model on the board with specific labels. She also indicates the ions and complex molecules that are involved in this phenomenon.

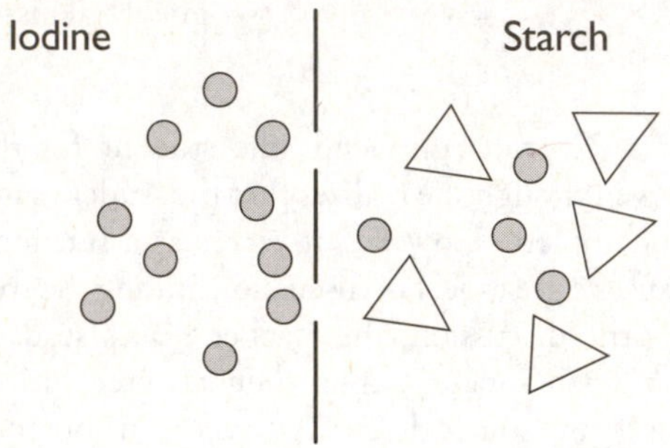

Now Mrs. Norton engages the students in a laboratory exercise on diffusion. They design an investigation, collect data, and present evidence of how diffusion is taking place. At this point in the instructional process she feels that her students have developed a mind set to construct models that represent a phenomenon. Further, she is confident that the students have increased their interest about this topic to the point where they will stay on task. Here are some of the ideas that the teacher will use to guide her modeling to learn instruction:

- Get students to build their knowledge construction from firsthand data collection.
- Encourage students to talk, write, and diagram their ideas of what is taking place during an event.
- Try to withhold information, terms, and explanations of the concept or principle until the students understand what is taking place.
- Organize students into small groups to carry out laboratory work or investigations to promote collaboration, dialogue, argumentation, and support for their ideas.
- Urge students to support their assertions and explanations with model diagrams and evidence they have gathered and organized from data.

Stop and Reflect!

1. Describe what the teacher did to initiate the study of diffusion. What did she do that might not be observed in a traditional biology or chemistry class where modeling to learn is not used? Compare your description with that of other class members.
2. Explain why or why not this modeling approach may be effective in helping students to better understand diffusion or other science concepts or principles.
3. How do the elements of this teaching and learning example reflect the conceptual change process of constructing scientific knowledge?

Motivation

Motivation is a central element of instruction that affects affective and cognitive learning outcomes. According to Brophy (1988, p. 205), a student's tendency to find schoolwork meaningful and worthwhile and to try to benefit from it is the essence of the motivation to learn. In science, students are motivated to engage in activities for the personal satisfaction gained from them and for the rewards or punishment that may be linked to them. Motivation that comes from personal satisfaction, interest, or curiosity is called intrinsic motivation. Motivation that has little to do with the activity itself, but rather with the associated rewards or punishment, is called extrinsic motivation. It is important for teachers is to encourage students to engage in activities for the intrinsic benefits derived from them and to also recognize that extrinsic motivation should not be discounted because it can lead to student learning and possibly to personal satisfaction and sustained interest.

By observing a student's behavior, it is impossible to determine if the motivation for engaging in an activity is intrinsic or extrinsic. Only by understanding the student's reasons for his or her action can it be determined whether the action is prompted by personal satisfaction, interest, curiosity, or by rewards or punishment. In some cases, teachers can develop intrinsic motivation in students by stimulating their interest in a topic or by gradually increasing the difficulty level of lessons to ensure continued success. For example, biology teachers are often successful in creating intrinsic motivation among their students to learn genetics by having them investigate family pedigrees. It is also true that at times teachers must rely on rewards and external inducements to achieve their instructional objectives, such as when a reminder about slipping grades is used to encourage a student to work harder. However, teachers should always be looking for ways to help students shift the emphasis from extrinsic incentive to intrinsic satisfaction.

According to Woolfolk (1995), intrinsic motivation is only one attribute that contributes to student motivation to learn. Four others are challenging learning goals, involvement in the learning task, achievement based on mastery learning, and feelings of control over effort and ability. All five attributes of motivation should be considered when planning instruction to achieve both affective and cognitive objectives.

In summary, the affective domain is an important dimension of science learning. Students need to leave science classes not only with science understandings, but also with favorable feelings toward science learning and the scientific enterprise and with commitment to some science-related ideas and actions. Motivation to learn is an important affective concept because of its role in mediating the achievement of both affective and cognitive objectives. It serves science teachers well to be familiar with aspects of the affective domain in order to better address this dimension of learning in the science classroom.

Assessing and Reviewing

Analysis and Synthesis

1. What have you learned from this chapter about cognitive psychology as it pertains to teaching and learning science?
   a. Without referring to the chapter, write a paragraph presenting the major ideas associated with constructivism.
   b. Compare and contrast a constructivist approach to learning science with a traditional approach.
2. How would you use the Piagetian ideas of equilibration and contradiction to engage learning? In brief form, outline an activity to teach a science concept, principle, or law using a:
   a. discrepant event situation with concrete materials
   b. verbal or written statement that contradicts the beliefs of many people

   Share these examples with others so that everyone expands their knowledge of how to stimulate learning in the science classroom.
3. Compare the conceptual change instructional sequence with the 5E Instructional Model presented in Chapter 8. How might each of these teaching sequences aid students to restructure their ideas about abstract science concepts and laws?
4. Construct a concept map to represent the major ideas presented in this chapter on learning.
5. Develop an analogy that you might use to teach a concept to a middle or senior high school group of students. Refer to the teaching-with-analogies model discussed in the chapter. Present the analogy to a group of peers, and get their feedback regarding the effectiveness of the instruction. Pay special attention to the potential for introducing misconceptions or incorrect notions about the target concept.

Practical Considerations

6. Find a teacher-developed or commercial instructional unit for a middle or high school science course. Examine the activities to determine the potential the unit holds for promoting conceptual change among the students who will participate in it. For this exercise, consider the conceptual change model discussed in this chapter. Focus on:
   a. eliciting ideas
   b. clarifying knowledge
   c. examining conflicting views
   d. constructing new ideas
   e. applying new knowledge
   f. reviewing the knowledge restructuring that might take place
7. Construct an observational checklist for studying the extent to which conceptual change might be taking place among the students in a science classroom. Then, identify a middle or high school science teacher to observe. Take notes on the instruction and determine the potential for producing student understanding of the topic under study. More than one observational session will be necessary in order to make a valid assessment of the type of teaching (constructivist/conceptual change or traditional) and learning taking place.

Developmental Considerations

8. Obtain some textbooks and paperback books that discuss behavioral and cognitive principles of learning. Summarize the descriptions of these approaches and techniques for incorporating them into your teaching. Focus on strategies and techniques that you intend to use.

Resources to Examine

How People Learn. 2000. Edited by John D. Bransford, Ann Brown, and Rodney Cocking. Washington, DC: National Academy Press.

This paperback book is a compendium of research that explains effective teaching and learning that has been informed by cognitive science research. The book discusses many of the ideas addressed in this methods textbook such as student-centered instruction, building conceptual knowledge, formative and continual assessment, and contextualizing the learning. Many of the chapters or sections of chapters can be used for reading and discussion in order to enhance science teacher understanding of student-centered learning.

Learning Science and the Science of Learning. 2002. Edited by Roger W. Bybee. Arlington, VA: National Science Teachers Association (NSTA) Press.

This paperback edited by Roger Bybee provides short, easy-to-read descriptions of learning strategies and techniques for science teachers. It addresses many topics, such as how students learn, inquiry and learning science, making connections, learner-centered teaching, assessment and student learning, and selecting curriculum materials.

Ready, Set, Science: Putting Research to Work in K-8 Science Classrooms. 2008. Michaels, S., Shouse, A. W., & Schweingruber, H. A. Washington, DC: National Academies Press.

The authors have written a short, easy-to-read paperback that elaborates on many of the ideas presented in this chapter and elsewhere in the science methods textbook. They present background information as well as many cases of classroom and laboratory instruction that inform good teaching practices and sound approaches to learning. Some of the topics addressed in this paperback book are: a new vision of science education; foundational knowledge and conceptual change; making thinking visible through talk, argumentation, modeling, and representation; and learning from investigation.

References

Anderson, C. W. (2007). Perspectives on learning. In S. K. Abell & N. G. Lederman (Eds.), *Handbook of research on science education* (pp. 3–30). Mahawah, NJ: Erlbaum.

Ausubel, D. P. (1963). *The psychology of meaningful verbal learning.* New York: Grune & Stratton.

Brophy, J. (1988). *On motivating students.* In D. Berliner & B. Rosenshine (Eds.), *Talks to teachers* (pp. 201–245). New York: Random House.

Dagher, Z. R. (1995). Analysis of analogies used by science teachers. *Journal of Research in Science Teaching, 32,* 259–270.

Driver, R. (1988). Theory into practice II: A constructivist approach to curriculum development. In P. Fensham (Ed.), *Development and dilemmas in science education* (pp. 133–149). Philadelphia: Falmer Press.

Driver, R., Asoko, H., Leach, J., Mortimer, E., & Scott, P. (1994). Constructing scientific knowledge in the classroom. *Educational Researcher, 23*(7), 5–12.

Driver, R., Squires, A., Rushworth, P., & Wood-Robinson, V. (1994). *Making sense of secondary science.* New York: Routledge.

Duit, R. (1991). On the role of analogies and metaphors in learning science. *Science Education, 75,* 649–672.

Duit, R., & Treagust, D. F. (1998). Learning science—from behaviorism towards social constructivism and beyond. In B. J. Fraser & K. G. Tobin (Eds.), *International Handbook of Science Education, Part One* (pp. 3–26). Dordrecht, The Netherlands: Kluwer.

Fosnot, C. T. (1996). *Constructivism: Theory, perspectives, and practice.* New York: Teachers College, Columbia University.

Furth, H. G. (1969). *Piaget and knowledge.* Englewood Cliffs, NJ: Prentice-Hall.

Glynn, S. (1995). Conceptual bridges. *The Science Teacher, 62*(9), 25–27.

Glynn, S. M., Duit, R., & Thiele, R. B. (1995). Teaching science with analogies: A strategy for constructing knowledge. In S. M. Glynn & R. Duit (Eds.), *Learning science in the schools: Research reforming practices.* Mahwah, NJ: Erlbaum.

Greca, I. M., & Moreira, M. A. (2000). Mental models, conceptual models, and modeling. *International Journal of Science Education, 22*(1), 1–11.

Kasschau, R. (1986). A model for teaching critical thinking in psychology. In J. Halonen (Ed.), *Teaching critical thinking in psychology.* Milwaukee, WI: Alverno College Institute.

Kosslyn, S. M. (1980). *Image and mind.* Cambridge, MA: Harvard University Press.

Lawson, A. E. (1994). Research on the acquisition of science knowledge: Epistemological foundations of cognition. In D. L. Gabel (Ed.), *Handbook of research on science teaching and learning.* Upper Saddle River, NJ: Merrill/Prentice Hall.

Novak, J. D., & Gowin, D. B. (1984). *Learning how to learn.* New York: Cambridge University Press.

Piaget, J. (1964). Cognitive development in children: Development and learning. *Journal of Research in Science Teaching, 2,* 176–186.

Piaget, J. (1971). *Biology and knowledge.* Chicago: University of Chicago Press.

Sternberg, R. (1995). *In search of the human mind.* New York: Harcourt Brace College.

Thagard, P. (1992). Analogy, explanation, and education. *Journal of Research in Science Teaching, 29*, 537–544.

Von Glasersfeld, E. (1995). Radical constructivism: A way of knowing and learning. London: Falmer Press.

Vygotsky, L. S. (1978). *Mind in society: The development of higher psychological processes* (M. Cole, V. John-Steiner, S. Scribner, & E. Souberman, Eds.). Cambridge, MA: Harvard University Press.

Wandersee, J. H., Mintzes, J. J., & Novak, J. D. (1994). Research on alternative conceptions in science. In D. L. Gabel (Ed.), *Handbook of research on science teaching* (pp. 177–210). Upper Saddle River, NJ: Merrill/Prentice Hall.

Wells, M., Hestenes, D., & Swackhamer, G. (1995). A modeling method for high school physics instruction. *American Journal of Physics, 63*(7), 606–619.

Woolfolk, A. E. (1995). *Educational psychology* (6th ed.). Needham Heights, MA: Allyn & Bacon.

Chapter

11

Discussion, Demonstration, and Lecture

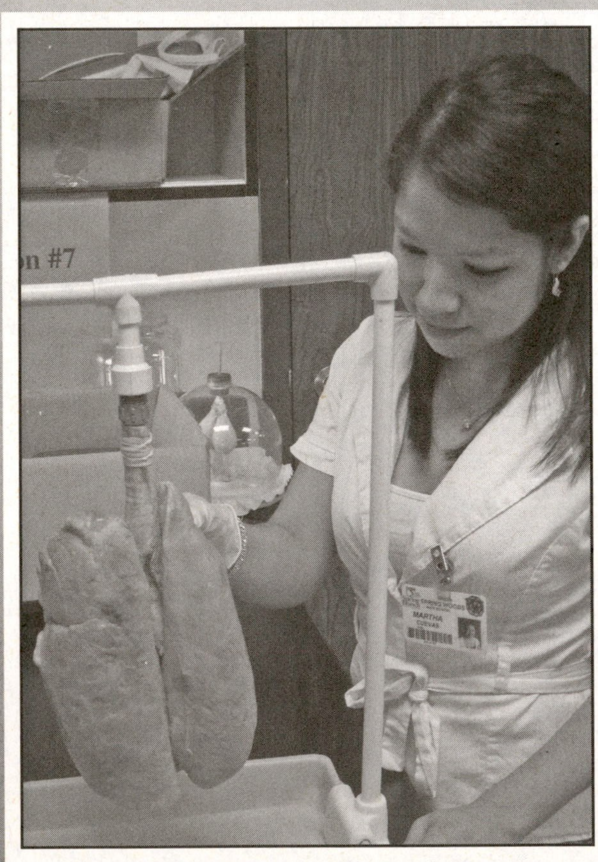

Teacher demonstrations can be used to engage students and promote scientific discourse.

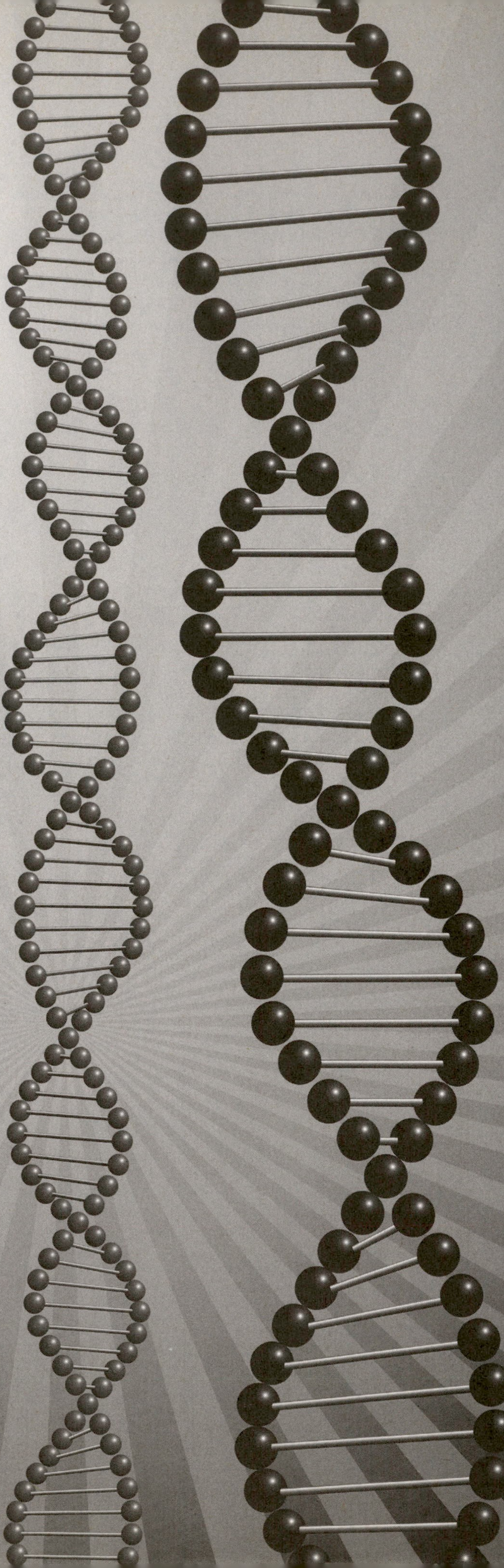

Talk and argumentation are important ways through which students learn science. Discussion, demonstration, and lecture are instructional strategies that provide students opportunities to productively engage in these forms of oral communication. Typical classroom practice suggests that these instructional strategies tend to be teacher centered and may do little to advance students' scientific understandings and reasoning powers. But this should not be the norm. When using these instructional strategies, teachers can do much to guide students toward understanding the language of science, where commonly used words can have unique meanings. They also can help students understand how scientists use argumentation to achieve community consensus and advance scientific knowledge. It is clear that the understandings that students construct from science discussions, demonstrations, and lectures are affected by the classroom discourse patterns that teachers encourage and by students' prior science ideas. Use of these instructional strategies by science teachers can contribute to a classroom context that helps students to develop their powers of logical reasoning while building potent understandings about the world in which they live.

AIMS OF THE CHAPTER

Use the questions that follow to guide your thinking and learning about the instructional strategies of discussion, demonstration, and lecture:

- What is scientific talk and argumentation? What kinds of classroom discourse patterns encourage scientific talk and argumentation?
- How can discussion be used to promote students' science learning?
- What should a science teacher consider when planning and leading a demonstration to encourage students' science learning?
- When should a lecture be used to facilitate students' science learning? How should a science teacher prepare for and present a lecture?

Scientific Discourse

If you were to observe a science class participating in a discussion, demonstration, or lecture, what would you see? Chances are that you would see students sitting silently or mindlessly copying notes as their teacher talks. And, if you did happen to witness students talking, they would likely be participating in what is called an I-R-E sequence, where the teacher *Initiates* the conversation, one student *Responds*, and then the teacher *Evaluates* the student's response (Michaels, Souse, & Schweingruber, 2008). While this discourse pattern may enable the teacher to maintain class control, it seems to do very little to further the goal for school science to prepare scientifically literate citizens. To become scientifically literate, students must do more than learn science facts and theories. They also must come to understand the ways of sense making that are characteristic of scientific communities. Talk and argumentation are central features of sense making in scientific communities, and must be central features of science learning in middle and secondary schools.

Scientific Talk and Argumentation

Some of the students you teach will be native speakers of English, but none of your students will be native speakers of science. Put another way, students are largely unfamiliar with the vocabulary of science and must learn the meaning of words used in science. For example, the word *theory* has a very special meaning in science that is different from its meaning in everyday talk. In a science context, theory is a well-established and complex explanation based on evidence (NRC, 2007). The cell theory, the theory of electromagnetism, the theory of plate tectonics, and the theory of evolution are among the many scientific theories that students will learn about when studying science in middle and high school. In contrast, the word *theory* in everyday talk may mean a person's prediction, guess, or belief. Other words used in science that have special meanings include *hypothesis* and *law*; *solution*, *mixture*, and *compound*; *weight* and *mass*; and *bug* and *insect*. In science classes, students need to be introduced to the words that have special scientific meanings and helped to distinguish between the scientific meaning and everyday meaning of the same word.

Students also need to have opportunities to engage in scientific argumentation. When doing so, it is most important to help students contrast scientific argumentation with argumentation as practiced in nonscientific contexts. Scientific argumentation is not a heated exchange between rivals or a debate, such as that engaged in by political candidates, with a winner and loser. It is "logical discourse whose goal is to tease out the relationship between ideas and evidence" (NRC, 2007, p. 33). The primary vehicle of scientific argumentation is persuasion, where ideas and evidence are put forth in an effort to convince a community of the explanatory or predictive power of the ideas. When engaging students in scientific argumentation, their ideas should be valued as long as they comply with the conventions of science and logic. For example, when engaging in scientific argumentation about the lift on an airplane wing, students should draw on their ideas of gravity, force, molecular motion, and air pressure, and combine them with data they gather about lift on a wing and the evidence that they construct. Involving students in scientific argumentation that incorporates knowledge, data, and evidence will guide them to be critical thinkers rather than individuals who regurgitate poorly understood terms. Engaging in scientific argumentation may also help students recognize how some arguments, while persuasive, may not be scientific because they do not comply with the conventions of science and logic.

Promoting Talk and Argumentation in Science Classes

Teachers can promote scientific talk and argumentation by considering the kinds of discourse in which they engage students. As mentioned earlier in this chapter, all too often discourse in science classes follows the I-R-E pattern, where students seem to be trying to figure out the "right" answer wanted by the teacher. Some discourse patterns appropriate for science classes that correspond to particular scientific language functions are shown in Table 11.1 Teachers can change the discourse pattern in their classes by asking questions and using other "talk moves" and "talk formats" that encourage students to think deeply and share their thinking with classmates before answering (Michaels, Shouse, & Schweingruber, 2008, p. 90). The success of a science discussion, demonstration, and lecture often depends on a teacher's

- questions
- talk moves
- talk formats

Oral Questions

Questions should be stated so that students can grasp their meaning and intent immediately. Early in the school year, teachers may wish to structure questions using words familiar to students, but later on strive to build students' vocabulary as they help them develop conceptual understandings. The vocabulary of science should be used in the context of clear and simple language.

Original: What is your idea of an astronomical unit?

Improved: What is the definition of an astronomical unit?

In this example, the original question is cluttered. "What is your idea of" can be easily replaced by "What is the definition of," but the term *astronomical unit* should remain, regardless of how complicated it might appear.

TABLE 11.1 Discourse Patterns and Their Scientific Language Functions

Discourse Pattern	Discourse Pattern Example	Language Function
I think _______ will _______.	I think the metal will emit an orange color when placed in the flame.	Making a prediction
The _______ had _______ so _______.	The plants had received no water for four weeks so they died.	Relating cause and effect
The _______ is _______ because _______.	The substance at the bottom of the beaker is a salt because a salt forms when an acid reacts chemically with a base.	Drawing conclusions
This _______ is similar to that _______ because both _______.	The forelimb of the bat is similar to that of the human because both have the same kinds of bones—humerus, radius, and ulna.	Comparing
This _______ is different from that _______ because one has _______ and the other does not _______.	Eukaryotic cells are different from prokaryotic cells because eukaryotic cells have a nucleus and organelles and prokaryotic cells do no have these components.	Contrasting
The main idea from this observation/text passage is _______.	The important point for this demonstration is that sound waves produced from different sources at the same instant can cause constructive and destructive interference.	Summarizing
This _______ is needed for _______ because it _______.	A closed circuit is needed to light the light bulb because electricity cannot flow through an open circuit.	Identifying relationships

From F. Dobb (2005), Introducing English learners to the language of science: One discourse pattern at a time. *The California Science Project: Los Angeles. (http://csmp.ucop.edu/downloads/csp/scientificdiscourse.pdf)*

Teachers can also improve their oral questioning by learning to classify their questions and using a mixture of question types that target different levels of thinking. As shown in Table 11.2, each type of question has its place in science teaching, and one type should not be used exclusively in preference to other types. Students should be asked questions that encourage them to analyze problems, synthesize ideas, and make value judgments, in addition to being asked to recall scientific facts. More important, teachers should not be overly concerned about matching their questions to the taxonomic levels shown in Table 11.2, but should recognize that there are different cognitive levels of questions and that a relationship exists between teacher questioning and student thinking (Kindsvatter, Wilen, & Ishler, 1996). When teachers ask concise and clearly worded higher-level questions and teach their students to recognize key words that indicate the desired level of response, students engage in higher-order thinking when formulating their answers (Costa & Lowery, 1989).

Interestingly, teachers generally ask low-level questions at random but direct higher-level questions to more able students, the so-called *target students* (Tobin & Gallagher, 1987). Target students often raise their hands to be called on and are the students the teacher believes will give correct and meaningful responses to questions. When target students are called on frequently, they tend to reduce the cognitive demand of the work for their classmates (Tobin, Tippins, & Gallard, 1994). For this reason, it is important for teachers to ask questions of varying levels to all students and not favor selected students in a class.

Talk Moves and Talk Formats

Talk moves are teacher questions and statements as well as periods of silence that encourage detailed student talk and foster student cognitive engagement. *Probing* and *redirecting* are two talk moves. Probing questions and

TABLE 11.2 Taxonomy of Classroom Questions

Level	Cognitive Activity	Key Words	Sample Questions
1. Knowledge	Remember, recall, or recognize facts, ideas, information, or principle as they were taught.	Define, identify, list, recall, quote	• Define photosynthesis. • Who discovered a cure for rabies? • What is the autumnal equinox?
2. Comprehension	Comprehend, interpret, or translate information or ideas.	Describe, explain, compare, summarize	• How would you measure the distance between Earth and a planet in the center of a neighboring galaxy? • How can you explain the movement of the dye in the water?
3. Application	Solve problems, find solutions, and determine answers through the application of rules, principles, or laws.	Apply, provide an example, use, determine	• Determine the resistance in the circuit from the given data. • What is the molarity of the solutions, given their normality?
4. Analysis	Distinguish the parts from the whole, identify causes, find support and evidence, construct hypotheses, and draw conclusions.	Identify cause and effect, draw conclusions, provide evidence	• What are the effects of the two drugs on the mobility of the goldfish? • What evidence demonstrates that harm has been caused by nuclear power plants?
5. Synthesis	Produce, design, make, and construct products, synthesize ideas, produce ways, and determine how to.	Make, produce, create, write, build, design	• Produce a scenario to show life in your town if obesity were eliminated. • How would you design an experiment to determine if energy can be saved by adding insulation to your home's attic?
6. Evaluation	Judge, appraise, assess, criticize, or substantiate on the basis of criteria or standards.	Evaluate, judge, assess, substantiate	• Evaluate the government's research on tobacco from a moral and ethical point of view. • Judge the merit of the research based on your criteria for conducting scientific research.

statements encourage students to extend, clarify, and justify their talk. "What comes next?" and "Please add more to what you've just said" are examples of ways to prompt students to extend their talk. Encourage students to clarify their thinking by saying, "Please clarify your statement," or by asking questions such as, "What does that mean to you?" or "How can you put that into your own words?" Examples of ways to ask for justification include "What evidence can you offer for that?" and "Why do you believe that is true?" In contrast to probing questions and statements, when redirecting, the teacher asks a student to extend, clarify, or justify the talk of a classmate. "What evidence supports John's statement that some reactions of photosynthesis don't require light?" and "Jimmy, would you please expand on Caroline's answer about the relationship between adhesive forces and meniscus formation?" are examples of redirecting questions. Other kinds of teacher statements that can be used to enhance student talk and thinking are presented in Table 11.3

Another talk move is *wait time*, which is defined as the duration of time between speakers. The pause that follows a teacher's question is called wait time 1, and the pause that follows a student's response to a teacher's question is called wait time 2. Research conducted in many classrooms revealed that the average wait time between a teacher's question and a student's response and the pause that follows a student's response is approximately 1 second (Rowe, 1974). The term *think time* is sometimes used in place of wait time to clarify the "academic purpose and activity of this period of silence—to allow students and teacher to complete on-task thinking" (Stahl, 1994, p. 1). A wait time of 3 to 5 seconds is most advantageous when encouraging student talk. Careful study of teachers' use of wait time indicates the following benefits:

1. The length of student solicited and unsolicited responses increased.
2. The failure of students to respond to questions decreased.
3. Student confidence and incidence of speculative responses increased.
4. The number of questions asked by students increased. (Rowe, 1974; 1978; Tobin, 1984)

In contrast to talk moves, talk formats are ways of organizing students to facilitate talk. For example, students could be paired or grouped into three- or four-member teams to conduct a laboratory activity or understand a text passage. Alternatively, a teacher might have individual students present the findings of their investigations to an entire class or engage a class of students in a discussion of a video viewed the day before. The task-related talk engaged in by students in talk formats such as these can lead to enhanced cognitive engagement, even among students not usually academically successful (Michaels, Shouse, & Schweingruber, 2008).

Promoting talk and argumentation in science classes may initially be challenging because of the unpredictability of student conversation and the level of teacher content expertise required to feel comfortable while doing so. However, failure to engage students in scientific talk and argumentation deprives them of coming to an understanding of science as more than a body of facts and static theories. Discussion, demonstration, and lecture are excellent vehicles for promoting scientific talk and argumentation.

Stop and Reflect!

Respond to the following questions before reading further.

- What you would say to fellow teachers to persuade them to make student talk and argumentation features of their science instruction?
- What are talk moves and talk formats? Give examples of each.

TABLE 11.3 Teacher Statements Useful for Enhancing Student Talk and Thinking

Statement Type	Use	Sample Statement
Declarative	Responding to an idea embedded in what a student said	I know what you mean. I've also seen what a tornado can do to a mobile home.
Reflective	Recasting or rephrasing what a student said	So you think that the winds of a tornado rotate in a counterclockwise direction.
Interest	Indicating that you would like to hear more about what a student said	Tell me what else happened when you tried to outrun the tornado in your car.
Referral	Linking one student's statement with what another student said	Your encounter with the tornado is very similar to Sharon's, even though yours was in Kansas and hers was in Texas.

Discussion

A discussion involves the expression of viewpoints by teacher and students about a topic that all possess sufficient background knowledge to make contributions. Two discussion types that can contribute to the goals of science learning are the guided discussion and the reflective discussion.

Guided Discussion

In a guided discussion, the teacher is the interaction leader and primary questioner and the interaction pattern is varied and flexible (Wilen, 1990). Two or more students may respond to a single question and the teacher need not react to each student's answer. In some instances, students may ask questions of the teacher or classmates to extend an explanation or clarify something that was said. During a guided discussion students are given time to think about questions and formulate answers before responding. A guided discussion can be used to help students construct for themselves the science knowledge that scientists have already determined and agreed on.

The questions asked during a guided discussion require students to interpret, explain, apply, illustrate, generalize, and conclude (Wilen, 1990). "How does the Gram stain help a physician prescribe treatment for a bacterial infection?" and "What evidence suggests that plants evolved from green algae?" are examples of the types of questions asked during a guided discussion. Responses to questions may vary, as the students discuss their own ideas about the topic under consideration.

Reflective Discussion

The centerpiece of reflective discussion, or true discussion, is the open expression of ideas. Particular interaction patterns are not associated with this discussion type. A reflective discussion is initiated by the teacher, who, much like a news program moderator, functions thereafter as the discussion facilitator. The teacher's initial question must be carefully worded to trigger original and evaluative thinking on the part of students (Kindsvatter et al., 1996). Reflective discussion is slow paced, and student responses tend to be quite lengthy. The momentum of the discussion is not maintained by a series of teacher questions, as is the case with guided discussion, but by students asking questions of one another and statements contributed both by the teacher and students (Dillon, 1990).

Participation by all students is not critical to the success of a reflective discussion. Students whose thoughts on the topic or issue under consideration are not well formulated may choose just to listen. As is true for guided discussion, the success of a reflective discussion rests on student interest and background knowledge. If background knowledge is lacking, the discussion becomes what Roby (1988, p. 170) calls a bull session, where "participants ventilate their implicitly agreed upon right opinions with a certain passion but with little purpose and no reflection."

Controversial issues on which persons take a stand make excellent subjects for reflective discussions. In science classes, the issues may deal with matters of current interest such as evolution, genetic engineering, and health remedies. Reflective science discussions may also center on questions that require problem-solving skills to answer. Questions such as the following may serve this purpose well: Sedimentary rocks can be distinguished from other classes of rocks on the basis of bedding, color, fossils, ease of breakage, and porosity. Which do you believe are the poorest criteria to use as distinguishing characteristics and why? Excellent reflective discussions may also center on conflicting laboratory data. Topics that are concerned with indisputable facts are not well suited for reflective discussion in science classes.

Leading a Successful Discussion

Think of a discussion as consisting of four phases: entry, clarification, investigation, and closure (Kindsvatter et al., 1996). In the *entry* phase, the teacher identifies the discussion topic and tells the students what will be done and why. Many teachers use attention grabbers, such as questions, photographs, video clips, and personal testimonials, to cognitively engage students and to arouse their interest when initiating a discussion.

During the *clarification* phase, rules for the discussion are communicated and terms or concepts important to the discussion are defined and clarified. Students need to know how they will be recognized to speak and that showing respect for the views of others is expected. They also need to know what role the teacher will play during the discussion. Will the teacher direct student talk, serve as the moderator, or just listen? In an online discussion, students should be told whether it is acceptable to comment anonymously, how often to post comments, and if persons other than classmates and the teacher will read their comments.

The *investigation* phase is the heart of any discussion. The central elements of this phase are teacher questions, talk moves, and talk formats, all intended to encourage student engagement and learning. Probing and redirecting questions and statements that request elaboration and further explanation serve to enhance discussion, but too much teacher talk may stifle student contributions.

While it is impossible to anticipate all questions that should be asked or talk moves and talk formats that should be employed during a discussion, it is helpful for the teacher to have planned for their use during critical times of the discussion. Using wait time, expressing a personal point of view, adding to a student's contribution, and grouping students in pairs or teams are talk moves and formats that can be used by a teacher to keep a discussion rolling and focused. It is also important to consider how student ability level, language skills, and home culture might affect the success of a teacher's use of questions and talk moves. For example, White's (1990) work revealed that productive discussion in classes of native Hawaiian students tended to incorporate features of indigenous Hawaiian verbal interaction, including choral responses to questions and overlapping speech.

Closure, the final phase of a discussion, while critical to success, is too often bypassed due to time constraints or poor planning. It is during this phase that ideas are summarized, synthesized, and applied to situations not directly discussed and where meaningful learning often occurs (Kindsvatter et al., 1996). Closure also occurs when the outcomes of the discussion are related to previous lessons and lessons to come. In a reflective discussion, closure may include the evaluation of decisions arrived at during the discussion. Closure in small-group discussion is the time when the spokespersons present the results of each group's work to the entire class (Kindsvatter et al., 1996).

To lead a good discussion, a teacher should be able to do the following:

1. Seat students in a circle or horseshoe arrangement so that they can interact easily and can observe each other's facial expressions. Participants also use facial expressions to communicate. (Of course, this is not possible in an online discussion.)
2. Keep the discussion moving at a reasonable pace.
3. Keep the discussion pertinent to the topic or issues under consideration.
4. Encourage all students to participate. Do not allow a few students to monopolize the conversation.
5. Acknowledge all contributions that students make.
6. Reject irrelevant comments with tact.
7. Summarize at the end of the discussion, and do so frequently or permit students to do so as often as is feasible.
8. Terminate the discussion when students begin to lose interest.

Stop and Reflect!

Read the vignette presented in Classroom Snapshot 11.1, then answer the question below.

- Suppose that at the afternoon meeting Ms. Block recommended to her colleagues that they use a reflective discussion to address the objective about the costs associated with AIDS. Do you agree or disagree with Ms. Block's recommendation? Explain your reasoning.

Demonstration

A demonstration is a concrete experience that invites scientific talk and argumentation. The conversations associated with an effective demonstration can help uncover student misconceptions, illuminate key concepts and principles, and lead to heightened interest and further inquiry. When considering the use of a demonstration, it is important to first consider if it is the most appropriate instructional strategy to use and then how to go about preparing for the demonstration. Some sources of science demonstrations are presented in Table 11.4 on page 188.

Planning a Demonstration

Once the decision has been made to use a demonstration, the teacher's attention must turn to the needed materials and equipment, student visibility and attention, as well as practicing the demonstration before presenting it to students.

The materials and equipment for a demonstration should be gathered well in advance of the actual presentation. Last-minute preparation may prove frustrating and cause either a delay in the presentation or no presentation at all. For example, a teacher may find that the apparatus has been lost or damaged or that chemicals are too old, exist in the wrong concentrations, or are in short supply. The teacher or students can construct the equipment needed for many demonstrations. When students construct demonstration apparatus, they benefit from the experiences of planning and building the devices. When constructing demonstration apparatus, it is important to keep in mind that students are more likely to understand the demonstration if the apparatus used is closely related to things with which they are familiar.

When considering student visibility, simple and large-scale apparatuses are best for science demonstrations. But even when large equipment is used, the teacher must take care to ensure that small and important details are made visible to students. Before presenting a demonstration, it is a good idea to view the setup from various points around the classroom to determine whether there are problems in viewing it. Good overhead lighting that eliminates shadows will make any demonstration easier to see, but extraneous materials or events not part of the demonstration may divert students' attention. For example, when observing the classic egg-in-the-bottle demonstration, students may fail to see it as a demonstration of the effect of changing air pressure but as a show of fire or heat. This is because they are distracted by the flaming piece of paper dropped into the bottle to heat the inside air (Shepardson, Moje, & Kennard-McClelland, 1994).

To focus students' attention, consider beginning a demonstration with a clear demonstration table and then proceed to remove the needed items from a box or other

Classroom Snapshot 11.1

Decisions, Decisions—Teaching About Sexually Transmitted Diseases

Ms. Block teaches life science at a large suburban middle school. It's Sunday evening and she's looking over the section in her textbook about sexually transmitted diseases. The section will serve as the basis for a unit on the topic. After school on Monday, Ms. Block will participate in a planning meeting with three other life science teachers. These teachers are counting on Ms. Block to bring ideas for the most appropriate instructional strategy to address several of the unit's learning outcomes previously decided on at an earlier meeting. The learning outcomes for which Ms. Block is responsible are the following:

- Identify the ways by which HIV is transmitted.
- Describe the ways to reduce the risk of HIV infection.
- Relate the symptoms of AIDS to HIV infection.
- Evaluate the benefits of the care provided AIDS sufferers with their cost to society.

After looking over the chapter and other instructional materials, Ms. Block developed a plan to share with the other teachers. Before school on the day of the meeting Ms. Block runs into Mr. Castle, a member of the planning team, in the hallway.

Castle: Have you given any thought to how we can address those HIV learning outcomes?

Block: I have. If you've got a few minutes, I'd like to tell you what I've come up with and get your reaction.

Castle: Sure. Go ahead.

Block: Well, there is not a suitable demonstration or lab activity that I'm aware of to help our students achieve the learning outcomes. But I do know of a DVD that is in our media center that would work to address the first three. If we can get the DVD, working it into a lecture may be our best bet. I've written some questions that I think will engage the students and help them achieve the learning outcomes. I'll bring them and hopefully the DVD to our meeting this afternoon.

Castle: I'm a little concerned about the last learning outcome. How do you think we should have our students evaluate the costs of AIDS?

Block: That's a tough one. I thought about suggesting that we try engaging our students in a reflective discussion. How do you think Ms. Johnson and Ms. Green will respond to that suggestion?

Castle: I'm not sure. They'll probably say that our students need more information than presented in our textbook and on the DVD and may not be prepared to participate in a scientific argument without someone's feelings being hurt.

Block: There goes the bell. We'll have to continue this conversation in Ms. Johnson's room this afternoon. Thanks for listening.

source. Alternatively, assemble the apparatus before class begins, cover it with a cloth or a box before the students arrive in the room, and then unveil the setup to begin the demonstration. Demonstrations that include unusual noises, lights, or motions are useful for attracting student attention and maintaining interest.

The only way to be certain that a demonstration will proceed smoothly is to set it up beforehand, try it out, and then use the same materials and equipment during the actual presentation. The availability of back-up materials such as additional batteries, pulleys, and glassware will often allow a demonstration to proceed as planned without problems. When trying out the demonstration, it is also important to consider the questions that will be asked and take measures that will be employed to ensure student engagement and learning as well as practices that will guarantee student and teacher safety.

TABLE 11.4 Sources of Science Demonstrations

Science Snacks, the Exploratorium of San Francisco
The demonstrations described at this Web site are miniaturized versions of some of the Exploratorium's popular exhibits. (www.exploratorium.edu/snacks/)

Society for American Scientists
This site includes numerous physics demonstrations developed by William J. Beaty of Seattle, Washington and links to other Internet sites that contain descriptions of additional physics demonstrations. (www.eskimo.com/~billb/amasci.html)

Chemistry Department of Elmhurst College, Illinois
Many chemical demonstrations performed by Dr. Charles Ophardt are described by topic and presented at this site. (www.elmhurst.edu/~chm/demos/)

Science Education at the University of Nebraska–Lincoln
A collection of biology, chemistry, and physics demonstrations compiled by Dr. Ron Bonnstetter are presented at this site. (http://nerds.unl.edu/pages/mamres/pages/demos/demo.html)

Hawai'i Space Grant Representatives' Space Science Activities
This site includes more than 25 demonstrations presented at the 2001 NSTA convention. They are useful for teaching a number of space science concepts. (www.spacegrant.hawaii.edu/hi-nsta2001.html)

***Chemical Demonstrations: A Handbook for Teaching Chemistry* (Volumes 1–4)**
Written by Dr. Bassam Shakhashiri of the University of Wisconsin and his colleagues, this four-volume set includes descriptions of hundreds of demonstrations. (http://scifun.chem.wisc.edu/)

75 Easy Life Science Demonstrations* and *75 Easy Earth Science Demonstrations
Authored by Thomas Kardos, these paperback books are available from the Ward's Natural Science Company, Rochester, New York. (http://wardsci.com/)

Science teachers should make demonstrations visible to all students.

Presenting a Demonstration

A science demonstration can easily result in a teacher-centered instructional session, which focuses only on the "oohs" and "ahs" of a dramatic event. However, we recommend using a student-centered approach during demonstrations, one that engages all students from start to finish. This is possible by carefully selecting demonstrations, crafting questions, and selecting talk moves that cause students to wonder why and to explain how. It is also important to involve students in demonstrations that have three phases: an introduction, a presentation, and a conclusion (Kindsvatter et al., 1996).

During the *introduction*, the purpose of the demonstration is established and students become acquainted with the materials and procedures. Recognition by the students of the demonstration's purpose is essential to assure cognitive engagement. The purposes of a demonstration should be kept simple. Moreover, interesting problems for students to consider often arise from the actions of the demonstration materials themselves. The problem will often lead students to the demonstration's purpose.

The introduction of a science demonstration provides a perfect opportunity to engage students in a "position-driven" discussion (Michaels, Shouse, & Schweingruber, 2008). Position-driven discussion is initiated by showing students the demonstration apparatus, but before the presentation is begun asking students to make predictions and to offer arguments and evidence to support their predictions about what they think will happen during the demonstration. Position-driven discussion is most productive when the problem posed by the demonstration has more than one possible outcome. For example, asking students to predict how many standard-size paper clips can be dropped into a glass filled to the brim with water tends to generate responses ranging from zero to hundreds. The discussion that accompanies secondary students' predictions often involves energetic talk about adhesion, cohesion, and the polarity of water molecules that is rich with arguments, evidence, and reasoning.

The demonstration *presentation* must proceed in a logical and organized manner, and move along at a somewhat rapid pace. Procedures that may cause long delays or pauses should be avoided. To ensure that students learn from a demonstration, a teacher may ask questions such as, "What observations have you made?" or "What happened in the last step?" as the demonstration proceeds. If students disagree in their responses to the questions, it may be necessary to repeat the demonstration or step. To prompt student attention and learning, a teacher could periodically summarize what has occurred or ask a student to do so. Depending on the nature of the demonstration, it may be possible to have students physically manipulating materials or equipment in this phase.

During the *conclusion* phase of the demonstration, the teacher helps students construct new understandings about the concept or principle illustrated in the previous phase. One way to do this is by engaging students in a guided discussion of the application of the concept or principle to everyday life. This will make the instruction relevant to the students and make the purpose of the demonstration easier to understand. Be prepared to describe several common situations that illustrate the idea, just in case the students do not suggest any. Questions should be asked to facilitate student conversation and meaningful learning during this phase of the demonstration. Discussion that challenges students' ideas and stimulates argumentation is "necessary to promote a scientific understanding of a science demonstration" (Shepardson et al., 1994, p. 244). Too much teacher talk can squelch student conversation.

Research indicates that the quality of science demonstrations improves as teachers grow in their science content knowledge and their understanding of science instructional practices and student characteristics (Clermont, Borko, & Krajcik, 1994). Nevertheless, there is much that beginning teachers can do to ensure the effectiveness of science demonstrations. Suggestions for making demonstrations effective science learning opportunities for students are presented in Figure 11.1. In addition, Classroom Snapshot 11.2 presents a vignette of a science demonstration that illustrates the modeling to learn approach discussed in Chapter 9 of this text. The vignette emphasizes the large amount of interaction and engagement necessary to help students construct meaningful science understandings from demonstrations.

Stop and Reflect!

Before reading on, do the following:

- By yourself or with a classmate, plan a science demonstration that includes the elements—questioning, student talk and argumentation, and modeling—illustrated in the vignette in Classroom Snapshot 11.2. Then, analyze your plan to determine how interactive and engaging it would be for students. In addition, consider presenting your demonstration to peers or adolescents in a school setting to determine the effectiveness of your planning and teaching.

FIGURE 11.1 Suggestions for effective science demonstrations.

- Select a demonstration that clearly fits the context of the unit.
- If a series of demonstrations is to be used, make sure that the demonstrations address a single concept (Shepardson, 1994).
- Make sure that all materials and apparatus are available, are in good working order, and that proper safety practices are in place.
- Clear the demonstration table of extraneous and irrelevant materials and equipment so that all students can see the demonstration.
- Speak at a moderate pace, loudly enough to be heard by all students, and enunciate clearly.
- State the purpose of the demonstration at the beginning or at the appropriate time.
- Describe and simultaneously show the steps of the demonstration.
- Ask questions to stimulate student thinking, to help students draw their own conclusions, and to initiate further investigation.
- Allow for sufficient time to incorporate a position-driven discussion into the demonstration and to achieve the intended learning outcomes.
- Conclude the demonstration with a discussion and, if appropriate, link the demonstration to applications in everyday life.

Classroom Snapshot 11.2

Demonstrating Mixtures and Solutions

Mr. Pratt's eighth-grade science class is ready to study mixtures as well as homogeneous and heterogeneous solutions. He decided to begin the unit by helping students build their understanding of these concepts with demonstrations of reflection and scattering of light.

Mr. Pratt wrote the following question on the whiteboard:

Why is the sky blue during the day and red on the horizon where the Sun is setting in the late evening?

The question produced some responses from students, which Mr. Pratt wrote on the whiteboard. But when he asked students to explain their responses, he received little in return. Then he presented his first demonstration to illustrate reflection of light by small particles. For the demonstration, the teacher placed a half cup of baking flour into a fine-mesh kitchen sieve. Mr. Pratt darkened the room and turned on a flashlight. Then, he tapped on the sieve with his finger in order to release some flour from the wire mesh, causing it to fall down on the tabletop. After calling students' attention to the flour falling through the air, he directed the flashlight beam through the particles at a right angle to the class. The reflected light rendered the fine particles of flour very visible. This caught students' interest and they wanted the teacher to demonstrate this many times.

Mr. Pratt proceeded by asking the students why the particles are so visible, even when the light is shinning at a right angle to their field of vision. He guided students' responses toward the idea of reflected light. The teacher called students to the whiteboard to diagram light waves striking flour particles, illustrating light reflecting off particles and traveling in all directions, including toward their eyes. The diagrams were left on the board to serve as visual models of light reflecting off large particles in the air. Then the teacher prepared a second demonstration to illustrate light reflecting off large particles in water. He began by partially filling a glass jar with water and stirring in approximately one teaspoon of milk. Mr. Pratt called the students to the front of the classroom, forming a semicircle around him. He asked one of the students to turn off the lights in the classroom, lowered the glass jar until it was about 3 feet from the floor, turned on the flashlight above the top of the jar, and asked the students to identify the color of light reflecting off the surface of the water. The students were quick to identify the bluish color. Then Mr. Pratt placed a sheet of white paper in front of the demonstration table, lowered the jar a few inches above the paper, and asked the students to observe the color of light coming out of the bottom of the jar. Again, the students were able to identify the change in color of the light, which was reddish in color rather than blue.

Mr. Pratt asked the students to take their seats and proceeded to the whiteboard to draw a large circle representing Earth and a small one showing the Sun at about 1:00 p.m. Then, the teacher and students engaged in a lengthy discussion, using many diagrams to advance student understanding of sunlight passing through Earth's atmosphere during the day and in the late evening. The session involved a great deal of questions and challenging of ideas.

 Lecture

The lecture has certain strengths that make it useful for science instruction. A large amount of material can be covered in a short time by lecture, and it is an effective means for introducing a unit, clarifying understandings, and defining science terms (Flowerdew, 1992). A lecturer can also teach many students using few materials and resources. In general, the lecture can be as effective as other instructional strategies, particularly when the purpose is immediate cognitive gains (Gage & Berliner, 1992).

When science teachers speak of lecture they are most often talking about an interactive lecture rather than something resembling the presentation by a keynote speaker at a convention. Teacher and student questions and demonstrations punctuate the interactive lecture. The interjection of questions and demonstrations encourages students to attend to the topic or issue that is the focus of the interactive lecture. Questions and accompanying demonstrations prompt the scientific talk and argumentation necessary for students to further develop their science understandings. In addition, student questions about demonstrations and responses to teacher questions provide a check on student understanding.

The interactive lecture is often an underrated teaching strategy. But as Eick and Samford (1999) point out, it holds great promise for beginning teachers primarily for two reasons. Its use enables the beginning teacher to develop confidence in classroom leadership because the teacher remains the focus of classroom activity. Also, the interactive lecture can serve as a bridge for the teacher to more student-centered instruction. This bridging function is facilitated through the opportunities for student talk and argumentation present in the interactive lecture.

Preparing the Lecture

Lecture preparation involves checking your understanding of the content to be presented, preparing lecture notes to guide your presentation, and organizing the lecture in a logical manner for your audience. Suffice it to say that teachers should be comfortable with their content knowledge in order to present a good lecture. But knowing the content is not enough. Knowing how to present the science content knowledge you have to students is equally important (Gage & Berliner, 1992). This "how-to" knowledge, which Shulman (1987) called *pedagogical content knowledge*, is reflected in the teacher's ability to explain ideas in more than one way, provide persuasive examples, use helpful metaphors and analogies, and recognize where students will likely have difficulty when studying a science topic for the first time. Your own science learning experiences will provide the foundation for the pedagogical content knowledge that you will use as a beginning teacher. You can strengthen your knowledge base for teaching by talking with other teachers, reading, participating in science education courses, and teaching the same science courses multiple times.

Lecture notes serve to guide the teacher's presentation and may take different forms. Some teachers feel comfortable delivering a lecture only when they have written the complete lecture in prose form. Other teachers, usually with more experience, prefer a skeleton outline that consists of a title and main headings with key terms and ideas organized under the headings. Further, a teacher may choose to prepare visual representations of lecture notes to guide students through a lecture and to stimulate note taking. The visual representation may take the form of an outline or graphic organizer, such as a concept map. Visual representations do help students follow lectures and may improve student achievement. Moreover, note taking helps students remember the material when the notes are studied in preparation for a test, but note taking by itself does not aid student comprehension of the material (Gage & Berliner, 1992). This suggests that it is important for students to listen carefully during lectures and study their notes before tests and for a teacher to use visual representations to cue students to important aspects of a lecture.

Special attention should be given to a lecture's introduction since it provides structure for what will follow. Good and Brophy (1994) recommend the use of advance organizers for this purpose. Advance organizers help explain and interrelate the material they precede (Ausubel, 1963). The *expository advance organizer* places the information to be learned into context with other information that is conceptually related. For example, for a lecture on the circulation of blood, an expository organizer might include a brief description of other systems in the body such as the lymphatic system and the renal/urinary system. A *comparative advance organizer* for the same lecture might compare the circulatory system with a hot water system in a house. The simplicity of a hot water system provides a concrete analogy for students to begin the study of a similar concept involving the human body. Cronin Jones (2003, p. 456) also suggests that lecturers consider using *rhetorical advance organizers*, which involve posing "a series of questions that cue students into the important topics to be covered."

Presenting a Successful Lecture

A well-organized lecture has an introduction, a main body, summaries within the body of the presentation, and a conclusion. The *introduction* should serve to motivate students to attend to the lecture and cue them to what will be presented and emphasized. Explaining how the lecture topic is related to the students' personal lives is one way to heighten motivation. Teachers can use questions, statements, and important terms to cue students about what to expect in a lecture. The introduction also serves to help students ready themselves for the information presented during the lecture.

The *body* of the lecture is characterized by the presentation of content in an orderly fashion, the use of visual aids to enhance the presentation, and the inclusion of questions and talk moves to stimulate student attention (Kindsvatter et al., 1996). Remembering that the processing capabilities of middle school and high school students are not those of adults, it is best to have a simple plan of organization for a lecture. A complicated sequence can only cause confusion. The organization for a science lecture may show how a main idea is composed of several subordinate ones. It may show how ideas or events are related chronologically or through cause and effect, or show the relationship of ideas through a central unifying theory (Gage & Berliner, 1992). Line drawings, graphs, photographs, models, and demonstrations are examples of visual aids that can enhance any lecture. Henson (1988, p. 92) reported the most effective use of visual aids occurs when the "lesson is not pre-developed but built up in front of the students, who help develop the concepts . . . as the lesson develops." Nonverbal cues such as body posture, facial expressions, eye contact, gestures, and physical distance can help hold student interest and attention and stimulate their mental involvement in the lecture (Kindsvatter et al., 1996).

One other way to achieve these same ends is by telling stories. Knox (1997) recommends that science teachers consider using the storytelling formats of myth, historical narrative, and detective story to enliven their lectures and enhance student engagement. The myth of Frankenstein, the historical account of U.S. bomber pilots' discovery of the jet stream during World War II, and the Sherlock Holmes–like mystery that surrounds Watson and Crick's discovery of the structure of DNA are examples of stories that Knox believes students should hear in science classes. However, historical accounts of scientific achievements must be accurate and not overly dramatic.

Summaries within an interactive lecture are typically question based. An alternative to summaries are lecture breaks (Olmsted, 1999), where students are encouraged to share what they have learned with classmates and provide feedback to the teacher about his or her lecture. Lecture summaries and breaks are intended to motivate, provide time for reflection, establish the relevancy of the material just presented, and allow for formative assessment.

The *conclusion* of the lecture is the place for the teacher to summarize major points and to ask additional questions. The success of the lecture may be gauged from students' responses to these concluding questions. Emphasizing important points during the conclusion will help students identify relationships needed to undertake future assignments and to be involved in other activities. Unfortunately, too many lectures lack conclusions as teachers run out of time while presenting the body of their lectures, which usually implies that the lecture was too long. Your responses to the questions posed in Figure 11.2 should help you gauge the overall quality of your lectures and their likely impact on student learning.

Demonstrating Your Understanding of Instructional Strategies That Promote Scientific Discourse

As mentioned at the beginning of this chapter, discussion, demonstration, and lecture are instructional strategies that provide opportunities for students to engage in science talk and argumentation. It is through

FIGURE 11.2 Considerations for preparing a quality lecture.

- How will students be actively involved in your lecture? Will you ask and answer questions, employ talk moves, or have students engage in an activity?
- How will you make your lectures relevant and useful to your students?
- What will you do to increase student interest in your lecture? Can humor or demonstrations be incorporated into your lecture?
- How will you link students' prior knowledge to new content during your lecture? Is your lecture organized to move from simple concepts to complex ones?
- What will you do during your lecture to prevent cognitive overload and learner shutdown?
- How will you introduce scientific vocabulary and keep scientific jargon to a minimum?
- How will you incorporate summaries or breaks into your lectures?
- What strategies could you teach students to help them improve their note-taking skills?
- What misconceptions are students likely to hold regarding the topic of your lecture? How will you confront students' misconceptions?
- How will you structure your lecture to include visual and kinesthetic stimulation in addition to auditory stimulation?

Based on information presented in L. L. Cronin Jones (2003), Are your lectures a thing of the past? *Journal of College Science Teaching, 32*(7), 453–457.

these forms of science discourse that students can construct meaningful science knowledge. As a beginning teacher, you will be expected to demonstrate your understandings of how to use these instructional strategies to promote scientific discourse among students that will lead them to construction science knowledge in your planning and practice. There are two sections of the National Science Teachers Association (NSTA) *Standards for Science Teacher Preparation* that address these understandings.

Standard 2: Nature of Science states:

To show they are prepared to teach the nature of science, teachers of science must demonstrate that they:

c. Engage students successfully in studies of the nature of science including, when possible, the critical analysis of false or doubtful assertions made in the name of science. (NSTA, 2003, p. 16)

Standard 5: General Skills of Teaching states:

To show that they are prepared to create a community of diverse learners, teachers of science must demonstrate that they:

a. Vary their teaching actions, strategies, and methods to promote the development of multiple student skills and levels of understanding. (NSTA, 2003, p. 21)

You can demonstrate your understandings in these areas by planning for and engaging students in discussions, demonstrations, and lectures where they construct science knowledge while participating in discourse in ways similar to its use in the scientific community.

Assessing and Reviewing

Analysis and Synthesis

1. Write an example for each of the scientific discourse patterns presented in Table 11.1 Then develop a pattern template and example for one or more of the following language functions: hypothesizing, measuring, disagreeing, and sequencing.
2. Write two questions and describe a talk move that you could use during a discussion, demonstration, or lecture on a science topic of interest to you.
3. Create a table in which you describe the strengths and limitations of discussion, demonstration, and lecture as instructional strategies.
4. When students have difficulty learning from lectures, it is often because they are unable to organize the information presented by the teacher in a meaningful way. How could a teacher use the topic outline that follows to facilitate student learning during a lecture on the circulatory system?

   Circulatory System
   I. Heart
   II. Blood Vessels
   III. Blood

Practical Considerations

5. Locate a description of a science demonstration that is of interest to you. Practice the demonstration and prepare yourself to guide others through the demonstration. Then, organize a science demonstration Share-A-Thon event with students in your class and invite friends, family, and others to participate.
6. Arrange with a science teacher to observe an interactive lecture, a discussion, or a demonstration. Pay particular attention to the questions asked and talk moves and talk formats used by the teacher during the lesson. Meet with the teacher after your observation to talk about what you observed.
7. Choose a science issue having a social connection that lends itself to reflective discussion. Then develop a plan that includes (a) the question or questions to initiate the discussion; (b) questions, talk moves, and talk formats to keep the discussion going; and (c) strategies to bring closure to the discussion.

Developmental Considerations

8. Start a file of science demonstrations. Add notes to your file about your success with each demonstration after using it with students.
9. Videotape yourself leading a discussion, demonstration, or lecture. Then, analyze the tape for your use of questions, talk moves, and talk formats. Develop and enact a plan to improve.

Resources to Examine

Ready, Set, Science. 2008. National Research Council of the National Academies, Washington, DC. [Online.] Available at: www.nap.edu/catalog.php?record_id=11882#toc

Chapter 5, "Making Thinking Visible: Talk and Argumentation," provides a concise overview of the research on scientific talk and argumentation and how talk and argumentation can be used by science teachers to support the science learning of diverse classes of students. The authors of the book are Sarah Michaels, Andrew Shouse, and Heide Schweingruber.

Are Lectures a Thing of the Past? 2003. *Journal of College Science Teaching, 23*(7), 453–457.

The answer to the question that is the title of this article is a resounding "No," according to Linda L. Cronin Jones. In making a case for using lecture as an instructional strategy, she describes four components of an effective lecture and summarizes 10 research-based considerations for lecturers.

Teaching and Learning Through Discussion. 1990. Springfield, IL. Charles C. Thomas.

Read Chapter 8, "Involving Different Social and Cultural Groups in Discussion." Jane White reviews anthropological research on classroom interaction involving Native-American, Hispanic, and other cultural groups and suggests a variety of strategies teachers can use to engage students from diverse cultural backgrounds in productive discussions.

Invitations to Science Inquiry. 1987. Lexington, MA: Ginn Press. Address for ordering: Science Inquiry Enterprises, 14358 Village View Lane, Chino Hills, CA 91709.

To arouse student curiosity about science, consider using discrepant events. This teacher resource manual by Tik L. Liem includes over 400 author-tested discrepant events. Many of the discrepant events are suitable for demonstration. Presented for each discrepant event is an illustration, list of materials, questions for students, and an explanation of the science behind the counterintuitive adventure.

Questions Are the Answer. 1996. *The Science Teacher, 63,* 27–30.

Authors John Penick, Linda Crow, and Ron Bonstetter present an innovative questioning hierarchy for science teachers. The five levels of the hierarchy highlight question types that emphasize prior experiences, relationships, applications, speculation, and explanation.

References

Ausubel, D. P. (1963). Some psychological and educational limitations of learning by discovery. *New York State Mathematics Teachers Journal, 13,* 90.

Clermont, C. P., Borko, H., & Krajcik, J. S. (1994). Comparative study of the pedagogical content knowledge of experienced and novice chemical demonstrators. *Journal of Research in Science Teaching, 31,* 419–441.

Costa, A., & Lowery, L. (1989). *Techniques for teaching thinking.* Pacific Grove, CA: Midwest Publications.

Cronin Jones, L. L. (2003). Are lectures a thing of the past? *Journal of College Science Teaching, 32*(7), 453–457.

Dillon, J. T. (1990). Conducting discussions by alternatives to questioning. In W. W. Wilen (Ed.), *Teaching and learning through discussion* (pp. 79–96). Springfield, IL: Charles C. Thomas.

Eick, C., & Samford, K. (1999). Techniques for new teachers. *The Science Teacher, 66,* 34–37.

Flowerdew, J. (1992). Definitions in science lectures. *Applied Linguistics, 13,* 202–221.

Gage, N. L., & Berliner, D. C. (1992). *Educational psychology* (5th ed.). Boston: Houghton Mifflin.

Good, T., & Brophy, J. (1994). *Looking into classrooms* (6th ed.). New York: HarperCollins.

Henson, K. T. (1988). *Methods and strategies for teaching in secondary and middle schools.* New York: Longman.

Kindsvatter, R., Wilen, W., & Ishler, M. (1996). *Dynamics of effective teaching* (3rd ed.). White Plains, NY: Longman Publishing.

Knox, J. A. (1997). Reform of the college science lecture through storytelling. *Journal of College Science Teaching, 26,* 388–392.

Liem, T. (1987). *Invitations to science inquiry.* Lexington, MA: Ginn Press.

Michaels, S., Shouse, A. W., & Schweingruber, H. A. (2008). *Ready, set, science!* Washington, DC: The National Academies Press.

National Research Council (NRC). (2007). *Taking science to school: Learning and teaching science in grades K–8.* Washington, DC: The National Academies Press.

Olmsted, J. A. (1999). The mid-lecture break: When less is more. *Journal of Chemical Education, 76*(4), 525–527.

Roby, T. W. (1988). Models of discussion. In J. T. Dillon (Ed.), *Questioning and discussion: A multidisciplinary study* (pp. 163–191). Norwood, NJ: Ablex.

Rowe, M. B. (1974). Wait-time and rewards as instructional variables: Their influence on language, logic, and fate control. Part I. Wait-time. *Journal of Research in Science Teaching, 11*, 81–94.

Rowe, M. B. (Ed.) (1978). *What research says to the science teacher* (vol. 1). Washington, DC: National Science Teachers Association.

Shepardson, D. P., Moje, E. B., & Kennard-McClelland, A. M. (1994). The impact of science demonstrations on children's understanding of air pressure. *Journal of Research in Science Teaching, 31*, 243–258.

Shulman, L. S. (1987). Knowledge and teaching: Foundations for the new reform. *Harvard Educational Review, 57*, 1–22.

Stahl, R. (1994). Using think-time and wait-time skillfully in the classroom. ERIC Clearinghouse for Social Studies/Social Science Education, Bloomington, IN. Retrieved June 12, 2008, from www.ericfacility.net/databases/ERICDigest/ed370885.html

Tobin, K. (1984). Effects of extended wait-time on discourse characteristics and achievement in middle school grades. *Journal of Research in Science Teaching, 21*, 779–791.

Tobin, K., & Gallagher, J. J. (1987). The role of target students in the science classroom. *Journal of Research in Science Teaching, 24*, 61–75.

Tobin, K., Tippins, D. J., & Gallard, A. J. (1994). Research on instructional strategies for teaching science. In D. L. Gabel (Ed.), *Handbook on research in science teaching and learning* (pp. 45–93) New York: Macmillan.

White, J. J. (1990). Involving different social and cultural groups in discussion. In W. W. Wilen (Ed.), *Teaching and learning through discussion* (pp. 147–174). Springfield, IL: Charles C. Thomas.

Wilen, W. W. (1990). Forms and phases of discussion. In W. W. Wilen (Ed.), *Teaching and learning through discussion* (pp. 3–24). Springfield, IL: Charles C. Thomas.

Chapter

12

Science, Technology, and Societal Issues

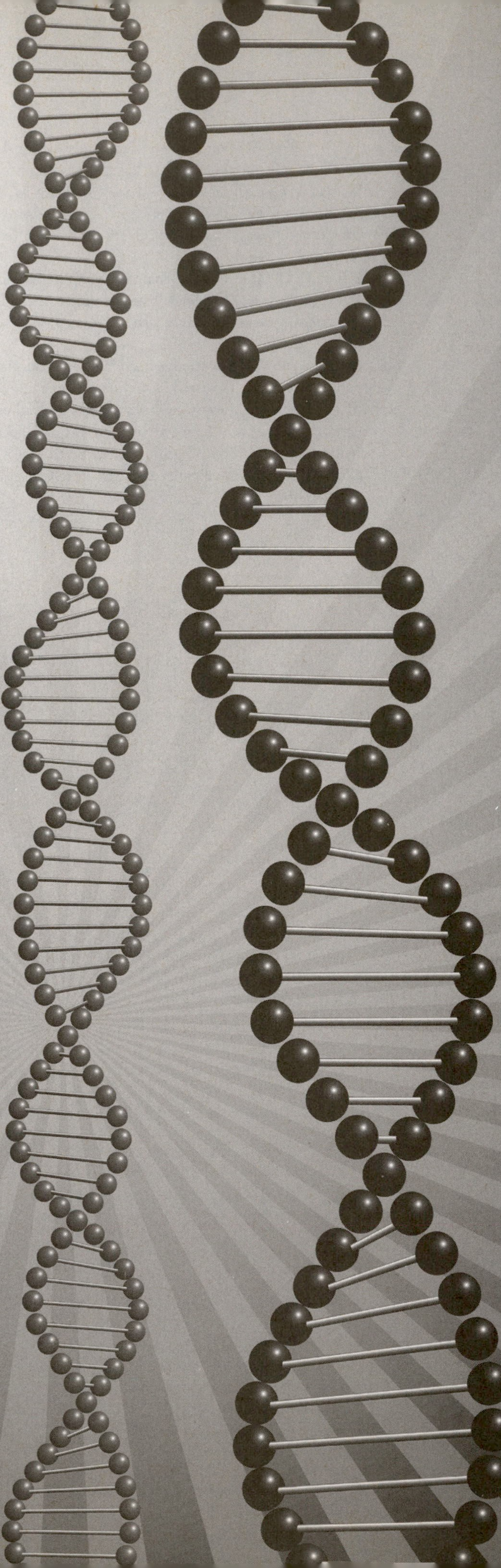

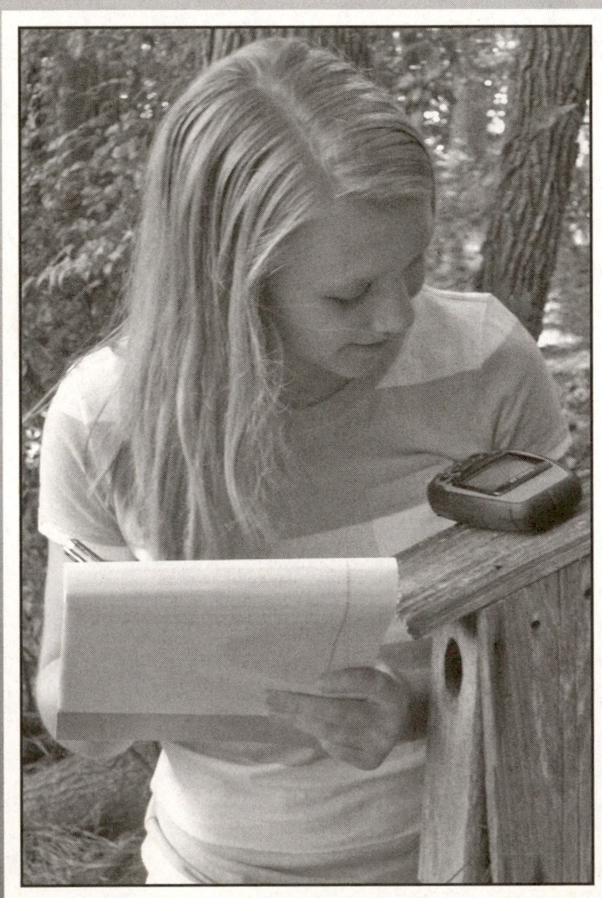

Students have many technological devices to assist them in investigating scientific issues.

Science is inextricably linked to technology and society. Science benefits from the tools and processes that technology provides, and technological solutions benefit from scientific research. Moreover, science and technology exist in a social context, where the work of scientists and engineers is influenced by the culture of their times and where scientific and technological advancements impact individuals and societies.

An important goal of school science is for students to understand the relationship between science, technology, and society and to use their understandings to examine and make thoughtful decisions about issues that involve their confluence. This goal calls for innovative instructional approaches that go beyond those that focus on traditional science content. The instructional approaches must link science and technology, and stress the application of scientific and technological knowledge to one's personal life and societal concerns. These approaches must highlight the work of engineers and scientists, and engage students in a variety of learning experiences, including those that involve the design and exploration of products, processes, and systems. The instructional approaches also must provide opportunities for students to analyze the impact of science and technology on society, and to determine the costs and benefits associated with important issues and problems. It is through instructional approaches with these emphases that students can develop scientific literacy.

AIMS OF THE CHAPTER

Use the questions that follow to guide your thinking and learning about teaching in ways to help students understand the relationship between science and technology and make informed decisions about science-related issues:

- What is technology? How is biotechnology different from technology derived from the physical sciences?
- How can technology be made a part of students' science learning experiences?
- What are socioscientific issues? How can they be addressed in middle and secondary school science classes?
- What should be considered when dealing with controversial issues and personal values in science classes, especially related to evolution and creationism?

Science and Technology

Every member of our society needs to understand and appreciate the interrelationship of science and technology. This is particularly true for today's youth, who will experience a multitude of scientific and technological advancements during their lifetime. A realistic understanding of the relationship between science and technology can be developed by first dealing with the unique attributes of each enterprise then addressing their implications for society. In addition, young people need to be presented with opportunities to engage in technological design. By proposing solutions to real problems and evaluating their consequences, students can further develop their understandings of the relationship between science and technology.

What Is Technology?

Just as science is not easy to define, neither is technology. Furthermore, the differences between science and technology are not clear-cut; science and technology are inherently intertwined. As a consequence, they convey different meanings to the professional and to the layperson. In general, *science* can be regarded as the enterprise that seeks to understand natural phenomena and to arrange these ideas into ordered knowledge, whereas *technology* involves the design of products, systems, and processes that affect the quality of life, using the knowledge of science where necessary.

Science is a basic enterprise that seeks knowledge and understanding. It is aligned with observation and theory. Technology, on the other hand, is an applied enterprise concerned with developing, constructing, and applying ideas that result in apparatuses, gadgets, tools, machines, and techniques. The products of science are often called *discoveries*, while the products of technology are referred to as *inventions*.

Technology preceded science in human history, beginning when humans invented tools to make work easier and life better. Early technology is simple compared with today's high-tech products. Simple tools were made by ancient peoples to aid in hunting, farming, and fighting. The technological products of today include complex devices, such as computers, and agricultural commodities, such as genetically engineered corn.

But technology is not limited to the artifacts of invention. Systems and processes are also technology. Navigation, medicine, and genetic engineering are technological systems and manufacturing, cloning, setting priorities, and implementation of the universal systems model are technological processes. After centuries of interplay between technology and science, there exists a myriad of designs, goods, and services that benefit humankind. Technology and science are often so intimately related that they rely on each other. This interplay of science and technology was as evident during the 1660s—when Robert Hooke used the simple microscope that he designed and built to see small chambers, which he called cells, in a slice of cork—as it is today in the work done in the laboratories of genetic engineers.

Technology Derived from the Physical Sciences

Technology is often associated with the physical sciences through the tools and machines that may be used to solve real-world problems and improve the quality of life.

Some modern technological achievements are computers, digital videodisc players, digital cameras, superconducting materials, nuclear power, cellular telephones, superhighways, plastics, and the Internet. Engineers design products and services that benefit society, often drawing on scientific information to assist in their work. Their products and services have constraints that range from safety and environmental protection to the limitations imposed by materials and the weather (National Research Council, 1996). Engineers are engaged in inquiry, use their imaginations, and figure out solutions to problems. They experiment, control variables, and make keen observations. These men and women possess a body of knowledge about their enterprise along with an understanding of many scientific disciplines. Most important, these individuals create products and processes.

In addition to the benefits of technology, costs also must be considered. Large-scale production of goods and services consumes valuable resources such as fossil fuels, minerals, and drinking and irrigated water. These resources are being depleted and are becoming more costly and difficult to obtain. Nations throughout the world must make decisions regarding the use of all resources so that this generation does not misuse valuable raw materials, leaving future generations without them.

Biotechnology

Today's vision of technology must also include the burgeoning area of biotechnology. The term *biotechnology* is used to refer to the applications of technology that make use of biological materials or systems to modify products or processes (National Convention on Biological Diversity, 1992). Biotechnology is closely aligned with the sciences of genetics, molecular biology, cell biology, and many others, and uses such tools as recombinant DNA, tissue cultures, and bacterial and virus vectors to transfer nuclear material into hosts. Men and women working in biotechnology also engage in inquiry, and use their understandings of the biological sciences to address the needs of humanity.

The applications of biotechnology are most evident in the health care and agricultural industries. Pharmaceutical production, genetic testing, and gene therapy are just a few of the application of biotechnology in the health care arena. Techniques of modern biotechnology in agriculture are used to improve crop yield, reduce crop dependence on fertilizers and pesticides, and increase the nutritional value of some food crops. But, just as is true for technology derived from the physical science, biotechnology can incite controversy. For example, genetic testing, because of its cost, is used almost exclusively in developed countries and there are fears that free access to genetic test results may lead to their misuse.

 Teaching about Technology

It is important for students to understanding technology and its relationship to science in order to function in a science-based society, such as that which exists in most countries around the world. Fortunately, many types of products, systems, and processes can be designed and investigated by students to develop their scientific and technological literacy.

Design and Build

Science teachers can engage their students in designing and building models of various technological tools and processes. The models will be simplifications of more complex designs and systems, but are invaluable in helping students understand how technologies function and their relation to science. For example, middle school students can design and build working models of electric motors, lightbulbs, can openers, egg timers, and other household items as well as string rockets and wind-powered toys. Secondary students can build robotic arms, radios, geodesic domes, and electric generators. Students also like to design and build zany machines like those depicted in the cartoons of Rube Goldberg. Goldberg's cartoon illustrations depict complex machines that involve very convoluted processes for accomplishing a rather simple task, and have spawned local and national competitions. More information about machines modeled on those presented in Goldberg's cartoons and machine-building competitions can be found at the following Web sites:

- Rube Goldberg, Inc. (www.rubegoldberg.com)
- Rube Goldberg Contest (www.rubemachine.com)

Students also enjoy the challenge of designing and constructing devices to achieve a particular engineering objective. Building a bridge using pasta, a wind-powered machine, a historic catapult using inexpensive hardware, or a container that will keep an egg from breaking when dropped from a three-story building are just a few examples of challenges that students enthusiastically pursue. When pursuing these challenges, students are presented with opportunities to design a solution to a real problem, implement and evaluate their designs, and communicate the stages of their work to classmates (NRC, 1996).

Other learning activities, such as planning a cafeteria menu to meet basic nutritional needs, comparing the absorbency of competing brands of paper towels, or the voltage of batteries, also provide students with experiences in design and analysis. Engaging in challenges of these types often leads to students apply their new understandings to other problems in their home and community. One example is Ashley Kling's award-winning invention. As a ninth-grader, Ashley invented a flashing firefighter's safety boot, which makes a firefighter more visible in smoky buildings and on ladders. Ashley's invention was prompted by her concern for the safety of firefighters.

Investigate and Improve

Reading, personal interviews, and site visits are forms of inquiry that many science teachers use to help students learn about technology. These forms of investigation are appropriate for learning about technological products as well as technological systems and processes. Students can find a great deal of reading material in libraries and on the Internet to improve their understanding and stimulate their interest about technological systems and processes. They will also find that many professionals are willing to discuss the technological systems that they use in their jobs or the processes that are the backbone of important businesses and industries. For example, students can investigate the relationship between research and development in a major corporation, how computers are used in the homes of classmates or in neighborhood businesses, the applications nanotechnology, or the process of priority setting used by emergency management teams at times of natural disaster.

Investigations of biotechnology can also take other forms. In addition to having students read books and articles about such topics as bioinformatics and genome mapping, teachers can involve them in laboratory activities and computer simulations that mirror the practices of the biotechnology industry. Students can play the role of a crime- scene investigator and attempt to identify a suspected murderer by comparing antigens and antibodies in immunoassay labs. In investigations and simulations that focus on the medical applications of biotechnology, students can examine genetic differences using DNA fingerprinting, identify genetic mutations using restriction enzyme analysis, and diagnose cancer using micro-array. Students can also investigate the effects of genetic engineering on crops by studying the DNA and morphology of regular cotton plants and genetically engineered Bt cotton plants. The fact that Bt cotton contains a bacterium that produces a toxin that kills insects can lead to interesting discussions about the ecological and evolutionary implications of genetic engineering. Online sources of other investigations and simulations that can be used to help students build understandings of biotechnology and technology associated with the physical sciences are identified in Table 12.1.

Through experiences with technology, students also can be introduced to the universal systems model:

- *Goal:* what the system should be able to do or produce
- *Input:* the ingredients that go into the system
- *Process:* the steps that lead to the intended goal
- *Output:* the result that is produced by the system
- *Feedback:* comparing the result to the goal and making changes to the Input or the Process (Forrester, 1961)

Using the model, student can develop understandings of how systems work and apply the model across the spectrum of technologies. For instance, the longstanding *goal* of the U.S. automotive industry is to manufacture safe and high-quality vehicles that the public wants to buy. To achieve this goal, the industry considers such *inputs* as the wants of potential customers, the facilities and workers needed to manufacture vehicles, and manufacturing costs and time. The industry constructs plants, employs workers, and obtains the raw materials needed for the *process* of manufacturing vehicles. The *output* of the manufacturing process is the cars, trucks, and vans that people buy. The decline in sales of vehicles that get poor gas mileage serves as *feedback* to the industry, prompting changes in the manufacturing process to produce smaller and more fuel-efficient vehicles.

As a result of their investigations of technology, students should be in a position to offer suggestions for improving technological products, systems, and processes like some of those identified below:

- *Products:* cellular telephones, iPods, and smart guns
- *Systems:* Internet, airport air traffic control, homeland security
- *Processes:* priority setting by students, technology use at school, distribution of community resources.

The desirable impact of integrating the study of technology into science instruction is illustrated by one physical science class's investigation of a local mass-transit rail system. In addition to students learning about energy, mechanics, motion and other science concepts, their investigation led them to offer much appreciated suggestions to the transit authority that projected increases in ridership and fuel savings.

TABLE 12.1 Resources for Teaching about Technology

Welcome Technology Teachers http://stlouis.missouri.org/501c/techteachers/index.html Examine the classroom resources presented by John Petsch at this site. In addition to many classroom technology context activities compiled by the American Society of Mechanical Engineers, this site provides links to design activities that focus on fiber optics, string rockets, robotic grippers, and newspaper acid rain shelters.
BIOTECH Project http://biotech.biology.arizona.edu Sponsored by the University of Arizona, this site is a portal to biotechnology resources and more than a dozen biotech laboratory activities.
Bay Area Biotechnology Education Consortium http://babec.org The curricula section of this Web site includes downloadable files for a number of laboratory investigations suitable for secondary students. The labs involve students in using the polymerase chain reaction (PCR) method to copy segments of DNA and fluorescent protein markers.
Iowa State University Office of Biotechnology www.biotech.iastate.edu/publications/ed_resoruces/biotech_curriculum.html Biotech curriculum units and modules developed for middle and secondary students are available at this Web site. Units and modules highlight the agricultural uses of biotechnology.
Using Technology to Study Cellular and Molecular Biology http://science.education.nih.gov/supplements/nih4/technology/default.htm This online unit is part of the National Institute of Health's Curriculum Supplement Series. Lesson plans and implementation support are provided at this Web site.
Engineering Education Service Center www.engineeringedu.com/students.html The student resources page of this Web site is a portal for information and investigations pertaining to a host of engineering fields, including electrical engineering, environmental engineering, ceramic engineering, manufacturing engineering, and metallurgical engineering.
American Society of Mechanical Engineers—Teacher Resources www.asme.org/Education/PreCollege/TeacherResources/ A number of engineering projects and activities suitable for middle and secondary science classes are described at this Web site. The Integrated Design Engineering Activity Series provides ideas for low-cost and fun engineering projects.
California Engineering and Technology Alliance—Engineering/Technology Curriculum for High Schools www.engineering-ed.org/modules.htm More than a dozen modules with topics ranging from mechanical design and robotics to semiconductors and civil structures are presented at this Web site. The lessons that compose each module are described in great detail, with downloadable materials available.

Stop and Reflect!

- Examine Classroom Snapshot 12.1. To what extent do you believe that Mrs. Johnson's class activities help students develop an understanding of the relationship between science and technology? Discuss your thoughts with a classmate.

Science and Societal Issues

In order for students to see science as relevant, they must be able to examine societal issues and problems and apply scientific processes and principles to them. They must be given many opportunities to discuss their beliefs and values and to investigate and propose solutions to real-world problems. It is through this type of instruction that students will be able to engage in meaningful discourse about science- and technology-related societal issues and problems and go on to make informed decisions.

From STS to SSI

The science-technology-society (STS) movement was born about four decades ago to promote change in science education. The change promoted was from school science as bound by the traditional science disciplines to

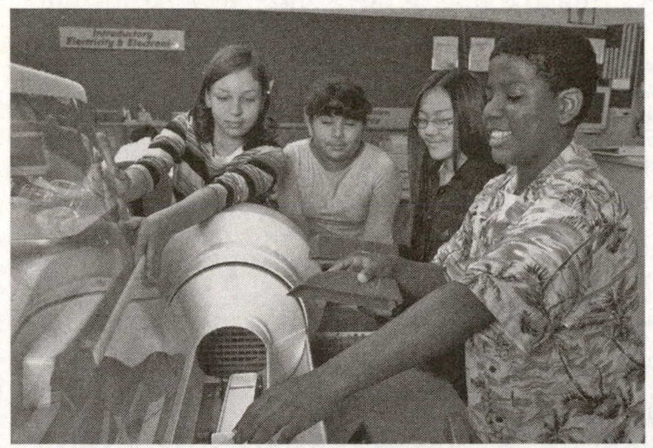

Classroom Snapshot 12.1

Building "Mouse Trap" Cars

Mrs. Johnson describes the instructional approach she uses in her eighth-grade physical science course:

More than half of my course centers on basic physics, which includes electricity, light, motion, and sound. I begin the study of each of these topics by asking students what they know about these topics and what they would like to learn about them. The discussions are followed by several laboratory exercises to develop fundamental concepts and principles. With some background, the students begin to participate in design projects. When we study motion, for example, I always involve students in the construction of "mouse trap" cars. These vehicles are powered by the basic mouse trap sold at hardware stores. The cars are made from scratch using simple materials or modified from toy cars and trucks. Since I attempt to link this car-building experience with the concepts of speed, acceleration, and friction, one of the objectives is to design a car that will accelerate the fastest from a stopped position to a line 2 meters away from the starting point. Another objective is to design a car that will roll the farthest. Students have the option as to which objective they wish to pursue. These activities are of high interest and they seem to reinforce the science concepts I want my students to learn.

I do not stop at the design phase of this activity because I want to further the investigative aspects of science and engineering. I ask all my students to write a short paper that requires them to analyze a real car and explain the features that contribute to its acceleration, speed, and efficiency. Some students use their family car for the purpose of analysis, while others go to automobile dealerships and get brochures on new cars, including hybrids. One of my students videotaped drag races from the Speed Channel and used the video to illustrate features of the cars that contribute to their acceleration. This activity also provides the opportunity for my students to invite local guest speakers, after obtaining my permission, to discuss how people design, maintain, and repair cars. A few years ago I took my classes on field trips to a local garage where race cars are built. Surprisingly, the girls were as motivated as the boys.

school science placed in a context of how it influences technology and, in turn, has an impact on society (Solomon, 2002). Consistent with this change, the intent of STS instruction is to increase students' interest in science through active involvement with issues and problems, thus preparing students for the role of active citizen in a democratic society. Scientific controversies and ethical dilemmas embedded in social contexts serve as important tools of STS instruction. Instruction guided by the tenants of the STS movement centers on such topics as water and air pollution, inappropriate land use, the depletion of natural resources, and personal health.

While STS instruction is successful in engaging students in the social dimensions of science and improving students' attitudes toward science, it has been criticized for not exploiting the science learning opportunities associated with the socioscientific issues (SSI) central to the instruction. Areas of pedagogical importance highlighted by critics of the STS movement that can be addressed through instruction that centers on SSI include:

- *Nature of Science:* Students' understandings of the nature of science affect their views of what counts as scientific evidence. (See Chapter 7 for an in-depth discussion of the nature of science.)
- *Issues of Classroom Discourse:* Students' science talk and notions of argumentation influence their views of and decisions about SSI. (See Chapter 11 for more information about science talk and argumentation in the science classroom.)
- *Cultural Issues:* As members of a diverse society, students' need to be tolerant of the views of others and recognize that their decisions about SSI are influenced by their culture. (See Chapter 9 for a discussion of how science instruction should respond to student diversity and culture.)
- *Case-Based Issues:* The investigation of issues through case-based pedagogy enables students' to resolve issues and examine how power can affect societal decisions and decisions of scientific communities. (Ziedler, Sadler, Simmons, & Howes, 2005)

Evolution from STS instruction to SSI instruction, which places emphasis on these four areas, functions to promote students' individual intellectual development in morality and ethics while developing their understandings of the relationship between science and society. Intellectual development in morality and ethics is viewed as vitally important to students' decision-making abilities related to SSI.

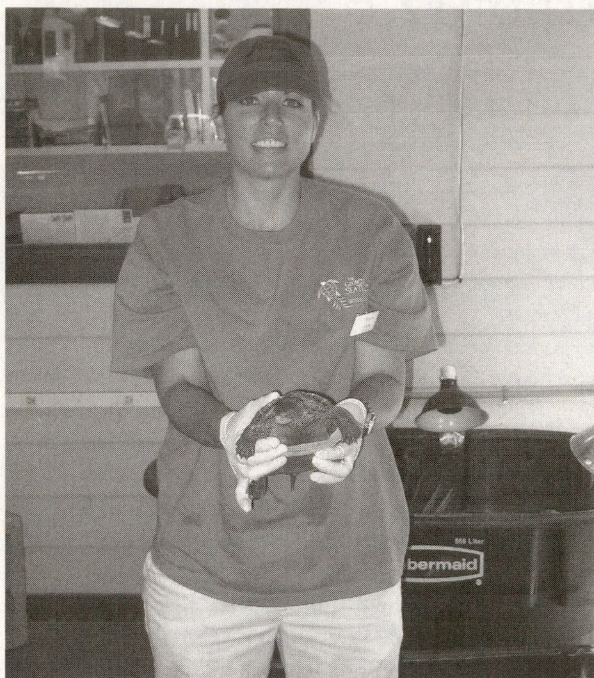

Teachers need to understand socioscientific issues in order to incorporate them into the science curriculum.

Issues Investigation

The investigation and analysis of SSI helps students develop deeper understandings of the issues and the underlying science. SSI investigation stresses the organization of factual information as well as the presentation of arguments and evidence. The investigation and analysis of SSI require students to engage in inquiry and to find out about ideas by doing library work and fieldwork, using the Internet, and determining other people's beliefs and attitudes. It also encourages students to separate fact from opinion and to become aware of the values held by individuals who disagree with them. The investigation of SSI culminates in students making decisions that affect their lives and the lives of others.

Two instructional models exemplify this approach to addressing SSI. They are the *analytical decision-making model* developed by Oliver and Newman (1967) and Johnson and Johnson's (1988) *structured controversy model.* Both models are extremely useful for guiding students' examination of SSI. For example, some U.S. communities are considering whether to use some of their land for long-term storage of radioactive waste from nuclear power plants. This is an important decision because of the impact the decision can have on the local economy and because radioactive waste triggers such strong reactions from people regarding the environment and public health. The community near any proposed storage site must weigh the risks and benefits of the land use.

Students who undertake assessing whether the storage facility should be built near a hypothetical community must investigate many aspects of the issue. They must learn about radiation and half-life, and study the safety record of similar facilities in other states and countries. They must compare the potential danger associated with nuclear power with that of other industries. This inquiry will likely lead students to study the hazards of using coal and petroleum to produce electricity and the problems of disposing of chemicals such as polychlorinated biphenyls, lead, arsenic, and other industrial waste products that have been going into landfills.

Students also must research the beneficial effects of a storage site to the community. How will this project benefit the community economically? Local business will increase tremendously, at least during the construction of the storage site, to provide food and lodging for the construction workers, technicians, and engineers. Perhaps roads and rails will have to be improved or built. Then there will be the maintenance of the facility once it has been completed and put into use.

The structured controversy model incorporates the unique feature of perspective reversal to help students focus on both the benefits and risks associated with a decision such as whether to make land available for the storage of radioactive waste. Students are paired and assigned randomly to learn either the pro or con position. After learning their assigned position and arguing forcefully in support of it, each pair is then required to learn and present the opposing position. By ensuring that all students understand both sides of the issue, reversing perspectives leads to collaborative decision making where the focus is not on winners and losers but rather on the best possible solution (Johnson & Johnson, 1988).

In order to move from factual learning to reasoned decisions, students should also investigate the attitudes and values of the people in the community regarding the long-term storage of nuclear waste. Although they cannot survey the citizens of the hypothetical community for which the proposed site is being considered, there are studies that have polled a variety of groups regarding their feelings about nuclear power, radiation, and waste disposal. These results will surely be a significant factor in the decision to accept or reject a nuclear waste storage site in the community. If students are, in fact, investigating an issue that will affect the community in which they live, interviewing people or asking them to complete a questionnaire in order to gather data on their knowledge of the issue or problem as well as their attitudes toward it would be in order.

An important outcome of issues investigation and analysis is decision making. Given all of the information that students have gathered, what will they decide to do regarding the issue they have studied? If students have been studying the feasibility of radioactive waste in their community, what do they believe should be done? Do they believe that another waste disposal site is needed but that the facility should not be constructed in their backyard? Decision making can result from a position paper prepared by students, as is recommended by Johnson and Johnson's (1988) structured controversy model, or from a discussion of findings and conclusions in class. Science students should be asked to make these and many other types of decisions. More information about the structured controversy model and the analytical decision-making model is presented in Table 12.2.

Action Learning and Service Learning

Two other approaches for students to learn science while exploring SSI are action learning and service learning. Action learning involves more than reasoning and decision making. It stresses collaboration, questioning, and community action, extending instruction beyond the classroom. In action learning experiences, students are given opportunities to take actions to resolve local SSI and to assess the effectiveness of their actions.

Action learning experiences involve students working in small groups and include the following components (Marquardt, 2004):

- *A significant issue:* The issue must be important to the students and provide opportunities for science learning. Issues that satisfy these criteria include the high use of water to maintain the school's landscaping and lawns, the daily soft drink consumption by the student body, and the unsightliness of a trashed-out stream near the school.
- *Process of questioning and listening:* Students generate many questions in order to frame the issue and understand its parts, they listen to each others' questions, and then propose various strategies to address the issue. Emphasis is given to the questions that lead to talk and argumentation, over answers.
- *Action taking:* The SSI chosen by students must be not only important to them, but one that they have the power to act on. It is through implementing their ideas that students learn. By seeing and reflecting on their actions, students can reframe issues, recognize that there are things that they did not consider, and propose new strategies and solutions.
- *Promise of learning:* The resolution of an issue can provide immediate benefit for a school or community. For example, students' actions of mulching landscaping and overseeding lawns with drought-tolerant grass seed can reduce a school's outdoor water use. However, of more importance is students' science learning that occurs as a result of questioning, listening, and taking action.

Service learning shares a number of characteristics with action learning; paramount among them are student activity and learning. Service learning marries service goals and learning goals with the intention that both

TABLE 12.2 Analytical Decision-Making Model and Structured Controversy Model Resources

Structured Controversy: A Case Study Strategy
http://ublib.buffalo.edu/libraries/projects/cases/teaching/controversy.html

Developed by Clyde Freeman Herreid, this site provides information about the strengths of structured controversy as an instructional strategy and an example of how to use structured controversy to engage students in a case involving the use of DNA fingerprinting in forensic medicine.

Applied Management Science: Making Good Strategic Decisions
http://home.ubalt.edu/ntsbarsh/opre640/opre640.htm

This Web site contains a comprehensive explanation of analytic decision making, as well as links to a host of other sites that address purposeful and strategic decision making.

Make Decisions
http://career.berkeley.edu/Plan/MakeDecisions.stm

Factors influencing decisions and decision-making styles along with several variations on the basic analytical decision-making model are discussed at this Web site. This site also contains an analytical decision-making worksheet.

For Teachers—Academic Controversy Primer
www.pbs.org/wnet/wideangle/classroom/controversy.html

Sponsored by the Public Broadcasting System (PBS), this Web site presents details about how to engage a class of students in structured controversy and includes student handouts and rubrics. A link at the site provides access to videos that highlight such issues as the spread of avian influenza A, the demise of Scotland's fishing industry, and the destabilizing effect of the AIDS pandemic on the African continent.

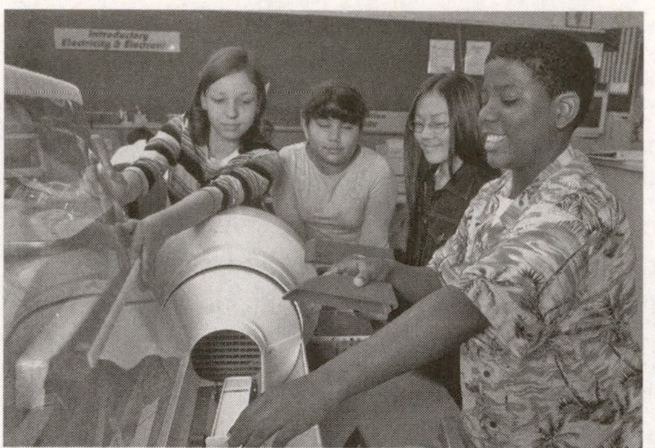

Classroom Snapshot 12.2

Mr. Bloom's Adventure

Mr. Bloom observed a great deal of water standing in a drainage ditch located several blocks from the middle school where he teaches life science. The ditch was an unsightly area because of the dirty water and the accumulation of trash. Mr. Bloom had a hunch that some sewage water might be seeping into the ditch because of the age of the city's sewer system, and that if they tested the water, perhaps fecal material would be found in it. When he proposed to students the idea of cleaning up the drainage ditch and analyzing the water for contamination, he got many volunteers who wanted to participate in the project.

On a Saturday in October, Mr. Bloom took a group of 30 students, along with several parents, to the ditch to collect the cans, cups, and paper products that had accumulated there. He also directed some students to collect water samples to be given to the city water department to analyze for contamination and to be examined in the school's science laboratory.

Mr. Bloom had made prior arrangements with the city public works department for the use of their rakes, shovels, and trash bags to aid in the cleanup operation. The public works department also picked up the trash that the students collected. The city water department tested their water samples for fecal material, and concluded that sewage was seeping into the drainage ditch.

The students derived a great deal of satisfaction from this project, especially when they observed the public works department digging up the broken sewage pipes and replacing them. They also benefited from examining water samples for microorganisms.

students and the community benefit from the experience. Science teachers have engaged students in service learning projects for decades. They have taken students to streams and beaches to clean up these areas and to collect samples of organisms to take back to the classroom for study. One example of service learning is student involvement in the reclamation of lands burned by wildfires. As students participate in revegetation efforts, they learn plant identification and physiology and the role of different plants in the environment in addition to learning about the ecological concepts of succession, habitat, and climax community.

Action learning and service learning are definitely ways to get students involved in learning with links to their lives and the communities in which they live. These approaches help students to become active participants in society and to learn science as they perform valuable community service. Considerable thought must go into the planning of action learning and service learning experiences. Some may need to be carried out after school or on weekends. Others may have associated hazards, and science teachers must weigh the benefits and risks of student involvement. Action learning and service learning offer science teachers wonderful opportunities to make science relevant and interesting to their students and enhance their understandings of science.

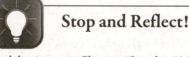

Stop and Reflect!

- Read the vignette in Classroom Snapshot 12.2 about Mr. Bloom's adventure. Which of the approaches of addressing SSI is exemplified in this vignette? Discuss the reasons for your decision with a classmate.

 SSI and Persuasion Analysis

When students interact with SSI via magazine articles, video documentaries, science instruction, or other means, they are experiencing persuasion. Persuasion is not an unethical process, but a means of purposeful communication used by the scientific community. Persuasion analysis can serve as a useful tool for systematically considering students' interactions with SSI in the context of science instruction. Persuasion analysis is important because the ability to evaluate as well as generate persuasive arguments to support or refute scientific claims is an important element of scientific inquiry (Sampson & Clark, 2008).

Commercial advertisements are the most familiar kinds of persuasive messages that adolescents are likely to encounter. This kind of persuasive message is quite easy to analyze. In contrast, persuasion associated with SSI is more difficult to analyze because it can be complex and may be emotionally charged. This persuasion is complex because the science concepts and theories aligned with the issues are complicated or abstract, and the issues themselves can be more remote than those targeted in the personal appeals of commercial advertisements. For example, consider the complexity and remoteness of messages about global warming, gene therapy, and energy conservation compared to ads for video games and candy bars.

Furthermore, most people, including adolescents, tend to be more emotionally involved in SSI than in the purchase of many of the goods targeted in commercial ads. SSI persuasion can touch our basic beliefs and our worldviews. For example, the belief that one is a "Christian" or an "environmentalist" might influence a number of personal actions. SSI persuasion that threatens beliefs such as these can be very emotionally charged, making dispassionate analysis of particular issues very challenging.

Science teachers can do much to enhance the persuasion analysis skills of their students. The analysis process can be guided by Hovland, Janis, and Kelley's (1953) question, "Who says what to whom with what effect?" This question highlights the persuasive message (what), its source (who), and the audience of the message (whom).

The Message

Students' analysis of SSI persuasion should begin with a consideration of what counts as science. This is an important starting point because some SSI persuasion, while seemingly convincing, may not apply epistemological criteria used by the scientific community to support its claims. Questions that may help students zero in on criteria used by the scientific community when examining persuasion include the following:

- What evidence is provided to support the claims made by the source?
- How believable or trustworthy is the evidence?
- How logical, straightforward, and sound is the reasoning used to argue in support of the claims?

Teachers can further help students' refine their analysis of SSI persuasion by encouraging them to examine features considered important by researchers who study students' science-related arguments. Features described by Sampson and Clark (2008) are the structure of the argument, the argument's content, and the nature of the justification used to support claims within an argument. Examine Classroom Snapshot 12.3 before reading further, as it will be referenced in the following discussion of these features.

- *Argument Structure:* Have students search messages for evidence that serves as the foundation for claims. Also encourage them to look for warrants, those statements that justify why the evidence is germane to the claim. Some warrants may be augmented by qualifiers and rebuttals, statements that provide strength for the warrants and statements that indicate limitations to the warrants, respectively. For example, in Classroom Snapshot 12.3, one piece of evidence included in the brochure to support the claim that all drivers should be riding on nitrogen-filled tires, is that nitrogen is safe. Warrants to support this claim are that nitrogen is a colorless, odorless, and tasteless gas, and that it does not promote combustion.
- *Argument Content:* A well-structured argument may be built on twisted science. It is important for students to check the science content used to support claims. A thorough understanding of the science related to an issue is vital to students being able to assess an argument's content. Classroom Snapshot 12.3 shows how a well-structured argument can contain twisted science. The statement "Nitrogen is a large molecule, keeping it from seeping out of tires as quickly as air" is presented as a warrant to strengthen the evidence that "Nitrogen helps maintain proper tire pressure." But, in fact, the molecular size of nitrogen, when measuring its covalent radius, is only about 3% greater than that of oxygen (Decelles, 2007). Following this logic, the seepage between a tire filled with nitrogen and one filled with air, consisting of about 78% nitrogen and 21% oxygen, is negligible.
- *Nature of Justification:* The content may be accurate, but is it relevant to the argument? The strength of an argument is dependent on the relevance of the justification used to support it. For this reason, encourage students to check the nature of the justifications used to support claims. Consider the statement in Classroom Snapshot 12.3, "Many car dealerships and large tire retail stores are inflating new tires with nitrogen." While it addresses the issue of nitrogenizing tires, it does serve as evidence that supports the claim, "All Drivers Should Be Riding on Nitrogen-Filled Tires."

When analyzing SSI persuasion, it is also a good idea to prompt students to consider how aspects of the issue are being intensified and downplayed (Rank, 1984). In Classroom Snapshot 12.3, the association with race cars, commercial airlines, and long-haul trucks is used to intensify the benefits of nitrogenizing tires. And the failure to mention that air is composed of about 78% nitrogen functions to downplay the practice of simply inflating tires with compressed air.

The Source

When analyzing SSI persuasion, it is important for students to consider the credibility of the message source.

Classroom Snapshot 12.3

Should Car Tires Be Filled with Nitrogen?

When Mrs. Coleman brought her car into the local garage for its regular tune-up, the service manager asked if she wanted to have the air in her car tires replaced with nitrogen. It would cost only $39, he said. Being unfamiliar with this practice, Mrs. Coleman asked for literature to read about the benefits of filling tires with nitrogen while she waited for her car.

The brochure given to her by the service manager included the following information:

All Drivers Should Be Riding on Nitrogen-Filled Tires

Fill your tires with nitrogen and they'll be safer, last longer, and give you better gas mileage. It is also good for the environment. Tire nitrogenizing is a service that this dealership is now offering to new car buyers and valued service customers.

- Nitrogen is safe. It is a colorless, odorless, and tasteless gas that does not promote combustion.
- Nitrogen helps maintain proper tire pressure. This is because nitrogen is a large molecule, keeping it from seeping out of tires as quickly as air.
- Nitrogen protects the environment. Tires at correct pressure improve gas mileage. This causes car engines not to work as hard and to release less waste CO_2 into the environment.
- Nitrogen does not contain the moisture found in the air. Moisture can cause wheels to rust, leading to costly replacement.
- Nitrogen is used in tires on race cars, commercial airliners, and long-haul trucks. People in these businesses recognize the benefits of nitrogenizing tires.
- Topping off low tires with compressed air does not harm them. The next time you bring your car in for servicing, the air can be easily purged and replaced with nitrogen.
- Many car dealerships and large tire retail stores are inflating new tires with nitrogen. Customers are pleased to get their tires checked and topped off when they return for scheduled maintenance.

Mrs. Coleman was not persuaded by what she read in the brochure. She chose not to replace the air in her car tires with nitrogen. As a chemistry teacher, she had questions about some of the information given for replacing the air in her car tires with nitrogen. However, she thought that the brochure would be useful for her students to examine. She wondered how her students would respond to the information presented in the brochure, and how their understandings of gas laws and nitrogen's atomic mass and bond length as compared to those of oxygen would affect their responses.

Does the source have special expertise regarding the issue addressed in the message? Source trustworthiness, attractiveness, or power, also may influence a person's response to SSI persuasion.

Trustworthiness is associated with having the best interest of the message audience in mind. The influence of attractiveness may be derived from the source's physical beauty or similarity with the message audience. Power may be linked to the sources ability to dispense rewards or punishment, but may also be associated with the source's legitimate authority, such as the authority exercised by teachers over students. For students not highly motivated to engage in issue-relevant thinking and scrutinize message arguments, what is believed about the source may have a decided effect on the persuasiveness of the message.

The Audience

The purpose of having students analyze the messages and sources of SSI persuasion is to prepare them to be better consumers. Informed consumers of SSI persuasion are better positioned to make decisions about issues that affect their personal lives and society. As potential recipients of SSI persuasion, students also must understand the motivational and knowledge factors that can affect their processing of this kind of persuasion.

Personal relevance is an important motivational factor that can affect students' processing of SSI persuasion. When personal relevance is high, students will be more likely to scrutinize issue-relevant arguments. For example, the issue of nitrogenizing tires may be personally relevant to high school students who are driving. For other issues such as oil drilling in uninhabited areas and genetic modification of food crops, the teacher will need to help students understand how these issues are relevant to their daily lives and futures and that of the society in which they live.

Students' issue-relevant thinking is also highly dependent on their understanding of pertinent science concepts and theories. Knowledge about the science associated with an issue tends to better enable message recipients to process claims, evidence and warrant, acknowledge a source's credibility, and detect when aspects relevant to an issue are being intensified or downplayed. Analysis of SSI persuasion should be considered a first step in preparing students to engage in argumentation about SSI.

Evolution versus Creationism in Science Teaching

"Nothing in biology makes sense except in the light of evolution."
—Theodosious Dobzhansky (1973)

The interplay between science and society is clearly evident in the long and heated battle over the teaching of evolution in science courses. Your understanding of the history of this controversy in U.S. courts, coupled with an understanding of persuasion analysis applied to SSI, will prepare you to teach about evolution and recognize attempts to undermine the teaching of evolution in public schools. To this date, the battle continues as fundamental religious groups challenge the validity of evolutionary theory. In spite of the centrality of evolution in biology, as stated by Dobzhansky in the above quote, and the extensive body of research supporting change over time, the intent persists to teach a creator-based explanation that life on the planet arose as we observe it today. These nonscientific ways of knowing have been called *creation science*, *scientific creationism*, and *intelligent design*. And now a new form of rhetoric is appearing to challenge the soundness of evolutionary theory, asserting that students should be taught *alternative views* so that they can develop critical thinking and learn about the strengths and weaknesses of evolutionary theory and decide for themselves. (Another, similar tactic is to ask teachers to "teach the controversy," and let students decide for themselves.)

Often, during the 20th century and into the 21st, state boards of education or individuals have challenged or defended the teaching of evolution, creationism, or, more recently, intelligent design (ID) in science courses. Some of the laws passed to restrict the teaching of evolution or promote the teaching of creationism have been rendered unconstitutional by the U.S. Supreme Court. Some of the most notable court cases concerning the teaching of evolution are summarized below.

The Scopes Trial, 1925. John Scopes assigned students some pages to read about evolution. In doing so, he was agreeing to test the merits of the Tennessee state law prohibiting the teaching of evolution in schools. This action resulted in a sensational event known as the "Monkey Trial." Scopes was found guilty and fined $100. However, this outcome was viewed as a victory for evolutionists. Subsequently, the verdict was overturned because of a technicality.

Epperson v. Arkansas, 1968. The U.S. Supreme Court invalidated an Arkansas statute that prohibited the teaching of evolution. The decision was based on the First Amendment to the Constitution that says the government must be neutral in matters of religion. Consequently, the Constitution does not permit a state to require instruction that is tailored to the principles or prohibitions of any particular religion.

McLean v. Arkansas, 1982. Judge William Overton ruled that a "balanced treatment" statute violated the Constitution, and teachers did not have to give equal time to creationism when teaching evolution. Further, creationism has no scientific significance, and creationism is not science; rather, it is religion masquerading as science.

Edwards v. Aguillard, 1987. Don Aguillard, a Louisiana biology teacher, challenged the equal time mandate in the state. The statute prohibited the teaching of evolution, except when it was accompanied by instruction on creation science. The U.S. Supreme Court held that the "Creationism Act" was unconstitutional, giving science teachers the right to teach evolution without addressing creationism.

Peloza v. Capistrano Unified District, 1994. John Peloza claimed that his First Amendment rights were violated by the school district's inclusion of evolution in the curriculum, because he considered evolution as a "religion of evolutionism." The Ninth Circuit Court of Appeals upheld a district court finding that the teacher's rights were *not* violated when the district appropriately required the science teacher to teach a scientific theory in biology.

Kansas State Board of Education, 1999. The Kansas State Board of Education voted to greatly restrict the emphasis on evolution in the state's science standards and, in doing so, ensured that evolution would not be a part of the state's assessment tests. The state board did not prohibit the teaching of evolution and it did not remove mention of evolution (microevolution is mentioned) from the state's science standards.

Kitzmiller v. Dover Area School District, 2004. The Dover, Pennsylvania, school board established a policy that science teachers would read a statement to biology students suggesting there is an alternative to Darwin's theory of evolution that is called intelligent design. The Dover high school teachers refused to follow the policy. Parents also opposed the board's policy and filed a lawsuit in federal court. The court ruled against the district policy that suggested intelligent design is an alternative theory to evolution.

Proponents of intelligent design claim that certain features or organs are too complex to have evolved naturally. Therefore, they must have been designed by an intelligent agent. Here again, a court's decision affirmed that religion under the guise of ID does not merit consideration in teaching of evolutionary theory. Highlights of Judge Jones's report (PBS-NOVA, 2007) are as follows:

- ID is not science.
- ID is the progeny of creationism.
- Evolution theory is not antithetical to religion.
- The disclaimer that the Dover, Pennsylvania, school board wanted read to students is flawed.
- The goal of the ID movement is to foment a revolution.
- It is unconstitutional to teach ID as an alternative to evolution.

Certainly, pressures from state mandates, parents, school boards, and religious groups have had and continue to have a strong influence on teachers' motivation to address evolution in school science in order to explain changes on Earth and in living organisms over time. Science teachers can find a good rationale and recommendations to teach evolution from U.S. Supreme Court decisions, science teacher organizations, and the scientific community.

The National Association of Biology Teachers and the National Science Teachers Association's Boards of Directors both support the teaching of evolution and discourage nonscientific ways of knowing in the science classroom. Below are statements about the teaching of evolution that these organizations support.

- The diversity of life on Earth is the outcome of evolution: an unpredictable and natural process of temporal descent with genetic modification that is affected by natural selection, chance, historical contingencies, and changing environments.
- Evolutionary theory is significant in biology, among other reasons, for its unifying properties and predictive features, the clear empirical testability of its integral models, and the richness of new scientific research it fosters.
- The fossil record, which includes abundant transitional forms in diverse taxonomic groups, establishes extensive and comprehensive evidence for organic evolution.
- Natural selection, the primary mechanism for evolutionary changes, can be demonstrated with numerous convincing examples, both extant and extinct.
- Adaptations do not always provide an obvious selective advantage. Furthermore, there is no indication that adaptations— molecular or organismal—must be perfect; adaptations providing a selective advantage must simply be good enough for survival and increased reproductive fitness.
- Although comprehending deep time is difficult, Earth is about 4.5 billion years old. Homo sapiens have occupied only a minuscule moment of that immense duration of time.
- When compared with earlier periods, the Cambrian explosion, evident in the fossil record, reflects at least three phenomena: the evolution of animals with readily fossilized, hard-body parts; a Cambrian environment (sedimentary rock) more conducive to preserving fossils; and the evolution from Precambrian forms of an increased diversity of body patterns in animals.
- Radiometric and other dating techniques, when used properly, are highly accurate means of establishing dates in the history of the planet and in the history of life.
- In science, a theory is not a guess or an approximation but an extensive explanation developed from well-documented, reproducible sets of experimentally derived data and from repeated observations of natural processes.
- Providing a rational, coherent and scientific account of the taxonomic history and diversity of organisms requires inclusion of the mechanisms and principles of evolution.
- Similarly, effective teaching of cellular and molecular biology requires inclusion of evolution.
- Specific textbook chapters on evolution should be included in biology curricula, and evolution should be a recurrent theme throughout biology textbooks and courses.
- Students can maintain their religious beliefs and learn the scientific foundations of evolution.
- Teachers should respect diverse beliefs, but contrasting science with religion, such as belief in creationism, is not a role of science. Science teachers can, and often do, hold devout religious beliefs, accept evolution as a valid scientific theory and teach the theory's mechanisms and principles.
- Science and religion differ in significant ways that make it inappropriate to teach any of the different religious beliefs in the science classroom.

Science teachers must understand the history of the issues and debates surrounding the creationism/evolution controversy over the last century. Without this background they will be intimidated and unsure of themselves in handling the teaching of evolution. One approach to teaching about the evolution of life is to begin the study of change over time in its many forms, including the universe, our solar system, Earth, bacteria, plants, and animals. What is the evidence for change over time and how have we come to understand the process? In addition, it is important to learn about the lives and scientific contributions of individuals who have contributed to this line of research. Because of the rich historical background and vast scientific evidence to support the evolution of Earth and its life forms, there is no research to bring in a debate or discussion on nonscience or religious-based ideas to challenge evolution. Below are aspects of evolution to consider in the teaching of life science.

- Study the life and accomplishments of Charles Darwin, especially his education, family, voyage on the *Beagle*, natural selection, and other contributions to biological science.
- Engage in the study of several different types of evidence for evolution. Add that the fact that so many different lines of evidence all converge on and support an evolutionary explanation for the unity and diversity of life on Earth, which strengthens our confidence in that explanation.
- Explain what is a *fact* and what is a *theory* as these terms relate to evolution.
- Summarize Scope's trial.
- Summarize several court cases in which the court upheld the right to teach evolution and ruled against teaching of creationism or intelligent design.
- Study the *Kitzmiller v. Dover Area School District* court case that ruled against the school board's requirement that teachers read a statement about intelligent design to students before teaching them evolution.
- Give the position of professional organizations, such as the National Association of Biology Teachers, National Science Teachers Association, and National Academy of Science, regarding the teaching of evolution in the classroom.

Considerations for Teaching about Technology and SSI

Addressing technology and SSI in the science classroom require careful planning and good judgment. You must select topics and issues that are directly related to your curriculum so that investigation of technology and the relationships between science and technology and society are viewed as educationally sound. You must also select topics that are relevant to your students and that will affect their lives.

Following the recommendations offered in this chapter will help prepare you to demonstrate your competence associated with both Standard 4: Issues and Standard 7: Science in the Community of the National Science Teachers Association (NSTA) *Standards for Science Teacher Preparation.*

According to Standard 4:

> *To show that they are prepared to engage students in studies of issues related to science, teachers of science must demonstrate that they:*
>
> *a. Understand socially important issues related to science and technology in their field of licensure, as well as processes used to analyze and make decisions on such issues.*
> *b. Engage students successfully in the analysis of problems, including considerations of risks, costs, and benefits of alternative solutions; relating these to knowledge, goals, and values of students. (NSTA, 2003, p. 20)*

According to Standard 7:

> *To show that they are prepared to relate science to the community, teachers of science must demonstrate that they:*
>
> *a. Identify ways to relate science to the community, involve stakeholders, and use community resources to promote learning of science.*
> *b. Involve students successfully in activities that relate science to resources and stakeholders in the community or to the resolution of issues important to the community. (NSTA, 2003, p. 25)*

The approaches to address technology and SSI discussed in this chapter offer a number of ways to help adolescents see how scientific and technological knowledge can enable them to become better informed about themselves and the communities in which they live. However, in order for any of these approaches to be successful, students' interests and abilities must be considered. For instance, middle school students may not be interested in the same topics that interest secondary school students, and middle school students will not be able to engage in argumentation at the same level as secondary students. Most important, you must also be knowledgeable about the technologies and social issues that you wish to address in the classroom and the science concepts and theories associated with them.

Assessing and Reviewing

Analysis and Synthesis

1. Distinguish between biotechnology and technology based on the physical sciences, then describe how the distinctions would affect your teaching about the relationship between science and technology.
2. For one of the topics listed below, describe a learning experience in which students would build a working model of a machine or gadget to further their understanding of technology.
   - motions and forces
   - chemical reactions
   - geochemical cycles
   - origin and evolution of the universe
   - the cell
   - structure and property of matter
3. Suppose you learned from your principal that parents believe that students in your classes are not learning the science content they should because of your efforts to incorporate the study of technology and SSI into the curriculum. Write a letter that could be sent to parents explaining your reasons for doing so.
4. Which of the following statements describe science instruction that has an SSI focus? Give reasons for your choices.
   - Textbooks guide instruction.
   - Students are active participants in the learning process.
   - Learning experiences include opportunities for scientific argumentation.
   - Instruction is teacher centered.
   - Students make decisions and take actions.

Practical Considerations

5. Learn about the machines described in the cartoons of Rub Goldberg. Then, design and build a Rub Goldberg machine. Demonstrate the machine to others and explain to them how designing and building such a machine can help students learn about technology and science.
6. Develop a learning experience to teach about an SSI in a middle school or secondary science class. Engage classmates or adolescent students in the learning experience. Then, write a critique of the experience, describing its strengths and limitations.
7. Arrange to observe a teacher lead students' exploration of an SSI. Talk with the teacher before and after the learning experience to understand the teacher's intended learning goals and the extent to which they were achieved. Try to determine how students' knowledge of the science associated with the issue contributed to their learning success.

Developmental Considerations

8. Start a collection of newspaper clippings, magazine articles, and Internet sites that address SSI.
9. Read the *National Science Education Standards* and the *Benchmarks for Scientific Literacy* to learn more about what these documents say about teaching technology and SSI in science classes. In Chapter 6 of the *Standards*, check out the Science and Technology as well as the Personal and Social Perspective standards; in the *Benchmarks*, examine the chapters "The Nature of Technology," "Human Society," "Historical Perspectives," and "The Designed World."

Resources to Examine

Beyond Discovery: The Path from Research to Human Benefit. [Online] Available at: www.BeyondDiscovery.org

This site, a project of the National Academy of Sciences, contains a host of cases that highlight significant recent technological and medical advances and traces their historical roots. Titles currently available include "The Hepatitis B Story," "Disarming a Deadly Virus," "The Global Positioning System," "Modern Communication," and "The Ozone Depletion Phenomenon." The cases can be read online or downloaded using Adobe Acrobat Reader. New cases on different topics are added each year.

Bulletin of Science, Technology, and Society. Journal published since 1999, available in paper copy and online. Available at: http://bst.sagepub.com

This journal is published bimonthly by Sage Publications. Each issue includes articles about teaching strategies, technological innovations, and science-related social issues and problems. Many articles speak directly to precollege science teachers and offer suggestions for infusing SSI into the science curriculum.

Shoestring Biotechnology. 2006. National Association of Biology Teachers, 12030 Sunrise Valley Drive, Suite 110, Reston, VA 20191. Order online at www.nabt.org.

This laboratory manual, edited by Kathy Frame, is a copublication of the Biotechnology Institute and the National Association of Biology Teachers. It contains a number of inexpensive teacher-tested biotechnology learning experiences suitable for high school students.

In the Light of Evolution: Science Education on Trial. 2006. National Association of Biology Teachers, 12030 Sunrise Valley Drive, Suite 110, Reston, VA 20191. Order online at www.nabt.org.

Written by Randy Moore, this book traces the history of the evolution/creation controversy from the 1925 Scopes trial to 2006.

Judgment Day: Intelligent Design on Trial. 2007. A PBS-NOVA presentation available online at www.pbs.org/wgbh/nova/id.

This exceptional presentation provides a great deal of information about the *Kitzmiller v. Dover Area School District* court proceedings in 2005. At this online site you can hear "In Defense of Intelligent Design," from Phillip Johnson, the father of ID; "In Defense of Evolution," by biologist Ken Miller; *Dover Board vs. Teachers*; "The Judge Speaks," by Judge Jones, who presided over the trial; "Defining Science," in how it differs from religion; "Fossil Evidence"; and other informative useful information for science teachers.

Teaching Engineering Made Easy: A Friendly Introduction to Engineering Activities for Middle School Students. 2006. Engineering Education Service Center, 1004 5th Street, Springfield, OR 97477. Order online at www.engineeringedu.com/store/tg1.html

This 208-page book contains activities and projects that can be used to teach students about technology and engineering. The activities are teacher tested and organized under civil, chemical, and mechanical engineering.

Nanoscale Science: Activities for Grades 6–12. 2007. Arlington, VA: National Science Teachers Association Press.

Written by Gail Jones and colleagues, this book includes 20 investigations organized around such themes as nanotechnology applications and societal implications. Background information and ideas for formative assessment accompany each of the activities.

References

Decelles, P. (2007). *Nitrogen for tires?* Retrieved August 4, 2008, from http://theforcethat.blogspot.com/2007/02/nitrogen-for-tires.html

Forrester, J. (1961). *Industrial dynamics*. Walthan, MA: Pegasus Communications.

Hovland, C. I., Janis, I. L., & Kelley, H. H. (1953). *Communication and persuasion*. New Haven, CT: Yale University Press.

Johnson, D. W., & Johnson, R. T. (1988). Critical thinking through structured controversy. *Educational Leadership, 45*(8), 58–64.

Marquardt, M. J. (2004). Action learning. *By George*. Washington, DC: The George Washington University. Retrieved July 12, 2008, from www/gwu.edu/~bygeorge/021804/actionlearning.html

National Convention on Biological Diversity. 1992. Article 2. Use of terms. Retrieved July 14, 2008, from www.cbd.int/convention/articles.shtml?a=cbd-02

National Research Council (NRC). 1996. *National science education standards*. Washington, DC: National Academies Press.

Oliver, D. W., & Newman, F. M. (1967). *Taking a stand*. Middletown, CT: Xerox Corp.

PBS-NOVA. (2007). The judge speaks. Retrieved July 21, 2008, from www.pbs.org/wghh/nova/id/judge.html

Rank, H. (1984). *The pep talk*. Park Forest, IL: The Counter-Propaganda Press.

Sampson, V., & Clark, D. B. (2008). Assessment of the ways students generate arguments in science education: Current perspectives and recommendations for future directions. *Science Education, 92*(3), 447–472.

Solomon, J. (2002). The dilemma of science, technology, and society education. In S. Amos & R. Boohan (Eds.), *Teaching science in secondary schools* (pp. 94–101). London: The Open University Press.

Ziedler, D. L., Sadler, T. D., Simmons, M. L., & Howes, E. V. (2005). Beyond STS: A research-based framework for socioscientific issues education. *Science Education, 89*, 357–377.

Chapter

13

Laboratory Work and Fieldwork

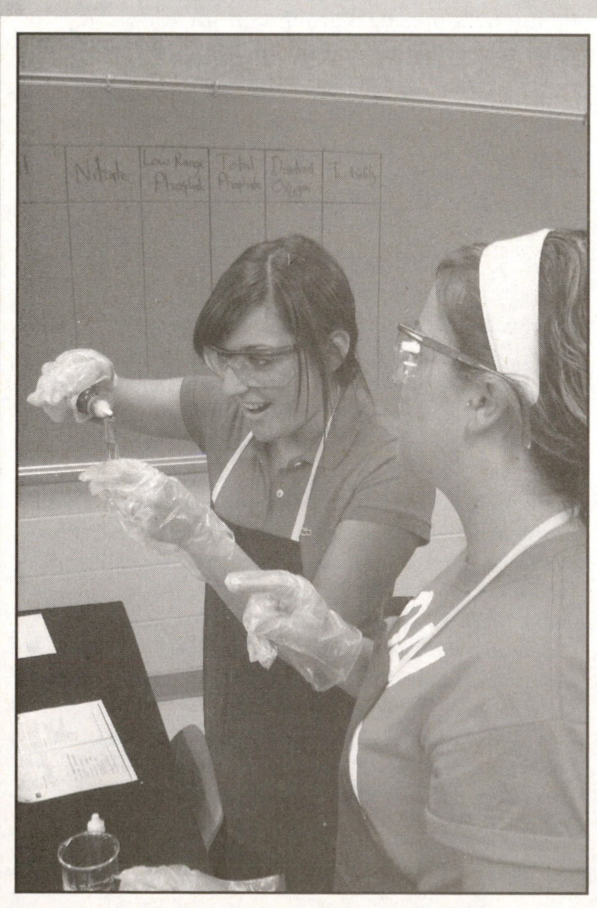

Laboratory work helps students to better understand scientific concepts and principles.

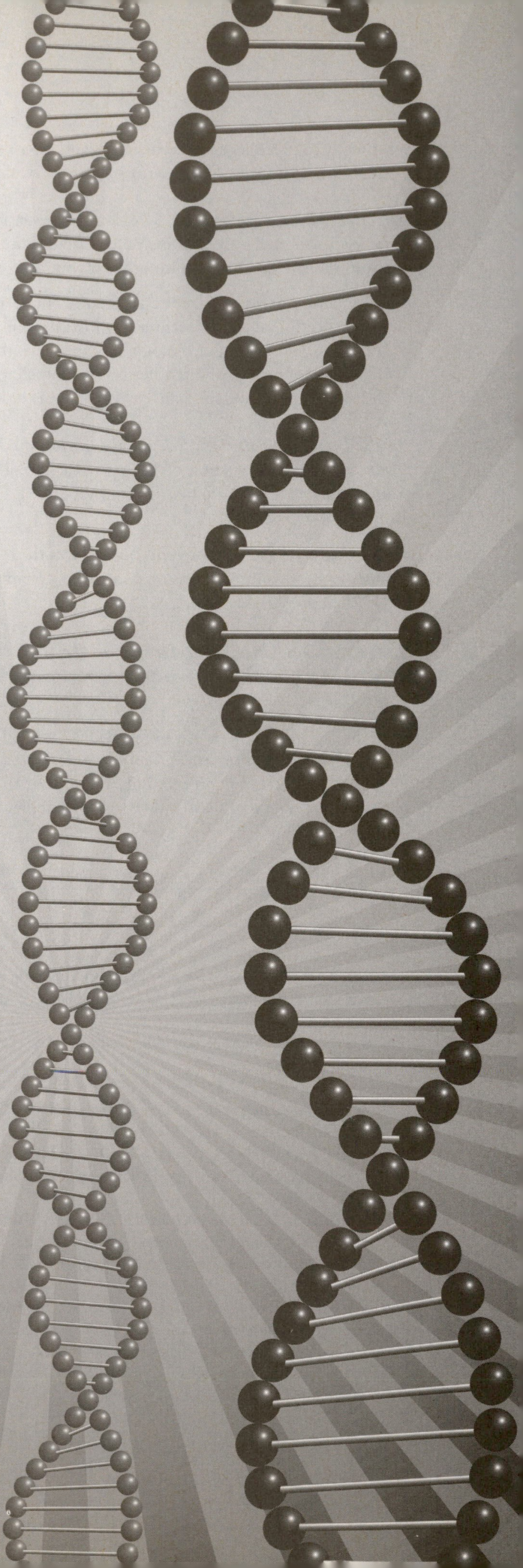

Laboratory work and fieldwork are unique types of science instruction. These strategies involve *firsthand* experiences, permitting students to participate in science as a way of thinking and investigating as well as developing a better understanding of science concepts, principles, and theories. They provide concrete, authentic experiences that aid students in comprehending phenomena that are under study in the curriculum and discussed in the classroom. However, in order for important learning outcomes to be realized from laboratory work and fieldwork, science teachers must plan them carefully and keep them focused on the specific learning outcomes. Further, science teachers need to know about the reasons why laboratory and field experiences often do not live up to their potential to achieve valued science education goals.

AIMS OF THE CHAPTER

Use the questions that follow to guide your thinking and learning about laboratory work and fieldwork:

- How precisely can you define the purpose of laboratory work and fieldwork?
- How many factors can you identify that may interfere with the implementation of laboratory and fieldwork in science programs?
- Can you explain at least five types of laboratory approaches that should be used in science courses and construct exercises that illustrate these approaches?
- What important elements should you include when conducting prelaboratory and postlaboratory discussions?
- Can you list many teaching tips that will promote successful laboratory experiences for students?
- How would you plan a field trip for a group of students that will be instructive and safe?

What Is Laboratory Work?

Laboratory work engages students in learning through *firsthand* experiences—interaction with the actual phenomenon being studied—not through simulation. This type of activity involves students in scientific inquiry by placing them in the position of asking questions, proposing solutions, designing experiments, making predictions, making observations, organizing data, explaining patterns, and so on. Laboratory work permits students to plan and to participate in investigations or to take part in activities that will help them improve their technical, laboratory, and cooperative skills. Some laboratory work involves hands-on activities in which students use specialized equipment. Other laboratory work requires only ordinary equipment found in our everyday environment. Certain laboratory work is best conducted in field and natural settings where little equipment is necessary and where no intervention from the observer is required.

The science laboratory is central to science teaching because it serves many purposes. Laboratory work has the potential to engage students in authentic investigations in which they can identify their own problems to investigate, design procedures, and draw conclusions. These activities can give students a sense as to how scientists go about their work, which in turn may influence their attitudes about the scientific enterprise. Along with attitudes about science, laboratory work can help students acquire a better understanding of concepts and principles as the result of concrete experiences (Freedman, 2002). In general, laboratory work can be used to promote the following learning outcomes:

- attitudes toward science
- scientific attitudes
- scientific inquiry
- conceptual development
- technical skills
- teamwork skills

Science laboratory work seems to leave a lasting impression on students. "Many of them [students] enjoy laboratory work and prefer it to other modes of learning. This is not, of course, the universal reaction of all students at all times" (Gardner & Gauld, 1990, p. 136). This statement is especially true of the middle school students who prefer active learning experiences to listening to lectures. Science teachers who are highly regarded by students frequently include laboratory exercises in their courses. These teachers believe that laboratory work enhances concept development and promotes scientific attitudes. They also realize that laboratory work breaks up the instructional period, which limits the amount of lecturing and adds variety to the course.

The laboratory has always been emphasized in science teaching, and during some periods in the history of science education, it has been given a dominant role. For example, during the major science curriculum reform movement of the 1960s, some science educators felt that a considerable amount of laboratory work should lead, rather than lag behind, the classroom phase of science teaching (Schwab, 1964). Today, science educators continue to value the importance of laboratory experiences, but view the laboratory as an integral part of a carefully planned science unit (Singer, Hilton, & Schweingruber, 2005). They think of science instruction as an amalgamation of laboratory work, lecture, discussion, reading, writing, and using the Internet.

If laboratory work is to promote productive learning experiences, many important science education goals must be incorporated into the instruction, such as the nature of science, science as inquiry, conceptual development, and safety. By merely participating in hands-on experiences, students will not automatically gain a good appreciation for authentic science. Therefore, science teachers must make *explicit* how each aspect of a laboratory/inquiry activity reflects science and how it is related to the subject matter under study. At many points before, during, and after laboratory work, science teachers must bring out how the activity reflects scientific investigation and how this relates to the course topic under study. This will require much more student talk and modeling to learn during the pre- and postlaboratory discussions.

Although most science educators promote laboratory work, this strategy does not necessarily produce all the outcomes expected by many educators (Blosser, 1981; Hegarty-Hazel, 1990) for a number of reasons. For example, a great deal of the laboratory work that takes place in schools is "aimless, trivial, and badly planned" (Hodson, 1985, p. 44). Laboratory work that is counter to what students expect does not necessarily produce new conceptions (Rowell & Dawson, 1983). Laboratory periods are often too short, and students do not complete their laboratory work (Gardner & Gauld, 1990). Of course, materials and equipment are a problem in some schools where limited resources are available for this type of instruction *America's Lab Report: Investigations in High School Science* (Singer, Hilton, & Schweingruber, 2005) echoes the sate of laboratory work in school science reported by researchers over the past 30 years. The report offers suggestions to enhance student learning from laboratory experiences with regard to instructional design perspective, which are to (a) specify the learning outcomes in measurable terms, (b) thoughtfully sequence laboratory work with other types of instruction, (c) integrate the process of finding out with learning the content under study, and (d) incorporate student reflection and discussion throughout laboratory work.

Science course laboratory work can be used to achieve many different learning outcomes. Some laboratory exercises, for example, might be employed to verify a concept previously discussed in class. Other types of laboratory exercises might be used to develop particular manipulative skills that are needed for subsequent laboratory work. Some laboratory exercises facilitate the attainment of concepts. The desired outcomes will dictate the type of laboratory needed. Each type of laboratory approach has characteristics differentiating it from other approaches. In general, most approaches can be classified into one of five categories: (1) science process skill, (2) deductive or verification, (3) inductive, (4) technical skill, and (5) problem solving. These categories are discussed after addressing how to prepare students for laboratory experiences.

Prelaboratory and Postlaboratory Instruction

Students must be prepared for laboratory experiences in order to benefit from them. They need to know *why* they are expected to participate in an activity and *what* they will derive from it. Science teachers who report dissatisfaction with laboratory activities often do not plan this unique form of instruction well or else do a superficial job of preparing students for this type of learning. Inexperienced teachers often believe that the laboratory activity itself will carry the students through this experience and automatically produce the intended learning outcomes. Experienced science teachers have learned to plan laboratory work carefully, conduct prelaboratory discussions, give important directions, and end with a thorough postlaboratory discussion.

Prelaboratory Discussion

The prelaboratory discussion prepares students for the laboratory activity. This phase of instruction informs students as to why, how, and what they will be doing. The prelaboratory discussion is critical because it gives the students a mind-set for the laboratory. However, it does not always reveal what students should discover. This step in laboratory preparation should explain how the activity relates to the topic under study in the classroom. If, for example, a principle is being discussed in the classroom, it should be made clear to the students that the purpose of the laboratory is to examine the principle under consideration (provided it is a verification laboratory). If an inductive laboratory exercise is planned, then the prelaboratory discussion should not present the principle, ideas, or patterns that students are expected to discover.

Consider the following discussion that might take place before a laboratory on qualitative chemical analysis to identify ions by the flame test.

Teacher: You are going to find out how chemists and laboratory technicians determine the presence of ions. We have been discussing ions in class, and now you have an opportunity to detect them in solutions. You might think of yourselves as chemists working in a crime lab. I will write the ions on the chalkboard that you will test for in today's laboratory: sodium, strontium, potassium, copper, and calcium.

Thomas, can you tell me what color will appear in the flame test for each of these ions?

Thomas: I'm sorry, but I can't remember them.

Teacher: It is not so important that you memorize the flame tests for each of the ions, but that you know where to find these tests in your textbook or on a chart, because these resources will be available to you when you are given a test on this subject. Will all of you look up the flame test in your textbooks at this time? [Pause.] Thomas, please give me the flame tests for the ions listed on the chalkboard. I will write them down.

Thomas: Sodium is orange, strontium is violet, potassium is purple, copper is blue, and calcium is green.

Teacher: Thank you. Now, let me show you how to test for these ions with this platinum wire. Pour a small amount of dilute hydrochloric acid into a clean watch glass. Dip the platinum wire into the hydrochloric acid and heat it in the burner flame. Why do I heat the wire first until it glows?

Student: To clean the wire so that it won't be contaminated.

Teacher: Good! Now, I dip the wire into the solution with an unknown ion and then put the tip of the wire into the flame.

Maria, what ion did I have in this solution?

Maria: Calcium!

Teacher: That's correct. Does anyone have a question about today's laboratory and how to proceed?

The prelaboratory discussion must give students the clearest possible picture and understanding of what they are to do in the laboratory. This will help the students concentrate to make the experience more meaningful. It also will prevent the experience from becoming a cookbook exercise in which the students must constantly refer to printed directions for guidance and become immersed in the mechanics of the laboratory instead of the excitement of finding out something for themselves. If special equipment and/or difficult procedures are involved, the teacher should show the students how to use the equipment and procedures and then call on some students to see how they perform these tasks. Prelaboratory discussions should be as short as possible, yet long enough to thoroughly orient the students to the laboratory.

Giving Directions

The directions for laboratory exercises must be explicit. They can be given orally and distributed in writing during the prelaboratory session. Oral directions may be adequate when one-step activities are involved and when the directions are simple enough to be remembered, such as:

The teacher advises her earth science class that diluted hydrochloric acid reacts with substances containing carbonates. She gives each pair of students a dispensing bottle of dilute acid and a tray of assorted rocks, minerals, bones, and shells. She directs the students to test the items for the presence of carbonates.

Sometimes summarizing directions on the chalkboard that have already been given orally is helpful.

The teacher sets out test tubes, medicine droppers, a soap solution, and a liquid detergent. She shows the students how to test the effects of these solutions on hard water. She then summarizes the directions on the chalkboard as follows:

1. *Fill two test tubes nearly full of water.*
2. *Add four drops of soap solution to one test tube.*
3. *Add four drops of detergent to the other test tube.*
4. *Shake each test tube well.*
5. *Hold the test tubes up to the light and observe.*

Written directions can be duplicated on paper and given to students, or they may be found in the laboratory manuals used in the course. Regardless of the form, the activities should be broken down into several steps. Each step should consist of a brief set of directions followed by some questions, as shown in the following example:

Strike one of the tuning forks against the palm of your hand. Observe the fork carefully.

1. *What observations can you make?*
2. *With which of your senses can you make observations of the vibrating fork?*
3. *Can you count the number of times the fork vibrates in one minute?*

Laboratory Safety

Safety should be a primary factor in laboratory work and addressed thoroughly during the prelaboratory instruction as well as in all phases of this experience. Science teachers must discuss safety in general with students and any potential hazards associated with a given laboratory before students are permitted to engage in this type of activity. They must go over general rules of laboratory safety and provide appropriate eye protection for all students as well as themselves. Some laboratory experiences will require aprons and protective gloves. No eating or horseplay is allowed in the laboratory.

Postlaboratory Discussion

The postlaboratory discussion is a critical component of laboratory work, and it must not be conducted hastily. Often, because of short laboratory periods, the postlaboratory discussion is rushed at the end of the period with little gain for students. The better approach is to hold off the discussion until the next science class period and to conduct the postlaboratory discussion in its entirety. Considerable thought, reflection, expression, analysis, and time must be given to the postlaboratory discussion in order for students to benefit from laboratory experiences.

The postlaboratory discussion presents an excellent opportunity to focus on important learning outcomes associated with laboratory work. For example, the following may take place in a postlaboratory discussion:

1. Students' *data and observations* should be placed on the board or overhead transparencies to be viewed and analyzed. Data should be placed in tables, charts, graphs, figures, or lists in a manner that communicates clearly what was observed.
2. The data, observations, and outcomes of the laboratory should be *critically analyzed* to determine what they mean and the extent to which they answer the questions or hypotheses under investigation. Students must *explain* the data and how it is related to the questions, methods, and interpretations. They should form *evidence* and structure *arguments* to support their conclusions. This will help students to become more logical in their thinking and cognizant of the importance of data in answering questions through scientific inquiry.
3. If the laboratory is designed to address *conceptual knowledge,* check on misconceptions and the extent to which these alternative conceptions are being affected. Students should be called on to state what they believed regarding a given idea before the laboratory was initiated and what they believe now as a result of their experiences and the data collected. Ask students to write out their ideas in clear, coherent sentences and to construct concept maps to show relationships between key concepts.
4. Call on students to identify the *science process skills* that they used to conduct their investigation and to speculate about how scientists and engineers might have conducted this laboratory exercise. These discussions will help students to gain a better appreciation for the *nature of science and technology*.
5. A science teacher can make the decision for students to *repeat laboratory work* and to perform certain parts of a laboratory over again. Performing some laboratory experiences only once may do very little to enhance some students' knowledge and skills. These individuals may need a considerable amount of *practice and exposure* to basic procedures and ideas, especially students who speak very little English. Also, many students do not have time to complete their laboratory work; therefore, they will not receive the full benefit of the learning experience.

Science Process Skill Laboratory

One purpose for conducting laboratory work is for students to develop their skills for collecting data and producing evidence to answer questions or to support or reject hypotheses. This aim requires that students use many skills to engage in their investigations. Some of the mental processes associated with science and, in particular, with laboratory work are referred to as *science process skills.* These skills include observing, classifying, using space/time relations, using numbers, measuring, inferring, predicting, defining operationally, formulating models, controlling variables, interpreting data, and experimenting. Table 13.1 provides a sample of science process skills that deserve the attention of science teachers because these are skills that middle and high school students should be capable of using. Let's look into the classroom of a science teacher who is focusing on taking thermometer readings and graphing the data.

Mrs. Swanson plans most of her laboratory exercises to increase students' graphing skills. She knows that the end-of-course science examination given to all eighth-grade students will have many questions that require students to construct or interpret graphs. One of the laboratory exercises that students carry out, during the study of physical properties of matter, is to graph the changes in water temperature over time as heat is added.

After placing her safety goggles and lab apron on, Mrs. Swanson sets up the apparatuses that students will be using on the front demonstration table—hot plate, beaker with ice, and thermometer. With the laboratory setup in view of all students, she discusses the purpose of this exercise. Mrs. Swanson explains to the students that they will be studying the temperature changes that will take place upon heating ice and water, resulting in steam. She demonstrates how to take the temperature readings in a safe manner so as not to knock over the beaker of hot or boiling water.

After the overview of the laboratory exercise—purpose, procedures, and safety—Mrs. Swanson addresses the recording of data and displaying it. After posing many questions, the teacher and students arrive at the form of a data table and graph that will be used to represent the information taken during the heating of water to its boiling point. The

TABLE 13.1 A Sample of Science Process Skills to Develop in Middle and High School Laboratory Instruction

Process Skill	Learning Outcome
Observing and inferring	Distinguish between observations and inferences. Make accurate observations that describe objects and events. Make plausible inferences that help to explain situations.
Measuring	Make measurements for length, mass, and volume, using SI or metric units.
Hypothesizing	Distinguish between inferences and hypotheses and know when to use each. Construct hypotheses that can be tested and for which enough data can be gathered for generalizing.
Communicating	Construct and label tables, bar graphs, and line graphs that are accurate and fit the situation. Keep a laboratory notebook and journal of activities with reflections. Write laboratory reports that are coherent and present procedures, results, and conclusions.
Experimenting	Test hypotheses and answer questions through controlled experimentation where independent and dependent variables are accounted for and properly controlled.

data table and graph are shown in Figure 13.1. Mrs. Swanson makes sure all the students are clear regarding the purpose and procedure of the laboratory and how to treat the data. She conducts the session using science talk with terms like physical properties, data, data table, graph, axis, labels, *and* independent *and* dependent variables.

Perhaps no science course is complete unless each student has been given the opportunity to conduct an experiment. Experimenting is the most complex of the integrated process skills and one that requires students to use many process skills to test out an idea. A true experiment tests a hypothesis that states a relationship between variables. Experiments can range from simple to very complex procedures. In science teaching, experiments can be valuable activities for which students are prepared and understand their purpose. Quite often, the term *experimenting* is used loosely to mean simply "trying something out" or "messing around." Although trying something out and messing around might be encouraged, these activities should be distinguished from a true experiment.

FIGURE 13.1 The representation of data taken from heating ice and water to its boiling point.

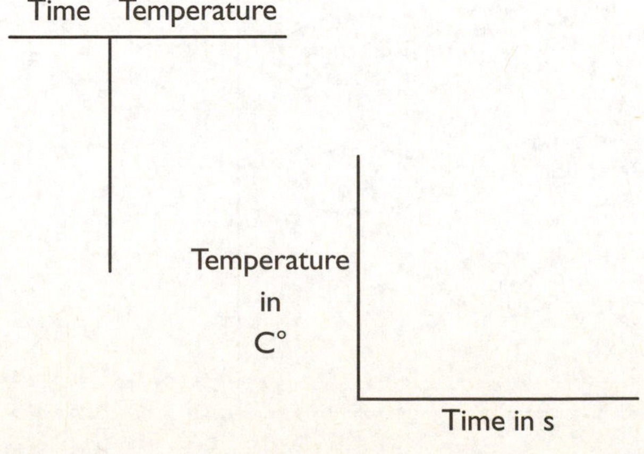

Some science educators prefer to restrict the term *experiment* to the type of investigation known as the *controlled experiment,* in which every effort is made to control the variables involved. All factors, except for the independent variable, are held constant, and the effects of the independent variable on the dependent variable are observed. For example, to determine the effect of ammonium sulfate on plant growth, two seed flats containing soil from the same lawn are seeded using a standard lawn grass mixture. One flat is watered with rainwater and the other with rainwater containing a little ammonium sulfate. The flats are kept in the same area to ensure identical conditions of temperature and light.

In this experiment, the seed flat watered with rainwater alone is called the *control.* The seed flat watered with the rainwater containing ammonium sulfate (fertilizer) is called the *experimental situation*, and the ammonium sulfate is the *independent variable.* The *hypothesis* being tested in this experiment is that ammonium sulfate will increase plant growth. The *dependent variable* is the amount of plant growth.

Science teachers can use science process–oriented laboratories to great advantage if they are sensitive to the intellectual development of their students. It may take considerable time to identify variables and formulate hypotheses. Thus, the less cognitively demanding skills, such as defining operationally, interpreting data, and graphing, may be the initial focus of science process–oriented laboratory exercises for many youngsters. With some thought and planning, science process skill laboratories can be very effective in motivating students to be successful inquirers, helping them to develop important cognitive skills and subject matter knowledge. This type of laboratory may also promote the spirit of science, especially among middle school students.

Deductive or Verification Laboratory

The deductive or verification laboratory is perhaps the most common approach to laboratory work in science courses. The purpose for this type of laboratory work is to confirm concepts, principles, and laws that have been addressed during classroom discussion and reading. Most science teachers present major ideas first, through lecture, discussion, and reading, followed by laboratory work to illustrate examples of key concepts. A biology teacher, for example, might use the deductive approach to discuss different types of bacteria, such as rod-, spherical-, and spiral-shaped cells. The oral presentation might then be followed by a laboratory exercise during which students observe the different shapes of bacteria under the microscope. Or a physics teacher might use a verification laboratory to demonstrate to students how the intensity of light diminishes as the distance between the light source and the light receptor increases (Figure 13.2). In connection with the laboratory, a formula might be presented to students and problems solved on the board using various numbers to represent the distance between two points. Students are often convinced of the mathematical model of light intensity through verification of the law in the laboratory.

Many concepts, principles, and laws can be developed best through a deductive approach, whereby they are first discussed by the teacher, then followed by a laboratory activity to verify attributes and relationships. Many of the laws of physics and chemistry, which are represented by mathematical formulas, can be illustrated in laboratory work. When the formulas for these laws are first presented in class, students begin to realize their meaning. Greater meaning is acquired when students gather data and use the data with the formula to verify the law or principle under investigation.

Verification laboratories have a positive feature in that they tend to provide students with an advanced organization of an abstract idea. With this approach, students are given some notion of what they are expected to find out. Many students, especially middle school students, do not tolerate ambiguity well, and therefore need to know what they are looking for in their laboratory work. This is why many science teachers discuss a concept or principle before they take students into the laboratory to carry out an investigation.

Consider the deductive approach used by a high school physics teacher during the study of light and electromagnetism presented in Classroom Snapshot 13.1. You might agree from reading the description of this deductive instruction that the approach can help to reinforce subject matter content that is taken up in the classroom. In many instances, science teachers have found this method to be beneficial, first to give students a conceptual organization of the topic and then to provide them with firsthand experiences. Also, note how Mrs. Beck attempted to avoid making this experience a cookbook laboratory by helping students become familiar with the procedures, so that they would not be preoccupied with following written directions during the laboratory and by giving them some freedom to "experiment" with the angle of the incident light beam.

FIGURE 13.2 This concept map can help students conceptualize the behavior of light through discussion and verification laboratory exercises.

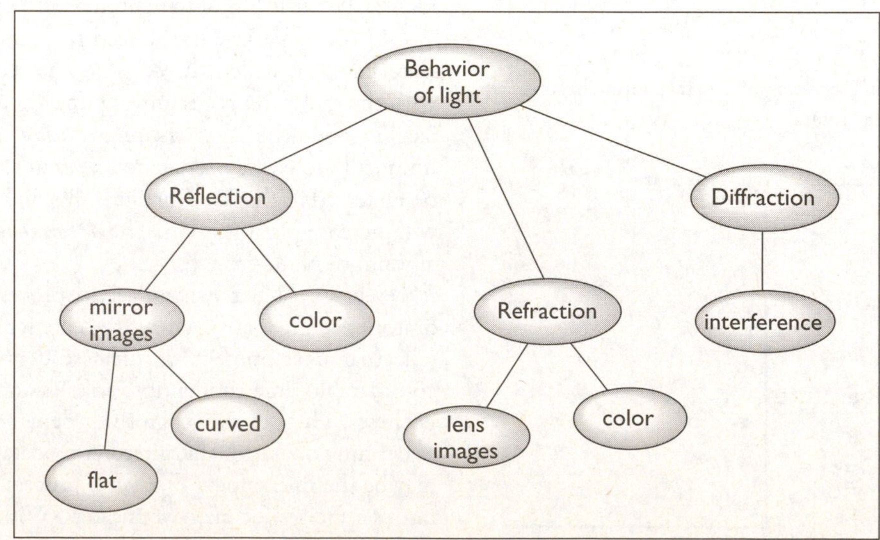

Classroom Snapshot 13.1

A Deductive Laboratory Exercise

Mrs. Beck begins her instruction on light and electromagnetism by providing students with a brief historical background and overview of this topic. She initiates this study with a lecture/discussion on three theories of light—particle, wave, and field. This segment is followed by a presentation on the work of the scientists who contributed to our understanding of these theories. Then Mrs. Beck carefully discusses the behavior of light, which she organizes in three main parts: (a) reflection, (b) refraction, and (c) diffraction. She provides students with a concept map to illustrate the order in which the behavior of light will be studied as well as the aspects of each that will be examined in the laboratory (see Figure 13.2).

After the background and overview, Mrs. Beck involves students in their first laboratory on the topic, which involves reflection. During the prelaboratory discussion, she calls on several students to explain reflection. Then Mrs. Beck specifies what the students are required to determine during the laboratory. A demonstration takes place on how to measure the angles of incidence and reflection. Again, she calls on several students to be sure that they know what to do during the laboratory experience so they will not need to constantly refer to the laboratory procedures.

The laboratory exercise requires students to work in groups and to determine the angle of reflection produced by imposing a beam of light on a reflecting surface. They are free to use many angles from which to strike the surface with a light beam. Although the students have a pretty good idea of what to expect as a result of their classroom discussions, they seem challenged by the activity because the teacher provides a variety of surfaces on which to study reflection. Some of the students display a lack of understanding about the principle, however, which is evident when they are asked to predict the reflection of a light beam that has a large angle of incidence.

Inductive Laboratory

The inductive laboratory is the opposite of the deductive laboratory. The inductive laboratory provides students with the opportunity to develop concepts, principles, and laws through firsthand experiences before these ideas are discussed in the classroom. The inductive approach places students in the position to search for patterns and to identify relationships among data, after which the ideas are discussed by the teacher and applications of the concepts are provided to reinforce the learning. However, the concepts to be studied by the inductive approach cannot be so foreign to students that they will not recognize any aspects of their features in a laboratory experience.

Although science teachers frequently use deductive laboratories, they should also use inductive laboratories to help students develop fundamental science concepts and principles. Examine the inductive approach taken by a high school biology teacher, Mr. Lefer, in Classroom Snapshot 13.2. Note how the teacher engages students and attempts to form their knowledge about reproduction in flowers.

Technical Skill Laboratory

Good laboratory techniques are essential for conducting successful laboratory activities and gathering accurate data. They require manipulative skills that involve the development of hand–eye coordination, such as focusing a microscope, sketching specimens, measuring angles, cutting glass, connecting meters, and setting up probeware. Good laboratory work also includes experimental technique and orderliness. Although laboratory work often relies on students' abilities to manipulate equipment, some is highly dependent on the use of special equipment and techniques; therefore, the emphasis of some laboratories should involve the development and use of these skills and techniques.

Science educators have placed too little emphasis on developing proficiency in laboratory skills and techniques (Hegarty-Hazel, 1990). All students and science teachers should master many basic laboratory techniques and manipulative skills associated with the science area in which they are involved. Science teachers who plan and organize laboratory experiences ahead of time can identify techniques that require special attention. For instance, the microscope is used a great deal in biology labo-

Classroom Snapshot 13.2

An Inductive Laboratory Exercise

Mr. Lefer, who teaches high school freshmen, realizes how easy it is to attempt to teach students too many terms in a biology course. He has observed new teachers as well as veteran teachers, teach biology as a body of vocabulary words rather than as inquiry-based science. Therefore, he initiates many of the biology course units that he has designed with an inductive laboratory exercise. One of his favorite inductive labs is on the sexual reproductive parts of the flower. On the day that he conducts this laboratory, the teacher brings dozens of flowers to school that he purchased at a local grocery store.

During the prelaboratory discussion, Mr. Lefer tells students that they are going to examine a flower, sketch its parts, figure out the function of each part, but most important to figure out the correct sequence of the fertilization process. He directs students to label the parts with the letters A, B, C, etc. and to provide the biological terms, if they know them, but not to refer to the textbook. On the bottom part of the sketch sheet, he tells students to provide the function for each part of the flower and to attempt to trace the process of fertilization that will lead to a new plant. The teacher goes on to provide a little background information to help students better understand the purpose of the laboratory—just enough information so that the students will take on the exercise as a challenge and not become disengaged. Then he asks class members to recall the study of sexual reproduction in vertebrates that took place earlier in the course. Mr. Lefer is careful to bring out the terms: fertilization, egg, sperm, and embryo.

With an idea of sexual reproduction in mind, the teacher assigns each class member a number from one to three. Then he sends the students to laboratory tables and asks them to take one flower from the pile corresponding to their assigned number. Mr. Lefer makes sure that each student has a pencil to draw with. During the laboratory, he moves around the room from student to student, providing cues and prompts to keep them on task. When the students have completed their sketches, labeling, and tracing the fertilization process, the teacher calls the students back to their desks for discussion.

For the postlaboratory discussion, Mr. Lefer asks for a volunteer from each of the three groups to place their sketches and labels on the board. Then he conducts a lively discussion with each of the three student groups whose participants argue about their labels and paths to fertilization. *Here is where students attempt to determine the pattern or sequence of the fertilization process in flowers.* At the conclusion of the group discussions for homework, Mr. Lefer asks the students to make a new sketch of their flower with correct labels and descriptions of the fertilization process, using what they learned today in the laboratory and with the aid of their biology textbook. He tells them to staple the new sketch sheet to the top of the one completed today, so that they can note the growth of their understanding, which is to be handed in tomorrow. The teacher also informs students that tomorrow he will quiz them on the how well they can label parts of a flower, give their function, and describe the fertilization process.

ratory work. Most adolescents have difficulty focusing the microscope and centering the specimen in the microscope's field. Experienced biology teachers provide their students with laboratory exercises on the care and use of the microscope. This work permits students to view such objects as newsprint and human hair under the microscope in order to learn how to focus this instrument and how to move objects into view. Because of the lens system, everything viewed is reversed, which confuses students; therefore, they need practice focusing the microscope. Beginners, for example, have a tendency to crush the glass cover slips under the objective lens when attempting to bring a specimen into clear view.

Psychomotor and mental practice with laboratory procedures is necessary in order to improve students' abilities to make accurate and precise laboratory measurements. Physical practice with laboratory equipment provides concrete experience with the apparatus and procedure. It gives the student a set of experiences on which to build images that represent the skill under development. Because time is always critical to laboratory work, firsthand exposure to the equipment is essential. Then, during class time and discussion sessions, mental practice of the skill and procedures under study can ensue.

In studying electricity, for example, experienced physical science teachers might say that it is essential to

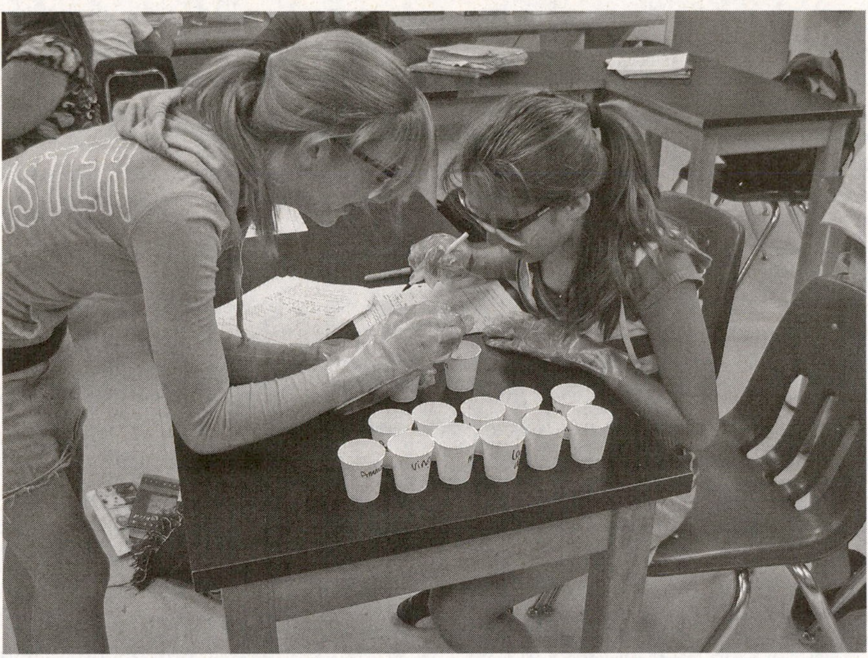

Students should be given many opportunities to make meaning from observations.

precede common laboratory exercises on electricity with one that focuses solely on measuring voltage and current, using the voltmeter and ammeter. It is often asking too much of teenagers to determine the current in a circuit before they are comfortable with the use of an ammeter. Remember, adolescents do not use electrical meters in their daily lives. What complicates this matter further is that many meters used in school laboratories have multiple scales, which can be very confusing to most people. Therefore, when laboratory work is carried out in stages, some designed to develop specific technical skills, students have a better chance of benefiting from this type of instruction.

For the concrete operational students participating in a middle school earth science class, constructing a profile map can be a challenge. Translating topographic information from contour lines to a vertical/horizontal profile is a task that requires considerable mental as well as manipulative ability. Most students need practice before they gain competence in this task and are able to realize the three-dimensional nature of a contour map.

Making sketches and drawings is an essential part of laboratory work. This type of activity not only provides a record of observations, but it reinforces visual images that pertain to essential concepts and learning outcomes in a science course. Here are some guidelines that can be used when instructing students to draw what they see in a biology class (or any other science course):

- Draw using a pencil and unlined paper.
- Make the drawing large enough so that important details are easily seen.
- Place the drawing near the left side of the sheet so that the labels can be placed on the right side.
- Print the labels one under the other.
- Use a ruler to draw lines from the labels to the drawing, and do not cross lines.
- Use light stippling or dotting to shade part of a drawing.
- Construct a title for the drawing at the top of the page.

The preceding discussion points out that many technical skills are necessary for improving students' ability to participate in and learn from laboratory work. Students need these skills to gain the unique learning outcomes associated with the science laboratory. If students have to struggle with basic manipulative procedures, they may lose sense of what they are trying to accomplish in the laboratory. Also, if students are so unfamiliar with basic laboratory procedures that they need to follow them by rote, they will lose much of the cognitive and affective benefits of laboratory work because they are preoccupied with following directions.

Small-Group Problem-Solving Laboratory

In some instances, science teachers should engage their students in problem-solving laboratory work where students are given opportunities to identify a problem, design procedures, collect information, organize data, and report the findings. This type of laboratory investigation can involve authentic inquiry experiences for students. This approach is also recommended on psychological grounds. Because students are involved in organizing their own learning, they may be inclined to better understand what they are doing. Students take more interest in their learning when they take part in organizing it.

Consider, for instance, a set of problem-solving laboratories at the middle school level in the life sciences. The teacher might recommend that students identify an insect to study over a one- or two-week period. The students select an insect they wish to study, then determine questions they wish to answer about the insect. Many students will be inclined to investigate what their insect eats. Most will attempt to determine their insect's reactions to various stimuli. For example, students who elect to study meal worms might determine how these insects react to water, vinegar, salt, soap, bran flakes, cola, sandpaper, glass, electricity, sound, heat, and light. The students can be encouraged to bring from home additional materials needed to study their insect. Some students may return to the laboratory after school hours to continue their inquiry beyond the regular time set aside for in-class laboratory work.

Some science teachers use the small-group problem-solving approach with students who wish to satisfy their curiosity about certain situations or with students the teacher wishes to motivate to study science. Science teachers can accomplish these ends outside of the regular laboratory time, usually after school when students can spend many hours engaging in hands-on experiences. For more information and examples on problem-solving instruction, study the section on small-group problem-solving approach in Chapter 8.

Ensuring Successful Laboratory Experiences

Science teachers must carefully plan and organize their laboratory activities in order for students to attain important learning outcomes from this work. They must give serious attention to the relevance of laboratory work, the degree of structure involved in activities, the methods by which students record and report data, classroom management, and evaluation of student work. Failure to give proper attention to these critical factors can undermine the value of laboratory activity in a science course.

Relevance of Laboratory Work

The association between classroom and laboratory work may not always be evident from their course experiences. Laboratory work often becomes a fragmented entity that seems to have little or no relation to the real world. This aspect of science teaching can become merely another activity to complete. Laboratory activities that incorporate commonplace devices and have immediate applications in the real world, however, are worthwhile to use. In laboratories where siphons, candles, electric bells, xylophones, household cleaners, mechanics' tools, over-the-counter medicines, and garden soils are studied, students rarely question the value of the work or its association with scientific principles.

Familiar objects provide a context that may be more interesting to students and serve to motivate their learning. The use of everyday materials demonstrates the applicability of science concepts and principles in daily life. These materials are usually inexpensive and easy to obtain. Often, students who are unmotivated in science classes are those who readily volunteer to bring in items for laboratory work. Also, when students study everyday phenomena in the laboratory, they are more inclined to acquire inquiry skills (Rubin & Tamir, 1988). If instruction begins with things familiar to students, the instruction is most likely to be related to the knowledge that students possess. Consequently, the instruction begins with what students know, which will facilitate their conceptual development as the instruction scaffolds their learning.

Degree of Structure in Laboratory Activities

Structure refers to the amount of guidance and direction teachers give to students. It usually takes the form of written directions or questions that are prepared on duplicated sheets or in laboratory manuals. Experienced science teachers often employ highly structured laboratory exercises, especially during the first part of a science course. Highly structured exercises provide students with a great deal of guidance, which helps the teacher to manage the instructional environment. Science teachers emphasize that when they must instruct large numbers of students, short exercises that provide students with plenty of direction seem to work best.

The following comments are from science teachers regarding the structure of their laboratories:

- "Our labs are highly structured and the answers seem so obvious, but not to these sixth-graders."
- "In physical science we use highly structured labs that focus on specific objectives and reinforce specific concepts. This is important to our ninth-graders who need help adapting to the high school environment."
- "The labs for many regular students are highly structured with specific instructions and questions that are close-ended because most of my students are not very science oriented. They get easily frustrated if they do not understand exactly what they are to do."

A note of caution is in order regarding highly structured laboratory work. There is a problem with using too much structure over the entire course. If the teacher uses highly structured activities throughout a course, problem solving, conceptual change, modifying misconceptions, and motivation may be limited. Structure can stifle self-directed learning and decision-making behavior. Consequently, toward the middle and end of the course, science teachers should vary the structure of their laboratory work.

After students have acquired basic inquiry skills and techniques, the teacher should give them the opportunity to identify their own problems and devise their own procedures. Over time, students will learn to conduct complete laboratory experiments. Some science teachers have suggested that students can be given more autonomy during the eighth and ninth grades than during the sixth and seventh grades, and many high school students are capable of conducting investigations with a minimal amount of guidance.

Leonard (1991) suggests that science teachers should attempt to "uncookbook laboratory investigations." He claims that too many procedures and written directions for students to follow can reduce advance organization by students, causing them to follow directions by rote and lose the meaning of the laboratory. Students can remember only so many directions and internalize only so much of someone else's procedures.

Student Recording and Reporting of Data

Students need assistance in recording and reporting their laboratory observations. When laboratory manuals are provided, the problem is somewhat reduced, because laboratory manuals usually provide space for student responses. When laboratory manuals are not provided, duplicated sheets or notebooks can be used to record data. Regardless of the form, recording must be kept simple. If students must devote too much time and effort to recording and reporting, they may develop an unfavorable attitude toward the laboratory.

Laboratory exercises vary in terms of their content and involvement. Consequently, recording and reporting these activities should vary. Some exercises focus on techniques and motor skills and require very little written activity. For example, exercises developing competence in using the balance, microscope, graduated cylinders, burettes, voltmeters, ammeters, force measures, and dissecting instruments require manipulative and mental skills, but little is required as far as reporting the outcomes in writing.

Exercises that involve students in a great deal of inquiry and open-ended investigations may require a more extensive type of report. In these situations, students may need to identify strategies that they will use to answer research questions. They should be expected to explain the procedures used to collect data when reporting their investigations. In addition, students must report data in a form that best communicates their value to the investigation. This usually requires the use of many communication devices used in science, such as graphs, tables, formulas, and figures.

Some science teachers require very little from students regarding the procedures used to carry out an investigation, because this information is usually written in the laboratory manual or on a handout. However, these teachers require their students to prepare a thorough explanation of: (1) the results, (2) the significance of the results, (3) how the laboratory relates to the subject matter content that is under study in the classroom, (4) how the laboratory reflects the nature of science, and (5) how the concepts and principles apply to other situations. Teachers indicate that students benefit greatly from these exercises when they are required to determine their importance and derive something meaningful from their laboratory work. They also mention that this assignment is very time consuming to grade.

A typical format for reporting science laboratory work includes the following six steps:

1. problem
2. materials
3. procedure
4. results
5. conclusions
6. applications

This format can become a rather rote form for reporting laboratory work—an unvarying format that may result in boredom and resentment from many students. Furthermore, students often mistake these steps as being synonymous with the scientific method. Science teachers are advised to vary their requirements for reporting laboratory work. Simple experiments require only simple records and reports.

Gardner and Gauld (1990) advise that teachers who emphasize correctness of data and conclusions might produce negative effects on students' laboratory performance and attitudes. They point out that students want to get the "right results" because their teachers use these results to grade them. Consequently, if students do not get good data or what is perceived to be the correct results, they may be penalized. This situation causes some students to copy data from other students so they will receive a good grade. Teachers should realize that getting the right answer can discourage curiosity and original thought. Science teachers must be acutely aware of the learning outcomes they are shaping from the type of laboratories they promote and the type of laboratory reports they require from students.

Management and Discipline during Laboratory Activities

Management is a critical factor for successful laboratory activities. This is especially true in the middle and junior high schools, where students are very active and perhaps cannot concentrate for extended periods of time. Laboratory room management may pose a special problem to the beginning science teacher, who may be a little lax in developing and maintaining rules for this type of activity. Some essential elements that need attention in the science laboratory include seating arrangements, grouping, discipline, and monitoring student activities. Desks and laboratory tables should be arranged so that they are not crowded, to allow for free flow of traffic. Keep students away from laboratory materials until they are ready to use them, especially during the time that the teacher is giving directions. Avoid placing worktables against walls.

Students can work individually, in pairs, or in small groups. The amount of equipment and materials usually dictates the working arrangement. Obviously, it would be best to have students work independently the majority of the time, but in most situations they must work in pairs or in small groups of approximately four students. Problems can arise when students within groups participate in very little laboratory work or when they interact between groups. Talking and fraternizing between groups usually result in a high noise level and disruptive behavior. It is best to require students to work and to talk only with those within their own group.

Noise level is a problem in open-space areas during laboratory activities. Noise creates distractions for classes in adjacent areas, causing fellow teachers to complain, and consequently resulting in negative reactions by administrators toward laboratory work. Science teachers instructing in open-space areas have had to work very hard to keep the noise level down. Those most successful at this task have instructed their students to speak quietly. These teachers help their students build a group esprit de corps, in which each group works quietly, guarding their findings, while remaining orderly.

Many laboratory activities can best be handled in groups. This is especially true for middle school students. Small-group laboratory activities will be most successful if every member is assigned a role. The following roles can be assigned to students within each group:

Coordinator: Keeps the group on task and working productively

Manager: Gathers and returns equipment and materials

Investigator: Helps conduct the investigation

Recorder: Records data and keeps notes on the investigation

Reporter: Organizes and reports the findings

The teacher should give students the opportunity to select roles that they wish to play in the investigation, giving them an opportunity to be actively involved in laboratory work. Students should rotate their roles, however, so that each is provided with a variety of experiences and takes responsibility for their learning.

Some science teachers are more successful than others at getting students to participate in orderly and productive laboratory experiences. Although successful teachers might begin laboratory activities with a great deal of control and structure, they soon begin to encourage their students to take more responsibility for their work and conduct in the laboratory. The most successful teachers are those who spend less time controlling their students and more time structuring them and giving them more opportunities to learn on their own as we have tried to explain in Chapter 6 on the science learning environment. These teachers maintain a classroom atmosphere in which students develop a sense of ownership and control over their work.

The teacher plays a major role in developing and maintaining a well-disciplined laboratory environment. This is essential in promoting student productivity and safety as well as avoiding complaints from other teachers and administrators. Consequently, the science teacher must keep students on task and maintain a reasonable noise level. Continuous interaction between teacher and students can facilitate this process. Walking from student to student or from group to group is also helpful. Such contact urges students to stay on track and gives the teacher the opportunity to help students with problems. It is important to move around the entire room so that all groups of students receive the necessary attention, rather than spending too much time with any single group of students. In addition, the well-managed laboratory room has all the necessary materials and equipment ready to be used. In some instances, the items should be arranged on a table where they can be taken and returned, whereas in other instances they can be placed on a cart that can be moved to where students are working.

Rules and policies regarding safety and behavior are essential to the success of the laboratory. They must be stated verbally early in the course, preferably during the first laboratory period. Once stated, they should be posted in clearly visible locations in the laboratory areas. Students should be aware that they will be expected to follow the rules consistently and without exception and that the teacher will be firm but fair about this expectation. The rules should include statements regarding conduct, safety, laboratory reports, use of equipment and materials, and grading; and they should be stated as positively as possible. Student input may be desirable when teachers are establishing rules of conduct; this will increase the probability that students will know the rules and, consequently, adhere to them. It may also be a good policy to provide a set of rules to parents so they know what behaviors the students are expected to exhibit in the laboratory. See Figure 13.3 for rules that can be used for developing a set of guidelines for science laboratory conduct. Please study Chapter 14, which addresses the important topic of providing a safe learning environment.

Evaluation

Evaluation of laboratory work as a part of the total science course grade is an essential part of a science course. There are several techniques to employ in this situation. Paper-and-pencil tests, laboratory reports, notebooks, practical examinations, laboratory behavior, and effort can all be used to determine the laboratory component of the course grade. At least 10 aspects of laboratory work can be used to evaluate students:

1. inclination to inquire and find out
2. ability to ask questions that can be answered in the laboratory
3. desire to design procedures to test ideas
4. competence and mastery of technical skills
5. competence and mastery of science process skills
6. ability to collect accurate and precise data
7. willingness to report data honestly
8. ability to report patterns and relationships and to explain their significance
9. thoroughness of laboratory reporting
10. inclination to behave properly in the laboratory

Short paper-and-pencil tests are often used to evaluate laboratory work. Few to many items can be used to assess information learned or reinforced in the laboratory. These assessments can also determine how well students gain the many learning outcomes possible from work in the laboratory. Laboratory reports and laboratory notebooks are used to assess students' ability to record data and report findings as well as to measure their on-task behavior.

The laboratory practical is an excellent way to assess students' knowledge of laboratory work. Laboratory stations can be set up where information or techniques can

FIGURE 13.3 This list of rules can be used to develop a set of guidelines for student conduct in the science laboratory.

Guidelines for Conduct in the Science Laboratory

1. Do your job well and assume your share of responsibility.
2. Keep the noise level to a minimum and speak softly.
3. Work primarily with members of your group; avoid interacting with other groups' members.
4. Raise your hand if you need help from the teacher. The teacher will come to you; do not go to the teacher.
5. Horseplay is not allowed in the laboratory at any time.
6. Eating or drinking is not permitted in the laboratory.
7. Follow all safety procedures that are posted.
8. Copy the rules concerning "Safety in the Laboratory" in your notebook for reference.
9. Carefully handle all equipment and return it to its proper place.
10. Report faulty or broken equipment immediately to the teacher.
11. Do not waste materials.
12. All dangerous organisms, chemicals, and materials must be handled as directed by the teacher. If you have any questions, ask the teacher.
13. Make certain that all glassware is washed and dried before being returned to storage areas.
14. Keep your work area clean and organized.
15. Clean your tabletop before leaving the laboratory.
16. Remove litter from the floor, particularly around the areas in which you work.
17. Strive for accuracy in making observations and measurements.
18. Be honest in reporting data; present what you actually find.

be assessed. The teacher must allow time to prepare the laboratory stations and must take care to ensure that students do not receive answers from their classmates.

Science teachers use direct observation to assess student behavior in the laboratory. Some middle school science teachers give a grade for each laboratory period for satisfactory or unsatisfactory conduct. The effort demonstrated by students in the laboratory should be rewarded whenever possible, particularly at the middle and junior high school levels. Giving credit for demonstrated effort can develop and maintain positive student behavior in the laboratory as well as reinforce the learning of science content and process. The teacher, of course, determines what part of the total grade should reflect effort in the laboratory. In general, laboratory work accounts for 20% to 40% of the report card or course grade, and effort should be a part of this percentage.

 Fieldwork

Science teachers should incorporate fieldwork into their curricula because it offers authentic learning experiences for students, giving them greater understanding of the natural and technological world in which they live. Field trips are perhaps the most enjoyable and memorable of academic experiences for students. Generally, field-trip sites are somewhat familiar to students which causes them to take a special interest in these events. Today, there is renewed interest in field experiences because of their potential to contribute to the improvement of scientific literacy.

Planning Field Trip Experiences

Field trips permit firsthand study of many things, both natural and human-made, that cannot be brought into the classroom. Hospital operating rooms, electrical power–generating plants, petroleum refineries, space centers, sewage treatment plants, observatories, and wildlife refuges are field sites that students can benefit from visiting. A trip to these and many other sites rivals any video presentation or in-class lecture that students might receive about the activities that take place at these locations.

The Curriculum

When science teachers entertain the idea for taking field trips in their courses, they must examine the curriculum and decide which experiences relate directly to their courses. Field trips require a great deal of time to arrange and conduct, so selection must be based on the goals and content of the curriculum. The question should be asked: Which topic(s) ought to be taught or reinforced by taking students into the field? If a science teacher can identify a topic in the curriculum that students should study outside the classroom, the chances are good that she or he can make a case for organizing a field trip to that location.

Surveying Possible Sites

Students should study indoors the things that are best studied indoors and study outdoors the things that are best studied outdoors. It should be obvious that far too much instruction takes place within the classroom walls. Fortunately, within and around most schools there are hundreds of things worthy of study—resources far more valuable than those available in the school science laboratories. Common objects and events are often the best to study in their natural environment. Science teachers can begin planning by making a list of field sites, beginning in the school, moving to the school grounds, streets, neighborhoods, community services, rural areas, small businesses, museums, hobbies, small manufacturing plants, and large industrial facilities. The places listed in Figure 13.4 present a large number of field sites, many of which are rather easy to access.

Administrative Policy

Field trips within the confines of the school property are usually easy to arrange. But, even for these experiences, it is advisable to consult with the school administration so that you are informed about school policy. Further, incidents may have occurred in the past that the teacher should be aware of, because these events may have caused the administration to be concerned about field trips, even on school grounds. Excursions off school property will certainly require administrative permission. Science teachers need to be fully informed of school and district policies regarding field trips to locations that require transportation. Liability is always a consideration. Policies governing trips away from school have usually been established. However, some principals may have negative attitudes about these events because of problems that they have encountered. Science teachers should be aware of these matters. Most school policies require written notice, which includes purpose, location, times of departure and return, and names of students. Written permission from parents is usually required as well. Figure 13.5 on page 229 presents a list of important considerations when taking students off-campus to participate in a field trip.

Conducting a Field Experience

Since taking a field trip is viewed as a big event, considerable preparation is invested in this undertaking. Planning and instructional activities take place prior to the trip so that students are well informed of what they will be doing. The

FIGURE 13.4 Examples of field study locations and related sites.

School Building

Heating and cooling areas: heat, condensation, temperature
Electrical system: safety, wiring, voltage, current
Automobile shop: batteries, engines, brakes, safety
Cafeteria: food, nutrition, diet
Kitchen: hygiene, cooking, fire
Music department: sound, music
Auditorium: acoustics

School Grounds

Lawn: plants, animals, habitats, ecology
Shrubs: effects of light and shade
Trees: seasonal changes, identification, classification
Flagpole: measurement, position of sun, seasons

Streets

Vehicles: types, stopping distances
Traffic: safety, patterns, intersections, lights
Pedestrians: patterns of walking and crossing
Streets: type of pavement, maintenance
Utility lines: service, safety

Residential Dwellings

Gardens: topsoil and subsoil
Flower beds: identification, classification, conditions
Lawns: organisms, fertilizers, shade and light
Insulation: type, amount
Roofs: composition, pitch

Community Services

Fire station: equipment, simple machines, ladders
Police car: computers, radar, engine, safety
Hospital: operating room, diet, sterilization
Nursery: plants, classification, seasons
Water works: purification, pipes, computer system

Small Businesses

Supermarket: food, labeling, refrigeration
Building supply: materials, machines, tools
Dry cleaners: chemicals, cleaners, safety
Electronic repair: electronics, computers, recorders

Manufacturing and Utility Plants

Bakeries: baking, receipts, packaging
Dairies: refrigeration, pasteurization, production, packaging
Chemical plants: refining, production, transportation, research
Electricity: furnaces, nuclear reactors, turbines, generators

Outside of the City

Beaches: wave action, marine life
Ponds: plant and animal specimens
Fields: flowers, birds, insects
Hillsides: erosion effects
Rivers: energy, sediments, movement
Woodlands: trees, classification, soil, succession

Other Sites

Botanical gardens: flowers, reproduction
Museums: archeology, geology, natural science, medicine, space science
Planetariums and observatories: planets, stars, solar system, universe
Zoos: ecology, diversity, evolution

teacher and the students need to know precisely what to do once at the site. After they return to the classroom, there are follow-up activities to maximize the value of the experience.

Preparation

Once a field trip has been decided on, considerable planning should take place to ensure maximum benefit. Instruction is part of the preparation phase so that students have a clear idea of what they will be expected to observe and learn. Students need to develop the proper mind-set for this event so that they will be concentrating and learning important skills, procedures, and information. Read Classroom Snapshot 13.3 to get an idea of how a high school biology teacher approaches a field experience.

Classroom Snapshot 13.3

Planning the Field Trip

Ms. Walker spent three class periods getting her students ready for a field trip to a large pond located on the grounds of the school district's Science Center. During the first period, she described the purpose of the field trip and informed the students that parental permission is required for those who would be going to the center by bus. In the second class period, Ms. Walker introduced the study of ecology with a brief lecture on some major principles of the topic. Then students were given practice in identifying a small number of organisms that they might collect on the field trip day. They seem to require a great deal of practice focusing on specimens under the microscope, especially those moving across the field of view. During the third period, the teacher organized the students into cooperative groups and gave all students a task to perform during the trip.

At the Field Trip Site

As soon as they got off the bus, Ms. Walker and her students entered the main building of the Science Center for a brief orientation by one of the staff members. Safety and student conduct were addressed. Then Ms. Walker reviewed the purpose for the trip and performed a check to determine if each student knew his or her task. Then students were taken to the pond and the center's staff member recommended techniques to collect specimens. When the students completed all of their work at the pond and returned to the center, they entered a large room with fifteen microscope stations where they could view macroscopic as well as microscopic organisms. The staff member and Ms. Walker circulated among the students answering questions and guiding them in their work.

After the Field Trip

Ms. Walker devoted two instructional periods to the pond trip back in her classroom. She used the first period for laboratory work to give each student more time to examine the organisms that he or she gathered, as well as those that others collected. Ms. Walker also set up four microscope stations with specimens for students to identify and for them to explain the role of living creatures in the pond's ecosystem. The second class period was devoted to group presentations to discuss the ecology of this aquatic biome. This session offered students another opportunity to construct more knowledge about important ecological concepts and principles.

FIGURE 13.5 A checklist of important field trip considerations.

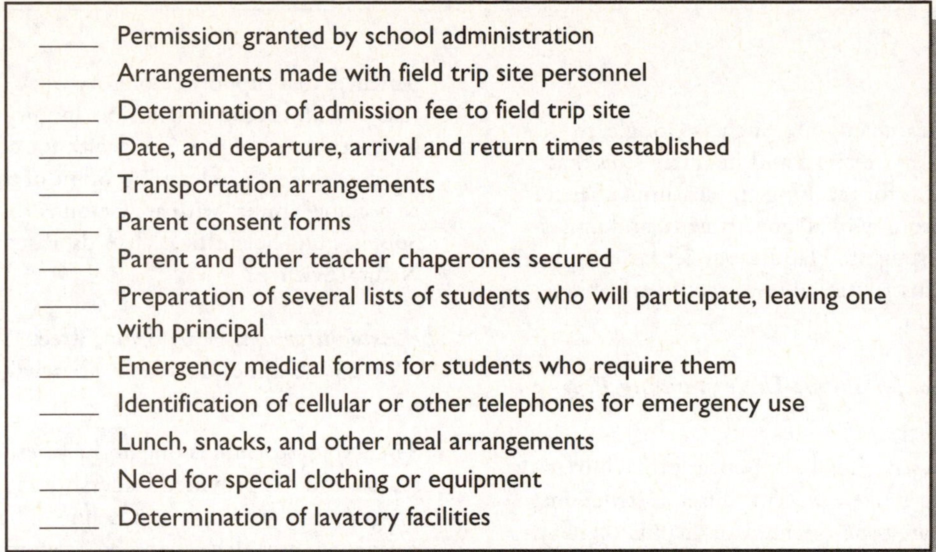
____ Permission granted by school administration
____ Arrangements made with field trip site personnel
____ Determination of admission fee to field trip site
____ Date, and departure, arrival and return times established
____ Transportation arrangements
____ Parent consent forms
____ Parent and other teacher chaperones secured
____ Preparation of several lists of students who will participate, leaving one with principal
____ Emergency medical forms for students who require them
____ Identification of cellular or other telephones for emergency use
____ Lunch, snacks, and other meal arrangements
____ Need for special clothing or equipment
____ Determination of lavatory facilities

Assessing and Reviewing

Analysis and Synthesis

1. Interview a few new and a few experienced science teachers to obtain their views on the purpose and importance of laboratory work in the courses they teach. Also, determine the frequency of the laboratory work conducted in their courses. Discuss this information with other members in your science methods class.
2. Analyze the laboratory activities for a science course and classify the laboratories into one of the following categories: process skill, deductive, inductive, technical skill, or problem solving. Evaluate the laboratory activities based on their variety and appropriateness for the students who are using them. Discuss your evaluation with other class members.

Practical Considerations

3. Develop an instrument to evaluate how a science teacher conducts a laboratory exercise. Include ideas discussed in this chapter, such as the prelaboratory and postlaboratory discussions, applicability, structure, recording/reporting, management, and evaluation. Establish a set of criteria from which you can make a judgment regarding the degree of inquiry that takes place during a laboratory exercise.
4. Survey how science teachers and science coordinators in a school district conduct inventories, order supplies and equipment, and maintain and store laboratory equipment, chemicals, and supplies.
5. Discuss science teaching facilities that you think are good laboratory learning environments with the other members of your methods class.
6. Develop a laboratory exercise illustrating one of the five types of laboratories described in this chapter. Conduct the laboratory with a group of peers or with middle or senior high school students enrolled in a science class.

Developmental Considerations

7. Plan a field trip for several science classes of middle or high school students to a site in your community. Address the aspects of fieldwork that are discussed in this chapter in order for the trip to be a productive and safe event.

Resources to Examine

The Internet

Use Internet search engines, such as Google, to locate laboratory exercises and field trip sites that offer many ideas for teaching and learning science. You will find commercial, government, and university sites with suggested laboratory activities and other science instructional resources to enhance a science program.

Science Education for Public Understanding Program (SEPUP)

SEPUP at Lawrence Hall of Science at the University of California at Berkeley has produced instructional materials that are issue-oriented and hands-on to improve the public's understanding of science and its relationship to everyday life. The SEPUP modules contain many hands-on laboratory activities for middle school and high school students as well as adults. Some representative titles are *Decision Making: Probability and Risk Assessment, Investigating Ground Water, Toxic Waste: A Teaching Simulation, Living With Plastics, Investigation Food Safety,* and *Household Chemicals.* These instructional materials are interesting and promote inquiry in the science curriculum.

Science Laboratory Supply Companies

There are a large number of laboratory/science supply companies that offer many publications and printed material to enhance active learning and firsthand experiences that support laboratory work. These materials provide excellent hands-on/inquiry-oriented instructional resources, along with the equipment to conduct this type of learning. Some of the companies to become familiar with are Carolina Biological Supply, Flinn Scientific, Lab-Aids, Pasco, and Ward's Natural Science.

The Exploratorium. 3601 Lyon Street, San Francisco, CA 94123. [Online] Available at: www.exloratorium.edu.

The Exploratorium is one of the finest science museums, and has provided leadership in educational programs of learning via museums. The facility has permanent as well as changing programs of high interest to teachers, students, and the general public. The museum provides an excellent field trip with hands-on activities that are based on Exploratorium exhibits, which include content discussions and classroom materials. This facility provides workshops and online support for inquiry learning as well as professional development for science teachers interested in ideas for inquiry-based science. Science teachers should visit this Web site and visit the museum if they are in or near San Francisco. However, there are dozens of other science museums across the United States, which are excellent field trip sites, providing educators with resources for laboratory investigations and demonstrations. Government organizations, such as NASA, also provide a wealth of science teaching resources.

References

Blosser, P. E. (1981). *A critical review of the role of the laboratory in science teaching.* Columbus, OH: ERIC/SMEAC Clearinghouse.

Freedman, M. P. (2002). The influence of laboratory instruction on science achievement and attitude toward science across gender differences. *Journal of Women and Minorities in Science and Engineering, 8* (2), 191–199.

Gardner, P., & Gauld, C. (1990). Labwork and students' attitudes. In E. Hegarty-Hazel (Ed.), *The student laboratory and the science curriculum* (pp. 132–156). New York: Routledge.

Hegarty-Hazel, E. (1990). *The student laboratory and the science curriculum.* New York: Routledge.

Hodson, D. (1985). Philosophy of science, science and science education. *Studies in Science Education, 12,* 25–57.

Leonard, W. H. (1991). A recipe for uncookbooking laboratory investigations. *Journal of College Science Teaching, 21* (2), 84–87.

Rowell, J. A., & Dawson, C. J. (1983). Laboratory counterexamples and the growth of understanding in science. *European Journal of Science Education, 5,* 203–215.

Rubin, A., & Tamir. P. (1988). Meaningful learning in the school laboratory. *American Biology Teacher, 50,* 477–482.

Schwab, J. J. (1964). *The teaching of science.* Cambridge, MA: Harvard University Press

Singer, S. R., Hilton, M. L., & Schweingruber, H. A. (Eds.) (2005). *America's lab report: Investigations in high school science.* Washington. DC: National Academies of Science Press.

Chapter

14

Safety in the Laboratory and Classroom

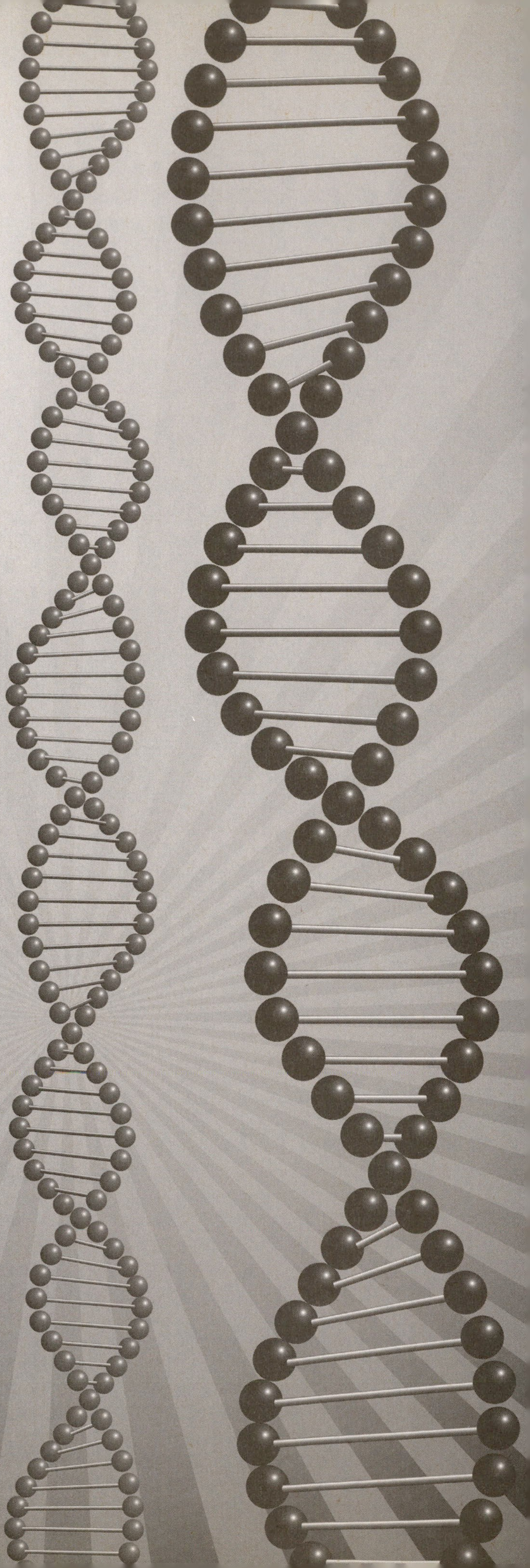

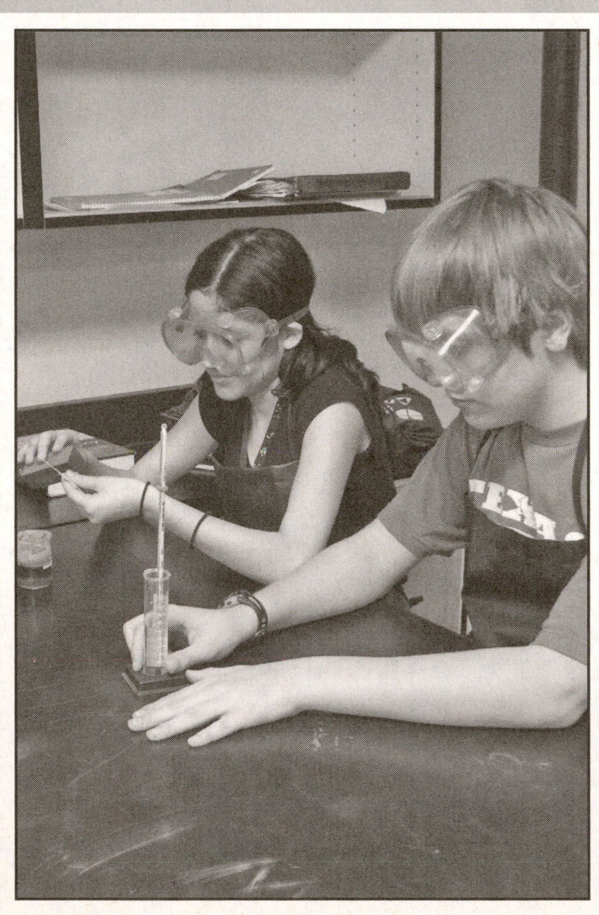

Appropriate eyewear is a critical consideration for science safety.

Science teachers must provide a safe learning environment for all students at all times. Safety is the law. The teaching profession requires teachers to keep students safe from injury. Providing a safe learning environment is one of the most important ethical principles of the teaching profession, and teachers have the moral obligation to uphold this standard. Science teachers are accountable for their actions and must develop a set of values that promote the safety and welfare of students and animals. The science laboratory and classroom are places where accidents can occur as a result of mishandling and use of apparatus, equipment, chemicals, and live organisms that are often maintained in these teaching environments.

A safety program must be in place that includes the training of teachers, students, and other personnel who may be involved in science instruction. Certain standard safety procedures must be implemented as a matter of course before, during, and after instruction, and these safety procedures must be given high priority to ensure a continuous and effective safety program. Not only must students be safe in school science activities, but they must also understand about safety and why there are certain rules and procedures.

AIMS OF THE CHAPTER

Use the questions below to guide your thinking and learning about school science and how you can be successful in providing a safe learning environment for students and ethical treatment of animals:

- Can you summarize what the laws state regarding the necessity to provide safe learning environments for students?
- Where would you find national, state, and district safety guidelines pertaining to where you are teaching or would like to teach science?
- What are the responsibilities of students and teachers for maintaining safety in the classroom, field, and laboratory?
- Can you list many preparations that should be made by science teachers before the school year begins to ensure a safe learning environment in the classroom and laboratory?
- Can you explain the safety guidelines for eye protection and wearing contact lenses during laboratory investigations?
- What are the safety guidelines for teaching biology, chemistry, earth science, and physical science courses?
- Where would you find Material Safety Data Sheets (MSDS) that provide information about the hazards and other pertinent information of chemical substances that you might use in the classroom, laboratory, and storeroom?
- Why is it important to teach a laboratory safety unit to students and for teachers to participate in safety workshops and seminars?
- Where would you find a safety contract for students and parents to sign?

Introduction

> ***Standard 9: Safety and Welfare.*** *Teachers of science organize safe and effective learning environments that promote the success of students and the welfare of all living things. They require and promote knowledge and respect for safety, and oversee the welfare of all living things used in the classroom or found in the field. To show they are prepared, teachers of science must demonstrate that they:*
>
> *a. Understand the legal and ethical responsibilities of science teachers for the welfare of their students, the proper treatment of animals, and the maintenance and disposal of materials.*
> *b. Know and practice safe and proper techniques for the preparation, storage, dispensing, supervision, and disposal of all materials used in science instruction.*
> *c. Know and follow emergency procedures, maintain safety equipment, and ensure safety procedures appropriate for the activities and the abilities of students.*
> *d. Treat all living organisms used in the classroom or found in the field in a safe, humane, and ethical manner and respect legal restrictions on their collection, keeping, and use.*
>
> (Standards for Science Teacher Preparation, *NSTA, 2003*)

As evidenced above by the Safety and Welfare standard developed by the National Science Teachers Association (NSTA) for Science Teacher Preparation, current national standards stress the importance of safety and that science teachers have an ethical obligation to promote safety in the science classroom, laboratory, and field. Consequently, they must recognize the legal implications when students are not properly supervised and when students are not trained to be responsible for their own safety and the safety of others. The teaching of safety and the use of appropriate laboratory procedures for safety should be an integral part of all science instruction. An accident or injury can spoil an enjoyable science learning environment.

 Safety and the Law

The science teacher must be knowledgeable about the legal responsibilities regarding safety in the classroom. The very nature of the science classroom and laboratory increases the probability of student accidents, and teachers must take every reasonable precaution to ensure the safety of the students and themselves. If an injury occurs in the classroom or in the laboratory, what do the courts commonly look for? First, the courts ask if there is a duty (responsibility) owed? And the answer to that is *yes*. Next, the courts want to know the standard of care that was provided. Three areas determine the standard of care in education. A teacher owes his/her students:

1. active instruction regarding their conduct and safety in the classroom
2. adequate supervision
3. consideration of foreseeable potential hazards

Merely posting rules in a classroom is not enough. Science teachers must instruct students about the rules, proper conduct, and potential hazards and assess their knowledge in these areas (Vos & Pell, 1990).

The teacher must be well acquainted with state regulations regarding liability. Each state has specific statutes and requirements. If an accident occurs as a result of a teacher's noncompliance with such regulations, then the teacher is vulnerable to a legal suit, which injured students may choose to initiate. Such procedures can result in heavy fines or even the loss of a teacher's job. In addition to state regulations, the local board of education may have explicit policies and rules regarding the teacher's responsibilities. Very often, courts uphold such policies, even though they may not appear in the teacher's contract, and the science teacher is held liable for breaches pertaining to the health and safety of students.

Science teachers should also *carefully read their contracts* and take special note of any responsibilities concerning student health and safety. The first and most obvious step the diligent teacher must take is to carefully investigate safety regulations that have been specified by state statutes, school board regulations, and the individual teacher's contract. Omitting this step is foolish because any accidents that result from noncompliance may leave the teacher legally responsible.

Another source of teacher responsibility with regard to safety is common law, which refers to law that has been established by judges in actual courtroom cases. The law of negligence (which is the primary governing standard) or fault derives mainly from common law. Because most states have waived common-law immunity, the school board is usually named as the defendant in a suit, although it is not uncommon for a teacher to be sued based on common law (Vos & Pell, 1990), especially where negligence is suspected; negligence usually occurs when a teacher's conduct falls below a standard of care established by the law to protect others against unreasonable risk or harm.

If an injured student sues the teacher on the grounds of negligence, the teacher can raise a legal defense called *contributory negligence*, which holds that the injured student behaved in a manner that contributed to the injury. The teacher must, however, offer evidence to show that the injured student's behavior constituted gross disregard for his or her own safety. If such behavior can be established, traditional common law would prevent the student from recovering damages from the teacher. However, in some states, this type of defense is being compromised by the doctrine of *comparative negligence*, which states that where negligence is involved, both the plaintiff and the defendant will be held proportionally liable for damages consistent with their respective shares or causation of the negligence. For example, if the plaintiff (student) committed 80% of the negligence, she or he could recover only 20% of the total damages from the defendant (teacher). Whatever the case, the teacher must be in a position to prove that he or she took every possible precaution to ensure the safety of the student.

Science teachers must always be prudent and demonstrate ordinary care in their teaching duties. During instructional activities in which certain safety hazards are known to exist, for example, in the use of corrosive or flammable chemicals in a laboratory exercise, teachers must use *extraordinary care* to avoid any mishap that could injure a student. The teacher must prepare students for the activity, pointing out the dangers and stressing the importance of behaving properly in the laboratory. They also must supervise students during activity so that they carry out their procedures safely.

The best way for a teacher to avoid legal suits is, of course, prevention. Teachers must make a calculated effort to anticipate accidents and potentially risk-laden situations. In addition, the teacher should keep complete records of maintenance work, safety lectures, and specific safety instructions given during particular activities. This time and effort can reduce the teacher's liability. More important, the teacher can reduce the occurrence of classroom and laboratory accidents.

All science teachers must become knowledgeable about teacher liability and indemnification (protection against damages, loss, or injury). They can begin by requesting to see documents in the local school district(s) pertaining to this area. In addition, they should acquire information on these topics from such sources as the *Laboratory Safety Workshop* (James A. Kaufman and Associates) and Flinn Scientific, Inc., which are described at the end of this chapter in Resources to Examine. *Safety in School Science Labs* (Wood, 1991) speaks directly to science teachers and is very informative with regard to liability and safety rules and procedures.

General Safety Responsibilities

Science teachers are responsible for safety in the science teaching environment; however, some may take the charge lightly. They should be aware that it is not unusual to find many potentially hazardous violations in schools such as inoperable fire extinguishers and safety showers, faulty overhead sprinklers and eyewash fountains, inadequate lighting, and unlabeled chemicals. In addition, they may find faulty equipment. Teachers must be aware of such problems in order to maintain a safe environment. They must be knowledgeable regarding what constitutes a safety hazard.

Accidents that occur in the laboratory are usually minor. The most common types are cuts and burns from glass and chemicals. Students will touch broken glass, handle hot vessels, and fail to wear safety goggles—all unsafe practices that can be avoided if teachers give students proper instruction and supervision. In addition, some students have a tendency to taste substances used for laboratory exercises. This is obviously dangerous. A general laboratory rule is no eating or tasting unless directed to do so by the teacher.

The teaching of safety must be done systematically and constructively. Many teachers introduce safety units at the very beginning of the school year. They instruct students on laboratory safety and how to conduct themselves during science classes. This approach is successful because it increases student safety knowledge and reduces the number of unsafe behaviors in the laboratory. Teachers should also become educated on safety and attend special courses and seminars on safety, enroll in first aid and CPR courses, talk with other science teachers about safety problems, and read articles on safety.

Preparation Before the School Year Begins

Before the school year begins, the teacher should inspect the classroom and laboratory to determine sites of potential danger. A checklist (inventory) such as the one shown in Figure 14.1 can serve as a guide for this purpose. A checklist ensures that the inspection will be organized and systematic, and that critical safety aspects will not be forgotten. At the same time, the teacher has a record of direct responsibility and concern for safety in the event that litigation should arise in the future.

Conducting an inspection requires the cooperation of the school principal and must be coordinated to include the services of maintenance personnel, electricians, plumbers, and other skilled individuals. The teacher, in concert with the appropriate personnel, should inspect the laboratory and classroom areas for malfunctions involving gas lines, water valves, electrical lines and outlets, exhaust fans and hoods, and temperature controls in storage and classroom areas. Eyewashes, fire blankets, fire extinguishers, and safety showers also require inspection. It is best to engage qualified individuals to detect and rectify problems in laboratory facilities. It is not the teacher's responsibility to correct electrical or plumbing problems. These problems must be handled by qualified personnel.

Before the school year begins, have fire extinguishers inspected and placed in areas where they are visible and accessible. Examine labels and seals on fire extinguishers to determine when they have been inspected and if they are perceived to be operable. Special types of fire extinguishers should be available in the laboratory—those that extinguish ordinary fires not due to electrical or chemical causes and those that control electrical and chemical fires. Fire blankets are important in certain laboratory situations—particularly the chemistry laboratory. Place these blankets in strategic areas in the laboratory and check them often to see that they are in good condition.

Safety showers and eyewash fountains that have not been used for a lengthy period of time tend to malfunction because of corrosion. The teacher is responsible for seeing that they are clean, functional, and available in various areas in the laboratory in case of emergency.

Sand buckets can be useful in case of fire. Periodically check them during the school year to see that they are clean, full of sand, and readily available in areas where fires are likely to occur. In general, sand buckets are considered standard equipment in chemistry and physics laboratories but not in the biology facility. We strongly recommend that sand buckets be standard equipment in *all* laboratories, regardless of the science discipline.

Inspect students' laboratory stations for gas leaks and electrical problems. All electrical outlets must be properly grounded and in good condition at all times. The teacher must correct electrical problems, preferably by engaging a qualified electrician. Gas leaks are detected by placing a soap solution around outlet joints and watching for the appearance of bubbles. Remember that merely "sniffing" the area is never adequate for detecting

FIGURE 14.1 Checklist for safety inspection of science facilities.

	No Attention Needed	Attention Needed	Comments
Gas valves and shutoffs			
Water valves and shutoffs			
Electrical lines and shutoffs			
Electrical outlets			
Exhaust fans			
Chemical storage 1. Temperature of storage area			
2. Aisles cleared			
3. Chemicals properly stored			
4. Age of chemicals within expiration date			
Fire extinguishers 1. Placed properly			
2. Label and seal show recent inspection			
3. Special type available for chemical fires			
4. Special type for electrical fires			
5. Type for ordinary fires not due to electrical or chemical causes			
Fire blankets 1. Recent inspection			
2. Strategically placed			
Safety showers			
Eyewash fountains			
Sand buckets			
Student laboratory positions 1. Gas outlets for leaks			
2. Water outlets for leaks			
3. Sinks have proper drainage			
4. Electrical outlets are functional and properly grounded			

small gas leaks. Do not try to rectify gas problems without the help of qualified personnel.

Teachers must have easy access to master controls for gas and electrical sources in the laboratory in order to prevent serious mishaps when it is essential to cut off the power or gas supply quickly. The design of older facilities may make it difficult to satisfy this requirement, but if controls are accessible, their location should be known to the teacher.

Safety Responsibilities during the School Year

The science teacher is responsible for promoting safety awareness once the school year begins. This responsibility has to be taken very seriously, particularly if students will be involved in activity-centered science. More accidents are likely to occur when students are exposed to hands-on activities during laboratory work. Consequently, more care and supervision is required when students are handling equipment, chemicals, apparatus, live animals, poisonous plants, and other hazardous items.

Class size must be considered when planning laboratory activities. Classes that exceed the recommended number of students for the available space pose a safety hazard. Unfortunately, few states have legislation that mandates class size in the science laboratory. Guidelines for laboratory space and class size are available from Flinn Scientific, Inc. (see Resources to Examine at the end of this chapter).

The first unit to be taken up at the beginning of the school year is safety. The instruction must be thorough and designed to help prevent accidents and unsafe practices as well as what to do in case of an incident. Some of the areas to address are: (a) safety rules that everyone, including the teacher, must follow; (b) familiarization with and location of the safety equipment; (c) demonstration of certain laboratory practices that must be carried out safely; (d) administration of a safety test to ascertain students' knowledge of the topic; (e) determination of which students wear contact lenses and have allergies or special considerations to be noted; and (f) safety contracts for students and parents to sign. The safety contract is meant to be proof that safety procedures were stressed in case such evidence is needed.

There are certain inexpensive general precautions that a teacher can take to ensure a safer instructional environment during the school year. The following are some suggestions regarding implementation of these procedures:

1. Develop a set of general safety rules to be in effect at all times in the laboratory. These rules should include a code for laboratory dress that requires safety goggles and gloves at appropriate times and should forbid careless activity, horseplay, and the wearing of contact lenses during certain activities.
2. Safety posters are necessary in the science-teaching environment. Posters that stress particular safety precautions are available commercially, but homemade posters may be more pertinent to the situation.
3. Schedule periodic safety inspections in the laboratory during the school year. Examine fire extinguishers, safety showers, fume hoods, and eyewash fountains. Check student laboratory stations to see that gas and water outlets and electrical sources are functioning properly.
4. Inspect storage areas regularly to see that aisles are clean and chemicals are properly stored and labeled. Remember to store chemicals by class and then alphabetically.
5. Have on hand Material Safety Data Sheets (MSDS) with information on all chemicals stored or to be used in the classroom and laboratory. The information will indicate hazards related to a given chemical substance as well as its properties.
6. Arrange laboratory furniture to allow enough working space for students to conduct activities. Inspect furniture to see that it is functional and not defective. Ask students to report any problems.
7. Inspect apparatus, equipment, and electrical devices before allowing students to use them. Electrical equipment and appliances must meet certain specifications and be approved by Underwriters Laboratories or another known organization. Homemade electrical devices can be hazardous.
8. Report problems in lighting immediately to the appropriate personnel. Good lighting is necessary for a safe working environment.
9. Monitor ventilation in the laboratory regularly. Again, report malfunctions as soon as possible. Do not conduct laboratory procedures requiring good ventilation while the system is functioning improperly.
10. Instruct students in the use of safety equipment. Point out the location of such equipment and periodically demonstrate the use of fire extinguishers, safety showers, and eyewash fountains. Allow students to practice using the equipment.
11. Teachers and students must wear proper eye protection and protective clothing when appropriate. They must use safety goggles whenever the possibility exists for an injury to the eye.
12. Require students to behave in the laboratory. Ask them not to engage in horseplay or other careless activity and constantly supervise students to see that their behavior is consistent with your expectations.
13. Demonstrate and stress the correct procedures before permitting students to use certain types of equipment, materials, and supplies. You should plan this carefully so that students grasp what they are expected to learn about the procedures and equipment.
14. Prohibit students from performing unauthorized experiments or activities. Do not allow them to use materials, equipment, or supplies unless instructed to do so. Never allow students to open chemical storage cabinets, refrigerators, and the like. Only the teacher has this privilege.
15. Perform potentially hazardous student activities as a teacher demonstration before allowing students to engage in the activity. Point out possible hazards and show students how to avoid certain behaviors and situations that may occur while they are conducting the exercise.
16. Report and describe all accidents, even minor ones, to the administration. Keep details on file for reference in case of future inquiries or litigation. Request witnesses to supply their signed versions of the accident, including the circumstances that caused the accident, if known. Ask them to include the names of the individuals involved and a description of the supervision the teacher provided during the time the accident occurred.

17. Do not allow students to transport chemicals outside the laboratory without permission. Chemicals, equipment, and apparatus should be used only in areas that are constantly supervised by the teacher.
18. Control the use of chemicals by storing them in safe places and allowing only required amounts to be available in the laboratory as needed.
19. Include first-aid kits as standard equipment in all science classrooms. Kits should include disposable sanitary gloves, sterile gauze for large wounds, medical tape and scissors, and bandages for minor cuts. Some students may be allergic to latex. They should not use latex gloves, especially during laboratory work. Vinyl gloves may be a substitute.
20. After reviewing first-aid procedures with students, post a list of the procedures near the storage rooms and other strategic areas. Do not allow students to use first-aid kits without permission. In the event of a serious injury, avoid the use of any medication or manipulation of the victim, immediately contact the school nurse or administrator for assistance. The materials in first-aid kits should be used only for minor injuries, burns, cuts, or other conditions that are not serious.

Eye Protection During Science Instruction

The eye is a precious organ and vulnerable to injury. Because the eye is formed of soft tissue and exposed to the environment outside the body, you must do everything possible to avoid situations that might result in any type of eye injury. Many laboratory and some field experiences require eye protection—this is *mandatory.*

Mr. Mason conducts a science demonstration at the beginning of the school year when the students are instructed about safety. Using the overhead projector and wearing his safety goggles, the teacher places the contents of a chicken's egg into a Petri dish, which he centers on the stage of the projector. Then he places a few drops of concentrated acid or base on the albumin or white part of the egg, which causes the protein to coagulate and become opaque. This makes an impression on the students regarding the damaging effects that corrosive substances can have on the tissues of the eye.

Eye Protection

For many laboratory and some field activities, appropriate eye and face protection is necessary. However, you may have difficulty identifying the proper eye protection for your students when you take a teaching position, because you may get little assistance from colleagues or administrators. Many "science teachers and school administrators may not fully understand the relevant safety regulations and standards to be able to correctly identify the various types of eye protection devices" (Kaufman, 2006, p. 26). There are three types of eye protection to consider in laboratory settings: safety goggles, safety spectacles, and face shields. In schools, safety goggles are usually required for eye protection. Flexible fitting safety goggles are the standard eyewear protective device that must be used for:

- corrosive gases and fumes
- irritating vapors
- corrosive liquids
- hot liquids
- sharp objects
- small particles and dust
- fire and heat

The first four situations involve chemical splash that can get into eyes. Sharp objects, small particles, fire and heat must also be kept from entering the eyes.

Some school districts may permit middle and high school students to wear safety spectacles with side shields in certain situations. These can protect eyes from sharp objects and small particles. You are advised to read the district and state policies on this matter and ascertain when safety spectacles are permitted for eye protection. Although we rarely see a face shield in school science laboratory settings, a science teacher may have the necessity to use one for, say a science demonstration. However, if the demonstration is so dangerous and risky, maybe it should not be part of the instruction.

Science teachers *must require* students to wear the appropriate type of eye-safety protection whenever the possibility exists that foreign material can come into contact with the eye. *That is the law!* Safety goggles or safety spectacles must be available, in good condition, and fit students properly. In the case of safety goggles, when the elastic bands break or become stretched so that they no longer hold the goggles to the face, the bands should be replaced or new goggles purchased. After students use the goggles, they should be placed in a goggles sanitizer that uses ultraviolet (UV) radiation to destroy organisms that may be transferred among the students. If a UV sanitizer is not available, use an appropriate disinfecting agent to clean the areas of the goggles that come in contact with the skin. Remember, in the event that corrosive material gets into a student's eye, the eye should be rinsed *immediately* with water for a minimum of 15 minutes followed by consultation with the school nurse and an eye care professional.

Contact Lenses

Many years ago a general policy existed that prohibited individuals from wearing contact lenses in science laboratories (Segal, 1995). The reason was that vapors, liquids, and tiny particles can lodge between the contact lens and the eye, causing irritation and even damage. Also, soft contact lenses present a risk because they can absorb and retain chemical vapors. In addition, when foreign materials are splashed into the eye, removing the contact lens may become a problem. Irrigating or washing the eye can be a problem if a person is unconscious and you are not aware that he or she is wearing contact lenses. Therefore, science teachers must know which of their students wear contact lenses by keeping a list of those who wear them. However, the policy for wearing contact lenses in school and industrial laboratory settings has changed.

Today contact lenses are generally accepted in laboratories, along with the appropriate eye protection. This guideline is supported by the American Chemical Society, the National Institute for Occupational Safety and Health, the Prevent Blindness America, and the American Optometric Association (Kaufman, 2006). Nevertheless, you should determine the school, district, and state policies for wearing contact lenses. Remember, regardless of the decision about wearing contacts in the science laboratory: *appropriate eye-safety protection must be worn in the laboratory and other settings whenever there is a risk of eye injury.*

Specific Safety Guidelines for Biology

> *The study of organisms, including nonhuman animals, is essential to the understanding of life on Earth. NABT recommends the prudent and responsible use of animals in the life science classroom. Biology teachers should foster a respect of life and should teach about the interrelationship and interdependency of all things. Classroom experiences that involve nonhuman animals range from observation to dissection. As with any instructional activity, the use of nonhuman animals in the biology classroom must have sound educational objectives. Any use of animals must convey substantive knowledge of biology and be appropriate for the classroom and for the age of the students. Biology teachers are in the best position to make this determination for their students. (The Use of Animals in Biology Education. Position Statement of the National Association of Biology Teachers, May 2003)*

Precautions for Using Animals

As stated above in the position statement by the National Association of Biology Teachers, the instructional use of live organisms in the biological science is essential. The study and care of animals provides authentic learning experiences not possible through textbook readings or viewing video presentations. However, this form of instruction necessitates that the teachers possess a great deal of knowledge concerning the handling of animals and specimens. They must know what to do with organisms in the classroom from start to finish.

Guidelines for maintaining animals in the science classroom must be followed.

Animals, microorganisms, and plants come into science classrooms in planned and unplanned ways. Both situations necessitate knowledge and preparation. For example, what would you do if a student brings to class a brown recluse spider or a coral snake? Would you keep these animals in the classroom for discussion purposes, even if you prohibited students from handling them? The uninformed biology or life science teacher may not realize how to handle a situation in which poisonous animals or specimens are brought into the classroom.

Animals that are poisonous or known carriers of disease are illegal to use for instruction. Avoid using poisonous snakes, scorpions, and gila monsters. If snakes are used, be certain that they are not dangerous to individuals concerned. Only those who know how to handle animals should be responsible for them. Most students must be instructed on the proper care and maintenance of animals.

A teacher should have good reason for keeping animals and insects in the classroom or laboratory. Safety, feeding requirements, replication of natural environments, and unjustified confinement must be considered before using animals in classroom work, all of which make the proper maintenance of animals in cages a problem. Maintain all animals in clean cages and feed and water them on a daily basis or as required. Make provisions for feeding animals on weekends and vacation periods. Often, teachers or responsible students take animals home over extended periods of time to ensure their proper care.

All animals used in teaching must be acquired and maintained in accordance with federal, state, and local laws. Most states require permits to acquire and maintain wild animals in captivity. If permission is granted to maintain a wild animal in the laboratory, it is important that the animal be returned to its natural environment as soon as its use is not required.

Animals such as rats, mice, guinea pigs, hamsters, and rabbits must be handled gently and with thick rubber or leather gloves. There is always a danger that animals will become excited as they are being handled, particularly if they are injured or pregnant, or if foreign materials are being introduced into the cage. Animals should not be provoked or teased. If animals feel threatened, they will defend themselves, sometimes to the point of biting or scratching. Animals will exhibit violent behaviors if poked with fingers, pens, and other objects. Discourage such actions because they can result in the injury of an individual or an animal.

Perhaps the best known set of guidelines for animal use in precollege education is from the Institute of Laboratory Animal Research (ILAR). The ILAR has published the 10 principles that are shown in Figure 14.2. These principles clearly delineate the responsibilities of those desiring to use animals for instructional purposes. You should note the restrictive use of vertebrates for animal study. The *Principles and Guidelines for the Use of Animals in Precollege Education* from ILAR is endorsed by the National Association of Biology Teachers (NABT). Although the ILAR guidelines are rather restrictive, NABT acknowledges the importance of animal studies and their use for science instruction. See NABT's Web site for its position statement on the use of animals in biology education.

Obviously science teachers must become more knowledgeable about the use of animals, particularly vertebrates, in the study of biology. Only then will they be able to guide instruction that achieves optimal educational value, but not at the expense of inhumane treatment of animal life. Orlans (1995) encourages science teachers to acquaint themselves with a large range of animal investigations that do not involve harming or destroying life.

Precautions for Specific Biology Procedures and Activities

Certain procedures and activities carried out in the biology laboratory require special mention. Activities involving the use of dissection instruments, sterilizing equipment and instruments, decayed and decaying plants and animal material, pathogenic organisms, and hypodermic syringes must be carefully monitored by the teacher. Activities involving blood typing and field trips also have unique problems that can cause them to be potentially dangerous.

Care During Animal Dissection

Certain cautions and procedures must be observed when conducting animal dissections. Use only rust-free instruments that have been thoroughly cleaned and sterilized. Dirty instruments are not safe and may cause infections. Instruct students thoroughly in the proper use of the instruments. Scalpels are generally used for dissection; if none are available, single-edge razor blades can be substituted. Some teachers recommend using scissors instead of scalpels. The teacher should demonstrate the proper techniques for using scalpels and dissecting probes before permitting students to use them. It should be stressed when students use a cutting instrument such as a scalpel that the direction of the incision must be away from the student's body.

Cuts can occur during the cleaning of scalpels and needles, so use care during the cleaning process. The use of protective gloves while cleaning equipment will protect the student against cuts and infection.

Using Live Material

The following list describes procedures and precautions to follow when using live material in the biology lab:

1. Do not use decayed or decaying plant or animal material unless every precaution is taken to ensure its proper handling. Improper handling may lead to an allergic reaction, infection, or accidental ingestion.
2. Warn students not to touch their mouths, eyes, or any exposed part of their body while using decayed or decaying material. Disposable gloves and forceps should be used to prevent physical contact.
3. Store decayed or decaying material in the refrigerator if it is to be used over a period of several days.
4. Use fungi with care to avoid the release of spores into the classroom environment. Spores may cause some students to have allergic reactions upon exposure.

FIGURE 14.2 Ten principles for the use of animals for instructional purposes.

The humane study of animals in precollege education can provide important learning experiences in science and ethics and should be encouraged. Maintaining classroom pets in preschool and grade school can teach respect for other species as well as proper animal husbandry practices. Introduction of secondary school students to animal studies in closely supervised settings can reinforce those early lessons and teach the principles of human care and use of animals in scientific inquiry. The National Research Council recommends compliance with the following principles whenever animals are used in precollege education or in science fair projects.

Principle 1

Observational and natural history studies that are not intrusive (that is, do not interfere with an animal's health or well-being or cause it discomfort) are encouraged for all classes of organisms. When an intrusive study of a living organism is deemed appropriate, consideration should be given first to using plants (including lower plants such as yeast and fungi) with no nervous systems or with primitive ones (including protozoa, planaria, and insects). Intrusive studies of vertebrates with advanced nervous systems (such as octopi) should be used only when lower invertebrates are not suitable and only under the conditions stated under Principle 10.

Principle 2

Supervision shall be provided by individuals who are knowledgeable about and experienced with the health, husbandry, care, and handling of the animal species used and who understand applicable laws, regulations, and policies.

Principle 3

Appropriate care for animals must be provided daily, including weekends, holidays, and other times when school is not in session. This care must include

a. nutritious food and clean, fresh water;

b. clean housing with space and enrichment suitable for normal species behaviors; and

c. temperature and lighting appropriate for the species.

Principle 4

Animals should be healthy and free of diseases that can be transmitted to humans or to other animals. Veterinary care must be provided as needed.

Principle 5

Students and teachers should report immediately to the school health authority all scratches, bites and other injuries, allergies, or illnesses.

Principle 6

Prior to obtaining animals for educational purposes, it is imperative that the school develop a plan for their procurement and ultimate disposition. Animals must not be captured from or released into the wild without the approval of the responsible wildlife and public health officials. When euthanasia is necessary, it should be performed in accordance with the most recent recommendations of the American Veterinary Medical Association's Panel Report on Euthanasia (*Journal of the American Veterinary Medical Association*, *188*(3): 252–268, 1986, et seq.). It should be performed only by someone trained in the appropriate technique.

Principle 7

Students shall not conduct experimental procedures on animals that

a. are likely to cause pain or discomfort or interfere with an animal's health or well-being;

b. induce nutritional deficiencies or toxicities; or

c. expose animals to microorganisms, ionizing radiation, cancer-producing agents, or any other harmful drugs or chemicals capable of causing disease, injury, or birth defects in humans or animals.

In general, procedures that cause pain in humans are considered to cause pain in other vertebrates.

(Continued)

FIGURE 14.2 Ten principles for the use of animals for instructional purposes *(Continued).*

Principle 8

Experiments on avian embryos that might result in abnormal chicks or in chicks that might experience pain or discomfort shall be terminated 72 hours prior to the expected date of hatching. The eggs shall be destroyed to prevent inadvertent hatching.

Principle 9

Behavioral conditioning studies shall not involve aversive stimuli. In studies using positive reinforcement, animals should not be deprived of water; food deprivation intervals should be appropriate for the species but should not continue longer than 24 hours.

Principle 10

A plan for conducting an experiment with living animals must be prepared in writing and approved prior to initiating the experiment or to obtaining the animals. Proper experimental design of projects and concern for animal welfare are important learning experiences and contribute to respect for and appropriate care of animals. The plan shall be reviewed by a committee composed of individuals who have the knowledge to understand and evaluate it and who have the authority to approve or disapprove it. The written plan should include the following:

a. a statement of the specific hypotheses or principles to be tested, illustrated, or taught;
b. a summary of what is known about the subject under study, including references;
c. justification for the use of the species selected and consideration of why a lower vertebrate or invertebrate cannot be used; and
d. a detailed description of the methods and procedures to be used, including experimental design; data analysis; and all aspects of animal procurement, care, housing, use, and disposal.

Exceptions

Exceptions to Principles 7–10 may be granted under special circumstances by a panel appointed by the school principal or his or her designee. This panel should consist of at least three individuals, including a science teacher, a teacher of a nonscience subject, and a scientist or veterinarian who has expertise in the subject matter involved.* At least one panel member should not be affiliated with the school or science fair, and none should be a member of the student's family.

April 1989

* In situations where an appropriate scientist is not available to assist the student, the Institute of Laboratory Animal Research (ILAR) might be able to provide referrals. For more information write to the ILAR, National Research Council, 2101 Constitution Avenue NW, Washington, DC 20418, or call (202)334-2590.

5. Avoid weeds and plants that may induce hay fever and other pollen allergies. Large amounts of plant pollen can produce adverse effects.
6. Do not maintain cultures of pathogenic bacteria, viruses, or fungi in the laboratory. To do so may expose students to infection, particularly if they are not trained in proper laboratory techniques for handling microorganisms.
7. Avoid the use of blood agar, which can induce the growth of pathogenic bacteria.
8. Avoid the use of viruses in the laboratory because they may infect other living organisms in the school building.
9. Do not allow students to inoculate bacterial plates with human oral material. This simple exercise involves certain risks because it could lead to the production of pathogenic organisms.
10. Warn students to be extremely careful when using pipettes to transfer microorganisms. It is best to use safety bulbs instead of pipettes.
11. Use precautions when transferring by inoculating needles or loops. When a heated needle or inoculating loop is placed in a culture medium, the material tends to splatter and produce aerosols, causing the release of microorganisms into the air. Instruct students to remove as much of the culture material as possible before sterilizing the loop or needle.

Sterilizing

An autoclave is the best tool for sterilization. However, because most schools do not have an autoclave, other means of sterilization must be used. Some biology teachers use a pressure cooker to sterilize materials. When used properly and only with certain materials, they can be useful. You must be familiar with the use of a pressure cooker and thoroughly understand the directions for operating it before attempting to use it. Clean the safety valve on a pressure cooker and make sure it is operable before using it. Strictly follow the safety limits indicated in the directions or on the pressure gauge. Turn off the heat so that air pressure in the cooker will gradually be reduced to normal level before removing the cover. Do not remove the cover until the pressure is at a safe level. Do not allow students to operate a pressure cooker without proper supervision. That said, please note that "pressure cookers can become bombs, releasing superheated steam, and we strongly recommend against their use" (Texley, Kwan, & Summers, 2004, p. 71).

In the absence of an autoclave, sterilize glass Petri dishes and test tubes that have been used for culture growth by placing them in a strong solution of Lysol, Clorox or household bleach, or other chemical disinfectant for a period of time before washing. Wear rubber gloves when washing glassware or instruments used for inoculation. The disposal of cultures in glass Petri plates can be a problem if an autoclave is not available. Use disposable Petri plates instead of glass plates for laboratory exercises in which students carry out their own procedures. Nevertheless, these items must be disinfected before they are discarded.

Body Fluids and Tissues

The use of human body fluids and tissues for biology laboratory investigations is a risky practice and not recommended, given potential problems with AIDS and hepatitis. The collection of blood and tissues can lead to infections and the spread of disease. Conducting blood typing on student subjects is risky.

Precautions During Field Trips

Field trips have inherent problems that require special attention to safety. Biology field trips take place in different types of environments, each of which has a unique set of problems. Consequently, it is essential that the teacher must realize beforehand what precautions are needed to conduct a safe field trip. This requires that the teacher first visit the area to evaluate it for potential hazards.

Students need a list of specific rules of conduct to follow during the course of a field trip. Each trip will probably require the development of a specific set of rules. The following are some general safety guidelines for a biology field trip:

1. Brief students about the area they will visit. Instruct them about the areas that they are prohibited from visiting without supervision, such as ravines, cliffs, and bodies of water.
2. Tell students the type of clothing they are permitted to wear or take with them. Appropriate footwear is essential to avoid accidents.
3. Instruct students about the plants they should not touch, such as poison sumac, poison oak, poison ivy, and certain mushrooms. Familiarize the students with poisonous plants that they may encounter on the trip. If possible, bring specimens of such plants into the classroom before the trip so that students can learn how to identify them. Warn students not to touch specimens in the classroom.
4. Warn students not to touch or pick up reptiles or other animals or touch dead carcasses of animals or birds.
5. Caution students about eating any plant material in the field unless it is identified by an expert as safe. Poisonous plants often appear very similar to edible ones, and even experts can make serious mistakes in identification. Alert students not to touch fungi and decaying material unless they are informed to do so.

Additional Considerations for Safety in Biology Teaching

Some additional safety considerations that apply to biology teaching are listed here:

1. Use indirect sunlight or a lamp when viewing with a microscope. Avoid direct sunlight on the mirror, which could cause damage to the eyes while viewing.
2. Avoid the use of alcohol burners in the laboratory; they are hazardous. Use Bunsen burners or hot plates instead.
3. Require that appropriate clothing be worn during the laboratory period and especially avoid long-sleeve or loose garments. Lab coats or aprons are advisable when students are working with caustic materials.
4. Require students to wash their hands after using chemicals and at the end of every laboratory session to avoid ingestion of chemicals.

Specific Safety Guidelines for Chemistry

A number of activities that are commonly carried out by students in the chemistry laboratory are potentially hazardous. The teacher must weigh the risks involved before allowing the students to perform certain activities. If the risks are too high, there are alternatives. If alternatives are not possible, then abandon the activity or perform it as a teacher demonstration. In some cases, even as a teacher demonstration, the risks might still be too great.

Chemistry Safety Precautions

The majority of accidents during science instruction involve activities in the chemistry laboratory or the use of chemicals in other teaching areas. Many accidents occur because teachers are careless about requiring students to wear goggles. In some instances students might be requested to remove contact lenses, but required to wear safety goggles, during laboratory activities. Proper dress and use of laboratory aprons are often disregarded. The teacher should check students' attire to see that they are not wearing loose jackets, neckties, or sandals.

The precautions listed here are further suggestions for a safe environment when using chemicals in the laboratory.

1. When inserting glass tubing into a rubber stopper, always lubricate the glass with glycerin beforehand. Otherwise, the glass tube is likely to break, possibly sending tiny glass fragments into the eyes or skin.
2. When bending glass tubing, keep the burner flame low and heat the material gently. Do not force the glass to bend; it may suddenly break or shatter, possibly causing injury to an individual.
3. When using a match to light a Bunsen burner, always light the match *first*, then turn the gas on *slowly*. Turning on the gas before lighting the match can result in accumulated gas, which might be explosive. Keep arms, hair, face, and other body parts as far away from the burner as possible while it is being ignited.
4. When heating any substance in a test tube, point the mouth of the tube away from the body. Boiling often occurs quickly and without warning, causing the boiling substance to spew the hot vapor on individuals in the vicinity.
5. Clean used test tubes meticulously. Residue left in test tubes could sabotage future experiments, either by altering results or, worse, by causing unexpected dangerous reactions.
6. Clean chemical spills immediately. There are potential dangers if laboratory tables are not cleaned. For instance, if spilled hydrochloric acid is not cleaned from the surface, an individual could lean on the table, causing burns to clothing or skin. A spilled substance also could accidentally be mixed with another spilled substance, which may result in a violent reaction.
7. Make absolutely certain that students do not attempt to remove a beaker, test tube, porcelain dish, or other glassware from a flame without using proper utensils. Tongs, test tube holders, and heat-resistant gloves are designed precisely for this purpose. No student should use bare hands during these tasks.
8. When diluting acids, always add the acid to the water, and not the reverse. The reaction of acid with water is exothermic, that is, large quantities of heat are released. If water is added to the acid, the water will tend to remain on the surface of the acid because it is less dense and, consequently, will not mix. It may produce a violent reaction, which in turn may cause the acid to splatter into the eyes or onto the skin of individuals nearby. To add the acid to the water safely, place a stirring rod in the water and hold it at an angle. Pour the acid slowly down the length of the rod above the water. This procedure prevents splashing while pouring. Be sure to wear safety glasses.
9. When heating materials, always use open vessels during the heating process. Do not heat vessels that have been sealed. When heating liquids, it is good practice to use boiling chips to prevent bumping.
10. When evaporating a toxic or dangerous solvent, use a well-ventilated fume hood.
11. Avoid subjecting flammable materials to any open flame. Open flames are dangerous in the presence of flammable substances.

All laboratory activities or demonstrations, whether performed by students or the teacher, must be considered potentially dangerous. Before using an activity, the teacher must first weigh whether the educational benefits are worth the risks that may be involved. The teacher must exercise extreme care no matter how many times he or she has performed the demonstration or conducted the laboratory.

Storing and Using Chemicals Safely

"The dose makes the poison. All things are poisonous and nothing is without poison, only the dose permits something not to be poisonous."
(Paracelsus, Wikipedia, 2008, p. 1)

Many accidents occur in the classroom or laboratory because of improper storage and use of chemicals. Those who use chemicals in their teaching must be knowledgeable about which substances are potentially dangerous. To avoid unforeseen problems, know what facilities are required for storage of chemicals, the safety procedures to employ when using them, and the safety procedures to use to properly dispose of them. Remember the words in the quote given above by Paracelsus, who was a physician and alchemist living in Europe during the fifteenth and sixteenth centuries.

Today, many chemicals should not be used or even stored in a science laboratory because of the growing concern for people's health and better understanding of the potential risks involved with these chemicals. Science teachers who are not experienced with chemicals should discuss their use and storage with experienced chemistry teachers, and they should become familiar with the literature recommended at the end of this chapter.

Combustible substances, poisonous materials, acids and bases, and other dangerous chemicals have special storage requirements and, in most cases, must be securely stored to avoid potential accidents. Always securely lock combustible substances, such as methanol and ethanol, in metal cabinets. Acids and bases should be stored on the proper type of shelving, in cabinets, or in a closet. Do not store chemicals that may react with each other in the same area; their caps may corrode so that they cannot be removed. In addition, acids and bases must be stored close to the floor to minimize the possibility that they might fall, crashing onto the floor, spattering their contents on someone. Glycerin and nitric acid, acids and cyanides, potassium chlorate, and organic substances should not be stored in close proximity.

Science teachers must refer to accepted schemes for organizing and storing chemicals, for example, the one developed by Flinn Scientific (see Resources to Examine at the end of this chapter). Teachers must not organize a chemical storage area by placing chemicals in alphabetical order because some chemicals can react with each other. The categorization of organic and inorganic compounds, volatile liquids, and acids and bases has been worked out by experts and should be followed.

There is a list of poisonous substances that by law cannot be maintained or used in the lab, including substances such as Benzedrine, benzene, arsenic, vinyl chloride, and asbestos. Other poisonous substances that are considered to be carcinogenic cannot legally be part of the chemical inventory, including formaldehyde, carbon tetrachloride, phenol, xylene, and lead compounds. Again, refer to the sources at the end of this chapter to determine what chemicals to use and store and how to inventory them.

Teratogens cause physical or functional birth defects and should not be stored or used in the science curriculum. Teachers must warn students of possible harmful effects of these substances. Some teratogenic substances include aniline, phenol, carbon tetrachloride, and xylene. A list of toxic substances, teratogens, and carcinogens is given in Table 14.1.

Carcinogens are cancer-causing substances. Do not store or use chemicals that are suspected of mutating cells. Warn students of the possible harmful effects of such substances.

Other Suggestions for Safety

All chemicals must be treated as if they are potentially dangerous. Do not downplay the problems that can result if chemicals are exposed to the skin or caustic fumes are inhaled. Neither should the teacher allow situations that may result in explosions or fires. The precautions needed to avoid potential hazards require knowledge about the nature of the chemicals stored in the laboratory as well as common sense in their use. The following suggestions can help prevent potential problems:

1. Keep the laboratory and other areas where chemicals are stored or used well ventilated and maintain a relatively cool temperature.
2. Use approved safety cans and metal cabinets to store flammable liquids.
3. Store cylinders of compressed gases by type and mark them as highly toxic, corrosive, or flammable. Store in cool and well-ventilated areas. Limit the amount of flammable liquids and gases maintained in the laboratory.
4. Store large bottles of acids and bases on shelves that are no more than 2 feet above the floor, and store them away from each other to prevent corrosion and other chemical reactions.
5. Inspect chemicals annually to see whether they are properly identified or outdated. Properly dispose of contaminated, unlabeled, and deteriorated chemicals.
6. Do not leave chemicals in areas where students are working unless they are going to use the chemicals.
7. Keep chemicals in storage until they are ready to be used.
8. Store only small quantities of flammable substances in areas where they will be used. Large quantities are difficult to handle in case of a fire or accident.
9. Do not concentrate large quantities of flammable substances in any area in the laboratory.
10. Do not store chemicals in hallways and other heavy-traffic areas. Students are often curious about what is stored in boxes and cabinets. Mishandling can cause accidents.
11. Do not store chemicals on shelving above eye level unless there is easy access with ladders or stools. Individuals trying to remove chemicals from out-of-reach shelves run the risk of dropping chemicals and causing mishaps.

Disposing of Chemical Wastes

To avoid unnecessary risks, remove from the laboratory waste materials that accumulate as a byproduct of scientific investigations and become useless because they are improperly labeled or have aged. Chemicals that are no longer used or needed also must be properly removed from the inventory.

Disposing of chemicals requires certain important procedures. Before disposing of chemicals, consider the federal, state, and local rules and regulations, the effect of the chemicals on the environment, their level of toxicity, and the degree to which they are hazardous. In addition, consult with an experienced chemistry teacher, a science supervisor, or use the reference information given at the end of this chapter. The following suggestions might be useful when disposing of chemicals:

1. Do not pour acids and flammable liquids down a drain without first diluting them. Do not dilute acids by pouring water into them; pour acids into the water for dilution. Neutralize or dilute all hazardous wastes before disposing of them.
2. Do not pour volatile substances and chemicals that produce obnoxious odors down the drain. They may lodge in interconnected drains located

TABLE 14.1 Some Hazardous Chemicals

Toxic Substances	Teratogens
Ammonium dichromate	Aniline
Ammonium thiocyanate	Benzene
Arsenic and arsenic compounds	Carbon tetrachloride
Barium salts	Lead compounds
Benzene and benzene compounds	Phenol
Beryllium	Toluene
Bromine	Xylene
Cadmium and cadmium salts	Irritants
Carbon disulfide	Ammonium dichromate
Carbon tetrachloride (also possible carcinogen)	Borane
Chloroform	Ether
Chromic acid	Hydrogen peroxide
Chromium trioxide	Methylene chloride
Cyanides (water soluble cyanides)	Nitrogen dioxide
Dimethyl sulfate	Toluene
Hydrogen chloride	Xylene
Hydrogen fluoride	Zinc chloride
Hydrogen iodide	**Carcinogenic Substances**
Hydrogen sulfide	Asbestos
Lead and lead compounds	Benzene
Manganese compounds	Carbon tetrachloride
Mercury and mercury compounds	Formaldehyde
Molybdenum compounds	Lead compounds
Naphthalene	Nickel and nickel compounds
Nickel and nickel compounds	Phenol
Nitrogen dioxide	Xylene
Styrene	
Corrosive substances	
Bromine	
Hydro-halogens	
p-dichlorobenzene	
Sodium	

in other areas of the building, causing odors in these areas.

3. Always label solid wastes as such and place them in suitable containers, making certain that the containers will not react with the wastes.
4. When there is doubt about the proper handling of solid wastes, seek advice from scientists at universities or nearby industries or call commercial disposal firms. Chemical supply houses also are good sources of information.
5. Use care when disposing of carcinogens, radioactive materials, and other hazardous substances. If you do not know the procedures for handling these materials, seek help from the science coordinator, principal, or local fire department. They may provide the proper disposal method or suggest someone who knows.

Material Safety Data Sheets (MSDS)

All science teachers must be familiar with the Material Safety Data Sheets (MSDS). They must know where to find them and how to access one for each chemical they store and use. The MSDS contain information about each chemical substance produced and schools must have them on hand for all chemical substances that are used in school science programs. The Hazard Communication Act requires this documentation for all chemicals stored and used in industry, schools, and universities. If you are unable to locate a MSDS for a particular chemical in the school in which you are teaching or observing, search for it on Google by typing in MSDS and the name of the chemical. You can even find MSDS information on vinegar, which is a common chemical found in many science teaching environments. Below is some of the useful information that can be obtained from a MSDS.

- chemical name and common name
- chemical formula
- chemical properties
- physical properties
- health hazards
- fire and explosion data
- spill and disposal procedures
- storage and handling procedures

Safety in the Earth Science Laboratory

In addition to safety practices normally involved in all secondary science laboratories, possible hazards associated with the teaching of earth science require special attention. Teachers are under the misconception that nothing dangerous can possibly be associated with the activities that occur in the earth science laboratory, but rocks and minerals commonly used in the laboratory can and do present certain health hazards. The tasting of minerals and rocks, chemical procedures and analysis, crushing procedures, and the mere handling of rocks and minerals in the laboratory are potentially dangerous activities.

Minerals containing arsenic and several that contain calcium, copper, lead, or zinc arsenates are poisonous (Puffer, 1979). Acute arsenic poisoning can produce gastrointestinal disturbances, muscle spasms, dizziness, delirium, and coma. Minerals containing lead also present health hazards because lead is poisonous in all forms. The ingestion of lead minerals in large quantities can produce cramps, muscle weakness, depression, coma, and even death. Lead poisoning can be cumulative, and effects can range from moderate to very severe (Puffer, 1979).

Inhalation of certain mineral and rock dusts also can cause health problems. Minerals containing manganese, asbestos, and quartz are hazardous in dust form, so avoid inhalation. Manganese dust can induce headaches, weakness in the legs, and general irritability when inhaled. Silica dust can cause silicosis (a lung disease), which has symptoms similar to those of tuberculosis. Asbestos dust fibers are known to cause cancer and asbestosis in human beings.

The following safety guidelines pertain to earth science laboratory practices. The teacher should use them whenever appropriate:

1. The teacher and students should wear goggles when crushing rock with a hammer or other instruments.
2. Do not crush rocks or other minerals unless they are wrapped in a cloth. This precaution prevents rock fragments and dust from being dispersed in the laboratory area and may prevent injuries to the eyes and other parts of the body.
3. Require students to wear gloves when handling large rock samples, particularly when moving or crushing the samples. Jagged rocks can produce both surface and deep wounds.
4. Do not allow students to lift heavy rock samples alone. Instruct students to help each other when lifting large or cumbersome samples. Use dollies or other equipment to move large and awkward objects.
5. Warn students not to wear open-ended shoes or sandals during field trips. Require them to wear long pants for protection. Gloves are essential when collecting materials on field trips.
6. Before taking a field trip, provide a special set of rules regarding the conduct of students during the trip. Oral directions are not substitutes for written directions. Written rules are constant reminders to students and ensure proper behavior in the field.

Care must also be taken when working with soil. Dirt can be contaminated with bacteria, mold, and other potential pathogens. Some soil samples may also be contaminated with heavy metals like lead and mercury. You should be sure that this material is handled carefully and disposed of properly. In addition, students should wash their hands after working with dirt.

Safety Guidelines for Physics and Physical Science Laboratories

Accidents from electrical sources in physics and physical science laboratories are not uncommon. The mishaps can range from minor burns to death. Burns caused by electrical sources are usually slow to heal and often require several months of treatment for recovery. Thermal burns caused by high temperatures near the body, such as those produced by an electric arc, are similar to sunburn and are usually not severe unless the body has been exposed for long periods of time.

Impulse and electric shocks are not only unpleasant; in some cases, shock intensities produced by higher currents passing through the chest or nerve centers may produce paralysis of the breathing muscles. Excessively high currents will cause death. Currents that blow fuses or trip circuit breakers can destroy tissue and produce shock and damage to the nervous system. It only takes a small amount of current passing through the heart, on the order of 0.1 ampere, to stop the beating of the human heart. The following safety procedures are guidelines for working with electricity:

1. Know the total voltage and current of the electrical circuit before using a piece of electrical equipment.
2. Use extension cords that are as short as possible, properly insulated, and of a wire size suitable for the voltage and current involved.
3. Service electrical apparatus and devices only when the power is turned off. Make certain that power is not accidentally turned on during servicing.
4. Do not permit students to service electrical equipment or apparatus.
5. Do not permit students to be in the vicinity of electrical apparatus or equipment being serviced.
6. Do not turn power on after servicing until all students are moved to a safe area. Notify students when it is safe to return to their positions.
7. Use properly insulated, nonconducting tools that are in good condition when working with electrical equipment. Use only appropriate tools—those that have specifications indicating that they can be employed for servicing electrical devices.
8. Properly mark all electrical equipment, using letters that are 2 or 3 inches high to indicate the voltage.
9. Make sure electrical contacts and conductors are enclosed at all times to avoid accidental contact and check them periodically for compliance.
10. Periodically inspect electrical outlets to see that they are in good order. Constant use may cause wear and loosening of outlets.
11. Avoid using metallic prongs, pencils, and rulers when working on an electrical device.
12. Do not wear rings, metal watchbands, or metal necklaces in the vicinity of an activated electrical device.
13. Never handle activated electrical equipment with wet hands or while the body is wet or perspiring.
14. Do not use highly volatile or flammable liquids to clean electrical equipment. There are cleaning solvents that can be used safely, but investigate whether they are suitable for electrical devices.
15. Allow only qualified electricians to perform electrical wiring and maintenance of electrical outlets and devices. Do not allow students or unqualified teachers to perform these functions.
16. Do not store volatile and flammable liquids in the vicinity of activated electrical equipment. The heat generated by equipment may cause a fire or explosion.
17. Do not handle electrical equipment that has been in use for a long period of time. It may be very hot and could cause serious burns; or the hot equipment may be dropped, causing damage to some of its parts.
18. Use electrical appliances that are approved by Underwriters Laboratories or another known laboratory.
19. Have homemade equipment inspected by a licensed electrician before using it. Always regard homemade equipment as potentially dangerous until checked by the electrician.
20. Use indoor equipment inside, not outside. The same is true for indoor and outdoor outlets, and indoor and outdoor electrical wires. Do not use outdoor equipment or wire when the ground is wet or when it is raining.
21. Service tools that have shocked anyone or that have emitted sparks. Do not use such tools until they are in good working order.
22. Have all electrical devices properly grounded. Grounding can be complicated and must be done by a licensed electrician.
23. If possible, have ground fault interrupters (GFI) installed to prevent possible electrocution. Many state electrical codes now require outlets to have a GFI.
24. Teach electricity concepts in the laboratory using low-voltage sources in the range of 1 to 6 volts.

Radiation Safety

Secondary school biology, physics, and chemistry courses include topics that involve radiation. Physics and chemistry courses involve experiments that deal with radiation emission of radioactive isotopes, X-ray diffraction apparatus, Crookes tubes, laser beams, ultraviolet rays, infrared rays, and microwaves. Biology courses sometimes involve experiments exposing biological materials to radiation sources. Apparatus and materials that generate radiation can be hazardous.

The inclusion of laboratory activities that involve radioactive materials in secondary school science is controversial; some feel that such activities are inappropriate at this level. This is not the place to discuss the pros and cons of such activities. However, the teacher should carefully weigh the benefits of these types of activities against the potential dangers of subjecting students to radioactive sources.

In any event, it is imperative that teachers know how to handle apparatus and materials so that the laboratory is a safe place for teachers and students to work.

Teachers should be properly trained in the use of materials and apparatus before attempting to use them in the laboratory. Self-taught teachers must be certain that their teaching techniques are safe and appropriate. Radiation experts and scientists, university professors, and other qualified individuals can provide invaluable assistance for formally trained and self-taught teachers. Furthermore, permission from the school administration to use radiation sources in teaching may be required. Some school districts have regulations that prohibit the use of such materials.

Suggestions for Use of Non-Ionizing Radiation

Using non-ionizing radiation requires special precautionary measures (Mercier, 1996). A list of these measures follows, including some special recommendations for using laser beams:

1. Laser beams are very dangerous. If the intensity is high enough, severe burns can result. Preventive measures are extremely important because laser beams can cause blindness in less than 1 second. The teacher must become skillful in handling the equipment and know the safety measures required. The following are safety recommendations for the use of laser beams in the classroom.
   - Keep students away from all sides of the path of laser beams.
   - Warn students and other individuals not to look into the laser beam.
   - Do not aim laser beams directly into the eyes.
   - Do not allow laser beams to hit the exposed skin of an individual.
2. Ultraviolet radiation is harmful below 310 nm. Mercury arcs and other sources can produce radiation below 310 nm, and the teacher should take care to use proper shielding and adequate filtering materials.
3. Radiation from microwave ovens can cause severe damage. Although high frequencies cause heat sensation on the skin, low frequencies do not, and an individual is not aware that tissue damage is taking place. Microwave ovens should be equipped with adequate interlock mechanisms.
4. Ultrasonic beams of high intensity also can be extremely harmful; use them with caution.

Science teachers and students should become knowledgeable about the various types of UV light because of its prevalence in our everyday surroundings and potential danger, and in some instances this form of radiation may be used for a demonstration or laboratory exercise. Ultraviolet radiation is a common form of energy in the world in which we live. It is one component of the Sun's radiation. Because this form of energy is invisible, humans are unaware of its presence. UV light is part of the electromagnetic energy spectrum, with wavelengths less than visible light and greater than X-rays. Conversely, UV light is electromagnetic energy that is greater than visible light and less than X-rays.

There are three types of UV radiation: ultraviolet A, long wave or black light (UVA: 400 nm–315 nm); ultraviolet B, medium wave (UVB: 315 nm–280 nm); and ultraviolet C, short wave (UVC: 280 nm–100 nm). Because some materials "glow" or fluoresce interesting colors under the influence of black light, it is used to achieve special effects in the entertainment industry and on clothing that is washed with certain detergents. While UVA does cause sunburn, it can damage collagen fibers and destroy vitamin A in the skin.

UVB is another component of the sun's radiation and because of its electromagnetic energy it causes sunburn, which can lead to melanoma—a very serious form of cancer. The UVB radiation that is used in tanning salons produces a suntan, but this method of sun tanning is not recommended by the American Cancer Society. However, UVB also has a beneficial effect in that it induces the production of vitamin D in the skin, which along with calcium produces healthy bone tissue. UVC can have injurious effects on skin and eye tissues because it is a higher form of electromagnetic energy than UVB and UVA.

 Safety Units for Students

The work of Dombrowski and Hagelberg (1985) suggests that a unit on laboratory safety increases students' safety knowledge and reduces the number of unsafe behaviors. Safety units that can develop student awareness and responsibility toward safety are best presented during the early stages of a laboratory course. Throughout this period, students can learn how to use safety equipment such as safety showers, fire extinguishers, eyewash fountains, and fire blankets. They can be indoctrinated to use laboratory aprons, eye goggles, and gloves at appropriate times. They can be shown how to handle broken glass, chemicals, and electrical equipment and how to light a Bunsen burner. Stress the importance of housekeeping as well as the necessity of maintaining a clutter-free work environment. During the course of the unit, the students can develop a set of safety rules, which the teacher can supplement.

The unit can vary in length, but two or three class periods would probably suffice. The unit should be general, dealing with aspects of safety that apply to the laboratory course that will be offered. The use of visual aids, demonstrations, and hands-on activities will meet the unit objectives. Active student involvement is necessary to make this unit an effective experience. Other safety considerations specific to a laboratory exercise can be dealt with as the course progresses.

The teacher can administer pretests and posttests using questions similar to those in Figure 14.3 before and after the unit to determine whether the unit improves students' safety awareness, knowledge, and sensitivity. The same questions can be used for both tests, or questions can vary, depending on what has been stressed.

After teaching the unit, require students to sign a safety contract such as the one in Figure 14.4. The students should not take the signing of the contract lightly. It is an agreement that the students will behave as required to maintain a safe environment. To make the document more meaningful, it is suggested that the parents read and sign the contract as well, so they also, understand the implications of its contents. The safety contract is a valuable record for the teacher to have in case of future litigation. It will show that the teacher has been responsible in attempting to instruct, promote, and maintain a safe learning environment for all concerned.

The teacher can effectively teach safety only with the proper background. Units cannot be presented in a haphazard fashion; they must be well organized and taught by knowledgeable individuals. A teacher's background knowledge should be extensive before embarking on a safety unit. Safety knowledge can be strengthened by attending courses, workshops, and lectures as they are offered by safety experts. Background also can be acquired by talking with science teachers, scientists, fire marshals, and others who have the expertise on particular aspects of safety.

Stop and Reflect!

Examine the learning outcomes in Table 14.2, which correlate with the *Standards for Science Teacher Preparation* (NSTA, 2003). You should be able to present evidence that you can exhibit the knowledge and skills indicated on the rubric, which will show that you can provide a safe science learning environment for students.

FIGURE 14.3 Sample laboratory safety quiz.

Laboratory Safety Quiz

Directions: The following questions are either true or false. In the blank to the left of each statement, write the letter *T* if the statement is true, or *F* if the statement is false.

_____ 1. It is required by law to wear safety goggles in the area where chemicals are stored.

_____ 2. When diluting acids, water is always poured into the acid.

_____ 3. A chemical is considered dangerous only if it is toxic or flammable.

_____ 4. The teacher is the only individual responsible for safety in the laboratory.

_____ 5. A fire that involves a solvent should be extinguished with a carbon dioxide fire extinguisher.

_____ 6. The disposal of chemical wastes produced from an exercise should be done by flushing the material down the drain.

_____ 7. Prescription glasses can be used instead of safety glasses when working in the laboratory.

_____ 8. It is permissible for students to use beakers for drinking purposes after they have been sterilized.

_____ 9. It is permissible for responsible students to remove chemicals from the storage areas.

_____ 10. The student should be able to operate various types of fire extinguishers.

_____ 11. In general, it would be permissible for students to substitute one chemical for another in the case of a shortage of a particular substance.

_____ 12. It is permissible to store reagents and chemicals in student lockers.

FIGURE 14.4 An example of a student science safety contract for teachers to consider using.

Sample Student Safety Contract

I agree to follow all the teacher's instructions and school policies regarding safety procedures during laboratory work and conduct myself in responsible ways at all times in the classroom and laboratory, and not to participate in horseplay in these facilities.

While in the classroom and laboratory I will do the following:

1. Act responsibly at all times.
2. Follow all safety and instructional guidelines given to me by the teacher and the school.
3. Keep my work area clean.
4. Not eat in the laboratory unless directed to do so.
5. Wear shoes with closed ends at the heal and front, and tie back long hair.
6. Wear safety goggles and protective clothing when instructed to do so.
7. Indicate if I wear contact lenses and if my parents have given permission to wear them in the laboratory.
8. Know the location of fire extinguishers, safety showers, eyewash stations, and safety blankets, and learn how to use them.
9. Know where to get help in case of an emergency.
10. Not enter a storage area unless asked to do so by the teacher.
11. Not take chemicals or equipment out of the classroom or laboratory unless asked to do so by the teacher.
12. Take and pass the science safety test given by the teacher.

I, ________________________________ have read each statement above and agree
Print Your Name
to follow them and all safety regulations given by the teacher, school, and school district.

________________________________ ________________________
Student Signature Date

________________________________ ________________________
Parent Signature Date

TABLE 14.2 Safety Unit Rubric*

NSTA Standard	Unacceptable	Acceptable	Target
9a. Understand the legal and ethical responsibilities of science teachers for the welfare of their students, the proper treatment of animals, and the maintenance and disposal of materials.	Does *not* discuss (a) the legal responsibilities, (b) contributory and comparative negligence, and (c) ethical responsibilities of science teachers concerning the welfare of their students. (0 pts.)	Mentions (a) the legal responsibilities, (b) contributory and comparative negligence, and (c) ethical responsibilities of science teachers concerning the welfare of their students, but doe *not* provide reasons for this compliance. (4 pts.)	Discusses (a) the legal responsibilities, (b) contributory and comparative negligence, and (c) ethical responsibilities of science teachers concerning the welfare of their students by providing *reasons* for compliance. (8 pts.)

(Continued)

TABLE 14.2 Safety Unit Rubric* *(Continued)*

NSTA Standard	Unacceptable	Acceptable	Target
9b. Know and practice safe and proper techniques for the preparation, storage, dispensing, supervision, and disposal of all materials used in science instruction.	Does *not* describe proper storage and disposal of chemicals, such as flammable solutions, acids, bases, solids, and powders. (0 pts.) Does *not* describe how an MSDS provides valuable safety information concerning the maintenance, use, and disposal of chemicals. (0 pts.)	Describes proper storage and disposal of *some* chemicals, such as flammable solutions, acids, bases, solids, and powders. (2 pts.) States that the MSDS can give valuable safety information concerning the maintenance and disposal of chemicals. (1 pt.) Includes the analysis of *one* chemical's MSDS for a chemical likely to be found in a science teaching area. (1 pt.)	Describes proper storage and disposal of chemicals, such as flammable solutions, acids, bases, solids, and powders. (3 pts.) Describes how an MSDS can give valuable safety information concerning the maintenance, use, and disposal of chemicals. (3 pts.) Includes the analysis of *three* chemicals' MSDS for chemicals likely to be found in a science teaching area. (3 pts.)
9c. Know and follow emergency procedures, maintain safety equipment, and ensure safety procedures appropriate for the activities and the abilities of students.	Does *not* list appropriate safety equipment, safety rules, and at least one safety resource that can be used in the science classroom. (0 pts.) Does *not* include (a) safety contract and (b) a safety quiz. (0 pts.)	Lists appropriate safety equipment, safety rules, and at least one safety resource that can be used in the science classroom. (1 pt.) Includes (a) a safety contract and (b) a safety quiz. (2 pts.)	Lists appropriate safety equipment, safety rules, and three safety resources that can be used in the science classroom. (3 pts.) Includes (a) safety contract, (b) a safety quiz, and (c) a lesson plan that can be used to teach safety to students. (4 pts.)

*This is an example of a science safety rubric that might be used to measure knowledge of NSTA's Safety and Welfare Standard from the *Standards for Science Teacher Preparation.*

Assessing and Reviewing

Analysis and Synthesis

1. From recall, make a list of safety hazard inspections you would undertake before the school year begins. Check your list with what is described in the chapter about these safety hazards and modify your list accordingly.
2. Design a safety contract that would be suitable for students taking middle school science. Compare the contract you have designed with the one found in this chapter. What are the differences? Discuss the differences between the two contracts with the students in your methods class. What did you stress in the contract you prepared that was not stressed in the one found in this chapter?
3. Write a few paragraphs stating the safety precautions that must be taken to protect eyes. Be sure to include the guidelines for wearing contact lenses.

Practical Considerations

4. Prepare an inventory of the possible storage hazards associated with any one or more of the following courses: physics, chemistry, biology, earth science, and physical science. After preparing the inventory, visit a local school and seek permission to examine the storage areas associated with the course you chose to teach.
5. Outline a safety program that you would institute if you were the chairperson of a science department in a middle or secondary school. Ask a science chairperson in a local school to critique the program. Discuss the results with your methods class.
6. Prepare the safety rules you would post in a prominent place in one or more of the following areas: (a) a chemistry laboratory, (b) a physics lab-

oratory, (c) an earth science laboratory, and (d) a biology laboratory. Prepare an example of the poster you would use for one of the areas. Ask a member of the class to make suggestions for improving the poster.

7. Observe a middle school or high school science laboratory activity while students are performing hands-on activities. What safety practices are obviously in effect? What safety hazards are evident while students are working? What precautions do students take to avoid accidents? Discuss the observations with members of your methods class.

Developmental Considerations

8. Make a list of questions regarding science safety that you would like answered. Go to the Web sites given in Resources to Examine at the end of this chapter. Determine the answers to your questions from these sites, and gather other information as well.

Resources to Examine

American Chemical Society. 1155 16th Street NW, Washington, DC 20036. Phone: (800)227-5558. [Online] Available at: www.acs.org.

The American Chemical Society provides a wealth of information regarding chemical safety. Their pamphlets and books are useful resources for science teachers who desire to learn more about the proper use and storage of chemicals.

Flinn Chemical Reference Manual. Obtain the most current edition. Flinn Scientific, Inc., P. O. Box 219, Batavia, IL 60510-0219. Phone: (800) 452-1261. Fax: (708) 879-6962. [Online] Available t: www.flinnsci.com.

Flinn is a recognized company that provides schools with equipment, information, and assistance to make their science program safe and successful. Some of the information and supplies that a science teacher can obtain from Flinn's catalog or by contacting the company are the following:

- safety equipment, such as goggles, cabinets, sanitizers, eye washers, showers
- student safety contracts, labels for chemicals, safety posters
- MSDS that provide important information about chemicals
- federal Right-to-Know Law or Hazardous Communication Standards
- standards and designs for school science laboratory facilities
- a scheme for organizing, labeling, and storing chemicals
- procedures for identifying unlabeled laboratory chemicals
- suggested laboratory chemical disposal procedures

Laboratory Safety Institute. James A. Kaufman & Associates, 101 Oak Street, Wellesley, MA 02181. Phone: (617) 237-1335. Fax: (617) 239-1457. [Online] Available at: www.labsafety.org.

Professor Kaufman has produced many useful materials to help science teachers and industrial workers better understand hazardous materials and situations that place people at risk. He and his associates conduct safety workshops across the country to educate workers and professionals about safety in the workplace. Dr. Kaufman visits school districts to assess their lab facilities and chemical inventories. He also publishes a safety newsletter.

National Safety Council. 1121 Spring Lake Drive, Itasca, IL 60143. Phone: (708) 285-1121. [Online] Available at: www.nsc.org.

This organization provides a large assortment of printed matter regarding many aspects of safety that pertains to schools, the workplace, and homes. They produce magazines and pocket handbooks that are appropriate for the lay audience. The site provides information and data on safety from vehicles to chemicals.

National Association of Biology Teachers. 11250 Roger Bacon Drive #19, Reston, VA 22090-5202. Phone: (800) 406-0775 or (703) 471-1134. [Online] Available at: www.nabt.org.

This is an important organization for providing information regarding the use of animals and all organisms. Periodically the NABT Board issues position statements on teaching biology, such as the use of human body fluids and tissues, products in biology teaching, the use of animals in the classroom, and dissection of animals. Their periodicals, *The American Biology Teacher* and *News & Views* (a newsletter), are very informative.

Investigating Safely: A Guide for High School Teachers. (2004). Juliana Texley, Terry Kwan, and John Summers. National Science Teachers Association Press. 1840 Wilson Boulevard, Arlington, VA 22201-3000. [Online] Available at: www.nsta.org.

This is a handy guide to classroom, laboratory, and field safety. It discusses many aspects of proper and safe conduct in science programs. The book addresses setting the tone for safety, equipping the lab, living organisms, field studies, and many other topics related to science safety.

Occupational Safety & Health Administration. 200 Constitution Avenue, Washington, DC 20210. Phone: (202) 523-7075. [Online] Available at: www.osha.gov.

This governmental organization has produced many regulations and guidelines for safety in the workplace. OSHA has many documents that pertain to all aspects of safety hazards. In some states, OSHA's regulations hold for public schools, whereas in other states OSHA's regulations are superseded by the state's Hazardous Communication laws and standards. There are many regional offices across the United States that a science teacher can contact for assistance.

Texas Safety Standards: Kindergarten through Grade 12. (2006). A publication of the Charles A. Dana Center at The University of Texas. [Online] Available at: http://www.utdanacenter.org.

The Charles A. Dana Center provides a large number of resources for science teaching. This 300-page resource addresses many important topics related to school science safety. Among the many areas addressed in this publication are laws, rules, and regulations; laboratory investigations and activities; field investigations and activities; facilities; safety equipment and supplies; chemical safety; health concerns; and safety training. In addition, this large-format paperback book includes a useful appendix that supports and supplements the chapter information. The information in this publication is organized well and easy to read.

References

Cullen, A. (1995, January–February) Contact lens emergencies. *Chemical Health & Safety,* 22–24.

Dombrowski, J. M., & Hagelberg, R. R. (1985). The effects of a safety unit on student safety, knowledge, and behavior. *Science Education, 69,* 527–534.

Kaufman, J. (2006, Summer). Eye and face protection in school science. *The Science Teacher,* 26–29.

Mercier, P. (1996). *Laboratory safety pocket guide.* Natick, MA: James A. Kaufman & Associates.

National Science Teachers Association (NSTA). (2003). *Standards for science teacher preparation.* Washington, DC: NSTA Standards for Science Teacher Preparation.

Orlans, F. B. (1995, October). Investigator competency and animal experiments: Guidelines for elementary and secondary education. *Lab Animal,* 29–34.

Puffer, J. H. (1979). Classroom dangers of toxic minerals. *Journal of Geological Education, 27,* 150.

Segal, E. (1995, January–February). Contact lenses and chemicals: An update. *Chemical Health & Safety,* 16–21.

Texley, J., Kwan, T., & Summers, J. (2004). *Investigating safety: A guide for high school teachers.* Arlington, VA: National Science Teachers Association Press.

Vos, R., & Pell, S. W. (1990). Limiting lab liability. *The Science Teacher, 57*(9), 34–38.

Wikipedia. (2008). Paracelsus. Retrieved July 4, 2008, from http://en.wikipedia.org/wiki/Paracelsus.

Wood, C. G. (1991). *Safety in school science labs.* Natick, MA: James A. Kaufman & Associates.

Chapter

15

Computers and Electronic Technologies

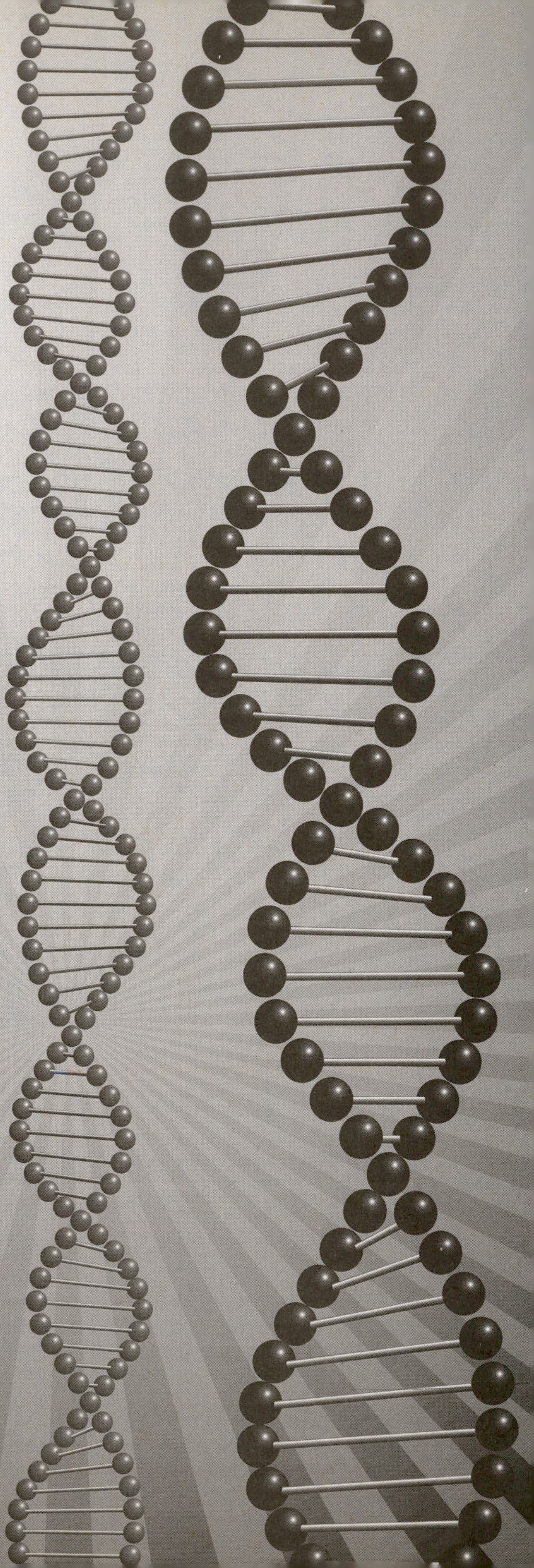

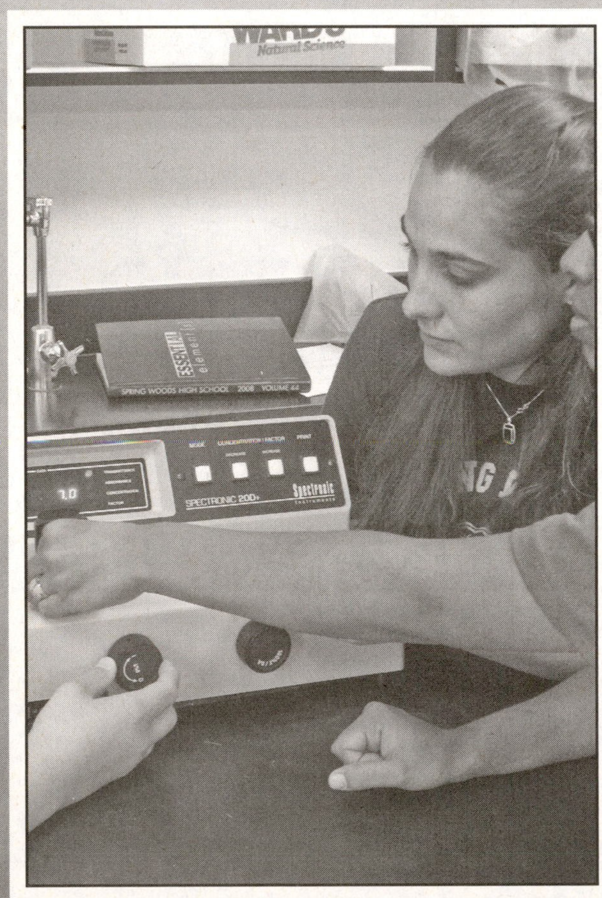

Electronic technology can help students to refine their understanding of science.

Computers and other electronic technologies are changing the work of science teachers as much as they are changing the work of scientists. Today, technology can support science learning in a multitude of ways, from information source to data organizer to communication tool. The power and versatility of computers have been significantly enhanced with the proliferation of multimedia systems and telecommunications capabilities. The amount of software available for use by science students continues to grow exponentially, and the science learning resources that can be accessed via the Internet are virtually limitless. In addition, advances in video, audio, and photographic technologies have extended sensory experiences associated with science learning. It is important that science teachers learn about the capabilities of computers and other electronic technologies and consider how best to use them to enhance the science learning experiences of their students.

AIMS OF THE CHAPTER

Use the questions that follow to guide your thinking and learning about some important aspects of using computers and other electronic technologies to support your students' science learning:

- What are some matters that a teacher should consider when integrating technology into science instruction?
- How can different media forms be used to enhance science instruction?
- What kinds of computer-based technology can support students' collection and analysis of scientific data?
- How can technology be used to encourage students' scientific communication and collaboration?

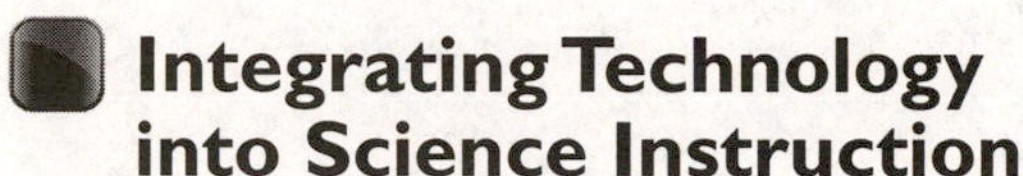

Integrating Technology into Science Instruction

The benefits associated with integrating technology into science instruction are many, and the list of benefits continues to grow as teachers explore new uses for emerging technologies. When computers and related technologies are coupled with appropriate pedagogy by teachers, students' science achievement improves and students view computers and other technologies favorably (Berger, Lu, Belzer, & Voss, 1994; Flick & Bell, 2000). The improvement in science achievement is most pronounced for authentic, complex learning experiences. It is in these learning experiences that students are challenged, engage in productive inquiry, make use of prior knowledge and higher-order thinking skills, build conclusions from data, collaborate with other learners, and reflect on their experiences (Papanastasiou, Zembylas, & Vrasidas, 2003; Stern, 2000).

Given the possible benefits associated with using technology, suppose you have just scanned a new Internet site or explored the potential of a new probeware package. You find yourself overwhelmed by the capability and potential of the technology. Should you integrate this computer tool into your science instruction? In order to make this important instructional decision, we encourage you to think about whether integrating the technology into your instruction will help students learn science.

Classroom observations reveal that when new computer-based tools are introduced into classrooms, much of the instructional time is spent learning the nuances of the tools. Little time is devoted to learning Science. Consider the teacher who naively thinks that students are learning science when preparing PowerPoint presentations for the first time. Rather than achieving the intended science learning outcomes, the students are learning the "bells and whistles" of the technology and the learning experience takes much longer than expected. This scenario suggests that technology use in the science classroom must be purposeful, supporting specific learning outcomes, and long term. It is also important that the purpose served by the technology be very clear, both for the teacher and students.

The work of Flick and Bell (2000) may help guide your thinking about when it is appropriate and worthwhile to integrate technology into science instruction. Their suggestions, worded as questions, are presented below:

- Is the technology used to help students learn important science content and skills in pedagogically sound ways?
- Are the unique features of the technology used advantageously in support of science learning?
- Does the technology help reveal students' science misconceptions and guide students toward more scientifically acceptable ones?
- Does the technology enable students to engage in science learning in ways not possible without it?
- Does the technology help students develop understandings about the relationship between science and technology and the interplay between science and society?

Guided by responses to these questions, middle and secondary school science teachers can position themselves to justify the time, effort, and financial expense associated with integrating computer-based technology into science instruction.

Framework for Integrating Technology

The nature of science provides a conceptual structure for considering how technology can be integrated into science instruction. Recall from Chapter 7 that science is thought of as a body of knowledge; a way of thinking; a way of investigating; and in terms of its interactions with technology, society, and the environment.

Computer-based technologies can be used to enhance students' understanding of the body of scientific knowledge through multimedia, providing access to complex concepts and unfamiliar forms, objects, and events. Computer-based technology can also facilitate students' engagement in authentic science investigations, where they work with data that they generate themselves or that are made available through simulations and from scientists. When participating in science investigations enhanced by technology, students often work in groups. The collaborative efforts of group work lead students to engage in scientific talk and argumentation, which provides evidence of their scientific thinking. Moreover, students derive meaning from science investigations enhanced by computer-based technology when they are linked to societal issues and problems, many of which, such as global warming and petroleum availability, have technological and environmental implications.

A framework based on the work of Bull and Bell (2008) that outlines the capability for integrating technology into science instruction is shown in Figure 15.1. This framework reveals a snapshot of the ever-changing palette of technological tools and their links to applications that support science instruction and enable students to better understand the nature of science.

Teaching Science with Multimedia

There are a number of media formats available for use to enhance science instruction, including still images, animation, audio, and video. They are available on the Internet and some can be generated using digital still and video cameras and audio recorders. In addition, some of

FIGURE 15.1 Framework of integrating technologies into science instruction.

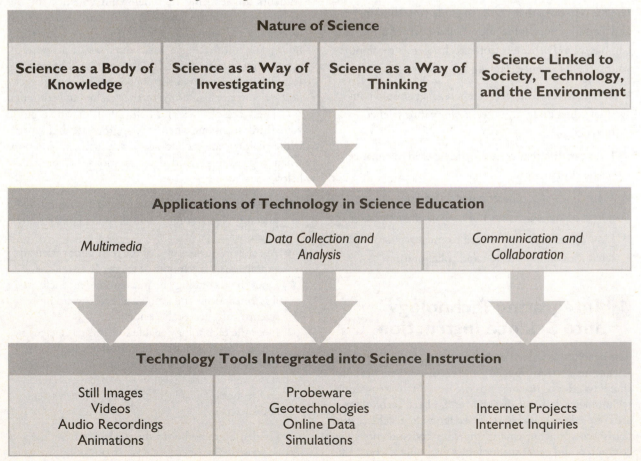

Nature of Science			
Science as a Body of Knowledge	**Science as a Way of Investigating**	**Science as a Way of Thinking**	**Science Linked to Society, Technology, and the Environment**

Applications of Technology in Science Education		
Multimedia	*Data Collection and Analysis*	*Communication and Collaboration*

Technology Tools Integrated into Science Instruction		
Still Images Videos Audio Recordings Animations	Probeware Geotechnologies Online Data Simulations	Internet Projects Internet Inquiries

the media formats can be easily edited using free or inexpensive editing software. Each of these different media formats can make a unique contribution to students' science learning. Collectively, multimedia can help you be successful in the classroom by enabling your students to use the modalities that are the most comfortable to them and by increasing their motivation for the subject and for learning (Tileston, 2004).

Still Images and Animation

Science teachers have long used photographs, drawings, and diagrams to communicate understandings that words alone cannot convey. The images used to support student science learning were often ones that the teacher had gathered over time or those provided with textbook programs.

Today, a plethora of science-related images can be accessed easily on the Internet. By using the Images option available on search engines such as Google (www.google.com) science teachers can access still images in a matter of seconds. In addition, you and your students can use a digital camera to capture still images to integrate into science instruction. All digital cameras have some means for transferring the images as electronic files to a computer, where the images can be viewed, incorporated into a multimedia presentation, or printed on paper.

Animation is the product of sequencing still images that show different positions of inanimate objects. Often built to simulate events and structures that cannot be seen or easily experienced by other means, animations can be particularly useful for helping students construct understandings about difficult and abstract science concepts. Animations that illustrate DNA transcription and translation, hydrogen bonding, muscle contraction, carbon-14 decay, and evaporation are among the many that are available at commercial, government, and university Web sites. Students also can create animations using the option on some digital cameras that permits the capture of a series of images over time (Abisdris & Phaneuf, 2007).

Audio

There are some things that students just have to hear to comprehend. The call of a mockingbird, the growl of a black bear, and the sound of a tornado are among the many audio recordings available on compact disk (CD). In addition, these audio recordings are accessible on the Internet, as are many others, including interviews with famous scientists such as the astronomer Carl Sagan and the ecology guru Rachel Carson.

A search for audio recordings that can be used to support students' science learning can be easily conducted by clicking the audio button on Dogpile (www.dogpile.com) or another Internet search engine. To enable all students to hear the audio recordings, consider connecting a set of classroom speakers to a computer or using headphones attached to an MP3 player for individual students.

Video

Video is perhaps the most compelling of all media systems available to science teachers. Middle and high school students have grown up surrounded by video, in games, at the movies, and on television. Many videos useful for science instruction are available in digital videodisc (DVD) format and can be shown using a DVD player to a class on a large monitor or through a projection system. Individual students or pairs of students can also watch videos on laptop or desktop computers equipped with DVD player software.

With the growing availability of fast Internet access and free video player software, most science teachers are also incorporating video from the Internet into their science instruction. There are video clips and full-length videos available on the Internet related to just about all science topics. In addition, students can capture video of demonstrations and investigations with video cameras for repeated viewing on computers or video iPods. And, when using video analysis software, students can mark the location of moving objects, such as a ball or model rocket, frame by frame on the video to calculate velocity and acceleration (Bell & Park, 2008).

Table 15.1 presents Web sites that have images, animations, audio records, and videos useful for science instruction. Key to realizing the benefits of multimedia found at these Web sites and others in science classes is coupling their use to sound instructional practice. For example, consider how showing images or video helps achieve intended learning outcomes of a unit as discussed in Chapter 3 of this text. Also, think about how multimedia can be used to engage students in scientific discourse as discussed in Chapter 11 and to assess students' science understandings as discussed in Chapter 4.

Stop and Reflect!

- Select a life, physical, or earth science topic that interests you. Then, craft a plan for using multimedia to teach the topic.
- Explore one of the Web sites identified in this section about multimedia. Write a brief description about what you found and share it with classmates.

TABLE 15.1 Sources of Science Images, Animations, Audio Recordings, and Videos

Animation Library
A collection of free animations for physics, biology, and human anatomy is found at this site. (www.animationlibrary.com/c/6/Science_and_Body/)

Botanical Society of America
Images accessed through this Web site are the contributions of society members and those printed in *The American Journal of Botany*. (http://botany.org/plantimages)

National Aeronautics and Space Administration
Video clips and movies about Earth and space exploration can be found at this site. (http://eartheducator.gsfc.nasa.gov/Video_Clips_or_Quicktime_Movies/)

National Geographic Society
Images and video clips related to many science topics are available at this site. (http://science.nationalgeographic.com/science)

Science Hack
This site is a source of science videos that have been screened by scientists. (http://sciencehack.com/videos/index)

Sounds of Science Podcast
From the National Academies, the audio podcasts available at this site address a number of contemporary science issues ranging from evolution to water use. (http://media.nap.edu/podcasts/)

Data Collection and Analysis

National and state standards documents indicate that scientific investigation and critical thinking should be the centerpiece of science learning. These documents emphasize the need for students to be able to analyze data collected from their own scientific investigations and investigations conducted by others, including scientists. Computer-based technologies provide the necessary tools for enabling students to collect, analyze, and display data, which, in turn, can stimulate their exploration and learning. Instruction that involves the integration of technology to support these functions can help students see science as more than a body of knowledge to memorize. Computer-based technologies that facilitate scientific investigation and critical thinking include probeware, geotechnologies, online data sources, and scientific simulations.

Probeware

In the laboratory and field, probeware can be used to provide students with firsthand experiences with the processes of data collection and analysis. The term *probeware* is used to describe electronic sensors that can be connected to a computer, calculator, or handheld device to collect different types of information. The electronic sensors, or probes, translate physical readings into electronic impulses that are presented as recognizable scientific data, with the aid of computer software. Probes available from commercial vendors can measure almost 40 different variables. For example, a gas pressure sensor can be used to measure the pressure of an air sample at different volumes, and a temperature probe can be used to measure air temperature or the temperature of liquids. Settings built into most probeware also allow users to select the start and stop time for an experiment and the rate at which measurements are taken. Several probes and the science concepts and principles that they can be used to investigate are identified in Table 15.2.

Probeware can be quite pricy, but the cost continues to come down as improvements are made to both hardware and software. We recommend that you, as a new teacher, first check to see what probeware is available at your school that can be used to support your instruction before considering the purchase of new technology. We also recommend that you practice with the probeware before using it in class, and consider organizing students into laboratory groups and rotating the groups through stations if sufficient probeware is unavailable for all to work at the same time.

Also, keep in mind that the use of probeware does not guarantee student learning, but it does promote student motivation and inquiry by allowing for the rapid collection of data, the collection of more accurate data than possible with manual instruments (e.g., thermometer, meter stick, etc.), and the presentation of results in tabulated and graphical forms (Hisim, 2005). Another very important benefit of probeware is that its use can allow students to discover mathematical relationships among measured variables (Park, 2008). Vernier Software and Technology (www.vernier.com) and PASCO (www.pasco.com) are two leading commercial venders of probeware and instructional materials useful for integrating probeware into science instruction.

TABLE 15.2 Sampling of Probes and Science Concepts and Principles They Can Be Used to Investigate

Probe	Concepts and Principles
pH sensor	• acid–base titrations • water quality
Colorimeter	• concentration of a solution • change in concentration
Conductivity probe	• total dissolved solids • salinity of water
Motion detector	• velocity and acceleration of a rolling object, person walking, or cart
Light sensor	• reflectivity • solar energy
Microphone	• waveforms of sound from music • speed of sound
Photogate	• free fall • collisions • pendulum motion
UVA and UVB Sensor	• absorption of UV radiation by sunscreens • UV intensity under different weather conditions
Current probe	• Ohm's law • phase relationships

Geotechnologies

Geotechnologies are relative newcomers to the science classroom, and include the following tools:

- global positioning system (GPS)
- remote sensing (RS)
- geographic information systems (GIS)

When integrated into science instruction, these tools enable students to collect, display, and analyze data that project spatial relationships.

GPS is a navigation system made up of a network of 24 satellites placed in very precise orbits and that transmit microwave signals to Earth. When a GPS receiver locks onto the signals from at least four satellites simultaneously, it can calculate the user's longitude, latitude, and altitude. When the user moves and the multiple satellite lock is maintained, the GPS receiver can also calculate other measures, including the user's speed, bearing, trip distance, and change in altitude. Handheld GPS receivers can be purchased for less than $100, making them an increasingly common tool in science classes.

RS is about detecting objects from a distance. RS is now the principal means by which the surface and atmosphere of Earth, planets, stars, and other parts of the cosmos are observed, measured, and interpreted. In addition to aerial photography, RS involves the use of satellite-based sensors that collect data in some form of electromagnetic (EM) energy. The energy is expressed as wavelength bands within the EM spectrum, including the ultraviolet, infrared, and microwave segments, and can be transformed into numerical data and images. Satellites equipped with RS devices can collect information about several areas of the EM spectrum at once across vast areas. Interpretations of data collected via RS can reveal much about objects and materials. The image shown in Figure 15.2 is a product of RS.

FIGURE 15.2 A product of remote sensing.

GIS are computer-based layered information programs, composed of maps and other forms of geographical data. The data used in GIS are collected from a number of sources, including GPS and RS. GIS data are thematically organized and can be positioned one layer on top of another to project such features as roads, buildings, surface water, vegetation, slope of the land, population density, and spread of infectious diseases. Figure 15.3 illustrates the layers of information that can be accessed via GIS and applied to science-related issues and problems.

The science investigations that can be conducted using geotechnologies are almost limitless, given the vast stores of data available at government and commercial Web sites and that which students can collect on their own. Baker (2008) advises that when integrating geotechnologies into science instruction that teachers begin by teaching students how to read and analyze maps and then gradually phasing in the use of geotechnologies to support science learning goals. The phase-in period may involve students exploring with a GPS or GIS software and data after being introduced to the tools, leading to investigations that have a local focus and involve collaborations with state or county officials responsible for mapping and GIS. When using geotechnologies, students can investigate questions of interest to them and gain a sense of the data collection and analysis techniques used by scientists. Sources of information useful for integrating geotechnologies into science instruction are presented in Table 15.3. Two examples of ways that geotechnologies have been used to support science learning are presented below.

- Students collect, document, and map lichen species diversity and density as bioindicators of air quality, specifically the quantity of atmospheric sulfur dioxide. The locations of lichen species are documented, longitude and latitude are established using a GPS receiver, and a lichen index is calculated. Using GIS technology, data collected by students are accessed in combination with other pertinent data as overlays, allowing the exploration of a host of questions related to air quality (Baker, 2008; Beeching & Hill, 2007).

FIGURE 15.3 Layers of information accessible via GIS.

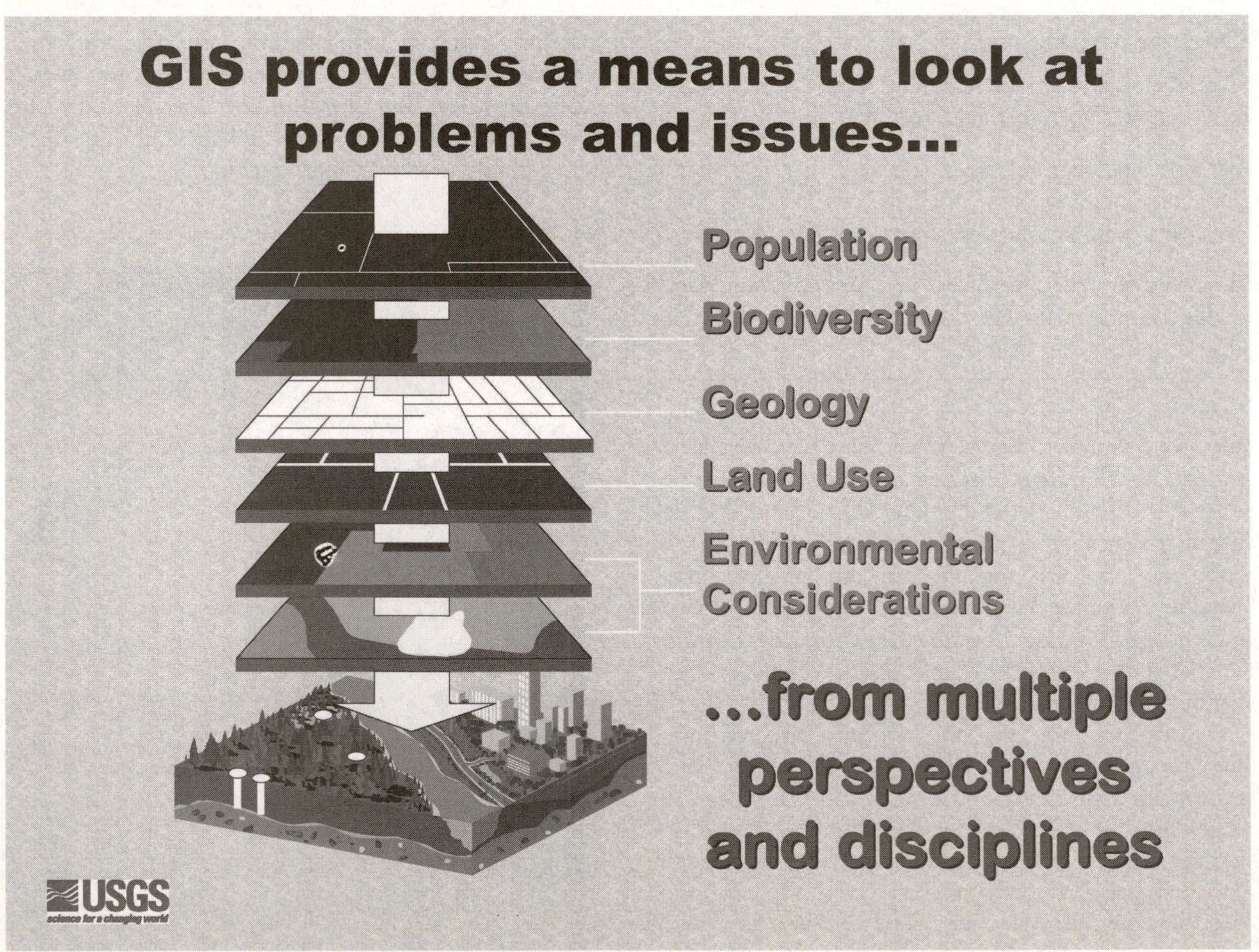

Used with permission. See PowerPoint from J. Kerski. Permission given for use in *Science Instruction in Middle and Secondary Schools.*

TABLE 15.3 Sources for Integrating Geotechnologies into Science Instruction

ESRI: GIS Educational Community
Environmental Systems Research Institute is a leading GIS company with unique services for the education community. Information about GIS software, such as ArcGIS Explorer, and lessons are available at this site. (http://edcommunity.esri.com)

Event-Based Science: Remote Sensing Activities
A series of lesson plans are provided that use remote sensing to teach science understandings. (www.ebsinstitute.com/rs.index.html)

Georgia Lichens Project
Information and teacher resources are provided for using GIS, remote sensing, and GPS methods to study lichens as bioindicators of air quality. (www.crms.uga.edu/lichens.htm)

Global Positioning System Overview
Materials developed by Dr. Peter Dana are provided at this site with information about GPS and its applications. (www.colorado.edu/geography/gcraft/notes/gps/gps_f.html)

Google Earth
Free software at this site enables users to explore Earth via satellite imagery, maps, terrain, and three-dimensional buildings. (http://earth.google.com)

KanGIS: K12 GIS Community
This site is a source of technical and instructional support for teachers using GIS, GPS, and RS. (www.kangis.org)

NASA's Remote Sensing and Information Page
Found at this site is information about remote sensing and lists of remote sensing resources about weather and climate, space and astronomy, as well as details about specific remote sensing instruments. (http://rsd.gsfc.nasa.gov/rsd/RemoteSensing.html)

Online Remote Sensing Guide
Made available by the University of Illinois, this site includes two modules that provide information about the types of images produced by radar and satellites and how they should be interpreted. (http://ww2010.atmos.uiuc.edu/(Gh)/guides/rs/home.rxml)

Total Ozone Mapping Spectrum—Resource Materials for Science Educators
This site contains a number of lessons that make use of data from the Total Ozone Mapping Spectrometer to study local and global ozone amounts and change. (http://toms.gsfc.nasa.gov/teacher/teacher.html)

- Students use GIS with GPS receivers to collect coordinates and chemical and biological constituents of a location streams, such as pH, dissolved oxygen, vegetation, and surrounding land use. They collect data from the same stream sites monthly to document changes and coordinate their investigation with local officials (Baker, 2008; Kerski, 2006).

Online Data

The location and intensity of global earthquakes over the past 25 years, the migratory patterns of loggerhead turtles, road test data for the year's five top-selling cars, and tomorrow's weather forecast for the capital cities of the 50 states. These kinds of data are ideal for science investigations because they enable students to answer questions of interest to them, but they are not data that can be collected by teachers and their students. Fortunately, data sets useful for answering a host of science-related questions are made available online by various scientific communities and government agencies. The data sets are collected via a variety of means, and may be made available in real time or archives and in different formats. For example, oceanographic data are collected using sensor-packed buoys, undersea monitors, ships at sea, and satellites and are reported as graphs, tables, maps, and images (Petrone & Lawrence, 2006).

When using online data to support students' science inquires, Trundle (2008) recommends helping students formulate questions that can be answered using data in addition to allowing students to devise their own protocols for analyzing data and drawing conclusions. Many students may have had little experience constructing questions that can be answered using data and working with data sets that included more data points than that collected by a class of students.

Online data sets are available for all science areas, and some are specially packaged for instructional purposes. Sources of online data include the National Oceanic and Atmospheric Administration (www.noaa.gov), the National Aeronautics and Space Administration (www.nasa.gov), the U.S. Environmental Protection Agency (www.epa.gov), and the U.S. Geological Survey (www.usgs.gov). Consider the following Web sites as places to begin your exploration of ways to integrate online data into science instruction:

- *BRIDGE: Sea Grant Ocean Sciences Education Center* (www.vims.edu/bridge/): Found here are links to real-time oceanographic and meteorological data sets that are packaged for instruction. A collection of teaching activities offers suggestions for using the data to enhance science learning.
- *U.S. Geological Survey: Wandering Wildlife* (http://alaska.usgs.gov/science/biology/wandering_wildlife/index.php): Data gathered using radio telemetry show the movement of six artic animals. The data are presented in animated videos that also provide information about the study from which the data were generated.

Simulations

Simulations are computer-generated models of real-world events, objects, or phenomena that enable students to engage in meaningful and interactive science experiences (Bell & Smetana, 2008). By changing the rate at which an event occurs, the parameters that affect a phenomenon, and by making small objects visible, simulations help students focus on what is to be learned. The Internet provides access to a host of free and low-cost simulations to help students learn science, some of which represent science phenomena in three-dimensional forms. Simulations can be found online to teach heredity and genetics; Earth, Moon, and Sun relationships; atomic structure and chemical bonding; energy, matter, and their interactions; magnetic induction; human anatomy; chromosome structure; and many other concepts.

Simulations are very powerful instructional tools to use when trying to help students learn abstract science concepts. They can also help students refine science understandings gained through hands-on experiences and observation, as demonstrated by students' learning outcomes about Moon phases when working with a planetary simulation to augment their observations of the Moon in the night sky (Bell & Smetana, 2008). Because of their very nature, simulations may distort or misrepresent aspects of the phenomenon, object, or event being simulated. For this reason, it is important to tell students where these distortions or misrepresentations are in the simulations that they are using so that they can consider this in their learning. For instance, colored balls in simulations of chemical bonding are not accurate representations of molecules.

We recommend that you build a collection of simulations for the science courses that you are teaching or hope to teach. Think about these simulations as tools to augment your instruction rather than replacements for other instructional strategies. Use the online sources in Table 15.4 to begin your collection of science simulations.

TABLE 15.4 Sources of Information for Science Simulations

Chemistry Collection
Organized by a group from Carnegie Mellon University, this site is a portal to many chemistry lab simulations and scenario-based learning activities. (www.chemcollective.org/)

Kent National Grid for Learning: Science Simulations
Found here are several simulations for teaching science concepts related to plants, forces and motion, electricity, food chains, and the environment. (www.kented.org.uk/ngfl/subjects/science/simulations.htm)

Physics Education Technology (PhET)
Supported by the University of Colorado at Boulder, this site provides interactive simulations for teaching many physics concepts, including sound and waves, light and radiation, and quantum phenomena. (http://phet.colorado.edu/simulations/)

IGCSE Biology Simulations
This site contains a collection of highly interactive simulations on genetic breeding, plant growth, and ecosystems. Each simulation has different challenge levels. (www.cambridgestudents.org.uk/subjectpages/biology/igcsebiology/igcsebiologysimulations)

Web-Based High School Chemistry Simulations
This site contains links to more than a dozen simulations and is supported by the Education Development Center. (http://cse.edc.org/products/simulations/catalog.asp#sodium)

Molecular Expressions
Simulations enable the exploration of images captured by different microscopes, and include stereoscopic and laser-scanning confocality. (http://micro.magnet.fsu.edu/)

MedMyst
Students learn about human body systems and the spread of infectious diseases as they engage in interactive medical mysteries. The site is sponsored by the Center for Technology in Teaching and Learning at Rice University. (http://medmyst.rice.edu)

Classroom Snapshot 15.1

Technology in Motion

The presence of computers and other electronic technologies is not a novelty at Eastside High School. The use of computers and technologies has been strongly encouraged by school administrators and well supported with local monies and several private donations. The high school media center and science department are well equipped when it comes to technology. The latest probeware and multimedia programs have been purchased in recent years for use in science classes, and teacher professional development has emphasized uses of computer-based simulations, GIS, and online data to support the teaching of science. All science classrooms have at least three computers, Internet access, and a SMART board. Parents and visitors marvel at the amount of technology available at the school for science instruction.

Despite the plethora of equipment, most Eastside High science students see the use of computers and other electronic technologies as "just a different way for teachers to teach the same boring stuff." Given this prevailing student attitude and their own professional development, most of the school's eight science teachers have become disillusioned with the promise of computer-based technology and are using it less than they were even a year ago. Many of the school's science teachers ask, "Why incorporate technology into science instruction if it does nothing to motivate students to learn science?"

Ms. Roper is one teacher who does not share this view. Her thoughts are about how she can get students interested in using technology to learn about motion and forces, the next topic in her curriculum. She is concerned about connecting abstract science concepts with what her students know and have an interest in. She knows that the technology available at her school can help her, but she doesn't want to use it in a way that will turn students off. Since many of Ms. Roper's students will soon be getting driver's licenses, she wonders if she can couple the school's technology and her students' interest in driving and cars to develop a set of learning experiences to teach motion and forces.

Stop and Reflect!

- Examine the vignette in Classroom Snapshot 15.1. What recommendations can you make for enhancing the learning experiences of Ms. Roper's students by using probeware, geotechnologies, online data, or simulations?
- How can your recommendation also help Ms. Roper teach her students about science as a way of thinking and as a way of investigating?

Communication and Collaboration

Science as a way of thinking and investigating involves more than using technology to collect and analyze data. It also involves working as a member of a science community to find answers to questions and sharing data and insights gained from investigations. Communication and collaboration are important aspects of the work of scientists, and should also be part of the science learning experiences of middle and secondary school students. Communication and collaboration are particularly important to the investigation of many problems that relate science to society, technology, and the environment. Web-based investigations provide students with opportunities to experience science as a process of thinking and investigating.

Web-based science investigations generally take two forms. One is Internet projects and the other is the more open-ended Internet inquiries. The structure provided by Internet projects suggests that students experience them first, before attempting Internet inquiries. Characteristic of both Internet projects and Internet inquires is students pursuing scientifically oriented questions, collecting evidence, drawing conclusions based on the evidence, and justifying their conclusions, in addition to communicating and collaborating (Bodzin, 2008).

Internet Projects

Internet projects involve groups or whole classes of students collaboratively investigating real-world problems. Some projects can be completed in a class period or two and involve little preparation, while others necessitate a larger commitment of classroom time and the purchase of special equipment for data collection or reporting. Through participation in Internet projects, students strengthen their understandings about the nature of science and improve their communication skills.

Internet projects take many forms, ranging from those coordinated by university researchers to those developed and facilitated by a single teacher. A number of projects, such as The International Boiling Point Project (www.ciese.org/curriculum/boilproj) and The Albatross Project (www.wfu.edu/biology/albatross), take advantage of the ability of the Internet to facilitate data sharing around the globe by focusing on phenomena that vary geographically. When selecting Internet projects for classes, it is a good idea to make sure that a project's driving question is (1) meaningful to students, (2) based on real-world experiences, (3) worthwhile in terms of the science content that can be addressed, and (4) open ended (Krajcik, Czerniak, & Berger, 2003). Questions around which Internet projects have been developed are: What is the effect of acid rain on our rivers? How do airline pilots find their way? How do pollen types and counts change with the seasons?

Internet projects can be found at many Web sites. For example, *A*ccess Excellence's Classrooms of the 21st Century (www.accessexcellence.org/21st/TE/AO/) and NASA's Online Interactive Projects (http://quest.nasa.gov/) provide indexes and access to dozens of ongoing projects. In addition, the CIESE Online Classroom Projects (www.k12science.org/currichome.html), the Globe Program (www.globe.gov), and Web-Based Inquiry Science Environment (http://wise.berkeley.edu) are good sites to search for partners and projects that match your interests and those of your students.

Internet Inquiries

In Internet inquiries, students seek answers to their own questions, often working in large collaborative groups. Internet inquiries provide students with opportunities to take full advantage of the Internet along with other electronic technologies. Students can gather information from Internet sites and other sources, analyze and make sense of the information, and then develop a presentation of their findings and conclusions (Leu & Leu, 2000). The findings and conclusions of the inquiry could be communicated to others and debated via e-mail or at a blog or school Web site.

Student participation in Internet inquiries usually requires additional scaffolding beyond that provided when engaging in Internet projects. Students need help to generate questions from phenomena they find interesting and to develop their questions into ones that will lead to meaningful and sustainable inquiries (Feldman, Konold, & Coulter, 2000). Students also need help searching for information using online search engines, finding resources pertaining to their questions, and analyzing and synthesizing the resources they find on the Internet (Hoffman, Krajcik, & Soloway, 2004).

To help address these challenges, Hoffman and his colleagues recommend that teachers model search techniques, talk with students about the appropriateness of search terms, and allow class time for students to demonstrate and discuss their online search strategies. They also recommend that students be reminded of the loosely configured organizational structure of the World Wide Web, the complex nature of research, and that answers to research questions often emerge from synthesizing information found at multiple sites and in other resources, including books and journals. Finally, they encourage teachers to support student evaluation and synthesis of online resources using the following strategies:

- Provide contradictory articles from the World Wide Web for learners to evaluate.
- Model and discuss appropriate evaluation and synthesis skills.
- Encourage learners to share resources and content summaries with peers.
- Require multiple information sources from students' final reports. (Hoffman, Krajcik, & Soloway, 2004, p. 220)

Central Science Sites

So far in this chapter, we have discussed several ways to use computer-based technologies to enhance science instruction. Access to the majority of these technologies and information about how to integrate them into science instruction is through the World Wide Web. However, for many science teachers and their students, searching the Web for these resources using Internet search engines can be at times frustrating and nonproductive. For example, the results of a search for *bird migration* using the search engine Google returned more than 551,000 hits, and the vast majority of these would be of little immediate use to middle and secondary school science students and teachers. A more effective strategy for science teachers who wish to begin using the Web with their students is to start by exploring a few central sites that provide information and resources specifically for science education (Leu & Leu, 2000).

Computers provide students with access to the world beyond the classroom.

Central sites have much in common with the large department stores in a shopping mall. By visiting one or two department stores, shoppers can find much of what they are looking for and save time in the process. By using a few central science sites, you can realize similar benefits. Some of the most useful central Web sites for science education are associated with federally funded projects and provide a number of resources for science teachers and their students. Others are the products of private efforts or the work of local or regional consortia that involve partnerships between museums, businesses, and schools. Presented in Table 15.5 are several central sites that are highly recommended by many who have carefully examined the Web with science education in mind.

TABLE 15.5 Central Science Sites

National Science Digital Library This site is a portal to many multimedia resources that have been carefully scrutinized for their scientific merit. (http://nsdl.org)
National Aeronautics and Space Administration (NASA) This site contains a wealth of information about the many NASA projects, a multimedia gallery that features some wonderful photographs and video clips, details about upcoming broadcasts by NASA television, and an education section. (www.nasa.gov)
Frank Potter's Science Gems Initially launched as a resource for earth science teachers, this site has expanded to include thousands of links to teaching resources for all science subjects. The resources are organized by topic. (www.sciencegems.com)
San Francisco's Exploratorium The Exploratorium site includes a number of highly engaging activities through which users can explore the science of various sports, build geodesic structures with gumdrops, or investigate the inside of a floppy disk. In addition, more than 100 scaled-down versions of the Exploratorium's exhibits, called *Science Snacks*, are presented. (www.exploratorium.edu/)
Access Excellence Affiliated with the National Health Museum and the pharmaceutical company Genentech, this site is for biology and life science teachers. The site includes an activities exchange, online science mysteries, directory of online projects, and a separate section for Advanced Placement biology. (www.accessexcellence.org/)
Science Learning Network Supported by Unisys and the National Science Foundation, the site's guiding theme is inquiry-based science education. Contained within the site are links to "Ten Cool Sites" that are updated monthly as well as activities and other resources from an international network of science museums. (www.sln.org)

Demonstrating Your Use of Computers and Technological Tools

As discussed in this chapter, computers and electronic technologies can be used in a variety of ways to enhance and support students' science learning. In fact, it is necessary in some cases to use computers and electronic technologies to help students understand aspects of modern science and recent advancements in a number of science fields.

Consistent with the National Science Teachers Association (NSTA) *Standards for Science Teacher Preparation*, you must develop understandings of how technological tools can and should be used to facilitate students' science learning and demonstrate these understandings in your classroom practice. Specifically, *Standard 5: General Skills of Teaching* states that teachers of science must demonstrate that they

> *successfully use technological tools, including but not limited to computer technology, to access resources, collect and process data, and facilitate the learning of science (NSTA, 2003, p. 21).*

Assessing and Reviewing

Analysis and Synthesis

1. How can integrating technologies into science instruction enhance students' understandings of the nature of science? Explain your answer in a brief paragraph.
2. Indicate your agreement or disagreement with each statement below. For those with which you disagree, rewrite the statement in a way that supports your vision of integrating technology into science instruction.
   a. All science teachers need to develop a basic level of understanding in using probeware to collect science-related measurements.
   b. When selecting multimedia, science teachers should begin by asking the question, "What concepts and skills can my selection help me teach?"
   c. Sooner or later, science teachers will need to be able to program software.
   d. Computer-based technologies should be incorporated into science instruction at least once a week.
   e. GIS and RS will become less useful to science teachers and their students in coming years.
3. Identify three to five possible shortcomings that you associate with using computers and electronic technologies to support science teaching and learning. Then develop strategies for overcoming these shortcomings.
4. Describe the differences between Internet projects and Internet inquires. What student learning outcomes would you expect from an Internet inquiry that you would not expect from an Internet project?

Practical Considerations

5. Use probeware to collect and analyze data from the laboratory or field. Discuss your experiences with a classmate and decide on strategies that could be used to overcome any problems you encountered.
6. Assemble a collection of images, audio tracks, and video clips that you could use to aid your teaching of a particular science unit. For each image, audio track, and video clip, briefly describe how you would use it.
7. Work with a classmate to interview two middle school or high school science teachers about how they integrate computers and electronic technologies into their instruction. What did you learn from your interviews that you would make a part of your own teaching practice?

Developmental Considerations

8. Work with a classmate to set up a blog for your science methods class. Encourage all of your classmates to use the blog during student teaching and beyond to discuss their uses of computers and electronic technologies to support science instruction.
9. Keep a log of your favorite Internet sites. Include in your log the Web address for each site and how you used the site to support your teaching.
10. Participate in professional development workshops that address uses of computers and electronic technologies in science teaching.

Resources to Examine

Technology in the Secondary Science Classroom. 2008. NSTA Press, Arlington, VA.

Edited by Randy Bell, Julie Gess-Newsome, and Julie Luft, this paperback book includes 10 concisely written chapters on uses of technology to support science learning. Chapter topics range from computer simulations to probeware to online assessment, and include listings of URLs for further exploration.

Vernier Software and Technology. 13979 S.W. Millikan Way, Beverton, OR. [Online] Available at: www.vernier.com.

Vernier Software and Technology has been in business for more than 25 years and is a premier supplier of science probeware. Probes available from Vernier can be used with desktop computers as well as with calculators and handheld devices. Some of Vernier's newest probes connect directly to a computer's USB port. In addition to an online catalog and purchasing directions, the Vernier Web site provides access to technical support, information about future training sessions, downloadable sample programs, and an online discussion board for users of Vernier products.

Science on the Internet: A Resource for K–12 Teachers. 2003. Merrill/Prentice Hall, Upper Saddle River, NJ 07458.

Prepared by Jazlin Ebenezer and Eddy Lau, this four-chapter handbook is a valuable resource for science teachers because of the hundreds of science-related Web sites identified and briefly described. The topics of Internet surfing strategies, ways of using the Internet for science instruction, links to science activities, and science curricular frameworks serve as organizing themes for the chapters.

Making Your Own Mashup Maps. 2008 (April/May). *Science Scope*, 58–61.

This article describes how to make "mashup" maps by combining data or technology from several different sources to support science learning. Authors Robert Lucking, Edwin Christmann, and Mervyn Whiting use Google Maps to illustrate how students can easily build personalized maps that include features associated with GIS.

References

Abisdris, G., & Phaneuf, A. (2007). Using a digital video camera to study motion. *The Science Teacher, 74*(10), 44–47.

Baker, T. R. (2008). Extending inquiry with geotechnologies in the science classroom. In R. L. Bell, J. Gess-Newsome, & J. Luft (Eds.). *Technology in the secondary science classroom* (pp. 43–52). Arlington, VA: NSTA Press.

Beeching, S., & Hill, R. (2007). *A guide to twelve common and conspicuous lichens of Georgia's piedmont*. Retrieved June 29, 2008, from www.crms.uga.edu/lichens/files/Lichen_12_Guide.pdf.

Bell, J. L., & Smetana, L. K. (2008). Using computer simulations to enhance science teaching and learning. In R. L. Bell, J. Gess-Newsome, & J. Luft (Eds.), *Technology in the secondary science classroom* (pp. 23–32). Arlington, VA: NSTA Press.

Bell, L., & Park, J. C. (2008). Digital images and video for teaching science. In R. L. Bell, J. Gess-Newsome, & J. Luft (Eds.), *Technology in the secondary science classroom* (pp. 9–22). Arlington, VA: NSTA Press.

Berger, C. F., Lu, C. R., Belzer, S. J., & Voss, B. E. (1994). Research in the use of technology in science education. In D. L. Gabel (Ed.), *Handbook of research in science teaching and learning* (pp. 466–490). Upper Saddle River, NJ: Merrill/Prentice Hall.

Bodzin, A. M. (2008). Web-based science inquiry projects. In R. L. Bell, J. Gess-Newsome, & J. Luft (Eds.), *Technology in the secondary science classroom* (pp. 63–74). Arlington, VA: NSTA Press.

Bull, G., & Bell, R. L. (2008). Educational technology in the science classroom. In R. L. Bell, J. Gess-Newsome, & J. Luft (Eds.), *Technology in the secondary science classroom* (pp. 1–7). Arlington, VA: NSTA Press.

Feldman, A., Konold, C., & Coulter, B. (2000). *Network science, a decade later: The Internet and classroom learning*. Mahwah, NJ: Lawrence Erlbaum.

Flick, L., & Bell, R. L. (2000). Preparing tomorrow's science teachers to use technology: Guidelines for science educators. *Contemporary Issues in Technology and Teacher Education* [Online series], *1*(1). Retrieved June 25, 2008, from www.citejournal.org/vol1/iss1/currentissues/science/article.htm.

Hisim, N. (2005). Technology in the lab. Part II: Practical suggestions for using probeware in the science classroom. *The Science Teacher,* October, 38–41.

Hoffman, J., Krajcik, J., & Soloway, E. (2000). Using the World Wide Web to support student inquiry. In T. Koballa & D. Tippins (Eds.), *Cases in middle and secondary science education: The promise and dilemmas* (pp. 216–221). Upper Saddle River, NJ: Merrill/Prentice Hall.

Kerski, J. (2006). *Geotechnologies in education blog*. Retrieved June 26, 2008, from http://education.usgs.gov.

Krajcik, J., Czerniak, C., & Berger, C. (2003). *Elementary and middle school classrooms: A project-based approach*. New York: McGraw-Hill.

Leu, D. J., & Leu, D. D. (2000). *Teaching with the Internet: Lessons from the classroom* (3rd ed.). Norwood, MA: Christopher-Gordon.

Papanastasiou, E. C., Zembylas, M., & Vrasidas, C. (2003). Can computer use hurt science achievement? The USA results from PISA. *Journal of Science Education and Technology, 12*(3), 325–332.

Park, J. C. (2008). Probeware tools for science investigations. In R. L. Bell, J. Gess-Newsome, & J. Luft (Eds.), *Technology in the secondary science classroom* (pp. 33–42). Arlington, VA: NSTA Press.

Petrone, C. J., & Lawrence, L. A. (2006, September). Monitoring the oceans for the classroom. *The Science Teacher*, 74–76.

Stern, J. (2000). The design of learning software: Principles learned from the computer as learning partner. *Journal of Science Education and Technology, 12*(3), 325–332.

Tileston, S. W. (2004). *What every teacher should know about media and technology*. Thousand Oaks, CA: Corwin Press.

Trundle, K. C. (2008). Acquiring online data for scientific analysis. In R. L. Bell, J. Gess-Newsome, & J. Luft (Eds.), *Technology in the secondary science classroom* (pp. 53–62). Arlington, VA: NSTA Press.

Appendix

Little Science Puzzlers

A Drop Of Water

A Puzzling Situation

Purpose

Many aspects of science involve problem solving. Scientists often attempt to figure out how nature acts as it does or how things work. Further, they must explain what they find out. Water is an interesting substance that can stimulate curiosity, provide a context to learn more about fundamental science, and engage students in problem solving. For example, if you place a drop of water on a piece of wax paper and ask the question, "Does the drop of water roll or slide across the paper?" you will have a puzzle that needs to be resolved and explained.

Materials

a piece of wax paper (approx. 8 cm × 8 cm) for each student

water and a dropper to distribute one drop to each student

a small amount of black pepper

liquid detergent and a toothpick for each student

Procedure

1. Distribute a piece of wax paper to all students and request that they place a drop of water on the paper.
2. Instruct students to tilt the wax paper so that the drop of water moves across it. Pose the question:

   Does the drop of water roll or slide across the paper?

   Encourage students to work on this puzzle by themselves to find a way to support their answer to the question and to determine for certain how the drop of water moves across the paper.
3. Circulate among the students to observe how they are examining the movement of the drop of water across the wax paper. Ask them to give a statement regarding how the water moves—rolls or slides—and to demonstrate that this is, in fact, the way it occurs.

   HINT: By placing a speck of black pepper or chalk dust on the drop, one can readily see that the drop is rolling.

Discussion

When most or all the students have solved the puzzle, ask them to explain the reason why the water rolls across the wax paper. Discuss the following concepts:

- **Adhesion:** the force of attraction between unlike molecules
- **Cohesion:** the force of attraction between like molecules

In this situation, we observe the cohesive effects of water molecules permitting a drop of liquid to form and maintain a spherical shape that will roll on a surface without breaking apart.

1. What happens when you place the tip of the toothpick into the detergent and then touch it to the drop of water?
2. How do you explain what happens to the drop of water?

   HINT: One end of the detergent molecule bonds to the water molecule and disrupts the adhesion between water molecules at the surface of the drop, causing it to break apart.

HOT IS HOT!

A Little Puzzler

The Sun is a gigantic fireball approximately 93 million miles from Earth. This star produces enormous amounts of heat generated by its nuclear furnace, where hydrogen fuses to form helium. These nuclear reactions produce high temperatures in the core of the Sun and a spectrum of radiation that spreads out into space. Humans can detect some of the sun's radiation in the form of white light, which makes it possible to see during the daylight hours. We can also detect its heat, especially during the summer months.

If you could extract a pinhead-sized portion of the superheated material from the sun's core, would a person feel this heat source on Earth from a distance of 1 mile, 10 miles, or 100 miles?

ANSWER: At 100 miles, the heat would be so intense that it would kill a person.

Source: Adapted from *The Cosmic Mind-Boggling Book* by N. McAleer, 1982, New York: Warner Books.

HOW STRONG IS STRONG?

A Science Puzzler

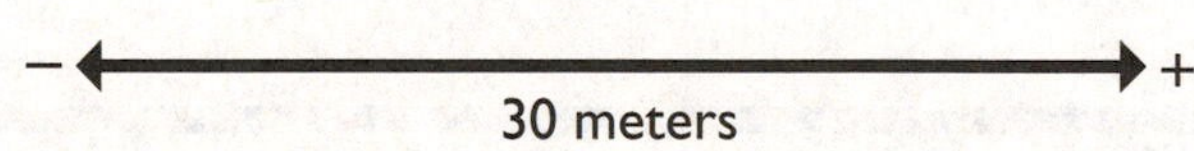

Ask students to tell you what they know about electromagnetic force. They should indicate that electromagnetism is one of the four fundamental forces that have been ascribed to nature by science. The four forces are called *gravity*, the *weak nuclear force*, the *electromagnetic force*, and the *strong nuclear force*. These ideas are used to describe the interactions that take place between the various types of matter: protons, neutrons, electrons, and so on.

Conduct a thought experiment whereby you ask students to visualize two bits of very dense matter, each with a diameter of 1 millimeter. Imagine that you can transform all the particles in one of these bits of matter into negative charges and all the particles in the other bit into positive charges, as indicated in the diagram. Further, you separate the two bits of matter by a distance of 30 meters. Ask the following question:

At 30 meters, will there be an attraction between the two bits of very dense matter?

ANSWER: Solicit responses from different students. Most will say that there is a small attraction between the two bits of matter. However, they will indicate that the force of attraction is very small because of the distance. They may mention the relationship that holds for gravity and electrostatics, which says that the force of attraction is equal to a constant times the product of the masses of the two objects divided by the square of the distance between them. These are small pieces of matter, and the distance of 30 meters is rather large.

Students will be shocked when you tell them that the force of attraction between the two bits of matter, each with an opposite charge, is 3 million tons. Yes! Three million tons of force is pulling the bits of matter toward each other. Wow! Now do you believe that electromagnetic forces are STRONG?

Thick and Thin Light Bulb Filaments

A Little Science Puzzler

Have you ever wondered how light bulbs are constructed so that some give off more light than others? The bulb on the left is rated at 40 watts and the one on the right is 75 watts.

Tell which bulb gives off more light and explain your answer.

ANSWER: The 75-watt light bulb produces more light. The main reason for this is the size of the filament inside the glass bulb. The 75-watt light bulb has a slightly thicker filament than the 40-watt light bulb. The larger-size filament permits more electrical current to flow through it; thus, it uses more energy and produces a brighter light than a lower-wattage bulb. Examine the filaments inside light bulbs rated at different wattages and note the thickness of each filament.

The Eggciting Egg Hunt

A Puzzling Situation

Context

It was the week before Easter and Mrs. Barefoot and her 5-year-old daughter, Caroline, were decorating eggs for the annual Easter egg hunt. They had just hard-boiled a dozen eggs and w\ere preparing to boil a dozen more when the phone rang. Mrs. Barefoot went to answer the phone while Caroline stayed in the kitchen. Upon her return to the kitchen, Mrs. Barefoot saw that Caroline had mixed the hard-boiled eggs with the raw ones.

How can Mrs. Barefoot tell the difference between the hard-boiled eggs and the raw eggs?

Materials

hard-boiled eggs

raw eggs

Procedure

1. Spin each egg on a smooth flat surface.
2. Quickly stop each egg from spinning and then at once allow it to spin again.
3. Observe the behavior of each egg. Group the eggs into two piles based on their behavior.
4. Raw eggs spin when released, whereas hard-boiled eggs do not.

Questions & Answers

How can you explain the different behavior of the raw and boiled eggs?

ANSWER: When the shell of the rotating raw egg is briefly stopped, its fluid will still be rotating.

Raisins on the Move

A Puzzling Situation

Context

It's snack time and two friends, Jan and Mike, are enjoying their raisins and sparkling soda as they sit and talk. All of a sudden, they are bumped by a passerby and some of Jan's raisins spill into Mike's cup of sparkling soda. Within a few minutes, they witness a strange occurrence. Raisins are moving up and down in the cup of sparkling soda.

What causes the raisins to behave like this?

Materials

raisins

clear plastic cup or drinking glass

sparkling soda (club soda, Sprite, or 7-Up)

Procedure

1. Fill the plastic cup about two-thirds full of sparkling soda.
2. Gingerly add four to six raisins one at a time to the cup.
3. Watch the raisins and write down what you observe.
4. Come up with an explanation for the movement of the raisins.

Discussion

When the raisins are first put into the cup, they sink to the bottom. While at the bottom of the cup, bubbles in the sparkling soda attach to the raisins. These are carbon dioxide bubbles. As the bubbles attach to a single raisin, they function like tiny life buoys, bringing the raisin to the surface. The carbon dioxide bubbles burst when they reach the surface, causing the raisin to sink. This process is repeated over and over until most of the carbon dioxide gas escapes from the sparkling soda and the soda becomes flat.

Appendix

Science Demonstrations

Bernoulli's Principle

A Discrepant Event Science Demonstration

Purpose

Discrepant events create surprise and cause students to concentrate on what is taking place. Many science demonstrations present contradictions in our thinking, because they illustrate laws and principles that are not immediately understood by observation. Bernoulli's principle, which pertains to air pressure, is such an idea. Fortunately, there are many discrepant event demonstrations that can be conducted in the science classroom to help students learn about Bernoulli's principle and many other principles.

Materials

two thick books of similar size and one sheet of 8 1/2-by-11-inch paper (for "Blow under a Sheet of Paper")

one shoe box (or any container or bowl of similar size) and several playing cards (for "The Falling Card Trick")

a spoon and a water faucet (for "Squirting Water on the Spoon")

Procedure for "Blow under a Sheet of Paper"

1. Set the two books on a table so they are approximately 5 inches apart.
2. Place one sheet of paper lengthwise so each end rests on one of the books. Center the paper between the two books (see figure).

3. Ask students to predict what will happen when someone blows hard between the two books and under the paper. Record their answers on the board.
4. Ask for a student volunteer to blow under the paper.

Questions & Answers

1. **What happened when the air passed swiftly under the paper? Is this what you predicted?**

   ANSWER: The paper bent down toward the table. Many students will have predicted that the paper will rise up or be blown off the books.
2. **Why did the paper bend toward the table?**

   ANSWER: When someone blows under the paper, that air is moving much faster than the air above the paper. The air moving rapidly across the underside of the paper produces less air pressure than the air above the paper, according to Bernoulli's principle. This action results in more air pressure above the paper, which forces the paper to bend down to the table. Bernoulli's principle states that the faster air moves across a surface, the less pressure it exerts on that surface.
3. **Predict what should happen if you hold a sheet of paper to your chin and blow across it. Why do you think so?**

   ANSWER: The paper should rise. Let students try this out for themselves at their desks. The moving air on top of the paper has less air pressure than the air underneath the paper, thus the paper will lift.

Procedure for "The Falling Card Trick"

1. Place a shoe box (or other container) on the floor directly in front of you.

2. Hold a playing card horizontally directly over the box and drop it into the box. Do not point out to students the angle at which you release or hold the card.
3. Ask several students to come up and try to drop a card into the box.

Questions & Answers

1. **Which cards fell into the box and which cards did not?**

   ANSWER: The observant students should see that the cards that were initially held horizontally and dropped fell straight down into the box. The cards held vertically or at other angles drifted away from the box.

   Some students might have trouble seeing this. You could make this a game where you predict whether each card dropped will fall in or not. After doing this a few times, through questioning, invite students to discover how you are holding each card as you drop it.
2. **Why do the cards that are held horizontally drop straight into the box?**

   ANSWER: As the card falls, the air pressure above the card drops. Since the card is horizontal, the air pressure affects the card uniformly. This can be drawn on the board as follows:

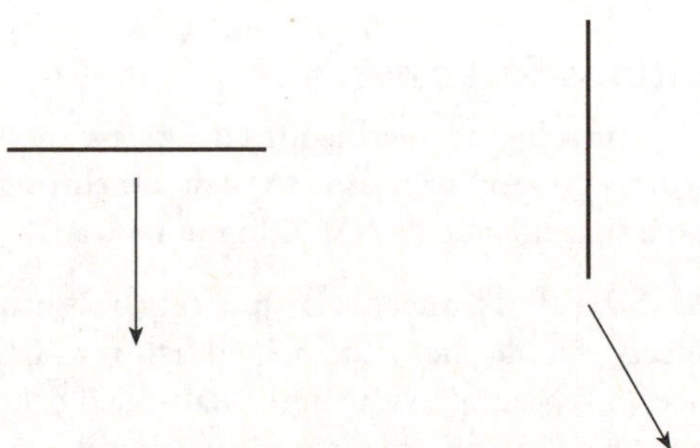

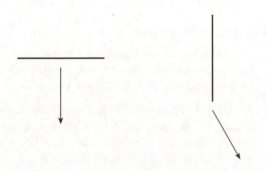

3. **Why do the cards dropped at an angle drift away?**

   ANSWER: As in the example, when the card is released horizontally, the air pressure above the card decreases as it falls. However, when the card is at an angle, there are differences in air pressure around the card. The air pressure is the lightest over the lowest part of the card. The lighter pressure does not cause that end of the card to lift because it is still falling, but the lighter pressure does cause that end of the card to fall more slowly than the other end. The difference in the speed at which each end of the card falls causes it to drift away and often to tumble end over end. This too can be illustrated on the board.

Procedure for "Squirting Water on the Spoon"

1. Turn on a water faucet to get a fast stream of water.
2. Loosely hold a spoon by its handle with the curved end 3 or 4 inches away from the stream of water. Ask the following question:

   What will happen when I bring the curved underside of the spoon in contact with the fast-moving stream of water?
3. Let several of the students hold the spoon and feel it jump into the stream of water.

Questions & Answers

1. **What caused the spoon to jump into the water?**

   ANSWER: The fast-moving water causes a decrease in the air pressure on the *bottom* of the spoon. Because the pressure on the bottom of the spoon is less than the air pressure on the top, the greater pressure pushes the spoon into the water.

2. **Can you think of examples of everyday occurences that demonstrate Bernoulli's principle?**

   EXAMPLE A: Airplane wings, hang gliders, and so on. The wings of an airplane are curved to form an airfoil. This shape creates an area of lower pressure over the wing when the plane moves through the air. The greater pressure underneath forces the wing upward, creating lift for the airplane.

   EXAMPLE B: Baseball pitchers throw curve balls and drop balls by putting spin on the ball. When a great deal of spin is given to a baseball, it causes the air on one side of the ball to travel faster. This, in turn, causes a pressure change that pulls the ball to the side with the least pressure.

   EXAMPLE C: When a semitrailer rig travels down the highway, it creates an area behind its large cargo trailer that has lower air pressure than one normally experiences driving down the highway. When a vehicle travels at close proximity behind the trailer, the vehicle will be pulled along by the reduced air pressure that it experiences between it and the trailer.

   EXAMPLE D: Many internal combustion engines use a carburetor to mix air and gas together to facilitate combustion. The air traveling through the carburetor is channeled into a narrower passage, causing it to speed up. The reduced pressure in the air channels "pulls" the gas into the carburetor where it mixes with the air. Again, we observe Bernoulli's principle in effect.

The No-Pop Balloon

A Science Demonstration

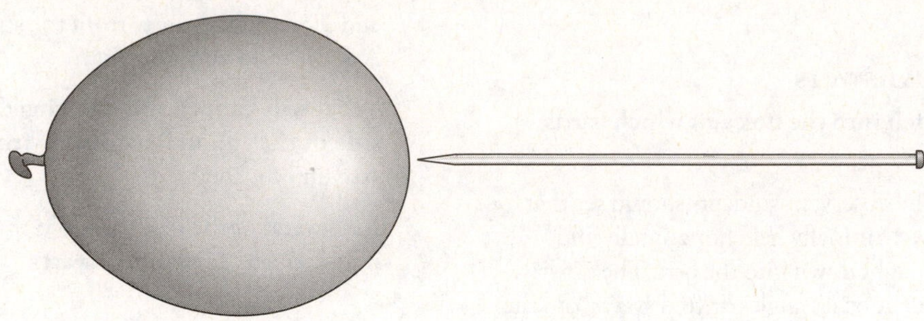

Purpose

You can demonstrate the property of a particular polymer by piercing a balloon with a sharp object and observing that the balloon does not pop. The rubberlike material that is used to manufacture balloons is composed of chains of carbon-based molecules. These polymers are very flexible and rather loosely structured, so a thin, sharp object can slip between the sheets of polymer chains and not disrupt the material. By following the directions and with some practice, you can present an attention-getting demonstration that will cause the audience to think more deeply about polymers and the wonders of human-made chemical products.

Materials

several large, good-quality balloons (i.e., balloons with heavy rubber walls)

a long, thin, sharp object to push into the balloon (e.g., an 8- or 10-inch length of coat hanger wire with one end sharpened or an upholstery needle)

some lubricant (e.g., cooking oil or liquid soap)

Procedure

Remember, you should practice this demonstration a few times before you present it to the class.

1. Inflate the balloon to only about one-half its capacity and tie the end. You do *not* want the balloon to be filled to capacity with air so that the rubber walls are stretched tight, ready to burst at the touch of a sharp object.
2. Take the wire or needle and lubricate the sharp end that will be pushed into the end of the balloon. You want to slip the point between the polymer chains.
3. Locate the end of the balloon, opposite the tied-off end. You may notice that this region is not stretched as much as the middle area. Now gently push the needle into the balloon with a twisting motion until it penetrates far into the interior of the balloon.

Questions & Answers

1. **Explain why the needle does not cause the balloon to pop or the air to rush out through the hole that the needle is making in its wall.**

   ANSWER: The needle is squeezing between the sheets of molecules that are held tightly against the needle. The air pressure in the half-filled balloon is not strong enough to disrupt this careful separation of rubber polymer.

2. **Do people bleed or feel the fine needles that are pushed into their skin when receiving acupuncture treatments?**

   ANSWER: Acupuncture is a similar process to inserting the needle into the balloon between the polymer chains. Skin is a polymer composed of protein-based tissue.

Bruising Fruit

A Science Demonstration

Have you ever wondered why an apple is sometimes brown on the inside when you bite into it or cut it open? If you examine the apple, in many instances you will notice that the skin has a slight indentation that indicates that the apple was hit or bruised, thus causing the flesh under that area to turn brown and mushy. When an apple or other fruit is bruised, oxidative enzymes are activated that catalyze oxidation-reduction reactions. These enzymes are found in the cells of fruit. They react with oxygen to decompose the cells of the fruit, which causes the darkening of the fruit. You can retard this process and illustrate it with a demonstration* by adding a common chemical to fruit.

Vitamin C, also called *ascorbic acid*, is well known as an important nutrient for humans. It is found in many citrus fruits and is used as a preservative and nutritional supplement. Vitamin C is a reducing agent. It belongs to the family of chemicals called *antioxidants*. As an antioxidant, vitamin C reacts with the oxidative enzymes in the fruit cell before they can destroy the fruit cell. The molecular formula for ascorbic acid is $C_6H_8O_6$.

Purpose

You can conduct the following demonstration to illustrate how to retard bruised fruit from browning.

Materials

vitamin C tablets
fruit juice
a few apples
six small beakers or cups

Procedure

1. Prepare the following setup of equipment and materials to illustrate how to retard the browning of bruised fruit with the addition of vitamin C. Either place a copy of the table on a chalkboard or on an overhead transparency to summarize the results and observations (see table on next page).

   Note that this is a set of experimental conditions that can be used for this demonstration. You can formulate other variables and conditions that may be even more illustrative of the ideas under study.
2. Slice an unpeeled apple (or pear) into six or more large pieces. Then bruise each piece of fruit by smashing it with your thumb. Place a bruised piece into each beaker and add the ingredients shown in the table on the next page. Then cover all of the beakers, except number 1.
3. Wait 25 minutes, then empty the beakers and make observations on the color of each piece of fruit.

Questions & Answers

1. **How does the fruit slice in beaker 1 compare to the others?**

   ANSWER: It should be darker in color.
2. **How does the fruit slice in the fruit juice compare to that in the vitamin C solution?**

   ANSWER: It should be about the same color.
3. **How does mother nature protect her fruit from the oxidative enzymes?**

   ANSWER: Apples and pears have protective peels or skins.
4. **If you make a fruit salad, how does squirting it with lemon or lime juice help prevent browning?**

   ANSWER: Lemon and lime juice both contain vitamin C, an antioxidant that retards the chemical reactions that lead to browning of fruit.

Source: Adapted from "The Chemistry of Bruised Fruit" by T. Anthony, 1987, in E. L. Chiappetta (Ed.), *Ideas and Activities for Physical Science* (pp. 2-14–2-15), Houston: College of Education, University of Houston with permission from Tom Anthony.

Beaker	Observation of Fruit: Beginning	Observation of Fruit: End
1—no liquid, uncovered		
2—no liquid, covered		
3—filled with water, covered		
4—filled with boiled water, covered		
5—filled with vitamin C solution, covered		
6—filled with fruit juice, covered		

Pull It or Yank It—What Is the Difference?

A Science Demonstration

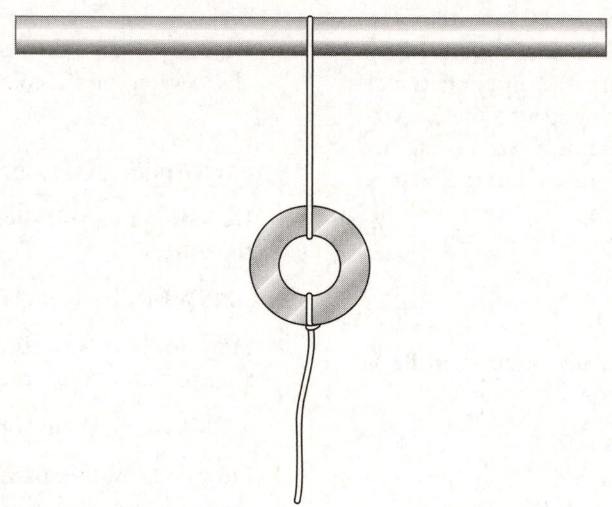

Purpose

Whether you pull or yank on a string that is attached to an object that you wish to move makes a big difference. In an attempt to move an object, you (the force) must overcome its *inertia*. According to Newton's first law of motion, or inertia, a body at rest tends to remain at rest and a body in motion tends to remain in motion unless acted on by a force. Certainly the mass of an object determines how easy or difficult it is to move the object or stop it if it is in motion. Here is a simple demonstration that illustrates the law of inertia.

Setup

Obtain some light string or heavy thread for this demonstration. You need a line that can be snapped or broken by pulling on it. Get a small barbell weight (a 2 ½-pound weight works well). Tie the string to the weight in two places as shown in the illustration. The top end must be secured to something strong, such as the end of a desk or a broom handle.

Procedure

1. Arrange the students so they are close to the apparatus and can see any changes that occur in the strings.
2. Alert students to observe the strings as you pull down slowly with an even force on the bottom string. The string above the weight will snap.
3. Alert students to observe the strings as you yank down quickly and forcibly on the bottom string. The string will snap this time between the weight and your hand.

Questions & Answers

1. **Why does a slow continuous downward force break the string *above* the weight?**

   ANSWER: When you pull down slowly, the barbell weight actually moves down with this force and it adds to the stress placed on the upper string. Thus, the upper string has more force on it than the lower string and consequently it breaks first.

2. **Why does a sudden increase in the downward force break the string below the weight?**

   ANSWER: When you yank on the lower string, the barbell weight and the upper string are at rest and tend to remain at rest. Therefore, the lower string has to overcome both of their masses or inertia, according to Newton's first law. The lower string absorbs the full force of the downward motion of the hand.

Call on students to repeat this demonstration to give them a feel for this inertial experience.

How Does a Weather Vane Work?

A Science Demonstration

Background

Knowledge of the direction from which winds are blowing is an important aspect of weather forecasting. In the Northern Hemisphere, winds move in a clockwise direction around centers of HIGH pressure and counterclockwise around centers of LOW pressure. Skies in a HIGH pressure area tend to be clear with generally fair weather, whereas skies in LOW pressure areas tend to be cloudy with stormy weather. By noting the direction from which the winds are blowing, the movements of HIGH and LOW pressure areas can be tracked and the next day's weather can be forecast.

Observations of wind direction can be made using a weather vane. Students are taught that a weather vane points in the direction from which the wind is blowing. This can lead to students forming a misconception about how a weather vane functions. Students tend to focus on the weather vane's pointing tip and neglect its size and shape. Which should be larger, the weather vane's tip or its tail? Does the shape of the weather vane affect its accuracy? These are the questions explored in this demonstration.

Materials

five 3-by-5-inch index cards
five plastic drinking straws
five straight pins
five pencils with erasers
scissors
cellophane tape
a metric ruler
a large fan or powerful hand-held hair dryer

Procedure

Weather Vane Construction

1. Cut one large and one small triangle out of an index card. The larger one should be about twice as large as the smaller one.
2. Cut two slits about 2 centimeters long at both ends of a plastic straw. Cut the slits so that the triangle index card pieces fit into the straw as shown in the illustration. Tape the index card pieces to the straw to hold them securely.

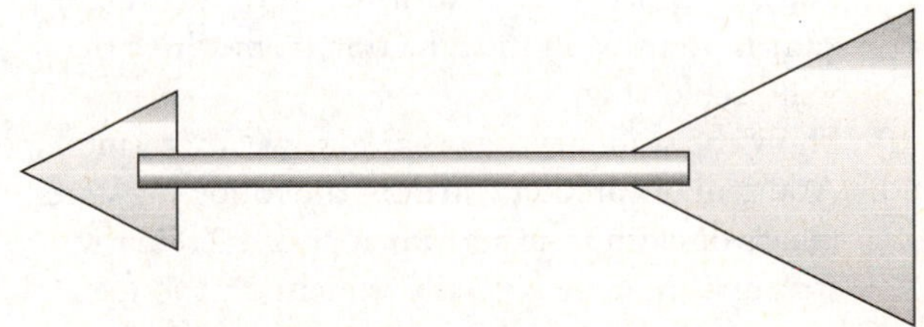

3. Find the weather vane's pivot point by balancing the straw on your index finger. Push a straight pin through the pivot point and into the eraser of a pencil. The weather vane should now spin freely on the pin and is ready to use.
4. Construct four more weather vanes that match the designs shown here. Mark the ends of each weather vane with the letters *a* and *b* as shown.

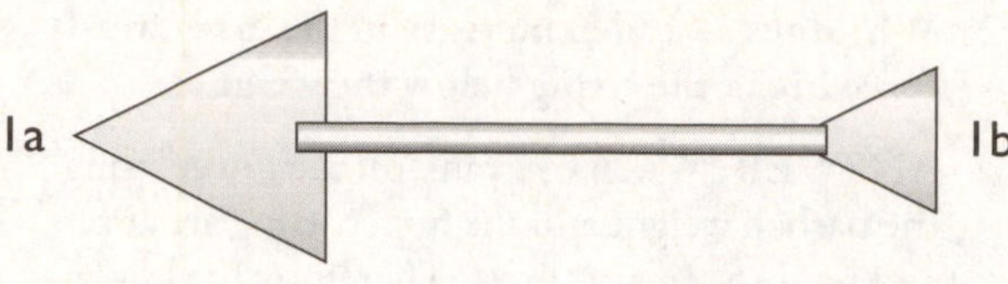

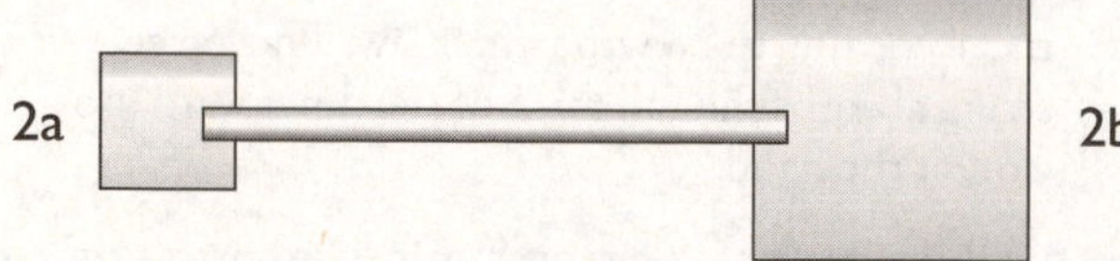

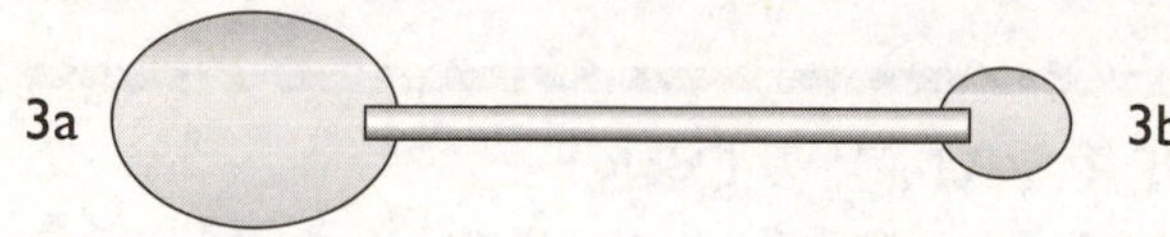

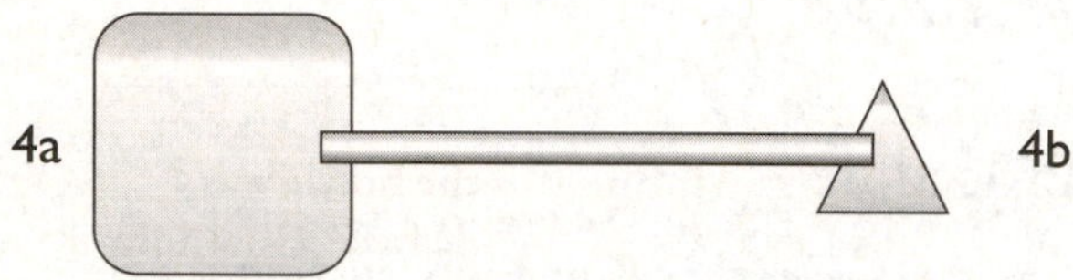

5. Copy the illustration of the four designs onto the chalkboard or prepare an overhead transparency of it.

Weather Vane Testing

6. Put the first weather vane constructed in front of a fan or hair dryer. Test it in the stream of moving air until its performance becomes predictable. Have students verify that the point of the weather vane is pointing in the direction from which the wind is blowing.
7. Show the students the other four weather vanes. Ask them to predict which of the following statements describes the performance of each in the stream of moving air. Tally students' responses.
   - With respect to vane 1, is the wind coming from direction 1a or 1b?
   - With respect to vane 2, is the wind coming from direction 2a or 2b?
   - With respect to vane 3, is the wind coming from direction 3a or 3b?
   - With respect to vane 4, is the wind coming from direction 4a or 4b?
8. Put each of the four weather vanes one at a time in the stream of moving air and observe its performance. Compare the students' predictions with the observations for all four of the weather vane designs tested.

Questions & Answers

1. **What happened when vane 1 was placed in the stream of moving air? Is this what students predicted?**

   ANSWER: End *b* pointed in the direction from which the wind was blowing. Many students will have predicted that the point of the weather vane, or end *a,* will point in the direction from which the wind is blowing.
2. **What happened when the three other weather vane designs shown in the figure were placed in the stream of moving air? Did the observations match the predictions?**

   ANSWER: For weather vane 2, the one with the squares, end *a* pointed in the direction from which the wind is blowing. For weather vanes 3 and 4, end *b* pointed in the direction from which the wind was blowing.
3. **Write a rule that fits the observations of the weather vane designs tested.**

   ANSWER: Examples of rules that fit the observations are:

   a. small end of the weather vane points in the direction from which the wind is blowing, regardless of the shape of the tip and the tail.
   b. The point is not the critical variable; the critical variable is the surface area of the ends of the vane.
4. **Compare the rules written by the students.**
5. **Build and test a weather vane design not presented in this demonstration that fits the rule.**

Making a Cloud

A Science Demonstration

Background

Clouds form when moisture in the air condenses. But what causes the moisture in the air to condense, and what does the moisture condense on? These are questions for which too few students have answers. In this demonstration the contributions of air pressure, condensation nuclei, and moisture to the formation of clouds are examined.

Materials

one clear, 2-liter plastic bottle with cap
water
matches
overhead projector (or other light source)

Safety

This demonstration requires the use of fire. Perform the demonstration away from flammable materials. Wear safety goggles.

Procedure

1. Seal the bottle with its bottle cap and rest it on top of a lighted overhead projector. Direct students to look into the bottle and not at the image projected by the overhead projector.
2. Repeatedly squeeze and release the bottle to change the pressure inside. (The air pressure inside is increased when force is applied by pressing on the outside of the bottle and decreased when the bottle is released.)
3. Add a couple of milliliters of water to the bottle, seal it again, and then repeatedly squeeze and release the bottle.
4. Put a lighted match inside the bottle and seal it. Then, repeatedly squeeze and release the bottle to change the air pressure inside.

Questions & Answers

1. **What did you observe?**

   ANSWER: A cloud did not form when the empty bottle was squeezed or when it was squeezed with water inside. Only after the match was dropped inside the bottle containing water and the bottle was squeezed did the cloud form.

2. **Did the cloud form when the bottle was squeezed or when it was released? How do you explain your observation?**

   ANSWER: The cloud formed when the bottle was released. Releasing the bottle causes the air pressure inside to be reduced.

3. **Based on what you observed, what conditions are needed for a cloud to form?**

   ANSWER: Moisture, condensation nuclei, and pressure change. (In this demonstration, smoke served as the condensation nuclei. Dust particles are the most abundant condensation nuclei in the air.)

4. **Explain how a cloud might form in nature.**

   ANSWER: Water evaporating from a lake or the ocean puts water vapor or moisture into the air. Dust particles and smoke in the air provide the condensation nuclei necessary for the water to condense on. With moisture and condensation nuclei in the air, a cloud would form when air pressure is reduced, such as when air is heated and rises.

Appendix

Science Laboratory Activities

The Diffusion of Molecules and Ions

A Laboratory Exercise

Purpose

Diffusion is a fundamental principle that is present in our everyday world. It is the tendency of molecules or ions to move from areas of higher concentration to areas of lower concentration until the concentration is uniform throughout the system. Diffusion explains how gases in the air spread out when released from one location where the concentration of their molecules is higher than in the space surrounding their source. Diffusion also explains how ions and molecules in solutions spread out through the liquid in a container or how nutrients move across a cell membrane.

Materials

bottle of perfume, cologne, or other odorous liquids, and cornstarch solution (rather dilute solution)

Lugol's iodine solution

plastic sandwich bags (fold-over type, not zipper type), one for each group

beakers or large cups, one for each lab group

Demonstration

Take a bottle of any perfume or liquid that students will be able to smell when you remove the cap and pour some on a cotton ball. Ask students the following questions:

1. How long did it take to detect the odor of the liquid once it was exposed to the air in the room?
2. How did the vapors of the liquid get from the cotton ball or the open container to your nose?
3. How do the molecules of the liquid travel from the source to your nose, in a straight line or zigzag path or some other type of motion? Require students to draw a diagram of the phenomenon.

In the discussion that follows these questions, bring up the term *diffusion,* explain it, and list many situations in which diffusion occurs in everyday life.

Procedure

Organize students into lab groups in order for them to carry out the diffusion exercise whereby iodide ions move through a plastic membrane.

1. Pour about 50 milliliters of cornstarch solution in each plastic sandwich bag and tie the top with a rubber band or string.
2. Place the bag of cornstarch solution into a beaker half full of iodine solution (Lugol's solution).
3. It will take about 15 to 20 minutes before you begin to see the cornstarch turn blue-black. If you wait 1 day, the reaction takes place to a greater extent and the color is more dramatic.
4. Ask students to devise tests to determine if other substances beside the ingredients that make up the iodine solution diffuse through the walls of the plastic sandwich bag.

Questions & Answers

1. **What does the color change inside the bag signify?**

   ANSWER: A chemical passed through the walls of the plastic bag into the starch solution. The chemical was iodine. The iodide ions were small enough to pass through spaces in the plastic and interact with the starch, giving the characteristic blue-black color that shows the presence of starch.

2. **Were the water molecules able to diffuse through the plastic bag into the starch solution?**

ANSWER: The water molecules are probably too large to diffuse through the plastic membrane.

Osmosis and a Chicken Egg

A Laboratory Exercise

Background

Life is maintained by an intricate balance of substances passing into and out of a cell through a membrane. Water, glucose, amino acids, carbon dioxide, and many other chemical elements and compounds pass through cellular membranes to maintain the proper nutrition that a cell must have in order to function. This dynamic process is partly explained by diffusion, which is the spreading of molecules from an area of greater concentration to an area of lower concentration. A type of diffusion associated with water is called *osmosis.* Osmosis is the diffusion of water through a selectively permeable membrane from an area of greater concentration to an area of lesser concentration. Osmosis is an essential process that takes place in all cells, with water molecules moving through the cell membrane.

Purpose

This activity illustrates osmosis taking place through the membrane of a chicken egg. A chicken egg is ideal for this exercise because it is large and has a cell membrane that becomes visible when you remove the shell in a particular manner. Although you may not have noticed, there is a membrane between the shell and the yolk/white part of the egg. If you remove the shell of an egg, the membrane can be observed surrounding the liquid material on the inside. With only the membrane to keep an egg intact, the effects of osmosis can be observed when the egg is placed in water where the concentration of water is greater on the outside of the egg than on the inside.

Procedure

This exercise takes approximately 3 days and can be conducted as a take-home laboratory exercise. During the first 24-hour period, the shell of one egg is removed by placing it in vinegar, which dissolves the calcified shell.

1. Each student should obtain two eggs of the same size and place each egg in a separate cup. In the first cup, pour in enough water to cover the egg. In the second cup, pour in enough white vinegar to cover the egg. The liquid level in both cups should be at least 3 centimeters above the egg. Let stand for 24 hours.
2. On the second day, make and record observations on both eggs. Remove the vinegar in the second cup and rinse the egg—carefully. Then pour in enough water to cover the membrane-exposed egg so that the water level is 3 centimeters above the egg. Leave for another day.
3. On the third day, make observations of the intact egg in the first cup with water and the egg with the shell removed in the second cup with water. What are the similarities and differences between the two eggs?

Conclusion

Write a few paragraphs describing what took place in this experiment and the science behind the events.

Radioactive Half-Life

A Laboratory Simulation Exercise

Purpose

The purpose of this laboratory simulation is to illustrate some concepts related to radioactive half-life. Radioactivity is an important process that occurs all the time in nature. It is occurring among some of the elements in our bodies every second of our life. The laws of chance are also illustrated in this simulation because radioactive decay is a random process similar to tossing a coin. This exercise is designed to review important background information that is necessary to understanding radioactivity and the atom.

Materials

shallow square cardboard boxes with covers (approximately 5-by-5 inches), one for every two students. (You can make square boxes from rectangular ones by cutting off the long dimension and restoring the sides with tape.)

unpopped popcorn, approximately 1 pound felt-tip pens

graph paper, one sheet for every two students

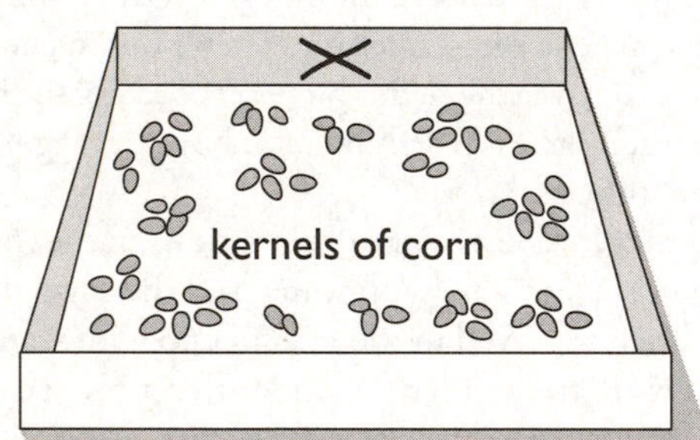

Preparation

Students will work in pairs. Each pair will be given one box, and 100 pieces of corn will be placed into each box. You can facilitate the preparation of this lab by asking a few students to help you count out the 100 pieces of corn for each box. A simple way to do this is to arrange the corn in rows and columns of 10, producing a 10-by-10 matrix, making it easy to see when you have 100 pieces of corn.

The boxes can be obtained at department stores, gift stores, or box stores. Mark an X on one of the inside walls of the box. Place a rubber band around each box to secure the cover so the corn does not spill.

Prelaboratory Discussion

Review some basic concepts related to radioactive decay with students by asking the following questions:

1. **What happens when a radioactive element decays?**

   ANSWER: The nucleus of the element gives off rays or particles. In some instances, this release of matter and energy changes the mass of the element by reducing the number of protons and neutrons in the nucleus, thus forming a new element with a lower atomic mass (equation A). In other instances, it results in the transformation of a neutron into a proton, thereby increasing the atomic number by one (equation B) while maintaining the same atomic mass.

   A. $^{226}_{88}\text{Ra} \rightarrow {}^{222}_{86}\text{Rn} + {}^{4}_{2}\text{He}$
   radium, radon, alpha particle

   B. $^{210}_{83}\text{Bi} \rightarrow {}^{210}_{84}\text{Po} + {}^{0}_{-1}\text{e}$
   bismuth, polonium, beta particle

   When a neutron transforms, it forms a proton and an electron (or a beta particle). Yes, it is strange to have a situation where energy and matter are given off, yet you end up with an element that has a greater atomic number—another unusual facet of nature.

2. **Why are some elements unstable and decay?**

   ANSWER: When elements have too many particles or neutrons versus protons in the nucleus, they have an abundance of energy in their nucleus. This excess energy causes the atom to be unstable and give up energy in the form of particles so that it can stabilize. Remember, everything in nature wants to become stable.

3. **How can you tell if a substance is radioactive?**

   ANSWER: Radioactive substances give off particles, rays, or energy that can be detected and measured accurately.

4. **What is half-life?**

   ANSWER: Since a radioactive isotope is constantly changing into something else, a very useful question is: How long will the isotope last before all the atoms in it have changed to something else? Half-life is the time it takes for one-half of the radioactivity to be given up. One way to tell how many atoms of a radioactive isotope are left is to use an instrument, such as a Geiger counter, that measures radioactivity by measuring the number of alpha, beta, or gamma rays emitted. Generally, the less radioactive material there is, the weaker the radioactivity will be.

5. **Why do radioactive substances behave this way?**

   ANSWER: Whether an atom is going to decay or not in the next second is a matter of chance. It might decay now, or it might not decay for another million years. As with flipping a coin, there are only two possible outcomes, the atom either decays or it doesn't. The chances that an atom will decay in the next second are a lot greater with an isotope that has a short half-life than one with a long half-life.

6. **How can you illustrate a 50-50 chance occurrence?**

   ANSWER: Flip a coin many times, each time recording whether a head or tail appears. What is the chance of getting a head or a tail? If you flip the coin only 10 times what do you get? Flip the coin 30 or 40 times and you will find that the 50-50 probability becomes more apparent. Radioactive decay is a similar process.

Tell students that they are going to perform a half-life laboratory activity using kernels of corn. Each box has 100 kernels of corn. Go over the following procedure before you permit students to begin the activity.

Procedure

1. Pass out the boxes, each containing 100 kernels of corn. Note that each kernel of corn has a pointed end. When the corn is in the box, the pointed end will point to one of the four sides of the box. What are the chances of a particular kernel pointing to the side marked X? (Answer: one in four)
2. With the cover securely on the box, shake it five or six times. Place the box on the table and remove the cover.
3. Remove the kernels that are pointing to the side with the X. Remember the kernels can be pointing to any part of the side with the X, not just directly at the X itself. If some of the kernels are pointing exactly at the X-side's corners, take one-half of those out. Do not put any of the kernels back into the box.
4. Using the table given, record the number of kernels taken out and the number left. Repeat this activity for 10 trials.

Data table of half-life graph

Trial	Started with	Took Out	Number Left
1	100		
2			
3			
4			
5			
6			
7			
8			
9			
10			

5. After the 10 trials, graph the results: number of kernels remaining versus trials. Ask the students to label axes of the graph; they need practice in this skill. Connect the points with a smooth line rather than using a ruler.
6. Use the figures from the class totals to construct a composite graph on the chalkboard from everyone's results.

Postlaboratory Discussion

1. Call on many groups of students to hold up their half-life graphs and compare the curves. Discuss the variation in the graphs. Point out that this is not due to students' errors, but to the fact that the smaller the sample, the greater the variation. Note that the composite curve produced from everyone's results is generally smoother because the number of trials is greater on this curve than on any individual group's curve. In an experiment measuring the radioactivity of actual materials, the curve would be very smooth because the sample of material would contain millions of atoms.
2. **Ask why a curved line was obtained instead of a straight line.**

   ANSWER: When you take one-half of a quantity, you get something even though it may be very small. In other words, you do not just end up with nothing quickly.

3. **Define half-life.**

   ANSWER: Half-life is the time it takes for one-half of the radioactive atoms to disintegrate.

4. **During radioactive decay, when does an element decrease its atomic number? Increase it?**

   ANSWER: When the nucleus of an element gives up an alpha particle, it loses four atomic mass units—two protons and two neutrons—and forms a lighter element. When one of the neutrons transforms into a proton and a beta particle, it forms a new element with a larger atomic number. (See the examples given earlier.)

5. **What is the significance of a long half-life versus a short half-life?**

   ANSWER: An element with a long half-life gives off matter/energy slowly; therefore, its radioactivity is not very intense. Consequently, it is generally not very dangerous but will be around a long time as a radioactive element. An element with a short half-life gives off matter/energy very quickly; therefore, its radioactivity is intense. It will not be around as long, but it may be very dangerous because of the rate at which it gives off radioactivity.

6. **How many trials did it take to use up half the kernels?**

   ANSWER: Usually two or three.

7. **How many trials did it take to use up half of the 50 kernels that were left?**

   ANSWER: Usually four or five.

Respiration in Yeast

A Laboratory Exercise

Background

Yeasts are single-celled fungi that form chains of cells. They belong to the class of fungi called *Hemiascomycetes*, which contains more than 30,000 species. The energy-releasing process that enables yeasts to live, grow, and reproduce is called *cellular respiration*. A principal source of energy used to carry on respiration is sugar ($C_6H_{12}O_6$), which may be derived from other multicarbon compounds.

Yeasts of the genus *Saccharomyces* are used to make alcohol in the production of cider, beer, and wine. Alcohol and carbon dioxide are produced when the yeast is grown in vats that contain little or no oxygen. Respiration under these conditions is called *fermentation*. A different strain of *Saccharomyces* is used in bread making. Here, the process is the same, but yields different results. As the sugar in the bread dough is used by the yeast cells, carbon dioxide is released, which makes the dough rise. Heat from the oven drives out the carbon dioxide gas and evaporates the alcohol, leaving the fluffy textured bread.

The equation for fermentation (anaerobic respiration) in yeast is

$$C_6H_{12}O_6 \rightarrow 2C_2H_5OH + 2CO_2 + 2{\sim}P$$

(2 phosphate groups)

Purpose

In the experiment that follows, yeast will be grown in the presence of little oxygen. The purpose of the experiment is to determine the effect of different amounts of sugar on yeast respiration rate.

Materials

- six 250-milliliter clear glass or plastic bottles
- six 200-milliliter clear glass or plastic cups
- six pieces of aquarium hose, each about 30 centimeters long
- two 6-ounce containers or bars of modeling clay
- 100 grams of table sugar
- two packages of dry baker's yeast
- 600 milliliters of warm distilled water
- 1/2- and 1-teaspoon size measuring spoons
- six graduated cylinders
- 50 milliliters Bromthymol blue (BTB) (*Caution:* BTB will stain clothes and skin.)

Procedure

1. Write the question, "What is the effect of different amounts of sugar on the respiration rate of yeast?" on the chalkboard.
2. Have students construct hypotheses related to the question before beginning the investigation. Ask them to provide reasons for their hypotheses. Proceed with the investigation once two or three hypotheses have been generated and discussed. An example hypothesis is: As the amount of sugar is increased, the rate of respiration will decrease.

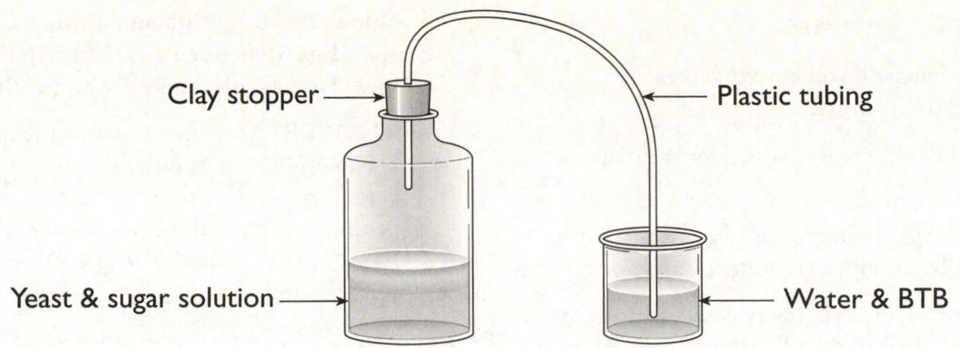

Assembling the Experimental Apparatus

3. Label the 250-milliliter bottles 1, 2, 3, 4, 5, or 6 to correspond with the treatment condition to which your group has been assigned. (Treatment groups are specified in the accompanying table. All treatment conditions should be represented in the class.)
4. Assemble the stopper apparatus for your bottle by rolling clay around the aquarium hose.
5. Pour 100 milliliters of warm distilled water into your bottle.
6. Add table sugar to your bottle in the amount indicated in the table. (5 grams = approximately 1 teaspoon)
7. Add 2 grams of yeast to your bottle. (2 grams = approximately 1/2 teaspoon)
8. Using the stopper apparatus, seal the top of your bottle. Make sure that the tubing is not touching the sugar solution.
9. Place the other end of the tubing in a cup of tap water to which two to three drops of BTB has been added.
10. Swirl the sugar and yeast solution in the bottle, then allow the experimental apparatus as illustrated to set for 10 minutes.

Data Collection

11. Count the number of bubbles released into your cup of water in 5 minutes. (All groups should start and stop counting bubbles at the same time.)
12. Then calculate the number of bubbles released per minute from the bottle by dividing the number of bubbles that you counted by five.
13. Copy the table and graph (as illustrated) onto a sheet of paper.
14. Record the number of bubbles per minute released from your group's bottle and the bottles of other groups in the appropriate spaces in the table.
15. Complete the graph using your class data.

Table

Bottle	Amount of Sugar	Number of Bubbles per Minute
1		
2		
3		
4		
5		
6		

Graph

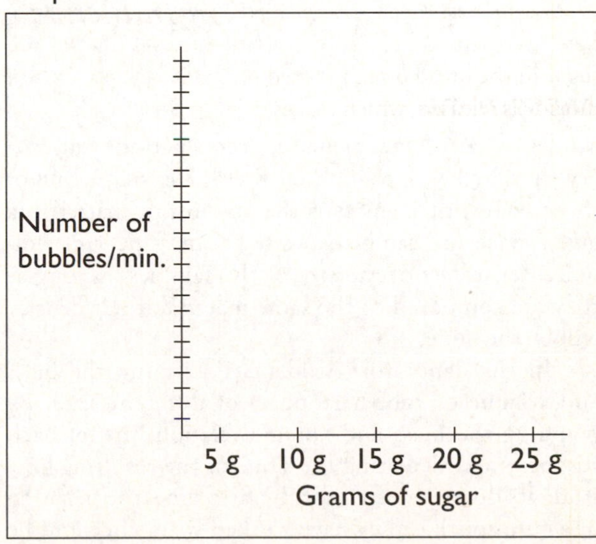

Questions & Answers

1. **What evidence do you have that a gas is produced in the bottles?**

   ANSWER: Bubbles are released into the cup of water.

2. **What is the gas being released from the bottles? What evidence supports your assumption?**

   ANSWER: The gas being released must be carbon dioxide because the BTB in the cup turned green or yellow, indicating that the water has become more acidic.

3. **How does the amount of sugar affect the amount of gas produced?**

   ANSWER: Answers will vary depending on results. The typical results show that more gas is produced when more sugar is added. A limit to the number of bubbles produced per minute is eventually seen when amounts in excess of 25 grams of sugar are added to the experimental apparatus. When the available sugar exceeds that which can be metabolized by the yeast in a fixed period of time, a leveling off of the respiration rate is seen.

4. **Do the results of the experiment support your hypothesis?**

   ANSWER: Answers will vary.

5. **What are the manipulated (independent) and responding (dependent) variables in this experiment? What variables were controlled?**

   ANSWER: Amount of sugar is the manipulated variable. Number of bubbles is the responding variable. Variables controlled include amount and temperature of water in the bottle, amount of yeast added to the bottle, and length of time bubbles were counted.

Extensions

1. Use the graph of class data to estimate the number of bubbles released per minute when 30 grams and 12 grams of sugar are added to the experimental apparatus. Check your estimates by repeating the experiment using these amounts of sugar.

   Note: Estimates beyond the range of available data are called *extrapolations* and estimates within the range of data are called *interpolations.*
2. Determine the approximate amount of sugar in grape or apple juice. Substitute 100 milliliters of juice for the sugar solution. After adding yeast and letting the apparatus set for 10 minutes, count the bubbles for 5 minutes and then calculate the average bubble count per minute. Using the graph prepared from class data, estimate the amount of sugar in the juice.

Mass and Volume Relationships

An Inductive Laboratory Exercise

Background

Students learn some science concepts better by discovery than by being told about them. Density is one of those concepts. Density is the amount of matter in a given space and can be expressed as mass per unit volume. Regardless of the size of the samples, as long as they are composed of the same material, their density will be the same.

In this laboratory students determine the mass and volume of rubber stoppers of different sizes. By graphing the mass and volume relationship for each stopper and calculating the slope of the resulting line, students discover, often for the first time, the meaning of a concept that they have worked with since middle school.

Materials

five solid rubber stoppers of different sizes (must be the same type) per group

two or three graduated cylinders per group, sized to contain the different stoppers

one balance per group

graph paper

tap water

Procedures

1. Tell students that the purpose of the laboratory is to determine the relationship between mass and volume experimentally.

2. Instruct students to copy the table presented below onto a separate sheet of paper.
3. Give five different rubber stoppers to each group. Instruct the groups to determine the mass and volume of each stopper and then record their data in the table. (Mass may be determined using the balance and volume by the displacement method.)
4. Next instruct them to construct a graph like the one shown below on a sheet of graph paper, making sure that the scales on the *x*- and *y*-axes are appropriate for their data.
5. Then instruct students to plot their mass and volume data for each stopper on the graph and draw a *line of best fit* through the data points.

Table

Stopper No.	Mass of Stopper	Volume of Stopper

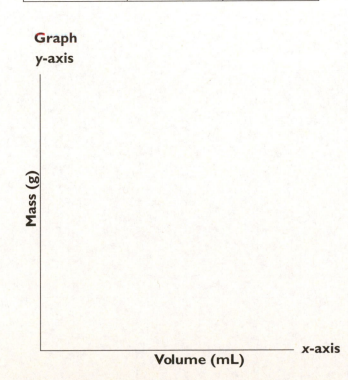

Graph

y-axis

Mass (g)

Volume (mL)

x-axis

Questions & Answers

1. **Describe the relationship between mass and volume shown on your graph.**

   ANSWER: Answers will vary, but should indicate that as mass increases, volume also increases.

2. **Calculate the slope of the line on your graph using two points on your line of best fit. Then calculate the slope a second and a third time using different combinations of points on your line of best fit. [Slope: $\Delta y/\Delta x$s $(y_2 - y_1)/(x_2 - x_1)$]**

   ANSWER: The slope of the line should be greater than 1 and all three calculations of slope should be the same, or nearly so.

3. **What science concept (physical property) does the slope represent? You may wish to consult your physical science, earth science, or chemistry text for help in answering this question.**

   HINT: You are looking for something that shows the relationship between mass and volume.

   ANSWER: Density.

4. **How do the data collected in this laboratory verify the definition of this concept?**

   ANSWER: The data show that the density of the rubber stoppers is the same regardless of the size of the stopper.

Appendix

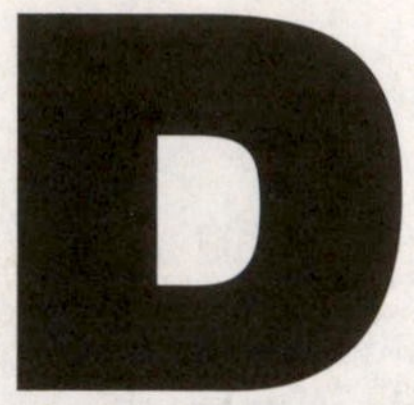

Scoring Key for Figure 1.1 Science Teaching Inventory

Directions

Circle your answers from the inventory in the following columns. Then, count the number of items circled in each column and multiply the total for each column by 8.33. Use the blanks below to record your column totals and product.

Column 1	Column 2
1A	1B
2A	2B
3A	3B
4B	4A
5B	5A
6A	6B
7A	7B
8A	8B
9B	9A
10A	10B
11A	11B
12B	12A

Total response in Column 1 _____ × 8.33 = _____

Total response in Column 2 _____ × 8.33 = _____

Explanation

The product obtained from your responses to Column 1 is an approximate percentage of how often your beliefs reflect an uninformed view of science teaching, whereas the product obtained from your responses to Column 2 is an approximate percentage of how often your beliefs reflect an informed view of science teaching.

Index

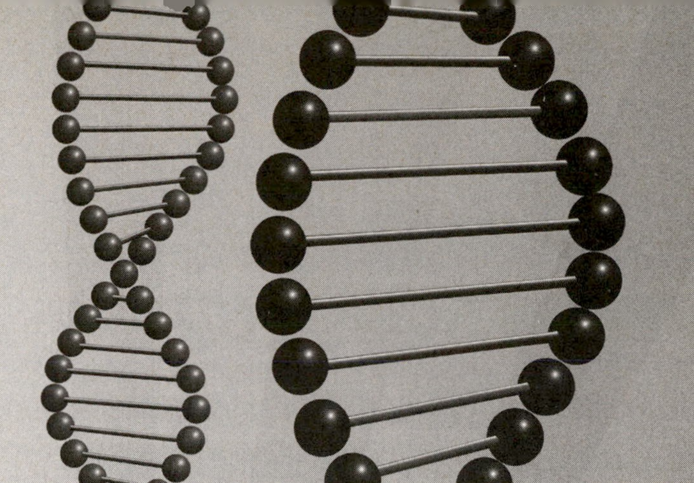